DOMINE DIRIGE NOS

Wool Exchange

Furniture

Guild Hall

Banking & Stock Exchange

THE
FINANCIAL
NEWS

PROSPECT
OF
The City of London
Being a Map for the
MERCHANTS, BANKERS, BROKERS
& other VENTURERS trading into
that City
19   34

ILLUSIONS OF GOLD

King Labour: The British Working Class, 1850–1914
The Secretary of State
The Chancellor of the Exchequer
Bobby Abel, Professional Batsman
Archie's Last Stand: MCC in New Zealand, 1922–23
The Financial Times: A Centenary History
WG's Birthday Party
Cazenove & Co: A History
The City of London, Volume I: A World of Its Own, 1815–1890
The City of London, Volume II: Golden Years, 1890–1914
LIFFE: A Market and its Makers
Phillips & Drew: Professionals in the City (with W.J. Reader)

THE CITY OF LONDON

Volume III

Illusions of Gold

1914–1945

DAVID KYNASTON

CHATTO & WINDUS

LONDON

Published by Chatto & Windus 1999

1 3 5 7 9 10 8 6 4 2

© David Kynaston 1999

David Kynaston has asserted his right under the
Copyright, Designs and Patents Act 1988 to be identified
as the author of this work

Endpapers: Rex Whistler maps of the City of London and the Stock
Exchange commissioned by the *Financial News* in 1933/4,
© the Estate of Rex Whistler. All rights reserved, DACS 1999.

First published in Great Britain in 1999 by
Chatto & Windus
Random House, 20 Vauxhall Bridge Road,
London SW1V 2SA

Random House Australia (Pty) Limited
20 Alfred Street, Milsons Point, Sydney,
New South Wales 2061, Australia

Random House New Zealand Limited
18 Poland Road, Glenfield,
Auckland 10, New Zealand

Random House South Africa (Pty) Limited
Endulini, 5A Jubilee Road, Parktown 2193, South Africa

Random House UK Limited Reg. No. 954009

A CIP catalogue record for this book
is available from the British Library

Papers used by Random House UK Limited are natural,
recyclable products made from wood grown in sustainable forests;
the manufacturing processes conform to the environmental
regulations of the country of origin

ISBN 0701161507

Typeset by Deltatype Ltd, Birkenhead
Printed and bound in Great Britain
by Mackays of Chatham PLC

This book is dedicated to Lucy

Illusions of Gold is the third volume of what is becoming a quartet of books about the City of London during the nineteenth and twentieth centuries. Framed by two disastrous world wars, it covers the years between 1914 and 1945 – years of a slowly dawning realisation, especially after the failed return to the gold standard, that there could be no easy way back to the golden years of the late-Victorian and Edwardian heyday. These were also the years in which the City's preoccupations started to become recognisably modern: the tussle with government for control over monetary policy; an increasingly deep involvement in the affairs of British industry; and a recognition that it could no longer take for granted public approval of its activities. As J.B. Priestley approached the end of his *English Journey* in 1933, a journey that had taken him through industrial desolation and untold wasted lives during the depths of the slump, he found himself unable to resist the conclusion that the City was probably the villain of the piece. It was not a charge that the City, with its tradition of secrecy, found easy to refute.

No one cultivated this mystique more deliberately or assiduously than Montagu Norman. There has never been a more dominant figure in the

City's entire history: Governor of the Bank of England for almost a quarter of a century, Norman suffuses this book with his brooding, enigmatic presence. Through his diaries, his letters and the often contradictory impact he made on his contemporaries, I have tried to provide the fullest portrait yet of the City's 'Pope'. Norman finally retired in 1944, believing himself to have failed, let down by nationalist demagogues, vote-grubbing politicians and ill-tutored democracies. Central bankers, however, can never escape parameters that extend beyond the purely financial, and the unfolding story of European monetary union will no doubt confirm this awkward truth.

There is another, more existential dimension. Norman himself would have found it impossible to go on living without his work at the Bank of England; yet for T.S. Eliot, who worked in or near Cornhill for eight years, the City became the embodiment of the waste land, a place of spiritual desolation. This continuing history of the City is, among other things, a memorial to all those who spent so much of their lives sitting at desks, trading on market floors, keeping the wheels of finance and commerce turning. Who are we to disparage their illusions of gold?

Contents

PART ONE

1914–31

Went to Mark Lane by train, then walked over the Tower Bridge, and back along Lower Thames Street to London Bridge, up to Whitechapel, St Paul's, Fleet Street, and Charing Cross, and so home . . .

A baby's funeral trotted briskly over the Tower Bridge among Pink's jam waggons, carts carrying any goods from lead pencils and matches to bales of cotton and chests of tea. In the St Catherine's Way there is one part like a deep railway cutting, the whole of one side for a long way, consisting of the brickwall of a very tall warehouse with no windows in it and beautifully curved and producing a wonderful effect. Walked past great blocks of warehouses and business establishments – a wonderful sight; and everywhere bacon factors, coffee roasters, merchants. On London Bridge, paused to feed the sea-gulls and looked down at the stevedores. Outside Billingsgate Market was a blackboard on an easel – for market prices – but instead some one had drawn an enormously enlarged chalk picture of a cat's rear and tail with anatomical details.

W.N.P. Barbellion, *The Journal of a Disappointed Man* (1919), entry for
24 October 1914

CHAPTER ONE

Very Convenient

The principal staircase was 'to be Honduras mahogany', and 'water closets throughout to have inch Honduras seats and risers on framed bearers', while elsewhere the carpenter's instructions were equally clear: 'All the timber to be Baltic fir of the best quality, of Riga, Memel, or Dantzig, well seasoned, and free from large or loose knots, shakes, and sap. The deals to be from Christiania, free from all defects. All nails to be wrought. The oak to be English of the best quality.' The mason also knew where he stood, with all window sills to be executed in the highest-grade brown Portland stone 'from the Waycroft, Maggot or other approved quarry, free from all flaws, vents, veins, sand holes, and large coarse shells, or other defects; the stone for carving to be especially free from defects, and of a fine even grain'. As for the slater, his instructions for the cisterns unambiguously concluded: 'Leave all clean and perfect at conclusion.' So ran the contract signed on 14 April 1871 between the merchant bank Frederick Huth & Co and the contractors George Trollope & Sons for the building of new offices at 12 Tokenhouse Yard, just to the north of the Bank of England. Almost half a century later, on 5 August 1914, the first day of the war, representatives of over a dozen of the City's leading merchant banks gathered there to discuss the unpleasant crisis in their affairs.[1] Their host was Frederick Huth Jackson, senior partner of Huths, and those invited included Rothschilds, Barings, Morgan Grenfell, Lazards, Hambros, Brown Shipley and Kleinworts, not to mention the still bravely umlauted Schröders and Frühling & Goschen. Thus was born the Accepting Houses Committee – 'accepting' as in guaranteeing bills of exchange. Over the years it would evolve as the innermost, and most mystique-laden, of the City of London's many clubs.

*

The crisis was recalled in January 1915 by S.F. Mendl, Deputy Chairman of National Discount Co, at the annual meeting at Cannon Street Hotel:

3

Towards the end of July the increasing political tension, the large withdrawals of gold, and the continued heavy fall on the Stock Exchange, indicated the approach of a storm, and, as we all know, a financial tornado burst on the 31st July, when the Bank of England rate was raised to 8 per cent, followed next day by a further rise to 10 per cent, and when the Stock Exchange was closed – an incident unparalleled in the history of this country. The situation, however, was at once taken in hand by the Government, assisted by the Bank of England, and the leading banking, financial and commercial authorities; and it was a fortunate circumstance that the Bank Holiday coming on the next Monday enabled the prolonged week-end to be made good use of. Before general business was resumed, an issue of paper currency had been arranged, the proclamation of a partial moratorium affecting bills of exchange had been declared, and the Bank Holiday was extended to the end of that week, by which time a general moratorium was in force. These unprecedented measures were, I think I may safely say, the salvation of the financial situation – (*hear, hear*) – and were absolutely necessary to maintain confidence, and to save the national credit from disaster. It is difficult to exaggerate the debt of gratitude owed by the financial and commercial interests, and by the nation generally, to the Government, to the Bank of England, and to those men of banking and mercantile experience and capacity who assisted, by their advice and co-operation, in evolving and bringing into effect the emergency measures referred to. (*Hear, hear.*) The success of those measures has been shown by their results . . .[2]

Mendl might have added that it was not only the various measures taken immediately before and after the declaration of war that saved the City's bacon, but also certain key decisions in the weeks and months following – above all, an extended moratorium and direct government assistance to the bill market, the accepting houses and the Stock Exchange, the latter of which stayed closed until the beginning of 1915.[3] Mendl's account was entirely authentic, however, in reproducing the City's self-congratulatory tone. It had apparently been a miracle on Lombard Street. 'While our Fleet keeps the trade routes clear,' the *Financial Times* applauded ten days into the war, 'the London Money Market, thanks to wise statesmanship, has been enabled to resume its accustomed function of granting credits, which is as indispensable as a safe sea passage to the smooth carrying on of our commerce.' Once again, the pink paper asserted, 'the Government and the leaders of the English banking world' had 'demonstrated their capacity for tackling boldly and effectively a national emergency'.[4]

Yet all was not really so smooth, Whiggish and morally uplifting. 'Business resumed,' Sir Charles Addis of the Hongkong and Shanghai

Bank noted in his diary on Friday, 7 August. 'An anxious day. Upon the whole it passed off quietly but men's hearts are full of doubt and fear and much is still obscure.' A few years later the bill broker Fred Gillett recalled that same day as one 'of the blackest gloom':

> Even the light hearted Gaggs saw no gleam of sunshine anywhere, he openly stated we were all ruined & spent a great part of the day hunting through the mass of securities he keeps in our safe to see if by chance he had passed over an unpaid coupon, to his intense joy he at last discovered one for 12/6; he reminded me of a sitting hen, coming late to the evening meal & scratching over the chopped straw in the hope of finding a grain of corn that had been missed. Mr B.S. [presumably a client] came in to see us, he had reached the very depths & informed us that all he saw in the future was a Pension at Lausanne.

A fortnight later, on the 21st, the stockbroker Paul Nelke candidly informed the Stock Exchange Committee that 'he had always traded on credit' and that 'he was a rich man on the 1st July but what he was now he could not say'. As for those closer to *haute finance*, Patrick Shaw-Stewart of Barings told a friend the same day that 'if you saw the length of the faces of those who know, you would realise this is one of the most terrific things London has been up against since finance existed'. Not just up against it but apparently cracking, to judge by the verdict of the Prime Minister, Asquith, on the City's leaders during the early weeks of the war: 'the greatest ninnies I ever had to tackle', in 'a state of funk like old women chattering over tea-cups in a Cathedral town'. Or, as Asquith's Chancellor of the Exchequer, Lloyd George, put it more mildly, 'financiers in a fright do not make an heroic picture'.[5]

Nor was the story of loss and redemption necessarily such a national triumph. 'I wish we could have got a more substantial *quid pro quo* from the bankers than the mere assurance of co-operation,' Sir John Bradbury of the Treasury wrote to the former Chancellor Austen Chamberlain on 13 August, implicitly criticising Lloyd George. Chamberlain himself added some revealing flesh in his diary that same day:

> The Chancellor explained to the representatives of the great accepting houses, to the bankers, and to the traders, his proposals in regard to the purchase of Bills by the Bank of England. He appeared to announce these as a decision already taken by the Treasury in conjunction with the Bank. At a late period of the sitting Lord Mersey [a Conservative with strong links with northern industry] protested vehemently against the release of the banks and holders from all liability, but it appeared to me that it was then too late to consider the matter, as the offer had already been made by the Chancellor to the parties concerned and accepted by them. It was

undoubtedly more favourable than any of them expected, and I think the
Chancellor went too far.[6]

Moreover, already looming on the horizon was the question of whether
the general moratorium, due to expire on 4 September and by which
payments arising out of contracts made before 4 August could be
postponed, should be renewed.[7] Questionnaires were sent out on the
19th to the nation's men of commerce and within a week 8,256 returns
had been received – 3,603 pronounced in favour of an extension, 4,653
against. Behind this vote lay a stark City/industry divide: whereas 78 out
of 81 London bankers were in favour of continuing the moratorium, and
157 out of 227 London export merchants likewise, only 973 out of
2,897 provincial manufacturers felt the same. Lloyd George chose to side
with the minority, explaining that 'the opinion, and an emphatic
opinion, was expressed, that to bring the moratorium abruptly to an end
might produce disaster, and we came to the conclusion that we would
prolong it for at least another month'. As the City's elder statesman,
Lord ('Natty') Rothschild, was honest enough to concede, in a memorandum written on 25 August for government consumption, 'the continuance of the moratorium in its present shape is for the moment very
convenient for a good many people'.[8] A good many people, but few of
them outside the square mile.

Significantly, many of those voting against the extension of the
moratorium gave as a reason that it had been abused by the banks. One
way and another it was the joint-stock clearing bankers – still for the
most part regarded as outsiders by the City, and indeed by the wider
Establishment – who took most of the flak during the crisis as a whole.
On 5 August, at one of the high-level conferences held at the Treasury,
the question arose of establishing a small plenary committee to arbitrate
over the working of Treasury notes, which were about to be issued. The
concern was that no bank should issue an excessive amount of these
notes in order to make profits out of advances at a high rate of interest.
The proposal was put forward that this committee should include two
bankers chosen from among themselves. With the bankers temporarily
out of the room, the Governor of the Bank of England, Walter Cunliffe,
was asked how many clearing banks there were: 'sixteen or eighteen', he
replied, 'but there is such jealousy amongst them that they would not
tolerate that.' The following morning he accused the bankers of hoarding
gold, a charge hotly denied.

Over the ensuing weeks the joint-stock men were attacked from within
and without the City, mainly on the grounds of their unwillingness to
help traders and manufacturers in what was, all agreed, an intensely

difficult situation. 'They do not seem to me to be playing the game on the evidence that we have got,' Edwin Montagu, Financial Secretary to the Treasury, told Lloyd George on the 15th. 'They had been treated with great liberality. They will probably make large profits during the war, and I think we have a right to expect more from them than they seem willing to do.' Morgan Grenfell's Teddy Grenfell, filling out his questionnaire soon afterwards, agreed: 'In my opinion the Banks which have been given protection as regards their portfolios, by the government, have not, in certain cases, given proper facilities as before the war, to merchants to encourage imports and finance exports, by which alone the food supply, foreign exchanges and general trade can be restored.' And on 26 August, in the Commons, Lloyd George himself declared flatly that 'some banks had not behaved well, and I think that it is better that that should be said'.[9]

Lloyd George spoke thus despite having heard two days earlier a strong plea of self-defence by the joint-stock banker *par excellence*, Sir Edward Holden, that remarkable self-made Lancastrian, now Chairman of the giant London City & Midland Bank:

> What I find is this. As I said here [i.e. at the Treasury] before, there is nobody so much in industry proper as I am. I am in it right up to the neck in all parts. Now, you have this condition of affairs, that there must be some contraction in the industry ... Whatever you do you cannot get the same level of business at the present moment that you had before the war ... I think we bankers may fairly claim, although we have had a severe criticism levelled against us, that we have, to a very large extent, done the very best we could. Speaking for myself, I know I have done the best I could.

And a little later there had been an interesting exchange:

> *Holden:* If the State came in and forced the Banks to lend a lot of money wrongfully then it must take the responsibility.
> *Lloyd George:* It takes the responsibility and also the control.
> *Holden:* We do not mind that so long as it takes the responsibility.[10]

Proper bankerly caution, no doubt, but Holden could not honestly have denied the charge, made not only by Cunliffe, that they were excessively divided amongst themselves. Traditionally Holden's great rival was Sir Felix Schuster of the Union of London and Smiths Bank, but he also kept a watchful eye on Henry Bell, General Manager of Lloyds. On 24 September Holden wrote a memorandum describing the previous day's

meeting at the Treasury to discuss extending the moratorium for yet
another month:

> I think Bell is nervous. I shall never forget him on that Sunday night [i.e.
> 2 August?]. He wants to be the Big Bank, and to come from under the
> Moratorium, yet he was the one who started it, and said he thought we had
> better go under the Moratorium for another month ... Then Schuster ran
> another hare, and that was the bills. He wanted all bills due on the 4th
> October extended for another month ... Then Cunliffe, who was at the
> top of the table, broke in and said 'What for?' 'What sort of bills do you
> mean?' Now Cunliffe is a very wily old man. He waits for you and when he
> sees a weak point in your argument he goes for it. When he attacks you you
> must always expect that he has found a weak point somewhere. He said
> 'What kind of bills are you talking about?' Well, he [i.e. Schuster] tumbled
> about and then had to come to the point, and it seems that they were
> Jewellers' Bills, that is to say the Amsterdam Diamond Bills at his Holborn
> Circus Branch. He could not, of course, go into the Bank of England with
> these as they were not approved acceptors in the sense of the class included
> in the Bank's offer. Therefore he wanted to get in here ...

Later in the memorandum, Holden noted how, speaking to Schuster and
the others, he had referred to 'Huth Jackson and that other gang round
the table of the Bank of England who have put the Chancellor in their
pocket'.[11] Enemies to his back, enemies to his front, by now Holden was
used to playing a lone hand, albeit with considerable financial resources
at his command.

*

For the 'very wily old man' in charge of the usually stolid rather than
guileful Old Lady, the crisis was his finest hour. Cunliffe had become
Governor of the Bank of England in 1913 and, as Grenfell (himself a
director) observed a few years later, 'as promotion is often by seniority
the Bank might very likely have had a brewer or wine merchant who in
ordinary times as governor could have quite well filled the place'. By
happy chance, however, in Cunliffe it had a Governor who 'had an
intimate knowledge of banking, bill broking, Stock Ex, accepting &
though not the greatest expert in all, yet he combined the knowledge of
all these spheres of finance to an unique degree'. He also had, Grenfell
went on, a 'wonderful physique enabling him to work as few younger
men could do'. Against that, 'he had no gift of public speaking, was
always at a loss for words, had very bad manners & suspected everyone
who differed with him, of having ulterior motives'. And, Grenfell added,

'he was rude & abrupt with his colleagues, the bankers & the ministers'. The main minister, on a day-to-day basis, was of course Lloyd George, and these two very different men got on far better than might have been expected. The loquacious Welshman's *War Memoirs* include an affectionate passage concerning Cunliffe:

> His sense of humour, which he concealed under a dour almost surly countenance, was an encouragement in those trying days. He was fond of little practical jokes to lighten the dismal anxieties of our common burden. He affected a deep resentment at our issuing the £1 notes as Treasury and not Bank of England Notes. He scoffed at the inferiority of our issue in the quality of its paper and its artistry as compared with the crisp £5 note of the Great Bank over which he presided. I can see his impressive figure with its rolling gait, coming one morning through the door of the Treasury Board Room. He had a scornful look on his face. He came up to my desk with a mumbled greeting, solemnly opened the portfolio he always carried, and pulled out a bedraggled £1 Treasury Note, dirty and barely legible. He said: 'Look at that. It came into the Bank yesterday in that condition. I told you the paper was no good – far better to have left it to us.' He had scrubbed the note in order to reduce it to this condition of effacement for the pleasure of ragging me. I told him so and he laughed. His manner was not propitiatory to strangers, but when you got to know him he was a genial, kindly man, and I liked him. I relied on his shrewdness, his common sense and instinct.

In the contemporary record of the crisis one sees Cunliffe in occasional but effective action, as when on 5 August he told a doubtful Bradbury that 'the best way to avoid a panic is to meet the situation like lions'. Presumably Asquith did not count this ultimate City man – pragmatic, inarticulate, relying on force of character allied to rank – as one of the ninnies. In early November, with almost all aspects of the crisis resolved and following a meeting about the imminent issue of a War Loan, he confided to Venetia Stanley:

> I like the Governor – a regular John Bull of the farmer type, but wonderfully shrewd & level-headed. When the others had gone, I told him (he is called Cunliffe) that the King had agreed to give him a peerage, and that I proposed to announce it at the Guildhall on Monday. He was not the least *émotionné* & simply said – 'Well, I obey orders'.[12]

CHAPTER TWO

Firing She££s

'Yes, we had to fight. But what a hateful necessity. I suppose Germany,
our best customer, will be beaten. And what then?' Addis, thinking City
man, asked the question on 9 August 1914 and found no comfort: 'A
hateful war. Even victory is only *less* hateful than defeat and *less* hurtful.
But hurtful and hateful our victory must be. After all Germany stands for
a great deal of what is best in civilisation. If she is wiped out the damage
moral and intellectual as well as economic will be enormous.' Independent thought rarely flourishes in wartime, and just over nine months later,
on 21 May 1915, unthinking City man spoke after the *Daily Mail* – no
less – had launched an attack on Lord Kitchener's conduct of the war.
The Stock Exchange's acknowledged tribune, the veteran jobber Charlie
Clarke, mounted a bench in the Grand Trunk market and submitted a
resolution expressing the House's confidence and indignation. 'The
resolution was carried with enthusiasm, and cheers were given for Lord
Kitchener, after which the ceremony of burning a copy of the "Daily
Mail" was carried out.' But whether thinking or unthinking, averagely
patriotic or super-patriotic, almost all the City men who stayed behind,
for one reason or another, shared a heaviness of heart as events
unfolded. Like everyone else they wanted it to end; like everyone else
they had no idea when it would. But as Gaspard Farrer of Barings put it
in the conflict's early days, 'how trivial our little City worries are
compared to our anxieties about the war and all those immediately
engaged in it'.[1]

Looked at in a more detached light, the First World War was the
worst thing that ever happened to the City of London. 'We cannot yet
reckon up losses,' wrote Maynard Keynes in the immediate aftermath of
the August 1914 financial crisis. 'I do not believe that anything has yet
occurred to derogate from the international position of London. Many
things will be done differently in the future, but no seeds of grass have
yet been sown in the City's streets.' He was wrong, for over the
following four years not only did Britain have to liquidate some 15 per
cent of its overseas investments in order to finance the war, but London's

position as the world's leading international financial centre was decisively eroded. The *de facto* suspension of the pound's convertibility, amidst an array of wartime regulations, in effect meant that Britain was no longer on the gold standard and sterling no longer globally pre-eminent; this in turn weakened sterling as the currency, and the City as the provider, of international trade finance; while as an international capital market, after a century of largesse, London was badly hit by a mixture of government restrictions and severe practical difficulties concerning transfers and remittances. Instead the baton, which London had once assumed from Amsterdam, now passed to New York. The international clout of that financial centre had been markedly on the increase since the turn of the century, but almost three years of American neutrality gave it a huge push, further enhanced by the dependence of the Allies on the United States for much of their wartime finance and supplies. The conditions were apparently ripe for the US to become, in the words of one American politician, 'the dominant financial power of the world and to extend our trade to every part of the world'.[2]

Just as unwelcome, and more immediate in its impact, was the omnipresent reality of government control over a wide range of the City's activities.[3] 'I do not think,' Farrer briefed a Kidder Peabody partner in Boston in March 1915, 'we have ever told you how Treasury-ridden we are in these days. No fresh loan can be made, and not even a renewal of an old loan carried out, without permission of the Government.' That old warhorse W.R. Lawson, journalist and Stock Exchange member, complained soon afterwards to the London Chamber of Commerce that 'the Stock Exchange was living under a system of Treasury tutelage'. There were, from a functional point of view, two particularly keen aspects to this enforced subordination. One was the existence from early 1915 of a Treasury-run Capital Issues Committee that soon took an increasingly negative attitude to applications for new issues, especially foreign ones. The other was the way in which the domestic money market (or discount market) lost much of its freedom of action, coming under government sway exercised through an arguably reluctant, but certainly obedient Bank of England. The crux was the system adopted from April 1915, by which Treasury bills were offered on 'tap' in such a way that the rate on these bills effectively replaced Bank rate as the arbiter of short-term interest rates. The market – perhaps short-sightedly – blamed the Bank rather than the Treasury. 'The rates may be altered daily & leaves the market completely in the hands of the Bank,' noted the bill brokers Smith, St Aubyn & Co on day one. And at the end of September 1915: 'The worst quarter we have had for many years. All caused by Cunliffe's money corner . . .' Yet for Cunliffe himself, in his fastness in Threadneedle Street but daily attending his masters in Whitehall, war had its difficulties. 'I remember Lord Cunliffe saying to me during the first few days of the war that while the war lasted the Bank would have to regard itself as a department of the Treasury,' recalled Bradbury years later.[4] Unfortunately, even for a lion – especially for a lion – this was easier said than done.

*

Four years of often fraught war finance began in a serious way in November 1914 with the first War Loan, for £350m at $3\frac{1}{2}$ per cent.[5] Holden, convalescing in Bournemouth, was unable to attend the key preliminary meetings; but his number two, Samuel Murray, kept him posted about what his rivals were up to, writing on the 12th:

> Mr Bell asked me at seven o'clock tonight to go over and see him. He told me they had just come back from seeing the Chancellor . . . The Chancellor enquired what amounts would the Banks undertake to subscribe for if necessary, and he said he expected the Banks would come down handsomely. He was told by one or two that they were quite unable to answer such a question right away and he jokingly said 'if you cannot answer for yourselves, perhaps you can answer for one another' . . . Mr Bell said that he was practically asking what the Banks would underwrite but nothing was said one way or another about remuneration.
>
> Mr Bell stated further that after leaving the Chancellor, the Bankers had a few words together. Leaf [Walter Leaf, Chairman of London County & Westminster] said that his Bank would take 5 millions but nobody else made any statement. Bell has since spoken to Mr Vassar Smith [his Chairman at Lloyds] and the latter suggested that they should think over during the night the question of whether Lloyds could say 5 millions, Bell taking the view with his Chairman that they ought not to mention anything like so large a figure.

Next day, through a series of wires, Holden persuaded the leading joint-stock men in London to take the line to Lloyd George that it would be better for the government to borrow on Treasury notes at 4 per cent; but at the decisive meeting that evening, Lloyd George privately consulted Cunliffe and then returned to the room to tell the bankers that (in Bell's words, as reported to Holden) 'the proposal for the finance to be done through the Treasury Note could not be agreed to as the Governor had pointed out an objection which was quite fatal, and that was that the

Bank of England would lose control over the rate'. At which point, according to Bell, everyone else gave in to Cunliffe.[6]

The loan was issued on the 17th, and six days later Lord St Aldwyn, former Chancellor of the Exchequer and now Chairman of the Committee of the London Clearing Bankers, offered a typically sardonic commentary:

> The newspapers have puffed it, as subscribed over and over again, etc. I don't believe this – and shall be quite content if it is well covered, when the result comes out. If it isn't, the Banks will have to do more. They adopted my suggestion of each subscribing a percentage of their deposits – and, with some difficulty, I squeezed them up to 10 p.c. for the Clearing Banks. Holden was amusing. His proportion wasn't quite as much as Lloyds' on the figures: but when Lloyds named their amount, he insisted on going for the same!

In the event the loan was undersubscribed, and the Bank of England felt impelled to step in and underwrite an additional £113m in addition to its original £40m, a decision taken by Cunliffe without troubling to consult his colleagues. As for Holden, at the bank's annual meeting two months later he had a good story to tell about how Midland had subscribed £10m: 'Under ordinary circumstances we should never have dreamt of taking such a large amount, but under the extraordinary circumstances of the war, it was our duty, as it is the duty of everyone, to show patriotism by making sacrifices. True, it will increase our profits, but we always contend that profits are not of the first importance in the administration of a bank.'[7]

For the City's merchant banks, involvement in high-level wartime finance was the prerogative of only a few. In particular the 'German' houses – above all Schröders, Kleinworts and Huths – were not only intrinsically suspect, but in such a parlous state that they were simply regarded as being out of the frame.[8] 'Houses trading with the Continent,' noted Teddy Grenfell as early as 7 August 1914, 'are in an awful position as remittances cannot come during the war', and those firms with a large accepting exposure to German and Austrian clients found that it was all they could do to repay the interest on their large, life-saving loans from the Bank of England. Rothschilds had no such problems – either ethnic or financial – but was equally out of the frame. Natty died in 1915 and his brothers Leo and Alfred in 1917 and 1918 respectively. 'A nice old boy' who 'required time to think, but in due course usually came forward with some sagacious proposal' was how Lloyd George described his old adversary, after attending Natty's funeral on Good Friday 1915. Natty's younger son Charles now became senior partner, against the wishes of his uncles, but the following year his own health gave way and he spent most of the rest of the war recovering in Switzerland. And, as Grenfell later noted, albeit with some exaggeration, the firm on Natty's death 'became of no a/c'.[9]

It was, however, a quite different story for Morgan Grenfell and Barings, both of which undertook a large amount of profitable as well as prestigious work on behalf of Allied governments. In January 1915 the British government signed the Commercial Agency Agreement with J.P. Morgan & Co, by which Morgans in New York acted as purchasing agent in the US for Britain and her allies. The inevitable go-between, mediating between the British government and J.P. Morgan, was Morgan Grenfell in London, a role that greatly enhanced its already high standing.[10] Over at 8 Bishopsgate, Barings continued, as it had done for so long, to service the needs of the Russian government. In the first year of the war it organised no fewer than four loans or credits, totalling £75m, and in the autumn of 1915 was involved in thrashing out a £300m, twelve-month facility somewhat reluctantly given by the British government. In fact the Treasury tried to squeeze Lord Revelstoke (senior partner of Barings) out of the transaction, but with Russian help Revelstoke was able to claw his way back in. 'The Treasury is inevitably unfamiliar with the details of banking arrangements,' Bradbury admitted to Revelstoke following a Treasury blunder over the details. Revelstoke's reply was graciousness itself: 'I am fully cognizant of the difficulties which attach to your desire to secure a closer control over advances, and I trust that in future the Treasury will not hesitate to let us know if at any time we may be so fortunate as to be able to be of any service to them.'[11]

By then much had happened in the home sphere of *haute finance*, although in the early months of 1915 Cunliffe continued to forge an effective axis with Lloyd George. 'His natural tendency to silence has been a good foil to the verbosity of the Chancellor,' Grenfell observed in January. 'They not only work well together but like each other.' And he added, following a recent conversation with Asquith, that the Prime Minister 'rightly put Walter Cunliffe very high'. A few days later Holden implicitly criticised the Bank of England when he told his shareholders that 'it is not too late to form a committee of the best practical financial men to be found in the City of London' and that 'this committee should sit constantly and should watch financial questions from every point of view'. But for the moment his close peacetime relations with the Liberal government seemed to count for nothing. Cunliffe and Lloyd George spent much of the first week of February together in Paris, at a major conference on Allied finance, and their relationship was further cemented. On his return Lloyd George 'spoke highly' of the Governor to a crony: 'His manner is unfortunate, but his advice good. When any proposal was made which L.G. thought doubtful, he turned to Cunliffe and asked his opinion. If he replied, "I don't like it", L.G. knew that it could not be accepted and acted accordingly.' Or, as Lloyd George himself recalled in his *War Memoirs*, 'when a question arose as to a transhipment of gold the Governor of the Bank of France expressed himself with great fluency. I then said: "The Governor of the Bank of England will state the British view on the subject". He rose slowly, and after a few preliminary puffs ['grunts', according to another account] he said: "We do not mean to part with our gold", and then subsided into his seat.'[12]

On the same visit Cunliffe declined to accompany Lloyd George on a visit to Béthune, which was under occasional bombardment: 'He said: "A predecessor of mine [Michael Godfrey, Deputy Governor, in 1695] was killed visiting the trenches at Namur. But he was there on business with the King, and the City said, 'Poor fellow!' but if I were hit in the stomach at Béthune they would all say, 'D—d fool – what business has he to go there?'".' Soon afterwards Cunliffe got rid of his own deputy, the port-wine merchant R.L. Newman, on the justifiable grounds of incompetence, and replaced him with the unexciting but efficient Brien Cokayne of the merchant bank Antony Gibbs. But by May, unfortunately for Cunliffe, the plates began to shift under his feet, with the war going increasingly badly and a major government reshuffle becoming inevitable. Lloyd George was interrupted in his shaving on the 20th by his maid, who told him that the Governor was downstairs wanting to see him. 'I went down. The old boy blundered out, "I hear they want you to leave the Treasury. We cannot let you go!" and then he quite broke down, and the tears trickled down his cheeks.' Lloyd George gently explained that Cunliffe must go to see the Prime Minister about the matter, and Asquith subsequently related the outcome. 'I couldn't get anything out of him, except "We don't want to lose our man! Don't take our man away from us!"'[13] It was to no avail, for a week later Reginald McKenna replaced Lloyd George as Chancellor.

The new man was in his early fifties and, before the war, had won the City's respect by carrying through the Dreadnought programme while at the Admiralty. 'It is said that McKenna owes his present position to the fact that he is an illegitimate son of Sir C. Dilke,' noted a Tory backwoodsman in 1910. 'Probably a mere fable, but it is difficult to explain advancement of such a very third rate man.' Margot Asquith found him 'cocky and cocksure to an irritating degree', but her daughter-in-law Cynthia liked him on the grounds that 'he is such a "Sunny Jim" and ripples on so easily'. Balfour would privately dismiss him as 'an able accountant', but Beaverbrook gave a rather more measured assessment: 'What is McKenna's character and nature? His abilities are brilliant and his logic remorseless. He is angular, emphatic, and positive. He likes to assert his view, and if you run against some projecting hump in his opinions you must merely nurse a bruise.'[14]

Unsurprisingly, McKenna proved reluctant to accept the disciplines of a learning curve. 'As regards Finance,' Grenfell wrote to Jack Morgan in August, 'undoubtedly McKenna is a very ignorant man and at first was inclined to try to appear wise.' By then Chancellor and Governor were at loggerheads. In late July Asquith sought to mediate, telling McKenna that Cunliffe had 'rendered us invaluable service during the past year' and that, though 'he has (like most people) limitations of outlook and faults of temper', his 'deliberate judgement' was 'always well worth taking into account' and that he was 'perfectly straight'. Asquith added that Cunliffe had expressed to him his wish to resign, on the basis that McKenna 'had lost confidence in him and in his judgement, and found cooperation with him difficult'. Things deteriorated still further during the rest of the year. On the one hand, McKenna was not really on top of his job ('he has a lot to learn, and we none of us can afford the time to teach him', Grenfell observed); on the other, Cunliffe was 'thoroughly overdone' and at one point went down with jaundice (diagnosed by Grenfell as 'the result of the strain of the last two years and partly I think the neglect of his teeth which have poisoned his system through inability to spare a few hours in time with the Dentist'). McKenna would, according to Beaverbrook's account, 'frequently urge Cunliffe the necessity of providing more bank balances for the government in the United States', to which Cunliffe 'would reply invariably, "Mr Chancellor, this is a matter of exchange, and the responsibility here lies with me"'.[15] Treasury/Bank relations had not been so strained since the days of Harcourt, another acerbic Liberal Chancellor.

The reference to the US and exchange was significant, for in the context of massive imports from America to Britain, the financial authorities in London faced an increasingly strenuous battle to maintain New York's confidence in sterling and thereby keep up the rate of exchange. The role of Morgans, on both sides of the Atlantic, was obviously crucial, but the London partners found it a frustrating experience. The politically incorrect Grenfell, in a section entitled

'Exchange Fall' from his invaluable retrospective notes, described the immediate outcome:

> The large purchases in USA of munitions, caused Sterling Exc^h to reach 4.47 Aug 1915 [having been £1 = \$4.86 prior to the war]. ECG [Grenfell] had made vigorous attempts since Feb & especially July to get governm^t to pay some attention to matter. Although ECG saw PM Asquith, L George, Grey & others they evidently thought him alarmist & paid little attention. It then became clear that the gov^t felt that they could do better without Morgans & in the autumn sent a mission Ld Reading [the former Sir Rufus Isaacs], Sir Edw Holden (of the Midland B^k), Babington Smith and Blackett of the Treasury to USA. Reading being a Jew & Holden being a cad & very tactless, were not happy choices. Holden conceived the idea that the proper way to treat Americans from whom he wished to borrow, was to insult them. He disliked Morgans & was very rude to them, trying to deal with others. This he found impossible & with great difficulty JPM & Co raised an Anglo-French 5 per cent loan for \$500,000,000m. JPM & Co took no remuneration.
>
> On their return Reading expressed his great thanks to Morgan but Holden strutted round telling the bankers how he had hoodwinked the Yankee & beat Morgan. Holden stated before his departing that he would be made a peer on his return but his conduct was such that he did not receive this reward!

It was probably a broadly accurate, if exaggerated account. Certainly Grenfell and his partners suffered from a growing dislike of undue American influence. 'Davison has a pleasant manner and a pleasant face, but he fills both John [Revelstoke] and myself with distrust,' Farrer wrote in early July after a visit from one of Morgans' New York partners. 'He is very clever, a real artist in exposition, and I should not be surprised to find that he completely got the best of our Government officials.' McKenna shared these suspicions, prompting Asquith to tell him later in the month that 'in regard to Morgans, while I do not doubt that they have made and will continue to make all that they can out of us, I see no reason to think that they have been acting unfairly, still less treacherously'. As to the presence of Midland's chief on the Reading Mission, Grenfell's explanation soon afterwards to New York was simple: 'Our Ministers and Officials are so frightened of an outcry against the Morgans influence that the Treasury, looking round for fresh advice, pitched on this man Holden. Our Joint Stock Banks are strong financially, but apparently run by small men and they have permitted this fellow Holden to get an ascendancy over them, and when the Treasury turned to the Joint Stock Banks for advice Holden put himself forward and got himself sent out to your side.' Moreover, if Holden did indeed strut around on his return, he was probably not justified in doing so. 'A real bad bargain,' Smith St Aubyn noted on 29 September, the day after the terms were announced; while, according to the most recent study of the mission, Reading and Blackett wanted to explore the possibility of securing a US dollar credit to supplement the loan, which would clearly by itself not meet the needs of the Allies, but were prevented from doing so by Holden's 'violent opposition'.[16] So masterful in pushing through bank amalgamations, Holden was perhaps less attuned to the delicacies of international finance.

These were difficult times for both antagonists, whatever their bravado. On 1 November Holden was compelled to address a meeting of members of the discount market, held at Union Discount, where (in Smith St Aubyn's words) he 'defended the action of giving such apparently high terms for the Anglo French Loan in the States'. A fortnight earlier, taking advantage of Holden's absence, Cunliffe had complained to a meeting of not unsympathetic clearers about the conduct of the financial situation. St Aldwyn privately reported the gist: 'McKenna turns for advice to Mr Keynes, who is held in the City to be a most untrustworthy adviser . . . the Governor's advice is not followed, and hardly even asked . . . Questions are in the air as to the future position of the Bank of England and its relations with the government . . .' Elsewhere in the City, however, patience with Cunliffe was starting to run out. The Smith St Aubyn diary, usually confined to sparse entries about market movements, burst into life on three successive days:

23 *November*. Minimum prices abolished for Consols, Colonials, Corporations & Foreign Stocks, whereby the bottom has of course fallen out of them. This masterpiece of finance is fittingly accompanied by sinister rumours of fresh monkeying with money by his 'Holiness', the Governor of the Bank.

24 *November*. Another charming Pin Prick from Cunliffe of the Bank. All the Clearing Banks have been ordered to charge $4\frac{1}{2}$ for call, notice & evening money, with what object is not clear except that Cunliffe hopes to get more money from the Banks at $4\frac{1}{2}$ to lend to the Government at 5 per cent. Of course this departure can have no effect on the American Exchange . . .

25 *November*. The 'Ukase' of Cunliffe came into force today . . . nothing can be done as we are simply dominated by a self constituted autocrat of very bourgeois type and the Banks crawl before him abjectly.

The next day Grenfell wrote to Jack Morgan: 'Cunliffe is getting very unpopular which helps Holden. Vivian [Grenfell's partner, Vivian Hugh Smith] saw Walter when I had the grippe last week and vows he will never go near him again, the same with Eric Hambro and Kindersley [of Lazards].' Nevertheless, if by the end of 1915 the City Establishment was finding the bullying Cunliffe insupportable, there was a limit to how much this was a 'help' to Holden. Almost certainly it was he to whom Revelstoke referred in a letter the following year, fielding an enquiry from the diplomat Sir Arthur Nicolson: 'I am not sure that you would be happy on the board. The chairman is an energetic individual of a coarse fibre. Badly bred, in fact, and not easy to work with. He is unpopular in City circles, and seems to have quarrelled with most of the personalities with whom he comes into contact. He has ability, but an unfortunate manner in its exercise.'[17] In short, neither Cunliffe's nor Holden's face fitted.

By November 1915 it was clear to everyone – whatever the jealousies and personal discord – that a new, more systematic approach to the financing of supplies from America was required. Accordingly, on the 18th McKenna appointed what soon became known as the London Exchange Committee, whose purpose was to ensure as favourable an exchange as possible, and which was empowered to take under its control all available gold as well as foreign currency and the proceeds of securities liquidated on foreign markets.[18] Its four members were Cunliffe, Cokayne, Holden and Schuster, and it was to be aided by a sub-committee of four foreign-exchange men, one each from London County & Westminster, Brown Shipley, Lloyds and London City & Midland. The main committee met at the Bank of England, but on the 29th the question was discussed of an office outside the Bank for the sub-committee's use, with its books, letters and so on to be kept at that office. However, this was 'a point which Lord Cunliffe stated that he was unable to concede as the business was Government business and the books should therefore be kept at the Bank'. Next day he added that he saw the sub-committee 'merely acting as an expert advisory Committee', to which Holden countered that, 'conducted in this manner, the business would be a fiasco and that Gold would continue to go out'. Having apparently been responsible for ensuring that the new body be given unprecedentedly wide powers, Holden now found himself in the frustrating position of not being able to use them, and on 3 December he wrote to Cunliffe that 'I cannot myself believe, as the Bank of England is the free Market for Gold, that it is wise for it to begin dealing in Foreign Exchange'. But, 'as you appear to have decided otherwise, which course in my opinion will result in failure and in losing our Gold, I am at a loss what to do'. Within a few weeks Holden had more or less stopped attending the London Exchange Committee's meetings, as it became clear that Cunliffe was determined to run the show, for all his protestations that 'as the Bankers' money was being used they had a right to know the method by which it was being used'.[19]

Cunliffe, recovering from jaundice, was not at the Bank on 1 January 1916 when one of his directors, Montagu Norman, spent his first day there since terminating his partnership with the merchant bank Brown Shipley. 'Free man today,' his diary recorded. Subsequently the firm's senior partner, writing to Brown Brothers in New York, put this departure in context:

> The functions of the London Office have been mainly in connection with credits, exchange and banking operations generally, as distinct from securities business. You will recall the many discussions which have taken place from time to time upon this subject, particularly those of the Spring of 1914 ... The principal point then before the House was whether the acceptance business should be entirely abandoned or to a great extent curtailed in favour of a security business on this side. We shall be within your recollection by remarking that Mr Norman urged a virtual adoption of the former course, but the consensus of opinion was against him ...

The outbreak of war merely delayed Norman's decision to leave Brown Shipley, and for most of the time before he finally did so he was working at the War Office, not in Founders' Court. On the sixth day of his freedom he received a welcome letter from Cunliffe's deputy, Cokayne, asking if Norman would 'be so kind as to come, regularly, and "devil" for me'. Cokayne added helpfully that 'it appears to be quite understood in the City that you have left your firm to devote yourself to public work, and if you come and help me here your action will be more "intelligible" still'. Norman replied gratefully – 'I shall try to be, or to become, your willing and cheerful fag' – and soon, having hitherto been only an irregular attender at Threadneedle Street, had his feet under his desk at the Bank. It was just a shame about the Governor. 'There goes that queer-looking fish with the ginger beard again,' Cunliffe once said loudly on passing Norman in a corridor. 'Do you know who he is? I keep seeing him creeping about this place like a lost soul with nothing better to do.'[20] Now at long last, in his mid-forties, Norman did have something in which to immerse himself.

Soon afterwards Benjamin Strong, Governor of the recently established Federal Reserve Bank of New York, paid a longish visit to London with a view to establishing closer Anglo-American financial relations.

Apparently the initiative was his, not the Bank of England's, but inevitably he would have to meet Cunliffe. Grenfell made an appointment, as well as preparing the ground. 'He tells me that Lord Cunliffe is very reserved, diffident, but nevertheless quite positive in his views,' Strong noted in his diary on 13 March. The following afternoon the two men met. 'Lord Cunliffe impressed me most favourably, relishes a joke, and likes to make one. He joshed me when I came in and . . . wanted to know why I had not let him know in advance of my coming over.' Strong then explained his scheme for more intimate co-operation in exchange matters, especially over gold shipments. Cunliffe asked for a little time to think about it. That evening Strong dined with Holden and a select group of City editors whom he had invited. 'On Sir Edward's invitation the meeting developed into a general "quiz" party – everybody asking questions. The last speaker, Mr Reeve [of the *Daily Telegraph*], made the astonishing suggestion (and I believe it was in all seriousness) that he believed it was a great mistake to have English speaking people separated into two political and financial organisations – that we ought to get under one roof again. That the Reserve Bank System was really the Bank of England . . .' And: 'This caused some amusement, but was roundly cheered. I did not find the gentlemen present at the dinner particularly well posted in regard to the American financial system.' A few evenings later Strong dined alone with Norman and then on the 21st took lunch with Cunliffe, who agreed to Strong's suggested arrangement. Towards the end, 'he emphasised again the fact that he was most anxious to conclude his term as Governor of the Bank'.

On the 24th the American was again at the Bank, consulting Padgett, 'Chief of the Bill Division', about the Bank's bill business. 'I asked him how they discriminated in the matter of finance bills. He said, that if he were to address that question to Lord Cunliffe he would say they could tell by the "smell".' Later that day, following a long session with Kitchener at the War Office, Strong dined with Huth Jackson and various prominent guests. Afterwards, in the library, his host 'told me a good many interesting incidents connected with the crisis here in 1914', causing Strong to reflect: 'There is no doubt but that these Englishmen are great fellows for criticising each other, but I constantly gain the impression that this is simply talk and when it comes to real business they generally get it done.' The 26th, a Sunday, he spent mostly with Norman, and the following morning he was at Barings, where he had 'a nice chat' with Revelstoke: 'Repeated my invariable story on the subject of American public opinion, with which he was polite enough to agree but subsequent discussion rather indicated that he, like the others, are rather skeptical of our good faith and protestations of good faith. He did not say this directly, but I thought his manner implied it a bit.'

Strong later called on Holden – 'Found him quite miserable. He is full of complaint about the Government . . .' – and then in the evening attended a Reform Club dinner full of City bigwigs. He heard there 'a good deal of criticism of the lack of flexibility in the English banking situation and apparently a growing desire to modify it so that the Bank of England would command a larger gold reserve', while 'after dinner a number of those present asked if some of the features of our new banking system were not applicable to the Bank of England'. On the 30th he was back at the Bank to make his farewells. He found Cunliffe 'just returned recently from a trip to Paris which he had made without anybody knowing it, and was in a frame of mind to criticise anything and everything the Banque de France did', accusing it of being 'distrustful' and generally uncooperative. Strong for his part was 'greatly amused at his humorous but expressive remarks about "the old bank". He admitted that the Bank of England was a museum, but that after all they could change when necessity required, whereas the Banque de France was much more a museum than the Bank of England and apparently did not have the capacity or courage to change.'[21]

Personal impressions aside, Strong's visit marked a turning-point in international central banking.[22] Prior to 1914 it had existed, and then only patchily, at times of crisis. Neither Cunliffe nor his predecessors would ever have dreamed of going abroad on Bank of England business. Now it was Strong who, in the circumstances of war, began to shape a dialogue; he and his new friend, Norman, were already implicitly looking ahead to a partnership in peacetime.

*

'Keep your eye on the prospects of the opening of the Dardanelles, for it will be an important point in connection with your Wheat, Barley and Oats operations,' Sir Archibald Williamson of Balfour Williamson instructed his man in Valparaiso in February 1915. For four years war was the ubiquitous fact of business life, benefiting some in the City and severely disadvantaging others. Sugar brokers, for example, virtually disappeared, as the government took early control of that particular commodity; but those dealing in timber enjoyed a three-year hiatus before the government moved in, and amidst high demand and sharply increasing prices there was plenty of profitable work. Rubber was another bull commodity, with firms like Lewis & Peat doing well.

Similarly, Antony Gibbs & Sons flourished through supplying Britain and her allies with nitrate of soda for munition purposes. Inevitably some attractive short-term gains were available. 'This firm has done very well indeed during the war,' a report for Kleinworts in February 1919 on the produce brokers Thornett & Fehr would note. 'They have speculated heavily in Tallow, Copra and Palm Oil which were all later commandeered by the Government, and Thornett, Fehr must have come out of the whole business with a very handsome profit.'[23]

Yet equally inevitably, especially with minimum prices operating for much of the period on the Stock Exchange, the day-to-day mood of the wartime City was generally downbeat. 'Conditions both as regards commercial business and the money market are entirely artificial,' Farrer observed in February 1915. And in September 1917: 'Business very quiet and getting quieter all the time. The City looks empty even in the streets and is deserted by three o'clock.' Of course, some of the low spirits were caused by the semi-permanent absence on war business of many of the City's leading figures. The energetic financier Jimmie Dunn announced as early as September 1914 that 'as financial business in London is for the time being at an end I must try and turn myself to the only business that can be done' – in his case making a more or less honest penny by supplying the British Army with horses from Canada. Or take the accountants Price, Waterhouse & Co, whose partners devoted so much time to government work that as many as five were knighted. Though they combined their work in various ministries with keeping the firm going at 3 Frederick's Place, they knew better than most that for the time being the City was no longer at the hub of the western world.[24]

Nevertheless, even in war the City could be a thrilling enough place, certainly to a youngster like William Winn, who began work there in about 1916:

A ship sailing downstream. A tug trailing a line of barges. Grim, weather-beaten warehouses yawning their black cadaverous welcome to the loads stuffed inside their jaws; the Tower of London in the background. On London Bridge, the crowd jostling along to the jingling of harness and the croaking of motor horns from omnibus and chugging taxi.

My regular route from bridge to office took me past the Monument, up Fish Street Hill, and thence along Eastcheap to St Dunstan's Hill. But when time permitted I would skip down the slimy stone stairway at the end of the bridge to teeming, smelly Billingsgate market: a tangle of swearing, side-stepping fish porters balancing boxes of marvellous-looking fish on their broad-brimmed flat leather hats. The boxes were loaded on to waiting wagons pulled by great Shire horses; their bulky-clad drivers, shoulders glistening with fish scales, perched high on small metal seats.

Unforgettable, the skilful street cleaners of London in those days: old and young men weaving among the traffic with pans and brushes to capture the steaming manure almost from under the horses' feet.

The office where I worked occupied the second floor of a narrow corner building facing a Wren church, St-Dunstan's-in-the-East.

'East India Merchants', inscribed in large black lettering on frosted glass panels in the main door, spoke of hot suns, warm oceans, minarets and jungles. The sign glamorised the flow of merchandise we traded in. Egg yolk and dried albumen imported from China, rare fruits in beautifully decorated pots and jars, fine teas, ivory, mica. Exports included shirtings, trouserings, gay cottons and threads; nails; consignments of corrugated iron; lead foil for lining tea chests; bicycles galore . . .

Office life was hectic; a last-minute bill of lading or insurance policy to collect, or a cable to code up and despatch. When work was finished, my thoughts would stray down river to Tilbury, where the great mailship which had claimed our day would be catching the ebb tide.

Every Thursday was 'Mail Day'. This notice, hanging outside the office door, leant importance and inviolability to a weekly event; 'No callers, No interruptions' was its message. For me it held the magic of 'tea money' – sixpence for the invariable two hours overtime up to eight o'clock, when the last registered letters and parcels of samples and late fees were handed over at Eastcheap post office just before it closed its doors . . .

From ABC to Chop-House, from sausage-and-mash and cups of tea to juicy grills and pints of porter, from shyness to confidence, I began slowly to win a grudging acceptance among men steeped in the subtleties of markets: custom, practice, contract; courage, success, failure.

To me, they were all the honourable upholders of the City I was so proud of . . .[25]

Winn was recalling these experiences three-quarters of a century later, in 1991.

If they had lived as long, or been so minded to memorise, would the clerks of the Bank of England have suffused their recollections in such a romantic glow? Probably not. 'All through these dark years there was a grim silence on the part of the authorities', Wilfred Bryant declared soon after the end of hostilities. 'I shall always regret the fact that on the anniversaries of the opening of the War, when we met and sang together *en masse* the National Anthem in the Lothbury Courtyard, no words from official lips were ever uttered of sympathy, appreciation, and encouragement . . . But, alas! the authorities seem to have looked upon us as mere machines.' And: 'We always lived from hand to mouth. Our domestic interests at home were never thought of. Sunday duty was often not officially announced till the last thing on Saturday night ... Such pin-pricks pierced into our very marrows.'[26] It all depended, as usual, on one's vantage point.

Back in the 1890s the Bank of England had pioneered the City's employment of female clerks, and during the war their number rose to well over a thousand, as the men went to the Front. Cunliffe was so unnerved by some of the colourful dresses he encountered that a rule was introduced confining permissible colours to navy, black and very dark grey. Elsewhere in the City the trend towards female labour similarly intensified – 'something over half our men staff have gone and we have now more young women than men in the office,' Farrer at Barings remarked in June 1915. Mainly employed by banks as typists and coupon clerks, the women earned significantly less than their male counterparts: at the Hongkong and Shanghai Bank, for example, an average of 28s 9d per week, which was 6s less than the male average. It was a differential that Sir Charles Addis there justified on the grounds that ladies were only two-thirds as efficient as men, taking 'due account of the inability of the female sex to stand a prolonged strain, their more frequent absence from work, and their liability to nervous breakdown in face of sudden emergency'. Sir Archibald Williamson was at first semi-inclined to agree. 'Don't blame us if mistakes or delay occur,' he warned Valparaiso in May 1916. 'Most of the invoices you get are now made up and written by women clerks. Look at them. They are quite well done. Surprisingly so.' But by April 1918 he had become a complete convert: 'We here find we can do a wonderful amount of good work with the assistance of women. Both in our book-keeping and clerical departments they have come to the front ... Up to the war we used them only as stenographers and secretaries, but there has been a great development, and they have come up to scratch and done well.'[27] Even so, he – like everyone else – assumed that the great majority would return to home and hearth once the war was over.

Male or female, one shared experience was the occasional, not unterrifying air raid. The City's first big one occurred on the evening of Wednesday, 8 September 1915, when the German naval airship *L13* started to come over the City just before eleven o'clock. In quick succession bombs fell on Bartholomew Close, Little Britain, Aldermanbury, Basinghall Street, Coleman Street, Moorgate, Salisbury House (Finsbury Circus), London Wall Buildings, Liverpool Street (leaving a crater there) and Liverpool Street Station. Altogether thirty bombs were dropped, six people killed, thirty-eight injured and over £0.5m worth of damage done. In 1917 the Germans began aeroplane raids directly targeted at the City. The most successful was on Wednesday, 13 June, coming late one morning out of a clear blue sky. Fifteen planes dropped bombs that killed over a hundred people and, as Grenfell wrote to Jack Morgan, 'in this crowded district, the bombs made a terrific noise as of course the sound reverberates amongst the high buildings and narrow streets'. He added that 'the nearest bomb to us failed to go off as it landed in a Churchyard, but the next one, just behind the Office, appropriately spoilt the Austrian Bank and missed Barings narrowly'.[28]

Two of the war's finest chroniclers were in the City that day. Siegfried Sassoon, on his way to Cambridge, needed to draw cash from his bank in Old Broad Street:

> When my taxi stopped in that narrow thoroughfare, the people on the pavement were standing still, staring up at the hot white sky. Loud bangings had begun in the near neighbourhood, and it was obvious that an air-raid was in full swing. This event could not be ignored; but I needed money and wished to catch my train, so I decided to disregard it. The crashings continued, and while I was handing my cheque to the cashier a crowd of women clerks came wildly down a winding stairway with vociferations of not unnatural alarm. Despite this commotion the cashier handed me five one-pound notes with the stoical politeness of a man who had made up his mind to go down with the ship ... I emerged from the building with an air of soldierly unconcern; my taxi-driver, like the cashier, was commendably calm, although another stupendous crash sounded as though very near Old Broad Street (as indeed it was) ... At Liverpool Street there had occurred what, under normal conditions, would be described as an appalling catastrophe. Bombs had been dropped on the station and one of them had hit the front carriage of the noon express to Cambridge. Horrified travellers were hurrying away ... In a trench one was acclimatised to the notion of being exterminated and there was a sense of organised retaliation. But here one was helpless; an invisible enemy sent destruction spinning down from a fine weather sky; poor old men bought a railway ticket and were trundled away again dead on a barrow; wounded women lay about in the station groaning. And one's train didn't start ...

An hour or two later, Vera Brittain was in Bishopsgate, to discover the fate of her uncle, who worked in National Provincial's head office there. She found him 'safe and quite composed, but as pale as a corpse', while the whole staff 'resembled a morose consignment of dumb spectres newly transported across the Styx'. Outside, the streets were 'terrifyingly quiet, and in some places so thickly covered with broken glass that I seemed to be wading ankle-deep in huge unmelted hailstones'. There were no bodies to be seen, though 'a crimson-splashed horse lying indifferently on its side', as well as 'several derelict tradesman's carts bloodily denuded of their drivers', suggested 'a variety of gruesome probabilities'. Like Sassoon, she concluded that such things 'seemed less inappropriate when they happened in France'.[29]

It was less than a month before the next round of unfriendly bombs. 'Great air raid on the City,' the Smith St Aubyn diary noted on Saturday, 7 July, '22 enemy machines come and return to the Coast before one is brought down! 37 killed. 141 wounded.' Addis recorded the event – 'It was an awful sight. There was no panic' – while Grenfell was typically laconic: 'The planes were quite low and just missed St Paul's and Northcliffe's Office. They got the GPO and the Swiss Bank and broke Speyer's best stained glass. Jimmy and Edgar not at home. All the women clerks stand the shocks extraordinarily well. They deserve several votes.' Serious preparations were soon under way in the expectation of further raids: 'I have not yet been told where my own funkhole is, but I intend to get there – at the double – when the time arrives,' Farrer admitted; but in the event the worst was over.[30] The largely intact City would stay thoroughly Victorian in appearance for a while yet.

Grenfell's Speyer reference was one among many, many manifestations of anti-German feeling that pervaded the City. Farrer at the outset took the civilised approach – 'it is right to draw a distinction between the German Government and the German nation, and I reserve my bitterness of feeling for the former,' he wrote to a colleague three days after war began – but if, which was doubtful, many other non-Germans were inclined to follow, that possibility vanished with the sinking of the *Lusitania* on 7 May 1915. Both the *Financial Times* and the *Financial News* declared that it was the 'crowning infamy' of what the *FN* called 'a series of cowardly crimes against humanity'. A few days later a mass meeting was held on Tower Hill, 'when in drenching rain thousands of City men assembled to support a resolution calling upon the Government to intern all alien enemies now in our midst, whether naturalised or not'. The anti-German mood did not abate. At Rothschilds, the German-speaking clerks continued for some time to talk German among themselves at the luncheon table, usually muttering '*Mahlzeit*' as they left it. Eventually in 1917, the story went, a thoroughly English clerk called Henfrey, 'able to stand it no longer, bore into the dining-room a *Daily Mail* poster bearing the words "Intern Them All", a message which he reinforced by shouting the words in the hoarse voice of a street-corner news-boy as he marched up and down the room'.[31]

Predictably there was a fair amount of name-changing: the London &

Hanseatic became the London Merchant Bank; the foreign exchange arbitrageur Robert Hecht became Robert Kay; even the ebullient stockbroker Max Karo temporarily became Max Kerr; and so on. The invidiousness of their position was summed up by C.W. Lagemann, a native of Hamburg but a leading figure in Mincing Lane. In June 1916 he resigned as Chairman of Czarnikows, telling his directors that 'my own record of 44 years' devotion to British sugar interests and of unstinted sympathy with the British cause has not obliterated the fact of my German birth'. Or take Helbert Wagg's Adolph Schwelm, a naturalised Briton but of German-Jewish origin. Before the war he had been a key figure in the firm's expansion; soon after hostilities began, he went to Argentina to look for business there; his return to Britain was delayed by the post-*Lusitania* emotional upsurge; eventually it was decided that he should stay in Argentina for the rest of the war; and shortly before it ended, Alfred Wagg wrote to him saying that his return to the City as a partner in Helbert Wagg was now unacceptable because he had not served in the British Armed Forces. Not surprisingly, an acrimonious parting ensued.[32]

Lloyd's and the Baltic Exchange had their demotic moments, but nowhere was hatred of all things German more hotly expressed than in the Stock Exchange. 'To say that the House was indignant at this latest dastardly outrage on the part of Germany is to put the state of affairs mildly, and members did not confine themselves to talk,' the *FT* reported, of the morning after the *Lusitania* news had come through. 'Few German or Austrian members had the temerity to enter the Stock Exchange, but the few who did put in an appearance were promptly surrounded by a hostile crowd and hustled out of the House again.' Under pressure, the Stock Exchange Committee posted a notice advising members of German or Austrian birth to 'keep away from the House at present'. Over the next few days a boycott movement spread, with a notice being posted in the Yankee market: 'Refuse to deal with German firms; do not put £ s d in front of patriotism'. As for individual members of German or Austrian birth, whether naturalised or not, many of them now made a public declaration of loyalty, as well as a condemnation of German methods of warfare, and by the end of the month well over a hundred of these declarations had been posted in the House. It was not enough. In November 1915, following a packed meeting of members, Charlie Clarke wrote to the Committee calling on it in the following March not to re-elect naturalised members of German and Austrian birth – 'with some few well considered exceptions' – in the light of the 'dastardly and inhuman acts perpetrated by the Enemy, which have outraged the moral sense of the people beyond expression'. The Committee, unsure of the legal position, managed to temporise. However, when in January 1916 a member called Ernest Breisach complained that a fellow-member, Adam Walker, had deliberately barged into him and called him 'a b—y German', it found 'that Mr Breisach having come into the House in spite of the Committee's warning has no grounds for complaint'.[33]

In March 1917 the Committee gave way. Following a petition from the Stock Exchange Anti-German Union – listing 142 members, mainly of alien enemy birth, and calling on the Committee not to re-elect them – it did indeed not re-elect about fifty, including such prominent members as Paul Nelke, Julius Stamm and Louis Fleischmann. One member, Edward Cuthbertson, bravely wrote a circular letter condemning the Committee's actions as 'a flagrant violation of the principles of justice and of freedom', placing 'in jeopardy the reputation of the Stock Exchange for integrity, fair dealing and justice'. It was not a letter that went down well with Alexander C. Scrimgeour, who from his home (Quaives, Wickhambreaux, near Canterbury) wrote direct to Cuthbertson:

> When your own wife, daughters and female relations have been raped to death by the huns, when your sons have been slaughtered by them, your house burned and your disgusting person driven into the ignominious slavery you so richly deserve, I hope you will see no occasion to change your views.
>
> Since you hold such views and have the beastly impudence to thrust them upon other people, I regret that there is no immediate prospect of your being put to the test by the sons, nephews and male relations of those friends on whose behalf you have indited such a nauseating and pusillanimous letter.

Presumably most German-born members concentrated on staying out of the way of the Scrimgeours of the House, but at least one worried also about posterity. In April 1912 the Managers of the Stock Exchange had agreed to grant an application by Alfred Schacht, a jobber in the Consol market, to be allowed to decorate the South African War Memorial on Empire Day. Just over six years later, in June 1918, that same jobber, now called Alfred Dent, wrote anxiously to the Managers: 'As the matter now stands on the minute book a member of German name initiated the decoration of the South African War Memorial. There is nothing to show that this member was British born and as wholly British in all respects as the most patriotic of his fellow-members. What the "House" of today knows and recognises might not be apparent to the future historian, were our archives ever to see the light of day. Can you see your way to prevent any possible misconception on the point?' The Managers responded by attaching the letter to the relevant page in the 1912 minute book, otherwise leaving it to this eventual light of day.[34]

The more eminent one was, the worse it was being of German origin, as Sir Carl Meyer, Baron Bruno Schröder and Sir Edgar Speyer all found. 'Poor Carl Meyer! he looks a broken man,' Addis observed in February 1915 of the Hongkong and Shanghai's director, a well-known City figure since the 1880s and with a son serving at the Front on the British side. In September 1916 he was asked to resign. Addis noted: 'I was sorry for him but advised him not to resist – the feeling against Germans, even naturalised Germans, is too strong.' Schröder's plight was equally unenviable. Within days of the war beginning he had been naturalised, his partner Frank Tiarks working closely in harness with Cunliffe to avert the threat of sequestration (as enemy property) of such an important firm. The move was widely criticised, including in Parliament, with sentiment not improved by Schröder's elder son being conscripted into the German Army. Then came the sinking of the *Lusitania*, prompting Tiarks to write to his brother that 'no institution with a German name ought to be tolerated in London', that this was the last straw and he had 'decided not to go on with JHS & Co after the war and to insist on a gradual liquidation' and would 'tell Bruno so tomorrow'. Soon afterwards, however, Tiarks was informed by Cunliffe that such a policy would be against the national interest, and Tiarks agreed to follow the Governor's advice and 'peg away in the direction he wants'. Even so, Tiarks told Grenfell in November 1915 that (in Grenfell's words) 'he felt Bruno S could never work here again nor did T himself think he could work with Bruno S'. Schröder himself avoided the City throughout the war, though at one point he was challenged to say whether he wanted Britain or Germany to emerge as victor. He replied, 'I feel as if my father and mother have quarrelled.'[35]

As for Speyer, he had never been popular in the City – 'he was able & kind but spoilt by prosperity & the management of the firm was not straightforward,' according to Grenfell. Nor had Speyer's Liberal inclinations helped. In 1914 rumours soon began to spread that his house at Overstrand, on the Norfolk coast, was being used to send signals to the German Fleet; and on 13 November Lord Crawford recorded in his diary that:

Robin Benson begged me to see him early this morning. I found him full of indignation. Several [the Portuguese Ambassador], his informant, says that at a recent dinner party in Downing St at which Mr and Mrs Asquith entertained him, Mr and Mrs Churchill, and *Sir Edgar and Lady Speyer*, the actual position and disposition of the Fleet was the subject of conversation. Several was horror-struck at this act of folly. Speyer is not trusted, his wife [Leonora, daughter of the banker Count von Stosch] makes no secret of anti-British sentiments – Speyer himself is actually being watched, so suspicious are the authorities. The man can't speak English, his brother [Jimmy] is one of our most violent enemies in the United States – and yet Asquith permits such a conversation at his table . . . One's blood boils at these things . . .

In the wake of the *Lusitania* incident and a fresh round of anti-Speyerism, the financier wrote to Asquith offering to surrender his baronetcy and membership of the Privy Council, but the Prime Minister declined, publicly sympathising with Speyer's 'sense of injustice and indignation' and referring to the 'baseless and malignant imputations' against his loyalty. Speyer, however, felt he could take no more, abandoning London as a place of business and moving to New York. By the end of the war Speyer Bros had ceased to be a presence in the City.[36]

Sad, embittering times too for Sir Ernest Cassel, who had left Cologne in the 1860s and had become by the end of the century the greatest financial operator the City had known since Nathan Rothschild during and after the Napoleonic Wars. Although in formal retirement after 1910, he kept in close touch with financial affairs, reassuring at least one person soon after the outbreak of war that he entertained 'no doubt of this country's solvency, whatever the pressure to which we might be subjected'. Yet even Cassel, in the prevailing febrile atmosphere, came under attack, and a fortnight after the sinking of the *Lusitania* he sent a letter to the press declaring that 'nearly half a century of my life has been spent in England, and all my interests – family, business and social – are centred here', adding that 'my unfailing loyalty and devotion to this country have never varied'. Nor had they, for over the years he had performed all sorts of important services, not least as Edward VII's trusted financial adviser. Later in 1915 there was an attempt to deprive him of his membership of the Privy Council. It failed, but hurt him deeply. And the following summer, after the Battle of Jutland, it was widely believed – entirely baselessly – that Cassel had actively conspired to maximise the adverse implications of that encounter in order to profit from a fall in the stock market.[37] He may not have been a lovable man, but he deserved better. And, taking the rabid anti-Germanism as a whole, the City was in danger of rejecting the cosmopolitanism that had been its single greatest strength.

*

The conduct of financial policy remained as sorry a spectacle after Benjamin Strong's visit as it had been before, though it was a spectacle hidden from public scrutiny. Norman, having quickly played himself in as a member of the Bank of England's inner circle, spent much of the early summer of 1916 at the Treasury, usually with the Chancellor (still McKenna) present. 'They neither grasp nor seem able to realise the true position,' he wrote in his diary on 30 May. A week later, after another visit: 'All muddle & getting worse & worse'. And the next day: 'C. of Ex seems utterly blind to Exchange position & inevitable dangers ahead, being filled with immediate politics . . . For some unknown reason he is sanguine of turning up a trump & refuses to face the position.' Finally, on 27 June: 'It's a thankless job going to Treasury. I shall do it no more, for tho' knowing jeopardy threatens us in N.Y. one might as well talk to an airball as to them.'[38]

Nor, as the year unfolded, did Norman derive much comfort from the Bank itself. An entry on 24 October was laden with meaning:

> Most of Treas Com [i.e. the Bank of England's Committee of Treasury, of which Norman was a member, but mainly comprising present and former Governors] having agreed to G. [i.e. Governor Cunliffe] for another year: he sh[d] make a point of regular full disclosure of Bk affairs & of his advice qua Gov. This is due to them as Treas Com (by long custom) & essential now to begin preparation of *united* front, as Enquiry after war is certain – & it will be engineered with main object of substituting State Bank. Such a Bank seems to be in minds of C [i.e. Chancellor McKenna] & whole Treasury as well as grumblers in City & busy bodies in Parl'ment.

Over the next fortnight Norman's hoped-for united front failed to materialise, as Cunliffe and his predecessor A.C. Cole quarrelled openly, the latter denying Cunliffe's accusations about breaches of secrecy. On 8 November, Norman recorded, Cunliffe 'accepted job for another year – but unconditionally'. Soon afterwards, however, Norman spent a weekend in Bath (staying at the Spa Hotel) and, in the course of 'long talks' with a for once 'entirely reasonable' Governor, managed to thrash out some sort of concordat. Cunliffe agreed that a female shorthand writer would attend Committee of Treasury meetings and provide a full précis; that those meetings would be more frequent; that all current business would be considered; that there would be a 'gradual bringing in of younger directors' into the Committee; and that in due course there would 'perhaps' be, on the Bank's Court as a whole, 'new directors drawn from Bankers &c'. The peacemaker's immediate reward came two days after his return from Bath: 'T. Com . . . Hatchet formally buried by G & ACC'.[39]

Meanwhile, Bank/Treasury relations continued to be deeply uneasy. Cokayne, Deputy Governor, said as much in his diary on 10 November: 'In evening saw Sir R. Chalmers (coming in with Grenfell, which was a mistake as it evidently gave the impression that I came to help him to get his way with the Treasury)'. Bad faith remained the order of the day, the exchange position deteriorated still further, and on 29 November, noted Norman, 'finance in U.S. now becomes a Cabinet question'. Over the next three weeks Britain lost gold at the daily rate of over $5m, as the Federal Reserve Board (in the absence of the ailing Strong) deliberately undermined Anglo-French credit in an attempt to get the Allies to end the war. By the time the worst was over, though gold continued to drain away over the next few months, there was a new government in London. Lloyd George replaced Asquith, to the pleasure of the *FT*, which anticipated a government 'to be run on business às distinguished from party lines'. The new Chancellor was the Conservative leader, and Norman noted in January 1917 that 'friction between Bk & Treasury has wonderfully lessened since Bonar Law became C'. The new year also saw the issue by Bonar Law of a major war stock – the Chancellor successfully exploiting patriotic feeling in his decision, backed by the Bank but not by the Treasury, to go for a long-term loan at 5 per cent rather than the more customary short-term one at 6 per cent. The *FT* called on the City to supply 'all the silver bullets it can turn out', while the *FN* greeted the War Loan launch as only it knew how: 'Every Cheque Is A She££ Fired At The German Trenches'. The exhortations worked, as Austen Chamberlain wrote to his sister in late February: 'The Loan is an even more marvellous success than I thought. You will see the figures in the papers. They exceed Bonar Law's wildest dreams.'[40] Almost £2,000m had come in, though the problem of how to service that mammoth debt now began to exercise more thoughtful minds.

The two global events that dominated 1917 were the Russian Revolution and America's entry into the war. Since 1914 Barings had been undeniably resourceful agents for the Russian government, but arguably could have done more to save Russian capitalism. 'I wish some upright Commercial House here could play the strong hand in Petrograd,' commented Grenfell in June 1916. 'Everything would point to

Barings doing so, but they seem unwilling to jeopardise what they have got by pushing ahead and yet are inclined to crab anyone who does try to push.' On 19 January 1917 Revelstoke left London as number two to Milner on an Allied mission to investigate Russia's claim to a new loan of at least £400m. In effect Revelstoke was representing the interests of both the Treasury and the Russian government, a position that seems to have caused him few ethical qualms. After the best part of a month, during which some determined bargaining was combined with a strenuous social programme, the delegation departed on 21 February with the outcome still inconclusive. Soon after Revelstoke's return the Tsarist regime fell. 'He thinks the army generally is sound for the continuance of the war', noted Addis on 29 March after a conversation with the Barings chief. Wishful thinking, but then a week later America at last declared war on Germany. The Governor was quickly across the herring pond. 'Cunliffe is for cash that fights' ran an American headline, and by early May he had helped to secure loans worth £300m.[41] Already hugely in hock to the United States, Britain was now in a state of dependency plain for all to see. The old country had become a debtor nation.

'We are expecting Cunliffe back any day now,' Farrer told an American correspondent at the end of May. 'He has been badly missed here; he is by nature so silent that until he disappears temporarily from the scene one hardly realises how good a man and how strong he is.'[42] Shortly afterwards, duly back from his acclaimed trip, Cunliffe was embroiled in an extraordinary episode of high-level rancour.[43] Beginning as a fierce campaign on his part against the Treasury (in particular against Chalmers and Keynes) over what he complained was interference in questions of exchange, it took the form by early July – at a critical stage of the war – of an almost mad attempt to block the government's access to the Bank's gold in Canada. Cunliffe did this entirely off his own bat. Bonar Law, writing to Lloyd George on the 9th, was incandescent. He described Cunliffe's telegram to the Canadian government as 'an act of extraordinary disrespect towards the British Government and a direct insult to me'. Next day Lloyd George summoned Cunliffe to Downing Street, reprimanded him severely and threatened (or so Cunliffe reported on the 11th to the Committee of Treasury) to 'take over the Bank'. He also gave Cunliffe a statement to sign, including the solemn words that 'during the War the Bank must in all things act on the directions of the Chancellor of the Exchequer'. Cunliffe, having consulted his colleagues the following day, refused to sign it. Lloyd George, after talking to Bonar Law, sent Cunliffe on the 13th a suggested letter of apology for him to send the Chancellor, 'the sooner the better'. It contained the offer of resignation in the absence of 'complete and harmonious co-operation' between the two men. Cunliffe's response – extolling the importance of a harmonious relationship between Bank and Treasury but declining to offer his resignation in the absence of such a relationship – failed to give satisfaction.

At this point, the 17th, the Governor went off to Scotland (Rhiconich Hotel, Lairg, Sutherland) on a fishing holiday, leaving Cokayne and Norman to try and mollify the Chancellor. Norman noted the next day: 'BL says half the trouble is because G's [i.e. Cunliffe's] head is swelled so much that he must have his own way on all matters. ? Result of going to the USA.' Cokayne on the 19th also saw Bonar Law. 'I have no animosity against him,' the Chancellor said about Cunliffe, 'but he is quarrelsome (which I am not) and I consider he behaved very badly to me. I gave him a good chance to put it right and he declined, so that is the end of it.' However, Bonar Law reluctantly ceded to Cokayne's request that the Deputy Governor try again to get a fuller apology out of Cunliffe, with Bonar Law clearly wanting an offer of resignation. Over the next three weeks Cokayne wrote along these lines to the absent Governor no fewer than four times. He warned that unless Cunliffe pocketed his pride, 'the position will become absolutely intolerable and there is bound to be a sort of public scandal'. Cunliffe for a time was adamant – 'let the Chancellor protest as he may, such a letter places my resignation in his hands and I simply become a Government Official under his orders' – but eventually, on 12 August, he sent Bonar Law the letter that Cokayne had most recently drafted. In it he made an 'unreserved apology for anything I have done to offend you', but did not as such offer to resign.[44]

Cokayne had persuaded Cunliffe to sign and send the letter not only by raising fears that the Bank's wings would be clipped after the war unless the dispute was settled, but also by mentioning that the person who was still really 'cross' with the Governor was his old ally Lloyd George, 'who, as I hear indirectly, was expressing himself very strongly about you the other day'; while in terms of the letter itself, the tactful Deputy Governor had persuaded Bonar Law to accept a formula of apology in lieu of a reference to resignation. Cunliffe was back in London on the 15th, 'looking very blooming', according to Farrer, and promising 'to be good'. Yet barely a fortnight after telling Bonar Law that 'I fully realise that I must not attempt to impose my views upon you', Cunliffe was informing his Committee of Treasury that he 'did not propose now or at any time to obtain the Chancellor's special sanction in regard to such changes as might be contemplated in the Bank Rate'.[45] He was not prepared, in other words, to concede that the recent bitter quarrel had altered the fundamental underlying relationship.

Cunliffe's days as Governor, however, were numbered. By September, with his behaviour becoming increasingly erratic, Cecil Lubbock (a Bank director) was telling Norman that Cunliffe was 'no longer sane – if ever he was'. Briefly he seemed willing to go quietly, but on 10 October he told Norman that 'it was in interest of Bk & Nation that he sh^d continue, that he could not continue once anyone else was selected, that he wished to go on until end of war & that he w^d be to me either a G. or an enemy'. Soon afterwards, at a meeting of the Bank's Court, he accused a former Governor, W.M. Campbell, of being against him because he had been denied facilities to borrow. This time Cunliffe's bullying failed to work, and on 8 November the Court elected Cokayne and Norman as Governor and Deputy Governor respectively from the following spring. Most men would have given up, but not Cunliffe. He now (in Grenfell's accurate words) 'changed his attitude to everyone outside the Bank. He toadied the press, the Bankers, the Treasury & the Gov^t. He tried to get the Bankers to move the Chancellor to ask that he Cunliffe should be retained at the Bank. He vilified Norman & the other directors.' So successful was Cunliffe in persuading his old enemies, the joint-stock bankers, to come to his aid that on 20 November they handed Bonar Law a resolution against the proposed change of Governor. Cunliffe professed that the resolution came as a 'great surprise' to him, but under questioning from Norman admitted that 'he had known about & seen resolution last week'. Somewhat superfluously, Norman added that 'he can't be trusted now'. The resolution failed to achieve its purpose, but by mid-December Norman was still noting that 'it seems more clear than ever that G. is consulting, if not intriguing with the Bankers – & esp Schuster'.[46]

Cunliffe was away in Spain for the whole of January 1918, but returned for a final acrimonious round. 'Clear case of megalomania,' Norman reckoned on 27 February, following a 'violent display' by Cunliffe at the Committee of Treasury, 'behaving like a spoilt child'. And on 22 March, at a meeting of the Bank's shareholders, he 'read a longish speech – of wh D Gov & Directors knew nothing – i. eulogising the Bankers. ii. bum-sucking the Press . . . feeling very hot, & even DG much disgusted with such an unfriendly finale. A dangerous & insane colleague.' It was a speech that made the worst possible impression on Grenfell, who found himself 'reluctantly compelled to agree that able & strong as Lord C is, yet he is selfish, disloyal to colleagues & the Bank.

He also has a bad yellow streak & is in no sense a white man.' The 'only excuse', Grenfell added, was that 'nearly all the members of the C family are slightly cracked & are not on speaking terms with each other'.[47]

The ex-Governor remained an oppressive presence in Threadneedle Street. 'Generally opposed all plans wh had been favoured by other members & brought discord where he found amity', was how Norman described Cunliffe's contribution to the Committee of Treasury meeting on 24 April. More importantly, political-cum-military discord threatened Britain's war effort, at the time of an ominous German offensive. In the Maurice Debate in the Commons on 9 May, Lloyd George faced the charge that his government had been deliberately withholding troops from Haig. He was no doubt comforted by a telegram from Charlie Clarke, assuring him that 'an overwhelming majority almost unanimous of the Members of The Stock Exchange desire to offer you and Mr Bonar Law their unflinching support at this critical time'. Clarke was in due course ticked off by the Committee for sending a telegram purporting to represent the views of the House, whereupon he 'addressed the Committee with considerable heat and said that he had spoken to groups of Members in his (the Consols) Market and in the Rubber and South African Markets and considered that his telegram expressed their views'. No action was taken.

By mid-July the military danger was easing but food supplies were still critical, and Cunliffe drew the attention of readers of *The Times* to 'the serious injury that is caused to asparagus plants by cutting down the foliage for the purpose of decoration'. Writing from his home at Headley Court, Epsom, he explained: 'Only last night my garden was entered and all the tops cut off and removed from six beds of asparagus, thereby ruining next year's crop. It is evident that there is a ready market for the foliage . . .' Early in August the Allies moved on to the offensive. 'Markets blazing good,' Farrer reported on the 13th to Revelstoke, who as usual – war or peace – was spending August at Aix-les-Bains. The following month Bonar Law tried to persuade Cokayne to lower the Bank rate. Mindful of the pre-war tradition by which (as one Treasury man later put it) 'a change in Bank rate was no more regarded as the business of the Treasury than the colour which the Bank painted its front door', the Governor refused. 'I feel strongly that it will be impossible to preserve our international credit unless we have comparatively dear money after the War and that the more we artificially cheapen it now, the more difficult it will be to revert to normal conditions,' he replied to Bonar Law.[48]

But when would that blessed period of 'after the War' come? 'The war has had a wonderful turning just lately,' the highly intelligent Robert Brand of Lazards wrote on 3 October to a New York correspondent, 'but we are still having a terrific struggle in France and it may be many months before the end comes.' Sir Archibald Williamson, an MP as well as a leading figure in the City, agreed, telling Lima two days later that he was not expecting peace 'until some time next year', for 'the German forces are still formidable'.[49] The outbreak of war four years earlier had come as an almost complete surprise to the City; now its abrupt ending did likewise.

*

It was not just in the obvious sense – the dislocation of the pre-1914 international economy, with its free movement of people, capital and services – that the First World War represented a difficult time for the City. For the first time in anyone's memory it started to come under significant pressure from an alternative socio-economic approach: one that stressed the interests of the provinces as against the metropolis, and of industry as against finance.[50] 'Business as usual' quickly lost its viability as a slogan, huge swathes of the economy came under temporary government control, and the establishment of the Federation of British Industries in 1916 was a key straw in the corporatist wind. Free trade, the gold standard, the balanced budget – all three were crucial props to City influence and, for the time being, all three were *hors de combat*. Briefly, and tantalisingly, the producer held the aces.

Inevitably, the war saw renewed criticism of the City's provision of industrial finance, sharply intensifying a debate that had begun in the Edwardian period. Tellingly, some of this criticism was internal, including an important survey published in December 1916 by Robert Brand of Lazards on 'Industry and Finance'. Although acknowledging that the British banking system was 'safer and more liquid' than the German, he emphasised how 'a reflective mind is constantly struck by the peculiar lack of contact between the chief financial centre of the world and the industry of its own country'. He went on: 'There are no first-class financial institutions in London which act as organisers or reorganisers of companies, or which issue on their own responsibility industrial securities . . . In a word, there are no financial institutions in London whose aim it is, as it is the aim of the German banks, to act as a kind of general staff to industry.' Accordingly, 'industrial issues, and particularly new schemes, are left too much to the company promoter', who inevitably looks 'to make as large an immediate profit as possible regardless of the future welfare of the business'. Then came a passage given added authority by Brand's knowledge of the square mile:

> There is a considerable body of opinion in the City, not necessarily very conversant with modern industrial developments, which thinks that our present system fulfils all reasonable needs. A large number of people regard our financial system, just as Burke regarded our Constitution, as something which grows and which is not made, and which has by natural evolution grown almost to perfection. It is argued that every country evolves the system which suits it, whether it be the British or the German or the American. To these critics it is presumably 'natural' that the Germans should build Zeppelins and we should not; that we should invent aniline dyes and the Germans exploit them; 'natural' too, that the German and American steel industries should increase by leaps and bounds and ours should remain stagnant. It is a form of argument strongly entrenched in the City, but it is not likely to exercise an undue influence on this and the next generation.

It was an optimism not shared by the economist H.S. Foxwell, who in a well-publicised lecture in April 1917 on 'The Financing of Industry and Trade' was highly critical of what he saw as an over-specialised City: on the one hand, 'the regular banks', though 'always ready to accommodate industry with temporary loans on excellent terms', refused to 'make a special study of industrial technique, or industrial problems generally, except so far as they affect short-loan business'; on the other hand, the issuing houses (i.e. mainly the merchant banks) 'fight shy of ordinary home industrial propositions' and 'prefer those put forward by foreign Governments, municipalities, or the very largest transport companies', for 'as a rule our English industries are too small in scale to attract the issue houses'. In short, he concluded, 'we are involved in a vicious circle which it will want some courage to break'.[51] The crux, as both Brand and Foxwell recognised, was institutional conservatism.

The City's response to two major developments was revealing.[52] In the summer of 1916 the independent-minded stockbroker and financier Lord Faringdon (the former Sir Alexander Henderson) chaired the Board of Trade Committee on Financial Facilities for Trade. The other members were Dudley Docker (the able, if self-publicising Midlands industrialist who had long criticised the City), Gaspard Farrer of Barings, and four other leading City bankers, W.H.N. Goschen, Walter Leaf, Richard Vassar-Smith and Frederick Huth Jackson. From the outset Faringdon stressed that 'there was no bank in England of any size that would offer to finance a new proposition of any magnitude', one able to look abroad and 'take in hand' something 'of the nature of the Victoria Falls Power Co, and say, "Here are a couple of millions for you in order that this contract may be placed with a British manufacturer". The Deutsche Bank and their friends did that operation in that way.' Accordingly, Faringdon 'urged that there was a necessity for the creation of an institution that could undertake business which the English banks at present cannot do'. Docker in particular was a forceful advocate of 'tied' loans, and he found support from the evidence of Sir Vincent Caillard of Vickers:

> I remember a loan, I think it was an Argentine loan, on which I sent to see a very first-rate British financier, known to *everybody* in this room, but I will not mention his name [Revelstoke?]. I put before him that it was very unfair that this money should be raised in England and that the whole of it should be spent abroad, as I knew it was going to be. He said, 'That does not matter to us; we make our commission, the British public gets a good investment, and we do not care about British industry'.

In September the Committee reported, supporting the establishment of an industrial trading bank, under Royal Charter, to seek to rival German and other foreign banks in their pursuit of exports. All signed except Farrer, who explained to Leaf that 'Lord Faringdon's scheme is too ambitious for my views and if I cannot commend it for my own money, obviously I cannot for that of others.' To Revelstoke, reporting on his 'most tiresome Committee', Farrer added that he could not 'help wondering to myself what my docile associates would do (all qualifying, I imagine, for a seat on the Board), if they found themselves in possession of £5,000,000 paid-up capital, and Henderson by ill luck removed to Abraham's bosom'.[53]

From the start, the City as a whole made a dead set against the proposed new institution. The exporters, Addis wrote in the *Economic Journal* in December, should be left by government 'to look after themselves'. In May 1917, after the British Trade Corporation had been incorporated (with Faringdon as its Governor), the House of Commons was told that 'the banks of the City are against this proposal' and heard it described as 'an official bucket-shop'. The *FT* mildly deplored the City's 'apprehension and jealousy' of the BTC, but saw it as inevitable, given fears that it might 'trench upon the ordinary legitimate business of banking, and upon that of the established financial and issuing houses, and to a certain extent perhaps even on that of the Stock Exchange'. The paper argued that these fears were 'exaggerated', reckoned that a lot would depend on how much business was given by government to the new bank, and noted of its board that 'that body comprises a number of first-class business men, including, of course, Lord Faringdon himself, but it is not very representative of the banking world, especially of that of London'. During the rest of the war the BTC was able to achieve little, but the City remained hostile. 'It may be necessary for us to open Branches down South and elsewhere when it can be arranged,' the Managing Director of the London & River Plate Bank wrote in August 1918 to his managers in Buenos Aires, 'but we have no idea of following up Lord Faringdon's suggestion to take any direct interest in any Trading Company – that would be quite contrary to any Banking Institution although the L. & B. [i.e. the London & Brazilian Bank] made a departure recently in that direction and raised a lot of hostile criticism from Merchants and others . . .'[54]

The other main wartime development, repudiating pre-1914 ortho-doxy, involved an explicit threat to the traditional primacy of the London Stock Exchange. This was the formation in 1916 of the British Stockbrokers Trust Ltd, an alliance of leading provincial stockbrokers. BST's first Chairman was the prominent corporatist Lord ffrench, and early in 1918 it publicly laid out its case:

> For many years before the war country brokers felt grave dissatisfaction with the conditions under which new issues of capital were offered for subscription by financial institutions in London. The issuing houses, most of which are not of British origin, were in the habit of telegraphing to country brokers giving them a few hours to decide whether they would participate in any imminent issues. The country brokers had but small opportunity of investigating the inherent soundness of new issues thus offered for subscription. They were not given the chance. Anxiety for underwriting, fear of being excluded from future issues, doubt that a refusal might play into the hands of a rival, were all factors the influence of which enabled the issuing houses to take this course.
>
> A still more important abuse which provincial brokers are convinced it is necessary to combat is in connection with issues for foreign concerns. In normal times vast amounts of British capital were subscribed for investment abroad. In most cases the plant and materials necessary for the establishment and upkeep of these foreign undertakings had to be purchased outside the countries in question . . . Issuing houses of German origin commanded the situation. They did so because they had channels of investment to deal with consisting of those who did not realise that they were being made the tools and servants of German economic penetration. The result was that, at inflated prices, many British investors, who were themselves manufacturers, provided money for the development of German industries . . .

The London Stock Exchange has never been happy in its official relations with country brokers. It has invariably taken up a high-handed and overbearing attitude, which appears to country brokers to have for its main purpose the preservation of what may be termed the vested interests of the dealers and brokers on the London Stock Exchange, regardless of the interests of the investing public, the provincial brokers, and the country generally.

BST described its aims as threefold: first, 'enabling country brokers to investigate the inherent soundness of new issues'; second, 'providing a source from which country brokers could obtain sound issues at fair prices'; and third, 'ensuring that British capital shall be applied to the development of British industries and not used for the purpose of German economic penetration'.[55]

Predictably, the new body ran into the London Stock Exchange at its most 'high-handed and overbearing'. Specifically, London ruled in January 1918 that no share of commission was to be given to provincial stockbrokers who were also shareholders in BST. Consequently, many provincial stockbrokers felt compelled to abandon BST, already criticised by the *Economist* for the way in which 'its remark concerning the foreign origin of most of our issuing houses smacks of the parish pump rather than of the world-wide finance which has grown with, and helped the growth of, our world-wide trade'. However, the organisation itself remained in existence, with offices at 3 Lombard Street deep in the enemy camp. 'London is the natural centre for investigation and inquiry,' it had told the London Stock Exchange. 'The evils which the B.S.T. proposes to remedy have their headquarters in London, and in order to counter and defeat them effectively they must be fought there.'[56]

With the City at large under attack, even the Bank of England accepted the need for a modicum of internal reform. In October 1917 – a few weeks after being attacked by the *Economist* on the grounds of excessive secrecy and inadequate use of industrialists and bankers – the Bank set up a committee under Revelstoke's chairmanship to consider 'the Direction and general working of the Bank'.[57] The others on it were Huth Jackson, Norman, Lubbock and Kindersley, and many years later Norman recalled that whereas Revelstoke 'took a great deal of trouble and used carefully to prepare his "case" before every meeting', Huth Jackson 'took little interest and seemed unable to distinguish gems from paste in the meetings'. Each director was asked to make a submission, with the question of whether the Bank's 'direction' should be broadened to include joint-stock bankers being of paramount concern. 'I do not think it would answer to have Members of other Banks, as it would create jealousies,' argued the merchant and former Governor W.M. Campbell. 'Their presence would give the Banks represented a preferential advantage.' Grenfell had no problem with the idea (wanting only bill brokers to be debarred from consideration), but according to Cokayne, 'so long as none of the banks are directly represented on our Court, our advice (e.g. to the Treasury) on matters concerning their interests will carry greater weight'. R.L. Newman, befitting 'the port-wine man', went further and said that he would 'deprecate' the election of any director who did not 'belong to a definite mercantile firm'. The committee itself was split. Whereas Huth Jackson 'considered that it was essential for the Bank to secure the best available men' and that it was therefore wrong to exclude the clearers, and Norman (for all his later criticism) argued likewise, Lubbock was essentially hostile to the idea, on the basis that the functions of the Bank of England and of the joint-stock banks were 'essentially different' and that 'no advantage would be gained by a quasi-fusion of the two'. Kindersley agreed: 'He considered that these Banks had too much power already and he viewed with alarm the growth of huge deposits under one control. It was his opinion that a man with such responsibility would naturally consider first the needs of his own Bank and that it would be impossible for him to give a fair and unbiassed opinion on the situation as a whole.'[58]

Before reporting, the committee heard the views of Hartley Withers, editor of the *Economist*. Rather cleverly he argued that the joint-stock men should become directors because this would benefit the joint-stock banks, having 'the effect of broadening their outlook, which is at present in almost all cases extremely narrow'. He also advocated the election of 'representatives of manufacturing districts in the provinces', saying that he 'did not anticipate that the Court would derive much direct benefit from their presence, but he thought it would have a good effect on the public, as it would create the impression that the Bank was becoming more a National Institution'. In the event, Revelstoke's committee decided against recommending a break with the Bank's traditional principle of debarring clearing bankers, let alone recommending industrialists; but it did successfully suggest that the Committee of Treasury become more youthful in composition and be elected annually by free and secret ballot. Unfortunately, the right candidates were not always elected. 'The inclusion of WMC [Campbell] than whom no one has been less useful, or more prejudiced or is more out of touch, shows how little value can be put on our plan for free ballot,' noted Norman on 28 March 1918, as the Cunliffe era of almost unopposed autocracy seemingly passed into history. And a few weeks later: 'Election to T.

Com of LHH [Colonel Lionel Henry Hanbury] . . . is an admission of seniority as agst brains! LHH admits as much & did not desire election. It shows that Democracy, ie a free ballot by Court, is not bold enough to supply best men . . .'[59] But to be fair to the Colonel, Norman and democracy would never be easy bedfellows.

As for the rejected infusion of new blood, perhaps (as Withers suggested) it would not have had such a rejuvenating effect on the Bank itself. 'They are too largely staffed, apart from the directors, on what in the Civil Service is called a second division basis,' Keynes wrote in October 1914 to Alfred Marshall about the clearing banks. 'Half of their directors, on the other hand, are appointed on hereditary grounds and two-fifths, not on grounds of banking capacity, but because they are able, through their business connections, to bring to the bank a certain class of business.'[60] Keynes was perhaps an unduly harsh critic of the men at the very top – notably Holden and Schuster – but his general point held.

Since the late 1880s the banks had been engaged in an almost continuous amalgamation movement, and in 1918 it reached its denouement. 'Time to Stop!' declared the *Daily Express* on 4 February, in response to newly announced mergers: between National Provincial and the Union of London & Smiths; and between the London County & Westminster and Parr's. A merger between the London City & Midland and the London Joint Stock was also on the cards. 'What does all this portend?' the paper asked. 'It is obvious that we shall see perfected in England a financial system equal to and even more powerful than that which the people of the United States found so tyrannous and irksome that in the end it had to be swept by the board.'[61] In response to this and other disquiet, Bonar Law appointed a committee of inquiry, to be chaired by Lord Colwyn, the former Sir F.H. Smith, an india-rubber and cotton manufacturer.[62] Bankers dominated both as members of the committee and as witnesses, giving evidence from mid-March to mid-April. 'I think it will be necessary after the war to have these big institutions to be able to compete with the fierce competition we shall meet with,' insisted Sir Herbert Hambling, the autocratic General Manager of the London Provincial & South Western Bank, specifically praising the German policy of creating big banks and thereby 'making themselves very strong'. Some dialogue ensued:

> Have you formed any view in relation to reasonable safeguards? – Against what?
> Against these amalgamations, for the protection of the public? – I do not think they want any protecting. The banks themselves live on their

customers. Their whole life depends on the good-will between the banker and his customer, and any endeavour of the banks to exploit the customers would be resented, would create opposition and would mean Government interference for a certainty.

Furthermore, Hambling decried the idea of a future body being created with the right of vetoing bank amalgamations: 'I have the strongest possible objection to Government interference . . . I think banks can do their own business better.' Stressing the post-war challenge, and above all the drive for exports, Holden likewise saw amalgamations as the absolutely necessary course:

> It is the only means of obtaining individual Banks of a size and power at all commensurate with those now being formed or developed in America and Germany . . . In view of the powerful rivalry with which we shall have to contend after the war in the arena of foreign trade, the real problem before us is not how to hinder and delay, but how to encourage and facilitate the development of big banks . . . I am not speaking of concentration carried to the point of monopoly. Far from it. There ought to be a sufficient number of powerful banks to ensure free competition amongst themselves . . .

A few, older City voices expressed opposition. 'We do not consider it wise for the benefit of the Stock Exchange at all,' observed that body's Chairman, O.C. Quekett. 'Our difficulty is that in normal times we are very large borrowers of money, and therefore competition is very much in our favour.' And Farrer: 'There may have been very good reasons perhaps from the joint stock inside point of view, which I do not know, but I do not see really that they were in the least necessary from the point of view of the public . . . I think you can allow a bank to become too powerful.'[63] Colwyn presented his report, broadly hostile to a further wave of mergers, at the start of May.

Over the next few months, to the surprise of some, Bonar Law waved through three amalgamations that were already in the pipeline – between the London City & Midland and the London Joint Stock Bank; between Barclays and the London, Provincial & South Western Bank; and between Lloyds and the Capital & Counties Bank – on the grounds of fair treatment between these banks and the ones that had already merged earlier in the year. In July, following the news that Holden's culminating predatory action had been sanctioned, *The Times* noted that 'outside what may be described as the amalgamating or would-be amalgamating circles themselves, the dislike of the City as a whole for this latest type of fusion among the already reduced number of large joint stock banks is made manifest whenever this question is under discussion'.[64] However, Bonar Law also made it clear that enough was enough. The 'Big Five' had been created, henceforth to be set in concrete. Barclays, Lloyds, Midland, Westminster and National Provincial had half a century of semi-oligopoly ahead.

'No doubt the motives before amalgamation, like most human motives, are mixed,' Addis wrote in the *Edinburgh Review* in July 1918. 'The element of fashion may enter into it; the recent marked tendency to trade combination; the propensity to do as others do. Personal vanity may count for something, a kind of megalomania; the desire to possess larger deposits, greater resources, more power than one's competitors.' All understandable, if not necessarily praiseworthy, but he warned that 'the bigger the bank the greater the danger that with the lapse of time it will become entrenched in a bed of vested interests, inimical to change, discountenancing the introduction of new ideas and discouraging the more efficient methods of young and vigorous competitors'. In short: 'The latent power of the amalgamated banks in sapping competition will be very great.'[65] An all too plausible forecast, but Addis himself had just become a director of the Old Lady. Now that they were *so* big, would the joint-stock men at last pierce the City's inner shield and achieve ungrudging acceptance?

Committees of inquiry proliferated during the war, mainly with a view to post-war 'reconstruction', and from a City – and indeed national – standpoint none was more important than the Committee on the Currency and Foreign Exchanges after the War.[66] It was jointly appointed in the autumn of 1917 by the Treasury and the Ministry of Reconstruction, after Cunliffe had made it clear that the City did not want to come under the sole sway of the latter authority. It was Cunliffe who suggested most of the names for the committee, mainly bankers; and, with Austen Chamberlain unavailable, it was Cunliffe who was asked by Bonar Law to assume the chairmanship.

The committee met regularly from February 1918, and much of the discussion turned on the role as well as the structure of the Bank of England. When W.H.N. Goschen suggested that a committee of the clearing bankers might be invited to meet the Governor weekly 'to discuss the situation with him', Cunliffe insisted that while 'such consultation was desirable ... it would not be possible to let such a Committee dictate a bank's policy'; and, supported by Addis and Farrer, he expressed his preference for 'a continuance of the present informal consultations'. The Hon Rupert Beckett, a prominent Leeds-based banker, renewed the suggestion (recently rejected by Revelstoke's committee) that the Bank's directorate 'should include representative bankers' and that 'with such representation the banks would surrender their gold with a better grace'. Cunliffe was predictably hostile, asserting that 'the Bank's first duty was to look after the gold reserve and there would be difficulty if bankers were responsible for the raising or lowering of the Bank rate'. Beckett also suggested that 'the period of service as Governor might be raised to five years', but Cunliffe was 'opposed to this', arguing that 'it was already difficult to get suitable men' and 'a longer period might leave a Governor too much power'. Holden gave evidence on 8 April: 'As you consider that the Joint Stock Banks should hold gold,' Cunliffe asked him, 'do you not think they should bear a proportion of the burden of the export of gold?' Holden replied: 'How are they going to do it? The export of gold is done through the Bank of England. You do not want us to begin issuing notes, do you?' There ensued a loaded exchange:

> Would you have the Joint Stock Banks return their gold, if we may call it so, to the Bank of England? – I would do so. I cannot speak for the Joint Stock Banks.
> And put it at the call of the Bank of England? – On condition. If your reserve had gone down so far as to put that reserve in a difficult position, then let the Bank have a call on so much of the Joint Stock Banks' gold as would put it right; but when you have got your gold back and it has got beyond that figure, let the Joint Stock Banks have it back again.
> It seems to me that if you hold gold at the call of the Bank of England . . . – Under an agreement. We should not let you call it whenever you liked.
> Then it would be no use? – We must have some agreement when it should be called. You must let us have a little bit of judgment in the latter.

Robert Benson was examined on 6 May ('made an awful ass of himself,' according to Addis), followed the next day by Christopher Nugent, by now the grand old man of the discount market and, Addis thought, 'good enough but sadly loquacious'. Perhaps Addis was disconcerted by Nugent's assertion in relation to the Bank of England that 'the support of the State, represented by gentlemen in the service of the State, seems necessary to my mind, having regard to the very different circumstances which have arisen in consequence of the war'.[67]

Taking the proceedings as a whole, none of the bankers, whether as witnesses or members of the committee, seriously questioned the assumption that the fundamental aspect of post-war financial policy should be a return as soon as possible to a fully operational gold standard, notwithstanding the probable deflationary implications of achieving such a return. The Federation of British Industries argued in its submission that the achievement of a favourable trade balance was the more important priority, but its views were ignored. The committee's report became public in late October, stating that 'in our opinion it is imperative that after the war the conditions necessary to have maint-enance of an effective gold standard should be restored without delay', for 'unless the machinery which long experience has shown to be the only effective remedy for an adverse balance of trade and an undue growth of credit is once more brought into play, there will be grave danger of a progressive credit expansion which will result in a foreign drain of gold menacing the convertibility of our note issue and so jeopardising the international trade position of the country'. By contrast, the FBI had insisted in its submission that the trade balance 'must ultimately depend on production in this country'. Elsewhere, the report had no suggestions to make about reforming the Bank of England and – in direct opposition to Holden's well-known views – advocated the maintenance of the Bank Charter Act of 1844, including its fixed fiduciary issue and the rigid separation of the issue and banking departments. It added that gold should be concentrated in the Bank of England for use as a reserve, with a minimum of £150m.[68]

City reaction to the Cunliffe Report was broadly favourable. 'It seems pretty clear already,' *The Times* reported on 31 October, 'that general financial opinion will firmly approve what is taken to be the governing principle of the report, namely, its making all its conclusions dependent on the main object of getting back, after the war, to an unimpeachable gold basis for our currency.' Two days later the *Economist*'s headline was 'Back to Sanity', while on 6 November the President of the Institute of Bankers, Sir Richard Vassar-Smith, stated that he thought 'there are few bankers who will not whole-heartedly agree with its main theses'. Holden was one of those few. Although not opposed to a restoration of the gold standard, he found otherwise little to applaud in Cunliffe's deliberations – above all not in the old-fashioned, paternalist notion that the joint-stock banks should hand over their gold to the Bank of England. 'Summing up,' he would tell his shareholders in January 1919, 'the Currency Committee have stated in effect that they cannot recommend anything better than the old system. They simply put us back to the old machine which has broken down before, and which may break down again. In consequence of this report not going far enough we may have a State bank, which is practically what the Americans have got today in their Federal Reserve banking system.'[69] Put another way, the

Bank of England, to Holden's exasperation, continued to rely on men, not measures; on intuition and crisis management, rather than elaborate hypothetical safeguards. And, in defence of that policy, at least Cunliffe was no longer the Bank's main man.

Implicit in the Cunliffe Report's conclusions was the belief that a speedy return to the gold standard would in turn help to ensure that London recovered her pre-1914 position as the world's leading financial and commercial centre. Earlier in 1918, replying to a letter from the venerable former *Economist* editor Sir Robert Inglis Palgrave, which included a communication from the Governor of the Bank of the Netherlands, Revelstoke surveyed the situation:

> Mr Vissering takes a pessimistic view of the future of the accepting business in London, and I allow that the considerations he advances are true in the main. I do not believe, however, that the moratorium proclaimed at the beginning of the war has been of any lasting prejudice to British credit. It was not every well-known accepting house which found itself obliged to take advantage of these legitimised facilities for delay, and I confess that, given the extraordinary prosperity forced upon neutrals by the very fact of the present world wide catastrophe, I am astonished that foreign countries should still continue to draw – as I have occasion to know they do – upon London, especially for goods which are not shipped directly to this country.
>
> We cannot expect that London will soon resume 'its old importance as financial centre of the world's commerce': but with all modesty I cannot but retain a perhaps optimistic conviction that the supremacy of British credit, with London as the clearing house of the world, may not necessarily be considered as a dream of the past.

It was a fair retrospective point, for London's acceptance business had declined gently rather than startlingly during the war, with even the more 'German' houses like Kleinworts and Schröders still ticking over. But of course the New York challenge loomed large. Was it a threat or was it perhaps an opportunity? Shortly before the war ended, the *Economic Journal* asked Robert Wyse, London manager of the Guaranty Trust Co of New York and soon to replace Nugent at the Union Discount, to give his views on 'The Future of London as the World's Money Market'. They were broadly sanguine, as he asserted that New York 'may perhaps take financial precedence of London, but that is not just yet'. And he went on: 'It is beyond question that Great Britain and the United States can co-operate in many financial ways at home and abroad to the advantage of both. The estrangements of old times are at an end ...' Perhaps, but he might have been interested in the private view of the American banker Willard Straight (much involved in Chinese finance) two years earlier, that the British idea of co-operation was that 'the other fellow does what the Britisher wants him to do, takes as much of the profit as he can get and for this, in the Englishman's mind, he ought to be thankful'. Above all, Wyse insisted, what London needed was a return to pre-1914 cosmopolitan finance: 'The League of Nations is only a fiction if all the great nations are not involved therein, and the world's money market does not answer its own description unless the motives of all its participants are free from suspicion and confidence is complete.'[70] It was, after the past four years, asking a lot.

*

Peace came at eleven o'clock on Monday, 11 November. Arthur Wrightson (in the absence of the indisposed Charlie Clarke) stood on an improvised platform and, holding a gold baton presented by his fellow-members, led the Stock Exchange in singing the National Anthem; Williamson informed Valparaiso that 'business is suspended' and 'crowds of excited and smiling people throng the streets, which are hardly passable'; Addis noted that 'the City was stunned and even awed' and that 'apart from hooligan lads & drunken lasses the restraint of the crowd was admirable'; and Sir John Ellerman, ship-owner, financier and Britain's richest man, told his daughter that 'the man who holds a similar position to myself in Germany has just committed suicide. I want you always to remember the War has been a very close thing'.[71]

C.H. Rolph, son of a City of London policeman, was seventeen years old and had been working for the past two years in 'the rag-trade warehouse' of Spreckley White & Lewis at 13–15 Cannon Street. It was, he wrote some sixty years later, a 'firm in whose service any honest and reasonably intelligent person could find a niche for life and settle down, happily enough, as a responsible citizen with satisfying leisure pursuits, a decent lawn mower and a family'. There, in the counting house, he sat at a high desk fitted with a foot-rail and 'wrote letters to customers and manufacturers in the "copperplate" script, downstrokes-thick-upstrokes-thin, which I suppose had really begun to die out with the dissolution of the monasteries but was taking a long time about it'. On Armistice Day, he and his colleagues 'all went mad':

> We had been told that the great news would be announced by the firing of maroons, which we had so long accepted as air raid warnings. It was ten past eleven when they went off in the City. Mr Edwards, our venerable cashier at Spreckley's, flung down his pen impatiently and made for the

basement. No, no, we called after him. This is not an air raid, this must be *peace*. But he had gone and, in the ensuing frenzy, he was forgotten. We all crowded into the big Cloth Department, which had huge ground-floor windows looking out on to Cannon Street. People from the five upper floors came running down the fine carpeted stairway at the back of the Department; men and girls from the Furs, the Mantles, the Skirts and Costumes, the Children's. Frock-coated men and shirt-sleeved juniors and immaculate saleswomen and beautiful models, all calling out incoherently and twittering and (incredible in those austere premises) actually embracing and kissing. Two or three people ran down the short flight of steps from the swing doors into the street, and then everybody followed, the building emptied as if someone had shouted 'Fire!' Work was over for the day, by informal mass resolution.

In Cannon Street a man on a bicycle was broken-windedly blowing the All Clear with a bugle he could hardly control as his cycle wobbled through the growing crowds. For some reason we all moved towards the Royal Exchange and the Mansion House, the very centre of the City. At the Royal Exchange someone had run up the Union Jack, and a stiff breeze filled it out. The Royal Exchange steps were black with people. Queen Victoria's statue was covered with clingers-on. Buses were accumulating in all the streets converging on the Royal Exchange, because the dense crowds had slowed them to the pace of the general movement, and eventually they all had to stop. They were all empty inside. Everyone was on top, far too many for safety. People were standing and sitting on the canopy over the driver's seat. One bus, a No. 11, was marked in chalk FREE TO BERLIN and was cheered madly by everyone. Men and women had taken off their boots and shoes so that they could bang them against the metal advertisement sheets on the buses' sides: anything, everything that could make a noise.

Hundreds of sellers of small flags appeared from nowhere. Individual buyers bought dozens and dozens of them, sticking them into every button-hole and other parts of their clothing and all over their hands. The flag of any one of the Allies was as good as that of any other. Huge military lorries came crammed with standing and cheering civilians. Then down came the rain, and no one cared a damn. Piano-organs appeared and people danced in the roads – the one adequate way, it seemed, in which to express excited joy and otherwise inexpressible relief. Those who couldn't dance rang handbells, banged trays, adding to the din of the Klaxons, the screaming whistles, anything and everything that could bellow, echo, vibrate, or shrill.

At last I reached Mappin and Webb's Corner, to find that a crowd later estimated at 100,000, crammed into the converging thoroughfares from every direction, had gradually stopped making a noise as the Lord Mayor, on the steps of his Mansion House, seemed anxious to say something to them. Inaudibly from where I stood, he said a few words that brought fresh cheers and tears, and then led three thunderous cheers for the King, followed by three more each for the Army and the Navy. And when he (or someone) began singing the Old Hundredth, it was gradually taken up by the thousands of rain-soaked revellers in the mightiest quasi-musical roar I have ever heard; and I was astounded that everyone near me seemed to know the words:

> Praise God from whom all blessings flow,
> Praise him all creatures here below;
> Praise him above, ye heavenly host,
> Praise Father, Son, and Holy Ghost.

It was a colossal sound, frightening, isolating; it was as though the God of Thunder himself had taken possession of that mysterious entity by which any crowd exceeds the sum of its constituent members. The very road and buildings seemed to shake with it. It's a hymn with only one verse, but what comparable crowd could sing it today?[72]

CHAPTER THREE

Facing Facts

'I have had one week of the City,' Conrad Russell wrote to his sister in January 1919. 'It is inconceivably horrible. War destroys all. The lucky ones are killed outright, the less lucky live on, mental wrecks . . .' The jobbing life no longer suited, and barely three months after his return to it he described his plight to the widow of one of the fallen:

> I think we are making money now for a bit. But it's very awful and I get more hopeless and useless every day. The Foreign Market is too difficult for me. It's as bad as one of Bertie's [i.e. Bertrand Russell's] books. Four or five times a day I blunder and my ignorance is exposed. Then I am ashamed and humbled to the dust. The survivors of the war are to be pitied. I did one dreadful thing and it came to the ears of the Committee which summoned Löwy who had to explain that his partner was poopsie and promise I wouldn't do it again. I can't even understand what I did. It was against the rules of the Exchange and also against some law made during the war. Löwy was sweet to me but he can't have relished the position and as I don't know and can't understand exactly what was wrong I may do it again. I've quite lost the little nerve I had. I suppose it's very unimportant to anyone but I don't like being a juggins. And that's what I am.

By the end of that year he had left the City and set himself up as a small farmer in Sussex. 'I like the feeling that the production of food is useful and honourable,' he wrote soon afterwards. 'I don't think a place like the Stock Exchange ought really to exist.' But – ineluctably – it did exist, and among the many who returned to Capel Court in the immediate post-war period were the Frisby brothers of the jobbers Ramsden, Frisby & Co. One had won the VC, the other the MC, and for ever after the latter was known in the House as 'the coward'.[1]

For war heroes and others, 1919 as a whole was a strange, disillusioning year of rapidly rising prices, Stock Exchange speculation, industrial strife and fear of Bolshevism. 'Every kind of industrial share is being hoisted up and numbers of companies are making fresh issues,' Farrer noted in April. As the domestic boom gathered momentum, the leading banks increased the level of their advances by well over half. 'We ladled out money,' Robert Brand of Lloyds (as well as Lazards) would recall. 'We did it because everybody said they were making and were going to make large profits, and while you had an uneasy feeling yet you thought that while they were making large profits there could be nothing said about ladling out the money.'[2] As for more creative finance, inevitably the company promoter was back in the thick of things. None more so than Clarence Hatry, born in 1888 the son of a prosperous silk merchant and educated at St Paul's School. Before the war he had been an increasingly high-powered insurance broker, but this was merely a prelude to the heady days of 1919, when he used the Commercial Bank of London (situated in due course in handsome premises on the corner of King William Street and Gracechurch Street, with a fine view over London Bridge) as his personal vehicle for virtuoso wheeler-dealing. Amalgamated Industrials was typical: Hatry floated it for £1.6m in June, as a ship-building, pig iron, coal and cotton-spinning combine with precious little industrial logic, and within four months sold the controlling interest for £5m. At this time Hatry also did very well for himself through major speculations in oil shares, such as Shell and Mexican Eagle. By the start of 1920 he was a very rich man, but in February had to leave business in order to undergo a serious abdominal operation, to be followed by several months of convalescence in South America. In the centre drawer of his desk he left instructions to (in his subsequent words) 'sell all speculative holdings and to keep the bank's resources liquid'.[3] He knew that no boom went on for ever.

It was not a boom that inspired universal joy, dominated as it was by inflation unparalleled in anyone's peacetime memory, but seen by the government for much of 1919 as preferable to the apparent alternative of mass unemployment. Organised labour flexed its muscles, and in August a group of bankers (including Addis) was summoned to Downing Street, given a statement on the industrial unrest, and asked for its co-operation against Bolshevism. The following month the railway strike brought the City almost to a halt, though when one day a few trains did run, this was (the Smith St Aubyn diary noted) 'to the great content of the Engine drivers who were showered with silver'. Hitherto unionisation had been almost non-existent in the City, but this now started to change, albeit slowly and tentatively. The nationwide Bank Officers' Guild was established in 1918, attracting many recruits in the joint-stock banks. 'A serpent has raised its head in banking' was Holden's temperate reaction, adding, 'I'll smash the B.O.G. or die in the attempt.' Salaries were raised and share participation schemes introduced, but the banks obstinately refused to negotiate with the Guild. So too did the Stock Exchange with officers of the Stock Exchange Clerks' Guild, founded in 1919 and soon representing well over 2,000 clerks. 'When one reads in a financial daily of S/E Clerks being paid less than dustmen, it is rather to the discredit of the "House" that such a thing should be possible,' the Guild's first Chairman, Sydney J. Love (of 79 Pascoe Road, Lewisham), very reasonably pointed out; but the Committee declined to recognise the body, even after its General Secretary, Charles H. Sykes, had stated that 'my Guild is pledged to the support of a just capitalism' and affirmed its 'loyalty to the forces of Law and Order'. Sykes was disappointed: 'The refusal to discuss our common problems must be taken as an expression of the unwillingness of the Stock Exchange to accept the co-operation of the staffs except upon terms of unconditional surrender.'[4]

The Bank of England adopted a more constructive approach.[5] On a Saturday afternoon in February 1919 a crowded meeting of the staff was held in the Court Room and addressed by Wilfred G. Bryant, a 1st-class clerk in the branch banks office. 'It has come to pass that because we are in the service of the Bank, the Bank claims the right to commandeer, if it thinks fit, the whole of our waking life and to recompense us for the sacrifice of all our leisure on its own terms,' he told his colleagues. 'Is it any wonder that human nature has rebelled against this worse than slavery?' And: 'For years past the whole system of promotions has caused comment and disaffection. Men are passed over without a cause assigned and are barred accordingly from legitimate advances.' And again: 'How many men in this room could give a complete list of our Directors? Or tell aught about their personalities? Not one in ten. Yet they are our masters . . .' However, speaking as a member of the self-styled 'Committee of Delegates', Bryant added a soft impeachment: 'We have not received from you, although we have been fighting your battles, all the sympathy that we deserved. There is a terrible amount of snobbery in the Bank. There is an extraordinary ability to sit upon fences. There is a remarkable shrinking from compromising your dignity or your fancied position with the authorities.' No doubt stung by his words, the meeting agreed to send a memorandum, 'respectfully addressed to the Governor and Directors of the Bank of England by the staff of the same', which demanded the establishment of a standing committee of directors and staff, on the grounds that 'in no other way does it seem possible that difficulties can be brought to light and alleged grievances ventilated'. In his diary Norman called it a 'Grumblers Meeting', but the Court as a whole responded by appointing a Special Committee on Grievances.

Over the next few months it heard many individual grumbles. From Harold W. Veasey, a superintendent in the dividend accounts office: 'I am afraid I must attribute my lack of promotion to some sinister influence; there is a general feeling on the Stock side that unless one is in with certain people one has no chance of promotion.' From Henry Onyon, a 2nd-class clerk in the dividend pay office: 'I was 11 years in the 4th Class, which was most disheartening, and I thought that once I got out of that Class things could not be worse; I have, however, been 13 years in the 2nd Class and I am still there. I am nearly 54 ... I believe my case is the worst in the Bank.' From Arthur J.F. Bond, a 4th-class clerk in the private drawing office: 'Since I was demobilised on the 12th December last, my average time of leaving on Saturday has been 3 o'clock ... I used to play Rugby football and often I did not arrive on the field until half-time.' From Henry H. Lempriere, a 1st-class clerk in the dividend pay office: 'I may say that I came into the Bank in 1882 and since then I have not spoken to a Governor or Director.' From James R. Sugars, a 3rd-class clerk in the accountant's bank-note office: 'A man never knows his character in the Bank. If a man wants to know his character he has to ask his Principal, who may or may not tell him. Any secret system is liable to abuse, as it places the Principal in an autocratic position ...' And from Cuthbert Pearce, a 4th-class clerk in the dividend accounts office, finding it difficult (at twenty-nine years old, married with small twins) to make ends meet on a basic salary of £290 p.a.: 'I have to work late on every possible occasion in order that I may be able to give my family the bare necessities of life ... The Bank have always been particular as to the type of men they elect into the Service; they come from decent homes and have the habits and tastes of gentlemen and I think the Bank should put them in the position to gratify those tastes.' Comforted by what Bryant described as 'the extreme repugnance among our men to have anything to do with Trade Unions', the Court in July set up an Advisory Council of directors and staff.[6] The Bank would remain for a long time a slow-moving and excessively hierarchical organisation; but the old days of seemingly arbitrary autocratic rule had gone for ever.

The year 1919 was also one of peacemaking, and in March, in a paper to the Institute of Bankers, Addis argued that 'the interdependence of nations makes it impossible to cripple Germany without to some extent crippling British trade'. In discussion, none agreed with the line that Herbert Gibbs had been taking – belligerently demanding £600m a year from Germany – but Henry Bell in the chair reckoned that Addis had gone a little too far, in that 'it was a human feeling that so far as possible the evils which a man had wantonly inflicted upon another should be made good'. Unfortunately for moderate opinion, Lloyd George looked to Cunliffe for expert advice as to the appropriate level of reparations. And Cunliffe looked to – what? 'A remarkable couple protected British interests, the Lords Sumner [a leading judge] and Cunliffe,' noted Keynes about the British representatives (sometimes called the 'Heavenly Twins') on the Reparations Commission at the Paris Peace Conference. It was as though, he went on, 'a vulture were bedfellow with a pig, the one tearing the flesh from the dying victim but it was the other who was gorged'. Cunliffe himself was less than gruntled. 'You are ordered here and ordered there,' he replied when asked how he was enjoying his time in Paris. 'Do this and do that. But no one ever says, "Good dog!"' £200m in gold was the first payment he wanted to be made by Germany, and Bradbury at the Treasury enquired how he had reached that figure. 'Because it's twice as much as they've got,' the unabashed ex-Governor told him. On another occasion he was asked how he had arrived at the preposterous figure that Germany should pay some £24,000m in a generation, about ten times what either the Board of Trade or the Treasury thought feasible. 'It came to me in church' was the answer. However, as Lloyd George remarked in later years, Cunliffe 'probably never put his nose inside a church'.[7] Of course Cunliffe was not solely responsible for the muddled, inconclusive position that the British government took over the whole question of reparations, but his crudely conceived advice did not help.

As for the peace settlement generally, the City seems to have been merely relieved that the war was over. 'I only trust that this definite signature of Peace may foreshadow the dawn of a happier era of prosperity,' Revelstoke wrote to a Paris banker in January 1920. Keynes's coruscating analysis of *The Economic Consequences of the Peace* had just been published, but Norman was probably correct when he described *Punch*'s reaction as 'a summing up of many people's attitude towards Keynes' diatribe', as he enclosed the relevant verses in a letter to Benjamin Strong. 'There was a superior young person named Keynes,' they began, and ended:

> Still we feel, as he zealously damns the Allies
> For grudging the Germans the means to arise,
> That possibly some of the Ultimate Things
> May even be hidden from fellows of King's.[8]

Cunliffe himself was already encountering some of those ultimate things, having succumbed to septicaemia less than a week into the new decade.

We have a final glimpse. In April 1919, after the New York investment bank Kuhn Loeb had suggested an international issue for Belgium, Anthony de Rothschild called on Cokayne at the Bank of England to ascertain his views. 'The Governor,' he reported to Rothschilds in Paris:

> repeated very much the same opinion as he gave us last month about the general situation and said that he did not think the London market was capable of handling any such operation, for the present at any rate. So long as we had to borrow money from the United States ourselves – and there was considerable uncertainty as to when we should have to meet our obligations in that country – it was most unsafe for us to lend money to other countries. He said that he could not definitely state that the Treasury would refuse permission for such an Issue but that he felt that it would be advisable to discourage the whole project from the London standpoint.

Following which, while Anthony discussed the matter with his cousin Charles, Cunliffe came in:

> He was informed of the telegram and of the opinion of the Governor of the Bank of England and asked to express his own opinion. He suggested that it would be advisable to consult the Chancellor of the Exchequer because he had had several conversations with Mr Chamberlain in Paris and he thought the Chancellor might have certain views on the matter. He particularly emphasised the fact that it would be most unwise to surrender our international financial position more readily than was absolutely necessary and pointed out that if an international issue was made Paris could subscribe nothing, London might make a pretence of subscribing a little and New York would have to find practically the whole of the money, but that it would be worth while for London to appear as a participant.

Chamberlain being unavailable, de Rothschild went to see Bradbury, who entirely backed Cokayne, not his predecessor, and 'stated definitively that at the moment the Treasury would not be likely to give permission for such an issue in London'.[9]

The fundamentals, it was painfully clear, had altered.[10] 'I have been making enquiries in the City and elsewhere with regard to the view held on the general financial situation to the extent to which assistance can be given by London to other European countries,' Brand a few weeks later informed Lord Robert Cecil, in Paris as Chairman of the Supreme Economic Council of the Allies. 'I find the general view is that if the problem is as big as it appears to be . . . it is far beyond the capacity of the British Banks and Accepting Houses.' Next day Brand wrote to a Lazards partner in New York, reflecting on his own recent stint as

Cecil's financial adviser: 'The longer I stayed in Paris, the more I was impressed with the enormous size of the financial and economic problem of Europe. Everything in reality depends on America's attitude and her willingness to lend freely and for long terms to Europe. Unless she does so the future is certainly very black and more than one country may be unable to escape a collapse.' The London market remained for the time being virtually closed to foreign loans, even for the best causes, and when in January 1920 Hambros approached Norman on the subject of a possible Danish issue, the Deputy Governor 'refused to hear the Danes or see them' and 'said the Danes sh^d go to N.Y.' Being a man of pre-1914 sensibilities, when London was the unrivalled capital market of the world, Norman added in his diary that 'this position' was 'generally unpleasing'.[11]

With the United States thus supplanting Britain as the world's creditor, how could the Americans be persuaded to deploy their abundant surplus capital on a co-operative as opposed to a competitive basis?[12] Strong was at least willing to oblige on a personal basis. 'I am sending you a shipment of "Lucky Strikes",' he informed Norman at one point in November 1919, those cigarettes apparently being unobtainable in London. Writing from Paris (where he was an American delegate) in June, Thomas Lamont of Morgans in New York had more ambitious co-operation in mind when he called on Brand to endorse 'a working partnership in business betwixt Great Britain and America':

> Let me make the concrete suggestion: America has ample credit resources, Great Britain has wonderful credit machinery all over the world. Why not make a combination of the two? Your people have splendid banks established in the Far East and all through South America. Now, we in America are right on the verge of duplicating every bit of that banking machinery by establishing banks of our own there and entering into very active competition with you. The result will be, you will make smaller profits, and so shall we, and we shall be very keen rivals. Why don't we avoid all that by our buying a half interest, no more, in a lot of your banks, and thus make a combination of your machinery and our credit resources? I suppose the very idea sounds fantastic to you. It did to Keynes when I sprang it on him the other night at dinner. His ready answer was, that your banks wanted to run their own business and didn't want any interference from outside. It was a very complete answer, because it showed the spirit of the whole thing.

As so often Keynes was on the money, for it would need more than a sudden change in the global pecking order to upset the assumptions of a lifetime. 'Senator Owen (Oklahoma) at Bk of E. Lunch,' noted Addis late in 1918. 'A typical Yankee politician; not attractive.' Or as Farrer, writing to a sympathetic Dutch banker, characterised Wall Street some years later: 'Everyone there is more or less out for everyone else's throat, and it is a case of devil take the hindmost.'[13]

Undeniably, irrespective of prejudice, these were difficult, challenging times. Austen Chamberlain was chosen by Lloyd George early in 1919 to be his peacetime Chancellor, not least because the City regarded him as reassuringly sound; yet within weeks Chamberlain was compelled to observe that 'when "the City" is acting by instinct and rule of thumb it is amazingly clever and sure, but when it is asked to advise on large new issues, it has no theory or policy to work upon, and is indeed a broken reed'.[14] The context was the debate about whether or not to continue to allow gold exports, and thus a theoretical gold standard, in the wake of the American decision no longer to support sterling. Cokayne and Norman saw the anti-inflationary advantages of maintaining a pegged dollar-sterling exchange rate at 4.76; the politicians feared the social and political consequences of deflation; and they received valuable backing from leading joint-stock bankers.[15]

Smith St Aubyn in the discount market was thoroughly browned off by the turn of events. On 16 March, Cokayne 'strongly advised us to sell our $3\frac{1}{2}$ War Loan which we proceeded to do', the firm duly selling £200,000 of stock. On the 28th it sold its remaining £400,000. Whereupon: 'After business hours an Order in Council was issued prohibiting the export of Gold. We should never have sold the stock if we had any idea of this, the dear money party have evidently been defeated.' It had indeed, Farrer soon afterwards referring to how 'the policy of the Government and the Chancellor of the Exchequer has established here a pernicious regime of cheap money, and the Stock Exchange and gambling public are cheerfully taking full advantage of it'. Put another way, the Bank of England had failed to recover the control over monetary policy that it had lost during the war. 'We feel to be living on a bubble which may burst sooner or later,' Norman wrote in June to Strong, almost certainly more mildly than he felt, adding, 'we are still hemmed in by War time restrictions as to rates of money'. The following month the Bank did win a significant victory with the so-called 'July Agreement' – ensuring that, despite rising nationalist opinion in South Africa, the sale of that country's gold was centralised in the London market, taking ritualised form from September with the start of the daily Gold Fix held at Rothschilds – but to orthodox eyes the government still seemed dangerously wedded to the debt-increasing, inflation-increasing idea of trying to build a world fit for heroes.[16]

Significantly, in this case, the City's best brains were on the side of orthodoxy. One of them belonged to Oswald Falk, a stockbroker who had trained as an actuary and had recently founded the Tuesday Club, a high-powered dining club for economists (including Keynes) and thoughtful financiers (including Addis and Brand). Early in September he circularised a 'Note on the Future of Interest Rates in London', in which he argued that the government's current 'inflationist policy' was 'helping to wreck our position as a financial centre', because among other evils 'the use of inflation involves the raising of commodity prices, encourages extravagance, causes industrial unrest and helps to depreciate the exchanges'. Later that month, on the 25th, Cokayne sent Chamberlain his grand remonstrance. He wanted him to raise the Treasury bill rate (still determining interest rates more than Bank rate did) and generally switch tack:

> The pound sterling is now quoted at a discount in all the most important centres . . . It is surely worth a temporary effort to recover the magnificent credit which the Country has so long enjoyed and which once lost could but slowly if ever be recovered . . . If the Bank had been free to exercise their proper functions they would long ago have taken steps to raise the value of money in this Country in order to protect the Exchanges. But while the present large floating debt of the Government exists the Bank are powerless to control the money market without the co-operation of the Treasury.

As for the domestic situation, Cokayne expressed his keenness to check the post-war credit expansion, 'which has inevitably led, or at least contributed largely, to a great increase in the currency and to extravagant living'. And in general, Cokayne warned Chamberlain, 'the Court regard the restoration of the gold standard and the resumption of free gold exports at the earliest possible moment as of vital importance to the Country as a whole and consider that it is well worth a temporary sacrifice to secure that end'.[17] The counter-revolution had begun.

In early November, to the City's surprise, Cokayne managed to secure an increase in Bank rate from 5 to 6 per cent – though Norman observed to Strong that, pleased though he was, 'at the same time I cannot regard the certainty of sound money as definitely settled'. In particular he was worried about 'the advocates of expansion and the printing press, which to a considerable extent is the view held by many political leaders'. Debate over monetary policy intensified during the winter, and Chamberlain found himself caught invidiously between the Bank and the banks. There was by now an important new player. Holden had died in

July, suddenly while recuperating in Scotland. Typically he had travelled there by car, not train, in order to inspect some branches on the way. 'His one hobby in life was banking and all that appertains thereto,' the *FT* justly obituarised. In his final year he had carefully trained the former Chancellor, Reginald McKenna, as his nominated successor, and McKenna was quickly into his stride, stoutly calling for national economy and an eventual return to the gold standard, but explicitly challenging the Bank's dear-money policy. 'Take my advice, don't run for the position of C. of E. when you enter Parlt,' Chamberlain wrote to one of his sisters in January 1920 after a wearying round of discussions. The clearing bankers have been accused of talking up their own books during this protracted tussle, on the grounds that higher rates would have led directly to 'damaging depreciation of their own and their customers' gilt-edged portfolios'; even if there is some truth in this, the fact remains that the joint-stock banks generally *did* have a somewhat wider grasp of the social consequences of dear money than that possessed by either the Bank of England or the Treasury.[18]

Praising dear money, and advocating still dearer, Cokayne in February commended the previous autumn's Bank rate rise to Chamberlain as having 'shown the attention of this country to face facts' – an early example of the Bank's ability to apply a sharp twist of emotional pressure in order to raise the stakes. The next round was recorded by Norman:

> 9 *March*. 4.45. Treasury. Long & pleasant meeting with Bankers – all strongly against Rate increase – except Leaf & Bell: nothing settled but they are to suggest an alternative (in the way of rationing credit or somehow limiting their advances) failing wh C of E. said clearly rates *must* go up at once. On the whole a financial failure, but social success. Low rates will someday ruin us.

Chamberlain himself was now privately backing Cokayne and believed the bankers to be 'biassed by their interest, timid & collectively selfish'; but several key Cabinet colleagues were still hostile to dearer money, and so he decided to 'disappoint the Governor & put the Bankers on their honour to behave better than they have been doing'. The promise of credit rationing failed, however, to do the trick. There still appeared to be an inflationary boom that needed dampening down; the pound was still making a poor fist of it, as international confidence in Britain's post-war economic prospects waned; and on 15 April, a fortnight after Norman had succeeded Cokayne as Governor, the rate was increased from 6 to 7 per cent.[19] Bank and Treasury (especially Bradbury) had proved a formidable coalition.

A revealing postscript to the rise was played out over the next few months. In fact the boom was already past its peak, and the depression setting in, but because of the poor quality of economic intelligence this was not generally recognised until the end of the summer. By July not only was Norman pushing for a rise to 8 per cent, for what was becoming the familiar mixture of domestic and exchange reasons, but Keynes was taking a stridently dear-money line, telling the Tuesday Club on the 8th that continuing inflation and fiscal extravagance demanded a tougher monetary stance. A week later Norman made his début at the Lord Mayor's annual Mansion House dinner for bankers and merchants. 'They had been for months past pursuing a steady and consistent policy, which he believed to be the one and only policy which would ultimately place this country again on that eminence which it occupied before the war,' he told the company (in his reported words). 'The object they had set themselves was, with as little delay as possible, to attempt to regain the gold standard, and to that end every movement had been directed.' But the next morning there appeared in the *FT* what was from Norman's point of view an ominous editorial, highly critical of the desire in some quarters for a further rise in Bank rate. After a reference to the 'dear money fanatics', it went on:

> Still the desire to shoot has not been abandoned. The old-time reputation of the Bank Rate as an arm of precision makes them anxious to load it up and let it off. Suppose they had their way and, aiming across the broad Atlantic, fired their 8 per cent shell. It would explode ineffectually in the air, but the recoil would react with incalculable injury on home trade and industry . . .

Norman may on the 17th have told Hawtrey at the Treasury that 'the City fears higher rates simply and solely because of the consequent depreciation in their securities', adding that 'this reason is never mentioned', but in reality there was a broader agenda at work. Chamberlain simply informed the Governor that another rise was politically impossible.[20] In the changed conditions of the post-war world – no 'automatic' monetary standard, volatile exchange rates, national and international financial considerations meshing far more closely than they had ever done before 1914 – it would become increasingly difficult for the high priests of the City to remain value-free technicians beyond criticism or even scrutiny.

CHAPTER FOUR

A Halfpenny Less

'Dined with Norman at his house Thorpe Lodge on Campden Hill,' jotted Addis in November 1919. 'Magnificently filled house for a lone bachelor.' And the following April, after Norman had become Governor: 'I like him. A clever fellow. I only hope his health will stand the strain.' Norman himself wrote to his mother, a difficult lady, after his election: 'I am never happy without work but now I expect to get more than I want and perhaps worry and kicks too, which take away from the quiet dignity that used to surround the position. All the same I am glad of the work.' The perceptive Addis, though occasionally critical, remained enamoured. In July 1921: 'Tea and an hour's talk with Governor at Bank of England. I like him.' And September 1922: 'That dear man Norman called . . . He is a friendly chap and singularly gifted with charm.'[1] It was at about this time that Anthony Blanche was telling Charles Ryder that charm was the English vice; in the hands of Montagu Norman, Governor from 1920 to 1944, charm was perhaps his most powerful weapon, and certainly his most insidious.

A handful of set-piece descriptions and reminiscences enable one to start to see the man in the round. Emile Moreau, a Governor of the Bank of France, first met Norman in Paris in 1926:

> He appears to have stepped out of a Van Dyck painting; elongated figure, pointed beard, a big hat; he has the bearing of a companion of the Stuarts. It is said that Israelite blood flows in his veins. I know nothing of this, but Mr Norman seemed, perhaps because of it, full of contempt for the Jews about whom he spoke in very bad terms . . . He adores the Bank of England. He told me: 'The Bank of England is my only mistress. I think only of her and I have given her my life' . . . Very mysterious, extremely complicated, one never knows the depth of his thoughts. Even so, he is very amiable, charming when he wants to be. That is the case when he tries to flatter me by telling me that the Bank of England was founded by French Huguenots . . .

Five years later Raymond Streat was one of a six-man deputation from the Manchester Chamber of Commerce who saw Norman at the Bank:

> The great man rose to his feet as we entered. If it had to be done in two words I should make my description of him that of 'a Spanish Grandee'. His beard and hair though greying are still mainly black or give that impression. His flashing eyes are probably brown but leave the impression of being black. His broad brow is of the kind one sees in the Dutch masters but rarely in real life. His movements are graceful and flowing and he has a voice of a singularly compelling and attractive timbre ... I doubt if this man has an equal, never mind a superior, at controlling situations and putting the men who come to meet him where he wants them firmly and kindly but ever so effectively. Towards the end of the interview this remarkable man spoke with intense and burning feeling about the obligations of the City of London to set such standards of integrity, not merely in action but even in thought, as would leave her reputation as untarnished in the future as it had been in the past. This note of high moral sentiment took me by surprise but it was in excellent taste and on the whole impressive.

All who knew Norman at all well were aware of the many contradictions in his character, and writing in the 1960s, the veteran economist Sir Theodore Gregory made a fair stab at encapsulating them:

> His physique and his voice were magnificent, he had great charm of speech and manner; at the same time, he was capable of great irritability and of violent fits of passion. He was an extremely hard worker and was yet subject to not infrequent bouts of nervous breakdown. He was both artistic and musical in his tastes and could be extremely kind. Yet, one of his oldest American *confidantes*, to whom he was obviously sincerely attached, could describe him as 'the most vindictive man I have ever known'. He could enlist warm friendships and elicit the most devoted service, yet he could seriously upset the nerves of some of his most faithful collaborators. He disliked politicians as such, but found a congenial soul in Baldwin. He was a mystic and read widely, but he had no clear-cut views on some of the profound issues of thought. Although he disliked explaining himself to more than one person at a time, his written communications were admirably expressed. He could never have been a success on television. He would have despised it ...

George Booth was a director of the Bank throughout Norman's governorship and, as the son of Charles Booth, had well-developed powers of observation:

> I never knew a person who was so feminine, so meticulous about his

person, so beautifully *soigné*, who was so ruggedly brave . . . He had funny little tricks, he was vain – but it wasn't the sort of vanity that mattered at all. And he was always using strange expressions. I remember he said to me once about someone, 'Your friend's a bit hairy in the heel, eh?' The one thing Monty never wanted to be asked was why he did anything. He didn't really know quite, but he had this extraordinary intuition . . . He used to walk down Campden Hill from Thorpe Lodge to High Street Kensington station to get the Underground to Mansion House. He wouldn't go to Cannon Street, the next station. He always went to Mansion House because it was a halfpenny less. And he would bow his head to the gentleman for him to take the ticket out of his hat. People said, 'What affection!' but it was agreeable humanity. He never made jokes or anything of that kind. He was just amusing. A continual bubble of wit.

Norman, befitting a one-time patient of Jung, has suffered more than most from being put on the psychiatrist's couch, but the Dutch banker J.W. Beyen, who got to know Norman in the 1930s, provides a genuinely insightful assessment:

He was profound and serious and at the same time playful and mischievous. He was courteous and kind but could on rare occasions be very cruel. He was immensely curious of all the facets of the human beings he met, of the events he had to cope with, though he had a profound disdain for details. He was full of contradictions and, nevertheless, a closely integrated personality. Though being uncommon, he was very normal, there was nothing eery about him. He was very much a product of England but by no means a typical Englishman. He was a great banker, banking was his life, he created the 'mystique' of the Central Banker. But he did not look like a banker at all. There was something of the actor in him – all leaders of men have that – but he did not act apart, he was very much his own real self. He had the touch of the artist in dealing with situations and people – he was not an artist. Intuition guided him but he was very rational and reasoned in his conception of problems. He was a traditionalist with an entirely unconventional approach. He exerted power but always through influence. He was, in every respect, immensely interesting.

All true, all somewhat tantalising. One needs to see the real man in real situations. 'Action is character,' F. Scott Fitzgerald remarked, and Norman would probably have agreed. A letter to Strong in 1922 is suggestive. 'I fear he is finding Schröder's Collection Department rather dull,' he wrote about Strong's son, temporarily apprenticed in Leadenhall Street. 'That is perhaps inevitable, because it is mechanical work;

but as I tried to explain to him, there is a world-reason in all these collections which he is putting through . . .'[2]

Even so, for all his personal qualities, one needs to explain how it was that Norman became the Pope of the City – a place that previously had tended to regard the Bank of England with at least as much scepticism as reverence. 'Experienced people in our market are not accustomed to regard the position of Governor of the Bank of England either as an assurance of intellectual or financial merit,' Kleinworts unequivocally, if ungrammatically, informed Goldman Sachs of New York in 1919. Nor on the face of it was Norman the City's type. According to Addis, his Mansion House speech of July 1920 had a 'strange' and 'mystical' quality to it – 'fine in its way but unsuited to his audience'. Clearly his length of tenure, conclusively ending the peacetime tradition of two-year gubernatorial stints, was crucial to achieving his ascendancy. Addis, writing in 1926 about the early part of the decade, gave a typically clear-sighted explanation:

> The orientation of our banking policy had been profoundly disturbed. The predominant industrial and financial position of England had been challenged and it was no longer possible for the central bank unaided to control the exchanges and prevent, as formerly, undue fluctuations in the value of gold by the accustomed use of the Bank rate. The only possible means of solving that question was to arrive, if that was practicable, at a common understanding with the central banks of the old world and the new in order to secure the adoption of a common monetary policy in which all could co-operate. The problem had become international. The Bank of England had ceased to be an insular institution. The suspension of the biennial rotation was justified by the necessity of securing continuity in the delicate negotiations required to adjust the administration of the Bank to the novel relations with the other central banks. This was not a matter of choice. It was a condition imposed by the war.[3]

So, inevitably with some acrimony involved, it was.

'At the beginning of next month, contrary to custom, I am beginning my third year,' Norman wrote to Strong in March 1922, following a forceful appeal from Strong that he stay on. 'What will happen after that I have not the least idea, but I must confess that there is no understudy at the present time ready and qualified to step into the gap.' Certainly his deputy since 1920, H.A. Trotter, was not the man to grasp the new nettle of international central banking. Anyway, the next in line for the chairs, Cecil Lubbock, had made it clear that he would not serve as deputy under Trotter. In October 1922 Trotter agreed to stand down ('he wishes to attend to his private business which is not doing well,' Norman informed Strong) and Lubbock in effect became Deputy Governor, formally from the following spring. Norman also told Strong: 'I continue as Governor. (& my so doing may raise some criticism, as it will be my fourth Year & people prefer the Rotation: But how swap horses just now?)' A year later, in November 1923, the question of a successor to Norman was seriously considered. 'Grenfell says No! to Lubbock,' noted Addis, who had already ruled himself out in a confidential discussion with Revelstoke. Lubbock was a capable man, but it would have been strange to have had a brewer (in his case Whitbreads) as Governor in the complex world financial order that was taking shape. 'I am engaged here for 1924/5,' Norman entered in his diary in February 1924. 'I am willing to be similarly engaged for 1925/6 and 1926/7.' Later in 1924 he put Strong in the picture:

> Lubbock is a loyal & good fellow & by next April will have done two years which, by tradition, is all that could be asked of him. He would have enjoyed & welcomed the dignity of being Governor but he has not the training as things are – nor at his age can he acquire it. So he is to be succeeded, practically speaking, by the next on the List – Anderson – who, like Lubbock, does not seem to have the training. But he is a masterful & strong man ...[4]

Sir Alan Anderson, a shipper, was indeed a tougher egg than the classical scholar Lubbock, and Norman would soon have to fight rather harder to keep his position.

Beyond the fact that the world had changed, beyond the City's seeming need for a single authority to help it make sense of that change, beyond that lodestar's longevity, there were Norman's considerable personal qualities, charm included. He made it his business to know what was going on in all the City's main sectors; his door was always open to the leading figures in those sectors; and by dint of 'moral suasion' – the dignified term for the raising of the Governor's eyebrows – he exercised greater authority over the City than any of his predecessors or successors. Every working day at the Bank he received a series of visits, each crisply (sometimes cryptically) recorded in his desk diary. For example, 6 December 1922: 'Rob Martin. Fluff.' 28 February 1923: 'Sir Rob Horne. Shall he join a Co as Chairman to take over certain of Tilden Smith's interests? I say certainly not.' 9 November 1923: 'Dufour: a miserable man "with a tale of woe".' 4 April 1924: 'Allan Cameron: I am hurt that he acted for Erlangers over Loan for Amsterdam – behind my back – too cheap.' 6 May 1924: 'E. Erlanger: to apologise for Issue of

Amsterdam Loan: he issued unwittingly, if at all.' 14 November 1924: 'Falk: I sh^d quite approve fresh capital & good management for Chalmers Guthrie & Co so as to make them into a first class accepting-house.' And so on. 'His requests were taken as commands, and complied with to the letter, often at a real sacrifice,' Lawrence Jones of Helbert Wagg later recalled. 'A summons would come to Alfred Wagg, who must put on a top-hat in which to obey it, for the wide-brimmed soft hat that hung outside Mr Governor's room would tolerate no rival.'[5] Perhaps some irreverent spirits hoped that Mr Governor's tube ticket was still sticking out from it.

*

'My own feeling is that the private firms are on their trial,' Farrer wrote shortly before the end of the war to a like-minded Dutch merchant banker, arguing that 'if they have not gone back during the war, they have at least not made the progress of the Joint Stock Banks'. The modified gloom was justified. Brandts, Raphaels and the two Sassoon firms were all well-known, essentially 'private' firms soon struggling to make adequate profits. Two merchant banks, both of which had provided Bank Governors, actually went down: Mildred Goyeneche & Co suspended payments in 1921 and Dent Palmer & Co two years later. The latter firm held a fiduciary position in relation to Turkish bondholders, prompting Norman to take an interest in the painful death-throes. In October 1922 H.G. Palmer introduced to him the firm's new partner, Nicholas Middard, who was apparently bringing in over £30,000 of fresh capital; but by the end of the year Middard had done a runner, apparently having withdrawn £73,000 belonging to the firm without telling his partners, and in May 1923 the firm failed. There were other firms that would have failed but for timely mergers, among them Frühling & Goschen, which joined with Cunliffe Bros at the start of 1920 (just before Cunliffe's death) to become Goschen & Cunliffe, though that firm also struggled.[6]

Or take Huths – from 1909 its senior partner was Frederick Huth Jackson, whom City opinion (according to Grenfell, writing in 1912) 'considered to be too theoretical & occupied with outside matters', one of which was his directorship of the Bank of England. However, help was at hand with the admission into the partnership in 1913 of Lord Leven, 'a young man lately in Guards', who offered a major infusion of capital. That capital, unfortunately, was withdrawn when Leven was killed in the war. Shortly before hostilities ended, Huth Jackson spoke

gloomily about his other partners, saying that neither Louis Meinertzhagen nor Lewis Walters 'was any good, having neither the character nor
imagination nor ability and that if the business was left in their hands it
would crumble away'. Huth Jackson himself died in December 1921,
leaving barely £100,000. Assessing the situation the following May,
Kleinworts stated that 'their German account acceptances have been
provided for under the Peace Treaty but unfortunately some fair
proportion of their pre-war acceptances represented commitments in
Poland, Austria, Russia & other countries not so protected'; that 'during
the last few years repeated efforts have been made to obtain a moneyed
partner, but without success'; and that 'they are very good friends of
ours & enjoy a prestige out of proportion to their real position, which is
obscure'.

Huths was such an inner-City house, having for so long provided
directors of the Bank, that Norman now felt the need to step in, with the
firm unable to meet the impending August 1922 deadline for repaying
the Bank of England's pre-moratorium advances of 1914. He summoned
Walters at the end of July, and over the next year Norman not only
advanced £1.5m, but also arranged for Huths to be taken over by König
Bros, though without losing its name. F.A. König became senior partner,
commended by Norman as 'an experienced and conservative Merchant
Banker of the very best class'. 'We understand that Koenig Bros brought
in some £750,000,' Kleinworts informed Goldman Sachs in 1925. 'In
confidence we have heard that Mr F.K. exercises very close control over
transactions, and in one quarter he has been reported to be not too well
pleased with his bargain. K. is not a popular man.' The truth was that
the firm was still being carried by the Bank of England. 'In the interests
of the Banking and Commercial Community,' Norman had told his
Committee of Treasury back in July 1922, 'Huth & Co must not fail.'[7]
Despite the underlying shakiness of the business, it seemed an incontro-
vertible proposition to fellow-members of the club.

Two 'German' firms, which had prospered greatly before the war,
remained under something of a post-war cloud that only gradually lifted.
Kleinworts, for all its sharp words about others, was the object of
Grenfell's suspicions.[8] He would recall that 'the brothers K' took in their
nephew Herman Andreae, who 'developed the business on more
speculating lines apart from the old merchant accepting business which
the K Bros have managed extremely well', and that Andreae 'became
very intimate with Sir M. Edgar of the very second rate house of Sperling
& Co', leading to the firm losing 'heavily' in 1921. In June 1920 Andreae
was quizzed by Norman about the firm's connection with Sperlings. 'All

serene & all clear,' recorded Norman, though without concealing his mistrust. Mackay Edgar was a more or less rogue Canadian financier, later described by the racing journalist Quintin Gilbey as 'a most genial host, as well as a most generous protector of the opposite sex', befitting both of which qualities he 'died penniless'; and in the heady atmosphere of 1919 he used Kleinworts' money to construct a shipping combine in the North-East that subsequently became a significant drain on the firm's resources. Nor was Kleinworts' situation helped by the continuing discord between the two brothers: Alexander was usually at 20 Fenchurch Street from Monday to Friday, while Herman would come in on Saturday. Not surprisingly, the succession question, and the future of the partnership, remained damagingly unresolved.[9]

Even so, Kleinworts in the 1920s was a fundamentally prosperous firm, recovering much of its old accepting business and even branching out into new areas more remunerative than shipping. The other side of Leadenhall Market, the same applied to Schröders, where it could never be quite the same again, although a creditable recovery took place.[10] Baron Bruno apparently did not return to the City until August 1920, and increasingly the running was made by the energetic, even exuberant Frank Tiarks, a director of the Bank of England since 1912 and closer than most to Norman. 'Very gifted, very dangerous – turning the charm on and off': Beyen's assessment was probably about right. Schröders also recruited cleverly (Albert Pam in particular), as well as having the perspicacity to establish in 1923 a New York offshoot, known as Schrobanco, showing a realistic acceptance of how the centre of gravity of trade finance, in the western hemisphere at least, had shifted across the Atlantic. 'They are doing a very large business with Germany,' Grenfell had reported the previous year about the London house. 'They are reputed to be still very rich and their general standing is high. In short, I should say they are the most influential foreign friends of Germany today, but entirely loyal to England at the same time.'[11]

Some things did not change. 'We only saw the young man for a few minutes and practically did not discuss business with him,' Gaspard Farrer wrote in a letter of recommendation to Kidder Peabody in New York in 1922, 'but he made a favourable impression upon us, looked one straight in the face, and seemed to me the kind of person who would be straight in his dealings.' If the face fits ... But at the highest level the question confronting Barings after the war was: whose should that face be? Farrer himself had only stayed on because of the war, while Revelstoke was in his mid-fifties. There was no one obvious at hand to assume the eventual leadership of the firm, and Farrer in 1919 appreciated that 'in the next few years we ought to be getting fresh blood in here'.[12] Happily, a figure was at hand comparable to Joshua Bates.[13] Three years later, in May 1922, Farrer wrote to Kidder Peabody in Boston about E.R. Peacock, who was about to sail to the States:

> He is well worth knowing. A Canadian by birth and I believe starting life as a schoolmaster, he took up Doctor Pearson's business interests when the latter was drowned in the Lusitania – Brazil Traction, Barcelona Light Heat & Power, Mexican Light Heat & Power, and sundry other interests all in the same state of utter impecuniosity, and has brought them through in a wonderful way. We made his acquaintance some years ago, took a great fancy to him, and John has since been instrumental in getting him on the Board of the Bank of England. He is absolutely straight, very level headed, not a talker, but goes and does things and does them well.

At the start of 1924 Peacock joined Barings, Farrer having recently explained to Boston that 'he has of course had a different upbringing from any of us here, but the set of his mind and all his ways are on the same lines as ours'. And by the end of February: 'Peacock is now established here, in good health and a great comfort to us.'[14] It was a thoroughly astute move on the part of Barings, comparable indeed to its recruitment of the Bostonian merchant almost exactly a century earlier.

New Court, by contrast, remained a closed shop.[15] Back in May 1919 Farrer had offered Peacock an introduction there – 'we have no idea what their attitude would be towards business, but we do know that some of the difficulties which existed in the past have now passed away' – but in practice Rothschilds in the 1920s was, if not quite as resistant to new ideas as it had been during the time of Natty and his brothers, far from being the force of old. Natty's son Charles suffered from sleeping sickness, with all its adverse side-effects, and in 1923 he killed himself. The firm was left in the hands of his cousins Lionel (who became senior partner) and Anthony, neither instinctively a businessman, though Anthony had the greater grasp. Lionel was at his happiest growing rhododendrons on his Hampshire estate, but one day stayed later than usual in New Court in order to address the City Horticultural Society that evening. The assembled clerks received some apposite advice. 'No garden,' he told them, 'however small, should contain less than two acres of rough woodland.'[16]

Rothschilds may have operated in a curiously cocooned world, but for most the ceaseless evaluations and evaluating were a way of life. In July 1923 the discount house Allen, Harvey & Ross pasted in its scrapbook three typical assessments derived from the Bank of England:

> *Erlangers.* Capital in 1921 (& now) reported to B/E to be £1,200,000. Their a/c is said by Westminster Bk to run very smoothly & they never seek accommodation. Said to be shrewd.
>
> *Seligman Brothers.* Capital about £2,000,000. Very cautious.
>
> *Higginson & Co.* B/E will not divulge capital, but regard them as strong owing to the certainty that Lee, Higginson & Co, Boston, would support them.

'Shrewd' was one word for Erlangers, but Grenfell the previous year wrote to Morgans in Paris about Baron Emile d'Erlanger himself that 'the man is a natural liar and a most unpleasant person, as I understand his father was before him'. As for Seligmans, the key figure there was becoming Louis Fleischmann. A particularly unpopular stockbroker before the war, he had left the Stock Exchange during it on account of the anti-German feeling, and by dint of ability was now emerging as a significant City figure. 'It is very good of you to express your approval of our Balance-Sheet,' Revelstoke wrote to him in 1921 (apparently unsarcastically), 'and any comment coming from a person of your experience is of all the greater value.'[17]

Arguably, though, the two main rising forces among merchant banks were Lazards and Helbert Wagg. From 1919 the London house of Lazards was part-controlled by the industrial, oil and contracting group S. Pearson & Sons, providing generous capital while allowing Sir Robert Kindersley to continue to run the show. 'The God of the City' was how Beyen would recall him. 'Bob Kindersley walking with a top hat into the Bank of England [where he was a director from 1914] was simply enormous – superhuman.' According to another central banker, Kindersley was 'a buccaneer in the City, and would try anything that was in the rules'. Tall, determined-looking and with bushy black eyebrows, he was, his obituary in *The Times* would assert, 'a man with whom it would be safe to go tiger-hunting and whom it would probably be unprofitable to oppose'. Kindersley's forceful characteristics were ideally complemented by those of the more cerebral Robert Brand, who combined a wide range of interests and correspondents with a sure business touch, informing Lord Curzon in 1921 that 'the activities of my firm have been rapidly growing' and that 'we have in the last two years opened Branches in Belgium and Spain'. The right mix of partners was also the key to the success of Helbert Wagg, in that issuing house's case a combination of British public school on the one hand, Jewish dealers on the other – the two elements knitted together by the paternalistic Alfred Wagg. One of those dealers was the gifted Max Bonn, after his small firm had been taken over in 1921; and on the public-school side, the coming man was the transparently honest, notoriously inarticulate Nigel Campbell.[18]

Perhaps Saemy Japhet should have employed a reticent Etonian as his front man. S. Japhet & Co 'are unquestionably active', Kleinworts told Goldman Sachs in June 1922, 'mainly in Stock Arbitrage & the exotic exchanges & have very lofty aspirations of becoming an International accepting house, but unfortunately the parties in control lack the personality so essential to the role they aspire to play, & we believe that some time will elapse before their acceptance is taken to any extent in this market'. The report added that Japhet himself had recently told Sir Alexander Kleinwort that 'in a few years they expected to be at the top of the ladder & to rank with the first & foremost firms of London'. Nevertheless, despite a lack of personal popularity, Japhets prospered sufficiently to be able to move in October 1924 into newly built, bigger premises at 60 London Wall, where at the celebratory lunch the guest of honour was the arms dealer Sir Basil Zaharoff.[19]

For most merchant banks accepting remained the backbone of their business, whatever the more glamorous, if hazardous, attractions of undertaking large-scale foreign issues on the London capital market. Trade finance recovered rapidly in the post-war boom, fell away alarmingly during the slump of the early 1920s, and then largely recovered again as the world economy picked up by the middle of the decade. Figures are available for only some firms, but by 1925 the market leaders appear to have been Kleinworts (£17.6m), Schröders (£13.9m), Hambros (£10.1m) and Barings (£10m). Acceptances mattered, in terms of prestige as well as profits. 'Our London credit business has kept up remarkably well', Farrer told a fellow-partner in October 1923, 'and we have joined Hambros in what looks like satisfactory Finland timber credits.' Some months earlier Brand wrote revealingly to Kindersley, who was in Madrid but about to visit Lazard Frères in Paris:

> We cannot deny that the losses on the acceptance business have been exceedingly heavy the last few years, and that we shall have to exercise great caution in the future. But we all here feel very strongly, and no doubt you will agree, that Paris do not recognise to what extent our whole position and business is based on our being an acceptance house. If we were to become in the future merely a finance house, the superior British, foreign and colonial corporation [a reference to the British Foreign & Colonial Corporation, a very active issuing house run by the Hungarian-born financier F.A. Szarvasy], instead of an international banking house, my interest certainly would wane a great deal. No doubt you will be able to explain the position to Paris.

Predictably the merchant banks disliked, even more than they had before the war, the clearers muscling in on their traditional territory. Back in 1916 Kleinworts, briefing Goldman Sachs about Barclays, had described that bank's venture into accepting as 'injudicial'; and in 1922 the equivalent report was that the results had been 'not always very happy'. For the clearers, however, there was also *amour propre* involved. In November 1924 Frederick Hyde, joint Managing Director of the Midland, received a courtesy visit from A. Hübbe, a director of Dresdner Bank: 'He said that it was not their practice to ask for accommodation, but if it could be offered to them they would be able to transact more business with us. I reminded him that our Acceptances were greatly sought for . . .'[20] Before 1914 the clearers had ducked out of them, but turf wars remained a serious possibility.

Certainly there was no exaggerated bump of reverence on the part of the City Establishment. 'We had the clearing bankers at lunch at the Bank of England,' noted Addis in May 1920. 'I am not impressed with their breadth of view.' And in November 1923: 'To Institute of Bankers to hear Hambling [Deputy Chairman of Barclays] deliver his inaugural address. Dull and pretentious.' The following year Farrer, reverting to his criticism at the time of the Colwyn Committee, wrote to a correspondent in Halifax that 'in my opinion the big Five Banks are altogether too large for proper supervision and control' and that 'the Directors and General Manager cannot begin to know personally their branch Managers, much less their customers'.[21] As the country's banking structure now began to assume a seemingly permanent, ossified form, there were inevitably many such criticisms voiced concerning institutional rigidities and cartelised complacency. The most searching analysis so far concedes a fair amount of retrospective ground to the critics.[22] Above all, there was an informal but effective agreement struck in the 1920s that depositors were to be paid 2 per cent below Bank rate, double the differential that had obtained for much of the nineteenth century. Admittedly there was still some competition for large deposits, but for most customers the unattractive reality was that of services being provided at a fixed monopoly price. Rates, accordingly, became broadly standardised for interest charged on advances. And, in terms of the City politics of the situation, the clearers in effect provided the Bank of England with an orderly, well-run, far from innovative banking system in return for being allowed to enjoy the fruits of something not far short of an oligopoly. In other words, stability above all things – and, granted the traumatic banking experiences in much of the rest of the world

during the inter-war period, there was something to be said for that
point of view.

Nonetheless, day-to-day relations between the Bank and the clearers
remained surprisingly prickly. This applied particularly to the two
dominant joint-stock men of the 1920s, Frederick Goodenough of
Barclays and Reginald McKenna of Midland.[23] Goodenough (Chairman
from 1917 to 1934) was one of life's autocrats, by the end of his career
rarely allowing a board meeting to last longer than twenty minutes. He
and Norman got on at best poorly, the Governor noting sardonically, 'I
guess his advances to Shipbuilders are growing oppressive', after
Goodenough had come to see him in September 1920 seeking authority
for a Norwegian loan. Two years later Kleinworts, in its hostile
assessment of Barclays, asserted that 'we think they have not been
considered conspicuous for their ability in dealing with new problems'
and 'we know of no personality in the Bank likely to make headway in
new directions'. Goodenough – for better or worse – was essentially
uncerebral, quite unlike McKenna. 'A clever debater & a bad witness,'
commented Addis in March 1925 after Midland's Chairman had
appeared before a National Debt inquiry. 'I do not like that type of
mind, always anxious to make a personal dash.' Norman broadly
agreed, telling Strong a little earlier that 'some people cannot avoid the
limelight'. McKenna – whose private view of Norman was that he was
'an intellectual without an intellect' – undeniably enjoyed a certain
amount of publicity; above all there were his great annual set-piece
speeches to shareholders at the Cannon Street Hotel in late January,
continuing the Holden tradition. As Keynes wrote after McKenna's
death, 'in a way that no other banker has ever attempted, [McKenna]
made the chairmanship of his great institution a pulpit from which to
instruct and educate public opinion'; and he was 'the one powerful
champion of the new ideas speaking from an unchallengeable position in
the City itself'. The most acute reading of McKenna comes from Wilfrid
Crick, a manager at Midland and the bank's first historian. Fully
conceding that McKenna 'was just as unpopular with other banks'
chairmen as with Norman' and that 'he knew his intellectual superiority,
but could display it sometimes in unpleasant ways', Crick added the
crucial rider that McKenna 'had a strong streak of compassion, and took
the cause of the unemployed very much to heart'.[24] At least once in the
early 1920s he almost returned to the chancellorship – and perhaps it
was a shame that he did not.

Keynes himself had now embarked on a difficult, even tortuous
relationship with the City.[25] He knew he needed the City, but he found

much of its culture and underlying assumptions intensely exasperating. 'Capitalist leaders in the City,' he remarked, 'are incapable of distinguishing novel measures for safeguarding capitalism from what they call Bolshevism.' The City, for its part, was often equally exasperated. 'A Professor, a man of theory, who has had no practical experience of business', was how Farrer described Keynes as early as 1917, 'a man who is governed largely by pure reason and thinks others are governed in like manner, and he is apt to omit the human equation'. As if in response, Keynes left the Treasury two years later and, though keeping his Cambridge position, plunged into foreign exchange speculation on a large scale. In the spring of 1920 the markets turned; and Keynes might have faced ruin but for a £5,000 loan from Sir Ernest Cassel, a year and a half before that aged financier's lonely death, and not his least service to humanity.[26]

Keynes never lost his taste for speculation, especially in commodities, and Norman wrote scathingly to Strong in 1924 about Keynes's 'position of trying to combine the position of financial mentor to this and other countries with that of a high-class speculator'. But there was also a more solid side to his practical involvement with the City, above all his position from 1921 as Chairman of the National Mutual Life Assurance Society. Working closely with 'Foxy' Falk, also on the board, Keynes was generally successful in his adoption of a more adventurous investment policy than institutional wisdom considered desirable. In 1924 Peacock was approached, via Revelstoke, with a view to becoming a director of National Mutual. 'I incline to think that you would hardly choose this opportunity to figure on a Board with these particular gentlemen,' Revelstoke wrote to Peacock (who was abroad), enclosing a list of the directorate. That same year Grenfell sent to Morgans in New York an article by Keynes on foreign investments, commenting, 'he always thinks and writes clearly but there is a want of practical knowledge which shows up at times and makes one fearful of his judgment'.[27] He was not, in a word, sound.

Yet was 'soundness', Keynes iconoclastically asked, any longer enough for the City and indeed the nation? He had a considerable regard for Addis (the feeling was mutual), but a marvellous letter of reproach that Keynes sent to him in October 1921, in response to a printed copy of Addis's inaugural presidential address to the Institute of Bankers, was timeless in its critique of practical man:

> You seem to sneer at the Economist for trying to consider these
> questions strictly on their merits and with the scientific object of

discovering which solution will most promote the prosperity of the world. You prefer instead 'the opposing interests, changing purposes, unruly affections and defective wills of ordinary men'. That is to say, you set up as criterion, not the general advantage, but the conglomeration of self-interest, ignorance, passion and general stupidity, which will in fact prevent a scientific solution from being adopted. And not only so, but you suggest that you are being much more high-minded in doing so.[28]

CHAPTER FIVE

Good Faith

Montagu Norman was, perhaps more than anything else, an internationalist – albeit one with certain strong prejudices about individual nations. During these post-war years, the governing tenet of his internationalism was that what the world needed was to return to the pre-1914 order of economic liberalism, with the global economy regulated by the benign dictates of free trade and free capital flows. London, he further assumed, would naturally revert to its position at the hub of that reconstituted financial and trading system. Accordingly, when Strong, visiting England in 1919, was told by Kindersley that the Americans had a moral obligation to forgive the huge war debt (almost £900m) owed to them by Britain – on the grounds that it had been a sacrifice for a shared cause – Norman unequivocally assured him: 'Pay no attention to Kindersley. His heart rules his head.'[1] In other words, Britain could not expect to be taken seriously as a commercial power if it reneged on its debts.

Eventually, in January 1923, Norman found himself in Washington advising the Chancellor, Stanley Baldwin, during the negotiations to settle the debt. Baldwin 'caught on from the very beginning', Norman was pleased to find, and was much influenced by the Governor's advice. The terms they returned with – a settlement spread over sixty-one years, interest of $3\frac{1}{2}$ per cent for most of that time – horrified the Prime Minister, Bonar Law, but received sufficient political and City support to ensure their acceptance. Addis demurred at the Bank, while McKenna briefly growled, before coming on board. Keynes was bitterly opposed, contending that whatever the international arguments in favour of the settlement (the prospect of American co-operation in future European reconstruction as well as the question of British financial honour), there were overriding national arguments against such onerous terms. Hitherto Norman had respected Keynes, even on occasion picking his brains, but his attitude now changed. A 'clever dilettante' was about the best he could say for the man from King's.[2] In reality, as Keynes had feared, a future beckoned of at least as much American rivalry as co-operation.[3] The dollar was strong, US vaults were flooded with gold, key markets (particularly in Latin America) had been captured from Britain – Norman knew all that, yet trusted to force of habit and personal charm to keep the new world in tow to the old. But at least he did not have to watch his back. 'I think it is extremely unfortunate that the City has failed as yet to formulate its view and express it,' Falk wrote at the start of 1923 to a concurring Brand about the debt question. 'I am afraid the City does not think sufficiently about these things.'[4]

Norman's charm came especially into play in relation to his direct American counterpart, Ben Strong. 'Whenever you do come to London,' Norman wrote to him in December 1920, 'let me remind you of your hotel, of which the address is "Thorpe Lodge, Campden Hill, W.8." The Booking Clerk tells me that an hour's notice will be enough to get your room ready, or, if you are in a hurry, this can be done after you have arrived.'[5] The two men kept up a voluminous correspondence throughout most of the 1920s, with illness (whether the world's or their own ailments) the dominant leitmotif.

By 1921 Norman and Strong were consciously formulating the principles of central banking, and the Englishman was comforting the American that 'if ever you should feel downhearted just you remember that, economically speaking, there is only hope through a community of interest & cooperation between all the Central Banks'. At the core of their shared conception was that central banks should maintain operational independence, free from government control, and should 'recognise the importance of international as well as national interests in the re-establishment of the world's economic and trade stability'. By early 1922 Norman's aspirations were ever loftier. 'I believe that the time is not far distant,' he told his Dutch counterpart Dr Vissering in February 1922, 'when Central Bankers presenting an united front will at last have an opportunity to play a part in the affairs of the world.' And the following month, to Strong: 'Only lately have the countries of the world started to clear up after the War, two years having been wasted in building castles in the air and pulling them down again. Such is the way of democracies it seems, though a few "aristocrats" in all countries realised from the start what must be the inevitable result of hastily conceived remedies for such serious ills.'[6]

The castles in the air were partly Norman's, for though the international conference at Genoa shortly afterwards explicitly endorsed the value of central banking co-operation and looked ahead to a full-blown conference of central banks later in the year, Norman was unable to convene such an assembly that would have sealed his very personal vision. The Americans in particular would not play ball, and Strong subsequently explained that the prospect of a conference where he would 'represent the only lending market, while the others would all be borrowers', had had little appeal.[7] Norman was disappointed but not deterred, continued to propagate his belief in the freemasonry of disinterested central bankers as a necessary counterweight to grubby, vote-catching politicians, and in Washington in January 1923 fully endorsed Strong's views as to unacceptable debt settlement, whatever the potential political consequences at home. He had a larger – and longer – game to play.

It was not, in the extraordinarily difficult circumstances of the time, an altogether ignoble vision. A letter to Strong in August 1922 was eloquent enough:

> I have never thought the immediate future of Central Europe looked blacker than it now appears to look. I cannot conceive how some sort of a break-up of Austria is to be avoided long before the end of the year; nor do I see how a condition very near to civil war can be avoided in Germany. It seems utterly impossible for the British Government to see eye to eye, or even to come to terms, with the French Government in respect of the methods to be adopted in dealing with the ex-enemy countries.[8]

Norman appreciated how important Central Europe had been in the pre-1914 economic scheme of things, and during the first half of the 1920s he managed to push through several major reconstruction loans for that part of the world, often with only muted City support.

'The Austrian situation is more than ever complicated,' Revelstoke told Farrer in June 1921, adding that 'our friend Monty is very anxious that something should be done' but that 'altogether it is a tiresome and exhausting affair, without any prospect of profit'. The following year, with 'the Austrian people' in London 'on a last desperate effort to raise the wind', it was Farrer who argued to Revelstoke that it was 'plainly an impossible matter for private people' and that it needed government support. A large-scale Austrian loan finally came off in June 1923. 'I suppose we shall have to lend a hand,' Farrer wrote to another colleague. 'Morgans are taking $25,000,000 for New York, but only did so with reluctance after hearing that Speyer had put in a firm bid for a similar amount. John [i.e. Revelstoke] truly remarks: even such a Jew as Speyer has his uses.'[9] The following year, a loan for Hungary seems to have happened only after Norman strong-armed Rothschilds and Schröders into undertaking it; though again, despite problems with the underwriting, it was a success, no doubt because its sponsors ('the Trinity' of

Schröders, Rothschilds and Barings) managed to insist on a yield double that of Consols.[10]

Arguably, though, it was the first of this issuing trio's reconstruction loans, for Czechoslovakia in April 1922, that was the most evocative.[11] 'We are still struggling, or are beginning to struggle, with the Czecho people,' Revelstoke informed Norman at the start of the year. 'A nice representative has appeared, a certain Dr Pospisil, who talks very indifferent French . . . I do not think that he perhaps appreciates how difficult the business will be, or how essential it is, in view of the state of flux in which these countries are, to have a real copper-bottom security which will induce investors to apply for the Bonds.' For some weeks Pospisil refused to provide adequate security – prompting Farrer to write at the start of February that 'we prefer to let others take the business' and that 'Czecho-Slovakia is but a state of yesterday, and all central Europe is in a state of fluidity'. However, the doctor himself made a favourable impression, being 'a regular professor, but so far as we can see, simple, and absolutely straightforward'. Eventually an agreement was reached over the revenues to be pledged, but shortly before the issue was made Farrer warned Hope & Co (responsible for the Dutch underwriting) that 'not one in a thousand of our public has heard of Czecho-Slovakia', and that 'it might as well be in the moon for all they know'. The loan itself was a success, against the background of a boomlet in the stock market, but the price of Czech bonds soon fell, prompting Farrer to admit in August that 'there is no getting over the fact that Czechoslovakia is a name that does not appeal to the British public, perhaps because they are too insular either to be able to pronounce or to spell it'. A far-away country, and although in due course a second tranche of the Czech loan was issued, this was not before Farrer had sternly told Pospisil that 'even in London millions do not grow like cherries on a cherry tree'.[12]

Germany, of course, lay at the heart of the challenging process of reconstructing Europe.[13] The crux was the seemingly intractable problem of reparations. 'This question plays the devil with us all and hangs like a sinister cloud over the world,' Peacock wrote to Norman in May 1922. He went on to argue that both the main parties were at fault – the French attitude 'technical & unyielding & exasperating', the Germans 'morally wrong', having 'not begun to do the possible' – and, Peacock concluded, '*we* pay the piper for the sins of both'. Norman, however, perceived only one villain, especially after the French occupation of the Ruhr. 'Here you have *all* the conditions of war except that one side is unarmed,' he told Strong in April 1923. 'How long can Germany continue thus?' On New

Year's Eve the newly appointed President of the Reichsbank, Hjalmar Schacht, visited London – being met by Norman at Victoria Station at 10 p.m. – and spent the first four days of 1924 in meetings with Norman and leading clearing and merchant bankers. 'Financially a man of sound and up-to-date views' was Norman's verdict.[14] Schacht was pressing for a large German loan, and Norman was fully prepared to back him.

On a visit to Paris in March he found the French 'still vindictive and unpeaceful',[15] and that same month organised a credit by central banks to enable the establishment of the German Gold Discount Bank. By the end of the summer there was international agreement behind the Dawes Plan, seeking to settle the reparations question – agreement that Norman much welcomed, though against his wishes the new German currency was to be put on a gold (in effect dollar) basis, as opposed to a sterling one.[16] 'It is the question of whether the dollar shall permanently retain a predominant position, or whether we are willing to surrender financial mastery to the Pound Sterling for good and all!' Paul Warburg of Kuhn Loeb in New York had written during the negotiations to an American member of the Dawes Committee. It is difficult to know how serious Norman was about seeking to establish a potential sterling bloc in Central Europe, especially granted the imminent likelihood of the world at large returning to a dollar-denominated gold basis. Even so, when at the end of May the New York banks at the last minute ducked out of the Hungarian reconstruction loan, Norman was palpably satisfied that Europe was able to go it alone and told Schacht that 'it would be ridiculous for Europe to be tied to the tail of America'.[17] Tied to that tail, however, Europe now was.

Integral to the Dawes Plan was the reconstruction loan for Germany. In July Farrer condemned 'the folly of people in this country lending money to Germany to put her on her legs', maintaining to a correspondent that 'it was the German State that was responsible for all the trouble, the German State that over and over again during the war showed the most cynical bad faith and dishonesty, and since the war repeated her conduct by wilfully depreciating the mark'. He added that 'it is quite certain that Germany as a State will never get a penny of my money, but I greatly fear that there are plenty in the City of London who do not share these views of mine'. In the event, though American investors took the lion's share of the huge 'Dawes Loan' issued in October 1924, London was responsible for some £10m. Norman struggled to bring the City into line, managing to persuade Rothschilds to participate secretly up to £1m, but noting in his diary on the 7th that the big joint-stock banks 'decline any official goodwill or support, unless all deposit Banks are named in prospectus'. However, on the 1st Addis had already correctly predicted that the loan would 'be a great success despite the adverse press – Daily Mail is gone mad in fermenting racial prejudices'. Addis had presumably read his *FT*, where the market report of the previous evening noted that 'the view that the loan would give a fillip to German competition has largely evaporated, giving place to a conviction that it may well act as a stimulus to world trade as a whole'. The underwriting was done easily enough on the 13th, though again, according to the *FT*, 'some few men there are who will have nothing to do with a German loan' on the grounds that 'the Germans, they say, have hoodwinked, cheated, damaged us in lives and pocket to an irreparable extent'. Farrer next day confessed himself 'rather surprised to find how easily the average Englishman has put sentiment aside in this case' and could only offer the explanation that 'one's experience is that investors are rather like a flock of sheep'.

That was on Tuesday the 14th, and the loan was about to be so enormously over-subscribed that, according to the *FT* on Thursday, 'many firms of brokers slept members of their staffs in City hotels on Tuesday night, and stories were current during the day that senior partners who had never before been seen in the City earlier than half-past ten or eleven caused something like consternation in outer offices by putting in an appearance yesterday morning in the neighbourhood of eight o'clock'. Without the loan the Dawes Plan was a dead duck, and the City as a whole – encouraged by the attractive 7 per cent coupon – was prepared to play its part, welcoming a concrete step in the long, difficult road back to 'normality'. Or, as the *FT*'s leader put it on the morning of those unwonted early arrivals, 'in the interest of Europe as a whole, we wish it well'.[18]

Soviet Russia remained beyond the pale. Predictably it was demonised, Norman for example confiding to Strong in 1921 his suspicion that that summer's coal strike was 'much more closely connected with Soviet activities than most of us have any idea of'. The following year, having attended the Genoa Conference, at which Russia was refused its request for a big loan, Brand told General Smuts in South Africa that he was 'of opinion that the chasm between the Bolshevik economic system and the system in force in Western Europe is too great at present to be bridged, and the Bolsheviks have to go much further in their return to such ideas as the sanctity of contract and the rights of private property before any trade worth speaking of is possible between Russia and the rest of the world'. He added that if it did receive a loan, 'the Russian Government would squander the money that it got'. In 1924, with a Labour government briefly in office, there was a semi-serious possibility of a British loan, but only if Russia was prepared to recognise the claims of pre-Revolution bondholders. The energetic stockbroker and financier Charles Birch Crisp, much involved in Russian affairs for almost twenty years, talked to Stock Exchange authorities and jobbers about a possible debt arrangement; 'not likely to be successful' was Norman's shrewd private assessment in July. Once (in relation to a Chinese loan) Crisp had been a popular hero in Capel Court, but no longer, especially after his recent change of political allegiance on account of the Conservative Party's anti-Bolshevism. 'When I resigned from the Carlton Club my firm lost many clients,' he would recall, 'and when I fought the Windsor division as a Liberal more clients fell away, and when my son stood [in October 1924] as a Labour candidate my business suffered an eclipse which led me later to leave the Stock Exchange.' A few others followed the pragmatic Crisp line (Kleinworts in 1925 granted the State Bank of the USSR £200,000 for reimbursement credits, a figure subsequently increased to £500,000), but Revelstoke was as usual close to the City pulse when he stated at about this time that 'any British institution which still possesses its sanity would be unwilling, I should apprehend, to trust these people as long as they do not recant their sins'.[19] The City would have little to do with that part of the world for another sixty years.

*

Elsewhere, one is struck by the global ubiquity of the City's tentacles during the first half of the 1920s – sometimes in spite of Norman's attempt to enforce an informal embargo on foreign (excluding colonial and reconstruction) loans, in order to prop up sterling and hasten the return to the gold standard.[20] Predictably the City's grandees genuflected. Farrer in February 1924 affirmed, in relation to foreign loans, that 'a hint from the Bank would suffice to deter all the leading houses who were not already committed and nothing much of importance could be done without them'; while a year later, with Norman opposing a proposed City of Paris loan, Vivian Smith of Morgan Grenfell wrote regretfully to Paris that 'we feel here that we have no option but to fall in whole heartedly with his views'. Others were less deferential, notably the Hongkong and Shanghai Bank, which in early 1922 pushed through a £2m Siamese loan against Norman's explicit wishes.[21]

Norman himself, as Brand explained in March 1925 to a Canadian banker, was in this respect anyway a reluctant policeman:

I have had one or two long talks with the Governor on the matter
recently, and I can tell you for your own private information that he
dislikes as much as anyone the necessity for restricting by artificial means
foreign loans here. He realises, in fact, that the procedure cannot last, and
that ultimately the rate of interest must be the deciding factor. However, he
thinks that his policy has been fully justified in the national interest during
the last year . . .

With British overseas lending through new capital issues running at this
time at around £130m a year, compared with the immediate pre-war,
pre-inflation annual average of about £170m, Norman and others in the
City were acutely aware of the ascendancy as an international capital
market that capital-rich New York was being allowed to establish.
'There is no getting away from the fact that the Americans will have the
field to themselves as far as Argentine finance is concerned,' Windham
Baring complained without exaggeration as early as 1919, 'as it will
certainly be some time before our Government allows us to take part in
any Argentine finance on a large scale'.[22] Neither the Treasury nor
Norman saw any alternative, and taking the post-war years 1919–30 as
a whole, the best calculation is that the total volume of foreign issues
made in New York was roughly double that of London. Admittedly
habit counted for something, borrowers had their loyalties, and many
international issues were shared between the two centres; nevertheless,
there was no disguising the fundamental shift.[23] 'A meeting with
Mackenzie King, the Premier of Canada in Bank parlour,' Addis
recorded in October 1923. 'Norman, Revelstoke, Peacock & I. King, a
willing intelligent man, realises danger of Canada getting too much
under control of U.S. financiers. They ought to borrow here.' Perhaps
they 'ought', but some of the old imperial certainties had vanished, as
Farrer acknowledged the next year in an assessment of a client's
investment: 'Years ago I heard Lord Cromer remark that Egypt was all
right as long as there was a British administrator and British bayonets to
back him; but alas, with the recent fashion of Mr Wilson's ridiculous
self-determination, British administration & British bayonets are considered out of date.'[24]

The City was still willing to fire financial bullets Down Under, long
seen as a place of fiscal irresponsibility.[25] In 1920 Queensland's Labour
Premier, E.G. Theodore, sought personally to persuade the City that his
state was a worthy borrower despite his policy of breaking up the large
pastoral estates, many of them British-owned and with close City links.
At a meeting in June with leading Stock Exchange members, he
complained that 'when he arrived in London he found a considerable

amount of antagonism to Queensland on the part of British capital and finance', adding that 'this feeling of hostility of capitalists to their Labour Ministry was widespread and damaging to their prospects'. Archibald Campbell, Deputy Chairman of the Stock Exchange, insisted in reply that his Committee 'were as jealous of the Credit of the State of Queensland as was the Premier but they were bound to interest themselves in the rights of British investors'. Herbert Marnham, a prominent jobber in the Colonial market, then stated that 'at a time when there was a scarcity of other Colonial issues, Queensland stocks were on offer' and that 'only today two buyers of Colonial issues had declined to look at Queensland Bonds'. Campbell concluded by hoping that Theodore would make a statement that 'would have the result of putting Queensland right with the British investor'. No such statement ensued, the London boycott continued, and Theodore defiantly told the Queensland press that 'I for one will not take money from England at the price of our self-government rights.'

The following year Farrer reflected that he had always thought of the Australasian colonies as 'a particularly vicious example' of 'spendthrift democracies', and fairly soon afterwards Queensland raised $22m in New York, though on expensive terms. It was not a development that Norman welcomed, and when in December 1923 the new Australian Premier, S.M. Bruce, raised with him the possibility of going to New York for a £10m loan, Norman 'strongly deprecated' the suggestion, referring with masterly vagueness to 'various difficulties, seen and unforeseen, which such a course would involve'. Theodore himself was back in London in 1924, seeking the conversion of a maturing £13m loan, and this time he submitted. Rents for pastoral leases were to be frozen, the City expressed satisfaction, and the conversion that spring was over-subscribed, though with the state having to pay a rather higher coupon than Theodore had expected. The *Daily Herald* condemned the episode as a case of 'direct action' on the part of London bankers; *The Times* remarked that if Queensland behaved itself for the next five years ('wise government' was the phrase), it would be able to come back to the London market for a long-term loan on more favourable terms.[26]

Resentment about financial control from London was also becoming a political issue in South Africa. Early in 1920 Henry Strakosch – London-based Managing Director of the prominent mining house Union Corporation, and in the confidence of both Norman and the Rothschilds – paid an important visit there, more or less successfully persuading the Smuts administration to delay any possible return to the gold standard until Britain herself was ready to return to it. During the same visit

Strakosch did much to ensure the establishment of a central bank (the South African Reserve Bank) based largely on private funding and, on the Bank of England model, independent of government. Moreover, its first Governor (holding the position for ten years) was W.H. Clegg, the Old Lady's chief accountant and a Norman nominee. Clegg, he assured Goodenough of Barclays, 'fully realises the importance of this matter to the City of London and to the Empire'. However, even before the new central bank opened its doors in June 1921, the South African gold producers were explicitly challenging the July 1919 agreement, inform-ing the Bank of England that they wanted 'to be free to send some of their refined product direct to India, some elsewhere, and as much or as little as they like to London'. Unsurprisingly, Norman told Clegg that 'to this I am unwilling to agree, mainly because I fear it would lead to the break-up of our gold control'. He added that 'the representatives of the producers in London are perfectly content and wish to continue the existing arrangement, but they fear political pressure from South Africa, very likely through the mouth of General Smuts'. But Norman no longer held the high cards, for South Africa by the end of 1921 had built its own refinery, and within a year he had been compelled to modify the 1919 agreement, in effect conceding freedom to South Africa's gold producers while retaining for the Bank (as he told the Treasury) 'the advantage of full information as to the manner in which gold is disposed of'. Clegg tried to comfort the senior Governor by telling him that the concession would have a 'good psychological effect', but in truth the locus of control had changed.[27]

Problems with local producers also pervaded the City's unhappy experience during the Chilean nitrate saga. The firm most centrally involved, with large-scale interests in the industry, was the merchant bank Antony Gibbs. Long established and undeniably part of the inner City, it was nevertheless reported by Kleinworts in 1919 as 'regarded to a certain extent as a "dark horse" in the Money market', the assessment adding that 'financially the firm is supposed to have had many ups and downs & their methods have also been subjected to criticism from time to time'. For many years the partner who had dealt with Chilean nitrate was the peppery Herbert Gibbs, who in practice devoted much of his time to his many outside interests, including from 1912 the chairmanship of the City of London Conservative Association. Indeed, the Gibbs family history would describe him as 'more intrigued by politics than business'. Chilean nitrate itself had been much in demand during the war, keeping the Allies in explosives, but demand slumped in the changed post-war conditions and by January 1921 Lord Cullen (the former Cokayne) was explaining to Norman that Antony Gibbs was so over-committed that it had sustained losses on nitrate during the previous year of around £660,000. That same month, at the request of the Chilean producers, a nitrate pool was organised in London, with Herbert Gibbs as Chairman.

It proved to no avail, with Gibbs reporting at the end of March to his main representative in Chile that 'the whole idea on which the Pool was based, as far as this season is concerned, has been rendered illusory by the bad consumption [especially in Germany and Russia, where the nitrate market had collapsed], and by the larger stocks in and shipments from the U.S.A. than those anticipated'. Therefore, 'we shall have to carry an enormous amount of Nitrate into next season [i.e. beyond 30 June] and some perhaps beyond it'. Other members of the pool, holding by this time about a million tons of nitrate, of which Antony Gibbs had just over one-third, included most of the leading merchant banks. By mid-May Schröders was evolving a scheme involving a government guarantee, Farrer reporting to Revelstoke that 'Tiarks tells me he has had Gibbs and his people in their office all the morning in a great state of worry'. By Saturday the 21st the pool had a letter ready to send to the producers' association in Chile. However, as Herbert Gibbs wrote to his representative there, it was not easy to get the letter off, 'as Rothschilds are not in the City on Saturday', though 'we caught one of them in the West End just starting to play golf'. He added that 'by turning Rothschild on' to the new scheme, 'we have called up our last reserves as I do not think that as yet at all events it would be wise to get the Foreign Office to meddle as they would certainly irritate & it is not likely that they would do any good'. Little immediate benefit accrued, and by early June Revelstoke was describing 'the nitrate position' as 'increasingly grave'. In July the producers tried to break away from the pool and (in Grenfell's subsequent words) 'sell 1922 production at a low price forward'. Inevitably, 'a great deal of friction ensued'.

At last, in September 1921, Herbert Gibbs sailed to Chile (probably for only the second time in his career) and managed to achieve an agreement with the producers, by which the pool received compensation of some £1.5m, the bulk going to his firm though by no means offsetting its total losses in the operations, estimated at being at least £3m. Subsequently, noted Grenfell, 'Guggenheims of NY who had made a great success of copper in Chili, started a large organ^n to amalgamate all the Chili nitrate producers'; 'this practically took away the whole of Gibbs' nitrate agency'. By July 1922 the firm was reckoned by Farrer to be 'in comparatively smooth water', but the frank advice of Kleinworts was 'would prefer abstain for the present'. In fact Antony Gibbs had received a body blow from which it would never really recover, and as early as February 1923 the word from Kleinworts was that 'we are given to understand that, except for insignificant amounts, they have ceased to accept for some months past'. That same year Herbert Gibbs was created Baron Hunsdon, and in July 1924 he was a witness before the National Debt inquiry on which Addis was sitting. 'A nice fellow but desperately stupid' was the crisp verdict of someone who had never had it to throw away.[28]

Brazil, more than other South American countries, remained in the British financial orbit during the 1920s.[29] Schröders, on behalf of 'the Trinity', lead-managed a loan for the state of San Paulo in March 1921, though there was a New York component to it that Speyers undertook. Morgan Grenfell was to have been a member of the London Group, but (Grenfell recalled) 'would not go in if Speyers were in any way associated with the loan'; and Vivian Hugh Smith 'considered Tiarks did not behave in a loyal manner to Morgans'. Norman seems to have waved that loan through, but could be less liberal. 'During the last two or three days,' he wrote in December 1921 to Reginald Johnston, the former Governor and still a director of the Bank, 'I have been repeatedly told that a "revolving" credit has been arranged by your Firm [E. Johnston & Co] on behalf of Brazil. I hesitate to believe this because such a credit is entirely contrary to the policy which the Bank has steadfastly followed for the last two or three years.' In May 1922, however, Rothschilds, Barings and Schröders were permitted to make a £7m $7\frac{1}{2}$ per cent coffee valorisation loan for the Brazilian government, reminiscent of the one of December 1908. London was the chosen capital market on account not only of habit but also the fact that American opinion was profoundly hostile to the coffee valorisation scheme itself. By the following year Brazil, in all sorts of economic difficulties, wanted to come back and raise a further £25m on the London market. Rothschilds responded by proposing a financial mission to scrutinise the situation on the ground, and the would-be borrower had little alternative but to consent.

The mission, which left shortly before Christmas 1923, was led by the former Liberal minister Edwin Montagu and included Addis, the financial journalist Hartley Withers and the tough-minded accountant Sir William McLintock. On the voyage out Addis kept a distance from his colleagues on the grounds that 'they like to gamble, and sports play such a large part of their existence'. In City terms there were two particularly interesting moments during the mission. At one point

Montagu toyed with the idea of using his financial leverage to try to get Brazil to agree to a most-favoured-nation commercial treaty with Britain, something that Brazil had always refused. 'Of course Addis would say the City has nothing to do with manufacturers [i.e. British manufacturers, who would have benefited],' Montagu reflected in his diary, 'but is not the time coming when the City would do well to protect itself by showing some identity of interest with the industrial classes?' Montagu also, in his keenness to detach the Banco de Brasil from the local politicians, suggested to New Court that the Brazilian government's shares in the bank be sold to Rothschilds 'or their friends'. With typical prudence New Court replied that 'while we agree with you that it would be an excellent thing for the Banco de Brasil to be independent from the Brazilian Government we think it would be most unpopular in Brazil for the national bank to be owned by foreigners, nor do we think it would be advisable for us to control such an institution as it might lead to grave difficulties between the government and ourselves'. This negative response perhaps explained the last sentence of Addis's diary entry on 2 April 1924, soon after their return: 'Dinner at Lionel Rothschild's to Brazil Mission. Very grand. Chambertin [?] 1869 &c. Brandy 1800. Jews. Ostentatious a little but kind and hospitable. Lionel spoke. Montagu very cold in reply.'[30] The mission's main recommendations – the usual City medicine of cutting government expenditure and eschewing monetary experiments, as well as giving independence to the central bank – were reluctantly accepted by the Brazilian government, and indeed were even partially implemented, despite a last-minute toughening of the loans embargo by Norman, which meant that Brazil would have to wait for another major loan.

The Far East was traditionally a significant area for the City, and soon after the war Addis personally reconstituted the London Group for possible future Chinese government loans, in the process flatly refusing the Foreign Office's demand that the price for its exclusive official support was the group's enlargement. 'It might be better to leave the joint-stock banks out of consideration altogether,' Addis thought in March 1919, shortly before an angry Vassar-Smith of Lloyds wrote to Curzon complaining about exclusion 'from business sought to be undertaken by a few favoured firms and institutions in this country to the exclusion of others'. Charles Duguid, financial editor of the *Daily Mail*, wrote a powerful article against the whole 'hidebound monopoly' approach, arguing that Foreign Office 'interference' with 'the freedom of finance' should be replaced by leaving the financial houses to fight it out among themselves for Chinese business. In a sense it was all academic.

Political instability in China in the early 1920s precluded any grand
international loans, Addis retired as London manager of the Hongkong
and Shanghai, and by September 1924 his successor, Sir Newton Stabb,
was declaring that 'the less the H&SBC is involved in political and
international matters, the better'.[31] Increasingly he and his colleagues
wanted to get on with the difficult enough business of exchange banking,
without being prey to the latest whims of the Foreign Office.

Japan, as usual, was a more rewarding experience for the City. In
January 1924 an enlarged London Group met at the Hongkong and
Shanghai's offices at 9 Gracechurch Street. The three old members were
the Hongkong and Shanghai itself, Yokohama Specie and Westminster
(having absorbed Parr's); the four new members were Barings, Rothschilds, Schröders and Morgan Grenfell; and Brand of Lazards was
subsequently told by Kengo Mori, the Japanese government's special
financial delegate, that the group's extension was 'mainly due to pressure
from Lord Revelstoke to be included' and that the 'members of the old
group were not anxious to increase the group'. The cause of their
deliberations was Japan's need for a £60m loan (half in New York, most
of the rest in London), following the dreadful earthquake of the previous
year. 'Japan has always kept faithfully to her engagements in the past,'
Farrer noted in February, and the issue proved a roaring success, though
Japan itself was critical of the relatively high 6 per cent coupon. Soon
afterwards the group tried to arrange an issue specifically for Tokyo, but
Norman insisted that in the wider context of the foreign-loans embargo
enough had been done, and he would not be moved.[32]

Unlike the old days, there was no longer automatically enough to go
round, as had been made graphically clear to the Whitehall Trust (a
subsidiary of Lazards) when it went to Midland in July 1923 wanting to
borrow £1m on behalf of the Tokyo Electric Light Co. 'The Bankers
were regarded as being a form of trust for British trade,' its man was told
by Hyde, 'particularly in view of the difficult times through which we
were passing, and if advances were to be made for finances of this kind,
it would limit the amount of money that might be wanted should trade
requirements spring up.' Priorities were starting to change, but only in
some quarters of the City. In August 1923, shortly after Hyde's remarks,
Farrer inveighed to a correspondent against the practice of tied loans,
arguing that 'such stipulations come perilously near to the practice of the
Hebrew money-lender, who insists upon part of his loan being taken in
old sherry and cigars'. He added darkly that 'I am afraid Baldwin,
Curzon & Co are being too much influenced by cries of distress from the
Midlands and north.'[33]

All was not quite back to normal at the Stock Exchange. Although its old noisiness returned from July 1919, following the removal of the wartime injunction against open bidding and offering, the House remained closed on Saturdays throughout the 1920s, initially at the request of the joint-stock banks, their staffs much depleted by the war. Moreover, the jobbing system (411 firms in 1920, down from some 600 on the eve of war) was now starting its long-run decline, though this was as yet masked by its sheer numbers.[34] One of those firms was Akroyd & Smithers. 'Your American market has practically ceased to exist,' the firm's founder, Bayly Akroyd, told his son as the younger partners returned after the war. 'You must find another market. There were 80 millions of Government debt before the war, now there are 800 millions; so there must be something to deal in.'[35]

The old man's advice was shrewd, for by 1920 over one-third of the nominal value of London's quoted securities comprised British government debt, a ratio that rose still further during the inter-war period. Norman naturally kept a close eye on the gilt-edged market. In April 1925 he was privately informed by W.H. Askew, of the dissolving firm of jobbers Gordon, Askew & Biddulph, that he intended to join Akroyds as senior partner: 'I say I have no objection ... *He* must decide on personal question with other Jobbers.' The Government broker was responsible for selling Consols and other gilt-edged stock to that market. Since time immemorial this business had been in the hands of Mullens, Marshall & Co, but back in February 1920 its senior partner, the rather dour J.A. Mullens, had returned from ten days' absence to be summoned by Cokayne and told that the Bank was unwilling to be left solely in the hands of Mullens's existing partners. 'Either MM & Co at once add a new & competent partner to assist & replace at times J.A.M.,' recorded Norman, 'or we employ another firm of Brokers concurrently with M.M. & Co.' Mullens took the hint and the next year merged his firm with the brokers Steer, Lawford & Co, the new firm being called Mullens, Marshall, Steer Lawford & Co, in due course finding its next senior partner not from the Mullens side.[36]

Mullens himself was at the top of an ill-appreciated profession. 'Why is a stockbroker less beautiful than a Homeric warrior or an Egyptian priest?' asked Christopher Dawson in a lecture to the Sociological Society in July 1923 on 'Progress and Decay in Ancient and Modern Civilisation'. The answer, according to Dawson, was self-evident: 'Because he is less Incorporated with life, he is not inevitable, but accidental, almost parasitic.' Nicholas Davenport, a young graduate who went to Rowe & Pitman in 1925 'to write the "economic stuff"', would probably have agreed: 'What struck me at first sight was the jolly vitality of stockbrokers. They were like healthy schoolboys, telling each other dirty stories, ragging around when the markets were dull, and occasionally de-bagging an outsider who intruded into the "House" . . . They were exceptionally quick-witted; their reactions to the ticker-tape were like lightning; they saw the future just a day ahead. Their intellectual level was about form four in the schools they had never really left.' It was true, Davenport went on, that 'to call their attention to the need for social change at that time would have been an unpardonable *faux pas*'. However, he added, 'what distinguished them from some of those who scoffed at and derided them' was that 'they were really prepared to fight and die for their Establishment'.[37]

Two episodes at this time reflected the aversion of the Stock Exchange as a whole to the uncomfortable forces of competition. One was the continuing awkward relationship with that provincial upstart, the British Stockbrokers Trust. In January 1921, at BST's annual dinner at the Savoy Hotel, McKenna proposed its toast and referred to the 'certain amount of opposition in the City' as lying in the past; but he was wrong. A Norman diary entry that November was suggestive: 'Scrimgeour & JAM [i.e. Mullens]. Straits Loan: no conditions as to method of underwriting, wh left to Brokers – but I advised them to give some to BST & attempted to smooth over troubles without giving up principles of "Sub-underwriting" barred.' The following spring Norman thought he had brokered a gentleman's agreement between BST on the one hand and Mullens, Nivisons and Scrimgeours on the other, by which BST would as an issuing house leave alone British government and colonial government securities, while the three firms (which traditionally enjoyed a monopoly in underwriting colonial loans) would not omit country brokers from their future underwriting lists. Leading figures at the Stock Exchange, however, declined to accept the compromise and continued to push that BST be advised to leave London, asserting that it represented a greater threat than solely in the underwriting of trustee securities, important though that was. Edgar Crammond, with a Liverpool Stock Exchange background and now Managing Director of BST, told Norman that to leave London 'would prevent their becoming, as he had always hoped, a leading Issuing House'. Eventually a settlement was achieved and BST stayed in London, but changed its name in 1924 to the much less threatening British Shareholders Trust and seems to have been gradually absorbed into the City Establishment.[38]

The other episode concerned commissions. Since 1912 there had been a fixed scale, introduced to benefit the smaller broking firms. Backed by the big brokers, a campaign to liberalise the scale got under way in 1922, and Claud Serocold of Cazenove & Akroyds told the Committee in November that the 'present restrictions' could not continue 'without seriously endangering the position of the Stock Exchange as the free market for the Securities of the World'. But in the course of 1923 the campaign petered out, partly because of the implicit opposition of the much more numerous small firms, partly as markets improved. It was not a wise long-term strategy. Writing shortly before Serocold's letter, Farrer perceptively identified 'the raising of the commissions, the insistence that all dealings should pass through the jobber, the proposal to insist that a broker's name must appear on the prospectus' as indications of the Stock Exchange's wish 'to look only to themselves and disregard the public'. Hardly an enemy in general to the City's long-established institutions, Farrer added that 'personally I do not believe the Stock Exchange as at present constituted is indispensable to the business of London' and that he knew 'no profession which is so well paid or anything like it, no profession in which money is earned more easily and with less risk, where the remuneration is so out of proportion to the services rendered'. Despite Farrer's characteristic rider that the Stock Exchange membership was 'the most generous body that I know of and the most undefeated in misfortune', this was a severe critique. And citing its 'too high' scale of brokerage, he concluded that 'the handwriting is on the wall and writ large'. So it was, for a decline lasting over half a century lay ahead for the Stock Exchange as a market for international securities – a decline undoubtedly accentuated by its restrictive practices.[39]

None of which much worried Walter Landells, a member since 1899, a partner with the brokers Zorn & Leigh-Hunt, and from April 1921 author of the 'Autolycus' column in the *FT*, which in humorous, gossipy fashion charted the day-to-day changes in the stock market. 'A birdlike little man, scuttling abstractedly about the floor, a great sheaf of papers invariably clutched beneath his arm' was how a fellow-member remembered 'probably the most famous financial columnist of all time'. Chosen at random, from July 1924, a few days' extracts give his distinctive flavour. The column on Monday the 7th included a tip or two for the week: 'The Tea market is one of the firmest round the House and scarcity of stock is again pronounced. Jorehauts, FINANCIAL TIMES readers will notice with interest, are £4 upwards, the price being still cum the dividend of 6s per share just paid. Among Nitrates, New Tamarugals at

66s offer a half-crown turn to those who bought them last week for the sake of a nimble profit . . .' More domestically, he featured an item on how members of the House 'keep afloat the colours of coaching, a form of thoroughly British sport which has been threatened by the advent of the motor-car'. Tuesday highlighted a self-proclaimed 'tip': 'Imperial Tobacco shares can be sold at 76s. Those holders who feel tempted to take their profit may find it pays them better to adopt the classical advice of *Mr Punch* to those about to marry.' On Wednesday he praised 'the real jobber, in whom is developed the instinct for market-making that is unknown to any other Exchange in the world' and who 'is prepared to take the rough with the smooth and to go on making prices as long as he possibly can'. On Thursday he turned to Jungles: 'The West African market ask what further startling reductions it can advertise in order to attract the people to a Bargain Sale. Only echo answers.'[40] It was hardly challenging stuff, but it was pitched at exactly the right level. Norman may have been the Pope of the City, but this unassuming picker-up of unconsidered trifles was its reassuring voice.

Essentially non-investigative, Landells was little help to his readers concerning the rogues who, as ever, periodically brightened up the City's life. Clarence Hatry never did make it to South America in 1920. Following his abdominal operation, he discovered that not only had his directors at the Commercial Bank of London not followed his selling instructions, but that they had made (in his subsequent words) 'further considerable purchases of speculative industrial shares' as well as entering into 'other commitments'. Accordingly, in 'a poor state of health' and with the market turning, he resumed his position as Managing Director in order to try – secretly – to clear up the situation. With the bank unable to meet its current liabilities, this involved Hatry in realising his own assets, including gilt-edged securities of over £750,000, in order to prop up the bank. As a purely cosmetic step he renamed it the Commercial Corporation of London in April 1921.[41]

Hatry was also in increasingly close contact with Gerard Lee Bevan, to whom he had sold the City Equitable Fire Insurance Co during the war. Bevan, fourth son of a former Barclays Chairman and by far the dominant force at the apparently staid stockbrokers Ellis & Co (established 1778), was in his biographer's description 'an elegant, plausible man who traded on his family connections and whose hereditary privileges left him arrogant, vain and irresponsible'. During the hectic post-war industrial boom he had used his broking firm as a convenient cover to enable him to make a series of highly speculative investments for the City Equitable, quite against the conventions of an insurance company. With the market now slumping, he – just as much as Hatry – needed an infusion of cash and in January 1921 visited Hyde at Midland, wanting a £600,000 advance, ostensibly to enable the City Equitable to extend its operations to the States. He returned in May, this time trying to get backing for his operations as part of a syndicate owning cattle ranches in San Paulo. July saw a successful City Equitable share issue – 'the shares have undoubted attractions and potentialities' commented the *FT*, and Kleinworts took almost 30,000 of them – but the following month Bevan had an uncomfortable quarter of an hour with Hyde. The banker complained that Bevan had broken his promise that money would be accumulated on deposit account in the name of the City Equitable, to which (Hyde noted) 'Mr Bevan said that this was not his understanding of the arrangement as there would be no object in asking us to give a guarantee if they had to give cash as security'. Hyde, clearly cross, referred to his diary notes of an earlier meeting, and Bevan promised to repay the loan within six months. 'I told him that on this understanding I would let the matter stand over.'

Six months was too long, for by January 1922 the skids were under Bevan. Acting on his behalf, Hatry saw Hyde on the 13th, 'explained that the affairs of the City Equitable Co had been criticised', and unsuccessfully requested a further £50,000 advance. With their price in free fall, 'Autolycus' noted cautiously on 1 February that 'dealing in City Equitable Fire shares is a matter of somewhat delicate negotiation'. Norman declined to intervene, as did McKenna, despite Hatry telling the investigating accountant, Frederick van der Linde, that Midland's Chairman was prepared to find a 'considerable sum' in order to save the City Equitable. In fact, the principal creditors were not the banks but the leading insurance companies. On the 3rd the City Equitable filed for bankruptcy; on the 8th Bevan vamoosed to Paris; and on the 16th Ellis & Co was hammered, apparently with £2m liabilities. An *FT* reporter managed to inspect the firm's offices at 1 Cornhill, looking across the Wellington statue to the Bank of England, and described how Bevan had 'occupied an expensively furnished room in the building, with oak panels decorated with exquisite wood carvings'. He added that 'the decorations above the fireplace included a design of an eagle feeding her young surmounted by the monogram "G.L.B."' Arrested in Vienna four months later, Bevan was eventually tried at the Old Bailey on sixteen counts, mainly of publishing false balance sheets, and given a seven-year sentence. Around the time of his release in 1928 the veteran company promoter H. Osborne O'Hagan analysed Bevan's career: 'He deliberately, when past middle age, did everything he could to forfeit his position and to ruin the fortunes of himself, his partners, his friends, and his clients, and what for? I don't see how he could possibly have benefited from any of his criminal acts. I ask, "What was his kink?" The only answer which comes to me is, "Vanity – pure vanity."⁴²

One of those ruined partners was Donald J. Pirie, who in May 1923 appealed to the Stock Exchange Committee to allow A.E. Ashford & Co to deal on his behalf: 'In common with everyone else connected with Bevan, I trusted him absolutely, and until my eyes were opened at the time of the failure I invariably found him worthy of that trust . . . I knew absolutely nothing of the affairs of the City Equitable.' He denied 'absolutely' the implication made during the bankruptcy proceedings of Ellis & Co that he had 'received sums from Bevan privately'; and, while conceding that he had 'saved a comfortable sum' from the post-war boom, he insisted that this was largely because he had 'no expensive tastes, and my personal and household expenses have never exceeded £1,800–£2,000 per annum' – the equivalent of, say, £50,000 in the late 1990s. Pirie's long letter (sent from Austen Mead, near Gerrards Cross in Buckinghamshire) wound up by stating that Ellis & Co had been his whole life, having worked his way up from junior clerk, and that 'at the age of 44 it is next to impossible to start on a new profession'. The Committee, often so unyielding in these situations, granted his application.⁴³ As for Hatry, his bank folded in 1923, but he still had plenty of schemes up his sleeve.

Before his fall Bevan also had a view of Lloyd's, still on the first floor of the Royal Exchange. There the grand old man was Cuthbert Heath, pioneer of non-marine insurance and one of those relatively rare City figures who combined mental agility with the utmost probity. Since the turn of the century he had been increasingly committed to the cause of credit insurance, in effect insuring merchants and manufacturers against the risk of bad debts, at a time when paying by instalment was starting to become the convention, not least for motor vehicles. Shortly before the war ended he formed the Trade Indemnity Co in order to provide cover against creditors abroad who defaulted. It began promisingly, so much so that on 1 October 1923 Norman noted: 'C.E. Heath, to explain use & excellent work of Trade Indemnity Corp (CAP to be £250ᵐ f paid): I greatly approve scheme.' Unfortunately for Heath, there broke later that month one of the great Lloyd's scandals, involving an underwriter called Stanley Harrison who was a leading exponent of credit insurance, especially in the motor field. 'Motor hire purchase – Guaranteeing bills – Heavy losses – Financed by more guaranteed bills – Cheque dishonoured – Chairman intervenes – Committee's action –

Meeting of Underwriters – Agreement to pay Harrison's losses': the chapter subtitles in the semi-official history of Lloyd's give the gist of the story. 'If we do not pay these bills,' Arthur Sturge, the Chairman of Lloyd's, declared when the scandal was uncovered, 'the name of Lloyd's will be seriously injured and will never recover during our lifetime.' The Corporation of Lloyd's itself put up £100,000, while £200,000 was subscribed by Lloyd's underwriters.

The instinctive reaction of the authorities at Lloyd's, and Sturge in particular, was henceforth to ban credit insurance altogether. There ensued a protracted, often acrimonious tussle between himself and Heath, the outcome of which was a compromise brokered in 1924 by which Lloyd's underwriters could only do the business indirectly, as re-insurance brought to them if approved by the Committee. There was no denying that a major loss of commercial freedom was involved, and Heath responded by recapitalising the Trade Indemnity Co with additional capital as well as the support of the large, non-Lloyd's insurance companies. Unable to shed its entrenched conservatism, Lloyd's had, like the Stock Exchange shortly before, shot itself in the foot. It was entirely appropriate that 'J.D. Marstock' – real name J.R. Parsons, the stolid, utterly conventional Wellington College contemporary of Harold Nicolson, immortalised in *Some People* – should have found a berth there as an underwriter after failing three times to get into the Foreign Office.[44]

Stagnation in Lloyd's and the Stock Exchange contrasted sharply with the rapid, turbulent post-war growth of the London foreign exchange market. Indeed, Farrer in his November 1922 critique of the Stock Exchange contrasted that market's 'too high' scale of brokerage to the low charges imposed by what he called 'by far the biggest and free-est exchange market in the world'. H.W. Phillips, in his authoritative survey a few years later of that market, recalled what had happened:

> With the unpegging of the world's exchanges in March 1919, there started one of the largest businesses the world has seen. A veritable orgy of dealing took place, and every centre seemed to be besieging London on long-distance calls. From early till late at night (6 p.m.) foreign centres called London and immense business was transacted. Brokers increased, and by 1920 there were about 40 different broking firms in the business of the banks and financial houses. There was business for all . . . The amounts turned over on the London exchange market were huge. Day after day the staffs of the brokers fed at their switchboards and went home exhausted.

Among the banks that took the plunge was the Société Générale, one of whose London dealers was a young man called George Bolton, son of a Baltic Exchange trader. 'Confusion reigned supreme as the brokers' direct telephones were massed together on a table,' he wrote many years later, 'and the only means of identifying any call was by altering the ringing tone of each telephone by stuffing paper, cardboard, metal clips, etc. between the clapper and the bell. Contract notes were delivered by hand, very often to the wrong bank, and it seemed miraculous that any business could be satisfactorily settled. Techniques were invented as we went along . . .' There had been a certain amount of foreign exchange dealing in London before 1914, but in the new world of volatile currencies and seemingly permanent political instability this was something different. 'Foreign exchanges and currency problems which in the old days were relegated to experts have lately become a topic of popular discussion,' the *FT* put it in January 1920, with perhaps a little exaggeration. Or as Winston Churchill wrote three years later to his stockbroker brother, Jack: 'What about selling a bear in marks. How can they keep this up long? It is a pure manoeuvre. France has got them by the balls.'[45]

By the early 1920s the foreign exchange market had settled down and no longer relied on improvising with metal clips. Noting that meetings in the Royal Exchange (anyway long superseded by the telephone) to deal in bills of exchange denominated in foreign currencies had finally expired in January 1921, Phillips described the market – a telephone market, with no physical meeting-place – in action:

> It is an extremely large and an astonishingly active market, swifter than stocks and shares and faster than cotton or wool. By a network of underground wires to the provinces; by sea-bed cables to Holland, Paris, America, etc.; by wireless to almost anywhere; by private wires to brokers and clients; the foreign exchange dealer finds himself a principal in a highly developed business. He is a telephone slave. Discs are dropping on his installation of private wires, and bells are ringing every moment of all and every day. He listens to the brokers making him prices, but his other ear takes in the requests and queries of his assistants. His voice is questioning the broker while his eyes and head are answering his colleagues. A spare hand is writing the cable to a foreign dealer, and his plug goes into the private line to a cable company, dictating as he writes. He is reasonably certain that his message has reached the cable company's New York office within 30 seconds, and the dealer to whom it is directed will soon after be at work on his order . . .

Not surprisingly, Phillips added, 'quotations are short and snappy' and 'conversations one or two words'.[46]

By the time he was writing (1925), some 120 banks were significant players in the market, serviced by thirty to forty broking firms (led by Harlow & Jones), which throughout the day quoted rates on all the main currencies. The banks included several leading merchant banks, such as Kleinworts, Schröders and Brown Shipley. It could be a tense business. Brown Brothers in New York cabled to Norman's old firm in April 1921 that 'a true friend of ours and yours tells us that your Exchange operations are creating comment in London even to the extent of the thought that you finance yourselves through them'. Edward Clifton-Brown replied indignantly, insisting that 'although figures are large', and that 'on occasions it has been advisable in order to bridge the gap in the "here and there" cash position to sell considerable lines of "cheque"', there was 'no warrant that we can discover for the suggestion made in your cable, the more so as our Operator absolutely assures us that our "cheque" has never been sold at any but the very finest rate' and 'has never been forced upon the market'. Even so, Clifton-Brown conceded, 'while we have been most particular about ensuring that no speculation was taking place in the rates of exchange, we have to a certain extent insufficiently appreciated the difficulties which might arise if actual dates of commitments are not closely matched'. In August the following year Brown Brothers reiterated anxieties about unmatched future positions, prompting Clifton-Brown to 'put on record our belief that our Operator has loyally adhered to the restrictions put upon him' and that 'every day and all day he has his exact position in front of him, and his figures are always ready for our inspection at any time of the day, and are brought into the Parlour for investigation at frequent intervals'.[47]

Almost certainly a less inhibited approach obtained at Helbert Wagg, following its acquisition in May 1921 of a foreign exchange capacity in the form of Bonn & Co. Two gifted young men dominated the firm's foreign exchange dealing in the 1920s: one was Lionel Fraser, the son of Gordon Selfridge's butler and in the process of starting to turn himself into a major City figure; the other, with an equally glittering future, was his deputy, Bolton, who had joined Helbert Wagg in 1920. 'Altogether, it was killing and frenzied work,' Fraser would recall, 'and except that the department was able to make a substantial contribution to the profits of the firm, I find it difficult to persuade myself that we were doing anything particularly constructive or helpful in those very disturbed times.' Perhaps so – but 'this unrestricted jungle warfare of the foreign exchange market' (Fraser's phrase) did offer a certain hum and buzz by now lacking in some other parts of the square mile.[48]

Not least in the City's traditional mercantile core. 'These are difficult times to live in – incendiary riots by Sinn Feiners in Liverpool, bombs thrown in the City today, Downing Street barricaded,' reflected Harry Williamson of Balfour Williamson in November 1920. 'Meantime there is a steady decline in the price of every commodity. This eventually will be all to the good; at present it is a sore trial to merchants!'[49] The historically crucial Anglo-German connection, in terms of people as well as trade, had been seriously eroded; war had also given American rivals the chance to replace London, not only in securing supplies but also in marketing finished goods; and between the wars, though British commodity trade generally waxed with the Dominions (though not India), it waned with western Europe, the United States, Latin America and China. Moreover, there took place a 'drastic slump in Britain's invisible income' – in other words from overseas investments, shipping, the provision of trade credit, and issuing.[50] One of many City merchants under pressure was Cecil Beaton's father, Ernest, who dealt in timber. By 1924 the family lived at 3 Hyde Park Street, and at dinner on Christmas Eve the usually good-humoured Ernest was in a thoroughly bad mood before he left to go to his City office. Cecil's diary entry offers a timeless vignette of commercial life:

> Mother sat in a chair and talked. 'We can't afford this house. We'll have to sell it and live in some cheaper place. Business has been bad. Ever since that brute of a Fox left, things have been getting slacker and slacker. Now you know Daddy has lost the American business. That brute Bowers has taken it away and given it to a man in Manchester. It'll make an awful difference: half of our income gone. No wonder your father's worried and edgy tonight. There's a cargo of stuff from Finland which may mean a dead loss of six thousand pounds. That's why he's gone to the office to see if any telegrams have come in.'[51]

*

Of relatively little interest to practitioners in the first half of the 1920s, but of consuming importance to Norman, was the long, difficult route march that was the British return to the gold standard.[52] Early in his governorship he began to appreciate the way in which monetary policy in general, and Bank rate in particular, was becoming politicised. Interest rates, he observed to Pierre Jay of the Fed in September 1920, 'are now a political as well as a financial question', while two months later he reproachfully told the Chancellor, Austen Chamberlain, that 'when I call to mind your remark to my predecessor (that an independent Rise in the Bank Rate would be an unfriendly act); when I remember our continuing desire for higher rates ever since last July and indeed long before it, and

your continuing unwillingness to consent, owing to political reasons . . .
I wonder what (in the spirit as well as in the letter) is the meaning of
"political pressure"'. But in the long run, however much Norman may
have wished otherwise, there was no avoiding this politicisation, with
the price of money now being seen as impinging directly on levels of
unemployment, housing policy and economic policy in general. The
clearing banks, with their traditionally greater domestic orientation,
remained at odds with Norman, whose fundamental belief was that
domestic problems required international remedies. It was not only
McKenna who pushed in the winter of 1920/1 for lower rates, but also
the far more conservative Henry Bell, General Manager of Lloyds.
Norman told the latter in December that 'tho rate reduction might affect
mentality at home it w^d not help sales abroad'. There was also
Goodenough, reported by Schuster to Norman in November 1921 as
being largely responsible for stirring up opposition to official policy.[53]
Eventually Bank rate did come down (to 3 per cent by July 1922), but all
too slowly and timidly, granted the dreadful industrial situation.

As for the putative return to gold, the prospects of which would
inevitably be hampered by an unduly cheap money policy that in turn
undermined sterling, this was explicitly considered by Addis in late 1921
in his presidential inaugural to the Institute of Bankers. He accepted the
need for further deflation in order to achieve it, seeing 'no hope of the
restoration of the old standard of living and of comfort for the great
middle class of this country until prices are further reduced'; called on
the country to 'take a long pull, a strong pull, and to pull all together';
repudiated 'the ingenious and insubstantial nostrums of claustral
economics'; and, calling for a return to gold as soon as possible,
beseeched, 'Let us have done with short cuts and by-paths and, *ohne hast
ohne rast*, bend our energies to return to the old standard.' Schuster,
seconding the vote of thanks, was conscious of the City's critics,
declaring that 'when we, as I believe most of us do, advocate a return to
the pre-war standard, a return to a lower level of prices, we have in mind
more than any other matter the well-being of our working classes'. Yet
undeniably there was another, albeit rarely articulated agenda involved.
Brand, clearly writing from the heart, touched on it in a letter to a French
correspondent in August 1922:

> It seems to me that modern international industrial civilisation is
> becoming too complicated for the democracies of the world to run. They
> do not understand its mechanism, and the popular press understands it as
> little, and merely inflames their prejudices. Popular politicians were all
> right as long as they were compelled to work, without their knowing it,

within the gold standard, but now that the delicate mechanism no longer works automatically, but must be kept at a pitch of reasonable efficiency by the politicians themselves, they are completely at a loss.[54]

Norman, with his profound aversion to the popular will and those who claimed to represent it, would have entirely agreed.

In July 1923 Midland Bank's *Monthly Review* cited the Federation of British Industries' recent call for a commission to reconsider the continuing deflationary monetary policy, as originally outlined in 1918 by the Cunliffe Committee with a view to restoring gold parity between sterling and the dollar. The anonymous article pointed out that the operations of the joint-stock banks were 'determined largely by the action of the central Bank without opportunity for discussion or approval' and stated that the FBI was under 'a complete misapprehension to associate the joint stock banks with the Treasury and the Bank of England in a criticism of this country's monetary policy'. On 5 July, at about the time this appeared, Bank rate was raised from 3 to 4 per cent. 'Said to have been put up on account of New York Exchange which has been falling for a month,' the discount house Smith St Aubyn noted. 'Came rather suddenly for us . . .'[55]

Keynes was intensely critical, writing in the *Nation* on the 14th that the rise was 'one of the most misguided movements of that indicator which had ever occurred', happening at 'a moment when the business world requires every scrap of stimulus and encouragement which can be given it'. He went on:

> What is the explanation? It is not the practice of the Bank of England to give explanations. But there is not much doubt that the explanation is to be found in the fall of the dollar exchange (not at all unusual at this time of year) of about 2 per cent. That is to say, the Bank of England think it more important to raise the dollar exchange a few points than to encourage flagging trade. They do this under the influence of the Report of the Cunliffe Committee, a document written several months before the Armistice, necessarily without any knowledge of all the extraordinary post-war developments . . .

A week later Keynes returned to the attack. In the context of having been supported, broadly at least, by the *Spectator*, the *Investors' Chronicle* and the *Economist*, he asserted that 'so long as unemployment is a matter of general political importance, it is impossible that Bank rate should be regarded, as it used to be, as the secret *peculium* of Pope and Cardinals of the City'. He also took comfort from the response in the

City columns of *The Times*, arguing that it reflected 'the divided mind between the old school and the new, very representative of the state of mind of the City generally'. In other words:

> It used to be our policy to restore the gold standard. It has become our policy to keep prices stable [i.e. not to deflate]. We have taken on the new doctrine, without, as yet, discarding the old, and when they are incompatible we are torn between the two ... We attacked the grandmother of Threadneedle Street, which was very improper, and we must expect a slight peppering. But *The Times*, like nearly everyone else, shrinks from the practical measures which the old doctrine would require from true believers.

The mind of the City was, as usual, reluctant to disclose itself, but there was surely a degree of wishful thinking on Keynes's part. Norman himself told Jay on the 19th that, despite 'adverse criticism from some quarters', the rise had had 'a salutary effect', not least 'the improvement, at least temporary, in the Dollar-Sterling rate'. Moreover, 'even the adverse critics probably realise now that their apprehensions on behalf of our trade were greatly exaggerated'. As for *The Times*, a leader in early August likewise poured cold water on Keynes's fears:

> No one, we think, with the lesson of the Continent before us, would advocate inflation as a remedy for our present difficulties. As for the opposite policy of an active and forcible measure of monetary deflation, we see no sign of its being adopted. All monetary systems have as their object the stabilisation of prices. Experience has shown that none can be so effective as the gold standard, because it links up, more or less automatically, the monetary policy of countries which use it.[56]

In short, hold on to nurse.

Norman, notwithstanding that support, found the autumn of 1923 particularly trying. Writing to Strong on 8 October for the first time in several months, he reviewed the various international troubles, expressed anxiety about continuing American isolationism and concluded: 'We can have & perhaps deserve nothing but troubles until we are again anchored to Gold. How & when can we do it?' The following evening a speech by the Minister of Labour, Sir Montague Barlow, badly upset the financial world by including an apparently sanguine reference to 'the possibility of the adoption of a policy of inflation as a means of financing schemes for the relief of unemployment'. Within a week Norman was telling the new Chancellor, Neville Chamberlain, that the speech had had an 'evil effect in the City', including bankers receiving 'several enquiries and protests . . . threatening the withdrawal of funds held here on behalf of foreigners'. A few days later Norman saw Bruno Schröder, who had been 'bombarded by people all over the world with fears of their stg balances'. Farrer, writing to an important client on the 24th, joined the rearguard action. Emphasising that the Chancellor was 'quite sound' over the fight against inflation, he went on:

I understand there is a number of young economists, among whom Keynes is included, very clever, very well informed but without experience in the practical management of affairs, who desire to get rid of the gold standard, and regulate our currency by an index number of prices, deflating as prices rise and reflating as they fall. I am not quite sure if I have interpreted their ideas correctly, but I believe that is the purport of them. However, in all times of stress we have currency faddists uprising with currency nostrums; I can only hope that before experiments are made in this country better trade will have returned and we shall then hear nothing more of them. The only person of note in the City who is flirting with the Keynes doctrines is McKenna, and among those who are best informed he is getting to be as much distrusted in the City as he was among his political friends.[57]

Barlow's regrettable speech was soon followed by the equally regrettable prospect of a general election, the result of Baldwin's quixotic protectionist initiative, which struck few instinctive chords of sympathy in the City but was seen by some as the only alternative to the even worse prospect of a capital levy, as apparently planned by Labour. 'The mere idea of bogeys brings about our present sufferings,' Norman complained to Strong on 13 November, and proceeded to list them as 'depreciation in Securities through sales, largely by foreigners: depreciation in exchange, favouring of course your dollar: instability of London: general unsettlement and cold feet'. It had been, he wrote next day to a colleague abroad, a 'sickening' experience. 'A few weeks ago we were through the worst of the autumn, with normal purchases of dollars and debt remittances finished and in exchange of 4.55: now we have sterling weak, below 4.40, Government Securities down 2 per cent or 3 per cent, and the foreigners whom we have been coaxing back to a belief in the stability of London, competing for dollars and grinding their teeth, if not cocking a snook at us!' The election was held on 6 December, and even a long-standing Liberal like Schuster voted Conservative and advised his friends to do likewise, on the grounds that a vote for the Liberals was a vote for Labour. However, the results pointed to a minority Labour government, prompting Ramsay MacDonald to ask a sympathetic journalist to sound out McKenna about likely City reaction. 'Reply favourable,' he noted on the 10th. 'Bankers now regard themselves as semi-officials & would not countenance panic. Would be fair ...'[58]

The following day Keynes's *A Tract on Monetary Reform* was published.[59] Dedicated – ironically or otherwise – to the Bank of England, and consigning the gold standard to oblivion as a 'barbarous relic', it advocated a system of managed money through which the central bank would be able to control the supply of credit and thus, in the words of one of Keynes's biographers, 'even out fluctuations in business activity'. Neither of the two main City insiders with whom Keynes was on friendly terms quite bought it. 'Almost thou persuadest me,' Brand wrote to him on the 12th. 'But I don't know what things will look like after a year or two of Ramsay MacDonald and Sidney Webb.' Addis responded likewise on the 21st: 'A managed currency may come some day, but I do not believe we are ripe for it yet. It would be ill to work except in an atmosphere of confidence and belief which at present is non-existent.' Among those who were wholly unsympathetic, Norman's only recorded comment was to tell Strong, 'I do not think that you need worry about answering any points in Keynes's book'; while Farrer sent a copy to a Kidder Peabody partner, telling him that 'it is brilliantly written and gives one much food for thought, indeed when it comes to the alternatives of stabilising prices or stabilising exchanges and suchlike conundrums it is all rather beyond me'. But he insisted on the central question that 'whatever criticisms one may level against the gold system, it has worked fairly well in the past and countries have prospered under it, and I believe it will continue to prevail ...'[60]

It was precisely figures like Norman and Farrer whom Keynes had in mind when, shortly after his book's publication, he gave a speech to the National Liberal Club. His notes survive, an extraordinary mix of stern vision and humorous cajolery:

> In the City of London there is a widespread belief that the pre-war system was as nearly perfect as the frailty of human nature permits, and that we need nothing but to return to it in every particle ... The Bank of England since the war has always done exactly the opposite of what the latest science recommends. I conclude from this that their opposition comes, not from mere obstinacy or conservatism, but from their not yet understanding the point. I am, therefore, optimistic about the future ... I should like to warn the gentlemen of the City and of High Finance that if they do not listen in time to the voice of reason their days may be numbered. I speak to this great City as Jonah spoke to Nineveh that great city. I prophesy that unless they embrace Wisdom in good time, the system

upon which they live will work so very ill that they will be overwhelmed by irresistible things which they hate much more than the mild and limited remedies offered them now.[61]

For the most part the 'gentlemen of the City' not only did not 'listen in time', they simply did not listen. They knew what they wanted – to get back to the old days, when the living was easy – and that was enough.

By late January 1924 the Chancellor was Philip Snowden, an instant victim of Norman's charm. 'I had seen caricatures in the Socialist Press of the typical financier – the hard-faced, close-fisted, high-nosed individual', he would recall. Instead, he found in the Governor someone herculean in his efforts, of international cast of mind and with 'one of the kindliest natures and most sympathetic hearts it has been my privilege to know'. Norman himself told Strong on the 30th that after 'the bark' of Labour 'had frightened all our respectable friends nearly to death, the bite does not seem to be as bad as was expected'. However, he went on: 'We here in the City have suffered fearfully from forebodings of Labour or Socialism or whatever you would wish to call it. I confess to you that the mere idea of a Capital Levy, for instance, has lost to London a deal of international business which has belonged here for a generation or two . . .' If there was a honeymoon on the City's part, it did not last long. Grenfell, writing in early April to a sympathetic coal-owner and describing Labour as 'determined to wreck every industry in England', looked wistfully abroad:

> I hear from all sides most extraordinary satisfactory accounts of the restoration of law and order and of the progress made in industry in Italy in the past three years . . . The middle class and the people with anything to lose have rallied under Mussolini in a most remarkable manner. The trains run punctually, the factories are prosperous and unemployment has been reduced from a million or more down to about 140,000 most of whom are wasters and unemployable . . . Unless the employers and the middle class, upper and lower begin to make a firm stand against Mr Bevin and Mr Maxten [*sic*] we shall deserve all we get or rather all we lose. In the bus strike last week the weather was bitterly cold though fortunately not wet and the clerks and employees in the warehouses and shops apparently showed no sort of resentment against the sympathetic bus strikers.[62]

Norman meanwhile, with both Snowden and MacDonald effectively in his pocket as far as monetary matters were concerned, could at last see the realistic prospect of a return to gold. On 16 April he wrote to Otto Niemeyer at the Treasury outlining the ideal composition of a committee to consider the amalgamation of the two note issues (Bank of England

and Treasury), a question that implicitly involved the far more important one of a return to gold. He wanted an ex-Chancellor as chairman; Treasury or ex-Treasury figures such as Niemeyer, Bradbury and Blackett; 'an Economist (e.g. Professor Pigou)'; and a banker. The eventual composition was Austen Chamberlain, Bradbury, Niemeyer, the orthodox Pigou and Farrer. There was no place for either Keynes or McKenna, the two leading critics of a return to gold. On 13 June, shortly before the committee met, Norman saw Walter Leaf. 'I approve his Draft Article for West^r Bks Review advocating higher BR as *definite* step towards free Gold mkt,' he noted, and Leaf duly warned that any delay could lead to the dollar supplanting sterling as the basis of international finance; indeed, could even 'hand over to Germany the financial sceptre in Europe as well as the commercial'. By contrast, Midland's review the same month argued that 'the expedient course for this country is not to take panicky measures to press a rapid return to the gold standard, but, while sedulously avoiding anything savouring of monetary inflation, to await a more general progress, less obviously attended by the evils of deflation'. So few, however, had a real grasp of the matter. The Bank of England's Committee of Treasury notionally grappled with it on 18 June, but Addis reflected afterwards that 'the gold question' was turning into 'a duel between the Governor and me', in that 'the others say little & scarcely understand the question and its bearings'.[63]

The first two to give evidence to Chamberlain's committee were, appropriately, Norman and Addis on 27 June. Having asserted that 'at the earliest practicable date you should recommend that gold for export be freely obtainable at the Bank', Norman addressed the possible sacrifice to be made in the short term by 'the trader' through a return to gold:

> I should think the thing is, in every country in the world and in every trade in the world unless he can obtain stability he will not prosper and in order to obtain stability through the only means by which I think it can be obtained, that is the gold basis, it is worth while for him to make once this sacrifice for the good of his business and for his future success, and if he does not make it he will be in a state of uncertainty and at the mercy of other countries until he does.

Norman also maintained that 'the danger of waiting is much greater than people imagine, much greater, not to currency, but to the trade of this country, to the financial standing of this country'. Following on in the afternoon, Addis took the line that 'people are very ready to see the advantages of a return to the gold standard', though he conceded that 'I am not sure that they are quite prepared to accept what it really means in the way of sacrifice'. Even so, that 'sacrifice' would 'not be too high a price to pay for the substantial benefit to the trade of this country and its working classes'.

Other witnesses over the next week or so included Schuster, who insisted that 'there cannot be a difference of interest between the City of London and the trade of the country', for 'the two go absolutely together', with both benefiting from 'an absolutely stabilised exchange' removing 'the speculative element of uncertainty'. He was explicitly hostile to 'the inflationary theories' of Keynes, expressed complete faith in gold as a standard of value, and wonderfully undercut fashionable nostrums of managed money by remarking that 'the Bankers have not the intellectual capacity to understand these problems'. Schuster did, however, want the time to be right before a return to gold, as did National Provincial's chairman, Sir Harry Goschen, prompting Chamberlain to comment privately on 5 July that 'having now heard the evidence of 6 bankers, I understand why we never chose a banker for C/E', for 'they would be paralysed with fear at such decisions as we have to take, & would spoil any policy by niggling pre-conditions when only courage can carry it through'.[64]

Two days later Norman spent an hour and a quarter with McKenna. The subject was 'Free Gold', and Norman's diary entry referred without comment to 'managed currency (which greatly dominates him), Chamberlain Com, &c'. McKenna gave his evidence on the 10th and was asked outright whether he wanted a return to a free market in gold. 'Well,' he replied, 'the argument is an extraordinarily difficult one. We know the pros and cons, but it is partly psychological, of which you cannot really form a definite estimate . . .' In the end, while stating that 'I would certainly not stand as in all circumstances a gold standard man', he seemed to come down tentatively in favour – at least if external conditions, as opposed to domestic deflation, made it possible to restore the traditional dollar-sterling rate and thus return to gold at the pre-war parity. It was a significant shift on McKenna's part, retrospectively perhaps justifying Norman's assertion to Strong the previous year that 'at heart I believe him to be much more orthodox than any of the others' and that his 'apparent heterodoxy' was largely due to his wish for attention.[65]

Keynes, however, remained broadly hostile to a return when he treated the committee to a seminar on the 11th, though not without ambiguities. Near the end he was challenged by Farrer over the notion of managed money:

Coming back to the rather practical point of this credit control, you gave Mr Chamberlain a great many reasons which ought to influence the Bank of England directors in making these changes. Do you think from past experience, looking over the past forty years, that we have had a breed of people who are capable of taking all those considerations and acting upon them, or do you think we shall have to breed a superman to do it? – My memory of events does not go back forty years, but I do not foresee any particular difficulty with it. I should not entrust this to the whole body of the Court.

You do not think you are anticipating Paradise in your suggestion? – No. I am not changing the methods. If the directors of the Bank of England are as stupid as some people think they are, our currency will break down in any case. I do not regard my system as intrinsically more difficult . . . I should not have the smallest hesitation in thinking that there would be always half a dozen persons in the City well competent to look after it. Once they have started it, they would not find any particular trouble.

Or as Keynes elaborated a little later, in the face of Farrer's well-grounded scepticism, 'at all dates there have been a considerable number of first-class men of the skilled central banking type of mind'.[66]

A fortnight later Keynes wrote a major, set-piece letter to Addis (undoubtedly one of the central bankers he had in mind), warning against 'the torments of a violent and sudden deflation' possibly resultant upon a hasty decision to return to gold. Moreover:

To risk all these misfortunes merely for the sake of linking up the London and New York money markets, and so facilitating the work of international financiers – for this in my judgment is all it comes to – is going to lay the City and the Bank of England open to popular attacks the violence of which might be very great. It seems to me most unwise to act in such a way at the present juncture as to suggest that the interests of industry are being subordinated to those of international finance. I think this, although I agree with you that our profits from international finance are very great . . .

Are you quite sure that the rigid linking up of the London and New York money markets is all honey? The magnitude of the New York money market is quite different in relation to ours to what it was in pre-war days and in pre-Federal Reserve Bank days. The chances of redundancy of credit there on a great scale are also increased. Are you sure that you want London to be at any time the dumping ground of unlimited cheap American money liable to be withdrawn at a day's notice? It means that we should become, without any power of helping ourselves, the victim of every inflationary boom that America may indulge in – and that she will indulge in such from time to time is surely a probability.

However, all this is much too big a matter to discuss in a letter. The more I spend my thoughts on these matters, the more alarmed do I become at seeing you and the others in authority attacking the problems of the changed post-war world with – I know you will excuse my saying so – unmodified pre-war views and ideas. To close the mind to the idea of revolutionary improvements in our control of money and credit is to sow the seeds of the downfall of individualistic capitalism. Do not be the Louis XVI of the monetary revolution . . .

I am now told by a good many friends that I have become a sort of disreputable figure in some quarters because I do not agree with the maxims of City pundits. But you know I ought not to be so considered really!

Keynes added a final, handwritten sentence, almost as an afterthought: 'I seek to improve the machinery of Society, not to overturn it.'[67]

Between late July and mid-September 1924 the Chamberlain Committee drafted its report, pro-return but advocating a wait of up to a year if necessary. This was wholly satisfactory in Norman's eyes, but then came another of those infuriating general elections. 'As a matter of fact,' he wrote to Strong on 16 October just under a fortnight before polling day, 'our sudden and unexpected political upheaval has come at the very moment when we had planned and expected to obtain an official decision about future gold policy.' And: 'The subject has not been overlooked these last few months when for the first time it has become a practical question. But you know how controversial a subject it is – how it is everybody's business – and how secretly it must be treated: so much so that not a word can be breathed until some decision has been reached . . .' In the heat of the democratic battle Grenfell told a New York banker that 'the only white thing' about MacDonald was 'his liver', and that 'the only portion of him that is not red is his blood'; but Norman was genuinely regretful about the imminent political change, telling Blackett at the Treasury that whereas Snowden 'would have followed sound advice' over a recommended return to gold, 'if the Tories come into power again, I am not so sure what they will do: they are apt to listen to the traders and manufacturers, who, while they profess a remote affection for gold and a real affection for stability, always want a tot of brandy (in the shape of inflation) before the level is fixed!'

The Tories did return, and Norman once again had to prepare to magnetise a new Chancellor. A letter from Strong in November, congratulating him on the public announcement of his reappointment as Governor for a sixth year, was some consolation: 'Probably you are the one person in the world who knows better than anyone else how anxious

I am that you shall succeed in everything that you set out to accomplish, not the least important being to leave the Bank of England with the pound sterling and the gold dollar firmly established as before the war. What a great achievement, indeed, will this be!'[68]

The legislation suspending gold payments was due to expire at the end of the following year, and Norman was naturally anxious to achieve a return to gold by then. Shortly before Christmas 1924 he sailed to New York, and spent a fortnight there arranging practical American support for when that time came. 'He has evidently swung round to an early return to the Gold Standard,' recorded Addis on 8 January 1925 after receiving a telegram from his chief. 'I am not in favour of going too fast. From being in the van of the restorers I now find myself in the rear.' And again, after a Committee of Treasury meeting on the 21st: 'Norman back from U.S.A. He is now as much in favour of an immediate return to the Gold Standard as formerly he was against. He goes too fast for me.'[69]

A vexed Norman sent Strong a handwritten note on the 24th:

> The last 3 or 4 days have shown here at the Bank a general approval in principle but a strange opposition in detail to the scheme you & I discussed. It is so easy for them to be critics of any scheme – as they are not called upon to produce another – & to cry for the best of both worlds! But with or without concessions I begin to feel that they will be worn down . . . & *then* will begin the real tug of war . . . parliamentary and political.

The Governor's confidence was not misplaced. Addis's diary entries for three successive days were telling, if not entirely grammatical:

> *26 January (Monday).* Lunch at Bk of England. Treasury Committee met at 2.45 & discussed Gold Standard from then till nearly 5. I am not in accord so Norman me to go together represent our different views to the Treasury on Wednesday.
> *27 January.* Lunch at Bk of England. A talk in Governor's room afterwards on South Africa, the U.S. and Germany. 'I love you when you agree with me' says Norman as he flung an arm over my shoulder.
> *28 January.* Treasury Committee at noon. At 3 Norman and I appeared together before Bradbury [now Chairman of the currency committee, following Chamberlain's return to office], Niemeyer, Pigou & Gaspard Farrer & made separate statements on Gold Standard policy. We were there a couple of hours and more. The discussion has been sufficiently prolonged. It is now time to act.

In their respective evidence Addis was somewhat more reserved than Norman, but the pro-return message was essentially the same. The committee now listened only to the two Bank of England men, and their report, sanguine about a relatively early return, was on the Chancellor's desk by 5 February. 'Discussions here have been so quiet and confidential that public are ignorant of the programme,' Norman was able to cable reassuringly to Strong on the 13th. 'Great majority seem to favour our return to gold as soon as we can safely do so, but have little means of judging when the moment will arrive.'[70]

Inasmuch as there was a debate in the public domain, the clearing bankers had all fallen into line. As usual the annual round of chairmen's speeches to shareholders took place in late January and early February. Goodenough saw the return to gold as certain, following the recent appreciation of sterling, with only the date in question, and emphasised that 'it was of the greatest importance that there should be an early return to a free gold market for London'. Leaf and Goschen broadly agreed, the latter asserting his belief, in line with 'the majority of people in this country', that 'the return to the gold standard and to a free gold market is most desirable in the best interests of all concerned'. J. Beaumont Pease of Lloyds concurred: 'There is in fact no controversy. The whole world, though guilty of infidelity in varying degrees and in divers places and in spite of some coquettings in other directions, is returning to its old love. There is no effective rival of any standing or consequence. Gold is almost universally recognised as the only practical international measure of values . . .'

Inevitably the keynote speech was McKenna's, delivered at the Cannon Street Hotel on 27 January. After some moderately positive words about the attractions of a managed currency, he turned to the gold standard's 'great and striking advantages', none greater or more striking than 'its moral effect':

> A nation will think better of itself, will almost regard itself as more honest, if its currency is convertible into gold. The fear of being forced off the gold standard acts as a salutary check in the extravagance of Governments . . . It is a real advantage to a nation to have a currency founded upon a value which is universally recognised: it inspires confidence and facilitates international transactions . . . So long as nine people out of ten in every country think the gold standard the best, it is the best . . .

Yet what did McKenna really think? Soon afterwards Goodenough told the new Chancellor, Winston Churchill, that he had had (as Churchill subsequently reported to Niemeyer) 'private confirmation' that McKenna was 'personally opposed to the Gold policy and regards it as unnecessary and unwise'.[71] Presumably McKenna's reservations were genuine, but perhaps he felt that the situation had reached a point where the Midland could no longer afford to be out on a limb.

If McKenna could not quite make up his mind, the same was true in spades of Churchill himself. On 29 January, the day after Norman's confident recommendation to Bradbury's committee of an early return to gold, the Chancellor had initiated what the Treasury somewhat sardonically called 'Mr Churchill's Exercise'. The four recipients of the Chancellor's memorandum were Norman, Niemeyer, Bradbury and Ralph Hawtrey (a key thinker at the Treasury). Churchill demanded from his advisers a policy based on national, as opposed to sectional, criteria:

> The whole question of a return to the Gold Standard must not be dealt with only upon its financial and currency aspects. The merchant, the manufacturer, the workman and the consumer have interests which, though largely common, do not by any means exactly coincide either with each other or with the financial and currency interests. The maintenance of cheap money is a matter of high consequence. If a return to the Gold Standard, when restored, could be defended only by an increase of the Bank Rate to 5% or even 6%, a very serious check would be administered to trade, industry and employment. If the Government took positive action to restore the Gold Standard and this were followed by a rise in the Bank Rate, we should certainly be accused of having favoured the special interests of finance at the expense of the special interests of production.

Niemeyer, Hawtrey and Bradbury all defended a return, as did Norman, who sent his reply on 2 February. It was imbued with characteristic moral certainties:

> National Credit needs not only a strict financial policy and healthy economic conditions but also good faith and a liquid Reserve.
>
> Gold is the guarantee of good faith.
>
> A liquid Reserve must be internationally valid: there is no internationally valid Reserve except Gold (or its equivalent).
>
> A Gold Reserve and the Gold Standard are steps in the evolution of Finance and Credit: as such they are necessary: so is a Police Force or Tax Collector: it is as dangerous to abandon the former as the latter . . .
>
> The restoration of Free Gold *will* require a high Bank Rate: the Government cannot avoid a decision for or against Restoration: the chancellor will surely be charged with a sin of omission or of commission. In the former case (Gold) he will be abused by the ignorant, the gamblers

and the antiquated Industrialists: in the latter case (not Gold) he will be abused by the instructed and by posterity ...

The interest of the U.S. in this respect is identical with that of Great Britain and the world. The Gold Standard is the best 'Governor' that can be devised for a world that is still human, rather than divine.

Churchill continued to hesitate – unable, Niemeyer reported privately in mid-February, to 'make up his mind from day to day whether he is a gold bug or a pure inflationist'.[72]

Then, over the weekend of the 21st/22nd, there took place a volley of argument and counter-argument. It began with Keynes in the *Nation* attacking a precipitate return, if return there had to be; Niemeyer at once sent Churchill a robust letter of refutation; and Churchill on the Sunday morning penned a long *cri de coeur* to Niemeyer. It was a remarkable piece of writing that would continue to resonate through the years:

The Treasury have never, it seems to me, faced the profound significance of what Mr Keynes calls 'the paradox of unemployment amidst dearth'. The Governor shows himself perfectly happy in the spectacle of Britain possessing the finest credit in the world simultaneously with a million and a quarter unemployed ...

This is the only country in the world where this condition exists. The Treasury and Bank of England policy has been the only policy consistently pursued. It is a terrible responsibility for those who have shaped it, unless they can be sure that there is no connection between the unique British phenomenon of chronic unemployment and the long, resolute consistency of a particular financial policy ...

It may be of course that you will argue that the unemployment would have been greater but for the financial policy pursued; that there is no sufficient demand for commodities either internally or externally to require the services of this million and a quarter people; that there is nothing for them but to hang like a millstone round the neck of industry and on the public revenue until they become permanently demoralised. You may be right, but if so, it is one of the most sombre conclusions ever reached. On the other hand I do not pretend to see even 'through a glass darkly' how the financial and credit policy of the country could be handled so as to bridge the gap between a dearth of goods and a surplus of labour; and well I realise the danger of experiment to that end. The seas of history are full of famous wrecks. Still if I could see a way, I would far rather follow it than any other. I would rather see Finance less proud and Industry more content.

You and the Governor have managed this affair. Taken together I expect you know more about it than anyone else in the world. At any rate alone in the world you have had an opportunity of a definite period of years of seeing your policy carried out. That it is a great policy, greatly pursued, I have no doubt. But the fact that this island with its enormous extraneous resources is unable to maintain its population is surely a cause for the deepest heart-searching.[73]

Niemeyer at once fired back a reply, positing inflation and all its damaging consequences as the only alternative to gold, but Churchill continued to ponder.

Monetary developments did not lighten his mood. In the face of an impending rise in the New York rate, Addis on the 23rd 'urged' Norman 'to raise Bank rate at once', but stated that 'he hesitates', presumably due to his awareness of how sensitive Churchill was becoming about the unemployment situation. But on the 26th, at the Committee of Treasury, Norman consented, with the Court to take the formal decision on 5 March. Niemeyer, fearful of the reaction, sent Churchill a minute on the 4th outlining in thoroughly pre-1914 terms the Bank-government relationship in monetary matters:

> It is not either necessary nor the practice for the Bank to consult the Government of the day, though the Bank is naturally well aware of the political reactions of its decisions. The Governor has on occasion mentioned to Chancellors that probably Bank rate ought to go up. I don't recollect that he has ever come and said that he is going to put it up tomorrow; and if he did, it would certainly not be with a view to seeking our approval. Our strong disapproval would no doubt have weight: but it would not be decisive. We have neither claim to be consulted nor power to enforce our views: and I think it would be generally recognised that in order to avoid political influence on these matters it is not desirable that we should have any such claim.

Bank rate duly went up next day, from 4 to 5 per cent, and on the 7th Lubbock (with Norman by now away, recuperating in the South of France) wrote complacently to New York that 'the raising of our rate to 5% while disliked by some people whose particular interests may be unfavourably affected by it is, I think, recognised by all competent judges to be the right thing to do'.[74]

On the 12th, however, the *Daily Express* launched a savage attack. 'What one 1% More Means: Dearer Food, Fewer Houses, Less Work' ran the headline, with the article concluding: 'Mr Churchill could have kept the Bank rate down had he wished. He did not do so, and he is responsible for the consequences.' Niemeyer at once sent Churchill a note repudiating the attack – 'the great industrial complaint against high Bank rate is precisely that it *prevents a rise* in prices, on which they expect to make profits' – and Churchill that afternoon in the Commons opted for discretion. Asked 'whether the Bank of England raised the Bank rate without conferring with him', he replied, 'Entirely independent action is taken in these matters by the Bank of England.' In private, however, he had been seething. 'W. will never realise that he is not Governor of the Bank,' Niemeyer at one point informed a colleague. 'He would be very foolish to dissociate himself from sound finance by denouncing the Bank. The effect on national credit *abroad* would be exceedingly bad . . .'[75] So Churchill bit his tongue, but his distrust of 'sound finance' merely deepened.

Elsewhere in his letter of 7 March, Lubbock asserted that 'there is no doubt that opinion here is strengthening in favour of the restoration of a free gold market', referring with satisfaction to the address that McKenna had given three days earlier 'at the House of Commons to a large gathering of Members, which I have no doubt will have a good effect'. He added that 'Mr Keynes appears to be left almost the sole advocate of "a managed currency".' In fact, in that address, McKenna had argued that a return to gold was desirable partly because it would *lessen* the Bank of England's power, in that whereas in the existing state of a managed currency 'the Bank of England, as the final authority in regulating the volume of credit in this country, has unfettered control over the quantity of currency', under the gold standard 'the control of the Bank of England is governed by the movement of gold'. It was an important point, for in recent years the Bank's 'contraction of credit has been too severe to permit of a real revival of trade prosperity'.[76]

On 6 March the financial section of the London Chamber of Commerce reiterated its long-standing preference for a return to a free gold market as soon as possible, and at about the same time Brand published an unequivocally pro-return article in the *Round Table*. 'A stable sterling exchange is of first-rate importance for the maintenance of London's pre-eminent position as the financial centre of the world,' he declared, arguing that 'that she could permanently maintain her supremacy with a fluctuating exchange, when there were other centres such as New York with a stable exchange, is more than doubtful'. More generally, he added: 'The gold standard, it may be owing to lucky circumstances, worked well before the war. It will have to show itself far less beneficial as a means of uniting the world in the bonds of one uniform standard of value than it has hitherto, before its abandonment will be seriously contemplated.' In sum: 'We have stable Governments both here and in the United States. If we really believe that the gold standard is worth some sacrifices, we should not hesitate too long. The whole world believes we intend to return to par. If we wait too long, psychological influences will turn against us, we may miss the moment and it may be many months before it returns.'[77]

Churchill could avoid a decision no longer. He invited to dinner on 17 March a formidable quartet, comprising Niemeyer, Bradbury, Keynes and McKenna. Norman was still away. On this occasion – for most of the evening anyway – Midland's Chairman was on the side of the doubters, to judge by the only eye-witness account we have, written some twenty years later by Churchill's private secretary, James Grigg:

> The symposium lasted till midnight or after. I thought at the time that the ayes had it. Keynes's thesis, which was supported in every particular by McKenna, was that the discrepancy between American and British prices was not $2\frac{1}{2}$ per cent as the exchanges indicated, but 10 per cent. If we went back to gold at the old parity we should therefore have to deflate domestic prices by something of that order. This meant unemployment and downward adjustments of wages and prolonged strikes in some of the heavy industries, at the end of which it would be found that these industries had undergone a permanent contraction . . .
>
> Bradbury made a great point of the fact that the Gold Standard was knave-proof. It could not be rigged for political or even more unworthy reasons. It would prevent our living in a fool's paradise of false prosperity, and would ensure our keeping on a competitive basis in our export business . . . To the suggestion that we should return to gold but at a lower parity, Bradbury's answer was that we were so near the old parity that it was silly to create a shocked confidence and to endanger our international reputation for so small and so ephemeral an easement . . .
>
> One thing about this argument comes back to me with crystal clearness. Having listened to the gloomy prognostications of Keynes and McKenna, Winston turned to the latter and said: 'But this isn't entirely an economic matter; it is a political decision . . . You have been a politician; indeed you have been Chancellor of the Exchequer. Given the situation as it is, what decision would you take?' McKenna's reply – and I am prepared to swear to the sense of it – was: 'There is no escape; you have got to go back; but it will be hell'.

McKenna, as Keynes would once remark, 'always lets one down in the end'. Two days later, back in harness, Norman recorded in his diary: '12.45. Chancellor for Lunch in Downing St. Gold return to be announced Apl 6 or 8.' And on the 20th: '2.30. PM, Chancellor, Austen C., Bradbury, OEN [Niemeyer]. Free gold statement to be in Budget about Apl 28.' Norman then returned to Threadneedle Street for tea and, Addis noted, 'much talk'.[78]

Addis himself still had reservations that he could not quite suppress. 'Much discussion with Governor of Bank on Gold Standard,' he wrote on 3 April. 'Chancellor will announce free export of gold in Budget speech on Apl 27. Too soon, I think. The risk is too great.' Yet the alternatives seemed worse, despite his considerable regard for Keynes, and on the 14th he wrote to Strong: 'Let us be thankful we have escaped the managed currency.' The budget was eventually fixed for the 28th, and five days before his speech an apparently convinced Churchill wrote to King George V putting the move into its imperial context:

> Canada is already on the gold standard, South Africa, Australia and New Zealand only await the British signal. The importance of a uniform standard of value to which all transactions can be referred throughout the British Empire and through a very large part of the world cannot be over-estimated. It benefits all countries, but it benefits no country more than our crowded island with its vast world trade and finance by which it lives.[79]

*

'Winston Churchill is about to deliver his Budget speech as I write,' Cecil Baring informed an American banker on that historic Tuesday afternoon. 'It is expected that he will announce the resumption of gold payments by this country. A great day for those of us who have such matters at heart.' Norman's diary entry burst into capitals: '3.45. Budget. H of C 3–6. GOLD STANDARD (about 4.5 pm)'. That evening he scribbled a congratulatory note to Churchill: 'Pray count on me to try to do my little bit.' The City as a whole seems to have been neither surprised nor made jubilant by the decision, but almost certainly few would have disagreed with the *FT*'s assertion, in its leader on the 29th, that 'the restoration of the free gold market had been anticipated and will bring far more permanent good than possible temporary inconvenience'; that, indeed, 'the decision is the best that could have happened in the interests of British credit and prestige'. In similarly positive tones, the City column in *The Times* greeted the announcement as 'a signal triumph for those who have controlled and shaped our monetary policy, notably the Governor of the Bank'.[80] Indeed it was arguably the apogee of Norman's influence, although almost twenty years of his governorship still remained.

The fullest account of 'the Norman Conquest' – the fateful return to gold in 1925 at the pre-war parity of \$4.86 to the pound – describes it as 'ultimately an act of faith in an incompletely understood adjustment mechanism undertaken for largely moral reasons'.[81] And so it was:

'incompletely understood' not least because of the wholly inadequate pool of expertise that Norman had to draw upon in the first half of the 1920s. In addition to higher morality, however, there was also naked self-interest at work on the City's part: not just a generalised wish to return to the prosperous verities of pre-1914, but, on the part of more analytical minds, a specific awareness that following the return to gold London would be able fully to resume its place as the world's leading international capital market. Inevitably the decision to restore the gold standard was, then and later, closely identified with the City. Industry was weak and divided in its counsels; the politicians in the end left it to the experts; and Niemeyer, the strongest single figure at the Treasury, seems to have had complete confidence in Norman's judgement. From the Cunliffe Report of 1918 onwards, it had been City assumptions that had largely shaped the framework of what debate there had been. Unfortunately, the City's contribution to that debate had rarely risen above the level of truism and platitude. 'That our bank chairmen should have nothing better to cry than "back to 1914",' commented Keynes after the round of speeches early in 1925, 'is not satisfactory . . . The "Big Five" have vast responsibilities towards the public. But they are so huge, and in some ways so vulnerable, that there is a great temptation to them to cling to maxims, conventions, and routine; and when their chairmen debate fundamental economic problems, they are most of them on ground with which they are unfamiliar.'[82]

Keynes's exasperation was understandable, yet on the part of the few more thoughtful City men there was an acceptance, even sometimes a public articulation, that simply to assume that the City's interests coincided completely with the nation at large was no longer intellectually sustainable – that, in short, there was a trade-off involved. Addis, so close to Norman and at one stage even more bullish about an early return, perhaps expressed it best. Speaking in April 1924 at the annual meeting of the Royal Economic Society, he conceded that the return to gold would, in the short term, lead to somewhat lower prices, with a knock-on deflationary effect on trade. But he asked: 'Is the comparatively small further drop, which is all that is required to bring us back to parity with gold, too great a sacrifice to ask of our people in order to restore the currency position on which the supremacy of this country in international trade and finance was formerly established? I do not believe it.'[83] Events after April 1925 soon showed the extent of the sacrifice that 'our people' – most of whom lived a long way from the square mile – would have to make.

CHAPTER SIX

That Man Skinner

'As you will have seen,' Brand wrote on 1 May to Paul Warburg in New York, 'we took the plunge as regards the gold standard two days ago.' He added, 'I think things will come all right.' A week later Norman told Strong that 'the transition to free gold has been easier and has caused not only less alarm but even less interest than could have been expected' – indeed, 'we rather prepared for a mountain and have (so far) brought forth a mouse!' The Governor attributed this anti-climactic reaction to 'the financial community' having 'lived for ten years in a dream'. If dream it had been, then the awakening was soon rude enough. On 15 July, at the Bank of England's Committee of Treasury, Addis tried to persuade his colleagues that the time was ripe to make the first shift in Bank rate under the gold standard a downwards one. 'Trade was very stagnant,' the Deputy Governor, Sir Alan Anderson, paraphrased Addis's arguments to the absent Norman, 'the tails of the traders were right down and the Bank of England would create a good psychological effect by showing that it was prepared to take some risk in order to give trade the fillip of a reduced Bank Rate. He did not get much support from the Committee on these views.'[1]

The very specific background, not spelt out by Addis/Anderson, was that the situation in Britain's coalfields had become desperate by the summer of 1925, with the recent catastrophic slump in foreign demand for coal having been exacerbated by the 10 per cent increase in cost that automatically ensued upon the return to gold at the pre-war parity. On 24 July, faced by the threat of a simultaneous cut in wages and increase in hours, the miners announced a national strike from the start of August. This was averted at the last minute only by government's promise of an inquiry and a short-term subsidy to the coal industry. The normally temperate Gaspard Farrer exploded on 4 August to an American correspondent:

> The decision of our Government to subsidise the coal trade fills me with
> alarm and disgust. Sooner or later the country will have to decide whether

it intends to be governed by the Trades Unions or by Parliament, and I think the sooner the trial between the two comes the better. Just at the moment every ill in every trade is put down to the gold standard, but my withers are unwrung.

In the eyes of the City, there was no doubt who spearheaded the campaign to blame everything on the return to gold. 'I have read your friend Keynes,' Farrer wrote on 7 August to Sidney Russell Cooke (a young, intelligent stockbroker on the fringes of the Bloomsbury set), 'and am very much amused, moreover dazzled by the brilliance and lucidity of his writing. The more I see of him the more I am impressed by his ability and intellect, but as to his wisdom and judgment, well, that is another matter.' The veteran merchant banker had been reading Keynes's just-published *The Economic Consequences of Mr Churchill*, an expanded version of three articles that had appeared in the *Evening Standard* on 22, 23 and 24 July. 'Keynes is fulminating in *Evening Standard*,' Anderson informed Norman the day after the final article appeared, while the Bank's comptroller, Sir Ernest Harvey, summarised their disagreeable thrust in a letter to the National Bank of Hungary: 'He imputes to the Bank the policy of deliberate intensification of unemployment, by credit restriction, with a view to reducing money wages and so bringing down prices and lowering the cost of living.' Two brief passages (of the pamphlet version) demonstrate that it was a fair summary:

> The Bank of England is *compelled* to curtail credit by all the rules of the gold standard game. It is acting conscientiously and 'soundly' in doing so. But this does not alter the fact that to keep a tight hold on credit – and no one will deny that the Bank is doing that – necessarily involves intensifying unemployment in the present circumstances of this country.
>
> On grounds of social justice no case can be made out for reducing the wages of the miners. They are the victims of the economic juggernaut. They represent in the flesh the 'fundamental adjustments' engineered by the Treasury and the Bank of England to satisfy the impatience of the City fathers to bridge the 'moderate gap' between \$4.40 and \$4.86. *They* (and others to follow) are the 'moderate sacrifice' still necessary to ensure the stability of the gold standard.[2]

To Keynes, as a tragic situation now unfolded, the Bank of England – and those powerful voices in the City who did not question the Bank – were guilty not of dishonour, but of narrow-mindedness. He had already said as much in his first article after the return to gold:

> The gold standard party have had behind them much that is not only

respectable but is also worthy of respect. The state of mind which likes to stick to the straight, old-fashioned course, rather regardless of the pleasure or pain and of the ease or difficulty of the passing situation, and quite regardless of particular interests and of anything except the public good as they understand it, is not to be despised. How much preferable is this mentality to that of the financiers of France!

But at the same time he was intensely frustrated – as he would tell the Manchester branch of the Federation of British Industries in October – by the refusal of his intellectual enemies to engage in open combat with him:

> Lenin and Mussolini have at least explained what they were at. But our despots are dumb. The veiled prophetess of Threadneedle Street speaks in the riddles of Bank rate, the City reverently accepts her word, but no one, it seems, has any idea what the old lady really means . . . It may be that the Bank of England has no steady or thought-out policy at all, but lives empirically day by day – by cunning rather than science. It is absurd that we do not know. For the immediate future of this country depends on the answer.

The remedy, however, did not lie in the nationalisation of the Bank, for Keynes believed – perhaps surprisingly – that it was already under effective public control, indeed that it had been so since the world at large had digested the lessons of Bagehot's *Lombard Street* back in the 1870s. Instead, what was needed was to *enlighten* that opaque institution. Keynes knew the City well enough to appreciate that its severe dislike of the concept of 'managed money' derived less from fear of government control over monetary policy (though that was not a negligible consideration) than from its profound, instinctive desire to return to the well-understood, still fondly remembered pre-1914 ways. Over the next few years he would compose *A Treatise on Money*, at the end of which he pinned his hopes on *rational* central banks, the antidote to investors who 'do not possess even the rudiments of what is required for a valid judgement, and are the prey of hopes and fears easily aroused by transient events and as easily dispelled'.[3] For someone who took such a dim view of Montagu Norman's intellectual talents, it was a typically imaginative prescription.

Did Keynes overstate his case about the damage inflicted on British industry by the return to gold at the pre-war parity? For almost three-quarters of a century the debate amongst economists and economic historians has rarely flagged, but at the very least few would deny that some significant damage was done.[4] In essence, the pound could only stay on the gold standard – and thus enable sterling to be perceived as a 'strong' currency, to the international benefit of the City of London – if foreign funds were attracted; and the inevitable price of attracting those funds was high domestic interest rates, or at least no possibility of a 'cheap money' policy. However, as Norman painfully discovered before 1925 was out, raising interest rates in order to protect an over-valued currency was no longer the simple, relatively uncontroversial matter that it had been in the classical era of the gold standard. Perhaps it was no surprise. In November, writing to Strong in the wake of two downward steps in Bank rate, Norman argued in defence of the 4 per cent rate that 'nothing else could have taken the wind out of the sales [presumably a Norman joke] of McKenna & Co as this has done or could do more to silence criticism of the Gold Standard' – an explicit admission that there was now a political dimension to monetary policy.[5]

By the beginning of December, with large quantities of gold leaving London and rates rising in America, Norman saw no alternative but to go back to 5 per cent. On the evening of the 2nd (a Wednesday), he called at the Treasury and informed Leith-Ross that there was every probability that next morning the Court would sanction this step. Whereupon (Leith-Ross related in a memo):

> I reported this to the Chancellor on the following morning and he at once telephoned to the Governor expressing his concern at the news. He told the Governor that if the rate were raised he would have to inform the House that it had been done without his being consulted and against his wishes. It was not fair to the Exchequer that action should be taken which affected all its affairs without an opportunity being given to him to consider it. He expressed an earnest request that action should be deferred at any rate for a week, to enable this to be done.

Addis privately noted the immediate outcome: 'Bank rate raised to 5% in spite of Churchill's protest on telephone. He is a —.' We will never know the epithet Sir Charles had in mind, but it was presumably not 'blighter'. Norman himself wrote to Churchill on the 4th, 'I can now only await the statement which you threaten to make in the House of Commons, but I may say that I believe your action to be unprecedented.' In the event, his bluff having been called by the Bank, Churchill stayed publicly quiet; but for Norman, who had handled the episode somewhat clumsily, it was a pyrrhic victory. Henceforth there was no possibility of Bank rate policy operating in a comfortably ring-fenced political vacuum. Or, in the words of Sayers, the historian of Norman's Bank, 'everyone knew that the political interest was derived from, and would last as long as, the obstinate million in the unemployment figures'.[6]

Unemployment was one thing, industrial warfare another, and without doubt the fact of an over-valued pound (with its direct impact on costs and therefore on wages) played a direct causal role in provoking the miners' lock-out, followed, in May 1926, by the general strike. 'An Assault on the Community' was the *FT*'s leader on the morning of Monday the 3rd, the first day of the strike, and it accurately reflected City opinion. 'The plain fact is that the coal-miners are attempting to hold the nation to ransom. Their undeviating demand is for the payment of wages which the industry cannot earn. They are completely indifferent on whose shoulders the burden is thrown, and what the toll of monetary loss, physical suffering, and industrial stagnation may be.' In the same paper, even the lighter tone of 'Autolycus' did not conceal Landells's bitterness about the miners: 'Apparently, the leaders prefer to follow the matrimonial example, so often set, in which one of the parties does all the giving, and the other all the taking.'[7]

The Stock Exchange stayed open ('The very idea of closing the House,' declared 'Autolycus', 'is scouted as being a sign of weakness, which, if adopted, would be construed as a concession to the forces of disorder'), and the Smith St Aubyn diary entry for the 3rd noted that the square mile had just about managed to go about its normal business: 'Tremendous crush of private cars trying to get into the City. Everybody late. Stock Exchange calm – prices are down but no pressure to sell.' Next day Addis eschewed the traffic jams – 'I pedalled comfortably by back streets on my trusty bicycle which I parked at the Bank of England' – while just to the north, in Tokenhouse Yard, the General Manager of the Bank of London & South America informed Buenos Aires that 'all our Staff, without exception, turned up today, most of them very late it is true, but it is a great feather in their cap, that despite the enormous difficulties, they were still able to attend to their duties'. Lack of transport was not the only problem. Staff at Kleinworts, for example, had bricks thrown at them as they passed through the East End on their long trudge in. Moreover, in the City itself, Lazards in Old Broad Street was probably not unusual in issuing emergency orders, 'in the event of rioting in the City, or danger of attack on Banks'. One order was that 'all female staff will proceed at once to the Second floor and arrange as may be possible to deal with any casualties'; another noted that 'the Directors' lift will be sent to the upper floor and will remain there'. In the Stock Exchange, meanwhile, the mood remained uncompromising, with the House believing that victory over the strikers would have, as 'Autolycus' put it on the 6th, 'the moral effect of showing that the nation is strong enough to defeat the poisonous doctrines chewed by foreign-bred firebrands'. And he added that 'passing from one market to another in the House, I hear a good deal of surprise expressed at the extreme moderation with which the Government are treating the ring-leaders and the rioters'. Transport problems gradually eased in the course of the week, and on Monday the 10th Revelstoke told Hugo Baring in Paris that 'it is possible that we may have some darker days before us, but the general tone here is quite confident'.[8]

The end came, quite suddenly, only two days later. 'At one o'clock,' recorded Addis on the 12th, 'as I sat with Strong in Bk of Eng. library, the Governor poked in his head. "General strike called off. Official." For this relief much thanks.' Soon afterwards, in the Stock Exchange, a waiter mounted his rostrum in the Consol market, lifted a megaphone to his lips and announced that the strike was over. 'Autolycus' described the memorable scene:

> Cheers rolled round all the markets of the House. Lines of men started off, at the double, to the telegraph offices and the telephone boxes . . . So general was the bidding all round the House for the various favourites that the volume of sound became welded on to a single note which rose, strident and triumphant, above all the uproar caused by the rushing feet, the staccato snap of the pneumatic telegram tubes, the shouting of the waiters, the electrified enthusiasm in the air, and the intense relief . . .

There was, however, no peace in the coalfields. Some six weeks after the strike, addressing from the chair the City of London Conservative Association, the former Herbert Gibbs, now Lord Hunsdon, conceded that 'there existed a certain sympathy with the miners', but declared that so far from sharing that sympathy, he believed that 'while they, the miners, were our enemies, we should not feed them'. Toughness similarly outweighed tenderness when Teddy Grenfell wrote on 23 July to a correspondent in India: 'I am beginning to have much more confidence that the men will now drift in fairly quickly. All the sob-stuff about starving women and children and the interference of the Bishops have been unfortunate. There are, of course, no starving women and children . . .' But the drift took a long time, and on 7 November, a Sunday, there was an intriguing entry in Norman's diary: '5.30. Steel Maitland [the Minister of Labour]. Will Bankers intervene in Coal Strike. I say No – too pol[al] & ind[al].'[9] Later that month, however, the miners' delegate conference did call off the strike. A grievous episode in British industrial history thus ended, but on the part of the City there had been little or no comprehension of the human suffering involved – or of its own responsibility for that suffering.

Over the next few years, with Keynes mainly concentrating on other matters, the two most persistent critics of the gold standard regime, and what they saw as the Bank of England's malign influence on monetary policy, were McKenna in public and Churchill in private. Addressing Midland Bank's shareholders in January 1927, and contrasting British depression during the decade with American prosperity, McKenna called for a monetary inquiry in order to redress the situation by which, for statutory reasons, the Bank of England's 'reserve, susceptible as it is to a drain occasioned by foreign demands for gold, is insufficient to permit open market operations with a view to increasing the volume of credit on anything more than quite a small scale'; and he demanded that the central bank be reconstructed on the same basis as the Federal Reserve Banks. The speech did not play well in Threadneedle Street, and antagonism between Norman and McKenna deepened in the spring when the latter refused to join a gold-pooling arrangement that Norman was organising. 'McKenna is *always* chasing the lime-light,' Norman told Strong in September, '& *always* making things difficult for me: he's a bad man.' Norman's view was entirely shared by Revelstoke, who in a letter to Peacock (away in Scotland) in October 1928 encapsulated the timeless City attitude to all those who dare to rock the boat:

> You will have seen the review of McKenna's new book in today's newspapers – a collection, I understand, of his speeches at the Midland Bank meetings throughout a series of years. If you happen to see it on the bookstall at Edinburgh tomorrow, it might amuse you to glance at the paper cover, which presents a photograph of the author in flaming colours, in a mode with which we are so familiar in Edgar Wallace's novels. On the back of the cover you will see in large letters the following quotation (or words to that effect):
> 'If Mr McKenna had been Governor of the Bank of England there would have been less unemployment,' etc, etc.
> (signed) J.M. Keynes
> We are engaged in preparing a frame so that an additional adornment may be given to the Governor's room.[10]

Relations were no better between Norman and Churchill. Tom Jones, Deputy Secretary to the Cabinet, watched an encounter between them at 10 Downing Street the morning after Churchill's budget in April 1927. He found Norman at first alone, 'looking thoroughly ill and disconsolate', and suggested to him that the Chancellor had 'bemused the public with a false sense of security'. To which Norman 'recalled Blondin and tried to recall the name of the famous juggler'. A few minutes later,

'Winston joined us, all smiles and buoyancy. "It was as good a get-out as we could get" was his salutation to the Governor, who made no reply.' The following month all Churchill's smiles had gone as he poured out his frustrations to the ultra-orthodox Sir Otto Niemeyer at the Treasury (but shortly to move to the Bank):

> We have assumed since the war, largely under the guidance of the Bank of England, a policy of deflation, debt repayment, high taxation, large sinking funds and Gold Standard. This has raised our credit, restored our exchange and lowered the cost of living. On the other hand it has produced bad trade, hard times, an immense increase in unemployment involving costly and unwise remedial measures, attempts to reduce wages in conformity with the cost of living and so increase the competitive power, fierce labour disputes arising therefrom, with expense to the State and community measured by hundreds of millions ... We have to look forward, as a definite part of the Bank of England policy, to an indefinite period of high taxation, of immense repayments and of no progress towards liberation either nominal or real, only a continued enhancement of the bondholders' claim. This debt and taxation lie like a vast wet blanket across the whole process of creating new wealth by new enterprise.

Churchill saw no way beyond this 'strict, rigid, highly particularist line of action' and now blamed the Bank for his intellectual captivity. Just over a year later, in June 1928, Churchill went volcanic again, this time at a Cabinet meeting. 'Winston to everyone's surprise suddenly exploded on Montagu Norman and deflation,' recorded Leo Amery. 'He is right of course about Norman's pedantry, but it is rather late in the day to undo the work of the last eight years ...' Indeed, according to his private secretary, 'he got into the habit of almost spitting out comments on the presumed enormities of "that man Skinner"' – Ernest Skinner being the private secretary in whose name Norman used to reserve his passages across the Atlantic. In later years Churchill would continue to brood over what he came to believe had been a betrayal. 'The biggest blunder in his life,' his doctor noted him telling the assembled company one evening in September 1945 as he convalesced by Lake Como, 'had been the return to the gold standard. Montagu Norman had spread his blandishments before him till it was done, and had then left him severely alone.'[11]

All of which left Norman distinctly nervous about deploying the traditional interest-rate weapon in order to maintain the gold standard. Sayers tells the story delightfully:

The Bank knew there would be trouble if Bank Rate went up, and it was almost as fearful of putting it down lest it should soon want to reverse engines and so again incur political wrath. So Bank Rate was almost frozen: no change at all through 1926; one only – a wee step down – in 1927; and no change in 1928. With his right hand tied behind his back Norman resorted to all the new devices he had been learning: he used all his blandishments with Benjamin Strong and other friends in New York; he exercised an iron control in the discount market; he kept a tight grip on overseas issues; he built up and ran down a secret reserve of dollars; he even stumbled into an old Bank trick of widening the gold points . . .

These were arcane, not unsuccessful manoeuvres, but by the start of 1929, with a boom raging on Wall Street, and gold being shipped in alarming quantities out of London and across the Atlantic, Norman could no longer refrain from using the big gun. He himself was in New York, but in the closest touch with the situation, when on Wednesday, 6 February the Bank's Committee of Treasury discussed Bank rate. 'Much talk,' noted Addis. 'Home to tea and rest. Lubbock [Cecil Lubbock, Norman's deputy at this time] telephoned that he was to see Winston Churchill at the House. Baldwin was present & all went well. It was agreed Bk must take responsibility of rise to 5½%.' The *Daily Mail* described an old-time City scene next morning:

> Long before the announcement of the Bank Rate was due to be made a large crowd of messengers, clerks, and silk-hatted City men collected outside the Bank parlour.
> In the Stock Exchange excitement was equally intense. Members stood in throngs around the Consol market and beguiled the tedium of the wait by registering bets on the announcement. Odds at 11.50 a.m. were 6 to 4 against any change.
> After a representative of Messrs Mullens, Marshall, the Government brokers, had announced quietly, so quietly that many of the members did not hear, 'Gentlemen, the Bank Rate is 5½ per cent', the special electronic indicators flashed the news through the Stock Exchange.
> There was, however, a pause between the figure 5 and the ½, and this is said to have resulted in a number of incorrect messages being despatched to provincial firms.

The absence of Norman and presence of Baldwin (the Prime Minister) at the crucial meeting had probably been decisive in getting through the rise. In any case Churchill, faced by some hostile press criticism and questions in Parliament, continued over the next week or so to play his usual public dead bat. 'Of course, if we were not on the gold standard,' he informed the Commons on the 12th, 'we might not have had a rise in the Bank rate on this particular occasion but, on the other hand, the financial position of the City of London and the country might stand very differently from what it does now.' And on the 19th: 'Decisions in regard to alteration of the Bank Rate are taken by the Bank of England on its sole responsibility. It has frequently been the practice of the Governor in post-war times to inform the Chancellor when a proposal to alter the rate is about to be considered.' With a general election pending, Churchill had gone far too far down his fateful road to play it otherwise. However, it did not take a lot of imagination to envisage another Chancellor wanting to establish his own control over monetary policy. Churchill himself bowed out of office with a thoroughly orthodox budget speech in April. 'I think Winston's defence of the gold standard is really well done,' Peacock wrote to Revelstoke in Paris on the 16th. 'He takes a line that is thoroughly sound and at the same time can be understood by the man in the street and will keep him straight.'[12]

*

Yet whatever its damaging influence on British monetary policy, there was no denying that in the course of the 1920s the City became far more deeply involved in the fate of British industry than had ever before been the case.[13] It was not, on the whole, an involvement that it instinctively welcomed. Writing in 1923 to the *Morning Post*'s Arthur Kiddy, doyen of City editors, Farrer expressed a continuing orthodoxy: 'The extent to which the big industrials of this country lean upon their bankers might easily become a danger, besides being bad for the industrials themselves. Banking arrangement of industrials is proverbially nerveless.' Two years later Norman saw the senior partner of the merchant bank Helbert Wagg, and made a crisp note in his diary: 'Wagg [i.e. Alfred Wagg], as to combining Acc. [i.e. accepting] business with trading & issuing Industrials and Secs. I discourage it.'[14] Larger circumstances, however, were inexorable. The commercial banks had badly over-lent during the immediate post-war boom and found it impossible to extricate themselves easily; the City's international business was no longer its free, unfettered pre-1914 self; and the high-profile problems faced by British industry – above all, the traditional exporting sector – made it politically impossible for the square mile to stand aside entirely. The depth of its involvement, let alone its beneficial or other effects, may remain matters of keen historical debate, but the fact of involvement and its unprecedented nature are indisputable.

For Norman himself, the turning-point was his increasing commitment from the mid-1920s to the affairs of Armstrong Whitworth & Co, the Tyneside armaments firm, which after the war had borrowed heavily from the Bank in order to diversify its business but was now in serious financial waters, particularly through a disastrous venture in a New-foundland paper mill.[15] A 'company doctor' was appointed – Frater Taylor, an unsentimental Aberdonian – and, with the help of Peacock of Barings, the three men tried to right matters. There began a costly (especially to the Bank) and seemingly interminable series of financial reconstructions, while from the start of 1928 Armstrongs and Vickers pooled their armaments and naval ship-building businesses to form Vickers-Armstrong. In August 1927 Norman spent a weekend with Peacock. 'He is full of plans and problems,' the latter reported to Revelstoke, 'and spoke particularly of the importance of bringing about closer relationships and a much better understanding between the City of London and the great industries of England, particularly iron, steel, coal and textiles.' Almost certainly two motives were uppermost in Norman's mind: the belief that there existed certain specific industrial situations in which finance could usefully and legitimately lend a helping hand; and the fear that unless the City assumed such a function, even on a strictly selective basis, then government might step in and try to do its job for it. There was no question of a blank cheque. In April 1928, for example, Norman was approached to form a finance company in order to assist the iron and steel sector, but he declined on the grounds that, as he noted in his diary, 'that trade now is merely waiting for protection & avoiding modernisation!'[16] Salvation, in other words, lay in the hands of industrialists, not financiers; but in the interests of material as well as spiritual health, he was sometimes willing to give a push – in the event, far more often than he could have originally envisaged.

Beginning with textiles.[17] By early 1928 the Lancashire cotton industry was in a poor way and, according to what was becoming the conventional wisdom of the day, in crying need of rationalisation. John Tattersall and John Ryan of the recently formed Cotton Yarn Association hoped to form a combine that would amalgamate up to five million spindles, possibly more; and the obvious port of call was Ebenezer Parkes, joint General Manager of Midland Bank. Not only was Parkes himself immensely experienced in the problems of Lancashire, but it was Midland that was far the most important creditor bank to the mills. Parkes recorded the outcome:

They wanted to know if they could tell their members that we viewed the proposal favourably. Told Mr Tattersall we could give no such general approval. We did not wish to take an obstructive attitude towards any efforts to get the Trade on to a better footing but our attitude was that in the first place we should use no coercion towards our customers and in the second place we should want to deal with the case of each Company on its own merits . . .

At about the same time, at the annual meeting of Martin's Bank, Robert Holland-Martin raised the question of the cotton industry and described the suggestion that the banks 'by enforcing combination should constitute an authority to control the industry' as 'entirely against all traditions of English banking'. By September, however, Norman was willing to oversee a cotton amalgamation, telling his Committee of Treasury that he:

> considered it necessary for the Bank to support and subscribe to a satisfactory scheme, partly to help the cotton industry, partly to keep the question away from politics, but more especially to relieve certain of the banks from a dangerous position. The growing advances of these banks to the cotton industry were already unduly large and unless they obtained relief there was danger that the Bank might be compelled to assist them.

In sum, industrial, political and financial motives all came into play; and in the short term, at least as important as any other motive was the financial, with the Bank of England being compelled by the end of the year to guarantee up to £1m to Williams Deacon's in order to cover that struggling Lancashire bank's advances to forty spinning firms.

By this time Sir Kenneth Stewart, a cotton goods merchant, was making the running – looking to form a combine that would merge up to ten million spindles – but there was one implacable opponent. Norman saw him on 14 November: 'McKenna. I implore him to accept Stewarts Scheme: heart not head – pro bono pub – not profit . . . He declares he is friendly, but Com & Board adamant in refusing & he agrees with them. 2nd Debs or nothing.' The price of Midland's support for the Lancashire Cotton Corporation was that the debentures to be created should be fixed-interest-bearing, and neither man would budge. As for Barclays, it disapproved of the LCC *per se*, with Niemeyer a few weeks later reporting a conversation that Stewart had had with Goodenough: 'His [i.e. Goodenough's] idea was that large amalgamation was a great mistake: that the proper course was to put together four sound firms and on that nucleus base a regeneration of Lancashire Cotton.' But with the Bank of England committed to making temporary advances to the LCC ahead of the intended debenture issue, Norman was determined to press ahead – believing, moreover, as he told a meeting of more or less sympathetic bankers and others, that 'the Cotton Industry was not the only in need of rationalisation, and he looked to any scheme for the rationalisation of the Textile Industry to lead the way and set the type for schemes of rationalisation in other industries'. The details of the LCC were announced at the end of January 1929, and in a not ungenerous response Keynes wrote that 'this incursion of the Bank of England – somewhat late in the day but wholeheartedly in the end – into the field of Rationalisation is in itself a matter of much interest and, in my opinion, of congratulation'. So perhaps it was, but crucially the Bank was unable to persuade the creditor banks that did theoretically support the LCC to refrain from an understandable policy of offloading on to it their worst cotton company accounts, thereby making the LCC little more than a combination of obsolete, uneconomic mills. Moreover, there was the question of managerial control over the new combine. All Norman's instincts were to adopt an arm's-length approach, but it was soon clear that management was the LCC's Achilles' heel. As with Armstrongs, a fairly bleak road lay ahead; and almost certainly Norman had not been insincere when he had told the bankers and others in December 1928 that 'he was not anxious for this business, which was entirely outside the normal sphere of the Bank of England'.[18]

Unwilling or not, Norman's new-found industrial emphasis mirrored the wider City trend – a trend epitomised by the accountants. Three in particular stood out.[19] Francis D'Arcy Cooper had only reluctantly before the war taken his articles with the family firm of City accountants, Cooper Brothers; but after the war he soon became its senior partner. One of his most important clients was Lever Brothers, the soap manufacturers, and it was to Cooper that the first Lord Leverhulme was confiding his increasingly serious business problems by 1920. Three years later, having successfully persuaded enough banks to keep Lever Brothers afloat, Cooper left his family firm and became Vice-Chairman. In 1925 he became Chairman, and at the end of the decade he played a key role in steering through the merger with Margarine Uni that created Unilever. Sir Basil Mayhew's career was less dramatic. Having founded his own accountancy firm before the war, his most important service to British industry probably occurred in 1926 when he steered Bowaters through a severe financial crisis. Undoubtedly, though, the king of the inter-war accountants in the industrial sphere was Sir William McLintock, whose father had founded Thomson McLintock, a firm that grew rapidly from its Glasgow beginnings. Merger and reconstruction were his special fortes, and by the late 1920s he had been intimately involved, at different times, with Explosive Trades Ltd, the British Dyestuffs Corporation, British Celanese, ICI, Beardmores and the Millers' Mutual Association. He also had his eyes on, not surprisingly, the British coal industry, as did others in the City. In December 1928 Norman saw Sir Henri Deterding of Shell and Vivian Smith and Teddy Grenfell of Morgan Grenfell: 'All favour idea of Rationalising Coal Industry: agree idea must be translated into a Scheme to amalgamate interests of Producers.' The following month, however, Smith informed Deterding that McLintock (who 'acts as Accountant for, I believe, something like 80% of the coal trade') had told Norman that 'it was quite impossible to hope to arrange any amalgamation in the coal trade', though in fact in the course of the year McLintock did merge twenty collieries to form Manchester Collieries.[20] The rise to prominence of the inter-war accountant is not difficult to explain. Industry, like economic life as a whole, was becoming bigger and more complex; in many cases the problems seemed intractable; and it was felt that the accountant was uniquely placed to see the big financial picture and even implement the necessary change.

For the merchant banks in the 1920s, it was generally a case of dipping their toes gingerly into the murky waters of domestic industrial finance, which they had largely left alone in the pre-1914 period. Most of the traditional élite summoned up the nerve. Barings took its cue from Peacock, who after his August 1927 weekend with Norman informed Revelstoke that the Governor had 'found a sympathetic listener, because I feel that it is a matter of vital importance to this country that there should be a much better understanding and more active intervention by the financial people, not merely the rather passive assistance afforded in the form of overdrafts by joint stock banks'. Armstrongs was a central preoccupation in this field, but Barings also acted as corporate financier for the brewers Taylor Walker, the British subsidiary of Goodyear Tyre and Rubber Co, and the Underground Electric Railways Co of London. Peacock even went on to the board of the last, where he waged an unsuccessful campaign against the large gap resulting from the curved platform at Bank tube station. 'I had a look at it again this morning,' he complained to Frank Pick in March 1927, 'and quite expect to break my leg there some day.'[21]

In the same year Morgan Grenfell made its first domestic issue (for Anglo-American Oil), but for several years it had been increasingly occupied by domestic corporate finance in general, including in 1925 arranging an important agreement between General Motors and Vaux-hall Motors. The house also acted for Gerrard Swope, President of General Electric of America, during his buccaneering attempt in 1928–9 to achieve control over the British electrical industry; though at one point Vivian Smith noted with some distaste that 'all this arranging of underwriting without consultation and agreement with us is very irregular and contrary to the methods and prestige of Morgan Grenfell'. Lazards also had an interest in electrical matters, especially after it had recruited the very able Percy Horsfall from English Electric in 1928 to run its new issues department. Schröders was making domestic issues from 1924, including two years later for the Pressed Steel Co of Great Britain, in which it had a significant managerial stake; while Kleinworts throughout the decade continued what was largely an unprofitable involvement in north-eastern ship-building. Finally, there were two of the less heavyweight (though perfectly respectable) houses. Helbert Wagg had been making issues for British companies since at least 1922, while Robert Benson & Co by spring 1929 was making a large (£1.6m), complicated issue for the British Power & Light Corporation.[22]

In sum, all this represented a significant shift of emphasis on the part of the merchant banks – yet the fact remained that not only was much of this terrain unknown and therefore difficult, but it was also often financially unattractive. Evelyn Baring's complaint in May 1928 about the Underground Electric Railways flotation would almost certainly have been echoed in other parlours: 'Compared with foreign Government loans, an issue such as this seems to involve a great deal more work at a great deal less profit.' That issue (made in conjunction with Rothschilds and Schröders) was for £4m, a far larger sum than most domestic industrial issues; and the received wisdom by the early 1920s was that any issue under £200,000 was almost certainly uneconomic for the issuing house concerned.[23] Inevitably, the merchant banks tended to retain their international orientation – including foreign issues – as much as they possibly could.

Equally inevitably, this left a gap in terms of domestic issuing, and during the decade several new respectable or semi-respectable entrants emerged to try to fill it. The British Foreign & Colonial Corporation, for example, was the creation of the Hungarian-born F.A. Szarvasy and, in addition to various capital reconstructions, handled flotations for companies as important as Imperial Airways, though in 1924 Szarvasy failed to see the potential of Marks & Spencer and passed up the chance of acting for it.[24] Charterhouse Investment Trust was formed in 1925 –

mainly by Sir Arthur Wheeler, the prominent Leicester-based stock-broker – specifically to undertake industrial issues; and when the ambitious Nutcombe Hume wrested control of it in 1928, Wheeler turned to his other issuing house, Gresham Trust, in order to make medium-sized issues of about £200,000 upwards.[25] Other new domestic issuing houses included Edward de Stein & Co, Dawnay Day and Ostrer Bros, the last specialising in film finance.[26] There were also a few stockbroking firms with aspirations to become reputable issuing houses, notably Myers & Co, for which the young Edward Beddington-Behrens began working in about 1927. 'Little Mossy Myers, as he was known, was about five foot three, but big in every other way. He was never petty in his financial dealings. The firm was making average profits of over £200,000 a year . . .' Myers had recently financed (via an £8m issue of preference shares) the purchase by the Berry Brothers of Allied Newspapers, and the new recruit soon added to the firm's new issuing business, with Richard Fairey as one of his first clients: 'He had gone round the City trying to raise new finance, but nobody would back anything so speculative as the aviation industry . . . I was able by telephone to get a sufficient American participation to induce the City institutions to hazard their money in the Fairey Aviation Company, which developed from strength to strength in future years.' In twelve months Beddington-Behrens earned over £27,000, becoming a full partner, and he would reflect in his memoirs: 'My first year in the City proved that one can make a success there without having any personal friends in City circles. People do business with you because it is to their financial advantage, and friendship does not enter into it.'[27]

Not everyone would have agreed, but what did become crystal clear in the late 1920s was that – despite the new-found interest of the merchant banks, and despite the crop of new entrants into domestic issuing – the domestic capital market was still almost as flawed, in terms of providing high-quality financial intermediation, as it had been during the 1890s when Hooley and Lawson enjoyed such a field day at the expense of British industry. The sorry story of the domestic new-issue boom, at its peak in 1928, was graphic testimony to the City's continuing institutional complacency and conservatism in this respect. Against the background of a raging bull market, quality control was conspicuous by its absence, as Revelstoke implicitly acknowledged in May 1928 in his overview of the Stock Exchange situation: 'The speculation has been mainly in these new industrial securities with which one is unfamiliar, and which certainly do not appeal to the representatives of higher finance.'[28]

A typical issue that autumn, as the boom reached its apogee, was for the Manchester-based British Dirt Track Racing Association (1928) Ltd, whose secretary and accountant went to London in October to ask Midland's Ebenezer Parkes why his bank was not willing to put its name on their prospectus. 'I told him frankly,' Parkes noted, 'that we could not see what the Public were to receive for their money, except licences. Nothing was disclosed as to the terms of the licences or their duration . . . We could not be associated with such an issue.' The following month saw the issue that became a byword for the boom, the £1m flotation of the Anti-Sag Parent Company. 'The ANTI-SAG Mattress Support,' boasted the prospectus, 'is an ingenious homely device which can be fitted to any bedstead in less than one minute. It will stand any strain, defies wear, rust and climate, and will treble the life of any mattress . . .' The *FT*'s comment was nicely under-stated: 'Obviously the shares can only be accounted an industrial speculation until prospectus expectations have been tested by commercial practice.' So frantic became the boom, and so rubbishy some of the issues, that according to a stockbroker looking back some twenty years later, 'there was even a concern whose main object was said to be the extraction (by a "secret process", of course) of essential fats from the contents of hotel dustbins and whose 1s shares (Dustbins Deferred, the market called them) were actually dealt in up to 40s'.[29]

In general, the boom was not the Stock Exchange's finest hour. Several of the leading firms stayed sensibly aloof, while Edward Lewis was not just broker to the Decca record company for its flotation in September 1928, but by early the following year was becoming the key figure in transforming its fortunes for the better; but for too many, the driving force was more or less naked exploitation. Firms making a great deal of easy money included such now-forgotten names as T. Gordon Hensler & Co (twenty-five issues in 1928 of generally poor quality, like Selecta Gramophones Ltd and Continuous Gramophones Ltd); Charles Stanley & Sons (twenty issues that year, epitomised by American and Dominions Unbreakable Records Ltd); Moy, Smith, Vandervell & Co (fifteen issues, including the notorious Anti-Sag); and Gibbs (John), Son & Smith (fifteen issues, including Worldecho Records Ltd and Colour Snapshots (1928) Ltd).[30]

A fascinated participant in the boom was the young John Kinross, whose character as well as background was strictly Scottish and who began working for the Gresham Trust in June 1928. New issuing houses were formed 'at a tremendous rate' in that year's boom, he would recall, 'and it was astonishing to see the number of broker-members of the

Stock Exchange who courted them. During this period practically any rubbish could be sold and the brokerages paid out on these issues were substantial.' Most of the financiers and company promoters who lay behind these evanescent issuing houses quickly became almost wholly obscure figures once the boom collapsed, but Kinross provides brief vignettes of two of them. One was Eugen Spier, who had made a paper fortune by floating Combined Pulp and Paper Mills Ltd in late 1927 through his Lothbury Trust. He acquired Claremont House near Esher, where Kinross visited him: 'I was shown into a beautifully furnished sitting room . . . The house itself was a superb period piece which Spier had filled with eighteenth-century furniture in excellent taste. He offered me a hand-made cigarette from what I think was a Fabergé box. Spier treated me with exaggerated courtesy . . .' In the event Combined Pulp, in which he had a large interest, soon went bankrupt, and it would be a long time before Spier resurfaced as 'a minor City character who possessed encyclopedic knowledge of Foreign Bonds and wrote about these for the *Investors' Chronicle*'. The other company promoter subjected to Kinross's clear gaze was Louis Jackson. In autumn 1928, when Kinross with his stockbroker friend Ernest Savory visited him at his Bishopsgate offices, Jackson had just successfully issued Wireless Pictures (1928) Ltd and was in the process of floating his second issue, Colour Snapshots Ltd:

> We were shown into a very long, rather narrow room at the back of the building which was almost entirely taken up by an enormous oak refectory table which I assumed had probably been supplied by Drages Ltd on hire purchase. There were some beautiful and extremely expensive flowers in the room and the huge table was piled high with applications for the new issue. Mr Jackson was sitting at the top of the table, flanked on one side by a distinctly over-decorative young secretary whose natural habitat was, at best, a film studio. On the other side were piles of telegrams – certainly several hundred – confirming late posted applications and the like.
>
> Having been introduced, he seized my hand and indicating the contents of the table he said, if memory serves me right, 'Seventy times over-subscribed, Mr Kinross – what price Rothschilds?' I got out as quickly as I could and took care never to see him again . . .[31]

Colour Snapshots was indeed over-subscribed, but within two years Jackson's Beaconsfield Trust had gone into liquidation.

It was all too easy. The market was rising, the public was eager and gullible, and *caveat emptor* remained the guiding principle of both company law and Stock Exchange surveillance. Nor did the excessively severe interpretation by the courts of the law of libel help. According to Oscar Hobson, editor of the *Financial News*, recalling some years later 'the flagrant "group finance" scandals' of the boom, 'it was only the fear of the law of libel (based upon a sound estimation of its dangers) which prevented the Press from exposing at least half a dozen of these scandals in time, at least, to save the pockets of a considerable proportion of the victims'.[32] Did it matter? Almost certainly it did, not only in that many good as well as bad ventures foundered as a result of the eventual sharp reaction against the excesses of the boom, but also in that during the boom itself it was practically impossible to differentiate between the good and the bad. Confronted by an incredibly strong tide of speculative froth, the City's most respected houses were able to do little more than look the other way. It was an understandable reaction, but hardly adequate. Towards one financier, however, their relationship was more complicated.

This was Clarence Hatry, now fully back in the thick of things.[33] Morgan Grenfell in April 1928 provided Morgans in New York with a résumé of his chequered career:

Mr Hatry is a man who became prominent as a promoter after the War. He was associated in those days with Mr Gerard Bevan and he floated several companies, most, if not all, of which met with disaster, and Mr Hatry is supposed to have lost most of the money he made during the boom.

During the last few years Mr Hatry has again become prominent. He has made a good deal of money in handling Municipal loans, and he has also been very much connected with the Drapery Trust, which bought up a great many drapery stores all over the country, and which recently practically sold themselves to Messrs Debenhams. We believe Mr Hatry is pretty well out of the business now, and we have no doubt that he made a very considerable sum of money.

Mr Hatry is very clever, and one or two of the people we know who have had business relations with him have always told us that they had nothing against him. He is a Jew. His standing here is by no means good. We should ourselves not think of doing business with him, but, as we have said above, he has made money lately and we should imagine he is probably more particular than he was some years ago.

Municipal loans had indeed been the vehicle for Hatry's return to prominence as a financier, as he set up Corporation & General Securities to enable him to bust open the monopoly over the placing of municipal issues, hitherto enjoyed by the three stockbroking firms of Mullens, Nivisons and Scrimgeours. To do this he had received the support of two other reputable stockbroking firms, Foster & Braithwaite and Cohen, Laming, Hoare (the latter increasingly driven by the young, distinctively aggressive Kit Hoare); and in three years from 1926 Corporation & General Securities made thirty-eight municipal issues to the value of £38m.

If the Stock Exchange was naturally split about Hatry's virtues, so too was the City at large. As early as October 1925, soon after Hatry's re-emergence, Norman noted that Frank Tiarks of Schröders had 'warned' Herman Andreae of Kleinworts 'of continuing to finance Hatry & thinks Kleinworts will go slow in having any dealings with him'. Tiarks was wrong, for over the next few years Kleinworts got ever deeper, and that usually very sensible merchant bank was not alone. George Greenfield, a literary agent who knew Hatry well in later life, gives a suggestive description of his appeal:

> He was a small bird-like man, with an enormous scimitar of a nose, a close-cropped moustache and the strangest pale blue eyes. He had a soft, sibilant voice – I never heard it raised in sorrow or anger – and a laugh that was a cross between a chuckle and a giggle. He had the quickest of minds and innate charm. A meeting with CCH, as he was known to friends and employees, was like drinking champagne on an empty stomach. You went in to see him, full of insuperable problems, and in quarter of an hour he had plucked out figures, juggled with them and then proved conclusively that the problems did not exist. Of course, when the bubbles subsided, you realised they had not gone away . . .

Hatry's personal vanity may have irritated some ('why,' remarked one of his secretaries, 'Mr Hatry even has the *soles* of his shoes polished'), but the combination of charm and mental agility will always go a very long way, perhaps especially in such a 'people' place as the City.[34]

Hatry's activities steadily expanded, against the background of a favourable stock market. In May 1927 he launched Austin Friars Trust, in his biographer's words 'a £300,000 finance house which was to be the linchpin of his later enterprises and the central company in a complicated network of interrelated investment and industrial undertakings'. The following year he floated both Photomaton Parent Corporation (operating photographic booths) and Associated Automatic Machine Corporation (operating vending machines, mainly on railway platforms). He also undertook the merger of most of London's private bus companies, before selling them to London General Omnibus Co, thereby helping to pave the way for what would become London Transport. Someone who worked in the Photomaton part of his empire, based in a sumptuous office in Lower Regent Street, was a young accountant called Roy Besch:

> One day Hatry telephoned to me and asked me to prepare a Balance Sheet showing the position at the present time and he wanted this the day after tomorrow! . . . By the following evening I had drawn up a Balance Sheet on very conservative lines, especially the valuation of Stocks of Materials &c. I took this round to Hatry at Pinners Hall [in Austin Friars], and glancing at it he said it was what he wanted; but would I come back the next day? When I went to his office again he said smilingly 'I have made one or two adjustments to your figures' and handed me a copy of his version. This was quite a fantastic document showing the amounts he *expected* to realise on the sale of Foreign Rights all over the world, which had the effect, naturally, of showing the value of the assets (and consequently the shares) at many hundreds of thousands of pounds. Having absorbed the figures I looked up to find Hatry smiling at me, and to his credit, said 'Don't worry, Besch, these will not go out over your name – they are my figures.' Well, that was a relief, and I confirmed that I could not possibly be responsible for them. He thanked me for what I had done and I left him on very pleasant terms.

By spring 1929, spurred by an undoubtedly sincere belief in the larger economic virtues of rationalisation, Hatry was seeking to achieve huge amalgamations within the British steel industry, both light and heavy. To do this, however, he needed serious backing, both financial (up to some £8m) and, as it were, reputational. It was not as if he had been without backing over the previous few years, but this was make-or-break.

Most of the leading joint-stock banks (with the notable exception of Midland) were already lending him considerable sums, and Kleinworts remained in his corner, but Hatry needed the support of at least one other major institution, preferably a blue-chip merchant bank. Kuhn Loeb of Wall Street had provisionally intimated that it would support steel reorganisation, but only with the right London partner; and its first choice was Barings. With Revelstoke away in Paris at a reparations conference, Peacock sounded him out, expressing no personal view either way. Revelstoke replied on 9 April:

> Personally I do not know C.H., but I know that he has a disastrous record. Was he not involved with Bevan in the iniquities of the latter? Was not the current opinion at the time that he too should have occupied the dock? I am aware that he is said to have 'made good' since that time: but I confess that I have grave doubts whether it would be right for us to have anything at all to do with him. Ask Serocold about him, if you will. The

man is undoubtedly clever and dextrous, but I doubt whether the 'Remember not past years' of the Hymn should be our motto in this instance.

If Peacock did ask Claud Serocold of the stockbrokers Cazenove's about Hatry, he probably got a dusty response; for at some point during the boom Hatry had approached Cazenove's with a prospectus that already had the firm's name printed on it as brokers, a piece of anticipation that Serocold's partner, Charles Micklem, did not appreciate, with the result that Hatry had to look elsewhere. In the event, Peacock replied to Revelstoke on the 10th: 'I am in complete accord with what you say as to the Steel business . . .'[35] The odds were starting to lengthen against this genuinely creative but flawed financier.

*

For all British industry's novel importance in the scheme of things, the fundamental orientation of the City remained international. London revived in the 1920s as a significant international capital market, while by 1928 its volume of acceptances (reaching a peak of some £170m outstanding) represented some four-fifths of the 1913 level.[36] Yet in a sense these were years of frustration and disappointment, especially once it became apparent that the return to gold had not automatically returned London to its pre-1914 place at the centre of the financial universe. There was no doubt where the object of Norman's resentment lay. Early in 1926 he wrote to his mother: 'England is part of Europe: Europe has quarrelled: Europe has thus reached poverty . . . America is detached and has thus become rich: so Europe is the "promised land" to America: to be possessed without even competition!' Brand, discussing with Kindersley in October that year the future strategy of their firm, did not disagree: 'New York is going to be in my opinion incomparably the most powerful financial centre in the world. Can Lazards maintain a first-rate position in Paris and London without being really strong in New York?' Over a century of experience could not, of course, be wiped out overnight – 'It is a great mercy for us that America has not got the knowledge and tradition as well as the money,' Norman a few days earlier sought to console Hjalmar Schacht of the Reichsbank, 'or there would be no place and no business left for you and me!' – but that alone was not enough. Or as Norman candidly noted not long afterwards, following a discussion with Edward Hilton Young, editor of the *Financial News* before Hobson: 'We agree the subservience of London to N.Y. market is better left alone in Papers.'[37] Yet, despite this failure to reverse the shift in the balance of financial power that had manifested itself during the war, the City of London – and indeed the British Empire at large – *did* stage something of a mini-comeback during the 1920s. 'The repute of the Sterling Bill, throughout Europe and perhaps the world,' Norman informed a correspondent in February 1927, 'has been wonderfully re-established since the return to the gold standard'; and if he somewhat exaggerated, that was surely pardonable considering the strenuous efforts he had made to achieve that return.[38]

Norman's plight in the second half of the 1920s, essentially the plight of a prisoner of circumstances beyond his control, was epitomised by his near-schizophrenic attitude towards foreign loans. On 3 November 1925, following a mixture of political and City pressure, Churchill announced the lifting of the formal embargo on foreign loans that had been in place since the previous November; and for the next few years Norman attempted to walk a tightrope – on the one hand, seeking to reassert London's standing as an international financial centre and not entirely give the game away to New York; on the other, fearful of what an avalanche of foreign loans would do to Britain's chances of staying on the gold standard, given that a high Bank rate was by now political dynamite. His diary shows him in action, the Pope of the City encouraging self-denial:

> *5 November 1925.* Glendyne & Nivison, as to freedom from Embargo. Go slow & avoid France, Italy, Russia . . .
>
> *2 December 1925.* 2 Rothschilds. ? Loan to Poland for Tobacco Monop & Exch. I say in confidence that they sh^d avoid all such transactions: not even worth discussion at present.
>
> *15 April 1926.* L de Rothschild. Brazil Loan: their opposition at Geneva does not incline me towards it – but free market & FO sh^d decide esp. as N.Y. can issue a loan.
>
> *8 October 1926.* Fleischmann [of Seligmans]: considering Loans here for 1. Central American Country & 2. Italian Industrial. I say free market – OK. BUT many more foreign issues – mean gold exports & higher B Rate & an end of such business.
>
> *22 April 1927.* 2 Rothschilds. Vivian Smith & CFW [Charles Whigham of Morgan Grenfell]. £6m Loan for Vienna. Officially nothing agst Issue here. Privately: a Socialistic city: an uncertain future as part of Austria of 20/30 years: not a 1st cl Loan! (worse than Buda P).
>
> *4 October 1928.* A de Rothschild . . . He protests bitterly agst continued embargo on French Loans . . .[39]

Norman's visitors well understood why he was behaving as he was, but undoubtedly the new rules of the game took some getting used to for all concerned. The more conceptually minded accepted, with reluctance, that economic internationalism now came in carefully circumscribed form.

The life and death of Captain Alfred Loewenstein, however, proved that there was still room in the City of the 1920s for an old-style, freebooting international financier.[40] He had made a fortune on the Belgian stock market before the war, especially through the placing there of Brazilian railway securities, and during the war had profiteered to considerable advantage, though Morgan Grenfell told Morgans in New York in 1917 that 'we see no harm in ordinary Banking transactions with this gentleman'. After the war he roamed the world looking for speculative opportunities, with the promotion of companies involved in tramways, electric power or artificial silk his particular speciality. 'Consider the potential of the artificial silk market,' he once told a journalist. 'Every man wants to buy silk stockings for his wife and silk underwear for his mistress and when he's bought this underwear for his mistress his conscience pricks him and he buys more stockings for his wife again.' Loewenstein worked ferociously hard, only took a bathe in the sea at Biarritz (his favourite residence) if he was accompanied by at least two valets and two or three secretaries, travelled everywhere with a large personal retinue, and when in the City based himself at Schröders, his particular friends there.

In 1926 it all started to go wrong. That March he lost control of British Celanese; not long afterwards, following a fall from a horse, his behaviour started to become eccentric; and by the summer Barings found itself dragged into his affairs. 'As I think you know,' Peacock wrote in September to Revelstoke, 'Mr Loewenstein is actively engaged in arranging for a large Canadian Holding Company to take over the Sidro and a great many shares and bonds that he and his friends have acquired of the Brazilian Traction Company, the Barcelona and the Mexican Companies. He is adopting his usual peculiar, theatrical methods which are very unpleasant to me and harmful to the business.' His holding company was Hydro-Electric Securities, while International Holding and Investment Co was the vehicle for his putative global domination of the artificial silk industry. By early 1927 he was in trouble and compelled to put his affairs in the hands of Barings. 'It involves having Loewenstein and his accountant in our office day by day, all day,' Peacock complained, 'and as he is in a state almost of collapse, and the accountant much the same, and as his accounts are of the strangest order, we are making the slowest kind of progress in finding out what the actual situation is.' Barings had the backing of Norman, anxious to avoid a dreadful public scandal.

Loewenstein was still a very active, prominent figure when, on 4 July 1928, he fell out of his private Fokker while crossing the Channel. The news made a huge impact in the City, with opinion divided as to whether or not it was suicide. Despite a recent sharp tumble in the value of Loewenstein's holdings, the journalist and former jobber Hubert Meredith was convinced that it was not, arguing that 'the fact that his collar, tie and pearl pin were found in the aeroplane lends support to the belief that he was suddenly taken ill, removed his collar to facilitate his breathing, maybe opened the door to obtain more air and fell out'.[41] But whatever the cause, it is arguable that over the previous two years Loewenstein had taken Barings for something of a ride. This time, however, that strangely susceptible streak in such a solid, utterly respectable house did not result in a Barings crisis.

And unlike 1890, there was no longer an automatic equation to be made between Argentine finance and 8 Bishopsgate. In both 1926 and 1927 the Argentine went for funds not to London but to New York, largely because the stamp duty imposed by the British Treasury priced Barings out of the market. In Brazil, however, London still dominated, largely because of continuing American dislike of coffee valorisation schemes. It was lucrative business, and inevitably there was a temptation to break up the traditional cosy monopolies. 'You will be amused to hear that Lazards have butted into the San Paulo business,' Farrer informed Peacock on the last day of 1925, 'and have a preliminary contract signed.' He added that 'our friends in Leadenhall Street are sweating blood', which was probably an under-estimate of the mood at Schröders. The spat passed into City mythology ('I remember when Baron Schröder crossed over the street to avoid meeting Sir Robert [Kindersley],' one banker would tell Anthony Sampson well over thirty years later, 'because Sir Robert had pinched the Brazilian coffee business from him'); but eventually the two firms made it up, with the partners being persuaded to share a toast – in coffee – at the end of a dinner of the Society of Merchants Trading to the Continent. The episode, however, did not enhance Kindersley's popularity, and in March 1929, in the context of Brazil wanting credit, Revelstoke told Peacock that if Lazards 'attempt to play any pranks with accommodation bills we could arrange that the cold hose should be played on them'.[42]

South America as a whole remained obstinately dear to the City's heart.[43] For example, that hugely influential investment figure Lord St Davids, controlling an important collection of investment trusts, could not be weaned away from South American railways as his principal investment counter, despite a certain economic logic to the contrary. So too with Lord Faringdon, who one way or another took a significant interest in most things going on in that continent. Yet, remarkably, he never once went there. On leave in London in May 1925, Harry Scott of the Bank of London and South America wrote feelingly to a colleague at the Buenos Aires branch: 'The Argentine dinner last night was a great success . . . Faringdon looks forward to the re-opening of the Caja de Conversion. It is extraordinary how shortsighted these London potentates are. I felt inclined to get up and tell him he did not know what he was talking about.'[44]

There was less emotional allegiance to Australia, but London remained the prime capital market, lending that country £35m between March 1927 and March 1928, compared to the £8m lent by New York.[45] In practice, somewhat concealed by these figures, relations between Australia and the City – rarely easy – deteriorated further in the late 1920s.[46] London feared profligacy, while the Australians by this time sensed incompetence as well as prejudice. For many years the stockbroker Lord Glendyne (the former Sir Robert Nivison) had been the key intermediary in Australia's borrowing on the London capital market, underwriting a series of loans; but as Norman's deputy, H.A. Trotter, confirmed to his colleague Sir Ernest Harvey (currently visiting Australia) in March 1927, 'there is no doubt of the truth of your statement that G. is showing signs of increasing age and does not have his old grip of the market or power to gauge the probable course of events'. He added: 'He is also more cantankerous than ever, a quality which has made itself felt in New York as well as in London . . . But even so, what opinion could you or I express now? G. is alive and kicking and it is not for us to bury him . . .' These thoughts, Trotter noted, 'emanate from the next room', and Norman himself wrote to Harvey soon afterwards to complain about how Nivisons was entirely mismanaging things: 'I see neither skilful nor tactful arrangements, and I think R.N. & Co must have missed several opportunities during past weeks . . . If in the future this sort of thing continues I hardly think that Australasia deserves £25,000,000 a year from the London Market.'[47]

All this was particularly unfortunate, from Australia's point of view, in the context of the City's growing criticism of Australia's external financial position and increasing doubts about the wisdom of holding Australian securities. Richard Casey, the Australian liaison officer with the Foreign Office, reported to his Prime Minister in July 1928 that Goodenough of Barclays was apprehensive about 'a lack of soundness in our methods of conducting ourselves', and he went on: 'This criticism was impossible to get away from. Rightly or wrongly, it was voiced daily by countless men in the City in the interminable discussions and conversations that go on with regard to the securities that are on offer in the City.' Early the following year a sharp twist was given to the chorus when Harvey, in characteristic Bankspeak, warned the authorities in Australia. 'They should not forget,' he wrote to the Governor of the Commonwealth Bank of Australia, 'that they are not the only borrowers whose needs have to be considered and if they make it a practice to disregard the opinion of their London Advisers, who alone have before them all the facts to form a correct view of the situation, they must not be surprised if they find that their appearances in this Market gradually come to be less welcome than we should wish them to be.' Crunch time was approaching, but meanwhile Glendyne staggered on, presumably with few – if any – of the relevant facts before him. Nor would his departure (he was about to be eighty) necessarily improve matters, as Casey informed his chief a few weeks after Harvey's letter: 'His son and heir, John Nivison, is a decent, honest, industrious sort of fellow but with, I think, very ordinary character and ability. I asked Montagu Norman some time ago what would happen when Glendyne died, and he threw up his hands . . .'[48]

In relation to the Far East, it was a case of playing the long game. There were few Japanese loans in this period, though Addis showed typical presence of mind when on a Tuesday in February 1927 he 'saw Norman & induced him to postpone Treasury Com. & go to Westminster Abbey service for Emperor of Japan', to be held the following day at noon. As for China, the Second Consortium had been in place since 1920, but was unable to act because of the disintegrating indigenous situation. Indeed, such was the growing strength of the nationalists there that in the mid-1920s the City was at the forefront of persuading the Foreign Office to abandon its one-China policy, predicated on support for the central government in Peking, and instead support the nationalist movement. The key figure at the FO was Sir John Pratt, and he observed in 1926 that 'whereas financial interests have men of great influence, ability and fluency to speak for them, trade interests are for the most part struck dumb'. These financial interests included the Hongkong and Shanghai Bank and Jardine Matheson, but irrespective of the shift in policy the latter seems to have wondered by 1928 whether the days of Chinese loans were over. From the perspective of 3 Lombard Street, David Landale of Matheson & Co sought to stiffen resolve at Jardine Matheson's head office in Hong Kong. However much the Chinese 'may consider Consortiums and Financial Groups are things of the past, and bugbears', he asserted in September, 'it is only through some organisation of the kind that they will be able to borrow any money on this market'. And: 'Why do you suggest that the organisation which we have ready made, and which includes the Bankers entitled to handle Far-Eastern business, should be liquidated, and what do you suggest should take its place? Do you wish to drop Chinese government business altogether?' His colleague Dallas Bernard agreed, telling Jardine Matheson the following spring that 'I do not consider . . . that our days in China are numbered – what we have got to do is to endeavour to stiffen up the British attitude, and no effort should be spared at your end to do this.'[49] Put another way, the City was not yet prepared to make the defeatist assumption that the old, cosmopolitan days had gone for ever.

Yet far more than in those fondly remembered days, it was Europe that now comprised much of the City's international orientation. Partly this was because there was so much to be done in relation to the post-war financial and economic reconstruction there; partly because, with various other parts of the world succumbing to the Yankee dollar, Europe was seen as a place where London could build up its financial strength relative to that of New York. Between 1926 and 1928, accordingly, Hambros made thirteen issues for continental governments, Barings twelve and Morgan Grenfell six. Russia, of course, was now largely outside the City's orbit. 'Hitherto we have on principle steered entirely clear of Soviet business,' Brand informed a Berlin banker in April 1926 about the attitude of Lazards, while later that year Revelstoke believed he was speaking for the English as a whole when he asserted to Hugo Baring that as long as Russia 'continue their infamous propaganda in Europe and in China, we shall refuse, as a body, to have anything to do with them'. But there was never a formal ban, and indeed when Austin Harris had asked Norman in May 1925 if he had any objection to Lloyds 'lending to Soviet Bks against platinum & other good security', the reply was that it was 'entirely for them to decide'. Portugal also failed to get the nod from 8 Bishopsgate, as Alfred Mildmay explained to an American correspondent in February 1927 after he and Evelyn Baring had returned from an exploratory visit there: 'We were told that a revolution was quite within the bounds of probability and, sure enough, we had hardly got home when the guns began to go off . . .' Mildmay graciously added that 'one is sorry to see a country of not unattractive people deprived of the advantages which might be theirs if only they could have stable government and their finances administered on Anglo-Saxon lines'.[50]

There were apparently no such problems about Germany – at the heart of European reconstruction – and Schröders led the way in a series of loans from December 1925: for the German Potash Syndicate, for the City of Hamburg, for the City of Berlin and for the Hamburg Waterworks Co. The Hamburg loan of September 1926, also involving Barings and Rothschilds, brought home how the larger world had changed. On the 13th, with Baron Schröder away in Hamburg negotiating terms, Peacock optimistically reported to Revelstoke (also away, in his case at Balmoral) that Tiarks had been telling him 'that a 6% loan at 94–95 would go here'; that Tiarks had been 'assured' by Walter Whigham of Flemings 'that the Trust Companies would take a large amount of it on those terms and he thought the Insurance Companies would also'; and that since 'New York cannot issue on such terms', the Baron was 'therefore hopeful of doing the whole loan'. Five days later the 8 Bishopsgate update to Revelstoke, this time from Arthur Villiers, reflected the underlying realities: 'The Baron's endeavour to oust New York has not succeeded and there are certain advantages in London sharing the business with New York. For one thing, £5,000,000 is a large amount for London, and competition between New York and London would result in the lender getting worse terms.' In the event, Schacht insisted on reducing the total amount and London finished by being responsible for only £2m. This disappointment led to an interesting but thwarted manoeuvre on the part of the always agile Tiarks. 'While I was talking to the Baron,' Villiers noted on the 22nd, 'Tiarks came in and is very anxious not to underwrite the Hamburg loan', on the grounds that there would 'only be a paltry sum for the brokers and that it will consequently cause more heartburn to underwrite than not to do so'. The next day, however, at the formal underwriting conference at 145 Leadenhall Street, Serocold of Cazenove's 'was asked his opinion and he was very definite that, however small the participation, the stockbrokers would much prefer to have some underwriting'. So it was, with Serocold being supported by Barings, and the five brokers each received £100,000 of underwriting at a commission of $1\frac{1}{2}$ per cent, which – since it was a hugely successful issue (over £35m applied for in London) – was easy money.[51]

There was also in these years a strong City commitment to Germany on the accepting side – for example, German commission earned by Kleinworts increased from £15,000 in 1921 to £117,380 in 1928. With demand for credit apparently inexhaustible, interest rates high and reparation payments being scaled down by the Dawes Plan of 1924, the logic was irresistible as Germany rebuilt her economy. Kleinworts obviously had a particularly strong German connection, but the same did not apply to Barings, where in 1925 almost half of the total income deriving from acceptance credits was earned on German account. The joint-stock banks also got keen, so much so that in the case of the Westminster, for instance, the bank's German commitments on acceptance credits were standing at about £4m by February 1929. At which point it was agreed by the board to make 'every endeavour' not to increase that figure.[52]

Belgium was another part of the European reconstruction jigsaw and, for all its sentimental associations, one of the more exasperating parts.[53] By 1925 the plan – in which Norman was increasingly closely involved, with Barings deputed to lead a London consortium – was for a large loan that would enable Belgium to stabilise her ravaged currency. It proved slow going, largely because London could not act without New York's backing, and for a long time Wall Street bankers took a decidedly dim view of Belgian financial soundness. Revelstoke sympathised. 'We had a long meeting with the Belgian Finance Minister etc on Friday here,' he told Hugo Baring in March 1926, 'and while we were in full discussion in quite a serene atmosphere, he got telephone messages from his own capital to say that there was a panic in exchange, etc, etc . . . I fear there is a strong party in Belgium who object to stabilisation, and who lean towards inflation. It is all very tiresome and unsatisfactory.'

Eventually, following a political reordering in Belgium, international confidence was adequately restored, and in October 1926 the London capital market put through a £7.25m loan as part of a long-term international loan package. Back in February, Peacock had conceded that possibly only a loan would prevent Belgium sliding into chaos and conceivably even into communism, but at the same time had expressed anxiety over 'the danger to Barings and our colleagues if we should issue something that is not sound that might come to grief in the very near future'. In fact, the loan was even more massively over-subscribed than the Hamburg loan a few weeks earlier. Barings had been joined in issuing the loan by Westminster Bank and Morgan Grenfell (important because of the crucial American connection), and at the end of the month the latter's Vivian Smith informed one of the New York partners that the London applications for the loan had 'amounted to £250,000,000, subscribed by 40,000 people', with 'many big applicants only getting about 1%'. Or as Smith's colleague, Charles Whigham, put it a few days earlier: 'I have seen subscriptions by individuals whom I know for an amount which is at least equal to, if not in excess of, the individual's entire wealth but there is no holding the public when they go wild over a particular issue.' Once again, underwriting the issue was the proverbial money for old rope; and for Barings and its friends these were salad days, though the £37 10s that Sir Edwin Lutyens made paled in comparison with Revelstoke's £15,000 through his various accounts, admittedly including those assets he managed for others.[54]

Italy was a more charged question – though rather more so inside the Bank of England than in the City as a whole. The Italian finance minister met Norman in December 1925 and deeply disturbed the Governor. 'Volpi said,' Norman reported to Strong, 'that he himself was going to direct Central Bank policy which should not be separated at all from general policy.' The following August Mussolini pledged Italy to a policy of deflation and exchange stabilisation, thereby opening the way to an international loan, but Norman would not be budged. Writing to Jack Morgan in November 1926, he admitted that 'Fascism has surely brought order out of chaos over the last few years' and that the 'Duce was the right man at a critical moment', but he went on: 'Opposition in any form is gone: freedom of speech, opinion, criticism and press – even private life as we understand it.' Moreover, the Bank of Italy was wholly lacking in independence, whereas according to Norman the state 'should surely permit a [central] Bank to "nag" its own Government even in public and to decide questions on other than political grounds'. It was an old song, but this time Norman's sensitivities failed to persuade the normally sympathetic Strong, who told him frankly that, in comparison to the relations of other governments with their central banks, the current Italian government had towards its own 'a record for fairness which is just as good, if not better than, any of the others'. Norman, also under pressure from Morgans in New York, took the point, agreeing to meet the Bank of Italy's governor, Bonaldo Stringher; and by early 1927 a London group had been formed for the handling of Italian government business.[55]

In October that year, in the context of serious negotiations being under way for an Italian stabilisation loan, Norman justified his change of heart to Strong:

> Italy is not a free country in the usual sense of the word, and certain things are lacking which in a liberal country like England are apt to be missed; for instance, freedom of speech, freedom of the Press, freedom of politics and so on. But the fact remains that she has made economic and financial progress and is probably making social progress too. It is difficult to know whether the present régime is becoming acceptable to Italians as a whole; but at any rate it has survived a period of strain and it continues.

Sir Edward Reid of Barings, writing shortly beforehand to a Kidder Peabody partner about 'the Italian situation', had altogether fewer qualms: 'The present Government's intentions as to the maintenance of industrial and financial stability seem to be good and as long as it continues in office it is to be hoped that the situation will be kept well in hand and that the period of healthy improvement will continue.' The loan went ahead at the end of 1927, with Hyde of Midland noting on 22 December that Grenfell had called on him and offered a participation of £500,000: 'Morgans were taking $2,500,000, and Schroeders, Barings & Rothschilds were taking $2,500,000 between them. The balance of the credit was being arranged among the Central Banks. The commission would be $1\frac{1}{4}\%$ for a year, and we agreed to take the participation.' That same day one of Grenfell's partners sent an effusive letter. 'We are all enormously grateful for your help,' Whigham thanked Norman, 'and I am sure that the Italians ought to be even more so, as without your efforts I am sure the business would never have been put through.'[56]

Even before giving ground, Norman's paramount concern was less with Italian liberty as such than with the prerogatives of central bankers as a breed apart.[57] Back in September 1925 he had outlined to the Bank of England's Harry Siepmann his most cherished dream:

> I rather hope that next summer we may be able to inaugurate private and eclectic Central Banks' 'Club', small at first, large in the future, with the following familiar sort of qualifications for membership – subscriptions in the shape of exclusive relations; appropriate balances with other Central Banks; proper ratio of free balances and earning assets in each market; no undue regard for profit; political freedom by right or by custom; credits when there is bad weather in any particular place; and so on.

By 1927, indeed, that dream came somewhere close to fruition, with currency stabilisation proceeding apace (well over twenty countries returning to the gold standard) and central bank co-operation starting to take on an institutional character. In July there assembled the so-called Long Island 'Club', a gathering of Strong, Norman, Schacht and the Bank of France's Charles Rist, the latter deputising for Moreau. 'World's Most Exclusive Club Meets Here for the First Time' was the headline in the *New York Herald Tribune*. In fact, the conference achieved little, if only because the four participants were seldom around the same table at the same time. And although Norman himself remained as attached as ever to his Olympian dream of central banking co-operation ('I want to make an umbrella, so that we can all get under it when it rains,' he would remark in December 1928), the fullest, most productive phase of that co-operation had passed.[58]

Partly this was because of the shift in American attitudes, especially with the long illness of Strong before his eventual death in October 1928; but undoubtedly the crux was France, which correctly identified a very strong bond between Norman and Schacht. Norman himself made no bones about it, telling Addis in 1927 that 'whatever complaints may be made against Schacht, and admitting that he is at times impetuous and may have been rattled, you will agree that when rock bottom is reached he is a MAN!' In the eyes of the Bank of France, Schacht was less a man than a monster, and inevitably this greatly coloured its attitude towards Norman. Its Governor from June 1926 was Emile Moreau, who during his two years in office became an increasingly formidable figure as a result of the *de facto* stabilisation of the franc and the Bank of France's accumulation of large sterling balances. He also kept a wonderfully readable diary:

> *29 July 1926.* Mr Norman arrived at eleven o'clock. At first sight, he is very likable . . . On the other hand, he seems to feel the deepest sympathy for the Germans. He is very close to Dr Schacht. They see each other often and hatch secret plans. Such an inclination is typical of the general attitude of the City . . . He is not a friend to us French.
>
> *26 March 1927.* I went to see Mr Poincaré to report to him on my trip to London. I told the prime minister that I came back with a favourable impression. The operation [concerning 'the immediate repayment of our debt and the return of our gold'] we proposed evidently embarrasses Mr Norman, but he will be unable to escape. Thanks to the strong financial position which we have regained, our roles have reversed and it is Mr Norman who is the petitioner now.
>
> *14 April 1927.* Mr Norman pretended [to Rist in London] that since he does not understand French very well, he had not grasped what I had told him at Calais concerning the exchange rate for the dollars which I intended to remit instead of pounds . . . In reality, the English hoped that we would overlook the ruse they were using to sell us pounds at a rate above their actual value. Their scheme frustrated and their little calculations revealed, they are now vexed.
>
> *21 April 1927.* The Bank of England has lowered its discount rate from 5 per cent to 4½ per cent. Is this a bluff or a sign of real ease? I lean towards the first interpretation.
>
> *6 February 1928.* I had an important conversation with Mr Poincaré over the issue of the Bank of England's imperialism. I explained to the prime minister that since England was the first European country to recover a stable and reliable currency after the war, it had used this

advantage to build the foundation for a veritable financial domination of Europe . . . England has managed to install itself completely in Austria, Hungary, Belgium, Norway and Italy. It will implant itself next in Greece and Portugal. It is attempting to get a foothold in Yugoslavia and it is fighting us on the sly in Romania. Should it be allowed to go forward?

28 April 1928. I find no candour among my British counterparts, only a hypocritical attitude with ill will at the core, fortunately tempered by fear . . .

The final entry was on 28 June 1928. 'Our work is not finished,' wrote Moreau. 'The essential tasks after the stabilisation will be to defend the results gained against the improvidence and demagogy of the politicians, to reorganise the Paris market so that it will become one of the premier markets of the world, and to co-ordinate and extend the activities of our banks abroad.'[59] Moreau and Norman may have agreed on the hopelessness of politicians, but otherwise the two financial powers they represented were set on a collision course. Should a hard rain fall on Europe as a whole, there was unlikely to be an umbrella in working order.

A loan to Romania was the episode that not only formed the flashpoint in the Anglo-French relationship, but also marked a significant decline in Norman's influence over the 'club' of central bankers.[60] By early February 1928, when Moreau referred to that country in his conversation with Poincaré, the matter was coming to a head: in essence, Norman wanted to pursue the customary procedure of making a reconstruction loan under League of Nations auspices; but in Moreau's eyes, the League was the thinnest of cloaks for London's financial imperialism, and instead he was determined to work with a New York issuing house (Blair and Co) in making a loan that would effectively squeeze out the Bank of England. Later that month, on Tuesday the 21st, Moreau travelled to London, despite having been told that Norman was ill. The illness, Moreau was convinced, was 'of a diplomatic nature'. On Wednesday, with Norman absent from the Bank, Moreau saw Lubbock, Harvey and Siepmann. The visitor took a tough line, claiming Romania and Yugoslavia as within the French sphere of financial influence; and he noted, 'I obtained a general declaration of complete equality and of mutual assistance between our two institutions'. Norman was back in the Bank by Thursday (as Moreau returned to Paris), but Addis recorded the following day: 'A talk with Norman after lunch about proposed French loan to Roumania. Poor man, he looked very tired and worn.' And three days later: 'A talk with Norman after lunch. He looks ashen gray & played out, poor man.' That was Monday the 27th, by which time Moreau had discovered not just that Norman was back in the Bank the day after he had been there, but that he was apparently reneging on Lubbock's promise that the Bank of England would stay out of the stabilisation of the Romanian currency. 'I am highly irritated by Mr Norman,' Moreau reflected, 'who is playing a game which is totally unfair. He refrained from seeing me, had me received by his subordinates, and then violated the commitments made by them.' Gallic indignation winged its way to Threadneedle Street, and Addis noted the next day: 'A word with Lubbock re his Rumanian blunder. He is very penitent. Governor back in bed.'[61]

In the end it came down to the attitude of Strong, and he supported Moreau, not Norman. He subsequently justified himself to Walter Stewart, an American economist who had become an adviser to Norman:

> As to the difference of view in this particular Roumanian matter, it really boils down to one very simple point. For some years past it has been more than current in Europe, both in political and banking circles, that Governor Norman desired to establish some sort of dictatorship over the central banks of Europe and that I was collaborating with him in such a program and supporting him. Possibly he and you do not realise the extent to which statements of this sort have come to us ... You can understand my hesitation in expressing this so bluntly to Governor Norman, and I think you can equally understand, better than anyone on this side of the water, how far it has been from my own intention to accept or assent to any such program ...

In June Norman wrote a letter of reconciliation ('think no more about Roumania or past remarks or misunderstandings'), and it was the last letter between them before Strong died.[62]

Yet if Romania was a lost cause, from London's point of view, the Balkans as a whole remained a contested area. Rothschilds headed a London group set up a year or two earlier to make loans to Yugoslavia, should the possibility arise, and in November 1928 there was an intensely suggestive entry in Norman's diary:

> L de Rothschild. I suggest that they sh[d] send someone to Belgrade as a 'warming pan': to act as Liaison between Group & Serbs: to remind latter that Ldn still exists: & to prevent French having a free field there (when Roumania rehabilitates). I say this concerns London, not merely the Group: & as a *private* and *secret* arrang[t] I will join with them in salary of the 'warming pan' ...[63]

This was an entry that would have confirmed all of Moreau's worst fears; it also confirmed Norman's penchant – sometimes so counter-productive – for the secret spinning of spiders' webs.

No amount of web-spinning by an intuitive, dedicated, but ultimately out-of-his-depth central banker could avert a pervasive feeling by the late 1920s that the world's monetary system specifically, and behind it the world economy at large, was heading for disaster. It was against this darkening backdrop that discussions began, in 1928, for what would eventually become the Young Plan on reparations and the creation of the Bank for International Settlements as an international clearing bank to facilitate further the reparations mechanism. No one imagined that these measures alone would suffice, and European eyes turned increasingly – and increasingly anxiously – to Wall Street and the extraordinary credit boom there. 'I had a long talk with M.N. this afternoon,' Peacock reported to Revelstoke on 18 February 1929, 'who tells me that on this occasion he had the hardest time in America that he has ever had. He is thoroughly unhappy about the situation there, as there is no leader and the F.R. Board are at odds with one another, drifting and not knowing what to do.' Perhaps earlier in the decade Norman could have knocked American heads together; now that was impossible. 'I do not know what to expect but the outlook is obscure and disagreeable,' Norman himself wrote to Kindersley on 7 March about the American situation and its implications, while three weeks later, to another correspondent, his sense of bafflement was palpable:

> I shall not attempt to write an essay on conditions here particularly as they change almost from day to day. But both financially and politically the prospect has rarely seemed to me more obscure than it does now. Picture to yourself that at one and the same time a Committee is laboriously discussing the whole question of German Reparations in Paris: that the rate of interest was yesterday 20% in New York where the Reserve System is not functioning and where the Stock Market is playing ducks and drakes with their own and other people's money: that three of the Central Banks in Europe have raised their rates within the last month, perhaps only as a beginning; and, lastly, that in a few weeks we are liable to be tossed hither and thither by a General Election . . .

Altogether it was not a happy prospect. Or, as Revelstoke had characteristically expressed it the previous May, taking the big view, the worry was that the ever-greater speculative fever in the US would lead to a raising of American interest rates, which in turn would be 'a serious matter for us in Europe, where the "reaction", to use a horrible

American phrase, may have a damaging effect upon our money market prospects'.[64]

The committee on reparations that Norman mentioned was an international body of experts that assembled in Paris in February 1929. The British expert was Sir Josiah Stamp, the statistician who had largely written the Dawes Report on reparations and had recently become a director of the Bank of England; he was seconded by Revelstoke. The latter's temper not improved by a severe bout of flu, he kept a diary that recorded his impressions of the others at the conference. Moreau, heading the French delegation, was intransigence itself and 'shuts his mouth like a steel trap when Schacht pleads poverty and inability to pay'. Schacht himself, 'with his hatchet, Teuton face and burly neck and badly fitting collar', reminded the diarist 'of a sealion at the Zoo, which is half out of the water on a rock, and is waiting to catch a fish thrown to him by his keeper'. Jack Morgan, on behalf of the Americans, was 'like a wild bison in a shop that sells Dresden china'. And the representatives of the British Treasury had a 'supercilious manner and sneering attitude for the whole of the rest of mankind'.[65]

The *real* problem, however, was Schacht, of whom Revelstoke declined to share Norman's good opinion. 'I do trust all these people will not be too lenient to that undoubtedly able and obstinate individual,' he wrote to Peacock at the end of February. He returned to the theme on 8 March:

> I try to persuade myself that Stamp and Addis [also in the British delegation] are not penetrated by a sub-conscious feeling of agreement with the Germans in their reiterated plea of misery, poverty, Bankruptcy, etc. They are so much more familiar with the figures, and so much more 'expert' than, Heaven knows, I pretend to be, but I do what I can to see through their eyes. But, quite between ourselves, I sometimes wonder whether a knowledge of men and of the world would not rather lead one to an inner conviction that these Germans can really pay and continue to pay a larger sum than they seem disposed to offer.

The attritional discussions continued over the next few weeks (though Revelstoke was able to pay a brief visit to London), and on 13 April he wrote plaintively to Mildmay from 27 Faubourg St Honoré: 'I have no sort of idea what is going to happen here . . . Best love to all at No. 8. How glad I shall be to see you all again.' Three days later, dutifully keeping Peacock posted, Revelstoke's spirits were no higher: 'We have had full sittings both this morning and this afternoon. The sessions have been lengthy, tiresome, and far from satisfactory. Schacht resumes his most negative attitude, is unhelpful to the last degree . . .' Two days later, on the 18th, the committee kept going until early evening, at which point the Germans stormed out, threatening to abort the conference. Revelstoke – still only in his mid-sixties, but seemingly around for ever, having as a young man righted Barings after the catastrophe of 1890 – summed it all up in his diary: 'Schacht was quite impossible today.'[66] The words were redolent of another, more congenial age.

*

Operating in a mental world a million miles away from the pleasures and pains of *haute finance*, and despite the occasional crisis of a timber merchant like Ernest Beaton, the day-to-day commercial City jogged along during the 1920s, in gradual decline but still for the most part making a more than adequate living.[67] It was an existence devoted to the filling of necessary if unglamorous niches, but occasionally some bit of this world – some cog in the machine – was jolted out of its complacency by a rude external shock. Indeed, with the larger world now singing the hymn of rationalisation and large-scale enterprises, the frequency of these shocks was starting to increase.

Three examples from the second half of the 1920s stand out. On the London Metal Exchange, the threat to its security came from Copper Exporters Incorporated, an American cartel formed in 1926 that included Rio Tinto. Against the background of American dominance in the world copper trade, it sought to control the production of that metal and thereby destroy the LME's powers of price-making. By 1928, with little physical metal available and the merchant trade all but eliminated, turnover on the LME was in steep decline; and over the ensuing winter, with prices rising fast, the American cartel took its opportunity to unload and make a handsome profit. It is a frustratingly ill-documented episode, but crucially the LME seems to have survived this major threat to its influence.[68]

Slightly further to the north in the City, the Baltic Exchange had its own problems, caused by the increasing tendency for the market's grain and oil-seed brokers to be eliminated in transactions between merchants and buyers. Most members wanted the employment of a broking intermediary to be made compulsory (along the lines of the Stock Exchange), but despite a call to action in 1928 the directors of the Baltic did nothing. By 1929, with the formation of the Millers Mutual, the situation had become desperate for the grain brokers in particular. That March, however, saw a fight-back, with the establishment by the

London Corn Trade Association of a futures market on the Baltic in Canadian wheat – in other words enabling transactions in physical Canadian wheat to be hedged; and for the grain brokers this was a vital shot in the arm.[69]

It was a somewhat similar story in the London sugar market, shaken to its core when Churchill in his 1928 budget prohibited the importation of refined sugar. It was, the sugar broker Gordon Hodge would recall, not only 'a paralysing blow to the White Sugar "Futures" Market', but also 'seriously interfered with the business of many brokers' firms whose livelihood was dependent on the importation of foreign White Sugar'. However, 'after a lot of thought and trouble the new "Futures" Market was formulated based on Raw Sugar c.i.f. London or Liverpool'. And 'although at first sceptics said the market was trying to do the impossible, actually it was started in 1929, and ran successfully for ten years'.[70] The City's markets, in other words, could still sometimes take an initiative if they had to, notwithstanding how extraordinarily deep the forces of conservatism ran.

Certainly there was, on the part of the merchant banks, a disinclination to engage in cut-and-thrust. 'I am afraid that as regards London,' Whigham of Morgan Grenfell conceded to a Paris-based colleague in June 1927, 'the position is as you say that the Greek Government having done its previous business here through Hambros it would not be possible for us to enter the field as competitor.' The following summer, sounding out various institutions about the possibility of participating in a £5m Spanish credit to be placed in London, Hyde of Midland hit an immediate road-block: 'Rothschilds – not interested. Schröders – always followed Rothschilds in Spanish matters, and, therefore, regret they would not be participating.' Nevertheless there *was* some movement, and a list of the merchant banks handling the most new issues (including joint issues) between 1926 and 1930 makes interesting reading. The top eight houses were Schröders on 33 (28 foreign issues, 5 home issues), Rothschilds on 32 (27/5), Higginsons on 25 (16/9), Barings on 22 (17/5), Hambros on 21 (21/0), and Erlangers, Helbert Wagg and Lazards each on 20 (17/3, 9/11 and 18/2 respectively). Rothschilds may have been flattered by its position, with a high proportion of its issues being joint issues led by another house, but perhaps its inter-war decline was not as precipitate as has usually been assumed; Higginson & Co was effectively the London branch of the leading Boston investment bank Lee, Higginson & Co; while Helbert Wagg was clearly becoming a serious force. The list did not include Cull & Co, a cross between a finance house and a merchant bank, very active in these years but not involved in accepting. As virtually a new entrant in the field, it formed Ultramar, acted for AEI and Courtaulds, did an enormous business in mining, celanese and oil shares, and made itself 'the shop' (thus controlling the market) in all the securities relating to the Chester Beatty mining empire. 'Never fail to give the public the shares they want' was the reputed dictum of one of its partners, Hugh Micklem.[71]

For the older houses – their prestige built up over decades – appearances mattered intensely. Vivian Smith of Morgan Grenfell was only behaving as he would have wished to be treated when he wrote in 1926 to Ernest Debenham of Debenhams Limited that 'what Kindersley means is that a Public Issue by our two Houses might be interpreted in the City as possibly casting reflections on Lazards as they did your last business by themselves'. He added that 'of course it would be quite possible for us to do the business jointly with Lazards without our name appearing, Lazards' name alone being on the prospectus as the Issuing House'. A year later, explaining this crucial matter to a Berlin bank, Kindersley's partner Brand was tactful but firm:

> We are most grateful to you for giving us the opportunity of issuing the Bremen Loan, and we very much regret that we have not been able to come to an agreement with Messrs Japhet about it. We felt that the business, while intrinsically very good, and one which we should have been glad to do ourselves, presented certain difficulties in the form in which Messrs Japhet presented it.
>
> In the first place, as you know, while Messrs Japhet are a highly respected and active firm, they have never before made an issue, or participated in one, and therefore their making a joint issue with us would undoubtedly have caused a very considerable amount of comment in the City. We have not informed Messrs Japhet that we should definitely refuse to make such a joint issue, but they must unquestionably understand that such an association would have certain draw backs for us . . .

Saemy Japhet had been in the City for some thirty years, but it was a thorny road that he indomitably trod. 'All right,' Norman replied later in 1927 to Colonel the Hon Sidney Peel, 'I will see your friend Mr Japhet, but you must please let me choose a day later on: for the moment my time is crowded.' A week later the great man did see Japhet, and it could have been a lot worse: 'Courteous visit & general talk: all satisfactory'.[72]

Japhet was but one of a trail of merchant bankers – eager or reluctant to give information, as the case might be – who found their way to the Governor's room. Again, one can do no better than quote Norman's own terse, telling diary entries:

30 August 1926. C.D. Seligman . . . I mention no figures but say that I *probably* hold as many of his Bills as any one & *certainly* as many as I wish to hold without looking at his figures. He will consider & probably bring the Bal Sheet after his holiday.

15 September 1926. C.D. Seligman. Shows me 30 June Bal Sheet, wh he has never shown anywhere but will show again to me if asked at any time.

23 March 1927. Olaf Hambro. All their acc^{cs} are eligible except £350^m [i.e. £350,000] – & possibly a Whaling Credit & Finnish Timber Credit wh if questionable are hallowed by long custom!!

27 April 1927. Sir Alex Kleinwort to introduce his 2 Sons as partners – very friendly – but no business.

10 August 1927. Konig . . . F.H. & Co [i.e. Huths] *are* short of cap for Ldn + NY . . . I ask him to study an amalgamation with some other firm: he can think of none but favours idea – provided he is still top dog.

26 October 1927. E.C. Brown. Rumour of heavy losses made by B.S. & Co [i.e. Brown Shipley]. He says only *one* doubtful a/c . . . Otherwise *all clean.* Acc. about £3 mil: Cap £780^m outside perhaps £200^m.

11 December 1928. H.A. Andreae [of Kleinworts]. I explain Bks position as Parent of Disc Mkt & large holder of their Bills: need for organised information for both reasons: retirement of Paget [i.e. as principal of the discount office]: Peppiatt as new Broom. He promises in Jan or Feb next to send Spicer [Ernest Spicer of the accountants Spicer & Pegler] (subject to Sir A's consent) to give adequate information as to Bal Sheet & to answer reasonable questions. I agree information will be secret & not disclosed & that same request is being made of firms in similar position.[73]

It was a tight little world, and such a degree of inquisitorial control – quite apart from the question of foreign loans – derived to a large degree from the strength of Norman's personality. Nevertheless, Lidderdale's forceful rescue of Barings in 1890 was still more or less within living memory; and the thought must have crossed some minds that, amid so much political and economic instability in the world at large, the Bank might again be looked to as saviour.

In the eyes of Norman, and those close to him like Revelstoke, Peacock and Tiarks, the village's real thorns in the flesh were the joint-stock banks and what were regarded as their overweening ambitions. Personal antipathy towards Goodenough of Barclays and McKenna of Midland undoubtedly played a part. J.W. Beaumont Pease, Chairman of Lloyds, was a welcome contrast. 'Perhaps he is not a great Banker,' Norman informed Strong in 1926, 'but he is certainly a real white man, maintaining a tradition in his Bank which excels the tradition of any of our other Banks. And he is a good friend of ours.' In fact, Norman had recently been thwarted by Lloyds, which had taken over the Egyptian offices of the Bank of British West Africa against his express wishes, but he was willing to semi-forgive. Lloyds took this action in 1925, the same year that Barclays merged three overseas banks already under its domination in order to form Barclays DCO (Dominion, Colonial and Overseas). Norman came out with all guns blazing, including in October 1925 making a formal appeal to the government, with the Bank contending that the clearing banks, 'having already sufficiently onerous liabilities at home, will be wise not to assume in addition the risks and uncertainties inseparable from business in overseas markets'. Churchill declined to intervene, but Norman still had powerful weapons at his disposal, refusing to open an account for Barclays DCO and letting it be known that that disagreeable creation would not be an 'approved' name for discount or advance at the Bank. The joint-stock banks had grown so rapidly over the past thirty years, and become so huge, that Norman's attitude – that of a private banker at heart – was understandable. The increasingly autocratic Goodenough would not, however, be bullied. McKenna seemed to be as intransigent in 1927, when alone of the clearing bankers he refused to renew a 1925 undertaking (on the return to gold) that they would not accumulate gold for their own purposes. With Midland, Norman complained to Niemeyer that May, 'neither argument nor abuse nor intercession seems to have the least effect'. And he added plaintively that 'the result of even one standing out is that the control of the gold market, of the central reserve of gold and, possibly, of the Bank Rate, is to be shared by the Bank of England with another Bank . . .' Finally, McKenna backed down to the extent of agreeing to a one-year renewal, and in 1928 the matter was resolved by legislation.[74]

There was also, of high importance to the merchant banks, the question of accepting.[75] Here the clearers became ever more aggressive competitors, culminating in about 1927 when (as Sir Edward Reid of Barings would recall in his memoirs) 'the Midland Bank caused a considerable sensation by coming to the conclusion that acceptance commissions were money for nothing and declaring that they were prepared to accept three months drafts for 0.125 per cent (or 0.50 per cent per annum)'. Not surprisingly, 'this caused considerable anger with Schröders, Lazards and other accepting houses'. Indeed it did, especially as the leading accepting houses were dragged into a costly price war, and when a few years later Tiarks of Schröders was invited to join the Midland board, he refused, stating curtly to McKenna that Midland's behaviour had been unsound as well as predatory. In fact, the traditional accepting houses greatly exaggerated the threat: at the end of 1928, *total* acceptances outstanding of the 'Big Five' were only £4.47m (Midland being the largest acceptor with £1.35m), less than a quarter of Kleinworts alone.[76] What mattered, though, was partly the price-cutting impact on profits, partly the symbolic challenge to hitherto largely – not entirely – sacrosanct territory.

One little City patch that the Bank of England was increasingly keen to protect and take under its wings was the exclusive, rather mysterious club that was the London discount market.[77] The market itself formed the Discount Market Committee during the war, and on 1 April 1920 almost Norman's first action on becoming Governor was to jot in his diary, 'See about weekly meeting with Ch'man of Discount Mkt'. Thursday afternoon was fixed as the time, a convenient midpoint between the announcement of Bank rate on Thursday morning and the Treasury bill tender on Friday. 'The Governor's tea-party', as it was called, became a ritual, but the DMC's chairman from 1925, Robert Wyse of Union Discount, became resented by other members of the market for talking to Norman alone and then not always conveying the information he had been given. The workings of the discount market were of considerable practical importance to Norman – requiring as he did through most of the 1920s to make money dear, yet without raising Bank rate – and from 1922 he had his own private source of intelligence, in the form of Seccombe, Marshall & Campion, specifically employed to conduct the Bank's bill business. It was a role analogous to that of the Government brokers, Mullens & Co, in the gilt-edged market.[78]

Occasionally, as in September 1927, Norman would summon representatives of the market as a whole and give them a stern talking to:

> He was not at all satisfied [the Principal of the Discount Office recorded] with the way the market had been conducted in the past six months – they had allowed 3-months' rate to be affected by temporary conditions – this would not do and they must keep it firm and stable. He knew how to deal with them if they didn't and could keep them in the Bank [i.e. when they needed to borrow, when money was tight] as long as he liked . . . Market could never force Bank either to raise or lower Bank Rate whereas the Bank could force the market to keep rates firm. Governor wants to know in course of the next day or two whether the market is willing and able to comply . . .

The market, as usual, was willing and able. Yet despite the sharp tone, Norman's broad sympathies lay entirely with the discount market. Later that year his deputy Lubbock, on the basis of a conversation with Norman, explained why to Leith-Ross of the Treasury:

We have a feeling that business is now being done by the Joint Stock Banks which formerly they did not undertake (at least to the same extent) and which tends to be destructive of the Discount Market as it used to exist and of the London Bill Market which has hitherto been unique. Thus New York and Amsterdam are probably making great strides towards a Bill Market in competition with London.

To be specific, I would mention e.g. the tendency of the Joint Stock Banks to substitute advances for bills: the reduction in their published Deposit Rate relative to Bank Rate: consequently their more or less 'pegged' rate for short loans: high deposit rates for special moneys over fixed periods, and so forth: all of which tend to mechanicalise the Discount Market, whereas its essence used to be dynamic rather than static and based on the demand for Commercial credit . . .'[79]

A large part of the problem was the huge increase because of the war in the volume of Treasury bills, but there was no doubt where the Bank also pointed a particular finger of blame. Here, as in most other areas, there was relatively little that Norman could do about the joint-stock banks; but if the going got really tough for the discount market, then he would do his best to preserve it, being driven by a strong emotional as well as practical attachment.

Norman himself was secure in his position by the end of the 1920s, though not without some continuing alarms on the way.[80] It had been a story of tangled motives ever since Norman 'should' have stepped down in 1922, and it assumed a new twist in October 1925. 'Rather a scare at Treasury Committee,' Addis recorded on the 7th. 'Alan Anderson will not go on as Deputy unless assured of being made Governor in a year. He finds his position intolerable, not consulted etc. I told him the Deputy's place is what its occupant makes it. He did not like that! He will retire.' Anderson (ambitious and able, if not a particularly attractive character) had had to put up with much from Norman during his brief tenure as deputy, but the Governor was imperturbable when he explained the matter to Strong on the 18th: 'The trouble is not that he is not clever & courageous & a good fellow but that his wishes are contrary to our ideas & the whole of our tradition & while we admit they may perhaps be suitable for a shipping business we are sure they are not suitable for a Central Bank.' Two days later, at a meeting of the Committee of Treasury held at Revelstoke's home in Carlton House Terrace, Trotter agreed to another spell as Deputy Governor, but only on the basis of a moral undertaking that he would become Governor in 1927. Norman did not resist, but from the start played down the firmness of the pledge. 'The idea is,' he wrote to Strong in November

1925 about Trotter, 'that he shall become Governor in April 1927 for the old period of 2 years: but this is no more than an idea & quite vague at present.' He added: 'There is also an idea that after April 1927 I shall be asked to continue to devote *all* my time to the Bank – as a sort of adviser for Foreign Affairs. But this too is quite vague . . .'[81]

Trotter duly became Deputy Governor in April 1926, and three months later Revelstoke reported to Peacock that amongst the Bank's senior directors 'the feeling is that H.T. and C.L. should be invited to take the Chairs in April next' – in other words, that Lubbock should become deputy to Trotter. Autumn was decision time. Addis's diary tells the story:

> *27 September.* Lunch at Bk of England. A long talk with Norman about the meeting tomorrow to discuss his succession. He declares he could not work with Trotter.
>
> *28 September.* At 12.30 meeting of Bk of Eng. directors. I propose Norman's continuance as Governor for another year. Arbuthnot seconded. An hour's discussion. We meet again on Monday.
>
> *4 October.* At 2.30 carried my motion for Norman to continue Governor for another year unanimously. Great victory!
>
> *6 October.* Treasury Committee & long talk afterwards with Governor. He will accept office again but only on assurance of Court's support and good will.
>
> *7 October.* At Bank of England Revelstoke & Cullen [the former Cokayne] broke to Trotter the break-down of the understanding that he was to be the next Governor. He took it well.

Perhaps he did, in the best mercantile tradition, but over forty years later his cousin Bob Boothby would relate how not becoming Governor 'broke' Trotter. In effect, Norman had won the day by raising the stakes, in particular rejecting outright the 'Foreign Secretaryship' compromise, stating not unreasonably to Revelstoke and others that such a role 'would be derogatory to the dignity of the actual occupant of the Chair'. But despite the apparent unanimity, the prevailing mood was almost certainly somewhat malcontent. 'If I am to continue as at present,' Norman wrote to Strong on the 10th about his colleagues, 'I ask their goodwill – & not merely their grudging support because they have got into a mess.'[82]

It was a mess caused less by personal hostility towards Norman than by the incompatibility of the new, post-war world with a natural wish to return to the old, pre-war methods. Opposing a return to automatic rotation of governors, Addis had summed up the matter in a typically lucid, and possibly decisive, memorandum to his colleagues at the end of September: 'We cannot go back even if we would. The old familiar ways of finance are abandoned, and it is mere illusion to suppose that we can ever return to them.' And, invoking a cluster of critical problems on the horizon (the German question, the statutory changes involved in the stabilisation of the Belgian, French and Italian currencies, the impending amalgamation of the Treasury and Bank note issues) as grounds for sticking with the present Governor, especially as 'the personal element has been enhanced by the urgency and secrecy of international negotiations', he concluded: 'We have reached a critical stage . . . There is much to be said for allowing a craftsman to complete his own work.'[83]

Trotter stepped down in April 1927, and Lubbock reluctantly returned for *his* second spell as deputy – 'I try to efface completely my own self & my own wishes,' he told Strong soon afterwards, while conceding that 'in moments of weariness my mind is flooded with the question: Why on earth did I come here?' Over the next year the question of rotation did not go away. 'Some heat generated with Kindersley, Grenfell &c,' noted Addis in June 1928 after a discussion by the Court, and at this stage they seem to have been the two most heavyweight figures seeking to bring Norman's governorship to an end. It was by now clear that the final chance was approaching for the principle of rotation to be reasserted, for Lubbock had made it plain that he did not wish to continue as deputy beyond 1929 and Norman was pushing hard for Lubbock's successor to be Sir Ernest Harvey, the Comptroller and former Chief Cashier. From the point of view of the pro-rotationists, the logic was inexorable: in the words of Sir Henry Clay (Norman's first biographer), 'an official who became Deputy Governor would become a permanent Deputy Governor, and the *de facto* continuity of the Governor's office would be reinforced'.[84]

For Norman it was the dream ticket, and in early September he spilled out his thoughts to Peacock, who duly reported them to Revelstoke:

> After dwelling upon the difficulties and dangers of the present position and the constant anxiety that had been caused him by the feeling in the Court Room, he referred to one or two special matters that, in his opinion, have a very serious bearing upon the position. He emphasised the folly of reverting to the Rotation system and said that he could not be asked to endorse this, as he entirely disapproves . . . He spoke of the political situation, and said that if, as was possible, we should have a Labour Government next year, he feared very much that they would not keep their hands off the Bank if the proposed return to amateurs were being carried

out. He reverted to his own rather unique position *vis-à-vis* Mr Snowden
and to the belief, which is shared by all leaders and very strongly held by
such leaders as Sir Josiah Stamp, etc., that the time is passed for such an
institution being in the hands of amateurs, and that it must be directed by
professionals . . .

The following month, on Thursday the 18th, the Court discussed
Cullen's resolution proposing a return to rotation. Revelstoke gave
Peacock the inside account of a memorable occasion. He described
Anderson's contribution as 'amiably damning and condemning M.N.
and all his works', whereas Whigham, 'with true Scottish brevity',
simply said that 'to his judgement this ridiculous proposal was perfect
nonsense'. Norman, according to Revelstoke, continued to go round the
table:

> Whitworth very well-intentioned, but long and tiresome; strongly
> against Lord C. Addis, a few admirable words calling the attention of Lord
> C. to the grave responsibility he was undertaking . . . Booth against M.N.
> Hanbury and Grenfell did not speak, and it came to my turn. It was then
> after one o'clock, the necessities of luncheon were becoming woefully
> apparent, and it was evident that a division taken at this juncture might
> end in trouble. I therefore asked M.N., without rising, whether it was
> intended to take a vote that day. If such a decision had been taken I should
> have thought it my duty to tell the Court what I thought of the whole
> matter – but my question raised a stream of technical discussion which
> resulted in reiterated chaos. The Minutes were then read, the Court was
> announced to be 'up', and my colleagues prepared for their midday meal.
> M.N. then told me that he had 'sensed', as he calls it, that a division
> would have resulted in a defeat. I did not agree with him . . . I had a long
> talk after the Court with Grenfell, and I think that he will re-consider his
> decision to support Cullen. But the whole affair is very unhappy and very
> preoccupying. I saw M.N. on Friday for instance. He told me he had
> passed a sleepless night . . .

Once again, the opposition crumbled. At the Court a week later,
Gladstone, Booth and Grenfell each (in Revelstoke's words) 'expressed
their regret that they had been led to support C's motion and added that
they no longer felt justified in doing so'. The motion was lost, after
which Norman made what Revelstoke called 'a most conciliatory
speech'. Norman would continue as Governor from spring 1929, with
Harvey as his new deputy.[85] It was unthinkable that an official (even a
knighted one) could become Governor, and henceforth the main internal

threat to Norman's position would be his health, psychological as much as physical.

The Bank itself was starting to become a rather different animal, as one of the more obscure directors, A.C. Gladstone, implied in his October 1928 remarks. Three years earlier, writing to Strong, Norman had referred to 'inadequate personnel' as a problem that 'we are seriously trying to remedy'; and during the interim he started to recruit (with the Court's somewhat reluctant consent) a group of specialist advisers, beginning with Harry Siepmann (with Treasury background and experience in India and Hungary), the American economist Walter Stewart and Sir Otto Niemeyer. Norman conceded privately in 1928 that 'we were late in building up a body of professionals drawn from outside', adding that 'we could not draw them from inside because the experience does not exist there'; but almost certainly he had to contend with worries that one day the Bank might be taken over by experts. 'The proper place for an expert is not in the Chair but behind it,' declared Addis, for all his anti-rotationism, to the Court in May 1928, as he opposed the concept of the Comptroller becoming Deputy Governor. 'It is for him to assist and advise, but it is for the Merchant Directors to determine the policy of the Bank, and it is the belief that that policy is so determined which has won for the Bank its traditional authority and prestige.'[86]

Moreover, in terms of those directors, there was still an abiding mistrust of the cosmopolitan, as the case of Sir Henry Strakosch demonstrated.[87] 'I am not sure if you know him,' Norman wrote to Strong in November 1927. 'Austrian origin: many years in Johannesburg; 20 years in this country: a student of economics: a gold producer with general financial interests . . . Full of public spirit, genial and helpful . . . and so forth. I have probably told you that if I had been a Dictator he would have been a Director here years ago.' The following February the Committee of Treasury (with Norman absent) discussed Strakosch's candidature as a director in place of Michael Spencer-Smith, recently killed in a motor accident. 'All for him especially Revelstoke,' noted Addis. 'I opposed. His name is against him.' And a day later: 'Revelstoke told me he had been thinking over my objections to Strakosch as a director & now agreed with me. It would not do.'[88] This was the ultimate condemnation, and Strakosch – for all his public spirit and unrivalled expertise in international currency – never did become a director of the Bank of England.

*

Irrespective of all the manoeuvrings in Threadneedle Street and elsewhere, the Stock Exchange remained, as almost always, the City's daily
pulse. It even enjoyed in the mid-1920s an old-fashioned rubber boom,
reminiscent of the legendary frenzy of 1910. One morning in July 1925
the broker-journalist 'Autolycus' found himself caught up in it, his
account incidentally reflecting the gentlemanly hours of business that still
obtained:

> Well before ten o'clock in the morning business was being done on the
> telephones, though many jobbers refused, naturally enough, to make prices
> until the market opened properly. A little before half-past ten, when prices
> were developing rapidly, there came a perceptible series of rushes from
> half-a-dozen parts of the House. They converged upon the Rubber market.
> It had the extraordinary effect of making business well-nigh impossible to
> execute, for the simple reason that around the principal dealers, there
> surged and shouted such a crowd as the market has not seen for a decade
> or two. You could not get near the man you wanted . . .
>
> I dropped a pencil, and wasted ten minutes to get out of the market in
> order to replace it, for to pick it up was impossible. In previous booms, one
> has heard stentorian bidding for shares going on all the time; but now there
> is no time for bidding. It is only occasionally that a buyer breaks into such
> lusty song. Everyone is far too busy to bother about anything except to
> book bargains as fast as possible . . .[89]

Another scribbler keenly interested in Stock Exchange matters, though in
his case as a non-member, was Sydney Moseley, who in an earlier life
had been incarcerated in the London Wall counting house of Waterlow
& Sons. His diaries reveal piquantly how his nominal expertise in the
subject failed to bear fruit in real life:

> *24 November 1925.* Busy as I am in journalism, I'm still fortune-hunting
> on the Stock Exchange. Have just lived through another critical financial
> period – saved at the last minute by a sudden, expected boom in rubber
> shares. But the storm isn't quite over yet. There has been a bad slump in
> French bonds.
>
> *14 December 1925.* Went to see one of my brokers, Smith, at the Stock
> Exchange. The rubber boom is still going strong, but Smith – to whom I
> give limited discretion – has bought me some mines and Home Rails,
> although he should have known that I have set my face against such
> speculations. I have had enough! Imagine my giving a broker 'discretion to
> deal'; yet that is what I have done!
>
> *31 December 1925.* I am quite resolved now to stop all this nonsense
> and put my money into safe securities. Though, Heaven knows what *can*
> be regarded as '*safe*' in this period of perpetual unrest! Even were I to buy

gilt-edged, who can say what they would be worth in the *next* war, or when a Labour government comes into power – as I imagine it will before very long. There is no golden rule to security these days . . .

8 March 1926. Success not only goes to the head but, as a result of the recent rubber boom, several jobbers actually went *off* their heads! One young man, exhausted after making a fortune, took his wife and children to Monte Carlo, played the fool there instead of recuperating, and, returning to London after four months, sacked his clerks and broke with his partner. He has, in fact, gone crazy. Another jobber, who got out with a fortune of £30,000, is now a nervous wreck, and a third, who made over £15,000, has gone into a mental home.

7 April 1927. Still trying hard to close down on my Stock Exchange dealings, and despite temptations, have made no move to buy anything recently. My last week's loss was £185! which is stupid. It does seem as hopeless as ever to make money by speculation.

June 1927. Money Making in Stocks and Shares is sold out. It has had a marvellous Press . . .

26 October 1927. Smith, one of my brokers, says with an odd trace of bitterness that I am one of the few good losers he has ever come across. As to that, I hate losing, but my philosophy comes to my aid. I don't show my feelings and I don't grouse, but what's the use of that if I can't stop myself from *quietly* worrying? In any case, good loser or not, everything seems to go wrong for me on the markets. Every account day I have to pay high interest for loan and contangos. It's a mug's game. I know it, and yet – hope springs eternal! So, refusing to cut my heavy losses, I keep waiting to sell out gradually 'as prices recover'. But, even when there *is* a recovery, I hope for prices still further, and so I hang on! What I find so heartbreaking is that the money I have made by hard work in writing is simply thrown down the Stock Exchange drain . . .

Moseley may have been his own worst enemy, but that sense that nothing could be relied on any longer, that there were no investment certainties left, was nicely put by T.S. Eliot in the *Criterion* in 1927: 'Everything is in question, even the fundamental dogma of modern society that debentures are safer than common stocks.' The time was not quite at hand for the cult of the equity, but later that year H.E. Raynes delivered to the Institute of Actuaries what would become a celebrated paper advocating institutional investment in ordinary shares.[90]

By this time, however, the burning investment issue of the day was becoming the sustainability or otherwise of the Wall Street boom. In 1924 Keynes and Falk had formed the Independent Investment Trust – given the rather derisive City nickname of the 'Brains Trust' on account of their stated intention to apply economic theory to investment management. Falk went to the States in 1928 and came back announcing that the credit position there was fundamentally 'unsound'; and as a result the company severely reduced its American holdings, especially in equities. At this point 'Foxy' Falk was ahead of the game, and should have stayed there. For lesser mortals, beset by doubt and difficulty, there was always the comfort of 'Autolycus'. On 16 April 1929 his 'Answers to Correspondents' column in the *FT* counselled its usual quota of caution to anxious punters:

A.R., Herne Hill. – I doubt if the company will go smash, but the shares you can only regard as being a highly speculative holding.

Blobs. – The prospectus struck me as being rather a sketchy affair, inferring that the shares are hazardous. If everything goes well, the company should make a lot of money, but the business is notoriously risky.

Unfortunate. – Your nom-de-plume is indeed appropriate. As the shares are unsaleable, I am afraid there is not very much option in regard to what you must do, at any rate for the present. The company has a sporting chance, and that is all one can say with matters as they stand at present.[91]

CHAPTER SEVEN

Smirched

The return to the gold standard an acknowledged disappointment, public discontent increasing about the Bank of England's apparent sovereignty over monetary policy, a Labour government in the offing, Hatry on the warpath, Wall Street potentially on the verge of imploding – the City in the spring of 1929 was a troubled place. Revelstoke timed his exit well, dying in Paris in the early hours of 19 April. 'It is just too sad and terrible, and that is all one can say,' Kiddy of the *Morning Post* wrote at once to Norman when the news reached London. 'A friend gone,' agreed Addis, himself in Paris. A few weeks later Alec Baring confided from 8 Bishopsgate to an American correspondent: 'One is positively bewildered at the thought that this terrible thing has really and actually happened. It will take a long time to realise that we have just got to carry on without him.'[1] Nobody had anything original to say about a man who, whatever his virtues and faults, never uttered an original thought in his life.

Revelstoke was still alive when in 1928 the Labour Party's policy statement, *Labour and the Nation*, proposed that 'the government of the Bank of England shall be vested in the hands of a public corporation, and shall contain representatives of the Treasury, the Board of Trade, Industry, Labour, and the Co-operative Movement'. With nationalisation of the Bank apparently on the cards, the City sought to mobilise. Hunsdon drummed up funds for the Anti-Socialist Union, in November that year for example receiving £5,000 from Lazards 'for the purpose of combatting the Socialist attack on the banking system'; that same month a lunch at the Savoy raised over £130,000 for the coffers of the Conservative Party. 'The way that I worked the City,' J.C.C. Davidson would recall of how he prepared the ground, 'was that I went down to a private meeting and told them that only big money was any good to me.' Despite the City's best efforts, however, it was Labour that emerged from the general election at the end of May 1929 with the largest number of seats. 'This means the beginning of the end of all the work we have been doing,' Norman apocalyptically observed to Skinner as the results came through on the Bank's tape machine. Ramsay MacDonald agreed to form a minority government on 5 June, and two days later, a Friday, Norman noted in his diary: '5.30. Tube to Ealing & thence Chequers for SB's last weekend.' Both Norman and the City at large regretted Baldwin's passing, but his Chancellor was another matter. Teddy Grenfell, writing later that year about Churchill to Morgans in New York, summed up the conventional wisdom: 'His opinions and views are as inaccurate as they are changeable. His record for thirty years has shown him to be the most unreliable of statesmen as well as the most unstable of friends.'[2]

MacDonald himself was not an unknown quantity, and at the outset his decidedly unadventurous choice of Cabinet prompted the *Economist* to remark on 15 June that he had 'spared Cheltenham and the City from alarm'. Even so, it was potentially a new dispensation, and on the 28th (three days after Alec Baring had noted that 'we are in the midst of a post-election slump here') there was an anxious tone to Harvey's report to the absent Norman of a recent conversation with Sir Richard Hopkins of the Treasury. The subject was Bank rate, and 'whilst disclaiming any desire or right to seek to influence the Bank's decisions, he expressed the hope that before the Bank took any action they would give serious consideration to the fact that an increase in the Rate at the present juncture might lead to the immediate raising of the question of the need for some control over the Bank's powers in these matters'. Harvey continued: 'I told him that the Bank are not unmindful of the views which have been expressed by members of the new Government on this subject but that they could not allow those views to stand in the way of such action as might seem to them necessary for the protection of the general financial situation.'[3]

The new Chancellor was once again Snowden, his personal admiration for Norman undimmed since he had written in the *Banker* in 1926 that 'his sympathy with the suffering of nations is as tender as that of a woman for her child', before going on: 'He is a friend. I know nothing at all about his politics. I do not know if he has any. A man's real politics arise from his temperament and feeling. And the Governor's nature is essentially democratic. I should say that he hates snobbery and class distinctions.' The inexorable fact, however, was that the question of control over monetary policy was approaching a moment of decision. Whatever his feelings towards Norman, and however much his disinclination (almost entirely shared by MacDonald) to nationalise the Bank, or indeed to veer from the path of financial orthodoxy, Snowden was acutely aware of the political sensitivity of Bank-rate decisions. On 24

July, at the Mansion House, he made his pitch. He not only expressed the hope that a rise in Bank rate might be avoided, but went further: 'I make an appeal to bankers and financial institutions to help the Government, to give the Government their confidence in the policy they were pursuing, because confidence is absolutely essential.' The Old Lady did not appreciate Snowden's speech. 'This public tendering of advice by the Chancellor of the Exchequer to the Bank of England is unusual, if not unprecedented, and its propriety is open to serious question,' declared the *Financial News* in an editorial entitled 'The Rules of the Game'; and, sending this cutting to Hopkins, Harvey noted that the paper's views 'seem to reproduce pretty accurately opinions which I gather are being expressed in most responsible City circles'. Snowden – like almost all Labour finance ministers would be – was under pressure from both sides; and on the 30th, in the context of the future likelihood of a Bank-rate rise, the *Daily Herald* argued bluntly that 'it is becoming increasingly urgent that the present position, in which the Bank of England remains almost the sole arbiter of the nation's economic fate, should be revised'.[4]

Crunch-time was also rapidly approaching for a virtuoso financier.[5] In April, late one evening, Hubert Meredith of the *Daily Mail* dutifully obeyed a summons:

Shortly after 11 o'clock, I arrived at Hatry's palace – I can call it little else – near Stanhope Gate. I was shown through a Palm Court, which seemed to me to be far more suitable to a luxury hotel than a private residence, into a magnificent billiard room, and I seated myself on a sofa near the fire on a raised platform at one end of the room. I was not kept waiting long; then in came Clarence Hatry.

He was in his City clothes and was smoking a pipe. He curled himself up on a sofa parallel to the one in which I was sitting and immediately plunged into an explanation of his great scheme for the steel industry.

I did not know Clarence Hatry well. I had met him once or twice before. His success had puzzled me, as he seemed to me a very ordinary individual with no outstanding personality, and I could detect no trace of that personal magnetism of which others spoke. I must admit that on this particular occasion, however, he impressed me rather more favourably than he ever had in the past. Perhaps this was because he struck me on that occasion as being really sincere in his belief that his efforts would lead to an enormous improvement in the steel industry of this country. He unquestionably felt greatly flattered at having the opportunity of showing what he could do. He seemed surprised at the support which had been promised him, without which (he explained) he could not have undertaken the scheme and which would enable him to find the necessary millions.

As he sat opposite to me, smoking away at his pipe, the financier disappeared and in his place there seemed to me to be a very vain man undertaking a colossal task, not with the idea of making money out of it, but with the object of showing the world what a great man Clarence Hatry really was . . .'[6]

Would the promised 'support' really come through? Not if Montagu Norman had anything to do with it. On 28 May his diary recorded a visit from the London partner of the New York investment bank Kuhn Loeb: 'Gordon Leith (at his urgent request). He begins, & I take a name out of his mouth & say "please don't ask me about Hatry or his schemes: I am ignorant of him & them". "A nod is as good as a wink" he says.' Next day Hatry himself – 'at his request by messenger' – visited Norman, in order to explain that it was 'now or never' in terms of his scheme for rationalising 60 per cent of the capacity of the steel industry. Norman was unyielding ('I make no promises,' he recorded), and shortly afterwards described his impressions to Tiarks of Schröders, a firm from which Hatry still had hopes of backing, hopes that Norman's letter effectively crushed:

> He has already bitten a scheme as large as (or larger than) he can chew: if he could further actualise a dream and join the two [i.e. for heavy steel as well as light steel] together on your and my backs, he would be relieved – and also successful. For the moment he is absorbed by the prospect of this relief and success – to it he would give up profit and leadership, just as he has already given up other good things. A dangerous and perhaps an ailing Mr Hatry.

Nor were Hatry's spirits helped by the election. Meredith ran into him at a reception on the 30th, as the results were coming in. 'The election had upset more than 90 per cent of those present,' he would recall, 'but I saw no one who had taken it so much to heart as Hatry. "This is ruination," he said to me. "How can I possibly carry through my steel scheme now?"' Hatry correctly anticipated that the value of his securities would take a hammering amidst the general bear market that was certain to ensue upon Labour's victory. A final hope vanished on 5 June when Whigham of Morgan Grenfell saw Norman. He had, noted Norman, been 'asked to finance Hatry's present & proposed deals in Iron & Steel cos', but was 'doubtful'. Norman's advice was unequivocal: 'I say he sh^d stand aside as long as Hatry controls.' Norman's advice was duly taken. The following week, on the 11th, Hatry paid his second visit to the Governor's room and, according to Norman, was 'largely a new &

moderate man today compared with May 29, wh he explains due to illness & strong medicine on former date'.[7]

Hatry had already probably taken the fatal step. Faced by a serious shortfall of funds in his proposed flotation of Steel Industries of Great Britain Ltd, he agreed at some point in June to the idea of one of his directors, an Italian called John Gialdini, that the immediate way out was through the forging of corporation scrip certificates (for Gloucester, Swindon and Wakefield), thereby providing security for the borrowing of further money from the banks until the steel combine was floated, whereupon the forged certificates could be redeemed. Hatry, in the words of his biographer, in effect 'intended to rob Peter to pay for Paul and to reimburse Peter from the profits of selling Paul'. It was fraud, undeniably, but not the most heinous fraud ever committed. In any case, Hatry's position remained perilous until the manoeuvre had been completed. By early August the flotation had still not taken place. 'We have, as you are aware, completed the purchase of the Shares and Securities of the United Steel Companies, as a result of which we have tied up a larger sum in cash than we anticipated would be necessary,' he wrote on the 8th to the Manager of Lloyds Bank at 39 Threadneedle Street. And, asking the bank to stand over until the end of the year its three loans totalling £750,000 – as well as explaining that in relation to the very recent temporary loan of £290,000 he was 'taking steps to liquidate this at the earliest possible date' – he held out a carrot: 'We take the opportunity to mention that now that the initial steps of the Steel Merger have been completed, we are in a position to arrange the transference of a further banking business to your goodselves, in which connection we shall be advising you more fully in the near future.'[8]

By this time, back in London after several weeks' absence, Norman had other things on his mind. Most pressingly, gold was continuing to drain at a disturbing rate to New York and Paris; and the question was whether Norman could implement the classic remedy of a hike in Bank rate, currently $5\frac{1}{2}$ per cent. His political master was engaged in the important conference on reparations taking place at The Hague, from where Addis reported on 21 August, following a conversation with Snowden that afternoon: 'I explained to him the financial position in London . . . It was only in order to avoid embarrassing his negotiations that Bank rate had not been raised . . .' Norman continued to stay his hand, until by the end of the month Snowden had more or less achieved his purpose at the conference. Would 'international' or 'national' considerations now prevail in terms of British monetary policy? The dilemma was nicely put by Addis, writing to Norman on the 31st: 'We are agreed that in the present condition of the foreign exchanges [i.e the drain of gold] it may not be possible to postpone much longer a rise in the rate, even although there may be little in the internal economic situation to indicate the expediency – indeed much the reverse – of such a step.'[9]

Addis himself, in terms of these competing priorities, was starting to shift his position, and on 4 September argued to Norman that 'with trade just a little better I still hope you may see your way to wait a little longer before raising Bank rate'. That same day Norman went, by invitation, to see Snowden at the Chancellor's country cottage in Surrey. There, according to Norman's memorandum of the conversation, they reached some sort of concordat:

> The Chancellor was persistent for a long time that a higher rate was no remedy; would harm trade; would be bitterly criticised; and would itself lead to still higher rates elsewhere and eventually here . . . The Governor said that his was the technical and financial side – the Chancellor's was the political and fiscal side. On this basis the Chancellor must now leave the Bank rate to the Governor, to which the Chancellor agreed, stipulating that the Governor should see him next week; the Governor promising that he would not this autumn put up the Bank Rate for fun but only when it was essential . . .

Put another way, Bank-rate decisions may still have remained formally with the Governor, but there was now an explicit acceptance on both sides that the political context was all-important. Norman duly saw Snowden the following Monday. 'We again agree on partnership,' Norman noted, '& leave it that BR *must* go to $6\frac{1}{2}$, but later rather than sooner if poss . . .'[10]

During their rural conversation on the 4th, Norman had 'described at length' the Bank's policy 'with regard to Rationalisation (Cotton and Iron and Steel)', stating that 'it was hoped to set up a separate Company to finance it and to have the best possible advice – including the best technical Steel man in the world'.[11] One implication was that Norman by this time clearly saw Hatry's ambitious steel rationalisation plans as a busted flush. Over the next fortnight the City's confidence in Hatry was palpably ebbing away, partly because of ugly rumours about the surprisingly large quantities of script certificates that were being dealt in in the Wakefield stock. By 17 September the shares in Hatry's concerns were starting to move into freefall, and not surprisingly his creditors took fright.[12] On Thursday the 19th a curt letter to Gialdini from James Gray of Lloyds Bank in Threadneedle Street informed him that, as far as the loans made to him and his colleagues were concerned, 'the Securities deposited with us, together with the credit balance on your [joint] account, are not available for any purpose until such time as the liability has been discharged'. Gialdini replied at once with an angry Marconigram: 'THOUGHT HAD IN YOU A FRIEND NOT AN ENEMY STOP . . . ANY BALANCE DUE WILL BE MADE GOOD STOP PROTEST EMBARGO SECURITIES AND BALANCE WILL HOLD YOU RESPONSIBLE IF ANY CHEQUES UNPAID'.[13]

These were fine-sounding phrases, but in fact Gialdini had already done a runner and was wiring from Lausanne. Meanwhile, that same day, Hatry and three youngish associates (Edmund Daniels, A.E. Tabor and J.G.G. Dixon) were meeting Hatry's tame guinea-pig Chairman, the 16th Marquess of Winchester, in Room 80 of the Charing Cross Hotel. 'We have sent for you,' Hatry said in words subsequently recalled by Winchester, 'to tell you we are all criminals.' Hatry and his trio then took a cab to the City, where at 3 Frederick's Place, home of Price Waterhouse, he made his confession to Sir Gilbert Garnsey, who had already started investigating the affairs of Austin Friars Trust on behalf of its worried bankers. Garnsey at once put Norman in the picture. By the Friday it was general knowledge that Hatry had crashed ('Stock Exchange depressed owing to Hatry scandals: very large amounts involved,' noted the Smith St Aubyn journal); Hatry himself made his formal confession to the Director of Public Prosecutions, vaingloriously (or selflessly, according to taste) taking complete responsibility for everything that had happened.

The *FT* on Saturday characteristically called for calm – 'It is desirable in the highest degree to realise that the ramifications and consequences of an isolated breakdown justify no general adverse reflection upon the business of the City as a whole' – but on Monday the atmosphere on the Stock Exchange was febrile, until it was established that the Hatry aspect of the impending fortnightly settlement, due on the 26th, would be indefinitely delayed. On Tuesday the 24th the leading joint-stock bankers assembled at the Bank of England, where Garnsey made a statement revealing that the total liabilities of the four parent Hatry companies amounted to some £21m, of which the Austin Friars Trust was responsible for some £15m. Among those present was Hyde of Midland, who recorded the discussion later in the meeting, after Garnsey had given details about the frauds in corporation scrip:

The Chairman [Archibald Campbell] of the Stock Exchange gave a statement of the number of bargains that were open for the present account which shewed that the group on balance had bought a fair number of the shares. The Governor stated that without committing ourselves to any particular line of action, the Banks should be sympathetic to the Stock Exchange customers and co-operate as far as possible with the Committee of the Stock Exchange. I said that while we would be sympathetic to all our customers with regard to the securities held at present, if sympathy was expected to mean we would be prepared to make advances against further blocks of shares of this character, I was afraid we should hardly be as sympathetic as that . . .

For all those who had gone too close to the Hatry flame these were intensely difficult, invidious days. 'I am sorry to hear of your losses but glad you have a goodly sum left in the business,' Norman wrote on the 27th to Percy Laming of the stockbrokers Cohen Laming Hoare. 'Of course this Hatry affair his smirched us all, especially in the eyes of foreigners, which we can ill afford, and I cannot but think that all who have been dealing with the group have knowingly been running an unnecessary risk.' The financier himself had been remanded in custody, and on the 30th Norman summed up his meeting that day with Garnsey in only seven words in his diary: 'I do not favour bail for Hatry.'[14]

The Hatry débâcle gave Norman the pretext he needed at last to raise Bank rate to $6\frac{1}{2}$ per cent, duly achieved on 26 September. Market reaction was subdued ('We have been expecting this for the last month,' noted Smith St Aubyn), but there was a distinct undertow of anxiety about the wider repercussions of the decision. In its leader entitled 'The Bank's Decision: Facing An Unpleasant Necessity', the *FT* whistled a familiar but nervous tune, defending the decision as taken 'in the interests not of any section, but of the country as a whole, which, as the great centre of international finance as well as of trade, can only be served by due consideration of all the surrounding conditions'; while the *Financial News* quoted a joint-stock banker remarking that 'it is hoped that the Labour Party will not make political capital out of the inconvenience caused by the inevitable change'.[15]

Although the trade union leader Ernest Bevin immediately referred to the Bank-rate increase as 'the challenge of the money-lenders to the State and to industry', the main immediate attack, perhaps predictably, came less from the Labour Party as such than from the press, especially the main Beaverbook papers. 'The Governor may be in touch with the volume of banking advances and trade bills,' the *Evening Standard* declared, 'but he is out of touch with the flesh and bones of industry'; and the *Daily Express* gave prominent billing to the views of various hostile industrialists, including the steel-and-coal magnate Lord Aberconway, who not only stated that 'the change will have decidedly detrimental effect on the principal industries of the country and it could not have come at a worse time', but added that 'I for one should like to know who precisely was responsible for the Bank's decision.' This and all the other reaction in the press – including a sharply hostile assessment from the *Daily Herald*, arguing that Bank rate would stay damagingly high as long as Britain needed to keep gold in order to stay on the gold standard – appeared on the 27th; and three days later Norman had a quarter of an hour with Claud Serocold of Cazenove's before he saw Garnsey. 'Dangers on Nat[1] Position of attacks by Beaverbrook, Melchett [chairman of ICI] &c' was apparently the theme of the stockbroker's visit, and his disquiet was symptomatic of the City starting to feel itself somewhat under siege.[16]

Within days that feeling was significantly heightened, when Snowden on 3 October announced to the Labour Party Conference at Brighton that he would shortly be appointing a committee to inquire into the relations between finance and industry. It was an announcement that had a specific history to it.[17] The burden imposed on industry by the return to the gold standard, the contrast between the continuing travails of the older industries and the relative ease with which overseas borrowers could come to the London capital market, the disreputable character of the 1928 domestic new-issue boom, recurrent controversies over Bank rate – all had contributed to an increasing general scepticism about the blessings conferred by the City of London. Or, in the words of the *Financial News* immediately after Snowden's announcement, 'noticeable in recent years' had been 'the growth of the belief that in some rather mysterious way "finance" is not organised for the general social advantage, but for the furtherance of the special interests of an inner world of financiers'. The possibility of a major monetary inquiry had been publicly discussed for at least two years before Labour returned to office in June 1929; and soon afterwards, on 12 July, Harvey sought to reassure the absent Norman:

> Questions are to be asked in the House as to whether the Government propose to hold an enquiry into the national systems of currency and credit, and I gather that if present intentions hold good the Chancellor will reply that if the question refers to the Gold Standard he has no intention of disturbing it, but that if it refers to an enquiry as to possible improvements in our system of banking and credit the matter is under consideration . . . Hopkins tells me in strict confidence that the Government are thinking of holding an enquiry of this nature and that the Treasury and the Chancellor

will endeavour to make the reference as vague and nebulous as possible and to avoid anything of an enquiry into the Constitution of the Bank. It will probably embrace such subjects as the direction of capital investment away from luxury trades and the extension of small banking facilities, co-operative and municipal banking, etc. We must not however lose sight of the fact that a demand may arise for the enquiry to include such questions as the Constitution of the Bank. Hopkins will endeavour to ensure that any Committee that may be appointed shall contain a preponderance of people whose currency views are known to be sound, or at least not unsound.[18]

Three days later Snowden made it clear in the Commons that any such inquiry would *not* consider the desirability, or otherwise, of maintaining the gold standard.

There the matter seems to have rested until late September. On the 27th, following the Bank-rate rise, the *Daily Herald* called urgently for an inquiry into credit policy; and three days later Norman – to whom the prospect of any inquiry, however diluted, was unpalatable – wrote to Hopkins at the Treasury in anticipation of likely attacks at the Labour Party Conference on 'the Bank Rate' and 'credit policy' and 'the effect of dear money on unemployment and other kindred subjects':

> Any such attack at Brighton or elsewhere can only be met in one way, namely, by a statement by the Chancellor or some other Minister that he regrets the Hatry incidents which do not affect the general situation and are in the hands of the Public Prosecutor: that he regrets the present Bank Rate but considers it unavoidable; that he has no intention of setting up any Committee on credit or kindred subjects: that he has no desire for any change in financial policy with which he is in agreement: and that the gold standard is an accepted fact and will by all means and at all times be maintained.

Norman added that 'the subject of a Committee' had 'never even been mentioned' to him by Snowden. This somewhat desperate attempt by Norman to hold the line worked only in part, for Snowden now came under strong pressure from Bevin in particular to announce an inquiry. This he duly did on 3 October – but in a mild speech influenced, and conceivably even semi-drafted, by Norman, to judge by the latter's diary entry for 6 p.m. the previous evening: 'Chanc^{or} at N° 11, about his speech at Brighton tomorrow'. Certainly, Norman on the 4th congratulated Snowden on his oration ('today it seems that you have got the extremists at both ends on your side'); while the City at large appears to have responded in a deliberately low-key way to Snowden's announcement. When an *FT* reporter sounded out 'a number of bankers', he found that

Two City Types:
1 ABOVE *Lord Cunliffe*;
2 RIGHT *Clarence Hatry*.

Life at 8 Bishopsgate:
Barings in autumn
1921.

3 *Lord*
Revelstoke
at his desk

4 *Lord Revelstoke's*
Secretarial
Department

5 *Typing*
Department

6 French Correspondence
Department

7 BELOW Postal Department

8 ABOVE Netball Team

9 Luncheon Room

10 Westminster Bank, Head Office at Lothbury, 1930s.

11 *Rebuilding the Bank of England.*

BANKERS

12 ABOVE *Reginald McKenna, seated,
chairman of Midland Bank, with his
vice-chairman and joint general managers.*
13 RIGHT *Sir Charles Lidbury*

14 ABOVE *Robert Brand*, right, *listens to his chairman at annual meeting of Lloyds Bank, 1930s*. 15 BELOW *Vivian Hugh Smith, 1st Lord Bicester.*

16 Billingsgate Market, 1937.

'it was only in exceptional cases that there was any disposition to question the wisdom of the decision, and even then the opposition took the form of merely doubting the efficacy of the inquiry and asking if it was proposed that the committee should teach bankers how to transact their business'.[19]

Nevertheless, the very fact of the inquiry was momentous, potentially putting the City under the microscope – and compelling it to justify itself – in a way that had not happened since at least the 1870s. Moreover, however much Snowden and the Treasury might seek to emasculate or ring-fence the inquiry, there could be no guarantee that they would succeed. There was also, approaching the tenth anniversary of Norman's rule, the personal element. 'Is there not some danger,' the Chancellor was asked by his private secretary (Grigg) a week after Norman's congratulatory letter, 'of giving the impression that the Governor is being put in the dock?'[20] For someone who dreaded the public glare, and was far from his best under it, this was an appalling prospect.

Even before the inquiry began, however, an era of capitalist history had ended. Throughout the summer of 1929 the bull market on Wall Street had continued to roar away, as the American financial authorities did too little too late to damp down the credit boom. It seemed a permanent state of grace, and in late July the very reputable stockbrokers Bourke, Schiff & Co of 10/11 Austin Friars sent out to valued clients such as Barings a four-page letter extolling 'the attractive investment opportunities which we believe are now afforded by the leading American Railroad Shares'. In addition, as a further come-on: 'We give you attached hereto a selection of some of the standard and most attractive issues, which we can recommend for substantial future appreciation in market value, and hope that the same may prove of interest and service to you.' Even some of those who had had doubts now stilled them – most famously Falk, who from June, following a further visit to the States, became what has been described as 'evangelically committed to the future of American securities'.[21]

The crash – one of the seminal events of the twentieth century – came in late October, with the immediate flavour caught by four *Financial News* front-page headlines between the 24th and the 30th: 'Wild Day in Wall St', 'Black Day on Wall Street', 'New Wall Street Debacle', 'New Big Break on Wall Street'. The overall atmosphere in the City itself was relatively calm, with no sightings of financiers throwing themselves off any of the few tall buildings, but for those intimately involved with American securities it was a dramatic enough time. A young clerk called

Marcus Colby, working for the small jobbing firm Halfhead & King, found himself in the thick of it:

Halfhead [i.e. the senior partner Robert Halfhead] was very friendly with an American firm, and used to do a lot of business in American stocks with this firm. About four days into the crash, at about 6 p.m., a cable came, and I was the only person left in the office dealing, and it said 'Repudiate all bargains done by a clerk without us telling him to do so'. So I rang up Halfhead, luckily I found him in and read the thing out to him. And he said, 'All right, go down and sell 5,000 Anaconda, which was a market leader, and 500,000 Steel'. Well, I rushed down to the market, battered my way into Bates [probably Harry Bates, a leading figure in the American after-hours street market] and sold the shares and I rang him up and said I'd sold and he said, 'Now go and liquidate the 8 shares which are open'. So I went round to Akroyd & Smithers [leading jobbers], and I said to the chap who I knew very well indeed, I said 'I want to sell these 8 stocks, and I don't want you to take an enormous turn out of me, I'll wait till you get the cable back.' You got a cable back in a minute in those days. And he got the cable back; I gave him a reasonable turn, went back, and by this time it was about a quarter past eight, and rang Halfhead, and told him what I'd done. He didn't even say 'thank you'. He said 'you can go home now'. I said 'thanks very much'. Well, that saved the firm from being hammered, I really do think, because they sold this bear; it was very clever, mind you, and I take my hat off to him. I think they made a profit in the end on the whole thing because we'd cut the losses which were fairly substantial, and they kept the bear going for about a week, and I reckon he was bloody clever . . .

I shall never forget, he said, 'I'd like to take you out to lunch for what you've done'. We went to Simpsons in the City and he said 'What would you like?' I said 'Roast beef and some potatoes'. He said, 'Don't bother about potatoes, you can spear one of mine.' That was the type of chap he was, having saved him from being hammered![22]

CHAPTER EIGHT

The Thrice-Tapped Nose

'It was, to begin with, a purely financial phenomenon,' the economic historian Sidney Pollard has written, 'but soon transmitted itself to the productive sectors, and as production and incomes contracted in the USA, this supply of dollars to the rest of the world fell drastically, and depression spread quickly to the rest of the world.' The profound consequences of the Wall Street Crash gradually sank in during the winter of 1929/30, with those having a large exposure taking the first hit. Falk paid for his folly in bulling New York by having to sell his country house, as well as falling out with Keynes over the running of their investment trust; while Kleinworts, so soon after losing almost £0.75m through Hatry, found its 'position' being 'discussed', in Grenfell's ominous words, on account of its close connection with Goldman Sachs of New York. The general mood in the City soon became distinctly downbeat, as a bear market set in and commercial activity as a whole declined. 'As far as one can see,' Barings told Kidder Peabody in December 1929, 'prospects are rather dreary', and a few weeks later Brown Shipley informed Brown Brothers that, according to the 'reports' it heard, 'most other businesses' had had to sustain 'considerable losses'. For at least a quarter of a million people working in the City the pervasive fear now became unemployment – the fear that runs through J.B. Priestley's sympathetic depiction of office life, *Angel Pavement*, published in 1930 – and even for those born above the salt these were somewhat anxious times, even as the generally untroubled tenor of day-to-day life continued. Writing from 28 Austin Friars on a Tuesday in February 1930, a young stockbroker, Frank Holt, reassured his father-in-law:

> I cabled you the glad news, a few minutes ago, it is a great relief to have it all fixed up, and they have dealt with me very generously. As I know you are interested in Yvonne & my affairs, I will explain the position to you.
> They are making me Junior Partner with a guaranteed minimum of £1,000 a year, and then a rising percentage of the profits, on a three year partnership contract, the reason being (all this is of course very private)

that one of the older partners wishes, at the end of 3 years, to retire. On the lowest profit figures that there have been for many years, I should get £2,000 my 1st year, £3,000 the 2nd, & £4,000 the 3rd. At the present moment business is dead all over the City so this year which is just finishing will be bad for all Brokers, but my interest does not start till 1st April and we will hope business in general will improve. At the end of 3 years we would make a new contract, which should be still more beneficial to me. However Yvonne and I are *very* happy and so are my Mother & Father.

Baby is in great form but is not talking much more . . . My old friend Eric is being married at St Margarets Westminster on Monday and I am to be the Best Man. Ion was to have been the smallest Bridesmaid (Eric is her godfather) but Yvonne thought she was *too* young . . .

Holt's father was Follett Holt, an important force in the South American railways world and a friend of Lord Faringdon, senior partner of the firm Greenwoods, which was now offering up such an attractive vista. Moreover, as was only reasonable to assume, business would soon be picking up. Indeed, the same month that Holt secured his berth at Greenwoods, another stockbroking firm, Cazenove's, felt confident enough to hold its first dinner party at the Savoy Hotel for partners and staff – a lavish six-course affair, complete with a cabaret of a comic man on a bike.[1]

*

Part of the City's malaise, funny turns on bicycles notwithstanding, was the reimposition of the informal embargo on foreign loans. The reason was the usual one – defence of the pound – and Snowden had made plain his wishes at the Mansion House in July 1929. Norman complied somewhat reluctantly. '"Embargo" may be a convenient but is not technically a correct expression,' he explained to Mildmay of Barings in January 1930. 'I am sure you know this well enough. But I do not wish the idea to get abroad that we in the City are as yet dominated by Westminster or Whitehall: we all prefer to accommodate ourselves to their views and so avoid such domination for the present.' But whatever the semantics, the reality was made clear to one merchant banker when he went to see Norman later that month: 'Wagg. No foreign Issues except by agreement with me.'[2]

Ineluctably, as the larger economic and financial situation deteriorated, the weight of influence shifted from the private financier towards the central banker, however circumscribed the latter was by the political process. The establishment of the Bank for International Settlements was an important symptom of this shift.[3] During their heart-to-heart in September 1929, Norman told Snowden that such an organisation 'seemed to be the only way for Europe out of financial chaos'. And: 'What was needed was a real understanding among the Central Banks, not for operations and cleverness in the early years of the Bank but from the Governors mixing on neutral soil at a B.I.S. Club. The Chancellor agreed to all this . . .' Negotiations and preparations continued during the winter, not always smoothly. 'The setting up of this B.I.S. seems to be continuous, controversial and troublesome and it certainly takes me *all* my time,' Norman wrote early in March; while a week later he conceded to another correspondent that 'there is no disguising the fact that, in some ways, the atmosphere in which the B.I.S. comes into existence is not what one might wish', in particular the fact that 'in Germany and in France the associations of the Bank with the Young Plan has led to its being mixed up, in the minds of the public, with politics and with Reparations'.[4] However, in April 1930 BIS did at last begin operations in Basle, and gradually developed into precisely that congenial, supra-political, European club of central bankers as originally envisaged by Norman: a club in which he himself was dominant.

A specific type of private financier now in steep decline was the British company promoter – and the last, larger-than-life specimen turned out to have been Clarence Hatry. He was tried in January 1930 and sentenced by Mr Justice Avory to fourteen years' penal servitude, the judge declaring that Hatry had committed 'the most appalling frauds that have ever disfigured the commercial reputation of this country'. According to Kinross, who was present, Hatry 'visibly reeled'. *The Times* the next morning was equally unforgiving: 'There have been rogues in finance before, but downright fraud and treason like this in the very citadel have not been known . . . A signalman has deliberately tampered with the signals. A rogue has traded upon the common expectation of integrity in finance . . .' But there was a fairly widespread feeling, in as well as outside the City, that the sentence was unduly harsh. That weekend there appeared in the *Sunday Express* under Hatry's name the first and, as it turned out, only instalment of 'The Road to Ruin':

> For the general public my sentence is the end of the Hatry crash.
> For me it is the beginning of the tragic years of isolation; the price of mistakes; the failure of my hopes, and the unhappy consequences of trying to achieve the impossible in the teeth of the fiercest opposition.
> In my life I have faced difficulties cheerfully; I have often carried through what others, less daring, have declared to be impossible.
> I have been vanquished within sight of the end of the most important

task an Englishman has ever undertaken. The motives that impelled me on this course were influenced by genuine desire to be of real service to the country . . .

For such irregularities as I was guilty of I have now to make amends. I have not made, nor do I make now, any attempt to shift the blame. As the head of the greatest individual financial enterprise in the City of London I accept my responsibility. I am no coward.

As soon as I realised that my hopes of rectifying what I had done were doomed to failure I informed the authorities of the true position. I saw the road along which it led, but I did not shirk.

Throughout the trial I have watched the icy features of the judge and wondered what he would have to say to me in the end. He speaks for the law, but I want the public to know that, as has been shown, I put in everything I possessed to save the situation. No man could do more.

In the course of my career I have made fortunes for many. I have been the friend of peers and men of distinction in the highest circles. The best are my friends still . . .

Petitioning from some of those friends, allied to impeccable conduct, eventually led to his being released from prison in 1939. During the war he borrowed sufficient money to buy Hatchards bookshop in Piccadilly. But one quarter in the City still did not forgive and forget. 'The idea that friend Hatry should have any influence in deciding what kind of books a large number of our fellow countrymen should read is repugnant,' the Bank of England's Deputy Governor, Basil Catterns, wrote indignantly to one of the Bank's directors, Isaac Pitman, after he had sent him a copy of the *Bookseller*, in which Hatry explained why he had taken up this line of business. In fact, for several years his new enterprise flourished, as he expanded and bought up various printing and publishing companies; however, he over-reached himself, as in the late 1920s, and in the end it all collapsed. Yet amazingly, after a period of retirement, he came back, and in the late 1950s was reported to be acquiring coffee bars in the West End, a ghostly figure in the world of *Expresso Bongo*. He eventually died in 1965.[5]

Back in the winter of 1929/30, Hatry had left a considerable mess behind him. The Stock Exchange settlement of his shares was postponed until 13 February, as Norman explained that day to Sir Osborne Smith, his representative at the Imperial Bank of India:

> The delay was due to the efforts made by a Stock Exchange Committee to draw up a scheme under which the general public should suffer no loss from a delivery of bad securities and to make a pool for professional losses . . . Of a total sum of £1,000,000 required for the pool, £800,000 was put

up by the brokers and jobbers interested, the remaining £200,000 being contributed actually or ostensibly by other Stock Exchange firms, etc. A considerable portion of it was in fact put up by the Banks, on the basis of contributions having no reference to whether, or the extent to which, they had suffered losses. The fund has been vested in the Royal Exchange Assurance, which will acquire all shares sold and in dealing with the genuine investing public will pay for them in full . . . While the scheme does not of course protect from loss any person who bought Hatry shares at an excessive price, it aims at protecting him from the further consequences of having acquired forged shares. It is an expression of the City's desire to vindicate its reputation for honest dealing and to maintain the trustworthiness of delivered shares.

Inevitably there had been considerable haggling behind the scenes, with the Stock Exchange firms originally asking the banks to contribute £250,000 and having to settle for about half of that. However, taken as a whole, the action was a notable one, reflecting a much sharper sense on the Stock Exchange's part that it was no longer just a private club, but had major public responsibilities. The Stock Exchange Committee had been moving in this direction since the war – prohibiting pre-allotment dealings, or dealing in new securities without permission – but this resolution of the Hatry crash had symbolic as well as substantive importance. There was still a long way to go, especially in terms of stronger disclosure rules prior to the listing of companies, but *caveat emptor* was no longer the ruling orthodoxy.[6]

Meanwhile, his efforts given a renewed urgency by the economic downturn, Norman continued to tread in industrial finance where no Governor had trod before. A significant innovation was the backing that he gave from January 1930 to hire-purchase finance, through a major injection of capital into the City-based finance house United Dominions Trust, run along consciously American lines by J. Gibson Jarvie. Norman's motive was partly to improve the national credit machinery, partly to keep government out of the money market. Jarvie himself, having been vetted by Peacock as to his honesty and prudence, had been summoned to the Governor's room the previous November: 'Jarvie. Generally as to *his* objects in instalment buying finance: a Crusade to marry Finance & Industry but *only* rationalised industry: no luxuries.'[7]

It was a deft card that Jarvie played, for rationalisation had become *the* Norman tune in the course of 1929.[8] Typical was his affirmation in September to Sir Hugh Reid, a leading figure in the locomotive industry: 'I am led to believe that the hope for industry in this country lies in Rationalisation. I do not attempt to define the word but I am a strong supporter of the idea to which I hope in one way or another to devote the prestige of the Bank of England.' The immediate problem was how to move from an *ad hoc* basis of attempting this to something more structured – or, as Norman had put it to Peacock a few weeks earlier, how to get all the various industrial questions out of his room 'and on a self-supporting and conducting basis'. Norman was extremely unwilling, however, to forgo ultimate control, as he showed in early October when he effectively warned off one merchant banker who was keen to take an individual initiative: 'A de Rothschild . . . Steel Industries: ?go into the Hatry position with idea of purchase of control. I advise him to go slow: complicated: management difficult: personal troubles: part of larger question. He will consider.'[9] Rothschilds controlling the British steel industry – it was a tantalising prospect, and one that would have confounded the usual assumptions about cosmopolitan finance, but it was never Norman's vision, least of all at this particular juncture. It was not that he was unconscious of the needs of industry; but he was at least as concerned that his own institution now justify itself to a wider constituency.

In November 1929 the Bank of England established Securities Management Trust, essentially a group of experts to advise Norman and see through rationalisation schemes. Its board included the leading industrialist Sir Andrew Duncan and the accountant Sir James Cooper, while its Managing Director from March 1930 was Charles Bruce Gardner, an experienced iron and steel manufacturer who, according to a *Financial News* profile, 'leaves the flamboyancy of the Staffordshire tradition to Mr Arnold Bennett'. SMT was a not unimpressive body, but it had only limited managerial resources and was further handicapped by its lack of someone familiar with the peculiar problems of the cotton industry.[10] Norman himself was Chairman and, even though the problems of industry had nominally left his room, was temperamentally incapable of not being closely involved on a day-to-day level.

The strain was considerable. 'The process of rationalisation – if indeed it is a process – is turning our hairs grey,' he wrote only half in jest to Walter Stewart on 8 January 1930, 'and will surely take mine in sorrow and disappointment to the grave.' The stakes could not have been higher. Two days later the Labour minister J.H. Thomas, who had been charged to deal with unemployment, gave an important speech in Manchester to local businessmen. A key passage in it had been drafted by the Bank:

> As a result of consultations which I have had, I am now in a position to state that the City is deeply interested in placing industry upon a broad and

sound basis and ready to support any plans that in its opinion lead to this end. Those in the City who have been studying this matter are convinced that a number of our important industries must be fundamentally reorganised and modernised in order to be able to produce at prices which will enable them to compete with the world. Industries which propose schemes that, in the opinion of those advising the City, conform to this requirement will receive the most sympathetic consideration and the co-operation of the City in working out plans and finding the necessary finance.

In a sense it was not just the Bank of England, or even just the City, but capitalism itself that was on trial. Justifying to the Court in November the creation of SMT, Norman had explained 'at considerable length the present position in regard to industry generally and his views as to the necessary steps to restore it to a healthy condition by private enterprise and without government intervention'. The credibility problem, not only on the left, was encapsulated by the thoughts of the twenty-seventh Earl of Crawford. In the context of his family firm, the Wigan Iron and Coal Co, being about to be 'rationalised' and become part of the Lancashire Steel Corporation, he visited Threadneedle Street in January 1930 (on the 7th, perhaps contributing to Norman's grey hairs) and was distinctly underwhelmed by the Governor and his colleagues: 'In their own affairs they have never given more employment than that vouchsafed to gardener, chauffeur, and valet. They are too much detached from the realities of production with its tremendous problems; they are usurers and nothing else ... The banks sail serenely above the tempests of industrial trouble.'[11]

Not long afterwards, on 22 February, Norman outlined to Sir Warren Fisher at the Treasury his plans for a new organisation to complement SMT:

It looks as if, within a couple of weeks, we should be setting up a new private Company to finance rationalised industry. This is a brief and particular object which should be accomplished within 5 years or never: therefore at the end of 5 years the Company will be liquidated. Moreover this object requires large credit but little money, so the Company will have a nominal capital of £4,000,000, £5,000,000 or £6,000,000 and a small paid-up capital. Thus it may come to be the outward and visible sign of what Mr Thomas describes as 'the City'.

The immediate process took rather longer, but over the next few weeks a name emerged – the Bankers' Industrial Development Company – and a board was chosen; it comprised Norman as Chairman, Sir Guy Granet of

Higginsons, Baron Bruno Schröder, Alfred Wagg, Peacock and Gardner, with Granet, Albert Pam and Nigel Campbell as alternates to Norman, Schröder and Wagg respectively. 'It is the Governor's intention,' noted his private secretary Ernest Skinner in early March, 'that the Directors of the new concern should work mainly by means of their alternates.'

Norman spent much of March reassuring and encouraging potential backers. He emphasised the finite nature of the commitment ('I believe that just as we must now go into Industry so we must be sure that we get out of it!' he wrote to one correspondent) and expressed himself 'hopeful that practically every domestic Bank and Issuing House will become a shareholder, thus showing their united willingness to recognise the conditions of today and to offer a way for the re-establishment of our basic industries'. Inevitably he encountered some prickliness, not only from Scottish banks, which tended to view rationalisation as a metropolitan plot. He saw one malcontent on the 18th: 'R H Brand, as to BIDCo complains of competition of firms with Directors on board. I say he sh^d see Granet – all bosh!' On the whole, however, the City saw no alternative but to fall into line, typified by the response from New Court on the 25th. 'I have now had an opportunity of consulting my brother,' Lionel de Rothschild informed Norman, 'and, needless to say, he is just as anxious as I am to do anything that is possible to meet your wishes and we shall be very pleased to take one share of £100,000 in your new company ...' The Bank itself subscribed £1.5m of BIDC's nominal capital of £6m, with the remainder coming from over forty other institutions, almost entirely clearing banks, merchant banks and issuing houses. 'I am not inviting the Prudential,' Norman told Granet, 'because their game is investment and not finance,' but otherwise there were few significant absentees.[12]

Norman's other, more traditional response to the onset of economic depression was of course through monetary policy.[13] At first the Bank reacted with commendable promptness, getting Bank rate down to 5 per cent by the middle of December 1929. Historically speaking, however, this was still a steep rate; and over the next two and a half months, despite palpable evidence of rapidly deepening depression, Norman's inherent mistrust of cheap money, his nervousness about jeopardising Britain's position in relation to the gold standard, and his largely unavailing wish to co-ordinate monetary policy with other central bankers all combined to create what was undoubtedly a damaging monetary stance. Hopkins at the Treasury was cogently pushing for cheaper money as early as 19 December; but although the rate was at last reduced to $4\frac{1}{2}$ per cent on 6 February, there was then another wasted month as Norman put back the lights to red. For Addis in particular it was a hugely frustrating experience:

> *12 February*. Treasury Com. A long argument on reduction of Bank rate, in which Stamp and I were defeated.
> *19 February*. Long Treasury Committee where I had Stamp's support in suggesting reduction of Bank rate, but Norman defeated us.
> *25 February*. Private talk about reducing Bank rate with Peacock, Cullen & Lubbock & Harvey, but could not persuade them in absence of Governor.
> *26 February*. A long Treasury Committee about the rate.
> *5 March*. Treasury Committee at 12. Bk rate reduced to 4% – at last!

A fortnight later another half-point was clipped off, but again it was too little too late. 'The Bank's policy seems to me quite inexplicable except by an unreasoning terror of cheap money,' Grigg had complained to Hopkins at the end of February, and it was a plausible assessment, applicable not only to the peculiarly fraught circumstances of 1930.[14]

*

By this time Norman was long used to such grumbles; what he was not used to was having to justify himself. The Committee on Finance and Industry cast a long, dark shadow after it had been announced by Snowden in October 1929.[15] The Scottish lawyer Lord Macmillan, a former Advocate-General, was appointed Chairman, while members included Lord Bradbury (of Treasury fame), Brand, McKenna, Lubbock, Keynes and Bevin. It was an intriguing mix, especially featuring as it did Keynes and McKenna, over the years the two most trenchant critics of monetary orthodoxy. But however apprehensive the Bank of England was, almost certainly the working assumption of most City grandees was that the committee would become the usual ineffectual talking-shop, of which seemingly there had been so many since 1914. Certainly that was Sir Alexander Kleinwort's assumption. 'Your Committees of Enquiry always make me smile,' he wrote to Brand on 8 November. 'The real trouble is that our cost of production is too high and neither the Conservatives nor the Liberals nor Labour can force the World to pay them . . . Let the Gov. economize and reduce taxation and drop all that nonsense abt maintaining the standard of living.' Nor were the committee's members themselves necessarily much more sanguine, with Brand telling Macmillan a fortnight later that he was 'inclined to agree' with Keynes that on 'fundamental matters the evidence we shall get from the ordinary banker and industrialist will be of very little assistance'.[16]

On 26 November, two days before he was due to be the first witness, Norman jotted in his diary: 'Bed: seedy'. Three days later he was sailing to the Mediterranean, for a convalescent cruise that lasted several weeks. The breakdown was real – 'I have been away for a month to get my fire-box patched because the fire burnt it through,' he would write in early January 1930 to Campbell of Helbert Wagg – but the timing was fortuitous and perhaps affected by the imminent ordeal. Instead, it was his deputy Harvey who took the stand, and in five days of evidence between 28 November and 14 December he made a more than capable job, concentrating mainly on explaining the mechanics of the Bank of England rather than attempting to elucidate or justify questions of high policy. 'On one important matter I think you may make your mind quite easy,' he wrote to Norman soon after his fifth appearance. 'To judge by what I have heard through one or two side channels, from a very charming letter which I have received from Keynes and from an hour's conversation which I had two days ago with the Chancellor, I think you may feel satisfied that whatever the outcome of the Committee may be, we at any rate have nothing to fear.'[17] Presumably Keynes had reassured Harvey that he did not question the importance of having a strong central bank; this did not mean that he endorsed the current or past behaviour of that central bank. Put another way, Norman's personal ordeal was only postponed.

As the committee got into its stride, perhaps the two most interesting early witnesses, either side of Christmas, were Goodenough of Barclays and Kindersley of Lazards. 'We have been going through a time of great world re-adjustments and there have been great possibilities and attempts to move the centre away from London to other parts of the world,' Goodenough responded, after being asked by Macmillan how far London was maintaining its pre-war position. 'My own opinion is, and always has been, that they could not succeed, largely because other markets have not the knowledge.' A little later he had a piquant exchange with another member of the committee, the economist Theodore Gregory:

> Have you considered at all the possibility of British joint stock banks undertaking the issue of long-term loans for British industry, acting somewhat in the manner of the German banks? – Long-term loans?
> Yes, public loans. – You mean to hold them?
> Well, you would have to hold them until there was a prospect of their

having some success, and you would then issue them to the public? – That, I think, would be very undesirable.

May I ask why? – Because it would bring us eventually into almost the control of an industry, a thing which we do not understand.

Kindersley, from his different vantage point, was similarly concerned to defend specialisation, in his case the accepting function of the accepting houses. Describing accepting as only 'a side line' for the joint-stock banks, he emphasised that 'it requires a very great deal of care, a very great deal of watching, a very great deal of travelling and a very careful study of world conditions, and it is the chief business of the partners of any acceptance house', in that 'they have not got other things equally important for them to do and they have to attend to it'. He was not overly upset about the recent failure of the Accepting Houses Committee to establish a central clearing house for information with regard to acceptances: 'My own view is that each acceptance house must depend upon its own skill and its own connections; but it is very difficult, owing to questions of disclosure of clients and so on, to get unanimity on that point.' And he insisted that London was still the accepting centre of the world: 'The sterling bill is still the best; the world much prefers it, everything else being equal, and London's discount facilities are so unrivalled; there is nothing like them in New York.'

Kindersley's belief in specialisation likewise shaped his reply after Macmillan had asked whether domestic industry was starved because of preponderant foreign investment:

> We do not come very much into contact with industry for this reason, an acceptance house must keep its funds liquid and it has to confine itself to the issue of what it believes to be first class bonds or debentures, it cannot assume liabilities which are going to mean a great locking up of monies, or it cannot father a particular industry. It cannot father a company; in my opinion, it should not.

Keynes pressed home to Kindersley the depressing implications of this unambitious attitude to industry on the part of finance:

> Take an English industrial concern of good credit but of small size which wants to raise, say, £50,000 on debentures, any larger sum being out of proportion to its scale. Is there any regular machinery through which its requirements can be satisfied? – Well, I am bound to say I do not know of any myself. I think it is a great weakness in the City of London that there is not such machinery. It is very difficult to place small issues . . . The average investor today does not like to have anything without a market, and you

cannot possibly have a market with £50,000 of stock or £100,000 of stock for that matter.[18]

The two Ks may not have been the first to identify this gap in the system, but it was an important moment of consensus in the history of industrial finance.

February was dominated by the evidence of some of the leading joint-stock bankers. Keynes and Frater Taylor (also on the committee) gave the palm to John Rae of Westminster Bank; but as Rae himself modestly added, passing this gratifying piece of news on to his Chairman, Hugh Tennant, 'I merely mention this as I have heard that the Bankers' evidence had not impressed the members too favourably.' Much of that evidence had been fairly defensive in character, especially in relation to the role of bankers *vis-à-vis* industry. Before going on to stress the absolutely paramount importance of liquidity to any deposit-taking institution, J.W. Beaumont Pease, Chairman of Lloyds, set the tone:

> I would like to say that on general grounds there has been a certain criticism of banks, that they ought to take charge of industry much more than they do, and that it is the function of a bank, if they see any particular industry is in distress from want of reorganisation, to take the initiative in dictating to that industry that some steps of that sort ought to be taken. It certainly is my view that that is not one of the functions of our English joint stock banks. I do not think they are qualified by knowledge, in the first place ...

Yet whatever the understandable concerns about illiquidity or ignorance, there remained no satisfactory answer to the fundamental complaint of E.L. Payton of the National Union of Manufacturers, giving evidence later in February:

> Where industry finds finance lacking is, that if we have quite a good business, we will say, in Birmingham that requires £250,000 capital, we cannot get it. The finance house, or the stockbroker, or the company promoter, say 'The business is much too small for us; we cannot bother about it; there is nothing to be made out of it; we cannot do it.' We go to the bank and they say 'No, we cannot lend you permanent capital in connection with this business.'[19]

£250,000 was at the very top end of the parameters of the existing gap in the provision of industrial finance, but again this was important evidence – and implicitly critical of the merchant banks at least as much as of the clearing banks.

Between 20 February and 21 March the committee also had six private sessions, not included in the official minutes of evidence. They mainly comprised lengthy tutorials by Keynes, but there were some interesting moments of discussion, if rarely featuring the former Deputy Governor, Cecil Lubbock. Looking ahead to the eventual report, McKenna spoke as chairman of the world's biggest bank at a time of increasing monetary delicacy: 'I would not discuss the gold standard if it is possible to avoid it, but I do think we might reasonably discuss certain remedies in the working of the gold standard.' To which Keynes agreed: 'One need not be supposed to have complete confidence in the remedies that one is recommending.' Another time, the question came up of the City's traditional bias towards lending overseas:

> *Keynes:* I think issuing houses could do an immense amount towards increasing home investment relative to foreign if they definitely took up a policy.
> *Brand:* I agree, if they found good home investments which looked profitable, but Mr Keynes's whole point, which I think is true, is that profits are too low.
> *Keynes:* Quite apart from that, I think that there is reason to suppose that they have not pursued a passionate policy of trying to find everything they could at home in preference to abroad.
> *Brand:* Quite, but it is a mistake to think that the issuing houses can do as much as stockbrokers.
> *Keynes:* Yes, I think that is so.

That same tension, between the international and the national, also preoccupied the committee in relation to the larger financial mechanism. 'Is the general position you are placing before us this,' Macmillan asked McKenna at the session on 21 March, 'that the method by which the Bank of England and the Treasury work our monetary system is dictated more by international considerations than by domestic considerations?' To which McKenna replied, with unusual simplicity: 'I should say solely by money market considerations.' But then, later in the session, he agreed: 'What I would like to ascertain is whether the tradition of the Bank actually takes into account the industry of the country or purely the money market? Following Sir Ernest Harvey's evidence right through, and I read it again and again, it seemed to me that the international money market was the sole guiding principle up to quite recently . . .' The last few words were a significant qualification, but Bevin made it clear that in his view the domestic consequences of monetary policy came a poor fourth in the Bank of England's eyes behind the defence of sterling, adherence to the gold standard and the position of London as an international financial centre.[20] For this trade unionist, more than for perhaps any other member of the committee, the prospect of the Governor at last giving evidence was particularly momentous.

Five days later, on the morning of the 26th, Norman was on the spot. He was fortunate to find in Macmillan a chairman who had no wish to embarrass his witness:

> In your opinion, I gather, the advantages of maintaining the international position outweigh in the public interest the internal disadvantages which may accrue from the use of the means at your disposal? – Yes, I think that the disadvantages to the internal position are relatively small compared with the advantages to the external position.
>
> What is the benefit to industry of the maintenance of the international position? – This is a very technical question which I am ill equipped to explain, but the whole international position has preserved for us in this country the wonderful position which we have inherited, which was for a while thought perhaps to be in jeopardy, which to a large extent, though not to the same extent, has been re-established. We are still to a large extent international bankers. We have great international trade and commerce out of which I believe considerable profit is made; we do maintain huge international markets, a free gold market, a free exchange market – perhaps the freest almost in the world – and all of those things, and the confidence and credit which go with them are greatly to the interest of industry as well as to the interest of finance and commerce in the long run.
>
> One of the criticisms which has been made is that while the policy pursued may have been excellent from the point of view of the financiers of the City of London, it has not benefitted the industries of this country, that the considerations which have moved that policy have been directed rather to the financial side than to the plain man's industry? – Yes. Of course, industry has had ill luck, shall I say, and has been in a very unfortunate position and from one reason and another has suffered particularly. I agree; I am sure that is true.
>
> There has been no doubt a conspiracy of causes at work? – Almost; yes.

Macmillan then asked Norman how far he thought the present 'abnormal' industrial situation was 'attributable to financial considerations'. The Governor declined to yield ground: 'Broadly speaking, I do not think that the financial machine is at fault. I think, to use your expression, that industry has had a series of misfortunes – was it?'

At this point Bevin intervened, pressing Norman to concede that one of those misfortunes had been the decision in 1925 to return to gold at the pre-war parity. 'I do not attribute the ills of industry in the main to that change,' Norman adamantly maintained. Keynes, with McKenna at his side, then got technical, seizing on Norman's contention that the impact of a rise in Bank rate was mainly psychological on the money market, with only a 'very small' curtailment to the overall mass of credit:

What would you call 'small'? Do you mean if securities at the Bank of England were reduced by, say, £5,000,000 you would call that 'small'? – I cannot name a figure of that kind, because the conditions change so often, and the whole volume changes so often, but what I mean is that the amount of security operations necessary to make a Rate effective is as a rule very small compared to the amount of securities which are in the market.

Of course £5,000,000 would be small in relation to that? – Very small. I am not thinking of £5,000,000 as an absolute figure.

If the amount of assets held by the Bank of England were reduced by £5,000,000 by how much would that reduce bank credit throughout the country? – I think your neighbour would tell you that best.

Mr McKenna: About £50,000,000 – ten times the amount? – I do not know that that is necessarily so.

Mr Keynes: You do not know? – Ten to one is an arbitrary reckoning based on the bankers' normal percentage of cash.

Would the curtailment of credit by £50,000,000 have no effect of any importance on industry? – I do not think it would; I would be surprised if it had much effect beyond the money market unless of course it had to be continued over an extended period.

In some discussions we have had in this Committee I began by setting forth what I believed to be the orthodox theory of the Bank Rate, the theory that I thought all authorities would accept. What you have been telling us today very nearly amounts to a repudiation of that theory? – I did not mean to repudiate it, as I understand it . . .

Bevin, less concerned to expose Norman's technical shortcomings, returned to the wider attack:

Having regard to the fact that the workpeople at home have to suffer the biggest blow of unemployment and the depression of their standard of life, can you see any way to separate the national and the international policies, so that the effect of restoring the gold position internationally can be in some way modified in its effect upon British industry? – I believe it is absolutely impossible to have two separate policies . . .

Supposing, for instance, you have to stop your gold flowing out, and therefore restrict credit, is it not possible to have a conscious direction of credit under those circumstances to the home market? – And to maintain, as it were, two separate supplies of credit at different rates?

Yes? – I do not think so.

Nor was Norman willing to offer comfort in another, related area:

> *Mr Keynes:* You would not expect rationalisation to increase employment until a very late date? – Until a late date.
>
> So you look forward to the present level of unemployment remaining for some considerable time to come? – I could not tell you; I do not know about that, but I agree that rationalisation would only deal with it at a late date.
>
> *Mr Bevin:* And would increase the progress of unemployment? – It is apt to do so.
>
> You have no suggestion to put to us how the Bank's policy can help us over that interim period? – No; none.

There was still time for McKenna to give the knife one last, sardonic twist. 'You do not think there is any certain relation between fluctuations in the volume of credit and fluctuations in employment?' he asked Norman. 'No, I am not sure that there is.' McKenna affected incredulity: 'You do not know?' To which Norman could only respond: 'There may or there may not be.'

The final stretch of Norman's longest morning was dominated by Bevin:

> I have listened to the evidence of the bankers to this Committee, and while industrialists have been urged to get out of their rut and to take a bigger view, I am bound to say that the very ugly feeling left in my mind is that so far as the City is concerned it is still within 'the mile' in the main, that it does not go outside its own financial 'mile' to consider these wider problems of industry, except one or two individuals like yourself who have been tackling the problem recently. I am wondering what has been done in the banking world in this matter, coincident with the inducement and the urge for industry to move beyond a single unit; how far it has received the consideration of the banking world and the financial world? – I cannot tell you. You are speaking generally, are you not?
>
> Generally, yes? – Are you thinking that the international knowledge and information which those who have come before have given has been inadequate; that is to say, they have not had due regard to the international position?
>
> No, I am thinking of their industrial knowledge. (*Chairman*): I think that what Mr Bevin really means is this. Industry is being urged to rationalise itself. Is it not time that the banks rationalise themselves? Is not that the

point, Mr Bevin? (*Mr Bevin*): Yes . . . – What I want to understand is what you are saying. The complaint against these bankers, of whom I am one, which I understand you to make – is it that their knowledge of international affairs is too little or that their knowledge of industrial affairs is too little, or is it that that knowledge is not sufficiently theoretical, not sufficiently technical, as you would have it?

It is not sufficiently collective: each is moving in his own little circle as far as I have been able to see it . . . As I have listened to bankers, they still talk of their customers in the limited sphere of firms and not industry, and no consideration, collectively or technically, or from the point of view of national economics, appears to have been given to the wider concept of the position and the part they have to play in it? – They are coming to it.

'That is encouraging,' responded Bevin, though possibly not in the most enthusiastic of voices. The concluding exchange was fruitless but revealing:

> *Norman:* May I say a word? Of course, you may complain of me, Mr Bevin, or of those bankers you have seen, that the evidence they have given you comes through their nose and is not sufficiently technical or expert. Of course, that may in some measure be true; I plead guilty to it myself to some extent, and it is a curious thing, the extent to which many of those who inhabit the City of London find difficulty in stating the reasons for the faith that is in them. Mr Keynes must know that very well.
> *Macmillan:* Of course, I suppose even a trade union leader sometimes acts by faith.
> *Bevin:* And finds that it has been misplaced.[21]

The time was ten to one, Norman had been giving evidence for over two hours, and he and Macmillan now repaired to the Athenaeum for lunch.

With his tail between his legs, Norman returned to Threadneedle Street in the afternoon. He was, according to Harvey, 'in a very depressed state', telling his deputy that 'he felt he had been quite unable to deal satisfactorily with the questions which had been addressed to him'. Next day Norman wrote to Gregory, inviting him to lunch and confessing that 'being ignorant of the individuals as well as of the particular subject, I found myself in some difficulty at yesterday's meeting of the Macmillan Committee'. In large part his problem had been, as he had conceded rather disarmingly to Bevin, that of articulating what was essentially instinctive behaviour. The secretary of the committee would recall how at one point, asked how he knew something, Norman simply replied by tapping his nose three times. Another moment not recorded in the minutes, but recalled by Brand, was when Macmillan told Norman that his committee would be very interested to hear the Governor's reasons for forming BIDC; to which Norman replied, 'Reasons, Mr Chairman, I don't have reasons. I have instincts.'[22]

In any event, it was not only Norman himself who was dismayed. 'Talk with Harvey & Lubbock about Governor's evidence before Macmillan's Committee,' noted Addis on the 31st. 'It fills us with consternation. It is deplorable. Difficulty is how to revise it.' Over the next day or two quite a few tactful amendments were made – for example, in answer to Bevin's question as to whether rationalisation would increase unemployment, the helpful word 'temporarily' was added to the original, more discouraging answer that 'it is apt to do so' – but, contrary to subsequent myth-making, no fundamental doctoring of the evidence took place. 'If the corrections appear at first sight to be rather numerous,' Norman wrote on 2 April, returning his copy of the transcript to the committee's secretary, 'you will see on examination that they are merely by way of re-arrangement of my answers.'[23] No amount of minor tinkering, however, could disguise the fact that it had been a traumatic experience – for the Bank as well as for Norman. Henceforth the Old Lady would take great care not to go into public battle again without very carefully prepared lines of argument.

Yet arguably it was as frustrating an experience for Keynes as for anyone. Part of him may have been motivated by revenge, the wish to humiliate Norman, but at least as large a part wanted to engage in constructive, hopefully persuasive dialogue with the man who really mattered. Virginia Woolf, four years later, would listen to Keynes recalling the experience: 'M. [Maynard] talked about Montagu Norman the Governor of the B. of E. an elf; an artist, sitting with his cloak round him hunched up, saying "I cant remember –" thus evading all questions, & triumphing . . .'[24]

*

Norman, commented Addis on 7 May 1930, 'grows more & more temperamental, freakish & paradoxical'; but a fortnight later a private meeting of the Committee of Treasury considered Norman's re-election as Governor from the following spring, and Addis could only reflect, 'of course he must go on if he wants to'. Norman did want to, however great the strain of continuing to play the gold-standard game in a fundamentally weakened condition. Even when there was a rare hopeful sign of a return to happier times, with a temporary improvement in the gold position leading to a relaxation in April of the embargo on foreign loans, it proved a false dawn. Not only did the gold position deteriorate (making it impossible for Bank rate to be lowered from the 3 per cent at which it rested from the start of May), but also, as Norman remarked in June to Sir Edgar Horne (Chairman of the Prudential), 'recently several foreign loans have been far less successful than it was hoped they would be and the outlook as you know is pessimistic'. Nor, in the context of the continuing bear market, did domestic issues flourish, though that same month one British company had no difficulty raising £2m. 'The name and business of Marks & Spencer are so well known as to need no introduction to investors,' the *FT* said when the prospectus was published. On the Stock Exchange itself, the depressed mood had been summed up in May by the findings of a sub-committee appointed to consider the re-election of persons of ex-enemy birth who had previously been not re-elected. It reported that such re-elections *en bloc* would be 'extremely unpopular' in the House.[25] Innate prejudice allied to a diminishing cake to share – it was an immovable combination.

One youngish stockbroker could see no way out. 'He is a bounder, a climber, a shoving young man, who wants to be smart, cultivated, go-ahead & all the rest of it,' Virginia Woolf wrote in 1928 of Sidney Russell Cooke, a pre-war pupil of Keynes who was now a partner in Rowe & Pitman. But to his friend Nicholas Davenport (also with Rowe & Pitman, though in a humbler capacity), Cooke was 'a highly sensitive young man beneath his acquired panache – he was in fact, an intellectual *manqué* . . .' Davenport would recall a classic City tragedy:

> I had been privileged to participate in a syndicate formed by the partners of Rowe & Pitman and Schröders to take up a block of Chase National Bank common stock – one of the high-flyers of Wall Street. For some weeks the shares sky-rocketed and we were counting our wonderful profits and then came the crash. The stock fell by 20 or 30 or 40 points a day. I saw the partners of Rowe & Pitman hanging on to the ticker-tape, their faces white and drawn, watching their money vanish into thin air. My participation was only the dollar equivalent of £500: the average partner lost over £5,000 in this little flutter . . .
>
> I could see that partnership worries were breaking his [Cooke's] nerve. One day during the nerve-racking bear market he said to his senior partner: 'Lancie, the time is coming when you will go into the market and not find a bid in a hundred War Loan' (meaning £100,000). The great man replied: 'Sidney, I think you are losing your judgement.' Turning his back on Sidney he walked out of the room. The young man, who had been the 'blue-eyed' boy of the firm, now found himself cold-shouldered by his senior partner. It was more than he could bear. A nervous breakdown followed soon after. After nursing-home treatment Sidney went off on a voyage. He came back

apparently restored to health. I went to dine with him alone in my flat in the Inner Temple which he then rented from me. He seemed calm, but a little distrait. We played bézique in silence. The next morning, 3 July 1930, he was discovered dead with his sporting gun beside him. I had lost my best friend, and Rowe & Pitman their most intelligent partner.

'Lancie' was the formidable Lancelot Hugh Smith, who had once had Jean Rhys as his mistress before brutally pensioning her off; it was the maid, Miss Violet Fancy, who found the body lying on the floor of the dining-room; Cooke's wife, daughter of the captain of the *Titanic*, was at the time in a nursing home in Norfolk Square. At the inquest on the 4th, at which Walter Monckton QC was 'present on behalf of the relatives', a cousin, Oliver Paget-Cooke, declared that Cooke 'had no financial worry, but absolutely the reverse'; while Fred Pitman (the nominal senior partner) declared that he had last seen Cooke on the afternoon of the 2nd in his office in Bishopsgate, where 'he seemed in exceptionally good health and had no worries'. The jury endorsed this optimistic scenario, returning a verdict of accidental death, after evidence had been given 'to support the theory that Mr Cooke was cleaning a gun when it accidentally went off'. The funeral was held at Brookwood Cemetery on the 8th, the memorial service at St Helen, Bishopsgate on the 10th; 'Lancie' was apparently present on neither occasion.[26]

Cooke's fate was timeless, but later on the day he was found dead there appeared the clearest sign yet of how the governing assumptions of an earlier age were now under fundamental threat.[27] 'While we retain the hope of an ultimate extension of the area of free trade throughout the world,' asserted a bankers' resolution that was made public that evening, 'we believe that the immediate step for securing and extending the market for British goods lies in reciprocal trade agreements between the nations constituting the British Empire.' The resolution followed a meeting at Hambros the previous afternoon, and signatories included three directors of the Bank of England (Peacock, Anderson and Walter Whigham), the Chairmen of four large clearing banks (Westminster, Lloyds, National Provincial and Midland), and Lancie's eldest brother, Vivian Hugh Smith of Morgan Grenfell. It was an impressive array. 'The import of the bankers' resolution has been avidly discussed in the City,' the *FT* reported on the 5th. 'Those dissenting from the views expressed were in a marked minority . . . It was insistently urged that banking interests had, within recent months, completely revised their view of tariff problems.' The impact was also considerable in the wider world, and Leo Amery was not exaggerating when he told Baldwin that the protectionist cause had received 'the biggest leg up since 1903'.[28] Two months later, diehard free traders in the City, including Addis, belatedly mounted a counter-resolution; but it lacked big names and failed to alter a general conviction that the traditionally free-trading City had decisively shifted its allegiance and was now far closer to industrial opinion (which in the first half of 1930 had become preponderantly protectionist) than had ever before been the case. Yet it is at least arguable that the July manifesto was essentially no more than a tactical retreat – that, compelled by harsh economic circumstances to choose between traditional economic internationalism on the one hand and the demise of sterling as a world-ranking currency on the other, the City preferred to jettison the former for the time being. In other words, the working assumption, as almost always, was that in due course it would be business as usual.

The City's mood in the summer of 1930 was not helped by the phenomenal exploits of 'the Don'; but on 14 July, three days after Bradman had rattled up 300 in a day at Headingley, the Bank of England's Sir Otto Niemeyer arrived at Fremantle to exact revenge.[29] With the Australian economy in particularly dire straits because of the world slump, and City suspicions of colonial extravagance at an all-time high, he had in effect been called in by Scullin's Labour government in order to recommend the steps that Australia needed to take so that its increasingly onerous financial obligations in London might be met with the assistance of the Bank. From the start Niemeyer proved an intensely divisive figure in Australia, but no one can have been surprised by the deflationary nature of the medicine that he prescribed. Certainly he had the City's full backing. Writing to an American correspondent on 8 August, Arthur Villiers of Barings did not deny that Australia had been 'hit very hard by world conditions', above all by the slump in commodity prices, but argued that that country's financial problems had been 'increased by the fact that the Labour element in Australian politics is very strong and has never had the courage or the wisdom to face the financial problem until now'. He added that 'one hopes that it is not too late', affirming that if the Australian government was 'strong enough' to follow Niemeyer's advice, 'they may turn the corner'.[30]

Niemeyer himself kept a diary that reflected something of his exasperation with the locals:

14 *August (Melbourne)*. At the Commonwealth Bank discussed the Victorian Budget with Pitt, Under Treasurer: like a codfish.

21 *August (Melbourne)*. Attended a meeting at the Melbourne Stock Exchange, including some rather amusing private discussion with the Stock

Exchange Committee, some of whose members were obsessed with the exploded doctrine of the enormous potentialities of Australia.

22 *August (Adelaide)*. Visited Treasury to interview the Cabinet. Emphasised to them that Melbourne Resolutions were a beginning and had now to be put into practice. In balancing Budget they must not forget question of dealing with maturities which, though difficult, provided them with the opportunity of converting on lower interest rates if finance properly managed. Much best man, Jelly, Colonial Secretary. Denny, Attorney-General and rogue, asked what would be the effects of repudiation.

24 *August (Adelaide)*. Official Lunch with the Members of both Houses of Parliament, after which Speech . . . Melbourne results were a scaffolding on which it remained for them to build. Charity began at home, and only Australia could save herself. It was their business to do this and no one else's.

25 *August (Adelaide)*. Dawes, President of the Trades Hall – a nervous youth, crammed with undigested economics. He disliked cutting down grants to Municipalities, etc. and wanted to have a capital levy. He had no idea what a capital levy would produce, or how much could be reconciled with needs for renewing maturities. Long and not unfriendly discussion – Inflation, Devaluation, etc. Not much of a creature, but also not vicious.

30 *August (Melbourne)*. Saw Phillips of the League of Nations Union: also Duggan, President of the Australian Council of Trades Unions and Duffy, Secretary of the Victorian Trades Hall, for about 2 hours. Their views as expressed, and on the whole I think sincerely, were moderate though confused. They were prepared to admit that costs would have to come down, but were not prepared to see wages go first without any guarantee that other things would follow. They hinted that the position would be different if there were what they called equal sacrifices all round.[31]

'Australia Faces The Facts' was the *Economist*'s confident headline on the 30th, but Norman soon afterwards was not so sure, replying to the prominent member of the Stock Exchange, Alfred Waley, who had sent the Governor a pessimistic letter he had received from his brother in Australia: 'I agree that as regards meeting the troubles in Australia it is largely a question of getting the right spirit, and I agree also that labour seems to be obdurate against wage cuts. I hope our good Niemeyer will succeed in converting these remote Australians to economic sanity and indeed to reason, but they have a long way to go.' Niemeyer by this time had sailed across the Tasman Sea, to spend a few weeks keeping the Kiwis up to the mark, but was back in Australia as his mission hit crisis point during October. The New South Wales election was waged over whether or not to accept the Melbourne Agreement of August, by which the Premiers had agreed to follow Niemeyer's advice that it would require a significant reduction in both costs and standard of living if their budgets were to be balanced. 'If Lang wins,' Niemeyer cabled Norman on the 24th, referring to the Labour leader, 'it will be impossible to hold the position.' Lang did win and Niemeyer returned home in November, his mission having apparently failed. 'Niemeyer was not the success he might have been,' reflected the senior British Trade Commissioner in Australia soon afterwards, having 'lost his head a bit', been 'tactless' and done 'some very stupid things'.[32] Eventually, in 1931, a compromise settlement was reached; but as increasingly on the home front, the Bank of England had found itself uncomfortably in the political firing line.

A central component of that home front was the increasingly alarming state of British industry. Early in April 1930, shortly before BIDC's formal launch, Norman's alternate on that body, Granet of Higginsons, expressed himself to Peacock as being dismayed about press coverage that portrayed BIDC as 'directly competitive with the issue houses'. This, according to Granet, was all wrong: 'Above all, its aim is not to be an issue house itself, and . . . it does not contemplate *initiating* schemes for amalgamation and rationalization itself; it will examine and pass schemes submitted to it and help to finance them.' By this time BIDC's sister, SMT, was holding regular meetings, and Skinner's notes offer an invaluable running commentary:

> 7 *April*. Mr Bruce Gardner has seen Sir William McLintock. No one speaks favourably of the L.C.C. (a concern for buying up bankrupt Mills), and Sir William wonders how much it is possible to do for the industry.
>
> 11 *April*. The Governor informed the Meeting that he had that morning, while at the Treasury, been induced to appear before the Committee which was enquiring into the Cotton Trade. He had expressed his faith in the L.C.C. although he knew that it was being sniped from all sides and had been described as an 'association of lame ducks'. But he had gone into the scheme after taking the best advice available: he had no regrets and still had faith in the idea.[33]

SMT/BIDC had several other matters on its industrial agenda, but cotton was its main focus during this first, critical year.

The commercial banks remained less than entirely helpful. 'Owing to the obstruction of the Midland Bank,' noted Skinner in June of SMT's latest discussions about the LCC, 'considerable difficulty was being experienced in obtaining the spindles for which they were responsible . . .' The following month, District Bank's Bruce Tulloch frankly admitted to Parkes of Midland that 'they had put most of

their less satisfactory Mills into the L.C.C.' BIDC itself dithered, and on
12 August a public letter was sent to Bruce Gardner from S.S.
Hammersley, Conservative MP for Stockport and a director of three
spinning companies. His particular grievance was the refusal to make
cash payments to existing interests in the cotton trade and thereby
facilitate amalgamations:

> This principle which you explained to me prevents the Bankers Industrial
> Development Company from finding finance for schemes similar to the one
> I have submitted, seems to me to show such a wilful lack of knowledge of
> the existing situation in Lancashire and of the practical difficulties that
> have to be overcome, that I feel it my duty to examine this principle – and
> to say without equivocation that in my judgement if it is persisted in the
> Bankers Industrial Development Company cannot be of the slightest real
> assistance in the effective reconstruction of the industry. The sooner the
> hollow farce of pretence that helpful finance will be forthcoming from any
> quarter over which the Bank of England has control, is done away with the
> better it will be for all concerned.

The Bank's Henry Clay privately conceded the following day that
Hammersley was 'right in suggesting that Thomas' speeches have excited
hopes that the Governor has no intention of satisfying', but the next
meeting of SMT conceded no ground. 'The publication of the Hammersley letter was discussed,' Skinner recorded. 'No personal reply to be
given but a selected Press to be given guidance ... B.I.D.Co to let
Hammersley stew.' Guided or unguided, the press gave much attention
to Hammersley's denunciation, and at SMT's meeting on 1 September
there was significant divergence of opinion. Whereas Gardner, according
to Skinner, argued 'that the L.C.C. could not at this moment make a
public issue as they had not a satisfactory case to present to the public',
Norman 'maintained that a public issue was the right policy if it were
practicable'.[34] Something, he was aware, had not only to be done by the
City, but to be seen to be done.

By autumn 1930, with Norman preoccupied by manifold anxieties,
Gardner innately cautious ('a moment's reflection will shew that a vast
amount of thought, investigation and negotiation are necessary before
any scheme of permanent value can result,' he counselled the Treasury in
October) and Granet offering indecisive leadership, precious little had
been achieved – or looked like being achieved – not only in relation to
cotton. One of BIDC's directors, Nigel Campbell, now broke ranks.
Early in November he circulated a memo arguing that SMT/BIDC was
going to need £10–12m almost immediately and up to £25m over the

next two to three years. He contended that 'it is essential that the "City" should carry the first risk, otherwise they will be accused of lack of good faith in the formation of the B.I.D. [as bankers tended to call BIDC]'. Later that month he returned to the charge, insisting to Peacock that BIDC had to take a chance and that 'I do not believe, quite sincerely, that unless some risk is taken much or anything will be accomplished.' After citing various steel companies (including Stewarts & Lloyds and United Steel), Campbell went on:

> For over six months Bruce Gardner has been pressing these men to rationalise and modernise. Is it unnatural that they expect some definite help? Personally, just as everybody in the City is marking time and proceeding with the utmost caution while waiting for the clouds to clear, so would I act if I were the head of a big industrial undertaking today. But the national need is that as quickly as possible these undertakings be put in order – and to accomplish it some considerable risk of what is going to happen in the world politically, industrially and financially has got to be taken . . . Granet remarked yesterday that if we offered these people their money and they refused it we had done our job. I cannot believe that is the right view . . . If I am right, and we are not going to get the security we should demand under normal issuing safety, and we accomplish nothing, will not the danger of the Government stepping in be greatly enhanced? . . . It seems to me that the whole situation calls so urgently for cooperation between the City and the Government and, if profits are made, a division of these profits . . . I think there is danger of our drifting into an impossible situation.

A fellow-director of Helbert Wagg would recall Campbell as someone who expressed himself poorly, and 'never read a book in his life except shockers', but who 'had the imagination to foresee broad combinations, and the ingenuity to make them practical', and whose 'simplicity and integrity made him trusted'.[35]

Campbell's views were made known to Norman and struck at least a partial chord. The steel situation was immensely difficult, but writing to Granet on 18 December the Governor returned to the cotton question:

> I want you to go further and to follow the Shipbuilding issue [the National Shipbuilders, due early in 1931] with a L.C.C. issue. It may be that the latter cannot make a pretty picture or a gilt-edged security but the interest is assured for five years, and this City has got to be prepared for certain risks in supporting industry: this issue, I think, is one of them though not a serious risk. Otherwise a Government will be forced to find money for industry, and one way or another will not escape without some

form of advisory or controlling position: indeed, this as you know is
actually being discussed. A purpose of the B.I.D. is to keep the Government
out of industry and to do so must be active and not passive.

'I almost entirely share your views and – without qualification – your
ideals,' Granet replied from the offices of Higginson & Co at 80
Lombard Street.[36]

The Macmillan Committee, meanwhile, had ploughed on during
1930, examining a variety of witnesses during the four months after
Norman's disastrous appearance. One of the most candid statements
came from Lionel Hichens, chairman of Cammell Laird and English
Electric. 'Whilst industry knows very likely all about the industrial side,'
he told the committee on 10 July, 'it knows very little about the financial
side, and the banker knows very little about the industrial side. They do
not come together enough.'[37] By the end of that month, following a
return appearance by Harvey, most of the evidence had been given, and
the members of the committee began to consider their eventual report.

Brand, from a position of particular authority, circulated to his fellow-
members in August a lengthy memo in which he stressed the need for a
closer finance/industry relationship. 'The City,' he argued, 'is very highly
and efficiently organised as an international and local money market, as
a market for first-class international issues and for granting short term
credit to home and also to foreign trade, and as a provider of all ordinary
banking facilities and advances to home industry, trade and commerce';
but, he emphasised, 'there are few of our bankers indeed in my opinion
who really know a great deal about industry'. This was a crucial defect,
for 'it is only by means of a close knowledge of industry that they will be
able to act properly in the very important rôle of financial advisers'. He
regretted, in passing, that the British Trade Corporation had failed to
take this job on, and instead become 'merely one more accepting house'.
What was to be done? He accepted that 'the big banks have no doubt
plenty of wits in their vast staffs', but 'the question is how to bring them
to the fore and give them opportunity and training outside the somewhat
narrow sphere of ordinary deposit banking'. However, he argued, that
was an impossibly large task ('the whole personnel of the big banks has
been brought up in a different tradition and would have to be trained
afresh'), and he therefore concluded that the best solution was for the Big
Five not to be expected to 'change its spots', but instead to co-operate
with a new finance/industry institution.[38] Primarily a merchant banker
but also a long-standing director of Lloyds Bank, Brand was a
thoroughly non-ideological intellectual who appreciated the deep conservatism, for good as well as ill, of British commercial banking.

That autumn he and his colleagues enjoyed some more private sessions, and on 31 October he drove home the need for a new institution, asserting that, because of the inadequate role of the banks, companies were often forced to resort to stockbrokers for advice. 'The stockbroker,' he plausibly claimed, 'knows as an expert just the condition of the market at that moment, but he knows nothing else.' The previous day the subject had been that hardy perennial, the Bank of England. Keynes called for it to engage in 'a more open discussion', and an instructive dialogue ensued:

> *Keynes:* If at every stage in the last ten years the Governor of the Bank of England had stated publicly what his object was and what he thought the things he was doing were likely to result in and how he assessed the advantages and disadvantages of his policy, if he told us what he was aiming at and what his method was and what he thought his method would cost in order to gain the advantages he was seeking, then it would be possible for public opinion of an informed kind to be crystallised on the point whether his policy was wise and successful. If it was obviously not wise and not successful the existing machine is quite capable of dealing with him.
> *Macmillan:* I think you might have a perfectly admirable Governor of the Bank of England who was incapable of expressing himself in terms of political economy.
> *Keynes:* He must be able to express himself in some terms.
> *McKenna:* He must know what he is thinking.
> *Brand:* He has great problems to deal with and must know what is in his mind and what he is aiming at.
> *Macmillan:* He must have a policy.

Early in December they returned to that reticent but indispensable institution:

> *Keynes:* I should like to see our Report centre round the magnification and evolutionary enlargements of the functions of the Bank of England . . . so that by the time her new mansion is ready for her [a reference to the physical rebuilding of the Bank], she must be no longer the 'Old Lady of Threadneedle Street' gathering her skirts round her, but some new image must be thought of appropriate to the occupant of the new palace.
> *Macmillan:* A bright young thing?
> *Keynes:* I hardly know what – perhaps Mr Lubbock can suggest something?
> *Lubbock:* Well, I am one of the old timers.[39]

So he was, and inasmuch as an old lady was belatedly starting to become a New Woman, it was little thanks to the former Deputy Governor or indeed most of his fellow-directors.

*

All such discussion was rather academic, in the context of the world outside during the autumn of 1930. Germany's 'position has been worsened by the results of the Election and her need for money, almost before the new Government has been formed,' Norman told the leading British overseas banker Sir Bertram Hornsby on 1 October. And, 'in general, feeling everywhere is not less pessimistic than it was, nor is there any light at the end of the tunnel . . .' Evelyn Baring, writing to New York a week later, was still gloomier. After referring to how 'all over the world, conditions seem to be as bad as they possibly can be from an industrial and commercial point of view', he added that 'now, to increase our troubles, Brazil seems to have caught the revolution complaint, and just when we thought that matters were settling down in that country the news comes of battles and insurrections to depress the price of all Brazilian securities'. So inconsiderate of the foreigners, but the position was little better at home: 'The number of unemployed shows no sign of decreasing and I believe that our Government is entirely at a loss to know what action to take. We hear rumours on all sides of a possible National Government . . . One thing is certain, and that is that no party is anxious to introduce the next Budget . . .'[40]

The sense of an impending crisis was gathering momentum, and the form it would take was presaged in mid-November when, as reported by Skinner, Norman told SMT of an exchange of views he had recently had with American bankers with whom he was on friendly terms:

> It had been said [i.e. by Norman] to them that if France and America did certain things it was certain to lead to trouble. They had replied that it was very likely that England would have to part with gold either to France or to the United States and if she did she would only have herself to blame. She had failed to rationalise; she had heavier taxation than anyone, to support social services and a dole on a basis that no country would pretend to sustain and which she also could probably not bear; there were likely to be three unbalanced Budgets running; wages also were too high and did not produce value for the amount paid. So long as this state of affairs continued it was useless for England to complain and no help would be forthcoming from across the way.

With the Labour government seemingly incapable of firm action, City eyes occasionally looked longingly elsewhere. 'It certainly reads to me to be good sound stuff,' Michael Herbert of Morgan Grenfell wrote shortly after Christmas to the bank's correspondent in Rome. 'Your Prime Minister seems to be endeavouring to meet the crisis with that courage and determination which I am sure are part of his character.' By the end of the year the registered unemployed in Britain totalled 2,660,000, compared with barely a million when Labour had returned to office in the middle of 1929.[41] A vast and dreadful human tragedy was being enacted, but what primarily concerned the City and the short-term holders of sterling was whether MacDonald's hapless ministry was capable of balancing the budget.

'Norman very nervous and depressed at business situation,' Addis noted on 7 January 1931, and a fortnight later Edward Clifton-Brown of Norman's old firm, Brown Shipley, reported to Brown Brothers on the 1930 balance sheet: 'For the first time for many years, we made a loss in London ... We feel that the loss is a temporary one owing to the disastrous world financial conditions ... The days of big profits for a private firm such as ours are, we feel, past ...' For Norman, it was the fundamental question of whether Britain would be capable of staying on the gold standard that was now the real worry, and on the 14th he reported to colleagues that he had informed Snowden that 'if loss of gold, Budget prospects, socialist legislation or any other cause' seemed likely to precipitate a flight from sterling, he would have no alternative but to increase Bank rate in order to bring public pressure to bear upon what he termed 'the unsatisfactory position'.[42]

The last days of January saw a perceptible heightening of the stakes. Norman's diary recorded an ominous visit from Granet (in close touch with Wall Street bankers) on the 26th: 'Dangerous prospect for stg: complaints on all sides'. Next day Norman himself wrote to Snowden's private secretary:

> I only pass on to you a tithe of what I get, but when I see in a personal letter from one eminent banker abroad to his counterpart in this country a phrase like this – 'the people on the Continent are quite apprehensive about England and feel that she must either make a very large loan in America or a general capital levy and that there is a distinct possibility of a revision of the value of the pound during 1931' – I think you ought to share it. And as a type of the steady drip and of the unseen pressure on us, you may care to whisper it to the Chancellor.

Also on the 27th a crowded meeting took place at the Cannon Street Hotel, convened by the so-called 'Friends of Economy'. In addition to the four Bank directors (including Peacock, Addis and Kindersley) on the platform, the chair was taken by Teddy Grenfell, who was not only a Bank director but also a Tory MP for the City of London. The clarion call was for retrenchment on the part of the government, with the demise of London as a leading international financial centre the probable consequence, if such a policy was not implemented. Even the level-headed Brand was seriously perturbed by the prospect of a flight of capital from London. 'It doesn't seem to me that our political leaders have any idea of it,' he told Keynes on the 30th. 'The trouble is that democracies seem unable constitutionally to make budgets balance.'[43] Over the next eight months or so, as the crisis of 1931 was played out, the City had no alternative but to operate within the confines of the existing political process; but such was the instinctive deference towards the City of most politicians – especially Labour politicians – when it came to financial matters that it was not too difficult for the City to apply the frighteners.

During February the gold position was particularly parlous, following large outflows since November, although Norman was able to tighten the market rate and thus avoid what would have been an explosive rise in Bank rate. The 'drip' of international opinion, meanwhile, continued. It was, to a significant if unquantifiable extent, City-fed – a reflection of the City's belief that, unless the politicians could be persuaded to change their ways, then the game was up. A prime example of the drip-feed at work was the private cable that Teddy Grenfell sent on 2 February to Jack Morgan in New York:

> I wish you personally to realise that this country is passing through a period of increasing financial difficulties and perhaps dangers.
>
> The general causes are of course well known to you and affect the whole world.
>
> The particular causes on the other hand are apt to be ignored but they are our responsibility and are deep and continuing. They are due, I think, to our fiscal and economic and industrial conditions such as extreme taxation and socialistic policies – the dole and a high standard of living – a bad spirit and obsolete plants and lost trade.

'Fundamentally,' concluded Grenfell, 'it's a long tunnel we are in.' Lord Bearsted of M. Samuel & Co, visiting Norman on the 5th, also saw darkness all around. The diary entry was contemptuous enough: 'Fear in his heart! wants to change £ for $, wh I say he sh^d avoid doing.'[44]

Six days later some possible light appeared at the end of the tunnel, when Snowden agreed to establish an Economy Committee that would search for places to make spending cuts. This committee, he emphasised to the Commons, would be bi-partisan (in the event, chaired by Sir George May, a distinguished actuary who had recently retired from the Prudential), and in the ensuing debate almost the only note of dissent was sounded by Lloyd George. Bringing back memories of his epic rhetorical battle against Natty Rothschild almost a quarter of a century earlier, he launched into a fierce attack on the City, declaring that it had Snowden in its pocket and that its deflationary obsession would ruin the country. Invariably reactionary, invariably out of touch with industry, the City had been found to be 'wrong every time' in its advice to government. And he remembered how, when before the war he had put forward his 'People's Budget', he had been 'received by City magnates with frigid and flopping silence, as if they were a row of penguins in the Arctic Ocean'.[45]

It was an attack that may have stung a few of the big penguins, but for the myriad little penguins, just trying to eke out a living amidst sharply reduced business, it was probably irrelevant. These included the ranks of half-commission men who, traditionally importunate, but charming and well connected, touted for business on behalf of stockbrokers. One such, working for Schwab & Snelling, paid a visit to SW3 on 22 February, which inadvertently led to the firm having to write an apologetic letter to the Stock Exchange Committee:

Mr Eals explains the circumstances in the following manner.

An old friend of his family is Captain Landon, late R.N. Mr Eals met him casually some months ago at a wedding in Sussex and Captain Landon said he would like to see him again some time. Mr Eals was himself in the Navy and served as a Midshipman on H.M.S. 'Warspite'.

Last Sunday afternoon Mr Eals wished to call on Captain Landon and had looked for his name in the telephone directory and found Captain Langdon R.N. at 54, Chelsea Park Gardens and thought that this must be the gentleman he was looking for. He called there and sent in his *private* card. He was then shown into the drawing room and there saw a lady and gentleman whom he did not know. He said 'I am very sorry! I think there is some mistake, I wanted to call on Captain Landon.' Captain Langdon said 'that is my name, but are you not by chance confusing me with Captain Landon also R.N.? That has happened several times before.' He was then asked to sit down and the conversation turned to Naval matters. It transpired that Captain Langdon was at one time connected with H.M.S. 'Warspite'. Later Mr Eals was asked what he was doing and he stated he was connected with the Stock Exchange. He was then asked his views on the general situation and also his views regarding certain shares. He stated that he did not know much about the shares mentioned but that his firm favoured International Investments Deposit Certificates. Mrs Langdon thereupon asked him if he would send her some particulars of the security, as she did not know it. This Mr Eals did on Monday . . .

Soon afterwards Mrs Langdon's own firm, Robinson & Glyn, found out that these particulars had been sent to its client and formally accused Schwab & Snelling of attempting to poach business. Schwab & Snelling got away with a caution.[46]

For Norman, an important part of the unfolding situation, although it hardly ranked with the fate of the gold standard, was what the report of the Macmillan Committee would say about his beloved Bank – 'Norman made an impassioned outburst in praise of his mistress The Old Lady,' Addis had noted after the Bankers' Dinner at Mansion House the previous October, adding that 'his qualities are I think more of the heart than the head'. Keynes, inevitably, tended to dominate the drafting committee, but it also comprised Macmillan himself, Gregory, Brand and Lubbock. The last-named fought a not unskilful rearguard action on the Bank's behalf. 'I agree with you,' he wrote to Brand at the start of 1931, 'that we must frankly face the fact that our return to our old par did help to make things difficult for our Export Industries.' However, 'the difficulty will be to assign to it its real proportion of trouble'. He added that 'we should do Industry a real disservice if we did not thoroughly disabuse its mind of the suspicion that its trouble has been due to the monetary policy of this country'. But, despite Lubbock's efforts, Norman seems to have been in something of a panic during January about the report's conclusions, so much so that he proposed to his colleagues that the Bank voluntarily modify its constitution and thereby forestall more drastic recommendations. He was persuaded, however, that he was being over-fearful, and he withdrew the suggestion.[47]

Norman's anxieties were probably allayed by his two final days of evidence to the Macmillan Committee, on 18 and 19 February, when he was accompanied first by Granet and then by Dr O.M.W. Sprague, his new American economist. Granet and Sprague fielded the majority of questions, and Norman was not remotely under the same sort of invidious spotlight as he had been almost eleven months earlier. The session with Granet pivoted, sometimes illuminatingly, on the contentious City/industry relationship. The City, Granet sought to reassure Brand, 'performs its duty generally to industry extremely well'. Brand was unconvinced: 'Take the year 1928, when large sums were raised from the British investor for what was called British industry. What guidance had the British investor from the City? There was a very large number of very bad issues . . .' To which Granet replied: 'Of course, one knows that that was a very unfortunate period in the history of the City; it had nothing to do with the ordinary financing of industry by the City . . .' The discussion then turned to whether the City had adequate machinery for helping industry to raise long-dated capital, and Norman adamantly insisted to Gregory that in normal times there was no problem at the supply end:

> You have spoken several times as if the issue houses could be filled up; but their business is only a very small business, and certainly only a part of the whole. I imagine in industry the mass of money is really found through some broker or another; and their capacity for finding money is very big. I myself feel, if we succeed in getting through this period, for which the B.I.D. was intended to function, we shall return to conditions in which the capital demands of industry, even if it should require large sums of money, will be supplied with no more difficulty than they have been supplied before. I am perfectly clear about that. I think there may be less investment abroad, but in future I think there will be adequate investment at home. I should think that the criterion whether or not that is to happen will be whether or not an industry can promise reasonable profits; and if it cannot, it is better without the money . . .
>
> The B.I.D. is only intended to fill a gap, not intended to make any permanent alterations in the structure of the City, or of credit. We have always found in the past, as I have been told, that, wherever the occasion for business existed, some institution or concern would find its way in and grow towards it. That has been the great difference between, for instance, ourselves and America. One has grown and the other has been made. Without any question, I believe that we shall grow again to fill any increasing needs.

There was just time, before the session broke up, for a final spat between Bevin and Norman, on the subject of whether those financing a rationalisation or reorganisation scheme should ensure that the labour aspect was satisfactorily resolved:

> My experience for what it is worth is this. The management deals with these re-organisations and just dumps them down without any previous consultation or without any attempt to get co-operation and then you have a dispute, or you do not get the scheme to work well? – That has not been my experience.
>
> It has been mine in both schemes I have had to deal with. – It has not been mine.[48]

With large-scale rationalisations already proving in practice distinctly difficult to pull off, Norman may well have felt that if bankers had to take into account industry's foot-soldiers, as well as its squabbling captains, then the task would become plain impossible. Put another way, he may have had a penchant for secrecy and even intrigue, but he was the very antithesis of a beer-and-sandwiches man.

BIDC itself remained largely unloved by its shareholders. 'The Governor is apt to call upon the Houses to take a share in certain industrial reorganisations which they would gladly refuse except for matters of public policy,' Grenfell told Jack Morgan in January, and few other merchant bankers, or indeed clearers, would have disputed the point; while it was probably by about this time, if not earlier, that BIDC received the City nickname of the 'Brought in Dead Company'. Moreover, in the early months of 1931, both the National Shipbuilders and the Lancashire Cotton Corporation issues flopped. The latter's £2m $6\frac{1}{2}$ per cent debenture issue, made under Bank of England auspices, was not unkindly appraised by the *FT* when the prospectus appeared in late March ('As an investment the stock may be described as offering an attractive return and as a useful mixer'), but 96 per cent was left with the underwriters.[49]

It was a depressing end to BIDC's first year, and Bruce Gardner's anniversary overview, sent to each director on 17 April, was far from upbeat:

> It would seem to me that the tests that we have been applying to all schemes are such as would be applied by any ordinary Issuing House and if this is to be the accepted policy then the B.I.D. is not going to give the increased help to industry that it was hoped and expected to do.
>
> Very large sums of money must be forthcoming if we are to make the slightest impression on the re-organisation of our basic industries and experience has shown that in most cases it will be impossible to help those industries to formulate schemes that can guarantee to the investor their interest and sinking funds on the money provided . . .

Peacock's reply three days later offered at best luke-warm comfort:

> The financial tests to be applied to schemes, whether they be those issued by bankers or by the B.I.D., must be in essence the same tests if they are to avoid misleading the public, the industry and ourselves; but the schemes that we finance must of necessity, it seems to me, be exactly those which would be dealt with by ordinary issuing houses . . . Our business is to come in earlier than the ordinary banker could, but we must come in only after we have applied the usual tests and satisfied ourselves that the scheme is in its essence thoroughly sound and likely to succeed.

As for the cotton industry specifically, which Gardner had emphasised, Peacock merely noted that it was 'a difficult and controversial subject to which we must give a good deal of thought before we make further commitments'.[50]

In general, both were agreed that the way ahead for BIDC did not lie in making new issues that would demand the broad-based support of investors, who invariably would not apply sufficiently long-term criteria to the industry in question; and the Committee of Treasury formally decided on 29 April that henceforth BIDC would, in the words of the Bank's historian, 'confine itself to schemes where its own resources could support reconstruction schemes that ought not to be left to the chances of governmental support'. Granted BIDC's limited capital, and the very difficult times through which its shareholders were now passing, it was hardly a recipe for that ambitious marriage between finance and industry that had seemingly been proposed in early 1930. If confirmation was needed that passions were cooling, it came soon afterwards, on 11 May, when Bruce Gardner wrote to the leading cotton spinner Frank Platt, architect of Allied Spinners (an ambitious would-be spinning amalgamation), seeking to merge some five million spindles owned by forty-four companies. The scheme, requiring £1.25m of new capital, was intrinsically sound, but Gardner told Platt that financial support would be forthcoming only if 'the world's trade and in particular the cotton trade of Lancashire was to show a satisfactory upward tendency' – in other words, financial help would only *follow* profitability. Nor was Midland (the main creditor of the forty-four companies) willing to back the merger, and consequently the scheme foundered.[51]

*

On its more traditional beat, taking advantage of a brief respite in the embargo, the City had been putting through a rather spluttering series of foreign loans before the final curtain came down. Norman did not give up without a struggle. 'Just at present there is too much active thinking further west about public issues to make me entirely comfortable!' he conceded to Charles Hambro on 2 March, but still said that a Greek loan proposed by Hambros could go ahead provided that it was done in several markets, including Paris if possible. A fortnight later, writing to Kindersley about a Spanish proposal of Lazards, he almost accepted defeat: 'Under present conditions at home and abroad we cannot afford to make fresh foreign loans: this is not entirely logical but I think *necessary*. Therefore, apart from any question of merit, we should not participate in any Spanish credit, directly or indirectly. Will you be so good as to give support to this view.' The City's swan-song came at the end of the month. It followed a crisis since the late 1920s in the Chilean nitrate industry, which the Chilean government attempted to resolve by establishing the Compania de Salitri de Chile (COSACH). It was backed by the City, and Schröders now lead-managed the £3m component of a £10m international issue, with support from Barings, Morgan Grenfell and Rothschilds. Conspicuous by its absence was Antony Gibbs, once synonymous with nitrate. 'An attractive if novel holding' was the *FT*'s comment, but some 90 per cent of the bonds were left to the underwriters.[52]

These were of course dismal times, for domestic as well as foreign issues, yet remarkably the City was about to produce a genuine innovation – the fixed unit trust.[53] Largely the brainchild of the merchant, entrepreneur and Bank of England director George Booth (*A Man of Push and Go* would be the just title of his biography) and of the stockbroker Walter Burton-Baldry, the First British Fixed Trust was issued on 23 April at 31s 9d per unit. It had Norman's informal blessing, and Lloyds Bank agreed to act as trustees, but it fared poorly, crucially hindered by the decision of the Stock Exchange Committee not to grant permission to deal in its shares. 'We would respectfully submit,' protested one firm, J. Silverston & Co, 'that the creation of this Fixed Trust is bringing business to the London Stock Exchange, in a manner that can only be of benefit to both Brokers and Jobbers.'[54] But at least the principle of the fixed unit trust had been established – in explicit contrast to the pyramided investment trusts that had crashed in New York in 1929 – and the initial trust's parent company, Municipal and General Securities (the present-day M & G), would within a few years be reaping a rich harvest, fair reward for seeds bravely sown.

There was not much else to cheer about in the spring of 1931, even if the sense of imminent crisis had receded somewhat. Snowden's budget on 27 April did little more than provide a breathing space, pending the findings of May's Economy Committee. Soon afterwards Norman was invited to a small meeting at the House of Commons to discuss monetary issues with about a dozen MPs. 'With your permission,' ran his reply of acceptance, 'I propose to bring with me to the meeting Dr Sprague, an eminent banking economist from Harvard who has been helping us here for nearly a year now: I am only a banker.' So he was, and a deeply puzzled one, unable either through international co-operation or orthodox monetary measures to see a way out. A cable on 5 May to his counterpart in New York, George Harrison of the Fed, captured his mood of despair, of not knowing which way to turn: 'The general economic outlook appears in every way so discouraging that for my part I should like now to try the effect of reductions of $\frac{1}{2}$% in your and our discount rates . . .'[55] Neither man was even remotely in control of the larger situation.

CHAPTER NINE

Going Off

'The leading bank in Austria and most important bank in Central Europe, perfectly good for its engagements,' was the confident verdict of a report prepared by Lazards on 7 January 1931 for Westminster Bank. The bank in question was Credit Anstalt, which was indeed Austria's largest commercial bank and was controlled by the local Rothschild house, S.M. Rothschild und Söhne of Vienna. Its size was such that a host of other banks in London and elsewhere had some involvement in it, but a notable exception was Barings. Revelstoke had refused towards the end of his life to give it a credit, according to one colleague 'saying very firmly that we should not as he did not like the management of it and was sure that it would get into trouble sometime'.[1]

On 11 May, barely four months after the assessment by Lazards, it became known that Credit Anstalt was in serious trouble.[2] Over the next few weeks Norman acted as decisively as he could – taking the lead in organising a 100m schilling credit from BIS to the Austrian National Bank, helping to establish a creditors' committee in order to try to prevent precipitate withdrawals, and in June advancing direct a 150m schilling (£4.3m) credit to the Austrian central bank. 'Un acte très audacieux,' the French Ambassador in London grudgingly conceded of this last action. Norman's grave warning to Harrison on 25 May – 'a monetary breakdown in Austria might quickly produce a similar result in several countries' – accurately reflected his overriding motive behind these steps. For obvious reasons, no house in London was more involved in the Austrian situation than Rothschilds, and it was at New Court that representatives of some forty banks gathered on 29 May in order to decide who should represent London on the international committee of creditors. The chosen three were Lionel de Rothschild, Kindersley and Charles Whigham of Morgan Grenfell, all merchant bankers. Among those present was Westminster Bank's foreign-branch manager, and on his report of the meeting, in which he noted who had been chosen, Westminster's combative chief General Manager, Charles Lidbury, scribbled, 'by whom?' Soon afterwards Kindersley went to Vienna, and years later the Dutch banker J.W. Beyen would recall how he 'made an awful proud English speech condemning Austria & the interpreter took all the bad out of it'.[3]

But if the City had acted impressively, for all its haughtiness, the fact was that its claims in Vienna were now frozen, thereby intensifying the fundamental problem of London's illiquidity – in essence, the accumulation of a mass of short-term liabilities that had resulted from the City's post-1925 policy of courting 'hot money' from abroad in order to keep the pound on the gold standard. With simultaneously a return to seminormality as an international capital market, disbursing foreign loans, the City had in practice been lending long while it borrowed short. International mistrust of a Labour government might alone not be enough to have the world's creditors knocking at London's door, but the freezing of a high proportion of London's European credits surely would.

So in a sense it proved, as financial instability in Austria spread rapidly to Hungary and Germany. The latter, owing to London's particularly high exposure there, was crucial.[4] 'I think probably we are the only prominent merchant banking firm who are doing nothing direct with Germany,' Vivian Hugh Smith had remarked to Grenfell back in May 1926, but thereafter even Morgan Grenfell had entered the fray in offering commercial credits to German business. In 1931 itself, runs on German banks began in late May, soon exacerbated by the insistence of many American banks on repatriating short-term loans; but Norman – heavily committed to the international economy – applied strong pressure on London banks to keep credits running. His diary recorded a visit on 10 June from Eric and Charles Hambro: 'Germany – sh^d they withdraw Credits &c as others are said to be doing: I say Germany is a good bet in the long run & needs help & comfort rather than worrying.' Nine days later Norman saw Beaumont Pease, in the latter's capacity as Chairman of the Committee of London Clearing Bankers: 'I explain European position & all that has happened. He is not withdrawing Credits. He is satisfied & has no complaint or suggestion about conduct here.'[5]

Norman would later be criticised for not having done more during June to protect the City's interests; but in the authoritative judgement of Sayers, 'it was simply that implications for the financial structure of the City appeared, in the early summer of 1931, to be secondary to the maintenance of international trading relations'; therefore, in the mind of Norman, 'if only an international trading collapse could be averted, London creditors could in general be left to look after themselves'.

Moreover, by late June the German situation seemed to have stabilised somewhat, in the wake of not only President Hoover's proposal of a one-year moratorium on inter-governmental debts, but the provision to the Reichsbank of a three-week $100m credit from the Bank of England and other central banks. Norman, far from being unduly sanguine, put Clegg in South Africa in the picture on 1 July: 'You can really have little idea of the times through which we have been going here lately, during which as near as no matter Austria, Hungary and Germany – indeed Eastern Europe – went over the dam; and we are not by any means clear of trouble yet . . .'[6] That same day began a new run of foreign withdrawals from German banks, and by 8 July the news from the Reichsbank was of the German financial system in a state of crisis. For all Norman's reassuring words of recent weeks, the City was by now extremely worried, and on 10 July the clearing banks and accepting houses established a Joint Committee to represent their German interests. It was in for a very long haul.

Almost everywhere, it seemed, required special attention by the early summer of 1931. India, to Norman's considerable anxiety, appeared to be on the brink of insolvency; the situation in Chile was critical; and to Brazil, following its upheaval the previous autumn, a trusted lieutenant was sent in order to seek to impose financial stability. 'In my belief,' Norman wrote to Lionel de Rothschild on 6 June, 'Brazil would already have defaulted but for the presence of Niemeyer and, apart from other misfortunes, it is possible that so long as he stays there default may be postponed or reduced to a minimum.' Or as he put it a week later to a fellow-central banker: 'The services of Sir Otto Niemeyer were lent by me to Messrs Rothschilds because I was anxious – as I remain anxious – to avoid a serious débâcle in Brazil. We have more than enough problems on our hands as it is.'

At home, the sense of, if not apocalypse now, certainly apocalypse soon, was nicely caught by one stockbroker, Vernon Laurie of Heseltine Powell, in some snatches of correspondence to his client Colonel Francis Whitmore. The Colonel was clearly attached to his Fine Cotton Spinners preference shares, but Laurie kept up a persistent, eventually successful campaign to persuade him to sell them. 'I hope I have made myself clear and not said too much,' he wrote on 26 May. 'These are very difficult times and many pre-conceived ideas and values seem to be crumbling.' And on 17 June: 'The main difficulty of these times is that all previous conceptions of what is good and bad appear to be wrong.' And two days later: 'I do not want to harass you about the Fine Spinner Pref shares, but

I do rather feel that if any thing is going to be done it should be done now or soon.'[7]

At least neither the Colonel nor his broker was in Ramsay MacDonald's unenviable position. 'You will readily understand that to the practical political and to the practical business man alike this is a policy almost of despair,' he wrote in a long, worried letter to Norman on 18 June, in the wake of recent gloomy speeches by the Bank's Professor Sprague. Wondering if the central banks could not do more, co-operatively, to stabilise prices, he went on: 'I hope you will not resent my intruding in these technical fields. I scarcely dare to contemplate, however, what it will mean for the world, and for this country in particular, if all prices and wages have to be forced down to meet the fall in commodity prices.' Norman in his reply a week later saw the prospect of central banking co-operation raising commodity prices as a chimerical solution: 'My experiences at Basle have convinced me that, even among a party which comprises only a few of the European Central Banks, the clash of opinions is insistent.' As for his economic adviser, Norman stated flatly that 'if his utterances may seem to some to have been on occasions hard, crude or ruthless, may it not be that having convinced himself that the true facts and difficulties of the position have too long been unperceived or faced in this and other countries, he finds it necessary to paint the colours with a heavy brush if he is to succeed in forcing home on unwilling minds the facts as he sees them?' The task was getting politicians, that regrettable necessity, to face facts; and Norman was determined that there must be no relaxation in the softening-up process. MacDonald's reply on the 29th could hardly have been more deferential:

> I am constantly being bothered about this matter, and it is a subject which I have never really studied and therefore know nothing about.
> I am sure you must be very worried just now, and, if it is of any help to you, pray be assured that I often think of you and the burdens you are carrying.[8]

All through this early summer May's Economy Committee was beavering away, likely – as Norman well knew – to produce the ultimate facts that the politicians would have to be compelled to face.

The other report that was pending, and came out first, was the Macmillan Report.[9] Having been told by Macmillan on 23 June that the committee had signed the Report and handed it to Snowden, Norman in reply three days later had speculated somewhat self-pityingly on its contents:

Can it be that the Committee have designed for me an easy road by which to withdraw from a position which from year to year becomes increasingly difficult and exacting and has already been occupied far too long by

Yours sincerely,

M. Norman

The Report was published on 13 July, and it turned out that he need not have worried. The main criticism concerned the inadequacy of the information publicly provided by the Bank; and, far from seeking to truncate the Bank's powers, the conclusion reached was that it was the central bank's function 'to keep the financial structure upon an even keel', using whatever means were at hand. These primarily comprised altering Bank rate, conducting open-market operations, managing debt, dealing in the foreign exchange market, and exercising moral suasion over the rest of the monetary system – the last weapon specifically endorsed when the Report referred approvingly to 'the use of the Bank's personal influence over, or advice to, prominent elements in the money market'. The Bank itself remained tactfully silent when the Report was published, but Peacock on the 15th sent Norman a copy of a gratifying note he had just received from Frater Taylor: 'I am sure you will agree that the Macmillan Report represents an honest effort to be constructive and that the B. of E. emerges triumphant, as it should.'[10]

The Report as a whole – which had been largely written by Keynes, though he had by no means been given entirely his own way – was to a large extent taken up by a detailed analysis of the workings of the gold standard, monetary control and international trade. It is largely remembered, however, for its closing pages, dealing with the domestic capital market. Noting that 'the relations between the British financial world and British industry, as distinct from British commerce, have never been so close as between German finance and German industry or between American finance and American industry', it lamented the relative absence of sound issuing houses for domestic industrial issues:

There are, it is true, one or two first-class houses in the City which perform for certain first-class companies the same functions as the older issuing houses perform for foreign borrowers. In addition these latter are to a limited extent entering the domestic field ... Again, the advice of stockbrokers, when asked for, may be a safeguard but it is scarcely sufficient to take the place of the responsibility of a first-class issuing house. With these exceptions the public is usually not guided by any institution whose name and reputation it knows.

The Report did not deny 'the fact that industry, having grown up on strongly individualistic lines, has been anxious to steer clear of anything which might savour of banking control or even interference'; indeed, the Report made it clear that 'we have no sympathy with the idea that the banks should in any way manage industry'. Nevertheless, there was no denying that 'in some respects the City is more highly organised to provide capital to foreign capitals than to British industry'.

Who, then, should do the job of providing that capital and financial advice? The joint-stock banks, the Report assumed, were unsuitable, though no reasons were given; while as for the merchant banks, they were too bound up with acceptances, for 'it has always been recognised that acceptance business necessitates the maintenance of a high degree of liquidity and is not consistent with serious liabilities in respect of industrial financing'. Instead, the Report pinned its hopes on BIDC, which 'might form a nucleus for that closer co-operation between finance and industry which we think is required'. Right at the end there was one further suggestion, when the Report identified what would become known as the 'Macmillan gap': 'To provide adequate machinery for raising long-dated capital in amounts not sufficiently large for a public issue, i.e. amounts ranging from small sums up to say £200,000 or more, always presents difficulties.' And the proposal was made that there should be formed 'a company to devote itself particularly to these smaller industrial and commercial issues'.

Reaction to the Report from the City at large was distinctly muted. 'Preliminary perusal appears to have left a feeling of disappointment,' noted the *FT*'s money-market column. 'From the academic viewpoint it is regarded as a useful compilation; from the practical standpoint it takes us no farther forward than we were before the Committee began its deliberations.'[11] It would of course take some time for the Report to be digested. At this particular moment, the City – never partial to such reports at the best of times – had rather a lot else on its plate.

*

The 13th was a Monday, the start of a traumatic week that July. On the same day that the Macmillan Report was published, news came through that one of Germany's largest banks, the Darmstadter, had suspended payments. The Reichsbank's warnings had been vindicated. Next day Norman returned, tired and dispirited, from a BIS meeting at Basle to discover that Kindersley urgently required to see him. English pride, in the case of the senior partner of Lazards, had come before a fall.[12] It transpired that fraud in the Brussels office of Lazards had resulted in a loss of £6m; and Norman was told that, even though help was likely to be forthcoming from both Pearsons (the main owner of the London house) and the bank's Paris house, the London business would not be able to continue without a major subvention from the Bank of England. There must have been at least *some* temptation on Norman's part to let it go. 'His is a difficult firm to deal with – only seem to look on business from just *one* angle,' he had written to Strong back in 1927, in the context of Kindersley being in Brazil and 'making a deal of trouble by promising Credits & discussing Schemes for valorising Coffee – certainly more than we want to carry & probably poor policy'. Kindersley had also been talked about in the late 1920s as a possible successor to Norman, and Revelstoke had surmised in 1929 that 'some of the French intrigues against Norman might probably be traced to the jealousies of the Lazard lot, who would give a good deal to see M.N. deposed from his present position'. On the other hand, even if there was that temptation, not only was Kindersley a director of the Bank and an undoubted member of the City's inner circle, but the larger situation was becoming potentially so serious that the failure of Lazards might easily lead to outright panic in the City. 'Kindersley a ruined man,' noted Addis on the 17th, but over the weekend the Bank agreed to lend £3.5m to Pearsons in order to keep Lazards going.[13] Lazards, for its part, agreed to close its foreign offices, though there remained the close connection with the Paris house. Astonishingly, even the barest outline of what had happened would not become public knowledge until the publication in 1967 of Andrew Boyle's biography of Norman.

Yet for Norman himself in the middle of July 1931, the plight of Lazards was only of secondary importance. 'Germany and Europe in Suspense' was the title of the *FT*'s leader on Wednesday the 15th, and 'Autolycus' described the effect on the Stock Exchange that day of the German situation: 'Nebulous, vague and obscure apprehensions over-hung the markets, preventing clarity of thought and trailing all kinds of side issues across the broad aspects of the case.' That afternoon Norman had to waste time listening to Sir Felix Schuster, once so important a banking figure but now virtually forgotten: 'Has a plan a fund Am deposits with German to be for 5–10 yrs under Reich guarantee. (Seems to think he must be busy, suggesting or helping . . .!)'[14] By this time the Joint Committee of clearing banks and accepting houses was asking Norman, in some desperation, to allow them in effect to call in their credits; his response was that, quite apart from the fact that to do so might not actually be possible, even to attempt to do so would almost certainly make the German situation far worse. His hopes, by the end of the day, were pinned on a political solution to the German crisis, in the form of an international conference to be held in London from the 20th; but in the event, before that conference could begin, the plight of the British banks with a large German exposure was sealed when short-term credits were frozen by the German government, which also forbade the repatriation of foreign deposits. The diplomatic conference, anyway, achieved little or nothing.

The accepting houses most affected were Schröders, Kleinworts, Huths, Japhets, Goschen & Cunliffe, and Arbuthnot Latham. Norman, to the dismay of Kleinworts for one, declined to bale them out, though he did ask their own banks to look sympathetically upon requests for assistance. Accordingly, gladly or otherwise, Westminster lent £3.5m to Kleinworts and also gave substantial assistance to Schröders. For both these hitherto flourishing houses, their entire capital was now locked up – an unappetising prospect. Yet no one in the City had greater 'bounce' than Frank Tiarks of Schröders, and between late July and early September he masterminded the first Standstill Agreement, which guaranteed the interest on London's frozen credits to Germany. Much of his work was done in Berlin, from where S.M. Ward reported to 8 Bishopsgate on 31 July: 'Tiarks showed me the scheme for dealing with existing foreign credits, which will be in the hands of all central Banks this morning . . . Tiarks was not very clear about the machinery and as it was past midnight I didn't worry him. He preserves a delightful air of detachment – all done to try and help others!' And a fortnight later, again writing to Villiers, Ward recalled how Tiarks had come in one evening to the Hotel Esplanade, 'showed me the Stillhalte plan "in strict confidence" and said that he had settled everything . . .' Unquestionably it was a major achievement on the part of Tiarks, who received important support from William Mortimer of the solicitors Slaughter and May, once the negotiations moved from Berlin to Basle.[15] Schröders and Kleinworts were down as a result of the German financial crisis, but not quite out.

Even before Tiarks began his work, however, the focus of the City as a whole had turned away from the German situation and towards what was developing into the long-expected, full-blown British financial crisis.[16] 'We are concerned and surprised at sudden drop of sterling today,' Harrison wired Norman on Wednesday, 15 July. 'Can you throw any light on this?' The immediate cause, not wholly clear to an even more concerned and surprised London, was twofold: worries about German exposure; and the publication two days earlier in the Macmillan

Report of figures showing, with unprecedented starkness, that London was a net short-term debtor of £254m. For some, as gold flowed out over the next few days, it was confirmation that the perils of economic and financial internationalism were starting to be exposed. 'Norman has sacrificed our industry and our production for the sake of a bill-market which may plunge us into disaster at any moment,' the strong tariff reformer Leo Amery declared at dinner on the 19th. 'We have preferred to be moneylenders to being manufacturers.' By the 22nd the Bank had lost £22m of gold in the course of a week. The Smith St Aubyn journal entry that day summed up the through-a-glass-darkly mood in the City at large: 'Outlook not too cheerful, but no real news from anywhere.'[17] Next day Bank rate, which had gone down to $2\frac{1}{2}$ per cent on 14 May, was increased by one full point, but this most conventional of moves barely checked the outflow of gold.

By the following weekend it was time to look elsewhere for support. The French authorities were starting to worry that it would be their turn next, and on Saturday the 25th Kindersley – apparently the French choice – was despatched to Paris to discuss a possible French loan to the Bank of England. Aid from America was instinctively more acceptable, and the following day Norman met Jack Morgan, who had just arrived in Britain. When he duly popped the question about a possible American credit, Morgan replied (as he reported back to New York):

> I said it seemed to me that before they could safely borrow in the USA, the Government would have to show at least some plan of restoration of financial stability and should at least have expressed the intention to reduce the expenditures to come within their means. This he [Norman] agreed was quite right and told me he had Snowden's permission to discuss the subject with me and report to me on the result.[18]

Norman's agreement that Britain could hardly expect American support without first making it clear that it would get its own financial house in order was entirely sincere. He had recently seen, ahead of publication, the May Report, indicating that the budget deficit was likely to be £120m – an alarmingly large figure in the era before deficit financing.

Part of Norman's diary entry for the next day, Monday the 27th, adequately conveys the sense of crisis:

10. Ch. Ex & RH at N° 11
11.15 C. Treas^y & ECG & R. Hopkins – till 1 pm
12. Cl. Bankers with EMH till 12.50
RMKs proposal from Paris of Credit £25m: similar credit

fr FRB: all fully discussed (also suspension)
    6. Pease, Goschen & RHM. Danger of suspension of gold payments.

These were lucid enough jottings, but Norman's own mental condition was starting to cause increasing concern to those around him, and indeed elsewhere. 'Can't he be persuaded to quit his panicky talk?' Russell Leffingwell of Morgans in New York implored Jack Morgan on Tuesday the 28th. For once he was probably not in the mood to savour the latest joke from just across the road in Capel Court. 'A member of the House just back from Spain, was describing in the market a bull fight he had witnessed,' recorded 'Autolycus'. '"The bull," he concluded, "has not got a chance." "Probably more chance than he would have in the London Stock Exchange," one of the listeners commented feelingly.'[19]

Amazingly, at this of all times, the City was intimately involved in one of the most well-publicised criminal cases heard at the Old Bailey between the wars.[20] Lord Kylsant, autocratic Chairman of the Royal Mail group of shipping companies, based in Leadenhall Street, was accused of having issued a false prospectus in 1928; his fellow-defendant, Harold Morland of the accountants Price Waterhouse, was accused of having aided or advised him in the publication of false statements concerning the Royal Mail's accounts in 1926/7. The background to the case was immensely complicated. The group had long been the dominant force in British shipping, but by the late 1920s it was seriously over-extended; and in the course of 1930 it required much assiduous high-level action, involving Norman and the Treasury as well as Hyde of Midland, Brigadier-General Arthur Maxwell of Glyn Mills, and the leading accountant Sir William McLintock, to enable the group to be kept going. By the end of the year, with Kylsant effectively removed from control, it seemed that catastrophe had been averted.

So indeed it had (though a long and painful reconstruction of Royal Mail still lay ahead), but scandal was about to break. Kylsant was the former Owen Philipps, and for well over a decade he had been at odds with his brother John, now Lord St Davids, of investment trusts fame. Early in 1931, and seemingly acting on behalf of the shareholders, the latter publicly queried the basis of the rescue plan, in particular why shareholders had not been warned about the real nature of the group's profit and loss allocations; and following questions in the Commons, the Attorney-General had no alternative but to bring forward a prosecution. The case began on 20 July. 'Public interest, especially in the City, in the trial was particularly intense and several hundred had applied for seats,' noted the *FT*; though in the event, the public gallery was filled 'by thirty or forty individuals, mostly of the type usually seen at the Old Bailey'.

Kylsant made a stiff, unyielding witness, while Morland tried to rise above the proceedings. When a fellow-partner asked him how he was coping, he replied, 'Well, they treated Christ much worse for much less so why should I bother?'

Much turned on whether the secret transfer of hidden reserves was acceptable, commonplace practice, and expert witnesses broadly confirmed that it was. At one point an exchange between Morland and the Attorney-General, Sir William Jowitt, revealed the extent to which auditing remained rooted in the *caveat emptor* assumptions of the nineteenth century:

> *Jowitt:* Do you think that when an ordinary, intelligent member of the public or shareholders . . . looked carefully through the accounts for 1926 and 1927 he would have a true picture of the company's position?
>
> *Morland:* The balance sheet gave him a perfectly true position of the company's position . . .
>
> *Jowitt:* It is very important for a shareholder to know . . . what current earnings his company is making?
>
> *Morland:* I do not see why.
>
> *Jowitt:* Do you agree that one of the most material circumstances which every shareholder has a right to know is the earning capacity of a company?
>
> *Morland:* Of course, I do not agree with that.

The case lasted for a week and a half, and the story went that as the jury pondered its verdict, Mrs Morland rang the court to ask if her husband would be late for dinner. 'Yes, Madam,' replied the solicitor, 'I should think about 12 months late.' In the event, Morland was acquitted, though never forgiven by some of his partners for having failed to consult them; but Kylsant was found guilty of issuing a false prospectus and sent to Wormwood Scrubs for a year. 'If he was guilty,' thought the *Economist*, 'then most of the chairmen of large public companies would today be in custody,' and in general much sympathy was expressed towards him. After his release he and his brother 'chose', in the words of their biographer, 'to ignore the existence of one another'.[21]

The day before the end of the Royal Mail trial on 30 July, Norman had buckled. '12.30 about – left C. Treas^y & went home about 3 o'clock. Queer.' So noted his diary on Wednesday the 29th, and thereafter Norman was only a bit-player as the crisis unfolded. His capable deputy, Sir Ernest Harvey, stepped into the breach, and on the 30th Bank rate rose from $3\frac{1}{2}$ to $4\frac{1}{2}$ per cent. That same day the Joint Committee of the British Bankers' Association and the Accepting Houses Committee (i.e. of clearing bankers and merchant bankers) sent a strongly worded appeal to MacDonald and Snowden. In the eyes of the nine signatories, who included Beaumont Pease, Sir Harry Goschen, Brand, Olaf Hambro, Robert Holland-Martin, Anthony de Rothschild and Tiarks, the solution was as clear as the problem:

> London has for many years, and, indeed, until quite recently, been regarded as the most stable monetary centre in the world, and is the repository, therefore, of huge sums of short foreign money, which are placed here in order to obtain the unparalleled advantage of the freedom and liquidity of the London Money Market. In the Macmillan Committee's Report these foreign deposits were there estimated at about £400 million. They can be withdrawn at short notice, and, if the foreign investor once loses confidence in the stability of our exchange, they will be withdrawn, just as similar deposits have recently been withdrawn from Germany . . . If we were to pursue a sound budgetary policy and show reasonable elasticity in adjusting ourselves to world economic changes, we should be able to maintain our exchanges without any difficulty . . . Every effort should immediately be made to restore confidence both at home and abroad. What we have urged other nations to do, we must now do ourselves, namely, restrict our expenditure, balance our budget, and improve our balance of trade.[22]

The publication on Friday the 31st of the May Report, with its disturbing budgetary projection and accompanying recommendation that government achieve a cut in unemployment benefit of £67m, served to fortify the bankers' argument.

Even Sayers, the most sober of financial historians, has argued that the Report 'presented the government's deficit in grossly exaggerated fashion', but what mattered was contemporary perception, which broadly speaking took May's findings as gospel. Not least MacDonald and Snowden, especially after the former had been told by Harvey on the Friday afternoon that the Bank's reserves had fallen by £55m since the middle of the month. By the Saturday it seemed that the point had been carried, as MacDonald announced the appointment of a Cabinet economy committee, which would meet for the first time on 25 August in order to make a detailed policy response to the May Report. Moreover, also on the Saturday, the Bank announced that it had had made available to it for three months two major foreign credits, in the form of £25m each from the American and French central banks. As almost all the great and the good departed or prepared to depart for their summer holidays, it seemed that the crisis had been postponed, pending a reasonable examination of the budgetary situation. For the City, the underlying objective remained unchanged. 'Whether we returned to the gold standard too early or not is debatable,' Peacock wrote to a correspondent on Saturday the 1st, 'but is no longer a matter of more than academic interest. To go off the gold standard for a nation that depends so much upon its credit as we do would be a major disaster.'[23]

With such its fundamental and, for the time being, unwavering priority, the City naturally viewed the May Report as a welcome stick with which to beat the government. Not surprisingly, some in the Labour Party viewed matters rather differently. Beatrice Webb, in her diary note of 4 August on the Report, anticipated the eventual political outcome: 'Luxury hotels and luxury flats, Bond Street shopping, racing and high living in all its forms is to go unchecked; but the babies are not to have milk and the very poor are not to have homes. The private luxury of the rich is apparently not *wasteful expenditure*.' The following day, the second business day after the Bank Holiday weekend, Norman struggled back to the Bank for the regular weekly meeting of the Committee of Treasury. 'Governor suffering from nervous dyspepsia,' Addis noted. 'Better but not well.' Keynes, writing to MacDonald the same day, touched on what he saw as the 'lack of clear guidance' coming from the City: 'The Accepting Houses, who constitute the major part of the Court of the Bank of England, are many of them more or less insolvent. The Governor is probably near the end of his nervous resources. It is now a problem for the Government rather than for the City.'[24] In a sense he was right, in that ultimately it was a government problem; but in fact, over the next fortnight, the City – and in particular the Bank – would give increasingly clear advice to the beleaguered politicians.

Even as Keynes was writing, sterling was coming under a renewed bout of severe pressure. This new and, as usual, international run on the currency seems to have been prompted partly by alarm at the grim findings of the May Report; partly by abiding doubts about the willingness – or even ability – of the Labour government to take tough remedial action; and partly by a tactical error on the part of the Bank itself, which failed to use its new credits to defend the pound when it came under attack in the foreign exchange markets of Paris and London. This failure, in the subsequent words of one Bank official, 'completely confused the market, created chaos in the continental exchanges, and administered an irreparable blow to confidence in the pound'. On this fateful day, Wednesday the 5th, the Bank lost no less than £4.5m of gold and foreign exchange. Next day Harvey sent a major letter to Snowden, one that took the crisis into a new, still more serious phase:

I wish to explain to you that in less than four weeks we have to date lost more than £60 millions in gold and foreign exchange and, apart from the credits, we have virtually no foreign exchange left. If the flood does not abate we cannot maintain ourselves long.

What particularly impels me to write to you at this moment is the discussion we had in our Committee this morning and the view of the situation taken by the Bank's most trusted advisers – men in intimate touch with the foreign markets – was, I cannot disguise the fact, extremely grave. However black the Governor may have painted the picture in his discussions with you, his picture cannot have been more black than theirs today.

I feel compelled to write to you to tell you this. We are doing all that we can but our power to act is rapidly diminishing. As I tried to explain to you last week, the reports which reach us all show that the sign which foreigners expect from this country is the readjustment of the budgetary position, and this attitude on their part has again been forcibly expressed today in messages from both Paris and New York. I am most anxious not to step beyond my province but I feel I should be failing in my duty if I did not say that with the prospects as they present themselves today the time available for the Government to reach decisions on this subject (as a means of safeguarding the value of sterling) may be much shorter than recently seemed likely.

Norman, feeling 'queer at home', would surely have endorsed his deputy's tactics.[25]

Norman was still 'sick at home' on Monday the 10th, as Harvey wrote a more cautious letter, this time to Hopkins at the Treasury: 'As regards your request to be informed of the Bank's views on the course to be pursued, it is of course difficult to form any opinion until some indication is forthcoming as to whether the Government are going to take any early action likely to restore public confidence at home and abroad.' And he added that 'the state of public opinion will decide what is likely to be possible and what impossible, and until therefore we have some signs from them it is impossible to form any definite conclusion regarding the matter'. When did financial advice turn into political interference? Harvey, who in many ways had the character of a top-class civil servant, was determined not to overstep the mark, invisible and shifting though it was. At the same time, he could hardly rely solely on his blast of the 6th, for as he told the Committee of Treasury on the 11th, 'he feared that neither the Prime Minister nor the Chancellor were yet prepared to face the position and from certain information which he had received he feared that the Chancellor might even be considering the advisability of an abandonment of the Gold Standard'. Villiers, writing the same day to Ward in Berlin, had some sympathy with the government's position: 'It knows the justice of what is written in the May Report and yet it knows that its followers will not support the carrying out of the recommendations.' However, he went on, 'an increasing number of people are beginning to realise that we must restore the confidence of the foreigner in the pound, and this cannot be done unless genuine attempts are made to make the Budget balance'.[26]

Wednesday the 12th saw much activity: the Cabinet's economy committee starting work earlier than had originally been envisaged; the Stock Exchange 'thick with rumour', according to 'Autolycus', including the rumour of an ultimatum from the bankers to the government 'threatening that, if something drastic were not done in the way of retrenchment and reform, the banks would refuse to accept Treasury bills'; Harvey making to the Committee of Treasury what Addis, who had been recalled from his holiday on the Scottish borders, termed 'a grave & disturbing statement'; and the Deputy Governor also keeping up the pressure on MacDonald, telling him that if losses continued on their present scale, 'the £36 millions left to us in our Credits will not last us very much more than a week'. That letter ended with a classic injunction from banker to politician: 'I cannot express too strongly my feeling that any apparent hesitation to supplement your encouraging words to the Press by definite action might speedily undo the good which you have already achieved.' Would MacDonald and his colleagues do the decent thing? Addis thought so. 'Politicians at last appear to realise the urgent gravity of situation & growing distrust abroad of our financial position,' he noted on the 13th, before returning to his holiday. Norman was not so sure. It was probably a day or two before he sailed for Canada and convalescence on the 15th that he was asked by Grigg's wife if the country would 'pull through'. To which he replied, 'Yes, if we can get them frightened enough.' Without doubt, 'them' referred to the government. Or, in the equally expressive words of Harvey, the unexpected man of the hour, writing to Bradbury on the 17th: 'We are having a desperate struggle in the hope that the Government, on whom we are keeping a strong pressure, will adopt and announce this week a programme of financial reform which will sufficiently restore confidence abroad . . . At the present moment it looks like being a neck and neck race . . .'[27]

The Deputy Governor was not inclined to drop the whip at this critical stage. On the afternoon of Tuesday the 18th, almost certainly in the knowledge that the Cabinet's economy committee was in the process of completing drawing up its proposed programme of cuts, Harvey sent another, stiffening letter to Snowden:

> Reports from both the Stock and Exchange markets say that whilst things are somewhat quieter today there is a general atmosphere of nervous hesitancy, everybody anxiously awaiting the announcement of the Government's programmes. I earnestly hope that it may be possible for such announcement to be made as soon as possible as markets are meanwhile the prey of all sorts of rumours, and so long as the present tension lasts there must always be the danger of a sudden break taking place in some quarter and becoming the signal for a general sauve qui peut.

There were no fancy foreign phrases in the Smith St Aubyn diary entry, probably written an hour or two later: 'A filthy day both in weather and money'. The following day – while the Cabinet wrangled fruitlessly – Grenfell informed Jack Morgan, by now on his Scottish estate, that MacDonald was still hopeful that a loan 'could be placed in New York if satisfactory promises of good behaviour were made here'.[28]

By Thursday the 20th, MacDonald was starting to be squeezed hard from both sides. He was told that day that Harvey 'definitely feels that much of the uneasiness arises from the impression that proposals for economy are being ousted by proposals for increased taxation' (an uneasiness reflected locally by the recent deathless assertion of the City editor of *The Times* that '"equality of sacrifice" has an ominous sound in the ears of the investing classes'); but at the same time the TUC announced its opposition to most of the envisaged cuts, an opposition that in turn significantly hardened the resistance of at least several members of the Cabinet, especially towards a reduction in unemployment benefit. The City as a whole was becoming increasingly exasperated. 'Nothing transpired,' noted 'Autolycus' at the end of another day's depressed trading on the Stock Exchange, 'to remove the unpleasant impression of the Government's reluctance to grasp, with any degree of courage, the necessity for putting retrenchment before taxation.' Harvey, however, sensed victory. 'I have no information yet as to how matters are likely to swing in the West-end,' he wrote to Bradbury that day, 'but from one or two indications which have reached me today I am hopeful that they might go in the right direction.' At the same time, he now sanctioned a cable that Grenfell sent in the late afternoon to Morgans in New York. It canvassed whether the British government might be able to place there a $250m loan – if it first made a 'satisfactory announcement as regards balancing Budget', an announcement 'which appeared to you and us indicative of real reform in finance and one permitting you to paint a satisfactory picture'.[29]

By Friday, with Addis again being recalled from holiday, and £33m of the £50m credits having been used up, the Bank was increasingly looking to the possibility of a private American loan to get it out of its immediate hole, after Morgans had told Grenfell how problematic it would be to place a long-term, public loan. MacDonald and Snowden, however, had only managed to persuade the Cabinet to accept cuts totalling £56m, over £20m less than had been provisionally agreed two days earlier; and on being told this, Harvey and Peacock informed MacDonald and Snowden that not only would such cuts be insufficient to enable further credits to be secured from abroad, but also that such was the current flight from sterling, and such the desperation of the exchange-support operation, that the Bank's reserves were likely to be exhausted in only four days. The coming weekend, it was apparent, would pay for all, and at the Cabinet on Saturday the recalcitrant colleagues of MacDonald and Snowden were confronted with a proposed programme now totalling £68.5m, including a 10 per cent cut in the dole. That evening Grenfell wired his New York partners, in effect asking whether the proposed economy plan would be sufficient to persuade them to grant a large and immediate short-term credit. Addis, meanwhile, was completing his first full day back in harness: 'At Bank till 9. Dined at Basque restaurant with Peacock, Grenfell. Lafitte 1917!'[30]

'It is the financiers, British and American, who will settle the personnel and the policy of the British government,' Beatrice Webb noted in her diary on Sunday the 23rd, following the previous day's manoeuvrings. And she added: 'It certainly is a tragically comic situation that the financiers who have landed the British people in this gigantic muddle should decide who should bear the burden. The dictatorship of the capitalist with a vengeance!' That Sunday proved to be a momentous day, though not one that Addis much enjoyed: 'Meeting at Bank of Eng, morning and afternoon. Politicians ill folk to work with.' By early evening Harvey and Grenfell were waiting at the Bank for the response from the Morgans partners, deliberating on Long Island. Eventually it came, saying that an answer to a firm request for a short-term credit could be given within twenty-four hours and asking for confirmation 'that the programme under consideration will have the sincere approval and support of the Bank of England and the City generally and thus go a long way towards restoring internal confidence in Great Britain'.[31]

It was almost nine o'clock by the time the cable confirming the telephone message had been received. Thereupon, according to Grenfell's subsequent account: 'The Deputy Governor, who had been rung up three times by the P.M., took the message down to him at the Cabinet meeting. The P.M. seemed very flustered, came out, looked at it and rushed back and read the whole thing to the Cabinet . . . The Cabinet continued to sit and it was clear that there were very violent discussions.' There were indeed, as virtually half the Cabinet refused to support the proposed cut in unemployment benefit, by far the most important single item in the package before them. By quarter-past ten, intending to resign, MacDonald (accompanied by Harvey) was at the Palace, where King George V was dining with his financial adviser, Peacock. The latter, who was also Harvey's most trusted adviser during the crisis, would later claim – implausibly – that the main subject of conversation during dinner had been grain prices.[32] MacDonald was persuaded to defer his decision until the morrow, and Harvey and Peacock accompanied him back to Downing Street. There they tried to persuade him that he could still serve the country by taking his place at the head of a National Government – a government, of course, fully committed to the enhanced programme of cuts.

Would Norman have approved? Resting up at the Château Frontenac in Quebec, he had been telephoned that evening by Harrison of the Fed. 'Norman,' recorded Harrison afterwards, 'felt that the program was inadequate; that we must not fool ourselves now; that any inadequate program would cause trouble in a year or so and that it is essential that we must force an economic adjustment now and not in a year or so from now; that the program, in his judgement, must be sufficiently drastic to place the cost of output and wages on a competitive basis with the rest of the world and unless that were done he was certain that the program would not be adequate . . .' In short, 'if the Government attacked the situation courageously', then 'they would not need a credit at all'.[33] But for Harvey and Peacock, in London and dealing with the politically possible, their task remained not the long-term reconstruction of the British economy but the immediate one of saving the pound. And Norman, if he had been at the helm, would surely not have quarrelled with that priority.

At ten o'clock on Monday morning MacDonald was asked by the King to form a National Government. At about the same time Harvey told his Committee of Treasury 'that he had been asked whether the Bank and the City generally would view favourably the formation of a National Government, with Mr Ramsay MacDonald as Prime Minister, to carry through the proposals already prepared by Mr MacDonald and Mr Snowden'. Baldly, and without further explanation, the minutes recorded that 'the Committee were of opinion that this would in all circumstances be the best possible arrangement'. For the City it was a day of mixed emotions. 'Meetings, meetings, all day,' noted Addis at its eventual end. 'Leader in "Times" stating credits all exhausted has had a bad effect on the continent. We lost over £10 millions today. At this rate we can only go on for two or three days more.' On the other hand, once the news was out by the afternoon of an imminent coalition government, it undoubtedly served as a significant fillip to the City's rather battered morale. 'Things rather uncertain, with a better tone at the finish of the day,' Smith St Aubyn recorded, while according to 'Autolycus': 'the announcement appeared to lift an invisible weight from the Stock Exchange mind'. Joy was not unconfined, however, and Beatrice Webb's reaction early that evening to the news of the fall of the Labour government was suitably sardonic: 'A startling sensation it will be for those faithful followers throughout the country who are unaware of J.R.M's and Snowden's gradual conversion to the outlook of the City and London society.'[34]

That night, as the *Daily Herald* was being put to bed, the City editor Francis Williams announced to the night editor, 'It's nothing but a ramp'; and the following morning Williams's story on the crisis appeared with the headline 'Bankers' Ramp', and thus a deeply emotive catch-phrase was born. In the course of Tuesday – while 'Autolycus' 'heard from many directions in the Stock Exchange hearty appreciation of the courage shown by Mr Ramsay MacDonald in the stand he has taken for sound finance' – MacDonald himself found time to write a lengthy letter of self-justification to J.L. Garvin of the *Observer*. 'They will go out & say: "It was a bankers' ramp . . ."', he wrote about his 'late comrades' in the Cabinet, but he argued that such a charge would be without foundation:

> They were told by the Chancellor & myself, whom they entrusted to the contact between themselves & the representatives of the Bank of England, that there was no bankers' ramp in the affair & no bankers' hostility, & that further, the bankers never interfered with political policy. All that the bankers said was this –
> 'Trade is most alarming & it is owing to the fact that outside this country a long propaganda & so on have weakened confidence in our finance. We cannot get a foreign loan unless something is done to restore that confidence, & no one can do it except the Government. You will have to do two things, & you can do them in your own way:
> (a) You must balance your Budget
> (b) As the great weakness of your reputation is expenditure which is not

only vast but is steadily expanding & has been mainly met by loans which you do not confess in your Budget, you must also do something about that. You have created the most friendly feeling both in New York & Paris so that they are simply waiting to help us in every way they can, but you must enable them to do so by giving a little more confidence to the foreign investor.'[35]

MacDonald did not consider whether the City's doubts about the Labour government had accentuated the international crisis of confidence, nor whether the undue deference of himself and Snowden towards the bankers had allowed the latter to set the larger agenda, but in broad terms he was surely correct.[36] First and foremost, throughout the weeks leading up to his government's fall, the bankers' unwavering priority was to save the pound; and they saw no other way of doing this other than by major cuts in government expenditure. It was not their aim to force the Labour government from office; indeed they believed that such cuts as were necessary were more likely to be generally accepted if they were implemented by a Labour government. Sincerely convinced that there was no alternative but to strain every sinew in order to stay on the gold standard, and deploying to masterly effect that 'odour of sanctity'[37] so beloved of bankers, especially central bankers, they gave the politicians precious little room in which to manoeuvre. If politicians fail to challenge the assumptions of bankers, that ultimately – then as later – is their responsibility.

*

By late August 1931 this applied as much to Conservative politicians in the National Government as it did to MacDonald and Snowden, who stayed on as Chancellor. Briefly, though, it seemed that the tide had been turned. 'Bank lost £5 millions today which is a little better,' Addis noted on 25 August. 'Went to Proms. A Tchaikovsky night. Glorious.' And on the 26th: 'Coalition ministry formed with Ramsay MacDonald as Premier. Better feelings. Drawings in Bank much reduced.' Soon afterwards it became known that the Bank had received short-term credits from America and France amounting to £80m. But at best, as August gave way to September, the City's mood was distinctly edgy. Gilts fell sharply, and on the 1st, following an anxious visit from the Chairman of the Stock Exchange, Harvey used the Government broker 'to let it be known in the Market that it was considered most improbable that the Government's programme would include any discriminatory tax on fixed interest bearing securities or plans for a forced conversion of 5 per cent War Stock'. Two days after this morale-boosting move, a circular issued by the stockbrokers Rowe, Swann & Co of 24 Old Broad Street, in response to 'numerous enquiries we are receiving daily with regard to the advisability of disposing of Sterling securities and reinvesting the proceeds in securities expressed in Foreign currencies', might have come draped in the Union Jack:

> We now emphatically put on record our firm conviction that such a course is extremely ill-advised, for the following reasons:-
>
> Firstly, action of this kind is definitely unpatriotic, and can only serve to aggravate the difficulties of His Majesty's Government, who have the right to expect the support of every private individual and financial institution, however large or small.
>
> Secondly, we feel strongly that, bearing in mind the present extremely low realisation value of Sterling securities, any nervous investor will pay a heavy penalty for his timidity in sacrificing sound securities at the present 'scrap' prices.
>
> Thirdly, we view the general national acceptance of the true principles of thrift, economy and strict financial prudence as the turning-point in our Nation's post-war history, and that, therefore, we shall emerge triumphant from this period of crisis which is undoubtedly *international* in character.
>
> We are, moreover, firmly convinced that the inherent financial stability of our great country is unimpaired, and that the present time may afford a unique opportunity for the purchase of British Government securities, which we still regard as being the safest investments in the World.[38]

A day or two later, with general confidence reviving, Addis was able for the second time to resume his holiday.

Everyone was waiting for Snowden's emergency budget on the 10th. It more or less followed the lines of the package that the Labour government had failed to agree upon and received a predictably enthusiastic response from the *FT*, which claimed that the 'resurgence of confidence in sterling is now well on the way to re-establishment, thanks to adhesion to an open and honest policy'. However, at a dinner party on Sunday the 13th, Rudolph de Trafford of Higginsons asserted that (in the words of his diarist host, Robert Bruce Lockhart) 'we must have an election this year . . . there will be no confidence in the City until we can get a government which will be in for several years . . .' By this time Keynes was advocating devaluation, and next morning the *Financial News* turned on him savagely. To do so, it claimed, would mean losing 'the sheet-anchor upon which our place as an international monetary centre depends', and it asked: 'Is this country to plunge the nations of the world into a new chaos because we have not the force of character or the common sense to free ourselves from the tyranny of trade union opposition to a revision of nominal wages?'[39]

But devaluation or no devaluation, managed money or gold standard, some things did not change. Also on Monday the 14th the Stock Exchange Committee considered a letter (dated the 10th) that it had received from a member, Chas W. Goff:

> I have for some time hesitated to write you on the horse-play which takes place in the Stock Exchange, but as in the last fortnight I have been twice kicked in the ankle and have previously been pushed, I venture to complain to the Committee in the hope that some steps may be taken to put a stop to it. On several occasions I have been conducting my business when some one has been violently pushed into me and I know that this has been the experience of many other members of the Stock Exchange. Today it was not the fault of the man who kicked me, but the fault of some one else and this is almost invariably the case. I am informed that some of the men who are responsible for the horse-play are not even members. I earnestly hope that the Committee may see its way to issue some very strong notice in regard to horse-play of all description, as it is intolerable to feel that one cannot go into the Stock Exchange without running the risk of being injured.

Goff attended in person and was told, in accordance with usual policy, that 'if he would bring a definite complaint against any member or clerk the Committee would deal with the case'.[40] As usual there was no follow-up, with Goff knowing full well that the sneak was not one of Capel Court's favourite species. The following day, Tuesday the 15th, came news that put Stock Exchange horse-play into the shade. There had been, it transpired, 'unrest' among the naval ratings at Invergordon – protests about pay cuts, which press headlines quickly turned into the appearance of a full-scale mutiny. Almost six and a half years on, the final act of the ill-fated return to gold was about to be played out.

'It is now realised that this country is determined to do its utmost to avoid a depreciation of sterling,' Paul Einzig's 'Lombard Street' column in the *Financial News* declared on Wednesday the 16th; that afternoon, challenged by the reports from Invergordon, ministers made a poor show in the Commons of toughing it out over the announced cuts in government expenditure. The Bank's reserves, which had been gradually ebbing away during the month, lost £3.5m in the course of the day. Anxieties about a precipitate general election further drained away the last vestiges of international confidence in sterling, and on Thursday the Bank lost no less than £10m. Although some in the City thought that an early election would have a stabilising effect on the situation, the Bank itself decidedly did not and was pushing hard for that election to be delayed. However, during the course of the 17th it became clear that the dominant Conservative element in the coalition was – for fairly blatant party political reasons – committed to as early an election as possible.

'It is believed that withdrawals owing to distrust in the future of sterling have largely come to an end,' stated Einzig's column on the morning of Friday the 18th, in one of the more off-the-beam remarks in the history of financial journalism. In the course of the day the Bank lost £18.75m. It was an enormous sum, partly explained by the fact that at some point in the morning the Bank, apparently without consulting ministers, gave up on the gold standard and let sterling go.[41] Invergordon, the probable imminence of an election and a new, serious Dutch banking crisis all contributed to the decision – essentially a reluctant conviction that the game was no longer worth the candle.

Early that evening Addis was summoned for the third time from holiday (catching the night train from Howick) and MacDonald was recalled from Chequers, where he had just gone. At 9.45, at what MacDonald privately called the most solemn conference ever to have been held at 10 Downing Street, the Prime Minister met Harvey and Peacock. Harvey explained that the day's losses 'had exhausted the dollar credit', but that 'there was £15,000,000 available from France'. He added that he 'did not himself think that we could raise enough to save the situation'; that 'if the situation could not be saved it was merely waste of more money'; and that 'he did not see that it was worthwhile raising £100,000,000 if people were only going to draw it out'. To which statements MacDonald 'agreed that if one could not see one's way through it was better to acknowledge it now'.

The discussion then turned to practicalities:

The Deputy Governor stated that it was better to stop on Monday morning as that would give time to warn the press, and the public could be stopped from rushing the banks. It might be necessary to stop the Stock Exchange tomorrow – by an unhappy chance they were meeting on Saturday for the first time [i.e. since the war] . . .
The Prime Minister asked what would the effect be on things in general, particularly on the internal situation, of this upset? Mr Peacock replied that it would be an awful blow to everyone, but that the banks would loyally support one another in trying to keep working, and if the press played up, appearances at home might not be too bad. (The Deputy Governor interpolated that the shock would be felt most keenly by wealthy financiers: there were lots of people who had in fact said that this was the

one cure for our ills.) Mr Peacock went on to explain the shock to our people all over the world in Ireland, Egypt, India and so on: in every village a bill on London was looked upon as cash – and it would be cash no longer.

At the end of the meeting, Peacock remarked that 'no one could accuse this country of not having made every effort before letting the pound go'; and 'it was pointed out' – by Harvey? by Peacock? by MacDonald? – 'that by having balanced the Budget, whatever happened, this country had at least demonstrated her will to play the game at all costs'.[42] It was, no one added, a game that had wreaked enormous damage.

The decision to re-open the Stock Exchange on Saturdays had followed a campaign run by the *Daily Express*, and inevitably this particular Saturday, the 19th, proved a difficult day in Capel Court, though as yet no announcement had been made about going off gold. In the eyes of 'Autolycus', however, writing his column for Monday's *FT* after the announcement had been made, the House came through with flying colours: 'While Stock Exchange members are not of those who wear their hearts upon their sleeves for daws to peck at, it is impossible for them not to feel a quiet pride in the fact of London being able and ready to stand up to the flood of selling which took place.' And he added that 'if ever the jobber vindicated his claim to fill an essential place in the machinery of the world's financial hub, he did it in the Consol market last Saturday'.[43]

Over the weekend many high-level meetings were held, but they were all to implement the fundamental decision that had been taken on Friday evening. A formal announcement to the press was made on the Sunday, shortly after Harvey had sent a deliberately cryptic cable to Norman, who was returning home from Montreal on board SS *Duchess of Bedford*: 'Sorry we have to go off tomorrow and cannot wait to see you before doing so.' Norman, understandably, was somewhat puzzled. The press on Monday the 21st sought to bolster the City's confidence. 'Stated bluntly,' declared the *FT* in its leader about the enforced departure from the standard, 'the main reason is that foreigners for no cause associated with our own internal conditions have not only prevented gold from fulfilling its proper function in the settlement of international trade balances but have also drawn largely upon our supplies for reasons peculiar to their own territories.' The *FN*, still more patriotic, contrasted the 'panic-stricken scramble for gold' that had occurred abroad with the stoicism at home, 'where the development of the crisis has been faced with our characteristic coolness and good humour'. *The Times* found a silver lining: 'A suspension of gold payments by a Socialist Government would have been one thing. But suspension by a National Government committed to retrenchment and reform is another.' And it anticipated that once the trade account had been balanced in the same way that the budget had been, 'this country will return to the gold standard'.[44]

During that Monday, with the Stock Exchange closed, the atmosphere was far less troubled than some had feared. 'Mr Farrer was in this morning,' Villiers wrote from 8 Bishopsgate to Albert Gordon at Kidder Peabody, 'and he remarked how different the present crisis is from any previous one which he has seen because on the present occasion there seems a complete absence of panicky feeling.' Villiers was generally sanguine ('I feel quite certain that our Government has done the right thing'), but for Grenfell it was a sad, even dreadful day. 'You will see by this morning's papers that after all our struggles we are driven off the gold standard,' he lamented to Vice-Admiral Sir Aubrey Smith at Iden near Rye. 'It has been rather a losing fight for some time – one rung a day – until the Navy business knocked us clean off the ladder. England was represented to the foreigner by the Navy and the Bank of England. It is all very bewildering and distressing.' Keynes, by complete contrast, was in jubilant mood, described as 'chuckling like a boy who has just exploded a firework under someone he doesn't like'. Yet Virginia Woolf perhaps had the right of it. 'We're off,' she scribbled in her diary on the 21st, '& I write about Donne. Yes; & what could I do better, if we are ruined, & if everybody had spent their time writing about Donne we should not have gone off the Gold Standard – thats my version of the greatest crisis &c &c &c – gabble gabble go the geese, who cant lay golden eggs.'[45]

*

For Eric Blair, the future George Orwell, it was all an even more massive irrelevance. On Saturday the 19th, after two and a half weeks hop-picking in Kent, he and his new friend Ginger returned to London, going to a 'kip in Tooley Street', just south of the river. They stayed there for about a fortnight, and several mornings, while it was still dark, they walked across London Bridge and found some work in the fish market at Billingsgate. An integral part of the City – close to the Monument and barely quarter of a mile from the Bank of England – it was a world apart from Harvey, Peacock and the hereditary grandees:

> You go there at about five and stand at the corner of one of the streets which lead up from Billingsgate into Eastcheap. When a porter is having

trouble to get his barrow up, he shouts 'Up the 'ill!' and you spring forward (there is fierce competition for the jobs, of course) and shove the barrow behind. The payment is 'twopence an up'. They take on about one shover-up for four hundredweight, and the work knocks it out of your thighs and elbows, but you don't get enough jobs to tire you out. Standing there from five till nearly midday, I never made more than 1s 6d.[46]

PART TWO

Credits and Debits

Unreal City,
Under the brown fog of a winter dawn,
A crowd flowed over London Bridge, so many,
I had not thought death had undone so many.
Sighs, short and infrequent, were exhaled,
And each man fixed his eyes before his feet.
Flowed up the hill and down King William Street,
To where Saint Mary Woolnoth kept the hours
With a dead sound on the final stroke of nine.

T.S. Eliot, *The Waste Land* (1922)

CHAPTER TEN

Died Waiting

'There is,' wrote H.M. Tomlinson near the start of *Gallions Reach*:

> a region of grey limestone and glass, horizontally stratified into floors, intercepted by narrow ravines called avenues, and honeycombed by shipping and commercial offices, which lies between Fenchurch and Leadenhall Streets. Billiter Avenue is one of its intersecting clefts. This secluded corner of the city must be traversed on foot, because its narrow paths are marked out only for its cliff climbers; but nobody ever goes into it except they who are concerned with the secrets of its caves. The wealth of the cave of Sinbad, compared with that of most of the offices of this canton of the city, would have seemed but a careless disposal of the superfluous, yet within the guarded recesses of the cliffs of Billiter Avenue no treasure is ever visible. It may be viewed at all only by confidential initiates, and even they cannot see it except as symbols in ledgers, bills of lading, bank drafts, warrants, indents, manifests, and in other forms designed to puzzle moths and official liquidators in their work of corruption. It has no beauty. It is not like the streets of jasper. It does not smell of myrrh. Its gates are not praise. There is no joy in it even for the privileged. A life devoted to the cherishing of this treasure gives to a devotee a countenance as grave as would golf or the obsequies of a dear friend. One rose in the sunlight, or a snail on the thorn, is superior to its dry and papery fame. Still, its influence is there, powerful, though abstract and incredible. The hidden treasure of this region, if as baffling to innocents as the beauty of the innumerable brass name-plates at its doors, has command, nevertheless.

Unfortunately most of the rest of Tomlinson's novel, published in 1927, is set in Malaya. Three years later, however, there appeared the most systematic attempt yet at the great City novel. Ponderous and over-schematic though it is, J.B. Priestley's *Angel Pavement* has many virtues – above all its sympathetic, unpatronising delineation of various distinctive City types. His focus, like that of Tomlinson, is on the City's commercial as opposed to financial sector: Twigg & Dersingham of 8 Angel Pavement (first floor) is a small firm whose speciality is the cabinet-making and wholesale furnishing trades. The firm's senior traveller is called Goath, and Dersingham has often said to his veteran cashier Smeeth, and Smeeth has often said to Dersingham, 'that what Goath didn't know about selling inlays and veneers and the like was not worth knowing'.[1]

It was a perceptive orientation on the part of Tomlinson and Priestley. 'It is remarkable how some country and even suburban folk think that the City is the Stock Exchange and the Stock Exchange is the City,' Percy Harley noted with some bitterness a few years later, in his memoirs of a shipbroker; indeed, historians as well as contemporaries have rarely given adequate attention to the City's commercial side.[2] When J.A. Findlay, the long-serving Secretary of the Baltic Exchange, declared in 1927 that 'the facilities which London enjoys for buying and selling, chartering and financing, are unique' and that 'one cannot, therefore, see anything to disturb its importance as the commercial centre of Europe', the claim was one that few at the time or over the next decade would have challenged. The larger climate, admittedly, did become less propitious in the 1930s – as governments became protectionist and producers, especially of metals, increasingly sought to control the market, at the expense of the traditional role of the merchant – but even so the City would not have survived the 1930s, with a sharp downturn in international financial business, as well as it did without its impressive range of commercial activities. Floor-space figures are revealing. In 1939, when there were 84.4m square feet of floor-space available for use, offices were responsible for less than half (37.6m), while warehouses, industry and shops took 22.3m, 9.9m and 4.1m respectively. It was almost exactly a century since Surtees had depicted Jorrocks & Co's wholesale tea warehouse in St Botolph's Lane, 'full of hogsheads, casks, flasks, sugar-loaves, jars, bags, bottles, and boxes', but that historical continuity was about to be shattered.[3]

*

At the heart of the commercial City were the seven exchanges that the financial journalist Collin Brooks toured in about 1931 for his entertaining survey, *Something in the City*. Tucked away in Whittington Avenue, 'an unassuming little passage-way' next to Leadenhall Market, he found the London Metal Exchange. Trading took place twice a day (12 to 1.20 and 3.45 to 4.15) in a ring 'of well-cushioned and comfortable looking benches', with a monogram as 'a kind of magic focal point' in the centre of that enclosed floor-space. Membership was divided into forty ring members and just over a hundred other members, the latter of whom could deal only through ring members; the exchange dealt in only four metals – copper, tin, lead and spelter, otherwise known as zinc; and Brooks was struck not only by the very formal, concentrated way of doing business, so different from the more relaxed routine of the Stock Exchange, but also by the invisible power of the LME:

> It is an annex of America and the gorgeous – or, perhaps, not so gorgeous – Beast. From William Street, New York, where stands the National Metal Exchange, from the Malay Straits, from other centres at the outer ends of the world, the cables tick over prices and instructions to Whittington Avenue, bids are made, and over-bid, and on the initiative of men thousands of miles away the business of the ring goes on. Similarly, when Whittington Avenue has ended its morning session and fixed its prices, the ends of the earth, as America and Malay represent them, jump into new activity. The mastery of time is conquered, the disabilities of space; the action and reaction of one centre upon another is a matter of moments only.

Moving on from the domain of 'the Forty Just Men', Brooks walked south to Lower Thames Street to inspect Bunning's magnificent, elaborately decorated Coal Exchange. The exchange met thrice weekly, dealing mainly in British coal and 'attended by coalmen from all parts of the country'. A high proportion of its dealings were, as with most commodity markets, in future deliveries, and Brooks noted that 'as with so many commodity exchanges, the bargains are concluded by word of mouth'.

The London Wool Exchange in Coleman Street, Brooks's next stop, had a rather different rhythm: London wool sales were usually held only six times a year, each lasting about a fortnight or three weeks, and for the rest of the year the exchange was empty. During a sale, the morning was spent inspecting at the warehouses by the docks, the afternoon in boisterous bidding at the exchange's crowded auction room. Brooks quoted S.W. Dowling, author of a generally more restrained, academic survey of the City's exchanges:

> If the lot is in demand, almost before the broker opens his mouth, eager shouts ring out from different parts, anxious bidders emphasizing their calls by shooting out their arms and waving catalogues to attract attention. Many stand up, and sometimes one wonders whether in their keenness they will not lose their balance and fall on to the tiers below. How the broker manages to decide who is the first bidder when a dozen shouts in English or guttural foreign tongues ring out together it is difficult to say. But he does –

and apparently rarely makes an error. If there is a dispute, the lot is put up again. Another lot may not be favoured – there is little bidding; or perhaps a chorus of shrill whistles and a roar of laughter show that some one has got in at a pretty stiff price. But it is all very good fun and good-humoured battle, and the rapidity with which the lots are dealt with, and the keenness and efficiency of the brokers in carrying through the business fill one with admiration.

Much of the wool traded in London continued to come from Australia, and in the midst of the acute political and economic fluctuations of the inter-war years, Brooks remarked that among the wool brokers of Coleman Street 'a fool in Canberra or a fire-eater in Sydney or Melbourne is watched with anxiety'.

In Mincing Lane, traditional centre of the City's commodity markets, Brooks found two buildings. One was the London Rubber Exchange, dealing in rubber shares as well as rubber itself. Since 1928 there had been a catastrophic fall in rubber prices, following the British government's decision to abandon the policy of output restrictions that it had introduced in 1921, and business had suffered – a far cry from the booms of 1910 or even that of 1925. Brooks's hopeful spin, however, was that 'the testing time of low prices' would ultimately 'link more closely the interests of the primary producer and ultimate vendor'. Just along the lane, in the London Commercial Sale Rooms, there was strength in diversity, as Brooks marvelled at how 'in the large hall on the ground floor are bought and sold sugar, tea, coffee, pepper, ginger, spices of all kinds, drugs, cocoa, rice, tapioca, sago, jute, hemp, shellac, copra, soya beans, oils, honey, beeswax, vegetable-wax and ivory'. He noted that 'some goods are sold by auction in special rooms, others by private bargain in the great hall', but that all trading had to 'conform to a general code laid down by the London General Produce Brokers' Association'. Tea, coffee and cocoa all provided particularly active markets, but the market in the LCSR that most excited Brooks was in sugar:

> The technicalities of this market are such that they constitute almost a series of pass-words to a secret society. A broker dealing in raw sugar talks of bargains on a basis of 'beetroot first runnings, 88 per cent nett analysis f.o.b. Continental ports', or of '96 per cent cane c.i.f. London/Liverpool'. Dealers in white sugars are relatively intelligible with their talk of 'type B delivered in a public bonded warehouse in London'.
> A futures contract made for raw or white sugars can, if circumstances dictate, be filled by tendering other specified sugars at fixed premiums and discounts, but the bargainers must adjust their deals not at their own free

will, but under the rules and regulations of yet another powerful body, the Terminal Sugar Market Association. The Terminal market in sugar is conducted under very close safeguards . . .

Dealing in futures has a legitimate place in trading operations, but it is an operation which sometimes has all the inconsequence and all the thrill of a pure gamble. Officially, mere gambling in futures is discountenanced by all markets: unofficially it is condoned. There is a certain economic justification for the practice, which need not worry us at this moment. It may, however, be well to say that the number of gentlemen reputed to be walking the Thames Embankment, without adequate breeching to their posteriors, for not leading trumps, is only slightly less than the number so circumstanced through dealing in futures without adequate training and knowledge of their market.

Brooks's other two main 'commercial' stops were the Corn Exchange in Mark Lane, dealing mainly in grain and flour, and the Baltic Exchange in St Mary's Axe, which was a commodity market (grain, timber, tallow, flour, oilseeds and so on) as well as a market for 'the chartering of vessels and the sale and purchase of their cargoes'. There was also, in a class of its own, Lloyd's, the world's leading insurance market, both marine and non-marine. Recently moved to a new, purpose-built home in Leadenhall Street, it fascinated Brooks as much as it had done many earlier writers:

> The Room is an arresting sight. The corners are filled by a multitude of box-like desks, each with telephones. These leave two great gangways clear, crossing the Room at right-angles and intersecting where the rostrum, an ornate, rather funereal structure, stands in the centre . . .
>
> The underwriters are in the desks abutting upon the gangways, so that the brokers, who move about the room, find them easy of access. The gangways at the busy times are packed with men, some standing, others working their way through the concourse from desk to desk. In one gangway is a lectern on which rests a huge book in which are inscribed, in a large roundhand, the names of vessels that have become casualties during the day. Over the hum of general talk there drones perpetually the monotone of the crier [sitting in the rostrum, calling out the names of members wanted outside]. Over the head of the crier hangs a huge ship's bell, a bell of fame, a bell of ill-omen. It is the Lutine Bell, and it rings when news has to be announced of overdue ships, one stroke meaning bad news, a loss or a wreck, two strokes meaning good or hopeful news, that the vessel is safe in port or is known to be not badly harmed. At the first stroke of the Lutine Bell, there falls a sudden silence. The room waits for the second stroke, which comes or does not come, and those members who will be affected by the state of the overdue ship crowd to the rostrum to hear what tidings are to be heard . . .

When a loss occurs, and it is a partial loss, the policy and claim documents are handed to an expert known as an Average Adjuster. The Average Adjuster's Room at Lloyd's is a place of mystery to those outside the craft ... The principle is, at its simplest, that a loss incurred for all should be equitably borne by all. But the laws of various countries differ as to what is a General Average Loss or how that loss shall be apportioned, and liability to contribute may arise quite apart from any question of assurance ... The average adjusters work under the rules and regulations of their Association, which was founded in 1872, and which incorporated in its official practice the original customs of Lloyd's. The findings of the average adjusters, however, carry no legal sanction. If there is a dispute upon them a Court must decide, but it is significant that rarely indeed are they over-ridden ...

The vast amount of money at risk on a day's business at Lloyd's, the especial skill which is enjoyed by its various sections of practitioners, the history behind it, would none of them justify my claim that Lloyd's may be considered as a competitor for the title of 'the best club in Europe'. That is justified by such adjuncts as its library, its art treasures, its dining-hall, chairman's room, and committee room, with their marvellous panelling and superb decoration. The dining-hall, prepared for distinguished guests, its tables spread with the wonderful plate, which usually lives in a strong room in the basement, and its chandeliers with their lustres alight; the library, a haven of quietude, with its books and treasures; the smaller rooms adjoining the library, with their ancient relics and their prints and souvenirs of old sea fights; the collection of Nelson letters and the old swords of honour and medals – these are communal possessions in which a member may take a personal pride and delight. Even its more modern amenities, the little row of shops and stores tucked away from the outer world, its amateur dramatic and operatic societies, its sports clubs, are much more like the organized activities of a club than those of a business institution ...

In short, Brooks declared with perhaps pardonable hyperbole, 'the wonder is that any man whose happy lot it is to do his daily business in such surroundings ever goes home'.[4]

Thousands and thousands of small, usually specialist firms comprised this diverse City, which extended beyond the somewhat narrow confines of the Bank of England, the banks, the money market and the Stock Exchange. To take just the northern side of Eastcheap in 1927, on the fourth floor of Eastcheap Buildings at number 19 were the dried-fruit broker Geo Oliver, the shipbrokers Davies, Jones & Co, the wine and spirit merchants Howes & Edwards & Sons, the merchant Julius Grimaldi and the fruit merchants Boyes Virgil & Co. The City's fur traders were classic niche operators who held three sales a year, each lasting about a month, at the New Hudson's Bay Sale Room in Garlick Hill. The London Fur Trade Association was established soon after the war, and by 1934 its membership comprised a mixture of brokers (like Eastwood & Holt of Dunster House, Mincing Lane, and S.H. Murley & Co of 24 Garlick Hill) and merchants (like Otto E. Gottstein of 78 Upper Thames Street and I. Solnik of 7 Lawrence Lane). That year its annual report included 'Notes for Guidance in Describing Furs'. For instance, in terms of 'furs made from pieces and not whole skins', the guidelines insisted that 'should an article or garment be made from paws, heads, tails, gills or pieces, it should be so described'; while on another vexed question, 'as Squirrel Lock is an accepted term in the Trade, any article or garment made from the Locks (bellies) of Squirrel must be described as "Squirrel Lock" but must not be described as "Squirrel" only'.[5]

In more continuous action was the City's still very important textile sector, based largely around St Paul's and Wood Street. Essentially a cluster of merchanting businesses increasingly under threat from large-scale textile manufacturers and retailers, it was nevertheless sufficiently competitive for one company – Bradbury Greatorex – to have a staff of some 700 in the late 1930s.[6] There were also the City's many thriving shops. Among those that advertised in the 1927 edition of the City Corporation's *Guide* were Herbert E. Tyler, tailor and breeches maker of 76 and 77 Cheapside ('It is the well-dressed man who commands attention today!'); Selby Farm Dairy of 8 Jewry Street; T.E. Yetton of 83 Long Lane, Aldersgate ('The Oldest Established Bootmaker in the City'); and, situated close to Fenchurch Street Station at 66–72 Minories, the Minories Garage, which claimed that 'after purchase service is maintained to give satisfaction to ourselves as well as to the Car Owner – a point worth noting'. All these are, however, but names, and as always the insistent question asks itself: who were these half a million or so people, who each working day came and spent their eight or nine hours in the City?[7]

'Man Thousands Knew Is Dead,' declared an *Evening News* headline in 1938, the accompanying article reporting the death at the age of sixty-five of Ronald Struan Robertson, a tea inspector with the Mincing Lane tea and rubber brokers Chas Hope & Son. The claim to fame enjoyed by Robertson, who had lived at Sutton, was that for nearly half a century he 'had crossed London Bridge at the same hour every morning' and that 'thousands of Londoners knew him by his carefully brushed top-hat, the inimitable buttonhole and the courteous dignity of his bearing'.[8] Were his sighs short and infrequent, his eyes fixed before his feet? In his case probably not – but perhaps the larger poetic truth still holds.

H.V. Morton, near the start of his career as a travel writer, climbed the Monument on a gusty April day in the mid-1920s:

> What a medieval mass of smoke! Even on clear, windy days with the far spire of Harrow Church like a black pin on a green pincushion there is smoke over London ...
>
> Londoners do not notice this on the ground level, or perhaps they are inoculated, but from the height of the Monument London is a City bathed in smoke. The streets of the City end in blue mists. The spires of the churches push their gray heads above it, and any object more than half a mile away is obliterated by smoke till a wind springs up. The roar of traffic comes up to you. When you hold tight to the iron balustrading you can feel the vibration.
>
> Tiny omnibuses run below, tiny men cross the road, in offices, like sections of honeycomb, thousands of typists are tapping their machines in one big building. You explore the activities of thirty firms as your eye sweeps the frontage. Managers at lonely desks, secretaries coming in with papers, typists fluffing their hair and typing. In one room two office boys are having a fight. What a hive!
>
> On the roof of another building a man is pushing a roller over a golf course! Behind runs the Thames, gray and misty. Barges, tugs, cranes, here and there an anchored ship. A Lilliputian train puffs out from the huge, jet-black ugliness of Cannon Street Station. On the other side Tower Bridge is faintly visible. Immediately below, midgets carry fish in baskets, and a long line of carts twists down to Billingsgate.[9]

Nothing more 'City' than the Monument, built by Wren to commemorate the Fire of London and situated near the house in Pudding Lane where the fire started. Just over 200 feet high, it remained a striking presence on the City skyline.

Down below, young Francis Ommanney, working soon after the war for a leading firm of East India merchants, explored the City's 'black, smoky, jostling, exciting streets':

> Glass and steel egg-box architecture was still a long way in the future and soot-grimed, blackened façades, whitened towards the south-west where the rain struck them, elbowed each other for space along the narrow streets. There was every variety of degenerate classical style with gas lamps slung from wires across the traffic. In the crowds that hurried along and dodged between the traffic many City gents still wore the top hat and swallow-tail coat. So did the bank messengers, hurrying along with their despatch cases chained to their wrists. Buses had open tops and there were

many horse drays in the streets, striking sparks from the granite setts as they pulled up from Smithfield and Billingsgate, and filling the air with the scent of horse manure.

C.H. Rolph, working for the City police, similarly recalled how 'many of the City streets at that time were paved with stone "setts", a kind of rectangular cobblestone constructed on the principle of producing as much din as possible'. On them 'two kinds of vehicles competed for the distinction of making the more row: traction engines, which were numerous, and horse-buses, which were nearly but not quite extinct'. The prize went to the horse-bus, 'because even its iron-rimmed wheels could not drown the appalling rattle of its windows' – until at last, in 1934, horse-drawn vehicles of nearly all description were banned by the City authorities. That reduced the overall din somewhat, as did the gradual replacement of the stone setts, first by wood-blocks and then by the almost ubiquitous Tarmac.

Rolph was also struck by the City's 'submerged tenth', its 'watchmen, lamplighters, beggars, wandering evangelists, sandwich-men and street traders', although the City Corporation did not allow that latter class to sell fireworks, cigarettes or drinks. 'There were,' he added, 'quite a number of street beggars in the City in the twenties, particularly around Throgmorton Street, Copthall Avenue, Tokenhouse Yard, and Lothbury. The attraction, no doubt, was the daily "street market" run by the Stock Exchange, which every afternoon crowded the roadway of Throgmorton Street with prosperous-looking men in black jackets and striped trousers, their faces perennially sunburned by weekends of golf and yachting.' The latter-day perspective of Sir George Bolton, recalling his days as a dynamic young arbitrageur with Helbert Wagg, was more benign. Odd characters he came across included the newspaper-seller at the corner of Threadneedle Street and Cornhill, who told his customers their fortunes; 'the mysterious individual in a shabby but well-cared-for suit with an open-necked shirt and a carefully rolled umbrella and a mane of greying fair hair, who every evening walked down Cornhill and stood in the centre of the Bank Crossing for hours surveying his empire'; and 'the fat man in the tiny oyster bar opposite Liverpool Street Station who would give me a dozen oysters, brown bread and butter for half-a-crown'.[10] It may have been the 1920s, but the spirit of the City, with its ceaseless ebb and flow of variegated humanity, was still a lot nearer to Mayhew's London than it was to Laing's *Metropolis*.[11]

Certainly it was not yet the age of the staff canteen. One of Bolton's colleagues, Lionel Fraser, worked his way up from regular but frugal lunches at the Red House in Bishopsgate ('ruled over by Emmie, as attentive a waitress as ever existed') to '"the Throg", Lyons's in Throgmorton Street, which occupied a distinctly higher place in the lunch-time hierarchy' and where 'even the Government broker ate'. The Throgmorton restaurant was the largest in the City, but scattered across the square mile were plenty of humbler Jo Lyonses, ABCs and Express Dairies, with their main clientele comprising a mixture of office boys, the less well-paid clerks and the female typists and secretaries who were now starting to be employed in large numbers. The abiding literary image of a cheap lunch in the inter-war City is fairly grim – 'a meaty, vapourish smell of beef and mutton, sausages and mash, hangs down like a damp net in the middle of the eating-house,' Louis reflects in Virginia Woolf's *The Waves*, as 'I prop my book against a bottle of Worcester Sauce and try to look like the rest' – and perhaps it does not mislead. Ommanney's recollection of lunch at the ABC tea-shop in Bishopsgate was one of only modified rapture:

> Waitresses with sweaty armpits rushed to and fro between the marble-topped tables. On a counter a huge metal tea urn sent up sacrificial vapours which bedewed the window where the red buses slid dimly to and fro beyond a moving screen of heads or umbrellas. The waitress called you 'dear' and 'luv' but never waited long enough to hear your whole order. She dashed off to shout things like 'two poached eggs twice and a Cornish pasty', 'two egg-and-veg and a Melton Mowbray, luv!' . . . The décor was strictly utilitarian. Big spotted mirrors on the 'lincrusta' walls reflected the rows of people sitting at the marble-topped tables, many of them with their overcoats and hats on. Branched stands stood about like trees bearing more overcoats and hats like heavy fruit and foliage . . . Lunch was very cheap and I think I fed myself quite adequately, or at any rate with something that filled me up for the afternoon, on less than a shilling a day . . .[12]

Notwithstanding the rise of the multiples, choice was still ample. Take the densely commercial area around Mincing Lane. For those not wanting to spend over a shilling, tip excluded, there was the Colonial Restaurant buried deep behind 9 Mincing Lane and Eastcheap, offering a large portion of prime Scotch beef or English mutton; for those more impecunious, there was Lockharts in Fenchurch Street, with its boiled pork and pease pudding plus veg; and for the well-off, or for that special occasion, there was the justly famed London Tavern at the corner of Mark Lane and Fenchurch Street, a favoured place for City banquets and, in the words of an occasional habitué of the 1930s, 'commodious with snack bars, cocktail bars, oyster bars, grill rooms, restaurants'. Queen Elizabeth had reputedly had breakfast there on her release from the Tower, but in the immediate post-war period there was probably no more celebrated eating-place in the City than Birch's of Cornhill. In his *The London Perambulator*, James Bone stopped off in 1925:

> It is a little green shop of George III's date, with three round-headed windows and a round-headed door just large enough for a Lord Mayor, but hardly wide enough for his coachman, the woodwork all carved with innocent renaissance decorations. A plain wooden floor and narrow oak counter worn by generations of scrubbers, a small plain settee of Chippendale period, are the only furniture, but in the national convention of separating Englishmen whenever possible, there is a sort of open screen of an earlier period dividing the little place in two. The open beams under the ceiling have been hewn by the adze: In this little low-roofed bower you may see the soundest and stoutest men on the 'Change standing and eating a special three-decked jam sandwich and drinking sherry or whisky-jelly or coffee, while upstairs turtle soup and oysters at surprising prices are being consumed.[13]

The following year saw the demolition of Birch's restaurant (though the business was transferred to Old Broad Street), as Lloyds Bank acquired that and other leases in both Cornhill and Lombard Street in order to build a new, eight-storey head office. The symbolism was unmistakable.

Mass demolition was followed by deep excavations, to lay the foundations of the new building. These diggings had unforeseen consequences, for on 6 August 1927 – a Saturday, fortunately – they caused the collapse of the head office of Commercial Union, adjacent to the site in Cornhill. Cracks had started to appear and widen that morning, and at 11 p.m. the caretaker and his family made a hurried departure from the building, as a big crowd began to gather on the steps of the Royal Exchange opposite. *The Times* described the most dramatic scene in that area since the Royal Exchange itself had burned down in 1838:

> A few minutes before 12 fresh fissures were seen, people were urged to turn back, and then the top floor gave way. An electric light had been left burning and the wire fused as the masonry poured down. The whole building appeared to heave . . . and the [western] end fell away with a loud roar which was heard for a considerable distance. Clouds of dust filled Cornhill and spread over the Royal Exchange to the Bank of England. When they had subsided it could be seen that the end of the building had been ripped out as effectively as if a bomb had torn away the structure . . .

In an era before the invention of 'total war', the scene next morning was not unshocking:

> Rooms had been cut across their middle. A stack of chimneys stood untouched above the highest floor, where the wreckage of a kitchen had been left. An iron girder hung precariously from the roof level. Below was the wreckage of offices ... From the lower floors thick girders hung downwards, bent and distorted by the weight of stone which had crashed down upon them. Everywhere there was a tangle of pipes and wires ...

Cornhill was closed to traffic for some three months, Commercial Union had to move elsewhere while its head office was completely reconstructed, and Lloyds with good grace paid £80,000 compensation. Apparently it was all the fault of loose soil, with the Wallbrook having once flowed this way.[14]

The new head office of Lloyds was part of a remarkable wave of bank building.[15] The merchant banks, as usual nimbler on their feet than the clearers, began the process with four new buildings in the mid-1920s, though Rothschilds and Barings remained aloof, content with their Victorian homes. Schröders decided to stay at 145 Leadenhall Street, but built afresh and, to quote the bank's historian, 'the front elevation was in a Georgian style with unadorned Portland stone facings, presenting a sedate and dignified face to the world'. Inside, however, 'the decoration was sumptuous: the walls of the banking hall and the principal stairway were lined with barley-sugar coloured Siena marble; a Grecian frieze embellished the tiled floor and was echoed along the walnut wood banking counter, which was topped with a polished brass grille; walnut coffering ornamented the tall ceiling, from which was suspended large art deco chandeliers of opaque glass with bronze fittings'. Not far away, at 41 Bishopsgate, Hambros occupied new premises: a handsome, tall building by Niven & Wigglesworth that would be praised by Pevsner for its 'brick and stone dressings, simply and elegantly neo-Georgian'. Leyland Rubber Flooring subsequently used a photograph of the interior of Hambros to advertise its product: 'A rubber floor gives the sense of dignity to a building; the silence that gives atmosphere – the atmosphere of solidity and worth ...'[16]

Any merchant bank worth its salt frowned on unnecessary ostentation – certainly exterior ostentation – and at the new home of Lazards at 10 Old Broad Street (rented on its upper floors to James Capel and Cazenove's) the guiding wishes of Kindersley and his colleagues were that, according to the *Builder*, 'it should give the impression of a country bank moved to London', and they 'expressed a preference for red bricks, simple lines, and the elimination of unnecessary ornament'. Morgan Grenfell's new home was in a pleasantly quiet backwater at 23 Great Winchester Street – 'I do not regret the nervous strain brought on by the busses [*sic*] in O Broad St,' noted Teddy Grenfell at the start of 1927. The architects were Mewès & Davis, and they produced an adequately elegant building in what Pevsner would term their 'usual chaste frenchified Palladian style'. Writing at the time in the *Banker*, Professor Albert Richardson of the University of London praised the building itself ('Ornament is conspicuous by its absence, the lines are pleasantly related, the mouldings are simple, the counters unobtrusive'), but took the opportunity to discuss the general problems of City architecture:

> Until the centre of city life is changed it will not be possible for bank architecture to compete externally with the great palaces of finance which are features of the business side of New York. In America the conditions are so entirely different. English architects, when called upon to deal with awkward sites in congested streets, are faced with difficulties which would confuse those accustomed to fewer restrictions.
>
> The main issue in London is to obtain natural light, as much as it is possible to gain it from close courts and areas. There are restrictions regarding Light, the need to complement existing buildings, and many other factors . . .[17]

So there were, but almost certainly it would anyway be only the joint-stock men who would want to create 'great palaces of finance', not the private bankers.

By the late 1920s, a decade after the 1918 amalgamations, the clearers (with the exception of Barclays) were responding to the challenge, as almost simultaneously a cluster of new head offices started to rise in the City. An early, perceptive observer was Arnold Bennett, one Wednesday in September 1928:

> My ideas for continuation of 'God' book being not quite in order, I wanted a romantic change, and went off by Underground eastwards and got off at the Monument, and walked about the City for an hour and came home through Holborn in a 22 bus. The City is continually changing architecturally, growing grander and more ornamental; and banks seem to be increasing their premises more and more. The City is a symbol of the domination of the banks. Expense has not been spared in financial architecture in the City. There is grandeur, despite the lack of space.

Despite notable stabs by Westminster and Lloyds, the clearing bank that achieved the most 'grandeur' was undoubtedly Midland, whose new head office at Poultry, designed by Sir Edwin Lutyens in association with Gotsch & Saunders, opened for business in 1930. An enormous building, the biggest that Lutyens ever designed in England, it has been justly praised by Booker in his survey of *Temples of Mammon* for its 'exquisite sense of balance and proportion, to which a degree of imaginative classical detail added rhythm without impairing the originality of the design'. Conveying a sense of immeasurable authority and the deepest of deep pockets, it yet had 'a façade very sensitive to the banking traditions of the City' – for example, 'the banded rustication recalled Soane's perimeter walls of the nearby Bank of England'. It hardly made life easy for Sir Edwin Cooper, responsible for building next door, on the corner site of Prince's Street, what was in effect the new head office of National Provincial. His work, full of recessed giant columns and completed in 1932, earned a scathing verdict from H.S. Goodhart-Rendel: 'If the purpose of external walls in a city building were to display figure-sculpture and to keep out the light, those of the National Provincial Bank would be hard to better.'[18]

In general, the merchant banks preferred red brick, the clearers marble (usually lots of it), but in neither case was there any significant concession to twentieth-century modernism. During the 1930s C.H. Reilly, an architectural professor, grew to be a particularly exasperated commentator, for example in 1933, when Glyn, Mills & Co wished its rebuilt head office in Lombard Street to be given the appearance of a wealthy individual's private home:

> As a nation we love under-statements. It may be one of the reasons why we are so often called hypocrites by other nations. We like our millionaires, when we have any, to walk about in rusty old clothes. We like to find the treasures of a Duveen or a Worth behind a forbiddingly plain façade. Similarly therefore it may seem right to the partners of this bank that their Piranesi-like halls should be buried behind these plain eighteenth-century brick fronts even if such fronts have had to be stretched to a twentieth-century size. One can at least be thankful that they have not given us a nineteenth-century structure, or columns and the other top-hatted devices, with which this part of London generally arrays itself.

Six years later, on completion of the Prince's Street extension to Midland's head office, he likewise identified a strong element of the English vice:

> However fine it is of its kind, and there is no doubt about its quality, it is in the precarious position of someone who tells a half-truth and with half

the world knowing it. Here it is, a monumental building appearing to be built in stone in the solidest possible manner and with all the grandeur that can be gathered from a great tradition of stone building, and yet we all know that that stone is merely hung on to steel girders and stanchions like so much sugar-icing. My generation, brought up to such things, may still as a whole accept them as natural, but will the next generation or the next? I doubt it very much . . .[19]

It was a powerful plea, but in a sense a naïve one. In financial architecture it is the external appearance, and the associations and impressions it conveys, that ultimately counts. Arguably it was almost another half-century before, courtesy of Lloyd's and Richard Rogers, the City acquired its first truly honest major building.

In the inter-war years, no work of construction was grander or more portentous than that at the Bank of England.[20] The explosion of the National Debt during the First World War made it beyond contention that the Bank had outgrown Soane's building. In 1920 the firm decision was taken to rebuild, and the following year Herbert Baker, at the time assisting Lutyens in the construction of New Delhi, was chosen by Lubbock to be the architect. Gratified to accept the commission, Baker asked him what the Bank of England stood for:

> Not the amassing of money, I was told; but rather that invisible thing, Trust, Confidence, which breeds Credit . . . I was told that the Governor, Montagu Norman, took as his pilot star the ideal that in a world left impoverished after the war the Bank might do something towards the healing of the nations through the beneficial use of finance . . . My instructions, in which I rejoiced, were that the materials and workmanship should be of the highest quality, and the best artists and craftsmen employed, but that any decoration should not be for the mere sake of ornament, but should have some special significance to the work and ideals of the Bank . . .

In 1922, accordingly, Baker put forward a plan, broadly accepted, 'which by the preservation and incorporation in the new building of the old external wall, of the banking halls behind it and of many other old rooms of Sir John Soane's building should go far to meet the reasonable conservative sentiment of the public', while at the same time seeking 'to develop on its traditional site a new Bank which would be sufficiently large and efficiently planned to fulfil the new duties imposed upon it by the war'. The plan involved clearing the ancient graveyard of St Christopher-le-Stocks, which had long provided an attractive garden court within the Bank, and in due course the bones of its occupants were gathered into sacks and reinterred in vaults at Nunhead Cemetery. The rebuilding itself, reaching seven storeys at its highest point, proved a marathon task, virtually complete by the outbreak of the Second World War.

Baker's Bank did not, on the whole, get a good press. A building 'which was once majestic' had been transformed, Reilly asserted in 1937, into 'the overgrown private residence of some plutocrat of more than Rockefeller proportions'. He particularly regretted the reconstruction of the famous Tivoli corner at the north end of Prince's Street – 'It is now but an approach, an over-elaborate step, to a commonplace little cupola above a low dome. Before it was a surprise, a thing of complete and strange and unexpected beauty to find in the City' – and he even indulged in a fairly vicious pay-off line: 'I see nevertheless after all this, the Bank has erected a statue to Soane. When one has destroyed a man's best work, I suppose it is the gentlemanly thing to do.' Eight years later, shortly after the publication of Baker's self-justifying memoirs, which misleadingly emphasised the retention and incorporation of Soane's best features, that most aesthetically discerning of modern diarists, James Lees-Milne, was shown round:

> To my surprise there is absolutely nothing left of Sampson, Taylor or Soane's work inside, and outside only Soane's outer wall. And that has been mutilated by Sir Herbert Baker. I was disgusted by the re-erection of the Taylor court room, which Baker tampered with to suit his own devices. Had he demolished the whole building and built anew from the foundations I should have respected him more, but he has compromised by reproducing Taylor vaulting and Soane motifs in the basement. Yet Baker is a distinctive architect and craftsman. His lapses into Kraal detail are undignified in classical work.

The most notable of the public attacks was made in 1957 by Nikolaus Pevsner in *The Buildings of England*. He declared that 'Baker's superstructure is not only oppressive but – which is worse – lacks grandeur'. He bitterly regretted the destruction of 'Soane's interiors with their infinite variety of domes, every one original and interesting, and several of a very high and exacting beauty'. Overall, taking the first half of the century as a whole, he reckoned that it was, even allowing for the Second World War, 'the worst individual loss suffered by London architecture'. Had the architect duped his client? Pevsner castigated Baker's autobiography as 'a masterpiece of egregious diddling', and undoubtedly there does seem to have been a scale of destruction not apparently envisaged in the 1922 plan. 'All that is best in a self-effacing gentleman of high culture' was Baker's description of Lubbock; but perhaps it needed a tough-minded player to keep the architect in check.[21]

A handful of other new buildings also made an impact on the inter-war City. The head office of the Port of London Authority – commissioned in 1912, opened ten years later – was built by Cooper with an exuberance that was to desert him when it came to the National Provincial. Dominating Trinity Square, not far from the Tower, it was in Pevsner's words 'a lasting monument to Edwardian optimism, like a super-palace for an International Exhibition, showy, happily vulgar, and extremely impressive'. The great man was less impressed by the four-storey, tantalisingly curved Britannic House that Lutyens built in the mid-1920s for British Petroleum and Anglo-Persian Oil. 'Stone-faced with the few accentuated first-floor windows in niches flanked by recessed columns in a very Lutyenesque way,' admittedly, 'but there is no excuse for the wretched American vice of breaking out into grand columniation on the top floors.' Soon after this, Cooper returned to the fray with the new Lloyd's building on Leadenhall Street. The neo-classical exterior was restrained enough, but Cooper let himself go inside – so much so that, according to H.V. Morton, the Room, if it had been stripped of its underwriters' boxes, was the sort of place where 'Antony and Cleopatra might have staged one of their Alexandrian indiscretions'. Everyone knew Lloyd's, but many in the City, certainly to the west of Leadenhall Street, may have overlooked the completion in 1936/7 of Plantation House in Fenchurch Street. Constructed to house the Rubber Exchange and a variety of commodity firms (including Lewis & Peat), it was the City's second-largest building.[22]

Each of these constructions had its admirers, but none excited the interest that Adelaide House did. 'Spectacular in its very forbiddingness,' would be Pevsner's estimate of this large, seven-storey, 'faintly Egyptian' block built by Sir John Burnet & Tait in 1924/5 opposite the Fishmongers' Hall, just to the north of London Bridge. Contemporary reaction was suitably strong. 'The architects,' declared the architectural writer Vernon Blake in 1925, 'have made history', for 'they have given English commercial architecture a definite modern expression'; while Reilly was enough of a humanist to assert three years later that 'Adelaide House seems to imply a race of robots'. Priestley was also struck. When *Angel Pavement*'s hero, Mr Golspie, gazes across 'at the immense panorama of the Pool' from the south bank of the Thames, his eye is caught by 'the severely rectangular building boldly fronting the river and looking over London Bridge with a hundred eyes, a grim Assyrian bulk of stone'. Indeed, it may well have been Adelaide House that Morton had looked down upon from the Monument, observing the managers at their lonely desks and the typists fluffing their hair. A variety of businesses occupied its floors, mainly with such unsentimental names as National Metal & Chemical Bank Ltd, Oil Cracking & Refining Co Ltd, Russo-Asiatic Consolidated Ltd and Var Oil Co Ltd. Perhaps because of its robotic feel – and notwithstanding the palpable, up-to-the-minute improvements it offered, such as electric lifts, central heating and an internal mailing network – Adelaide House remained a one-off in the inter-war City.[23] Consciously or otherwise, the City deferred the joys of the modern office block.

Confirmation of the City's unwillingness to brave the shock of the new lay in the fact that between 1905 and 1939 only about one-fifth of its fabric was rebuilt. The 'old' City was almost everywhere: down towards the river from St Paul's, secluded courts and alleys like Pope's Head Alley, Honey Lane, Russia Row and Turnagain Lane; north of Paternoster Row, a labyrinth so impenetrable that Mrs Dalloway lacked the courage to 'wander off into queer alleys tempting bye-streets, any more than in a strange house'; in obscure courts buried behind Cornhill, seemingly timeless chop-houses like the George and Vulture (a favourite of Mr Pickwick) and the Jamaica Wine House (originally London's first coffee-house); near Eastcheap, the Georgian and early Victorian offices and warehouses of Love Lane; and nearby, in Great Tower Street, an almost unbroken mass of mainly undistinguished Victorian shops, offices and warehouses.[24] The list was almost endless.

Crucial to the continuity of the City's character were, of course, its churches, of which by the start of the 1920s there were just over fifty. In 1920, to the horror of the City Corporation, a Bishop of London's Commission recommended the destruction of no fewer than nineteen of them. A severe tussle ensued, with at one stage the Sheriffs, in the exercise of an ancient City of London privilege, presenting themselves at the bar of the House of Commons to protest against this proposed vandalism. Eventually, in November 1926, the Commons voted down the Church's plan by 124 votes to 27. During this battle the City's bankers and brokers stayed, for the most part, above the fray. Some years later the journalist Stephen Graham, as part of his investigation of London life, visited a timber broker's office. From it, he and his host looked down 'on the mouldering tombs of a Wren church'. He asked: 'Are business men generally in favour of the destruction of the City churches to make more room?' To which the timber broker replied: 'Absolutely'.[25]

It was not a sentiment shared by Virginia Woolf, who by the late

1930s was in love with the old City. 'To Southwark & Lambeth, walking, yesterday,' she recorded in her diary for 3 November 1937. 'A great autumn for long City walks this. I discovered St James Garlick hill . . .' A fortnight later she told Vita Sackville-West how 'almost every day I take my walk through the City. I like it better than Kent – Bread Street, Camomile Street, Seething Lane, All Hallows, St Olaves – Then out one comes at The Tower, and there I walk on the terrace by the guns, with the ships coming up or down – which is it?' The habit persisted – 'Walking in the City the great relief,' she noted in March 1938 – and on 30 January 1939, a Monday, there was even something of a City adventure:

> Took the bus to Southwark Bridge. Walked along Thames Street; saw a flight of steps down to the river. I climbed down – a rope at the bottom. Found the strand of the Thames, under the warehouses – strewn with stones, bits of wire, slippery; ships lying off the Bridge (Southwark? – no, the one next to Tower Bridge [presumably London Bridge]). Very slippery; warehouse walls crusted, weedy, worn. The river must cover them at high tide. It was now low. People on the Bridge stared. Difficult walking. A rat haunted, riverine place, great chains, wooden pillars, green slime, bricks corroded, a button hook thrown up by the tide. A bitter cold wind . . . So to Tower. Made a circuit: discovered St Olave's Hart Street: Pepys Church; too cold to explore; wandered about Fenchurch alleys, Billingsgate; walked through Leadenhall Market . . . saw a golden pheasant; so back by omnibus . . .

Three months later, on a bitterly cold, late April day, she took another City walk, exploring 'the fur quarter behind Blackfriars'. There she found 'men in white coats aparelled in silver fur skins' and 'a smell of fur', as well as 'some old City Company houses' and 'one of the usual 18th Century mansions tucked away', before she turned into Cannon Street and 'bought a paper with Hitler's speech', which she read 'on top of Bus'.[26] The fur quarter and Hitler's speech: it was an ominous conjunction. The City that Virginia Woolf got to know and love in these last years before the war was old, idiosyncratic and deeply reassuring. It was becoming, in fact, a part of herself and her identity.

One writer's reassurance was another's exasperation. In February 1932, Simpkin Marshall (based at Stationers' Hall Court) published Harold P. Clunn's truly monumental *The Face of London*, subtitled *The Record of a Century's Changes and Development*. Change and development were, in Clunn's eyes, to be embraced not shunned, as he indicated in a couple of passages on Walter Bagehot's old stamping ground:

Before the construction of the new Martin's and Lloyds Banks, a hideous row of tall brown-brick buildings stood on these sites, fronting Lombard Street, south of Birchin Lane. The various banks had their trade signs in metal, hanging above the street, which perhaps gave it an old-world appearance, but the houses themselves were more suggestive of the exterior of some prison or mausoleum . . .

The church of St Mary Woolnoth at the corner of Lombard Street and King William Street was designed by Nicholas Hawksmoor in 1716. If the retention of All Hallows Church is a sacrifice of good money which might well suffice to build a dozen churches in the suburbs, what shall we say to this much more glaring anomaly of the church of St Mary Woolnoth occupying what is perhaps the most valuable site in the whole city?

Two years later, in a supplement marking the golden jubilee of the *Financial News*, there appeared an article entitled 'What Would Wren Have Built Today?' After diagnosing the square mile as increasingly overcrowded, badly lit and generally impossible to work in efficiently and pleasantly, the answer was confident and uncompromising:

> We must give up the building rule which restricts the height of buildings, and we must not only do that, but we must build office blocks twice as high as St Paul's, and have green spaces and wide roads in between the blocks . . . Two dozen skyscrapers, though they would obviously dwarf St Paul's, would not take away from its beauty if they were beautiful themselves. They would alter the sky-line, certainly, yet we should not sacrifice health, time, and comfort to one skyline because we have not the courage to create another.[27]

The author of this clarion call to modernise the City was a young architectural writer called John Betjeman.

A personal gloss on this type of attitude – one that was soon to be immensely powerful – was provided in the 1970s by the architectural historian Sir John Summerson, in his concluding remarks to a survey of the Victorian rebuilding of the City, as he sought to recall from memory the still essentially Victorian inter-war City:

> I remember in fact precious little of it. As a student I was conscious only of its sombre intricacies, its multiplication of sad and sooty ornament and, more than anything, its nauseating excess . . . The eye of the 1930s saw the City as dead: a petrified theatre of bad architectural rhetoric. Today, half demolished and overwhelmed by a harsh and shimmering modernity, it begins to live again and to move . . .[28]

The later Betjeman, that doughty City conservationist living in Cloth Fair, would no doubt have nodded his head sadly.

*

What was life actually like *inside* these mainly dark, ill-lit buildings?

Jack Smeaton started work in 1915, as a junior clerk, at the solicitors Slaughter and May of 18 Austin Friars:

> All letters were copied in a 'press copy letter book'. Most of them were type written but some were still in manuscript. The flimsy pages of the copy book had to be damped with cloth sheets and the letters placed in the book underneath the page and then put in a press, kept there for a few minutes and taken out. If the pages were too damp the copy and the original letter were completely unreadable. If they were too dry the copy was unreadable; but this only served to add a certain amount of interest to our normal occupation . . .
>
> Mr C.H. Tolley was the cashier and the author of *Tolley's Income Tax Chart*. He also acted as Office Manager and ruled the staff with a rod of iron. He had a habit of requiring in writing the explanation of any mistake or misdemeanour on the part of any of the junior members of the staff. He also had envelopes (when advertising his *Chart* in the early stages) addressed by junior members of the staff – in their own time – at the rate of 80 envelopes for 1/-. I addressed only one lot of envelopes and Mr Tolley objected to my writing, whilst I objected to his 'rate for the job'. We accordingly parted company on that and he did not forgive me for a long time . . .
>
> If a senior attended a Summons before a Master other than in a morning coat and top hat it was considered insulting, and although as time went on the rules of dress were relaxed to some extent until about 1930 no one would dream of attending a Summons before a Master or appearing in Court unless dressed in a black jacket and striped trousers and with a wing collar. Such things as coloured shirts or soft collars were unheard of in the office. In fact, some years after the end of the 1914 War I won a 5/- bet by coming to the office on a Saturday morning in plus fours. It was considered that if any of the Partners saw me in that casual dress I would have been looking for another situation . . .

The firm's ruling spirit was the forceful, immaculately dressed William Mortimer. 'S and M,' he would instruct his juniors when a draft of a letter was placed before him, 'are never obliged and very seldom glad.'[29]

The young Francis Ommanney, commandeered by his family in the early 1920s to join a firm of East India merchants, arrived reluctantly each day at 'a very gloomy building in a narrow street not far from the Stock Exchange':

The room where I and several others worked was thick with black dust, and piled dog-eared papers, yellow with age, mounted up to the ceiling. A vast safe occupied one wall. The window looked out on to a dark well of soot-grimed lavatory bricks. The lights, obscured by fly droppings, had to be kept on all the time except on the brightest summer day when a rectangle of blue could, by craning one's neck, just be seen at the top of the well.

I found myself surrounded by Scotsmen. Mr Macdougall was my boss, a funny, crusty, white-haired old man from Edinburgh who sat at an enormous dusty desk in the middle of the gloomy, dusty room. I was in the Codes Department ('one of the toads from the Codes', as another office boy said). Our department dealt with the long tables which came in coded from the Far East and were sent out again in code at all hours of the day, but usually, it seemed, just as we were getting ready to go home. Incoming cables were decoded and outgoing ones coded by Mr Macdougall and a clerk. They were typed on stencils by the blonde typist who was unashamedly cockney in the midst of all this scotchery. She said 'Ta, ever so' and 'Pardon'. They were then duplicated on the Roneo machine by Miss Lewis, who wore pince-nez and glazed waterproof cuffs. Then I carried the duplicated sheets round to the various departments . . .

I began in the Rubber Department just across the passage. It was ruled over by a red-headed Scot, Mr Mactavish, who was always shouting down the telephone with his chair tilted back as far as it could safely go. His ash tray on the desk in front of him was piled high with cigarette butts and another cigarette waggled from his lower lip and spilt ash all down his front as he telephoned, pushing his fingers through his red hair. The floor all round his desk was littered with samples of sheet and crêpe rubber which smelt very faintly of pigs' manure.

And then to the Produce Department, presided over by Mr Rintoul, a tall, distinguished, military-looking man. He, too, was incessantly tele-phoning, sometimes with his chair tilted back, but usually standing up. He never paused when I came into the room, or took the slightest notice of me, except sometimes to say, 'For God's sake shut the door, boy!' He telephoned in a very quiet, level voice. 'No, no. No, I'm not buying. No, I shall hang on and wait. Oh yes, I know. That's what you said last time. Once bitten, twice shy, y'know! What? In vain is the trap set in the sight of the bird, what! Now look, my dear fellah, make it two and seven-eighths, eh? Then I might do business, but not otherwise, what! . . .' I stole out, shutting the door as quietly as possible and feeling less than the dust . . .

Then there was the Engineering Department through a glass partition where Mr Lycett, in shirt sleeves and green eye-shade, presided over a drawing office. Rows of clerks were working at drawings on illuminated tables. Mr Lycett was a very jolly man who always made funny jokes and sang ribald versions of opera arias –

Credits and Debits

I dreamt that I tickled my grandfather's balls
With a drop of sweet oil on a feather

I thought this was excruciatingly witty and had to pause outside and compose my features before descending into the more rarified atmosphere of the secretaries' rooms downstairs . . .

After a while Ommanney managed to persuade his family to release him from 'the gloom and the dust and the fact that all day long one never saw the sky'. Macdougall shook his hand. 'This is a sair mistake ye're making, mark my words, boy' were his timeless parting words to the future distinguished marine biologist.[30]

Would Ommanney have been happier in one of the City's several hundred stockbroking firms? Probably not, but there would have been plenty of characters for him to recollect. At Cazenove & Akroyds, occupying the third floor of 43 Threadneedle Street during the first half of the 1920s, a renowned disciplinarian among the staff was Kathleen Cross, who eventually ran the ticket account and the jobbers' ledger. Her memoirs, written some sixty years later, suggest a certain mellowing in old age:

> . . . Next came a room with a small old-fashioned telephone switchboard which was worked by Jack Shepherd. He had been a butler in very high society; he reprimanded anyone who did not answer the telephone immediately – even the partners. The door of this room was immediately opposite that of the partners' room; he would blast their door open and shout, 'Sir, don't you know I am calling you?'
>
> Half-way down the corridor on this side was an opening with a small counter. In this room sat old Joe Mead on inscribed stock and working out contracts. I remember the first comptometer arriving in 1921. Joe refused to use the B . . . thing and it was amazing how he got the answers out as quick as the machine, no matter what state of intoxication he was in! Every day at eleven he disappeared and went to Pimms who were next door to us. When in season he had his dozen oysters and brown bread and butter, otherwise he had a sole, with his pint of Pimms No. 1 . . .
>
> We did work very late hours, often until 10.00 p.m., when we were busy. As we were nearly opposite Finch Lane, it was useful when we were at the office late for the men to go over there for refreshments; I was left in the office and they brought a packet of sandwiches back for me. We were brokers to Martinez Gassiot, the port wine importers, and we always had some cases in the office; it was usual for port wine to be served in 'tumblers' during the evening. The first time I had it, I went to sleep over

my transfers, so they called a taxi and sent me home! After that I had a special small glass . . .

Other characters included the firm, but benign office manager George Hanneford, who would beam at each recipient as he handed out the quarterly bonuses; a spindly Ulsterman called Major Whittington, who had seen better days but became the firm's first statistician largely on the strength of his beautiful handwriting; and the dealer, Bertram Crosse, who with his fruity voice as well as choice anecdotes was in particular demand as an after-dinner speaker. In contrast, the atmosphere seems to have been less congenial – to judge by the firm's historian, on the basis of oral reminiscence – at Mullens, the Government brokers, in its dark offices in George Street:

> The partners would open their own mail. For Sir John Mullens [senior partner in the 1920s] this meant slitting open each envelope, removing the contents and dropping the envelope just *outside* the waste-paper basket; later, some menial would be summoned to sweep the results up from the carpet. The boys on duty in the hall would dread the continuous ringing of the partners' bell. One ring meant a call to a lesser partner; an impatiently repeated ring meant Sir John. He had the habit of murmuring his requests without looking up, and the boys did not dare to ask him to repeat himself . . .
>
> All members of staff were expected to wear a dark clerical grey suit, with a bowler hat, and to carry an umbrella. The partners, traditionally, wore black silk top hats. It was expected, also, that staff would wear starched white hard collars. One young clerk daringly adopted a soft white collar. Sir John, on his way into the office, noticed. A few minutes later, a messenger approached the young man and put a few small coins into his hand. 'Sir John's compliments, and will you please go and buy yourself a collar.'[31]

Probably more representative than either Cazenove's or Mullens was Phillips & Drew, in the early 1930s a typical small stockbroking firm almost entirely dependent on private client business. Dougie Phin, half a century after being recruited as an office boy at 12s 6d a week, would recall life at Palmerston House in Old Broad Street:

> It was a real Victorian pile – great echoing halls, scrappy old offices – it was a real Dickensian office. You went up in a great hydraulic lift where you had to pull the rope, and a young chap there in a scruffy old uniform, and then you went in the office, and it was a great old coal fire at one end – sixpence a bucket was the coal, and the office boy had to go down and get

it from the dungeons . . . It was very dark – dark paint and dark mahogany desk – and the usual slit in it where the boys put their stock in, and then they scribed on it, 'Died waiting, 1934', and then the office manager would see you and come round and clip your ear. Our desks were the old-fashioned sloping desks with the big brass rails across the middle. You sat on a very high stool, and believe it or not they were very comfortable because you had a foot-rest and a flap . . . The first duty of an office boy was to fill up the ink-wells – blue, red and copper [i.e. black] ink, because all the contracts were written by hand . . .

Though fully recognising the 'charm' of the ruling family, Phin was not inclined to be unduly sentimental: 'On the whole, a damned happy old office, although the Drews were bloody mean and you were expected to work your guts out.'[32]

Phillips & Drew was as yet barely a name in the City, quite unlike N.M. Rothschild & Sons. In 1925 that almost fabled institution took on a seventeen-year-old called Ronald Palin, who was the son of a Bank of England clerk and had been expected by his school, Rossall, to try for an English scholarship to Oxford. 'If you want to come, you'd better come now,' Lionel de Rothschild said to him at the interview, and more or less on the spur of the moment Palin agreed. From the start he was fascinated, particularly by some of the senior members of the staff. There was the correspondence clerk, George Tite, 'with his high collar and stock, his black jacket and narrow striped trousers, his thin cynical smile and his mordant wit'. Seldom arriving at New Court before eleven, he would point out that he had already '"bathed, shaved, breakfasted and crapped"', adding that '"other people may get here at ten, but if ever I am here early I notice that they then immediately disappear for about an hour, presumably for just those purposes"'. Also in the Correspondence Department was the Austrian-born, far more obviously industrious Ziffer: 'He did his job very thoroughly, holding up each letter as he checked it three inches from the thick lenses of his spectacles; so thoroughly, indeed, that he always began with the die-stamped address. "New Court, St Swithin's Lane," one could hear him reading to himself in a soft whisper if one were near enough. "Yes, that's right. London, E.C.4. Right."' Ziffer was reputed always to wear a dinner jacket when dining at home, after which he sat reading the *FT* until it was time for bed.

By his third year, Palin was in the Foreign Exchange Department under Percy Wingate: 'He was renowned for speaking his mind in a forthright manner and never hesitated to call a man a bloody fool if that was what he thought, always adding, however, the words "if you don't

275

mind my saying so".' Wingate, known to the foreign exchange market as 'the Great White Kaffir', was a formidable operator – unlike Shirley Snell, 'the most beautifully turned-out man I ever knew at New Court, or indeed outside it'. For all Snell's inadequate intellectual grasp, however, he was kept on, presumably because he added to the tone of the place. It was a place where Palin himself, by the time he came of age, was starting to be accepted:

> The slightest trace of uppishness would still invite the reminder that I had 'only been here about five minutes' but the tone of voice was without sting. And I was gradually but surely and permanently falling in love with NMR; with the building as I found my way about it, with its inmates as I got to know them and with my job. I enjoyed doing work which I felt I understood, taking pride in accuracy and in consideration of the effect upon others of what I was doing and how I was doing it. Above all I enjoyed the humour and the good humour; it was a happy ship.

In 1930 he was transferred to the Dividend Office, employing up to half the staff and responsible for the issuing and servicing of foreign loans. Palin more or less remained there for the next thirty years. Did he ever regret that moment of impulsiveness in 1925? 'It was not until much later,' he would eventually write in his delightful memoirs, 'that I began to realise what I had missed and to feel the ache which has been alternately assuaged and sharpened by the *splendeurs et misères* of life at New Court but has never completely left me.'[33]

Nowhere, though, can there have been a keener sense of regret, of life passing by on the other side, than on the part of many of those incarcerated in the Bank of England. There, the huge wartime rise in the National Debt caused in turn a huge rise in staff numbers – up from barely 1,000 in 1914 to some 4,000 in 1919 – with an accompanying bulge in the age-profile of employees, which gave birth within the Bank to the eloquent term 'the Hump'. Leslie Bonnet, who worked in the 1920s in the absurdly over-manned Accountant's Department, remembered the sharp tensions caused by this huge intake of young staff in the immediate post-war years:

> So every pre-war clerk became a person of great authority, wearing a top hat in the office, enthroned in a raised stall; and able to make or break any junior at will. Results were ludicrous. Some of these old men were of feeble intellect. Some were more numerate than literate. Many were just plain stupid. And why not? They hadn't been chosen for initiative, or intelligence. Good handwriting was their best commendation. And so,

confronted by this seething cauldron of ambitious, clever, young men, it is little wonder that they feared and hated the newcomers.

Someone who did manage (in 1926) to get away from the Bank was George Chambers, who had gone there on leaving Dulwich College:

> After a couple of years, going up to the City by the same train every morning and coming back home by the same train every evening, the thought of continuing that existence for the next forty years or so seemed a dreary outlook. I began to think that life might be more interesting if I were to see a little more of the world before it was too late. So, what about exchanging life in the Bank of England for, say, life in either the Chartered Bank of India, Australia and China or the Hongkong and Shanghai? So, deciding to take the bull by the horns, I walked one day into the Secretary's Department of the Bank of England and asked the first-class clerk there (a big shot) if it would be possible for me to see Mr Alexander. After looking at me with mingled amazement and scorn he managed to say, 'Do you mean Mr Alexander, the Assistant Secretary? What the hell do *you* want to see him for?' He didn't add '. . . a miserable squirt like you'. He didn't need to, the look on his face was quite sufficient. As for a mere probationer wanting to see a *really* big shot like the Assistant Secretary . . . well, well, well. The long and short of it was that a few days later a flunkey came into the sub-Treasury and told the Principal that I was to report there and then to the Assistant Secretary. The Assistant Secretary was even more astonished when I explained to him that my ambition was to join the H&SBC (in other words, to leave the high and mighty Bank of England) and that, in order to achieve that aim, I solicited a nomination from Sir Charles Addis. After a couple of gulps he must have thought that if anyone were crazy enough to *want* to leave the Bank of England the best thing to do would be to help him on his way. So, to my surprise, for by now I was beginning to feel a bit panicky, he said he'd speak to Sir Charles about it. He then told me to get back pronto to wherever I'd come from. Which I did, taking care to keep a safe distance from the first-class clerk on the way . . .[34]

*

At the time, it was easier for some than for others to express disenchantment. Reay Geddes, ambitious youngest son of the businessman and politician Sir Eric Geddes, and educated at Rugby and Cambridge, managed via Sir Guy Granet to get a berth at the Bank of England, starting in March 1933. 'Wants to come because he thinks there must be a great opening on the foreign side,' stated the initial report on him. 'Does not think of coming into the Bank in the ordinary way nor of going through the mill at the ordinary pace.' Over the next eighteen months he spent time in various parts of the Bank and achieved good reports for his aptitude and attitude. By December 1934, however, Geddes had decided to leave, and he took the opportunity to send to the Chief of Establishments his observations.

He noted at the outset that 'the boys who the Bank enlist have a good general standard of education, no experience other than that of school and holidays, and no definite bent', and that 'the vast majority do not come at their own express request, but on the choice of their Fathers, who are glad to find a gilt-edged investment for the capital represented by a son who is "developing rather late"'. He went on to explain how, because of the policy of deliberate over-manning (in order to be able to cope with the occasional brief rush), the new recruit found himself not only quickly bored but also corrupted:

> It is quite inevitable that the recruit should start work in one of the outer offices. There he meets and works beside 'Disappointed men' who are always willing to tell what dreadful luck they have had at the hands of God, disease, the war and the Bank's complete disregard for merit. These gentlemen have one curious loyalty: if their superior winks at the custom of coffee or tea being taken during office hours, it is quite understood that each clerk enjoys these pleasures entirely at his own risk, if there are complaints from the 'case'. The recruit then learns that the foremen allow rules to be disregarded, but deny any knowledge of such transgressions. This cannot increase the recruit's respect for his superior. Apart from this loyalty, the disappointed ones have none. With their mocking of keenness, their obstruction of questions and their eyes on the clock, they are a strong and undesirable influence on boys fresh from school, during the latter's almost inevitable periods of doubt and apprehension.

Inevitably, disillusion sets in – exacerbated, according to Geddes, by older clerks often saying to the recent recruit, 'Does it ever strike you that you will be like me one day?' As a result, Geddes calculated, some 2,000 men, roughly half the Bank's total workforce, were condemned 'to work at which their education only serves to make them uncomfortable – either openly discontented or passively awaiting a pension'. In his view, it would be altogether more desirable if the work was done by those better suited to it:

> The objections to a cheaper grade of labour than the Bank employ at present are behaviour, appearance and intonation. A visit to the Clearing House would show how difficult it is to pick out Bank men. This is not to suggest that the Bank's standard is lower than in years gone by, but that

mass-produced clothing and general knowledge have spread a certain 'savoir faire' which used only to be obtainable in conjunction with expensive education.

'While the men are here,' Geddes concluded, 'let them work. If they are temporarily surplus, they are better playing golf at home than dominoes in a "Mecca" cafe.'[35] Geddes himself had a notable business career ahead, while his report was carefully filed away, to gather dust.

The Bank merely led by example, for almost everywhere in the City was run along rigid, hierarchical lines. 'I shall have failed to convey the feudal atmosphere of the place,' Palin memorably remarked in his memoir of inter-war New Court, 'if I leave the impression that the partners were regarded simply as ordinary human beings whom an accident of birth had placed in control of a great business and thus also of the lives of a number of other human beings.' Rather, 'they were a higher order of creation', so that 'it was in the nature of things that a young male Rothschild should inherit a partnership in the family business when he attained a suitable age in the same way as he inherited material possessions and it did not enter anybody's head that any other qualification could ever achieve the same result'. In 1931, when Rothschilds decided to recruit a Cambridge graduate called Michael Bonavia, he was unequivocally told by the staff manager that however well he did, there was absolutely no prospect of becoming a partner.[36]

In many firms the partners had their own separate entrance, as well as dining room and lavatory; while at the Lombard Street office of Guaranty Trust Co of New York it was permissible for staff to nip out for tea and a bun to the nearby ABC or Lyons tea-shops, but Fullers in Gracechurch Street was strictly off-limits, being for management only. Autocrats – not merely of the breakfast table – abounded. One such was Robert Wyse, the Scot who in 1922 succeeded the legendary Christopher Nugent as Manager of Union Discount. 'I had to choose between my family and my business – I chose business,' he was once heard to say, and he made sure that everyone suffered with him, as the Union's historians eloquently describe:

Promptly at ten each morning, he would arrive at the office, smartly dressed with a high, stiff, butterfly collar, a rolled umbrella on his arm, a small attaché case in his hand, often with his pipe in his mouth. The Head Messenger would trot behind him to catch his coat and umbrella as he tossed them on one side. His 'boy' or assistant would be standing at the ready with the morning mail placed open on Wyse's desk in front of him. After a cursory greeting to the other Managers, he would go through the mail, marking it liberally with one of his innumerable red pencils, which had to be kept ready sharpened for him; woe betide the messenger who forgot to sharpen them; the pencils would be thrown at him.

'Men now!' Wyse would announce to his 'boy' who would call in the heads of departments, then Managers and the Market Men. He would then give his daily conference at which he would fix rates and lay down his policy for the day.

'Bills now!' would be his next command and his 'boy' would produce the previous day's bills discounted and their information cards, which he would then examine and mark liberally with his red pencil . . .

An episode one Saturday showed Wyse at his very worst, after he had summoned one of the male typists to type out a lengthy letter (three pages of foolscap) that he had just finished drafting:

Harry Mann noticed that there were some spelling mistakes so, while typing it, he spelled the words correctly and took the letter down to be signed. Twenty minutes later, he was summoned by the buzzer. Wyse was furious at having been corrected: the letter was to be typed exactly as he had written it. Mann typed the letter again and took it back with the Manager's notes. Half an hour later, the buzzer went again. Wyse wanted the letter typed again; all the mistakes which had been corrected by the typist on the first letter were now corrected by Wyse on the second and Harry Mann had to type it a third time. In those days the office closed officially at one o'clock on Saturdays but it was four o'clock in the afternoon by the time Mann had finished and could go . . .[37]

In general, as organisations became bigger, the Manager – whether senior manager, departmental manager or office manager – was an increasingly powerful figure. Whereas the partners of, say, a merchant bank or a stockbroking firm concentrated on the 'front end' of the business (in other words, the deal-making and the securing of clients), the settlement of business (in the 'back office') was left in the hands of trusted subordinates. That subordinate tended to be omnipotent in his own kingdom. At James Capel, for instance, the staff had no access to the partners except through the office manager. Or take Kleinworts, which by the mid-1920s had a staff of almost 400. Henri Jacquier had the misfortune to fall foul of a manager over some South American accounts. 'Trivial really,' he would recall. 'I had three differences with him for which he castigated me pretty strongly . . . I should have known that you must never put a big man in the wrong.' Jacquier's punishment, unquestioned by the partners, was no increase in salary for fourteen years. The most feared of the managers at Kleinworts was Stirling Karck, a man whose harsh streak probably derived from his not unreasonable hopes of becoming a partner having been dashed. 'You don't want to worry about your friends – stand on their neck and get a bit higher,' was his declared philosophy, and at 20 Fenchurch Street it was acknowledged as a wise move to avoid the French and Belgian Departments.[38]

Paternalism ran deep, a relationship typified in many firms by that unquestioned boon, the annual staff outing. Quite often this took the form of a day trip to the senior partner's country house. For example, the employees of the solicitors Clifford-Turner & Co twice in the 1930s left Old Jewry at 9 a.m. in a motor coach bound for Heathfield Park, the large house in Sussex, with an estate of nearly 350 acres, that Harry Clifford-Turner had acquired. There, after lunch, they enjoyed an afternoon of games, tournaments and competitions, the latter on one occasion including a ladies' ankle competition judged by the office manager, Horace Skuse. There followed tea and dancing, in a specially erected marquee. On a more week-to-week basis there was increasingly systematic provision of sporting facilities, and when in February 1921 the women's section of The Barings Sports Club held its inaugural meeting at 8 Bishopsgate, it was unanimously agreed that the colours for the first netball match should be yellow and black, 'the idea suggested by the colours of the Bank Messengers waistcoats!'[39]

Implicit in paternalism was job security, and there is no doubt that the prevailing City culture remained that of one berth lasting a lifetime. Michael Verey has recalled the sixty or so clerks whom he got to know during his early days at Helbert Wagg in the 1930s:

> They were the most splendid people for integrity and hard work and devotion to duty. Not probably madly ambitious, as I was, they were content to have a good steady job with a patron like Alfred Wagg. They were better paid and looked after than their equivalent in any merchant bank. One or two of the clerks were literally found on doorsteps in the East End. The firm never had to advertise for staff. If somebody retired or died – they practically never resigned – the head of department already had a list of people who had applied for jobs.

Nevertheless, in practice it all depended. At Kleinworts, for instance, the extremely difficult situation in the early 1930s meant that staff numbers were more or less halved, through a systematic programme of dismissals each Friday. The commissionaire's dreaded words, 'The staff manager would like to see you', became the stuff of nightmares, especially as the chances of a clerk who had been made redundant finding another job were at best slim. At Bensons, by contrast, there were no redundancies.

'In all the partners' discussions about economising,' that firm's historian notes, 'it was the one option never once considered. The attitude was that Bensons was a family firm that stuck together through thick and thin, and everyone counted.'[40] This was indeed the acceptable face of family capitalism, fortified by the knowledge born of long experience that financial markets tend to be cyclical.

The regular working day was not, by the standards of the 1990s, all that long. 'I'll remind ye,' the fierce Macdougall told Ommanney, 'that your hours in this office are nine-thirrrty tae one and two tae five-thirrrty, and I'll thank ye, young man, tae keep tae these hours.' At Barings, the rule from March 1929 was that new clerks would henceforth have to start work by 9.30, clerks of less than ten years' service had to be at the office by 9.45, those with more than ten years' service by ten, and clerks over sixty years old 'do not sign the Attendance Book'.[41] Even so, in the City as a whole, there was not only the compulsory Saturday morning, but most contracts stated that an employee could not leave the office until the day's work had been completed – which, as Katie Cross discovered at Cazenove's, might not be until well into the evening.

Pay was adequate, rather than wonderful. At James Capel, for example, a new clerk would start at about £70 a year, receive annual increments of £5 or £10, and eventually break through the £175 barrier, at which point he was permitted to marry. At another stockbroking firm, Phillips & Drew, there was a striking comparison in the share-out for the year ending March 1936: whereas the five partners received an average of £1,530, even the relatively well-paid Tommy Tomkinson, sole telephone operator as well as responsible for the post and the jobbers' books, took home a screw of only £4 5s a week. Moreover, although many firms did in this period start to introduce profit-sharing schemes and thereby put bonus arrangements on a more orderly and equitable basis, there was still plenty of scope for individual capriciousness, as the unfortunate Jacquier of Kleinworts found to his cost. Also in Fenchurch Street, at Austin Reed's flagship branch, the young Philip Horton, who went there in 1923 from Watford Grammar School, made the mistake of asking the authoritarian manager, Percy Osborn, for a salary rise on the grounds that he thought he was doing his job well. 'Of course you do your job well,' Osborn replied. 'You wouldn't be here if you didn't. We don't give salary increases for doing your job. We give salary increases for doing more than your job!'[42]

There was also, of course, the whole question of pension arrangements, traditionally a case of grace and favour. H.B. Reynolds had retired from Barings in 1912, and on the last day of 1924 he humbly petitioned that bank's directors for an increase to his pension, in the context of the post-war increase in the cost of living. 'I am nearly 77,' he observed, 'and am not likely to trouble you much longer.' The request was granted (his pension being increased to £540 a year), and Revelstoke was suitably paternalistic: 'Any such representation from so old and so valued a member of our staff is entitled to our very particular sympathy . . .' Reynolds, from his home in Woodford Green, replied gratefully: 'I ought now to be able to get along comfortably, and can only hope that the ease of mind this gives me will not so lengthen my life that I may be looked upon as a nuisance by Baring Brothers & Co.'[43] By the mid-1930s most of the merchant banks had introduced pension schemes (usually contributory), but many other firms, including stockbrokers, had not. Thousands of clerks still worked until they literally dropped, or became physically incapable, and it was not uncommon to have a working span in a single firm of sixty years or even, in some cases, seventy. It was not yet, in fine, the era of the 'Bobo' – burnt out but opulent.

As for the work itself, if there had been a hint of mechanisation prior to 1914, between the wars it became more than just a hint. Stephen Graham, in his quickfire *Twice Round the London Clock* of 1933, was particularly struck:

> As I stand waiting to see the manager at a big bank in Bishopsgate, my ears are assailed by a sort of jazz, a rapid tapping and screwing, as of flat kettle-drums and toneless saxophones, the chorus of adding machines.
>
> No longer do innumerable pens waiver over the desks. The City is no longer full of penpushers, but of handle-pullers, tap-tap-tap screw, tap-tap-tap screw. It seems even more mechanical than pen-work, but the clerks are proud of their machines.
>
> They show me one which calculates automatically the price of drafts on New York or elsewhere, and others which do multiplication and division and work by electricity, numbers revolving and reassorting themselves as the motor whirls, and making me think of an arithmetical brain in a glass case with workings visible. Interesting little machines, each of them represents so many fewer clerks in the world . . .

By the time Graham was writing, there had indeed been a significant degree of mechanisation in the City's main commercial banks. Midland had led the way in the mid-1920s, installing ledger-pasting machines in what was still the head office in Threadneedle Street; Lloyds by the end of the 1920s was developing mechanised book-keeping at its head office; and at Barclays by that time adding machines were increasingly prevalent. Among merchant banks, Kleinworts was probably ahead of the game by the late 1920s. Not only was most of the correspondence typewritten (on huge Underwood machines, remembered by one female typist as 'heavy as lead, and when I had finished a day's hard banging on them all the veins were standing out on the backs of my hands'), but the accounting system had also been mechanised (using 'huge machines like locomotives which made a great noise – clank crank!').⁴⁴

Almost everywhere the use of the typewriter became prevalent, but inevitably the overall pace of mechanisation varied. At Cazenove's, for instance, old Joe Mead may have spurned the comptometer, but in about 1936 it was one of the first stockbroking firms to mechanise its accounts, using what was essentially a line-posting system; even so, at least one of the clerks, Walter Rudge on jobbers' ledgers, still found that in practice he had to write up the books as he had always done, in order to check what was going on. Moreover, whatever the clerks may have told Graham, there was in general considerable suspicion, and even hostility, towards the whole process of mechanisation, not least (especially from a male point of view) because of its employment implications. Union Discount was a graphic – perhaps extreme – case in point. The first accounting machines arrived at 39 Cornhill in the 1930s, and the staff at once made a dead set against them. 'They took jolly good care they didn't work,' Wyse's 'boy', H.F. Goodson, would recall. 'They didn't put sand in the machines, they just didn't press the right buttons.' One of those compelled to operate the new machines and finding the experience memorable, during their disastrous trial period, was Howard Planterose. Once:

> we had to work all night because we couldn't strike a balance. We had a bottle of whisky and bars of chocolate, and at five o'clock in the morning we went down to the Unsecured Deposit office and found a basket of slips that had been left and not collected. Finally we balanced and pushed off to the Charing Cross Hotel, where we had baths and shaved and had breakfast. We got back to the office at half-past ten and were ticked off for being late . . .

The pay-off came at the end of the three-month trial period: 'The message came out from the Managers' Room, "how long will it take you to get back to hand-posting?" We said "we'll do it tonight!" and we did too.'⁴⁵

There were plenty of City offices where the clerks still sat on high stools by long desks and where the concept of mechanisation, certainly extensive mechanisation, was no more than a faint rumour. The work often remained incredibly laborious. The future television newsreader Robert Dougall joined the accountants Deloitte, Plender, Griffiths & Co in 1931: 'Deloittes, being a traditional, long-established firm, would have no truck with new-fangled adding machines, so we clerks did all the casting of endless columns of pounds, shillings and pence by hand.' One of Dougall's colleagues was Roderick Leveson-Gower, who 'lived for horses' and 'had acquired the knack of breaking off in the middle of a column of figures and looking up to tell you what his fancy was for the "3.30" and then to pick up again with his adding at the exact point where he had left off'. Probably more typical of the balance between the old and the new was the Registration Department of the Lord St Davids group of investment trusts in the late 1930s, by now based at 117 Old Broad Street. There the basic discipline of the office remained manual – handwritten share certificates, registers and dividend warrants, as well as individually calculated dividends – but there was a belated, perhaps reluctant element of mechanisation in the form of 'two heavy Burroughs listing machines, operated by a casino-type lever, and an ancient addressograph machine for addressing envelopes and dividend warrants'. Nevertheless, and undeniably, mechanisation had come to stay. This was so even in the Bank of England, where Mercedes accounting machines were in widespread use by the mid-1930s, as well as special fanfold typing machines, using continuous stationery, and the Hollerith system of punched cards.[46] The Bank may not have been quite in the vanguard of mechanisation, but once it accepted the necessity for change it applied itself with characteristic thoroughness.

The gradual mechanisation of office life had the effect of significantly increasing (compared to pre-1914) the number of women working in the City, mainly as telephonists, typists and (from the late 1920s) machine operators. There is a scattering of figures about the women employed during the inter-war period: seventy at Barings by the end of 1923; thirty-four at Kleinworts two years later; about twenty at Linklaters by the mid-1930s; and seventy-three (out of a staff of 213) at the London office of the Hongkong and Shanghai Bank in 1936. Particularly striking was the Bank of England, where by the 1930s the experience of mechanisation was that two and three-quarter women plus one machine could produce the output of four men. There, between 1926 and 1939, while the number of men employed went up from 1,900 to 2,350, the female total increased more sharply from 1,200 to 1,700.[47]

Such figures, however, tell only part of the story, for it was a universal truth of the inter-war City that the women who worked there were paid at an appreciably lower rate than men, had to retire earlier and had few, if any, promotion prospects. Compelled in many places (including the Bank of England) to resign if they wished to marry, women in the City were, by and large, treated as second-class citizens. In 1922 Westminster Bank sought out the opinions of its managers on the question of female labour. 'Willing, neat workers and good writers but unsuitable in Departments where the work has to be finished to time,' was the view from head office. The Lombard Street Manager agreed: 'Being connected with the various clearings and so working "against the clock" is a strenuous office. It, therefore, should have the most physically fit and efficient staff. The ideal, and considered in the end the cheapest, being a male staff.' Or, more bluntly, from Aldersgate Street: 'I prefer a male staff for efficiency, drive and discipline.' The apartheid could run deep. At one insurance company, National Mutual, the annual staff dinner in the 1920s was invariably an all-male affair, with female members of staff each given two tickets for a theatre of their choice; while at Rothschilds, although the men were entrusted with a daily luncheon voucher, to enable them to eat out, the female staff were compelled to eat all together in the basement dining room. Even such a civilised and in many ways sympathetic figure as Sir Charles Addis found the quiet revolution hard to adjust to: 'One day at the Hongkong and Shanghai, where as usual he was wearing a morning coat, he refused outright to share the lift with two lady members of staff.'[48] One should not exaggerate, for undoubtedly in many offices there was a reasonable degree of integration, but the old City had been *such* a male place that inevitably this was a major shock to the system.

Recruitment, whether male or female, still tended to be conducted along strongly personal lines. Shortly before Christmas 1927 the head messenger at Barings was dismissed, after the uncovering of a minor scam involving the removal and sale of foreign stamps from envelopes. It was accepted that his involvement may have been unwitting, and he was granted a compassion allowance of £100 a year. In his late fifties, he found it impossible to secure another job, and in July 1928 he appealed to the bank's Alfred Mildmay: 'In my extreme unhappiness at being unable to find a situation, may I ask, that if, with your far-reaching influence you should hear of a vacant position you would let me know I should be very deeply grateful.' Mildmay replied, not unkindly, that if he could help he would, but that 'most employers have friends of their own, whose claims they consider before looking elsewhere for servants'.[49] Mildmay was surely right, and in practice this meant that, even at the City's humbler levels of employment, there was a strong and self-perpetuating bias towards the middle class (whether upper or lower) in terms of recruitment.

At this stage, however, it was not a bias that embraced any significant leaning towards graduates. At Barings itself, Sir Edward Reid was asked in 1928 by a Scottish correspondent about the possibility of 8 Bishopsgate recruiting one or two graduates of Scottish universities. 'A very important qualification is (in addition to the usual "steady & hardworking nature, good health & temper" etc) an *accurate and orderly mind*,' Reid replied somewhat discouragingly. 'There are many whose intelligence is completely nullified, as far as business is concerned, by the absence of this.' It is true that Lloyds in the 1930s did start a modest programme of graduate recruitment, but that organisation was very much the exception. Where personal connection counted above all was, classically, at the Bank of England: there it was possible to secure a billet *only* if one was first personally nominated by a director. Leslie O'Brien – son of a school-attendance officer and educated humbly enough at Wandsworth School – managed to get his nomination from Lord Revelstoke. The tenuous connection was that O'Brien's father had once played in the same cricket team as the Hon Guy Baring, but what may have tickled the great man's interest more was the fact that the O'Brien family lived in Revelstoke Road in south-west London. 'The large majority of the staff,' O'Brien would recall of the Bank that he entered in 1927 as a nineteen-year-old, 'came from the upper middle class with a public school education. I was one of the fortunate minority who started rather lower down the scale. I remember some of my father's friends being somewhat astonished that I had secured such prestigious employment.'[50]

Chance played an even larger part in the story of how Leonard Toomey, son of a first-generation Irish labourer and brought up in a Battersea terrace, reached the City. The decisive encounter was in 1938, when Toomey was fourteen: 'I was working as a page-boy at the Overseas League in St James's and I met a chap who was a member of the Club and who said did I intend staying there for the rest of my life? I said, "No, actually I'm looking for work." And he said, "Well, I work at Lloyd's and I know a firm at Lloyd's who are looking for an office boy" . . .' The young Toomey, perhaps not surprisingly, had never heard of Lloyd's, but from a field of about five or six boys who applied he got the job – the turning-point, as it proved, of his life.[51]

*

For the artistically ambitious son of a timber broker, the problem one harrowing fortnight in 1925 was not how to find a way into the City, but how to scramble out. Cecil Beaton came down from Cambridge that summer, without a degree, and after a few rather inconsequential months he reluctantly agreed to his father's suggestion that he should acquire a better grasp of business by going into the family firm and keeping accounts. Beaton's diary records the ensuing torture, not only in the offices of Tagart, Beaton & Co, on the fifth floor of Equitable House in King William Street:

20 November

I walked to the tube station with my father and a thousand other men, all smoking pipes, all carrying morning papers under their arms. I didn't buy a paper. I glared and glowered at the people in the train, intent on their papers and themselves. They never looked about them.

Daddy lectured me with earnest impatience: 'The first rule in business is . . . to put it another way . . . the simple plan is . . .' These expressions echoed over and over again in the midst of a long harangue I didn't understand at all. I replied dutifully 'Yes,' or 'No.' I was more or less resigned to my fate, except for one thing: I would never wear a bowler hat.

We arrived at the office. A series of nondescript men slid into my Father's room with letters, their expressions as dreary as their collars.

I had rather a headache. The radiator-heat atmosphere of the building didn't help any. I hadn't had time to visit the lavatory after breakfast, which made my depression total.

Then, abruptly, I heard Reggie [Cecil's brother, who had gone straight into the office from Eastbourne College] talking professionally and competently on the telephone. How important! I began to think the place wasn't such a farce after all . . . I had to read one or two typewritten letters, but I couldn't understand them any more than Daddy's pompous explanations. He created an aura of great hurry, kept tapping his fingers and became impatient with the poor clerks. I was made to do a lot of figures in a book. Each figure (feeguire as Daddy calls it) had to be put in exactly the right spot or else sharply rubbed out with an indiarubber. Daddy keeps one in a drawer of his desk, wrapped up in a piece of paper. Each time the rubber is used, the paper gets unfolded, then folded up again. By lunch time I had copied out a lot of feeguires. Reggie took me to the place where he generally goes. I'd imagined worse, but it was 2 o'clock and the crowd of young men at Birch's, as the place is called, had thinned out. We went downstairs, crossed a sawdust floor, stood at a counter and ate: ham in roll sandwiches, beef sandwiches, rock cakes, chocolate biscuits. We drank punch.

Afterwards, we went to the Jamaica place for coffee. This I did think revolting. The coffee couldn't have been worse, the bowler hats stiffened

my determination not to wear one. I had the impression of a lot of dirty
beetles fighting for existence.

Back at the office, I decided that the whole building smelled like an
underground lavatory. I wrote some more feeguires in the book and was
faced with the task of doing additions. I have always been bad at
arithmetic, finding it an agony to add anything up. Now I must needs do
the best I could. My head went round and round. Exhaustion overtook me.
I struggled for hours . . .

24 November

Up at the last minute; on with the clothes that lay crumpled by the
bed. My shirt was dirty, but what did it matter in the City! Nothing
mattered . . .

The same office, the same petty work, the same routine. I wrote out
receipts, filled up the ledger, wrestled with averages and sums until my
head was splitting and my hands clammy.

In the luncheon interval, Reggie and I were out over an hour. We ate at
Simpsons, a chop-house. We had a great lump of meat, beautifully cooked.
The men there looked dreary, everything seemed dreary. Worse, I felt more
resigned than yesterday. If it went on much longer, I'd gradually lose
interest in everything I ever hoped to accomplish.

However, Beaton's days in the City were mercifully numbered:

3 December

The pater stayed very late at the office and came home in a foul mood.
He turned Reggie out of the room, then ticked me off about the books. He
said I couldn't do work that a child of twelve could do. What with
mistakes, scratchings out and blanks, I'd put the files in a chaotic state. In
future, he would be afraid to let me handle them. Why, I couldn't do the
simplest addition of feeguires. The business would soon be bankrupt if I
continued. He even went so far as to say he didn't want me at the office
again, but at the same time wouldn't tolerate my doing nothing.

I felt untouched by his fury. It just seemed far away. Inevitably, of
course, I knew my work had to be checked; and I felt certain I'd made a
few slips. But in all ignorance, I couldn't have guessed it mattered so much.
Apparently, when something has been written down wrong, one must take
a ruler and put a ruled line through the mistake, not just draw a line
through it by hand.

7 December

At breakfast this morning I asked, 'Are you expecting me at the office
today?'

The question baffled my father. He didn't know. He had had to engage a

Dutchman (evidently of an unexcitable nature) to scratch out my mistakes and clear up the books.

I said, 'I have enough orders for photographs to keep me busy a whole week.' This was true.

'All right,' and he clicked his tongue . . .'[52]

That, to the relief of all, was the end of Cecil Beaton's City career.

Some nine years later the grandson of a former Governor of the Bank of England turned up at 20 King William Street for his first day at the family coffee business (E. Johnston & Co) and, again despite his pedigree, proved almost equally unsuited. 'I was not cut out for the City life,' Brian Johnston would recall of life on the third floor of Stafford House, 'and never understood its argot – draft at ninety days sight, cash against documents less $2\frac{1}{2}$%, etc.' A brief ray of sunshine was an exchange with the office manager. 'Mr Johnston, you should have been here at 9.30.' 'Why, what happened?' A year in the City office was followed by spells in Hamburg, Brazil and back in London, and during the five years before the war he grew to detest everything about the business of coffee. *It's Been a Lot of Fun*, Johnston would characteristically call his memoirs, but it had not all been cakes and japes.[53]

Of those who failed to last the course, however, the definitive City experience was that of T.S. Eliot.[54] In his late twenties, and as a seemingly more attractive alternative to school-teaching, he joined Lloyds Bank in March 1917, entering the colonial and foreign department at 17 Cornhill. 'Perhaps it will surprise you to hear that I enjoy the work,' he wrote early on to his mother, elaborating soon afterwards to another correspondent:

> I sit in a small office with a mahogany desk and a tall filing cabinet, and feel much more important than my salary warrants, as I have charge of all the balance sheets of their foreign correspondents, filing and tabulating and reporting on them. Not that I know anything about banking, but the business is so huge that I don't suppose more than half a dozen men in the bank know more than their own little corner of it. I share an office with Mr McKnight [the original of Eggerson in *The Confidential Clerk*], who lives in a suburb, polishes his silk hat with great care when he goes out, and talks about his eldest boy.

By 1920 Eliot had moved to the information department at head office, dealing on his own with knotty points – usually legal and international – arising out of the Versailles Treaty. The City itself, however, he now saw as spiritually null, redeemed only by the lunchtime haven of its churches;

as he had graphically written to Lytton Strachey as early as 1919, 'I am sojourning among the termites'. Eliot had a breakdown in the autumn of 1921, and that winter he wrote much of *The Waste Land* while convalescing in Lausanne.

He was back in the City by early 1922, and over the next few months often met the American writer Conrad Aiken for lunch, usually a rump steak in a Cannon Street pub. Aiken would recall how Eliot invariably had with him his pocket edition of Dante's *Inferno*. That October his poem appeared in the *Criterion*, whose publisher was R. Cobden-Sanderson of 17 Thavies Inn, EC1. The immediate acclaim for *The Waste Land* probably only intensified Eliot's despair. 'Of course I want to leave the Bank,' he told Ezra Pound in November 1922, 'and of course the prospect of staying there for the rest of my life is abominable to me.' The following July he returned to the colonial and foreign department, which by this time had moved to 20 King William Street. 'A little room under the street' was how a colleague would describe Eliot's new office. 'Within a foot of our heads when we stood were the thick, green glass squares of the pavement on which hammered all but incessantly the heels of the passers-by.'[55] Over the next two years Eliot wrote a regular, anonymous article on foreign exchange for *Lloyds Bank Monthly*, until at last, in November 1925, he left the Bank and took up a position with the publishers Faber and Gwyer. He had been in the City for just over eight and a half years.

Those nine lines in *The Waste Land* – 'Unreal City . . .' – remain the most haunting lines about the City in the whole of twentieth-century literature; they echo, consciously or otherwise, Herman Melville's description in the 1850s of 'that hereditary crowd – gulf-stream of humanity – which, for continuous centuries, has never ceased pouring, like an endless shoal of herring, over London Bridge'. Eliot too saw the crowd flowing over London Bridge and 'had not thought death had undone so many'. His extraordinarily grim lines, however, tell only one truth about the City. Priestley, some years later, told another, in the person of the middle-aged cashier, Smeeth, as with pipe lit he walks down 'the chilled and smoky length of Angel Pavement'. There, 'everywhere would be a bustle and a jostling, with the roadway a bedlam of hooting and clanging and grinding gears, but he had his place in it all, his work to do, his position to occupy, and so he did not mind but turned on it a friendly eye and indulgent ear'.[56] Eliot's vision or Priestley's? The City experience embraced both, and so, in a Forsterian connection, must we.

Yet at the time that remarkable politician-cum-writer Charles Masterman was not so sure. His study of *England after War* appeared in 1922,
the same year as *The Waste Land*; in it he described, almost equally
hauntingly, the inhabitants of an imaginary London suburb called
Richford:

> Every morning that terrific progeny of Free Trade, the City of London,
> sucks in from all the Richfords overcrowded trainloads, hurrying rapidly
> one after the other, of respectably and dingily garbed human beings. They
> spread themselves in that labyrinth from attic to underground cellar, with
> nimbleness and apparently without repugnance, to spend the best of their
> days in copying other men's letters, adding up other men's accounts, or
> distributing, in vast numbers, in written or printed instructions, the
> requests and demands of other men for the alteration of universes which
> they have never known. Every evening they trample their way back to
> Richford. And the evening and morning are one day. They are all either
> clerks in banks or shipping companies, or accountants, or insurance
> officials. And they are all rearing children to be insurance officials, or
> accountants, or clerks in banks or shipping companies.
>
> There are fifty or a hundred churches in that same City of London, most
> of them built by Christopher Wren on the sites of former churches
> consumed in the Great Fire. Their spires and domes flash upwards,
> pointing to the planets or the fixed stars: with the legend which Paul found
> at Athens, marked as if graven upon them: 'To an Unknown God'.[57]

CHAPTER ELEVEN

Toddling out the Tips

The Bank of England had the gravitas, the merchant banks had the mystique and the clearing banks had the assets, but the Stock Exchange remained – to the outside world – the most emblematic part of the City. It was not just a case of the daily fluctuations of the stock market being the most visible, high-profile example of the City in action. When the *Complete Limerick Book* appeared in 1926, it included seven pages of fairly blue limericks in a chapter entitled 'The Stock Exchange Variety'.[1]

That same year Virginia Woolf enthused to Vita Sackville-West not about limericks, but about spending a day being driven through Oxfordshire by her stockbroker brother-in-law, Herbert Woolf, and his wife Freda: 'I promptly fell in love, not with him or her, but with being stock brokers, with never having read a book (except Robert Hichens), with not having heard of Roger, or Clive, or Duncan, or Lytton. Oh this is life, I kept saying to myself . . .' A dismal Sunday with them in 1927, however, ended this particular romance. 'We had 5 hours,' she informed Vita, 'such talk you can't imagine: in damp drizzly woods for the most part – My passion for stockbrokers is dead.' For that serious-minded young Scotsman, John Kinross, getting to know the City in the autumn of 1928, there was never any such passion. 'I sometimes had my lunch in the ABC Cafeteria in Throgmorton Street in order to absorb the atmosphere,' he would recall. 'It was full of sharp young men from the Stock Exchange. Their talk made it clear that their main object was simply to outsmart the next man. I knew that I should never be able to compete with them, and I often felt depressed.'[2]

There may indeed have been some 'sharp young men' about, especially in the context of a boom, but most people continued to take a fairly dim view of the intelligence of the average Stock Exchange member. Some years later, as Peter Carrington (the future Foreign Secretary) was about to leave Eton, he received some timely advice from his housemaster. Mr Butterwick 'explained that for the really stupid boy, in his experience, three professions could be pursued with some hope of success: farming, soldiering and stockbroking'. It was also indicative that Osbert Lancaster coined the immortal tag 'Stockbrokers Tudor' to describe the mock-Tudor houses that had started to proliferate since the war, especially in south-east England. 'Soon certain classes of the community were in a position to pass their whole lives in one long Elizabethan day-dream,' he wrote in 1939 of the new lifestyle that accompanied these buildings, 'spending their nights under high-pitched roofs and ancient eaves, their days in trekking from Tudor golf clubs to half-timbered cocktail bars . . .'[3] The condescension was infinite, the term stuck and the Stock Exchange's already well-grounded reputation for middle-class philistinism was further cemented.

*

The ninefold increase in the National Debt caused by the First World War meant that British government securities – gilts – retained throughout the inter-war period a far more dominant position in relation to the stock market as a whole than they had done during, say, the thirty or forty years prior to 1914.[4] It is true that of the 5,629 securities officially quoted in March 1938, over a quarter were industrial and commercial; but in terms of market value, the British Funds comprised almost 40 per cent, industrial and commercial securities only 14 per cent. In a non-inflationary age, gilts continued to be seen as fundamentally more sound investments than equities, and few institutions included substantial holdings of ordinary shares in their portfolios. These institutions – above all insurance companies, but also investment trusts and (from the 1930s) unit trusts – were becoming an increasingly significant force. In 1933 the *Financial News* calculated that institutional investors had total holdings of about £1.7bn and generated around one-fifth of Stock Exchange turnover. Even so, the private investor was still king and, in the words of the *FN*, 'investors, on the whole, seem to prefer to have the fun of managing their investment themselves through their own stockbrokers rather than to entrust their savings to an insurance company, an investment trust or a building society'.[5] These individual investors tended to be much more willing to take a punt on ordinary shares and were less deterred by the general absence of reliable financial information about companies, especially the true value of their assets. The Stock Exchange itself hardly encouraged popular capitalism. As early as 1923, a year after it began, the BBC asked for permission to broadcast prices – a request granted, with the utmost reluctance, only three years later, a concession rendered almost useless by the stipulation that no prices were to be broadcast prior to 7 p.m., long after the end of trading.

Overall, whether in government or industrial securities, the market was becoming increasingly domestic in its orientation – in marked contrast to its essentially global character during the golden years prior to 1914. No longer, especially in the 1930s, did capital flow unfettered around the world; while in various ways the Stock Exchange did not help its cause, for example by its attitude to international arbitrage, which was at best indifferent and at worst hostile. Inevitably the result was that much of London's international business between the wars bypassed the Stock Exchange. 'When it is remembered that there must be taken into account exchange rates, commission charges, interest, cables, insurance, fluctuations in money, settlement days, and the possibility that a commitment entered into in one centre may not be successfully undone or closed in another,' F.E. Armstrong symptomatically noted in 1934 in his semi-official *The Book of the Stock Exchange*, 'it will be seen that arbitrage is a highly skilled and technical business.'[6] These were hardly words to enthuse the troops.

In 1938 the Stock Exchange's total membership was 4,132, of whom 2,491 members were brokers, 1,433 were jobbers and 208 were inactive. These 2,491 brokers belonged to 465 firms, working out at an average of 5.4 members per firm.[7] What qualities did these two and a half thousand brokers bring to bear? 'I found new faces but little advancement in stockbroking as a financial science,' George Aylwen would recall of his return to J. & A. Scrimgeour at the end of 1918. 'Most members were merely passers on of information and gossip, there was little or no attempt to sift information, to analyse prospects of equities, or indeed to justify the recommendation of the many and various tips toddled out by the market and the many outsiders who frequented clubs and other convivial places where people with more money than sense assemble.' Donald Cobbett, who as a young man in the 1930s combined financial journalism with working on the floor of the House, was no more flattering: 'The average stockbroker merely conjured a few current ideas out of his topper and trusted to the excellent fino sherry at Short's or the Jamaica to impart an impression of high promise. The compliant clients were then plied with the current inspirations . . . Few stockbrokers in those pre-war days boasted what could be dignified a statistical department; few even had a competent statistician . . .' Admittedly the shortage of reliable information on the equity side was a powerful discouragement to the development of investment analysis. When Foster & Braithwaite decided in 1934 to create a statistical department, the partners disarmingly noted that this was 'with a view to improving the publicity side of the business' – as opposed, in other words, to altering the approach to investment itself.[8]

Nevertheless, the Stock Exchange in this period seems to have made little or no effort to improve the general calibre of its members, one of whom, William H. Tapp, justifiably complained to the Committee in 1938. His particular beef concerned 'the so-called "three decker Members"'. These were the gentlemen who achieved membership of the Stock Exchange, as of other desirable London clubs, through a mixture of personal connections and money. Personal connections were needed in order to find a nomination (by which a new member replaced a retiring member) and three sureties, each by the mid-1930s putting up £500 in case of default. Money was needed to buy the nomination (about £300 at this time); to buy three shares in the ownership of the Stock Exchange (about £210 each); and for the entrance fee of 600 guineas. There would also be an annual subscription of 100 guineas. Tapp, almost certainly a broker himself, was indignant:

> There can be no doubt that an enormous amount of harm is done to the prestige of the Stock Exchange by people who are allowed to join as full Members even although they are under Sureties, without any training whatsoever for their profession. It is all ex the dignity and welfare of the Stock Exchange, and we could do a vast amount of good if under some statute the Stock Exchange could be reformed so that every Member had to have at least three years' training either with a Stock Exchange firm, or a Chartered Accountant before he could become a Member at all.
>
> I remember full well my astonishment in 1927 when I approached Colonel Sir Richard Eaton with a view to joining the Stock Exchange. I was then forty years old and I had had experience in nearly all the outposts of the British Empire, but it amazed me to find I could become a Member by paying certain fees, of what I have always considered to be a highly technical and difficult business.

'The majority of stockbrokers are decidedly an ignorant class who know very little more beyond 8ths, 16ths, and 32nds,' one witness had complained some sixty years previously to the Royal Commission on the Stock Exchange, and in the eyes of Aylwen, Cobbett and Tapp not much had changed.[9]

In a nutshell, whom one knew still mattered more than what one knew. In 1930, not long after one of his sons had secured a berth with the leading gilt-edged brokers Pember & Boyle, Sir Charles Addis 'dined at the Conservative Club' with the firm's Colin Campbell. 'He wants me,' the still strongly Calvinistic banker noted, 'to get George the entry to banks, firms &c, in other words business connexions for his firm which I will not do. I cannot tout even for my own son.' With the right sort of background, a few well-placed friends or relatives and an adequately attractive personality, it was not too difficult for a broker over the course of a few years to build up a reasonable connection and therefore business; what was far more difficult was to secure a foothold *vis-à-vis* the City's élite. When he was not being 'Autolycus', Walter Landells was by the 1930s a partner of E.B. Savory & Co, and in January 1939 he wrote painfully enough to Sir Edward Reid at Barings, following an order to purchase stock for the Infants Hospital, one of the bank's charitable causes: 'The fact is that for years past I had been rather hoping to get an introduction to your famous firm, thinking that perhaps one of these days we might be placed upon your list of Stock Exchange brokers . . . If we can do anything for you in stocks and shares we shall regard it as being an honour as well as a pleasure.'[10]

Most stockbroking firms did not rely just on their partners to achieve the crucial introductions to prosperous clients, for they also employed a wide range of half-commission men, who in return for bringing business from the West End and elsewhere would retain half the commission thus generated. One such was Gubby Allen. After Eton and Cambridge, he started in the City in 1923 with Royal Exchange Assurance, but over the next ten years his main preoccupation was playing as much first-class and club cricket as he could. He toured Australia in 1932–3 and, as a fast bowler, refused to adopt the controversial, ungentlemanly 'bodyline' tactic. On his return he joined the stockbrokers David A. Bevan & Co on a half-commission basis, becoming a member of the Stock Exchange later in 1933. From the firm's point of view, he brought with him not only his sporting reputation but also a host of friends and acquaintances whom he had made on and off the cricket field; and in 1936–7 he captained the next English tour to Australia, almost but not quite managing to wrest back the Ashes from another stockbroker, Don Bradman.[11]

During the voyage out Allen probably did not read Keynes's recently published *The General Theory of Employment, Interest, and Money*, with its celebrated Chapter 12 on the psychology of investment. 'The social object of skilled investment,' Keynes declared, 'should be to defeat the dark forces of time and ignorance which envelop our future.' In practice, however, 'the actual, private object of the most skilled investment today is to "beat the gun"'. And, in a particularly memorable passage, he went on:

Professional investment may be likened to those newspaper competitions in which the competitors have to pick out the six prettiest faces from a hundred photographs, the prize being awarded to the competitor whose choice most nearly corresponds to the average preference of the competitors as a whole; so that each competitor has to pick, not those faces which he himself finds prettiest, but those which he thinks likeliest to catch the fancy of the other competitors, all of whom are looking at the problem from the same point of view. It is not a case of choosing those which, to the best of one's judgement, are really the prettiest, nor even those which average opinion generally thinks the prettiest. We have reached the third degree where we devote our intelligences to anticipating what average opinion expects the average opinion to be . . .

A powerful indictment, and entirely compatible with the make-up of the average stockbroker of the period; but arguably there was another, even stronger reason why the Stock Exchange of these years, and indeed for a long time afterwards, was so poor at analysing economic fundamentals and distributing financial resources accordingly. This was the prevalence – barely recorded in the contemporary literature – of what would eventually be termed 'insider dealing'. It was, as Michael Verey of Helbert Wagg would recall, a process in which the stockbroker tended to be the crucial lubricant or middle-man:

Kit Hoare would have dinner with the investment manager of the Pru, and the investment manager of the Pru after dinner probably let a few secrets go that he, the Pru, had been told about this, that and the other. So Kit Hoare went round to his friends the next day and said, 'I think probably ICI or whatever it might be is a jolly good buy at this price'. A great deal of word of mouthing . . . And there was a good deal of directors in clubs with their friends, stockbrokers and, 'we're doing jolly well at so and so' – there was a good deal of that. So that this all percolated through stockbrokers to Helbert Wagg . . .[12]

Insider dealing began to be outlawed in the United States in the 1930s, but in Britain it was not until the 1960s that it started to be generally recognised as a form of theft, let alone made illegal. Instead, the reputation of many brokers stood or fell by their ability, on the basis of inside information, to provide their chosen clients with profitable tips. From a broker's point of view, moreover, there seemed little point in spending money on analysing the form – even if one had the ability or inclination to do so – when instead it was possible, for the most favoured brokers anyway, to go straight to the horse's mouth.

Did, for example, the partners of the Government brokers, Mullens,

indulge in insider dealing, either for themselves or for their clients? The
very thought was unthinkable – after all, as the car of the sartorially
implacable Sir John Mullens turned each day past Mansion House, at the
end of its journey from Belgrave Square, he would be saluted by the
policeman on duty. Inevitably we have no evidence either way. Mullens
himself, on retiring at the end of 1928, was succeeded as senior partner
by the more congenial Edward ('Eddie') Gosling, who had joined
Mullens as a result of its merger with Steer Lawford in 1921. His
successor in turn, in 1937, was Edward ('Ted') Cripps, recruited some
years previously from his family firm of Simpson & Cripps and,
unusually for Mullens, not an Old Etonian. Cripps would not have
joined Mullens had it not been for the premature death of Hugh
Priestley, successor-designate to Gosling and whose move from Wedd
Jefferson had been very much on the urgings of Montagu Norman.
Priestley was immensely tall, a lover of games, never went abroad and
sent his son James to Winchester, from where he went to his father's old
firm, Wedd Jefferson. 'What would the boys have thought about
someone going into the Stock Exchange for a career?' Jimmy Priestley
was asked many years later. 'I don't think the boys ever really discussed
that very much,' he replied. 'Certainly the City hadn't got a very
high name. I think most people thought the people who went there
were rather like me who had very little brain but hoped to make some
money . . .'[13]

Mullens itself did start recruiting the odd actuary in the late 1930s,
including Henry Milnes from Prudential, but far more typical of the
firm's ethos was the extrovert Dermot Berdoe-Wilkinson, a partner from
1921 to 1952. 'Flamboyant, wearing the largest button-holes in the City,
he was known to his irreverent juniors as "the Ringmaster",' the firm's
historian notes, adding that he 'blithely professed to know nothing about
the technicalities of the money market'.[14] Nevertheless, although 'no
intellectual', the fact remained that Berdoe-Wilkinson was responsible
for a considerable proportion of Prudential's broking needs. At a time
when the Pru was becoming *the* dominant force in institutional
investment, one can only surmise whether this continuing, very lucrative
responsibility was a reflection of Berdoe-Wilkinson's deceptive professionalism or the Pru's less than exacting standards.

Elsewhere, the triumph of breeding over brains was epitomised by
Rowe & Pitman and its senior partner.[15] 'I found myself in a snobbish
upper-class firm,' recalled Nicholas Davenport, whose presence as the
firm's statistician was tolerated rather than welcomed:

Lancelot Hugh Smith had royalty among his friends, his clients and even his relations. He was the father figure of the great Hugh Smith clan which had brothers, nephews and cousins entrenched in the merchant banks, investment trusts and other financial institutions throughout the City. For me Lancie stood for the Establishment as I had imagined it to be – pompous, powerful, upright, unbending, alert to defend the pound sterling to the last million of the reserves and to the last million of the wretched unemployed. All the immense Stock Exchange business of the Hugh Smith clan poured through Rowe & Pitman. In addition to this bread and butter the firm floated many company issues and handed out underwriting to the life insurance companies and banks whose Stock Exchange business it handled. The profits of the firm were therefore enormous. The partners enjoyed fabulous incomes . . .

'Lancie' had, as both Jean Rhys and Sidney Russell Cooke discovered, an unyielding streak. But he also had the knack of making himself useful to the very highest. 'My dear Lancie,' Norman wrote to him in March 1924. 'So many thanks for your note as to the sale at Sothebys. I do not seem to have heard about it but will arrange to make a bid if anything seems suitable.'[16]

It was, as Davenport observed with grudging admiration, a formidable money-making machine that Lancie oversaw:

I remember Hugo Pitman, one of Lancie's partners, calling me into his room one day to ask me to explain a balance sheet. There was really no reason why Hugo should have bothered to understand a balance sheet. His family's immense clientele was not built up on his understanding of company accounts, but on his integrity and charm. He had rowed for Oxford and was a friend of Augustus John, whose paintings he had collected. He was given the first issue of the Ford Motor Company to handle, because a Ford family connection had been up at Oxford with him and had rowed in his college boat.

Lancie's clientele was even more impressive than Hugo's for it included royalty and most of the dukes and earls. I was called to his office one day to hear him on the telephone saying 'Yes, Yes, Your Majesty; No, Your Majesty', but it was merely, he smilingly explained, the King of Greece. The Yorks used to come occasionally to lunch in the office – the late King George VI and our present Queen Mother – because one of Lancie's partners was Jock Bowes-Lyon, Elizabeth's brother, who was adored by the staff because of his perfect manners. Jock was never rude to clerks.

Bowes-Lyon had, however, been seriously wounded in the war and subsequently took to the bottle, dying in 1930.[17]

Someone else for whom drinking would become more than social was the young Ian Fleming, who through the good offices of Alfred Wagg (uncle of a friend) joined Rowe & Pitman in 1935. He himself was a grandson of the great Robert Fleming, who had died two years earlier, but Ian inherited little of his zeal for all things financial. Although personally popular in the firm, he was, thought a colleague, more attracted by the *idea* of money-making than by the mundane reality of it:

> Ian's job consisted basically in keeping contact with his clients, advising them, and bringing in fresh business. Normally he would take his client out to lunch – usually White's Club or somewhere in the City – and he'd take a great deal of trouble to make sure that the food was as good as he could get. Over the lobster or the tournedos he'd start talking rather knowledge-ably about what he called the strategy of investments – he used to enjoy theorizing about money. Then after lunch he would bring the client along to the office, turn him over to the client investment section, and that would be that.

Or, as Fleming himself ruefully conceded in his subsequent days of fortune and fame, 'I never *could* understand what was meant by a sixty-fourth of a point.'[18]

The strength of the partnership system is that it can attract a varying range of talents and knit them closely together – a dictum exemplified in the inter-war period by Cazenove's, rapidly emerging as London's leading firm of stockbrokers, especially in new-issue finance. Take Geoffrey Barnett, a partner from 1919 to 1947. Tall, thin and distinctly reactionary in bent, his main qualities were good connections (his father was on the board of both Alliance Assurance and Lloyds Bank), intense rectitude and an immaculate sartorial sense epitomised by his trousers always being adorned by spats with pearl buttons. He had his own room where, swathed in a huge travelling rug and protected in the winter by kid gloves and a fur muff, as well as a foot warmer, he would complete *The Times* crossword, then call for a cup of Bovril ('lukewarm again') and get on with his main task, which was signing the firm's contract notes on behalf of the partnership as a whole. In front of him was a huge blotting pad, which he never used unless completely clean ('always the danger of forgery'). Later in the morning he would leave his room and walk over in his top hat to the Bank of England office in Finsbury Circus in order to act as the client's 'attorney' for all the gilts inscribed there.[19] He was, in short, no business-getter, quite unlike the firm's two main partners, the remarkable duumvirate Claud Serocold and Charles Micklem.

Lionel Fraser's subsequent assessment was entirely accurate: 'They brought something new to stockbroking. One, shrewd and charming, opened the door, and the other, detailed and able, did the work. They laid the foundations of a fine business.' Serocold – charming, extrovert, Old Etonian – was more than just the perfect front man, however, for he also had a lot of practical-based knowledge, combined with a fruitful supply of inside information that, in the right company, he was willing to share. At Hambros it became a byword how, just as he was leaving the partners' room, he would pause and say, 'Well, there just might be one thing . . .' – at which point all the merchant bankers would, as one man, get up from their seats and walk towards the door. Micklem was very different. The son of a company secretary, he had gone to Wellington College, was a man of few words and always travelled third-class to and from Waterloo. Despite his military bearing, he possessed an acute financial brain, always at the service of his clients; and at Cazenove's he created an ethos of solidity, reliability and pride that would permeate the firm long after he had retired. As a direct result of his influence, there were by the 1930s two cardinal if unwritten office rules: that one did not discuss outside the office what one did inside it; and that Cazenove's did business only with those with whom it wished to do business.[20] Together he and Serocold turned the firm into a major force – but it was Barnett who not only did all the tedious and necessary contract-signing, but also at his home in St Albans held the first garden party on behalf of the staff.

One firm broadening its appeal was Joseph Sebag & Co, which before the war had had an almost entirely Jewish client base. The key figure in this process was Charles Sebag-Montefiore: nicknamed 'The Pirate' by Rothschilds, he was a stockbroker who combined some vision with considerable practicality. When his son Denzil went up to Cambridge, he was advised by Charles not to read economics, 'as I would have to unlearn before being useful in the firm'; and on Denzil duly joining the firm in 1934, and being briefed about the all-important morning visits to the parlours of the merchant banks, 'my father dinned into me that no one could be expected to have good fresh ideas every day and be respected, and that in general the fewer the ideas, the more effective they became'. One of the firm's new partners in the inter-war period, and doing much to expand its range of clients, was Arthur James, a great-nephew of the Iron Duke. He was, Denzil thought, 'the quintessential Englishman, never having held a passport in his life, much preferring to stay and shoot at most of the great stately homes of England'. Indeed, 'he was one of the best shots in the country' and, as a result, 'had friends everywhere'. Denzil also recalled how a rather different – but in its way almost equally important – role in the firm's rise was played by one of its main dealers, E.H. Burgess Smith:

> Smithy specialised in mining shares. Individual gold mines were floated on the London market by Mining Finance Houses, who were themselves quoted, and had themselves paid for the development of the new mines to date. The technical mining side was dealt with in Johannesburg, the financial side was done in London. Smithy used to tell us that the Mining Finance House dealers used to operate from City Bars where they seemed to stay all day long. Coates in Old Broad Street was a favourite. It used to be the duty of young men like Smithy to run to the appropriate bar and tell a dealer of changes in the price of shares he looked after, and hope to get an order to buy or sell . . .

Like most dealers, employed by stockbroking firms to execute their business on the floor of the House, Burgess Smith had no family money behind him; unlike most, however, he did eventually become a partner in his firm. In effect, stockbroking members of the Stock Exchange divided into two classes: partners who stayed mainly in the office; and non-partners who rarely left the floor. 'All have access to the same washroom,' Cobbett would note rather bitterly about these two types of Stock Exchange member, 'but that is about as far as the real equality goes.'[21]

There would always be a whiff of 'outsiders' about Sebags, and so there was also about Vickers, da Costa & Co. That firm's founder, Cecil Vickers, was only twelve when he began work in a broker's office in 1895. His abilities were such that by the war he had become a partner in Nelke & Phillips, flourishing stockbrokers specialising in South African gold shares. In 1917, however, the firm was driven out of existence by the feverish campaign against members of German birth, such as Nelke, and Vickers decided to start his own firm, in partnership with three others, including D.N. da Costa. Vickers provided stern, forceful leadership, and it quickly became a force to be reckoned with, employing up to seventy staff by the 1930s. Another of the original partners was John Millns (a big man remembered for his square jaw, frock coat and violent opposition to the creation of a statistics department), while an early partner was Jack Churchill, Winston's younger brother. Jack has been characterised as 'inoffensive and self-effacing', so the two brothers hardly resembled each other, but the relationship did bring useful publicity for the firm, as well as the future Prime Minister's business. One of Jack's sons, Johnny, briefly tried the City but did not enjoy it, and to paternal dismay left Vickers in 1931 and eventually became a not unsuccessful artist. 'If my father were alive today,' Johnny would later reflect, 'my painting would still be termed: playing the ass in the gutter.' According to Johnny's obituarist, 'his father could never understand why he preferred the artist's struggle to "an easy life" in the City, where the signing of a few documents could have kept him happily in port and cigars'.[22]

Some stockbroking firms were happier than others to employ licensed intellectuals. One was Buckmaster & Moore, where the dominant figure was 'Foxy' Falk, until in 1932 he left the Stock Exchange and started his own firm of American-style 'investment bankers', O.T. Falk & Co. He took with him a young economist called Thomas Balogh, who on behalf of Buckmasters had recently made some dazzlingly successful predictions about how the over-valuation of the Argentine peso would impact on the price of Argentine railway stocks. Buckmasters was, in relation to other stockbroking firms, in the vanguard of research and statistical analysis; even before Balogh left, it had already recruited a young Scottish actuary, Lewis Whyte, who would become one of the century's most authoritative writers on investment matters. Senior partner in the 1930s, in the wake of Falk, was another Scot, Ian Macpherson, a former barrister who became (in Whyte's words) 'a skilled stockbroker with a gift of persuasive exposition'. One of the firm's most important institutional clients was the Provincial Insurance Company, its head office far away in Kendal, and in the course of the 1930s Macpherson on its behalf kept an increasingly watchful eye on the usually brilliant, but sometimes troubling investment policy of the Chairman of the Provincial's finance committee, one J.M. Keynes.[23]

By this time, Buckmasters had a rival in terms of attracting intellectuals: Chase, Henderson & Tennant, of which Davenport, disenchanted by Rowe & Pitman, was a partner from 1933. Indeed, H.P. Chase himself had left Buckmasters in 1926 in order to start his own firm, which he did with James Henderson (who brought the Scottish investment connections) and John Tennant (who brought the capital). Chase 'had great strength of body as well as of mind,' Davenport recalled, 'and once threw the heavy volume of the *Stock Exchange Official Intelligence* at my head when enraged by some trivial political argument'. Having left Buckmasters because there was not room in the same firm for two characters as dynamic as Falk and himself, Chase was determined to introduce a new professionalism into stockbroking, and he largely succeeded. Unfortunately, as Davenport also recalled, he 'became addicted to scotch'; or, in the more tactful words of the firm's historian, 'even before the war his insensate appetite for work had left him a burnt-out shell'. Another partner from 1932, responsible for bringing Davenport to the firm, was Robert Boothby, at this stage of his life an ambitious MP permanently short of the readies. Davenport quickly discovered that Boothby 'would sooner gamble than do the hard work necessary for making money in the City', and that 'in fact the City bored him stiff'; as for Davenport himself, it was not long before he became frustrated by the limits being placed on his intellectual freedom, especially in relation to the financial column that he wrote for the *New Statesman*:

> They [the partners] said I must not criticise bankers, however stupid and deflationist they might be, because they might be clients of the firm. They warned me that I must never attack the Bank of England. On one occasion when I had done so in my weekly column, the senior partner called me in and said menacingly: 'You have been attacking the Bank of England again. Well, I've just had lunch with one of the managing directors (Humphrey Mynors it was) and he told me to tell you: "LAY OFF!"' Of course, I did not. My criticism of the Governor of the Bank as the arch-priest of deflation and unemployment was, as a Keynesian, my constant theme . . .

Professionalism, in other words, did not extend to dangerous iconoclasm. And, to make matters worse, Davenport found being a partner in a stockbroking firm even more of a bind than marriage: 'You could always walk out on your wife if you have such an inclination but you cannot walk out on your partners. There are too many legal documents in the way.'[24]

There were several hundred less well-known stockbroking firms, chugging quietly along and devoted almost entirely to private client business. With at most a handful of partners, and employing no more than two dozen staff, they could keep going provided there were sufficient clients to enable the modest office expenses to be met, those clients paid their differences, and above all the partners did not speculate unduly – or unduly rashly – on their own account. Phillips & Drew, for instance, was then a family firm, in which the Drews retained a strong presence and share of the equity; according to the recollections of David Drew, who joined in 1927, 'if we could scratch £100 commission in a day we were well satisfied – £300 and we almost went out and celebrated'. In the year ending March 1936, at a time when a leading firm like Cazenove's was returning a net profit of around £0.5m, the five partners of Phillips & Drew had to make do with a net profit of £7,651. Part of those profits had been generated by the firm's various half-commission men, who during the inter-war years included such diverse characters as Norman Walters, a well-to-do bachelor who became Chairman of Fortnum & Mason, rarely smiled and was nicknamed 'the screaming skull' by irreverent staff; Kenneth Dingwall, 'the Dingo', who was a former officer with the Gordon Highlanders and brought in several distinguished Army men as clients; E.H. Lacon Watson, a genial man of letters whose clients included Sir Arthur Conan Doyle; the Hon Alexander Archibald Douglas Wolston Dixie, a 'gay butterfly' of the 1930s who owned one of the original SS Jaguars; and John Cecil Stafford Charles, who belonged to a family of surveyors and property dealers, was renowned less for his stockbroking than for his skill at field sports, could be exceptionally rude to the clerks, and is remembered as 'very toffee'.

As it happened, however, March 1936 itself marked a fundamental turning-point in the firm's history. An unassuming, self-made, middle-aged actuary called Sidney Perry, who in appearance resembled most people's idea of a pork butcher, had found his progress blocked at David A. Bevan & Co, and rather than go to the trouble and expense of starting his own firm he had come to an arrangement with Phillips & Drew by which he would build up his own team within the firm, sharing the profits. Perry was one of the few actuaries working in stockbroking, and he appreciated that there were rich pickings to be had by adopting a more scientific approach, especially in relation to the 'switching' of gilt stocks, in effect a form of arbitrage. Perry set up his desk at Phillips & Drew in March 1936 and over the next three years began to recruit his own, qualified team of actuaries and accountants, able to speak to the investment institutions (especially the insurance companies) in their own language. One of the City's countless small, family-run outfits had taken the first step, however unwittingly, towards being turned into a notable meritocracy.[25]

So many stockbroking firms, so many stockbrokers . . . The formidable Kit Hoare, who with his great bushy eyebrows and closeness to the Pru built up Cohen Laming Hoare into a major, independent-minded company broker; the very religious Bob Carter, senior partner of Sheppards, who would growl to a vacillating client, 'you tell me which stock you want to buy and I'll buy it for you'; Richard Hart-Davis of Panmure Gordon, a man of extremes who once hurled a telephone out of the window on being given unwelcome news by one of his dealers about the price of a pet share; E.J. Podger of Windsor & Mabey, a man whose girth ensured that his surname was also his nickname . . .[26] All four were prosperous, all four were men of standing – unlike poor Norman Chivers, an almost instantly forgotten victim of the 1931 financial crisis.

It was a sad story. Having been severely wounded during the war and winning the MC, Chivers was in his mid-twenties when he began his Stock Exchange career in 1922, joining the small broker Herbert Blaiberg and becoming a partner. He continued to suffer from shell-shock, had frequent attacks of malaria and was also subject to fainting fits. In 1931 he moved to a bigger firm, Burtt, Jones & Hammond, and soon came unstuck. From his home at 'Bunree', Higher Drive, Purley, he wrote a letter of confession to Sidney Burtt:

> I have not slept for several weeks, and could not stand the anxiety of not having been absolutely truthful, any longer. I have done nothing criminal, and have in my enthusiasm only injured myself. I did exceed, to a degree, the discretion I had with the two or three clients, and assumed friends, little did I think when matters went against them, they would behave as they have done . . . Please don't give me too strong a cross-examination, I feel a little better already, and when I come up about 10.30 tomorrow, will tell you everything, and then do my utmost in future to regain your confidence, with whom I am so happy.

The Stock Exchange Committee read this letter on 13 October, the day after Burtt explained to it that 'on three occasions Chivers had opened accounts for clients without the clients' permission' and that 'the matter had been brought to light when the clients were pressed for payment'. In person on the 13th, Chivers revealed that the clients had been clients of his when he was a partner with Blaiberg. Over the next week both Burtt and Blaiberg spoke up for him. 'We can see no other motive for his action than that of wishing to create a favourable impression with us regarding his ability to obtain business,' Burtt asserted, while Blaiberg 'was sure that illnesses had had an effect on Chivers' balance of mind' and 'he felt that Chivers had missed, through no fault of his own, the training which was essential in the early years of a business career'.

There was also, as the Committee moved ponderously through the due process of passing and confirming sentence for dishonourable conduct, an avalanche of letters from Chivers:

> Gentlemen, my wife and I have been praying night and day you will give a reprieve for my foolish action. Since my days of leaving school, my service days and S.E. I have always enjoyed my share of popularity and respect. Any symptom of publicity would be a life long knock for me . . .
>
> Gentlemen, I feel I should not worry you any more, but the last evening, before the decision is made, I cannot help asking once more, your forgiveness, and the chance, to make amends, and become a happy fellow again . . .

I cannot realise that I am in such a predicament, a victim of circumstances . . .

Gentlemen, I have your verdict, I am sure you will forgive me speaking quite openly. I must as a fellow, well born, ask the question, as man to man, fellow to fellow, before you pass this sentence, have I no recompense? . . .

I have suffered severely already, I could face a great deal myself if necessary but it is so very hard for dependants. The old tale, the sins of the fathers etc. Perhaps you would give further consideration to one very repentant . . .

In fact the sentence – a two-year suspension – could have been a lot worse; but sin or not, it was enough to end this father's hopes of founding a stockbroking dynasty.[27]

*

Leading brokers like Charles Micklem or Lancelot Hugh Smith divided their working time mainly between their own offices and those of their clients, venturing relatively seldom into the House, but indisputably it was the lofty, domed, multi-pillared, teak-floored 'Gorgonzola Hall' that remained the heart of the Stock Exchange and arguably of the City itself. A financial journalist and a merchant banker as well as a jobber in the Jungle (i.e. West African) market in the course of his variegated career, Hubert A. Meredith in 1931 took his readers inside:

No matter how inactive the market may be, the ear is always assailed by a low rumbling sound which seems to emanate from all corners. It is caused by a mixture of bidding and offering of stock, conversation between members, calling of names from the various waiters' stands, the shuffling of feet as members walk across the floor, the rumble of the pneumatic tubes which convey telegrams to the Postal Department and the vibration of the never-ending traffic in Old Broad Street which can be distantly heard through the windows. The conglomeration of all these noises is impossible to describe. When once the ear is attuned to it, however, it is possible to detect particular voices in particular markets. Experience enables one on entering the House to be able, by the rumble of noise emanating from markets, to know whether the dealers who are calling out prices are bidding or offering . . . In addition to the noise, in normally active times there is an incessant bustle caused by the continuous movement of people, from the silk-hatted broker down to his bare-headed unauthorised clerk, walking about from one market to another, in busy times as quickly as possible, the whole scene being one of general activity and animation . . . Space is a serious problem, particularly in busy times, when a very large number [potentially up to some 10,000, including clerks as well as members] is engaged in active work inside the Stock Exchange. Although there is no question of reserving seats, certain members use certain seats and, having used them for so many years, no one else would jump their claims. The majority of members, however, have to stand all day long, and one of the trials of a clerk starting in the Stock Exchange is the fact that he is running about or standing all day long – a state of affairs which takes a lot of getting used to . . .[28]

One of those young clerks who had to cultivate physical stamina was Terrence Ahern, employed in the 1930s by the option dealers Baily, Mercer, Karo, the last partner being the by now celebrated Major Max Karo. He ran the Stock Exchange Cadets and each year at the start of May would appear on the floor in a new straw boater which, according to Donald Cobbett, 'seldom survived the joyous welcoming, ending up in perpetual passage over the heads of an hilarious mob in the Kaffir market'. It was a world that left a deep impression on the young Ahern:

> Standards were extremely high. Anybody that didn't play the game or was found out doing something that was not correct was ostracised and probably found it very difficult to deal. There was one, a very unpopular chap called 'The Slug'. He used to go round and round the market trying to check it with everybody so they called him the Slug. And they used to sing 'There's a long, long trail a'winding'. He was unpopular and he found it very difficult to deal . . . There was another chap called Richard Slazenger. In those days they dealt a lot in 32nds and 64ths and he got the nickname of Richard the 64th because he always wanted to deal a 64th different from anybody else . . . There were all sorts of nicknames for people there. There were people called 'The Fish' and 'The Goat', and another was a small and extremely ugly man and he was called 'Don't Tread In It' in the Mining Market. One particular chap was caught on the railways without a ticket so they all used to get round and sing 'Oh, Mr Porter, what shall I do, I got carried off the train at Crewe' . . . There was another person in the gilt market, he wasn't Jewish but he looked Jewish. They used to get round the gilt-edged market and sing 'Jerusalem' to him. Whenever there was a lull in the market and there was nothing doing, they always got up to some form of tricks to keep them amused. If it's a wet day and nothing doing, some chap would come in with a neatly rolled umbrella, and while he wasn't looking they'd undo the umbrella and tear up all these pieces of paper and then roll it up again very carefully. When he came out they all watched him open the umbrella, he got covered in all this confetti. There was always something that they found to amuse themselves. Of course as a junior clerk or a blue button you had to watch and look on because if you stood around too long they said, 'What are you hanging about for?' . . .

Cobbett offers some gloss. The small, ugly gentleman was, according to him, called 'Step-in-it', on the grounds that 'he affected a slow and dignified gait with head in air as if he had a permanent bad smell under his nose', with the result that 'he was always greeted by some of the more uninhibited members with the cry: "Mind you don't step in it, Sir!"' As for the singing of 'Jerusalem', this was led by two jobbers in the gilt-edged market, Charlie Lord and Arthur Rogers, and took place each Friday afternoon at about 3.15 on the appearance in the market of a top-hatted broker called Louis Pierce. The choice of him, Cobbett explains, was attributable to Pierce having once been heard to say to a jobber, as they disagreed about the price of a particular stock, 'I will wait till my brudder comes in.' Pierce himself, insists Cobbett, 'thoroughly enjoyed' the weekly serenade – and he adds that the adjacent Alliance Assurance (its offices overlooking Shorter's Court) would 'throw wide their windows to listen with evident appreciation'.[29]

There was plenty of other ensemble singing on the floor of the House. 'Abey, Abey, Abey my boy, what is your bloody name now?' would for years mark the appearance of a Kaffir jobber who during the war had changed his name from Abrahams to Austin. And what Cobbett recalls as 'a sonorous, measured rendition of the "Volga Boatmen"' would regularly mark the appearance of a broker who reputedly dealt with Transport House. As for the member who had a congenitally miserable face, he could expect nothing else than 'I've gotta motto – always merry and bright . . .' The floor's japes, meanwhile, ranged from the general – above all the throwing of paper darts, with the Kaffir market's highest ambition being to lodge them in the grilles of the ceiling – to the distinctly more personal. Every Monday morning a stockbroker called Horace Ryan, who had once foolishly boasted about the runs he would make for a parents' cricket team and then been out for a duck, was greeted with a round of orchestrated clapping and cries of 'Well run, Sir!' Johnny Johnson, a jobber who was a stalwart of the Stock Exchange Christian Association, was predictably nicknamed 'The Bishop' and regularly forced to endure an anointing ceremony, the water usually being poured from a fellow-member's fountain-pen cap. There was also the broker who, around lunchtime, frequently had his shoes removed and thrown up well out of reach on the wire racks covering the heating system. 'He always,' according to Cobbett, 'said he went along with it because "it helped his dealing".'[30]

The Stock Exchange was, undeniably, a club with a cruel streak; but like any good club, it made sure that age brought with it certain

privileges. Whereas a younger or middle-aged member could literally be
hounded out of the House if he dared, in Cobbett's words, attempt 'such
self-expressive departures as suede shoes or a checky suit on a relaxed
Saturday morning', their seniors had far greater freedom:

> I recall one jobber, an isolated figure on the fringe of the Kaffir market,
> solemnly sporting a high-skirted topper outdated by fully half-a-century.
> Several others attired themselves in frock-coats and sponge-bag trousers –
> one was even seen in snuff-coloured whipcord – while spats, cravats, and
> monocles were common accessories. Fergie, my jobber-boss, always kept
> his pince-nez, suspended from a black riband in his top, flapped waistcoat
> pocket. Response to any price enquiry involved quite a little ritual in
> extracting and adjusting this aid before ponderously perusing his long
> dealing book. One ancient, in a rusty, four-skirted jacket, used to scavenge
> in the huge, wicker wastepaper baskets positioned about the floor. You
> could see him secreting chosen lengths of string and discarded newspapers
> about his capacious clothing . . .

On or off the floor, there was no cult of youth. 'No one in the City will
listen to what you have to say for twenty years,' Serocold of Cazenove's
was wont to remark to his junior partners, and that may well have been
an under-estimate.[31] Many jobbers jobbed until they dropped: it was a
way of life as much as a way of business, and their jealously preserved
spot on the market floor represented – albeit invisibly – their deepest
identity.

The territorial imperative remained strong on the part of those
responsible for manning the Stock Exchange's dozen or so principal
markets. In November 1937 a jobber in the Foreign market, J.L.
Nickisson of Aubrey Spurling & Co, complained bitterly to the
Committee, in the context of an upsurge in the business of an adjacent
market threatening to destroy his own market's traditional boundaries:

> I should like to bring to your Notice the absolute chaos which daily takes
> place between the Foreign and American Markets from the hours of 10 and
> 11 a.m., and again in the afternoon about 3 p.m. making it at times
> absolutely impossible to transact one's business. This is very largely
> brought about by Clerks (blue button) who seem to be attracted by
> curiosity at what very often resembles a Football Scrummage and anyhow
> detracts from the amenities and smooth working of the markets of the
> House. Several suggestions have been made to better this state of things,
> one being that a partition or white line should be drawn between the two
> markets and a waiter placed there to keep a clear passage . . .

The Committee could only express its 'sympathy' to Nickisson, along with its 'regret that they were unable to afford him any material relief'.[32]

During the inter-war period the number of jobbing firms very gradually declined – 411 in 1920, 358 in 1930, 342 in 1938 – and by the eve of war there was an average of just over four members per firm.[33] According to the broker Marcus Colby, who began his career in 1926, 'the vast majority of the numbers of jobbers were two-men firms who had very little capital, and they were really not much good to you', in that 'they wouldn't take you on probably over 1000 shares anyway, so really they were ignored, as far as I was concerned'. Indeed, 'I think there were, probably all through the Stock Exchange, not more than twenty firms that I would deal with'.[34] Colby no doubt exaggerates somewhat, in that there were still considerably more than twenty large or medium-sized jobbing firms capable of making a price in a considerable quantity of shares, but his larger point about the continuing numerical prevalence of the small jobber is valid.

How did these two-man, or even one-man, firms manage to get by? The answer seems to have been that the small jobber would act as a dogsbody for brokers active in the particular market in which the small jobber specialised. 'He told them what was going on, he kept them posted in prices,' Ahern recollects, 'and if there was any change in the market, sent messages and rang up the office and told them the changes in the price, he would take limits and do them for the broker.' Ahern adds that although this small jobber, carrying either a very small book or possibly no book at all, 'may have been somewhat parasitical in the fact that he was making a price on the back of someone else in the market, at the same time he was performing a function in keeping the broker informed of what was going on in the market'. Cobbett confirms this analysis about the 200-plus firms of lesser jobbers, 'many trading like a species of pilot-fish, off the backs of their bigger brethren':

> Such small fry tended to be subsidised by a few friendly brokers prepared to give away a fraction in their dealing in exchange for a keen, up-to-the-minute price service before the days of internally televised changes. Their ability to survive lay largely in knowing the closest 'touch' in the prices of the market leaders – that is, the inside spread between the varying quotations of, as in those days, a wide choice of keenly competing jobbers.
>
> These book-and-pencil jobbers tended to proliferate under boom conditions, or they followed like the carpet-bagger of the mineral discoveries, the swings of activity – successively to mines, rubbers, tin shares, and so on – most rewarding at any given time. In hectic conditions, such as occasionally prevailed in the rubber market, where long queues of

impatient brokers would form at the jobbers' pitches, it was often impossible to reach the main practitioners, and consequently in the interests of speed, it paid to deal on the fringe of the market with some interloper, albeit on a wider price basis.

Cobbett himself worked for a time for one of these fringe jobbers, Fergusson & Bousfield, and over half a century later was proud to have done so: 'We knew the news. We knew the prices. We knew the touches . . .'[35]

The gilt-edged market, also known as the Consol market, was at this time by far the most important market, as a result of the wartime swelling of the National Debt, and in its prime location by the Capel Court entrance it also occupied the most space. Inevitably there was resentment, as in December 1932 when the gilt jobbers Wedd, Jefferson & Co led a movement to end the practice (re-introduced in September 1931) of opening the House on Saturday mornings. There was, argued the public-spirited Wedds, no real demand, and therefore not a true market, so that 'price manipulation is easy and "bear" raids on Government and other securities are by no means impossible'. There ensued a successful counter-campaign, including a letter to the Committee from the veteran jobber, still dealing in four different markets, Charles Pulley, who complained that the Wedd Jefferson memorial had been got up by dealers in the Consol market who now found it difficult to do their business. 'It is not right,' he maintained, 'that a section of the House which, since the tragedy of 1914, had enjoyed eighteen years of uninterrupted prosperity, should ask the Committee to close the Stock Exchange because there are difficulties in regard to their own particular business caused by the shorter hours during which the Banks are open.'[36]

During these years Wedds itself was generally recognised as one of the three leading jobbers in gilts, alongside Francis & Praed (which perhaps led the triumvirate) and Akroyd & Smithers. A contrasting trio of partners dominated the show at Wedds, which Jimmy Priestley joined in 1933. Jack Russell was 'a frightening character' who 'always wore a bowler hat' and, when he returned from lunch and put his hat on the rack, invariably induced 'a hushed silence'; George Wilkins was 'an absolute charmer'; and John Longuet-Higgins was 'very unpopular', but 'much cleverer and probably the brains behind them'. There were three or four other partners, about forty staff, the profits were considerable, and the young Priestley found the atmosphere fairly complacent: 'They all had money, those partners, and I think it's much more difficult when you've got money to be go-ahead and do it better rather than when you're hungry . . . They just wanted the quiet life. They had their money, they had their country houses.'[37]

The other main domestic market was the Industrial market, known before 1914 as the Miscellaneous market, and the focus for business in such shares as Dunlops, Courtaulds and Imperial Tobacco. The dominant firm, by common consent, was F. & N. Durlacher, of which the senior partner from 1936 was Esmond Durlacher, a jobber possessed of an unusually high analytical intelligence.[38] Beneath Durlachers there were some two dozen reasonably well-capitalised firms jostling for position, of which two that would become enduring presences in Industrials were Bisgood Brothers (later Bisgood, Bishop & Co) and Smith Brothers. At Bisgoods the two brothers, Eustace and Bertram, gradually eased down during the 1920s, and by the early 1930s the firm was in danger of winding down completely, until the arrival of Harold Strachan from a rival firm of jobbers, Hadow & Turner. He had had a distinguished war with the King's Own Scottish Borderers, had a reputation as a cricketer and possessed an attractive, independent-minded character. He proved an excellent chief dealer and did much to rebuild and indeed enhance the firm's reputation. The firm's particular speciality remained anything to do with the motor industry, while other partners in the 1930s included a forceful character called Henry Bishop, his brother Louis and Howard Taylor, whose claim to fame was that he had bowled Herbert Sutcliffe with his first ball in county cricket.[39]

There were fewer off-spinners at Smith Brothers. Founded in 1924 as Smith & Cutler, and changing its name five years later, its background was South African; but although at various times it enjoyed a strong presence in the Kaffir market, during most of the inter-war period its bread-and-butter was Industrials. Archie Jessep, straight from elementary school in West Ham, joined the firm in 1928:

> Charlie Smith [the senior partner] was a very grand man. You could talk to him like a father, and if he saw that you were making sense, he'd help you on your way . . . We were in 2 Angel Court. It was three floors, we occupied two floors of it. It was like a rat trap. It really was. A terrible office. I think it was something like £2 or £3 a week – very tiny . . . I learned through watching my senior partner. I stood by his side all day long. His prices were always seen to be closer than the rest of the jobbers. Say, if he bought 1,000 shares and sold 1,000 he was content to take three farthings on it, which was £3 2s 6d, where other people wouldn't look at it. You might put it down as the Jewish spirit. But he would take small profits and make large money . . . The Jewish firms always made the closest prices; the Jewish attitude, small profits, larger business . . .

Smiths, although still fairly small, was poised to become the market's permanent outsiders – skilled, aggressive and with no time for sentimental pieties about the purpose of its existence. 'I was competitive,' Jessep would recall when asked why Charlie Smith had made him his authorised dealer on his twenty-first birthday, 'and my idea was to make money. And that was the biggest thing in the Stock Exchange, to make money.'[40]

The Industrial market was neatly placed between the intense respectability of the Consol market on the Capel Court side and the exuberance of the various Mining markets on the Old Broad Street side. Rex Whistler, in his wonderful 'zoological' map of the floor, drawn in 1933, identified four distinct Mining markets: the Kaffir Circus; Rhodesians; Australian, Indian and Malayan Mines; and the Jungle (i.e. West African mines). The political, diplomatic and economic turbulence of the inter-war years meant that these markets generally prospered, especially those dealing in gold-mine shares, and there were several notable booms, though none quite as memorable as the Kaffir boom of 1895. Some jobbers, as ever, came unstuck. Higham Brothers, which as Hyman Brothers had done so well in 1895, failed early in 1937 when Kaffirs, in the words of the senior partner's nephew David Higham, 'took an unexpected sudden turn'; unfortunately Uncle Willie, who 'had charm, honour and an easy way with life', was 'away in Scotland and out of reach'. In the Rhodesian market, specialising in copper mines, the most powerful, intimidating jobber was undoubtedly Julian Berger, a renowned big bidder who (as recalled by Cobbett) 'suddenly galvanised into clamorous bidding for five thousand Rhokana at perhaps £20 a share was enough to daunt the most adventurous spirits, particularly if they happened to be short of a couple of hundred'. Sometimes Berger left the bidding to a partner, nicknamed 'His Master's Voice'.[41]

In this and the other Mining markets, most of the leading jobbers had an important, if rarely stated, relationship with the outside 'shops'. One of the best-known shops of the day, in its case specialising in West African gold mines and largely responsible for the jungle boom of the mid-1930s, was the Finsbury Pavement House group, controlled by the legendary Herbert George Latilla. 'H.G.L.', as he was generally known, was 'a broad-built, craggy, roughly affable man' whom Cobbett would occasionally visit at 120 Moorgate for orders, sitting 'at his vast mahogany desk' surrounded by a 'sea of carpet'. Latilla had grown up in Brighton, had reputedly served as bell-hop to the South African mining entrepreneur Abe Bailey, and for reasons unknown his left hand was invariably 'encased in a brown, leather glove', which 'he poised stiffly upwards, elbow on the desk'. His tame jobber was 'the ebullient Captain Martin', of the jobbers Martin, Donn & Co, nicknamed 'The Call of the Wild' on account of 'his penetrating tones pitched with feverish insistency, successive octaves above the steady clamour of the House'. Cobbett memorably describes Granville Martin in stentorian action:

'At a penny-ha'penny buy Marlu . . . Buy ten thou at three-ha'pence, Marlu . . .' then impossibly higher again, frantic in his urgency, winding his voice up to an incredible pitch . . . 'Tu'pence-farthing buy Marlu, BUY TWENTY AT . . .'

Then someone lurking inconspicuously on the fringe of the market would casually stuff him with a fiver (stuff, the market's colloquialism for suddenly taking advantage of an over-adventurous bidder). 'Sell you a fiver! [i.e. 5,000]' The broker – or maybe it would be a fellow-jobber apparently slumbering on a nearby seat – would snap out his offer incisively, noting it down immediately in a black, leather-bound dealing book whipped with a conclusive gesture from his jacket pocket. Momentarily the babble of surrounding dealers might be hushed; but not for long.

'Buy five at tu'pence-farthing!' Martin would snap back equally decisively, and be off like a shot to one of the half-dozen or so telephone booths adjacent to the market to report the bargain (and conceivably a number of others accumulated since his last call) back to the shop [i.e. the Finsbury Pavement House group]. From the shop, Martin would receive his booking instructions, be told to which of a coterie of favoured stockbrokers the wholly internal deals were to be put down. A great deal of shop business was done to bait the hook. And all this, of course, is what would have made the modern sleuths of the marketplace puce with righteous indignation . . .

Who comprised these shops? Latilla and Sir Edward Myerstein were, according to Cobbett, 'the joint props of the revised Jungle market'; in some of the Rhodesian copper-mine securities, the finance house Cull & Co exercised a controlling influence; while in such Kaffir shares as Geduld and East Geduld, Union Corporation was the undisputed shop. From the shop's point of view, the jobbers they employed had to be well known to brokers and have a good connection with them; had to be able to retail bull or bear information as it suited the shop; and, perhaps above all, had to be able to cushion bull or bear movements in the prices of a shop's stocks, knowing that if they – the jobbers – found themselves too long or too short, they could always go to the shop to relieve them. It was a delicate relationship, necessarily covert, granted that Stock Exchange rules specifically forbade jobbers from having direct contacts with outside interests – though it is hard to believe that the authorities could have been ignorant of these relationships. It was a situation hardly conducive to fair markets, and Ahern came to believe that the West African market in particular was 'basically rigged':

> If people like Myerstein and Latilla wanted to get a share up they went in and sold some stock and then bought it back – they sold it badly and then bought it back deliberately, 'oh the shop's buying', and then someone else came buying. And all the time as they sold it, they'd bought a bit back, sold it, sold it; when they'd finished selling the price came down.
> *What kind of period are you talking about?*
> Two or three months.
> *And did you as jobbers often feel that you had lost out through manipulations of the shop? I mean were you more often the victims rather than the beneficiaries?*
> Well, it's up to you to use your know-how . . .[42]

*

To be a successful jobber, everyone agreed, needed a mixture of flair, resilience and optimism. Roy Sambourne, a jobber for some forty years, inherently possessed neither flair nor optimism, but almost every weekday that he was in London he turned up dutifully in Capel Court.[43] Before the First World War, as a young man down from Oxford in 1900, he formed a partnership with an instinctively more adept operator, a German émigré called Ernest Pohl; but Sambourne himself flourished only moderately, despite his brother-in-law being Lennie Messel, a partner in the prominent stockbrokers L. Messel & Co founded by his father Ludwig. Their firm, by now called Pole & Sambourne, was still in existence after the war, but for Sambourne life on the Stock Exchange was increasingly a burden rather than a pleasure. 'I have just enough to scrape along with, but have to be most careful – no cigars or liqueurs, just simple living, dining alone at home,' he recorded (with no doubt some exaggeration) in his diary in February 1919; soon afterwards he declared, equally characteristically, that 'the Stock Exchange is a grievous disappointment, I feel so helpless there'.[44] So on the whole it went on, all dutifully recorded in Roy's relentlessly self-pitying diary – although the firm itself, standing in the Foreign market and specialising in the shares of the Venezuela Oil Company, always did enough business to carry on, sometimes in a mild way even prospering.[45]

The first half of 1925, in which as usual the clouds would occasionally but misleadingly clear, was as typical as any other six months:

7 January. CFM [Charles Maclachlan, a partner] leaves early & Orpen [Ronald Orpen, another partner] makes a sad mess of VOC. We lose over £100 & are heavy Bulls when I leave at 5 pm. All Orpen's mistake.

8 January. We have a good day all round in the City. VOC making back all we lost yesterday.

9 January. All day long I have a streaming cold – at its very worst. Ridge [Arthur Ridge-Jones, the firm's half-commission man] & I have sherry as usual. CFM makes a price in 3,000 Brit Cont [British Controlled, another Venezuelan oil company] pref & loses £70 or so & in addition we are bulls of Shell all round. Such a pity this running losses like we do.

13 January. Very disappointing business today. We get caught in & out of the VOC & do no good one way or the other. EHC [Ernest Cawston, another partner] flounders about – Pole & I do nothing. Lunch off sandwiches Lyons & no tea . . .

20 January. Orpen has one of his mad conceited fits which leads to trouble. He deals in 5,000 BC pref & sits & looks at them all day long – only selling 500 – Naturally I want them sold & at 4 pm there is unpleasantness. CFM is largely to blame. He does not take a firm hand – it is all a great worry to me. Periodically we have these troubles. There is little doing & Oils are out of favour.

27 January. Oils difficult today – the usual mysterious selling in face of better outlook for oil. House speculation & market punters responsible.

4 February. City not very exciting. Foreign market very idle. Oils good but no public. Railway strike threatening. Wisden's soon out now. Lunch at Pimm's. Lobster & No 1. This latter makes me sleepy, & I won't take it again.

5 February. City not very busy – but Oils again present features – & we do some business. This last a/c has been thank God a good one & I hope & pray we may continue to do well.

6 February. We do 2 wonderful deals in Anglo Egyptian 'B' – first 2,500 & then 5,000 shares. Our oil book at end of day shows well over £300 profit. It is like a fairy dream & Pole & I can scarcely realise it.

10 February. City very disappointing. Oils sag & recover after but no 'go' in them. VOC is très difficile . . . Lunch Lyons & tea Pilcher [Charles Pilcher, a one-man jobber who had joined the Stock Exchange the same year as Sambourne]. Up to office – poor business – & VOC close $3\frac{5}{32}$ – there is some mysterious selling about.

19 February. Much chaff as to my top hat [which he had worn to a funeral at Brompton Oratory before going on to the City]. I am annoyed – perhaps too self conscious at some of the bounders of the Foreign Market.

Things had not improved for Sambourne by early summer:

4 May. City disappointing. We get caught out badly in VOC. Ridge & self have sherry. He is an ass with his money.

8 May. Very little business. Most disappointing week. I am all day in a state of depression which I cannot shake off. It usually comes on me at this time of year. I feel so out of everything.

12 May. A very dull day in the City. Dearer money calls a fall in prices. No business. Lennie does not come near me. I see Linley – very full of his dances – as I was in 1904. Ridge & I as usual. Lunch Lyons. I still feel depressed. Tea Pilcher.

2 June. Nothing doing in S. Ex. I do puzzles all day . . . I wish I had some invitations for this week . . . CFM does a little in oils. I laze about. I wish Fitzgerald [presumably Evelyn FitzGerald of Panmure Gordon], Smith (Rowe & P), Serocold, Wilkinson, Hollebone, Labouchere [Charles Labouchere of Tritton, Labouchere & Caro, another leading firm of brokers] or a few more would come near me sometimes. There must be something about me which freezes people off. I wonder what it is. I haven't the knack of it. Even Burney [Albert Burney, formerly Birnbaum, of Grieveson Grant] who wanted to be friendly never carried out to any extent his intentions & there it is. Lunch & tea Lyons. Pilcher. I rather like him.

24 June. We do everything wrong in Oils – caught out & caught in – and I get in the dumps.

30 June. We have a rotten day in the City. VOC fall from $2\frac{23}{32}$ to $2\frac{17}{32}$ & we lose on the day – not much – but we have accounts open with doubtful Brokers . . . Pole in addition makes a fool of himself in taking 5 German 7% from 'the Yellow Peril' – who of course is no turn – & Cawston is rotten as always . . .

By September poor Sambourne's sense of isolation and failure was becoming almost obsessive. 'You see,' he explained to himself on the 7th, after compiling another long list of leading brokers who shunned him, 'I never will make advances to anyone who can help me for I hate to imply that I am trying to get something out of them. Were they all jobbers I should probably be more friendly.' Two days later: 'I feel depressed all day in the Stock Ex. No Broker seems to take the slightest pains to deal with me.' On the 14th: 'I do nothing in the City – and never look like it. Plenty doing in Foreign market – but no one comes near me.' And on the 21st: 'My standing in the Foreign market is more & more of a complete farce. No broker seems to think it worth while to come near me & one & all – Messel's included – avoid me. I know them all but they never come to deal. Even less than a few years since. The result is that I spend my time trying to do acrostics.'

Worse was to come, for that autumn saw Sambourne almost literally pole-axed by a short, sharp crisis. Over the previous year or two his trust in Pole had started to ebb, as his partner began to borrow extensively from the firm. Matters now came to a head, with Sambourne under increasing pressure from his junior partners to be – for once in his life – decisive. The diary served as a refuge, as well as a record:

30 September. Today culminates in fearful anxiety . . . It appears that Pole has £9,500 of his original capital borrowed. During the last 3 years or so he has borrowed chiefly from friends on the S. Ex. – £3,000 odd – including £250 from Rosen a money lender . . . CFM & I immediately cancel Pole's signature at the Bank much to the wonder of the clerks there – & we then go to see Pole in the office. His worst offence is that he has embezzled £700 of his Brothers. Naturally the interview is very painful & any decision is left in abeyance for the time being. Pole has deceived me & everyone. He is a base liar and dishonest & his presence is a grave danger to all of us. I go back to the House – where the news must leak out . . .

2 October. I see Pole & we have no further recriminations. Somehow I still like him . . . I leave the office feeling rather warm at 5.40 pm & walk down the Embankment as far as The Temple & take train Home [18 Stafford Terrace, Kensington] . . . Bath & dress. CFM & RCO turn up & we have a jolly dinner – the talk being normal talk till we reach the Drawing room – then we have a frank discussion. RCO less adamant than I thought. CFM & he both say we must exclude Pole from the Partnership – possibly taking him back in 3 months' time . . . I am kept awake till 2 am by motor car in mews . . .

7 October. CFM & I talk in office 12–12.30. He strongly of opinion Pole should retire from the Firm for a space of time & then perhaps return as $\frac{1}{2}$ book. I feel I am not strong enough to run a firm without Pole's assistance. CFM is honest but not clever. RCO is ambitious – & entirely out for himself. Personally I want to keep Pole.

8 October. CFM tells Pole very straightly that he must retire from the Firm. Unfortunately Pole seems entirely not to realise what he has done . . . I feel I cannot run the firm without Pole's strong influence. It is a crushing blow to me. I am no good on my own. In a word I do not think it expedient to let Pole go.

12 October. I am very worried all day & in no mood for business.

13 October. RCO walks with me at 5 pm to Tube & says 'If you keep Pole – you will lose me'. He is not a help to me. All out for himself.

14 October. I spend from 12 to 1 in the office with CFM. It now seems extremely doubtful if ever we can have Pole back. Certainly he must resign his partnership. There will be gossip & rumour on the S. Ex.

28 October. At 12 pm CFM & I go to office & find Pole awaiting us. He is busy tearing up papers of his in the filthy office drawers. At first he upbraids us – & claims as a right his share of the business to date – his £1,000 – but on CFM pointing out the absurdity of the line he is adopting, he takes up an altogether different attitude. It is all painful enough. He signs his resignation – and we part the best of friends. I say how happy we had been together & I think he sees the impossibility of his continuing as a Partner. He is to try & fix up with someone else & in a couple of months to return & try & make a living. He almost breaks down twice – & we agree to give him his share in full to date. I am greatly upset & so is CFM. The firm will now be Sambourne & Co & pray God we may succeed.

After this denouement Sambourne's anxiety levels gradually returned to normal, as did his self-fulfilling sense of being a pariah, for all his proud wearing of the Old Etonian tie. 'No one deals with me,' he noted mournfully on 1 December, the day of the signing of the Locarno Treaty and an accompanying strong market in Foreign Loans. 'A nice order in Austrians or Greeks would be Oh so welcome – & fill me with pride.'

Over the next decade he gradually came to terms with the fact that he would never be more than a peripheral figure in the Foreign market. And in his personal life, it became abundantly clear that he would never marry, as a series of apparently unconsummated affairs with younger women invariably tailed off because of his innate reluctance to pop the question. On that fateful weekend in September 1931 when Britain went off the gold standard he was in Paris, at the end of a holiday with a young professional dancer:

19 *September (Saturday)*. The news in the paper of ruination staring us all in the face is too much for me. I pull myself together . . . I settle up – & we have a final cocktail – & catch Golden Arrow. Good lunch – but I am intensely miserable.

20 *September*. Ghastly news in the papers – God help us all – I can only pray – God knows how I have hoped & trusted that there might be an end of it, acute worry for us all.

21 *September*. England off Gold Standard – what does all this mean? God help us.

Life, however, did go on; and by 1935, ten years after the drama with Pole, Sambourne was as weighed down by the fluctuations in Venezuela Oil Company shares, and by his partners, as ever:

7 *April*. Worries over the future of our firm. CFM has a down on Tom [Leveson-Gower, a young partner] – & he is not guarded in his speech. He lacks control – & he is liable to burst out at any moment. I suppose Breeding is wanting. I admit Tom is grasping & has his faults – but he is a great business getter.

11 *April*. VOC are a great worry . . . We have got far too many . . .

12 *April*. We do sell 170 VOC – but that is all.

13 April (Saturday). I am dreading our position in VOC & am so desperately afraid of bad oil news. I pray all may go well. If only some demand might spring up early next week. It looks steady now. I pray all may go well.

15 April. Thank God we sell 2,000 VOC @ 42/ – & have 3,000 left.

20 June. A very anxious & worrying day. We get VOC bumped into us & we cannot sell them. We have over 6,000 shares & they are only $2\frac{1}{4}$ & look like going lower. It is very worrying – but I pray things may take a turn for the better tomorrow . . .

19 August. Feel worried re City. Thank God I have something put by – liquid so to speak . . .

4 October. CFM gets very tiresome. He is obsessed with the idea of selling VOC – & doesn't try to get the utmost price. He is easily rattled – & we lose the opportunity of a real good day.

25 October. I get very red – I do not know why before the whole market over some silly bid being mistaken. It worries me.

18 November. All looks favourable & so it starts off. But alas heavy selling of Shell comes in the market. We get 3,000 VOC pf & 1,000 Burmah – none of which can we sell – & are in a parlous position when at 3.40 the Shell announcement is made of deferring decision as to Int Div. This is a heavy blow – & there is a slump all round. It is very sickening – and I pray God all may come right.

16 December. The City is awful. Prices fall & we do badly. The outlook is not good & I am rather nervous . . .

CHAPTER TWELVE

Team Spirit

'Dined as Duoro Hoare's guest with Merchant Adventurers,' the less than sybaritic Charles Addis noted in May 1920. 'It now lives apparently to guzzle. These 10 course dinners are an outrage.' In the late 1930s, while in London on behalf of Deutsche Bank, a future banking legend had no such qualms. 'I tried all the kitchens,' remembered Hermann Abs. 'The best roast beef was in Lloyd's, the best fish was with Olaf Hambro, the best coffee was with Schröder. The best general food, in accordance with the season, was Kleinwort. I knew the quality of all the luncheons in the City.' Presumably this culinary research included lunch at New Court, the most prized invitation of all. 'Into this lofty oak-panelled room, with its huge single window looking out on to the courtyard, and its long table which when fully extended would seat twenty people, have come the kings, princes and governors,' Palin would observe with pride. He added that, in those inter-war years, it was unknown for even the bank's General Manager to receive an invitation to lunch with the partners. One day, at the end of the morning, the firm's long-serving specialist in acceptance credits, Philip Hoyland, found himself in conference with Lionel de Rothschild and the solicitor Hugh Quennell, a partner of Slaughter and May. At 1.30 sharp, as Lionel rose from his desk, Hoyland waited for his marching orders. 'Come and have some lunch, Quennell,' Lionel announced, before turning to his faithful retainer. 'Hoyland, you'd better go and get your dinner.'[1]

*

The food, and the appropriateness of the table at which that food was eaten, mattered more than ideas. Lawrence Jones – at Helbert Wagg throughout the inter-war years, a director from 1923 and known to all as 'Jonah' – reckoned that 'during the whole of my career in the City I came across a mere handful of men who were in any sense students of monetary or economic problems' and that 'to the vast majority of those daily occupied with the manifold branches of financial business, theories and doctrines were of no concern'. Instead, 'what they did know was that they were in the City to make money'. Jones himself in his early years at Helbert Wagg kept up in his spare time 'a course of reading which might some day, I hoped, qualify me to talk on equal terms with the Robert Brands and the Oswald Falks'; but from the vantage-point of a desk in the partners' room he came to appreciate how rare figures like Brand or Falk were and the futility of his intellectual mugging-up:

> A stream of stockbrokers made regular morning calls upon our chairman, Alfred Wagg. They came, of course, in the hope of netting an order to buy or to sell, but they were always welcome, some for their cheerful and amusing company, and all for the information they could give about the movement of markets and prices. Of all these alert, friendly men I can call to mind only a few of whom it could be said that they were serious, thorough-going students of the intrinsic values of the securities they bought and sold for their clients. Nor were these few outstandingly prosperous. One of the most successful brokers, whose income in good times was said to touch six figures, was almost absurdly ignorant of the quality of his wares. I can remember an occasion when he had been pressing Alfred Wagg to buy a certain American share during the great boom in the late 1920s. When asked the nature of the business in which he was so anxious that we should become shareholders, he was almost indignant. 'I haven't the slightest idea,' he replied. But he kindly offered to ring up one of his clerks and find out. This man's prosperity was due, not to any professional knowledge, but to his wide social connections. He had a remarkable knack of getting rich people, with whom he dined or shot or spent his Saturdays to Mondays, to invest or to speculate through his firm. His fellow-brokers were not always kind about him.
>
> 'Good morning, X. How's the Duke?' inquired one of these, in ringing tones, on the floor of a crowded House.
>
> 'Er – which Duke do you mean?'
>
> 'Oh, any old Duke'.

It was not only stockbrokers, Jones recalled, that formed 'a constant stream through our partners' room or through our vaulted luncheon-room upstairs', but also jobbers, bill brokers, bankers, accountants and so on. 'Many were lively and amusing, some were dull; the majority were intelligent experts in their own line of business. But I cannot remember getting much enlightenment from any of them about the profounder movements of public affairs. It was rare, for instance, to hear the point of view of Labour. There was a very general confidence in the Conservative leadership, and a deep suspicion of all socialists . . .'

There was another important way in which the reality of the City confounded Jones's expectations. A lawyer and a soldier in previous incarnations, he had naturally imagined that the City, being inhabited by businessmen, would conduct itself along businesslike lines. Not so:

> Compared with the adjutant's Orderly Room in any cavalry regiment, or a barrister's chambers, or a man (not a woman) out shopping, the City is a place of hesitations and longwindedness. No doubt there are one-man businesses where decisions are made swiftly. But in houses where there are many partners, and at board meetings, the tempo is for the most part leisurely indeed. There is gossip and chaff and the latest good story before a conference or a board meeting gets under way: it is all friendliness and informality; the debate saunters off into by-ways; the real point is sometimes not reached until we are washing our hands for lunch. The comfort of our partners' rooms, the deep leather sofas, the open fires, the pictures on the walls, all encourage a rather cosy, lounging method of discussion. Accuracy, punctuality, and dispatch belonged to the counting-house downstairs, not to the partners' room. They were paid for, and amply supplied. For the execution of policy we depended, like Cabinet Ministers, upon a first-class Civil Service. Those rather dawdling methods, laced with fun, may be the reason that City men rarely have duodenal ulcers, unlike their American counterparts . . .

Altogether, despite sometimes being unable to get sufficiently worked up 'about the question of whose name should be printed first on a prospectus', Jones found the City of the 1920s and 1930s a congenial enough milieu: 'It was agreeable to work in an atmosphere where mutual liking played as large a part as the cash nexus. There was competition, but it was amicable, even generous.'[2]

Jones's memoirs, *Georgian Afternoon*, are essentially kindly; but those of two others who, like Jones, penetrated somewhere near the centre – though rarely to the very centre – of the City's inner core offer much harsher appraisals. Francis Williams was City editor of first the *Daily Express* and then the *Daily Herald*, and by the early 1930s had formed a clear view of the place: 'The City possessed a few people of great intelligence and ability and a small number of exceedingly stupid and unpleasant ones, but for the most part its higher echelons were composed of amiable and socially pleasant people who were living rather lush, comfortable lives not because they were possessed of ability beyond the ordinary, but because they came from the right sort of backgrounds, had been to the right sorts of schools, had the right sorts of connections and had inherited money from their fathers.' Nicholas Davenport, writing in the early 1970s, was still less complimentary. In 1930 it was with considerable gratitude that he accepted an invitation to replace his late friend Sidney Russell Cooke as a director of the National Mutual Life Assurance Society:

> The fact that my public school was Cheltenham and not Eton made a lot of difference to my prospects. To the Old Etonian, every financial door in the City was open. He had as a rule inherited great wealth and his mind was trained to think in terms of money and its management. He would not know how to make money out of manufacture or bourgeois retail trade. Eton would have destroyed that capacity although his father might have made his fortune out of such vulgar enterprise. The monied and Eton-educated son would turn his nose up at factories and shops and would drift naturally into the merchant banks, the discount houses, Lloyd's, the Stock Exchange and the investment trusts of the City . . .
>
> The City's Establishment at that time was, in effect, an old boys' racket. It was immensely respectable and enjoyable enough if you like to indulge at lunch in smoked salmon and white wine and trivial conversation. The millions spent each year on guzzling in the City board-rooms and guilds, and in the Lord Mayor's junketing, would amaze the under-privileged and enrage the poor. It was a sort of Mafia in reverse – a gang based on honest dealing instead of blackmail, on good 'hard' money (lots of it) instead of easy loot and on simplicity instead of cunning. The only rules were playing safe, resisting change, opposing new ideas, upholding the Establishment and being willing to dress up and go on the pompous dinner parade in the City halls . . .[3]

Davenport himself, it is worth adding, may have had left-wing leanings but was less a socialist than (like his hero Keynes) an intelligent capitalist. Allowing for a certain amount of rhetoric, there is little reason to doubt the essential truth of his analysis.

*

In May 1924 Brand was asked if he would like to become a director of the National Discount Co. The offer had an obvious appeal – the board, he was told, 'sits on Wednesdays at 12.15 at present, and half an hour is more than the usual period', with the recompense being 'fees about £500 free of income tax' – but in the event Brand, already heavily committed, turned it down. In modern values some £15,000, tax-free, for perhaps twenty hours' attendance a year . . . Not surprisingly, there were relatively few leading City figures who did not indulge in multiple directorships. 'The bankers of London,' Percy Arnold wrote in a pioneering, quasi-sociological analysis published in 1938, 'have a finger in many pies.'[4]

General Sir Herbert Lawrence – Chairman and Managing Director of the City's largest remaining private bank, Glyn Mills, during much of the inter-war period – was one such. Before the war he had, in his biographer's words, 'collected South African mining directorships'; from 1906 he was on the London committee of the Imperial Ottoman Bank, becoming its Chairman in 1925; from 1912 he was on the board of the Midland Railway; in 1921 a Vickers cash crisis saw him joining the board of that armaments concern, becoming Chairman for eleven years from 1926; and he was also in these years Chairman of the Anglo-Austrian Bank. 'He was an honourable, straightforward man whose word could be relied upon absolutely,' Peacock recalled a decade and a half after the General's death in 1943, adding that 'he was a man of good ability, but no genius'. Or take an associate of Lawrence's, the high-minded Guy Dawnay, who in 1928 formed the issuing house Dawnay Day. Over the years he was Chairman of Gordon Hotels (whose flagship from 1931 was the Dorchester Hotel in Park Lane), of the London board of Liverpool & London & Globe Insurance, of British Celanese, of Armstrong Whitworth, of the Army & Navy Stores and of Artillery Mansions Ltd. 'A fragile figure with something of exquisitely fashioned porcelain in the finely chiselled features of his small face' was how Compton Mackenzie described this champion of the boards.

There seem to have been few such flourishes about Colin Frederick Campbell, another with an exemplary City trajectory. Born in 1866 and educated at Eton, he started in the City with the family firm of East India merchants, Finlay, Campbell & Co. In 1903 the firm became Forbes, Forbes, Campbell & Co, and Campbell was to be its Chairman for many years. Other long-standing chairmanships during the first half of the century included London Assurance, the discount house Alexanders and the Telegraph Construction & Maintenance Co. Campbell was also an entrenched member of the board of the Chartered Bank of India, Australia & China. The focus of his banking career, however, was National Provincial, one of the 'Big Five' clearing banks after the war. Campbell was a director from 1903, became Deputy Chairman in 1929, and four years later succeeded Sir Harry Goschen as Chairman. His biographer makes no great claims for his abilities, but notes that at National Provincial 'his dignified and fair-minded presence appears to have engendered affection as well as respect'.[5]

This world of overlapping directorships and fingers in many pies was epitomised by the investment trusts, controlled during the inter-war years by a handful of groups or institutions, which both then and later received little scrutiny or publicity.[6] One was the '69 Old Broad Street

Group', its name slightly changing when it relocated to 117 Old Broad Street at the end of 1937. The group had begun in 1910 with six small investment trust companies initiated by Jack Austen in close liaison with Lord St Davids, the former John Wynford Philipps. The group specialised in investing in foreign railways, especially South American, and by 1936, having survived some difficult years, it controlled sixteen investment trust companies with a total capital of £21.1m. Solid City types manned these companies' boards, exemplified by the stock-broker Brigadier Keith Thorburn, a director of English & International Trust, formed in February 1929. 'He was a large man by anybody's standards,' the group's historian recalls, 'well over six feet tall, weighing in at 18 stone. He gave the appearance of being made of granite and about as malleable. His voice creaked from a great depth, but it could carry and was very deliberate.' The 'Robert Benson Group', run by Bensons, was rather smaller – seven trusts and £20.3m capital by 1936 – but more select in its composition of boards. The English & New York Trust, for example, which the young Rex Benson sought to revitalise from the late 1920s, included a representative from both Morgan Grenfell and Helbert Wagg, in the persons of 'Rufus' Smith (son of Vivian Hugh Smith) and 'Jonah' Jones. The trust's credibility was further enhanced by the inclusion on the board of Philip Fleming and Archie Jamieson, both of whom were partners of Robert Fleming & Co, which remained in the inter-war period *the* investment-trust house in the City. It was estimated in the early 1930s that some fifty-six investment trusts came under the sway, directly or indirectly, of Flemings; and it was commonly said that Flemings was one of two institutions that merchant banks or stockbrokers would invariably consult before deciding on the terms of a new issue (the other being the Prudential).[7]

But of course it was the merchant banks themselves – those family-run fiefdoms – that were increasingly coming to represent the very quintes-sence of the 'old' City. Hambros is an illuminating example. In 1921 it had the sense to merge with the Scandinavian-owned British Bank of Northern Commerce, as a result of which C.J. Hambro & Son was reconstituted as Hambros Bank Ltd, and over the next two decades it was a largely vigorous presence, especially on the accepting side in the 1930s. Nevertheless, a closed shop still applied, quite as much as it had done in the days of Carl Joachim or Everard (who finally died in 1925, still active and a director of the Bank of England). Norman, writing to Ben Strong in November 1927, enclosed a letter of introduction to Olaf Hambro (son of Everard) and John Hugh Smith, who were about to cross the Atlantic:

The former is now the guiding spirit; shrewd, industrious and gradually becoming entirely orthodox. (This, I think, for the same reason that your friend in the story recommended honesty as the best policy!) . . . You will notice that the law of Mendel has operated almost cruelly in the case of Olaf Hambro who alone among his family shows unmistakeable signs of an origin which had really been forgotten!! . . . John Hugh Smith has been only a short time with Hambros. An old friend of mine who, if you will give him a chance, can recount to you with great intelligence most of the best gossip in London: in other words, he is intelligent and well-informed.

To be a Hambro was to be a serial director. The 1931 edition of the *Directory of Directors* recorded that Sir Charles Hambro, Charles J. Hambro, Henry Charles Hambro and Ronald Olaf Hambro – all four of whom occupied prominent positions in the bank – between them sat on the boards of thirty-three other concerns, including the Bank of England, Royal Exchange Assurance, the Mercantile Bank of India, Westminster Bank and London Assurance. Nor was John Hugh Smith a slouch, notching up eleven outside directorships of his own. At 41 Bishopsgate itself, Olaf was Chairman from 1932. 'A tall, large man, dark-haired with a black moustache,' according to the bank's historians, 'even in middle age he had a stern, imposing and often forbidding countenance, a gruff voice and an autocratic manner.' And:

> He was a stickler for punctuality. From the depths of the chairman's office, at the north-east end of the 'partners' room' on the first floor, at 1.15 pm each day he would command his colleagues 'Time for lunch', and with one accord the four or five other directors present would leave their desks, gather in the board room for a glass of sherry, and at 1.30 pm precisely proceed to the dining-room, where the butler would be waiting . . .
>
> Olaf's pipe was his most trusted and devoted companion. Its permanent position – clenched firmly between his teeth – accounted for the inaudible mutterings which managed to escape the restricted exit. He always smoked a special blend from Robert Lewis' in St James's, and Olaf's characteristic half-pound tins of tobacco were left strategically in all the first-floor rooms of 41 Bishopsgate . . .[8]

There may have been cleverer Hambros at the bank, including his nephew Charles, but unarguably it was Olaf who personified the rock-solid image of Hambros in the eyes of almost all the rest of the City.

If anything, Morgan Grenfell was even more Establishment, arguably rivalling Barings. Teddy Grenfell (gradually winding down his day-to-day involvement) became the first Lord St Just of St Just-in-Penwith in

1935, while Vivian Hugh Smith became the first Lord Bicester of Tusmoor three years later. A family biographer would recall the latter's 'steady mind and sound judgement allied with a spirit of prudent enterprise', all of which acted in tandem with 'a charming and dignified presence', while his obituary in *The Times* in 1956 would describe Smith in glowing terms as 'a notable representative of the City':

> He had in full measure the best and most typical of its talents and abilities. Anybody thinking of Lord Bicester would think first of the reasonable and fair-minded attitude with which he approached every problem, his anxiety that in any transaction all concerned should not only get, but should feel that they were getting, a fair deal. This more than anything was the clue to his fame and success as a negotiator . . . Lord Bicester had the advantage of a charming and dignified presence and a natural gift for friendship; perhaps one of his most noticeable and valuable personal traits was the calm, reassuring, and unruffled manner which was the outward sign of an inner steadiness of mind and judgement. Indeed, in his work, his character, and his person alike, he was the very embodiment of the City at its best . . .

A flavour of this four-squareness comes through in a 1925 letter to George Whitney of Morgans in New York. Replying to a request for information about Rio Tinto, Smith told him that it was 'controlled by the Paris Rothschilds, but as it is an English Company the London Rothschilds, even though they have a very small, if any, interest in the Rio Tinto, control it on behalf of their French cousins'. Accordingly:

> If you are considering trying to obtain control of the Rio Tinto I think we should have to go to the Rothschilds and tell them quite frankly what we are proposing to do . . . It would never do for us here to try and take away the control of the Rio Tinto from the Rothschilds owing to our extremely friendly relations, but it is quite possible they might be willing to part with the control, if they still hold it.

Smith was also for many years Chairman of George Yule & Co (later Yule, Catto & Co) and Governor of the Royal Exchange Assurance, but Morgan Grenfell was always his main concern.[9] There, four new partners or Managing Directors were appointed in the 1930s: 'Rufus' Smith, Vivian's eldest son, inevitably Eton-educated and not particularly brilliant; Francis Rodd, Vivian's son-in-law, son of the diplomat Sir Rennell Rodd, and pigeon-holed by his sister-in-law Nancy Mitford as not only a 'bore' but also a 'cold fish'; Willie Hill-Wood, who had once won infamy through an appallingly slow, ugly batting display in a

Varsity match, but who had excellent connections, considerable charm of manner and was a close friend of Jack Morgan; and J.S. Morgan's great-grandson, the 2nd Viscount ('Bill') Harcourt, like the other three an O.E.[10] It was hardly a dynamic quartet, hungry for business, and Morgan Grenfell was about to move into a long period of conservatism, complacency and what its historian describes as 'gentle relative decline'.[11] Not that this, for a quarter of a century, adversely affected its reputation in the City.

Vivian Hugh Smith of Morgan Grenfell, John Hugh Smith of Hambros and Lancie Hugh Smith of Rowe & Pitman were all 'Financial Smiths', direct descendants of the seventeenth-century Nottingham banker Thomas Smith and members of the City's most ubiquitous family. An equally typical member, from another branch, was Colonel Bertram Abel Smith, who in the early 1930s, in addition to being a director of M. Samuel & Co and National Provincial Bank, was on the board of Shell, Atlas Assurance and various investment trusts. Or take the four Whigham brothers at this time: Walter, of Robert Fleming, was also involved with about a dozen other concerns, including holding a Bank of England directorship; Gilbert was a director of seventeen oil companies, including Burmah Oil and British Petroleum; Charles was a partner of Morgan Grenfell and on the London committee of the Hongkong and Shanghai Bank; and George was Chairman of British Celanese.[12] The Martin family similarly had tentacles that stretched: Robert Holland-Martin was Chairman of the London board of Martins Bank from 1923 to 1944, Honorary Secretary of the Bankers' Clearing House from 1905 to 1935, and President of the Institute of Bankers from 1929 to 1931, as well as being on the boards of Union Discount and the Corporation of Foreign Bondholders, and Chairman of the Southern Railway from 1935; Granville Bromley-Martin, his brother-in-law, was a fellow-director of Martins; and Edward (Ruby) Holland-Martin, one of Robert's six sons, was an executive director of the Bank of England from 1933.[13]

Many sons were happy enough to take their due place among the City élite, their lives virtually pre-ordained at birth. Ernest and Cyril Kleinwort, the sons of Alexander, were two such who, following careful if rather oppressive training, became competent merchant bankers. 'Never become emotionally involved in any business problem,' Alexander taught his boys, having had that dictum drummed into him by his own father; and on Alexander's death in 1935, Norman was able to receive reassurance from Herman Andreae of Kleinworts: 'Ernest & Cyril K are sound & safe & reliable. Most of Sir Alex[a] fortune is already

331

theirs . . . His death in no way affects standing of Firm.' For some sons, ultimately compliant, it was more of a wrench. Henry Vigne, born in 1898, joined the family firm of stockbrokers after serving in the First World War and having a spell planting rubber in Malaya. 'I wanted to see other countries,' he would look back rather wistfully near the end of his life. 'I was determined not to go into business in the City of London if I could possibly avoid it. My father wanted me to and I knew if I stayed in England that I should have to go there. And I did have to go there in the end but I'd had my little fling abroad by then.'[14]

Sometimes the pressure came from the father-in-law. Percy G. Mackinnon was Chairman of Lloyd's during the 1920s, and he managed to push his son-in-law from becoming a fairly unsuccessful architect into a fairly successful underwriter. Nevertheless, in the view of that underwriter's son (the journalist John Gale), 'there was something caustic and exasperated about him, as though he knew his life had taken the wrong turning'. It was not a turning that the young Victor Rothschild, on coming down from Cambridge, was prepared to take:

> It came as rather a shock at the age of twenty-one to learn that I was expected at least to try the life of a banker in the City of London. This I did, but the moment was unfortunate. In 1931 there was a world recession; the City seemed moribund, boring, rather painful. I did not like banking which consists essentially of facilitating the movement of money from Point A, where it is, to Point B, where it is needed . . .

So a man of much brilliance, the future third Lord Rothschild, was lost to New Court. Three moribund decades would ensue, as control continued to be vested entirely in the hands of other Rothschilds willing to put in the hardly strenuous hours.[15]

Almost as strong as the City's instinctive attachment to keeping things in the family was its urge to recruit Old Etonians. Schröders, for example, brought in a trio in the mid-1920s, each in his early twenties and none having a family connection with the bank. As the Master of Wellington College would ruefully note in January 1940, comparing his school's recent progress to that of Eton, one parent who had a boy down for both schools 'went so far as to tell me the O.E. tie was worth £200 a year in the City' – probably an under-estimate.[16] There are many to choose from, but Rex Benson, Oliver Lyttelton, Andrew Carnwath and Michael Verey were, taken as whole, a fairly typical quartet of Old Etonians, who in the inter-war period were starting to make an impact in the City.

Benson (born 1889) was the middle son of Robert Benson, had a distinguished war and stayed in the Army before becoming a partner of Bensons in 1924. He had an engaging, energetic personality, once privately conceded that he was 'a little frightened of myself as I get led away with enthusiasm', and did much to revitalise Bensons during the 1930s. Although not remotely an intellectual, unlike his father, he was capable of independent thought and was particularly good at identifying and attracting men of talent to work around him.[17] Lyttelton (born 1893) was the only son of Alfred Lyttelton, a lawyer and outstanding cricketer who also became a government minister. After the war, he wondered what to make of his life: 'I thought of my first cousin, Melville Balfour, a rich and successful stockbroker [with James Capel], fond of hunting and racing ... I said I fancied becoming a banker in the international field, and he smiled at this naïveté. He did more, however; through Sir James Leigh Wood he got me a place as a learner in Brown Shipley & Co.' Over the next year or so Lyttelton began to understand something of the wrinkles of banking and foreign exchange, before in August 1920 he was put forward by the partners for a vacancy at the recently established British Metal Corporation, run by Sir Cecil Budd and based in Abchurch Yard. From 1922 until the war Lyttelton was its General Manager, seeking with some success to make the British Empire self-supporting in non-ferrous metals. Ultimately his interests would move beyond the City – into politics and industry – but his City years, combining merit and connection in about equal proportions, provided the base.[18]

Carnwath (born 1909) could not have had a simpler route to the square mile. The son of a doctor, and a King's Scholar at Eton, he did not work hard enough to win a university scholarship. Eton, however, recommended him to Barings. 'I had never heard of Barings,' he would drily reminisce, 'but inquiries showed that I would probably be wise to explore the matter further.' He arrived at 8 Bishopsgate in December 1928, just in time to savour the back view of Revelstoke, who was descending the steps on his way to the fateful German reparations conference in Paris. A distinguished career lay ahead, especially in corporate finance, where in his obituary's words 'he remained a calm and relatively detached practitioner' and 'won and retained the confidence of corporate clients to a remarkable degree'.[19] Verey (born 1912) would be a rather more flamboyant merchant banker. Born into a family that invariably sent its sons to Eton, he came down from Cambridge in 1934 and began to look about:

I was anxious to go somewhere where, if I worked hard and it was a good firm, I would make some money. I was pretty sure that meant something in the City. I talked to my father [a solicitor] and he said, 'I will speak to my friend, Alfred Wagg'. He and Alfred had been friends since they were little boys at the same private school together and were very close friends at Eton and Cambridge and thereafter. There was a, for me, ghastly, agonising dinner party which was held in Alfred's very grand flat in Berkeley Square with a butler and footman (not things we had), which my father and mother and I went to. My father and I wore dinner jackets and I said to my father, 'I'll just stay doggo so that he can't take against me. You do the talking.' So my father was frightfully good and swept Alfred along . . .[20]

If the City had been opened up to competitive examination, as for example the Civil Service had been in the nineteenth century, which of these four would have won through? Each would prove himself to be able rather than otherwise; yet each had such a flying start, in comparison with the great majority of the City's actual and would-be intake – mainly, but not entirely, operating at a humbler level – that it is impossible to gauge accurately the extent of that ability.

Sometimes even an Etonian background did not guarantee that the face would fit. Arthur Grenfell, after coming resoundingly unstuck in 1914 for the second time in his career, was never quite able to reclaim his position. 'There are men who consider him a danger to the City,' his most powerful supporter, Lord Grey, conceded during the war, 'and think that he ought to be prevented at any cost from ever regaining his footing there.' Whigham of Morgan Grenfell, writing to a New York correspondent in 1928, confirmed the accuracy of that statement: 'Since the war Arthur Grenfell has been in various activities and I think quite probably has made a good deal of money as there is no question about his abilities. At the same time his record is such that we could not recommend any of your friends putting their affairs in his hands.' Such an attitude, of which he was well aware, did not break Grenfell's seemingly indomitable spirit, but made it much harder for him in his various new initiatives (many involving transport in Eastern Europe) to adopt the high profile, in terms of the investing public, that his natural talents and ebullience warranted.[21] George Wansbrough was a rather different sort of semi-outcast. After Cambridge, he had been deterred from going to Barings by Sir Edward Reid ('You must realise that not being a relative of the family, you cannot look forward to a partnership') and instead had gone in 1927 to the apparently more welcoming Bensons. His sympathies were left-wing, and in 1931 he was described by Hugh Dalton as 'an Etonian Bolshevik who stroked the Cambridge boat, went on the stage, married a Roman Catholic Jewess' and who 'thinks we ought to nationalise the Stock Exchange'. Four years later, in October 1935, a Bank of England memo recorded this rebel's fate:

> When Mr Wansbrough was nominated as a Socialist candidate for the next election the question was raised whether he could continue as a Director of R.H. Benson & Co, but it was decided to allow him to carry on for the time being. Earlier this summer he had certain domestic troubles and, as a result of these also of Mr Wansbrough's political ambitions, Benson & Co decided that it would be better to part company. They have parted on good terms and have allowed Mr Wansbrough to remain on his various outside Boards in which he continues to represent Bensons. These directorships bring him in about £1,200 a year. He has set up an office in the City entirely of his own responsibility and rather discouraged by Bensons . . .[22]

Such an outcome was perhaps hardly surprising, for ultimately what really counted in the day-to-day conduct of City business was trust and reputation – qualities that both, in large measure, derived from mutually shared values as well as background. The French writer Paul Morand, on the basis of a visit to London in 1933, tellingly described the money market in action:

> The first prices [on the Stock Exchange] quoted, gentlemen are seen leaving on foot going into the different banks, being received at once, advising clients, and returning to their own; they are negotiating money discounts. These journeyings are typical of London. They are the proper thing, because to use the telephone would be to appear badly brought up. After two o'clock in the afternoon it is difficult to find day money, but until then nothing is easier. Money abounds in London. It is a real country market in which the eggs and chickens are millions. You can get a million pounds in a moment, without any contract or immediate proof. But to do that you must be well known, well dressed, and well educated – at Eton, Harrow, Winchester or Rugby. Here the public school spirit comes in again. The money which these gentlemen go on foot to find, sometimes chewing a Canadian apple, does not circulate materially: it is merely a matter of accepted credits, merely the matter of a signature; but one only gives it to someone who is well shaved, with agreeable manners, who is quick on the ball or rides hard to hounds, whom one calls by his Christian name and with whom one has played cricket for fifteen years . . .
> 'Manners' have an importance in the City, undreamed of by the foreigner.
> 'And if a young man has bad manners?'

335

'Well, then he never gets a good rate of discount, and it is all up with him . . .'[23]

*

Was the inter-war City a more 'closed' world than it had been prior to 1914? There are some obvious grounds for believing that it probably was. In November 1930, some six months after it had become clear that the Stock Exchange remained generally unwilling to re-admit ex-members of German origin, and would continue to uphold its 1918 rule that anyone born in Germany, Austria, Hungary, Bulgaria or Turkey was ineligible for membership, the Chairman of the Baltic Exchange, John Parry, decided – probably somewhat nervously – to test the waters in his market. In a letter to members, he argued that the existing policy, which was similar to that of the Stock Exchange, 'is prejudicial to the interests of the Members inasmuch as it limits scope and volume of business that can be transacted on the Exchange'; he suggested that, twelve years after the end of the war, the time had come to open up membership to nationals of all countries, reflecting the fact of 'the business of the Exchange being international in character'. Ahead of an extraordinary general meeting called for 12 December, there ensued the predictable storm of protest, including an anonymous letter to the *Daily Telegraph*:

> The proposal amounts to nothing less than selling the birthright of the younger generation – the clerks who are budding principals and senior members of the room. Many of our clerks, as it is, are looking for work, and an influx of foreigners would make things much worse . . .
> If the measure is carried there is nothing to prevent the Soviet Government from being represented on the Baltic Exchange.

Accordingly, the meeting was first postponed, then adjourned and finally abandoned. The following year a watered-down reform was introduced, with naturalised British subjects being permitted to become clerks, but this hardly made it a market open to all talents. Nor, also in the City's 'East End', were things any more liberal in the sugar market, where the wartime exclusion of Germans, once such a powerful presence, was strictly adhered to in peacetime. 'At last it was brought home to the Mincing Lane fraternity,' the sugar broker Gordon Hodge would note with some satisfaction in his memoirs, 'that a foreigner really had no standing in this country.'[24]

Many of these excluded foreigners were, of course, Jews. That did not stop fevered fantasies (though mainly outside the City) about the Jewish conspiracy in international finance, fantasies that the leading financial journalist Paul Einzig implicitly addressed in an authoritative overview in the *Banker* in 1933:

> Those who talk about the predominant Jewish influence in British banking ought to be reminded that there is not a single Jew among the directors of the Bank of England, and hardly any among the directors of the 'Big Five'. Even among the banking firms the Jewish element does not by any means predominate. In fact, Jewish banking houses of international standing could be enumerated on the fingers of one hand; they are N.M. Rothschild & Sons, Samuel Montagu & Co, M. Samuel & Co, Seligman Brothers, and S. Japhet & Co. Most other leading banking houses are essentially non-Jewish. In the various sections of the London financial market, it is only the bullion market in which Jews predominate. Their relative influence in the foreign exchange market has declined to a fraction of what it used to be, as a result of the extension of foreign business by the joint stock banks. Though there are many prominent Jewish Stock Exchange firms, in the aggregate, they form a small minority. As for the money market, it is essentially non-Jewish.[25]

Would there have been greater Jewish representation – for example, on the Court of the Bank of England or on the boards of the major clearing banks – if there had not been widespread anti-Semitic prejudice in the City? Presumably there would, for undeniably there was such prejudice.

'They are very well known here, Jews but quite nice people to do business with,' was how Vivian Hugh Smith described M. Samuel & Co in 1925 to Morgans in Paris; while over the years it was plausibly believed at Sebags that the reason that stockbroking firm never got any business from Morgan Grenfell was because of an unwillingness to deal through Jews. The Pope of the City shared the prejudice. 'I refuse to see Baldry – who is a Broker & Jew,' Norman recorded in his diary in 1932; and although, inevitably, he accepted that there were some Jews in the City who were too important to be shunned, he rarely if ever seems to have established warm relations with them. Lionel de Rothschild, for instance, was always addressed by him in correspondence as 'Dear Mr de Rothschild', unlike the pet names Norman accorded to many other leading figures. Lawrence Jones, a humane as well as perceptive observer of those around him, saw the City's anti-Semitism as 'endemic' but 'mild':

> There were no fears of conspiracy: there were no accusations of corruption. There was an Anglo-Saxon suspicion of cleverness, a school-boyish contempt for people who cared little for fresh air and field-sports,

and a Philistine mistrust of taking the arts seriously enough to spend money upon them. But above all I believe most Anglo-Saxons are subconsciously shocked by the Jew's devastating commonsense and objectivity. We Britons like to wrap up both our aims and our means of achieving them in a comfortable vagueness. We hope to attain something, somehow. The Jew knows precisely what he wants, and exactly how to get it. And when he comes out with it, sharply, we are apt to shudder, as if the bedclothes had been whipped off as we lie in bed . . .[26]

The metaphor is apt, for over the centuries a series of remarkable Jews have come to the City, found it slumbering, given it a rude awakening, ignored the often emotive protests and bequeathed a wholly beneficial legacy.

Some firms, of whatever ethnic origin, were more open than others to the advance of merit. At Rothschilds there was no chance of a partnership unless one was born a Rothschild; at Cazenove's it was still unknown to come in at the bottom and rise to the partners' room; while at James Capel, out of the inter-war intake of ten partners, only one, the dealer George Rushton, was essentially self-made, and he had to content himself with becoming a salaried partner, unlike such full partners as Pleydell Keppel Stephenson, the Hon D.G. Fortescue and George Sholto-Douglas Pape. Elsewhere, however, there were signs of a less restrictive approach. At Glyns, under General Lawrence, the partnership began to be less dominated by the Glyn, Mills and Currie families; at Wallace Brothers, whereas during the sixty-three years from its establishment as East India merchants in 1862 only three out of fifteen partners and directors had not had a family connection, from the mid-1920s the pattern changed completely, so that over the next forty years only two out of eleven directors *did* have such a connection; and at Samuel Montagu, what that firm's historian describes as 'a narrow, conservative family business' was transformed in the 1930s by two key appointments to the partnership – one definitely a City insider, David Keswick, the other an outsider, a gifted Belgian called Louis Franck.[27]

Clearly there is a balance to be struck in the historical judgement, a balance perhaps embodied in the four-man partnership of the very successful finance house Cull & Co. Gilbert Russell was a cousin of the Duke of Bedford; Hugh Micklem (a brother of Charles Micklem of Cazenove's) and Eric Cull were former oil jobbers; and fourthly, offering the financial creativity, there was Hermann Marx, described in 1929 by one Morgan Grenfell partner as 'a Jew' with 'a reputation of being a pretty shrewd man'.[28]

That same year, after Revelstoke died in Paris, the new Lord

Revelstoke sought to reassure King George V. 'You will see,' Cecil Baring wrote to the private secretary Lord Stamfordham, 'that the concern remains, as a whole, a family affair, although it has always been laid down here, and we of the family constantly recognise, that there can be no place for one of our members unless he shews the requisite character and brains.' The last three words begged a fundamental question, but certainly no one was keener than Peacock to ensure that blood alone no longer provided an automatic entrée. In July 1937, a Barings memo recorded, he received a visit from 'Lady Lovat with her younger son, the Hon Hugh Fraser, with reference to an understanding she had had with the late Lord Revelstoke (Cecil) that Mr Fraser should come to No. 8 for a period as soon as he had finished his education'. Fraser was at Oxford, with two years still to go there. However, 'it was made quite clear [i.e. by Peacock] to Lady Lovat that anyone coming here came on six months' probation, and that the extension of such a period, in the case of people like her son, depended entirely on whether we considered them sufficiently promising to go through all the departments of the Office or not'. Moreover, 'Sir Edward made it clear that, unless a man could produce something quite out of the way in qualifications, he could not expect to spend his life at No. 8'.[29] This was, of course, only an ideal, but it was significant that it was articulated.

Peacock himself was a Canadian, one of many foreigners – though not as many as before 1914 – for whom the City still provided a profitable if not always entirely welcoming home. Already the power behind the throne in the 1920s, he in effect led the bank after Revelstoke's death, being particularly prominent in the areas of international finance and corporate finance. Cecil Baring may have privately called him 'The Paycock', but neither he nor the other active members of the family imagined they could do without him.[30] Another flourishing North American was the mining financier and entrepreneur Chester Beatty, whose London-based Selection Trust had been formed in 1914 in order to finance and develop new mining ventures, a task in which it was especially successful between the wars in relation to the copper belt of Northern Rhodesia. One of the more attractive figures in the mining world, Beatty does not seem to have pushed himself unduly hard, certainly by the time that Selection Trust moved in 1926 to new offices in Mason's Avenue, linking Coleman Street and Basinghall Street. Having taken the tube from Kensington, he would arrive shortly before noon and spend most of the next few hours either on the telephone or inspecting progress reports by his men in the field. If he lunched on his own, he was usually happy enough with beef hash and a bottle of beer.

He would leave at four o'clock, according to his biographer, 'buying his evening paper with a cheery word with the Cockney news-vendor outside Doctor Butler's Head before a chauffeur picked him up at the end of the Avenue'. Moreover, perhaps imitating the example of Lord Faringdon and South American railways, he never went to the copper belt in Central Africa, partly on the grounds of health worries, partly because he believed that his time was better deployed in London, with regular visits to New York.[31]

Of course, most of the City's immigrants still came from the Continent, and here the story of that dynamic outfit Singer & Friedlander was particularly instructive. Before the war it had been a stockbroking firm, with origins that were manifestly not Anglo-Saxon, and as a result of the Stock Exchange's policy during the war it turned itself into a banking business, with arbitrage, foreign stocks and bonds, and bill discounting as its main specialities. New partners from 1920 were Julius Stern, formerly with Japhets, and Max Ullmann, who would subsequently found his own merchant bank; while by the mid-1920s the driving force was increasingly the very young, very talented arbitrageur Marcel Pougatch, of Russian birth but educated in Paris. There were also the Hock brothers. The founder at the turn of the century of a Vienna banking house, Richard Hock in 1923 decided to take an interest in Singer & Friedlander and accordingly sent his son Francis to join it. Five years later Francis became a partner, and in 1932 he was joined as a partner by his elder brother, Dr Hans Hock, who had already been a partner in the family bank in Vienna, had trained as an economist as well as a banker and specialised in foreign bonds. A rapidly growing concern (incorporated in 1933, with a paid-up capital of £200,000), Singer & Friedlander would for a long time be positioned at some considerable distance from the City Establishment – reflected in the joke that, in a cricket team of merchant banks, Singers would keep wicket because 'it never misses anything'. In that same team, it was always assumed, Barings would bowl uphill into the wind, loyal and uncomplaining.[32]

Siegmund Warburg was presumably the all-rounder, as cultured as he was dedicated, as intellectual as he was ruthless.[33] The bare facts of his early life are that he was born in 1902; after university, took his place in M.M. Warburg & Co, the family bank that was based in Hamburg; spent time as a trainee in Boston and New York, as well as in London, where he was with Rothschilds; in 1930 became the bank's resident partner in Berlin; and, as a Jew, left Germany not long after Hitler came to power, taking up permanent residence in England in 1934. That October he was closely involved in the formation (or re-launching) of the

New Trading Company, operating out of three small offices in King William Street. There are various, somewhat conflicting accounts of how this came about, but according to Denzil Sebag-Montefiore, a reasonably inside source, Warburg on his arrival in England 'was befriended by the Rothschilds', who already owned the New Trading Co as a subsidiary that they 'used for transactions they did not wish to be directly associated with, usually because the transactions were too small for them'; accordingly, as an act of friendship, the Rothschilds 'sold him or, perhaps, gave him' the company. The problem with this version of events, and others in biographies of Warburg, is an entry in Norman's diary for 15 October: 'Sir A. Stern. "The New Trading Co" for Barter, anywhere except Germany. Majority held by Paris & Ldn Sterns in Engl & French Cos. Minority held by Dutch Cos of German connections. I say there is no objection.' Norman's visitor was 'Bertie' Stern, an old friend of Roy Sambourne, and by now helping to preside over the long, inexorable decline of Stern Bros, which in the middle of the nineteenth century had been one of the great Jewish merchant banks. This brief interview with Norman – in effect, enabling the Governor to give his blessing to the venture – may well have been Stern's single largest contribution to the City.[34]

What we indubitably know is that NTC's Chairman from October 1934 was Sir Andrew McFadyean, who had had a distinguished career at the Treasury, and that the joint Managing Directors were Siegmund Warburg and Harry Lucas. The latter, several years younger than Warburg, had made rapid progress after university to become Assistant Manager of National Discount, until tuberculosis enforced his departure and a year of convalescence in Switzerland. Almost certainly he was a match for Warburg, a tribute by the *FT* after his death reckoning that 'few men had a more acute analytical mind, which grasped fundamentals so rapidly and seized upon the most important points so eagerly'. Over the next few years NTC became an established rather than a major force, as Warburg took his measure of the City and spent much of his time enabling Jewish families to get themselves and their money out of Germany. Indeed, he took directly under his wing in King William Street three immigrants – one Austrian, Eric Korner, and two Germans, Ernest Thalmann and Henry Grunveld. In the long run the most important of the trio was Grunfeld (as he would soon become), who after a gruesome encounter with the Gestapo in 1934 had already established himself in the City before being recruited by Warburg in 1937 and becoming his utterly trusted right-hand man. Two things struck Grunfeld most forcibly, he would reflect half a century later, about the City of the

1930s: on the one hand, its prevailing ethos of trust, the reality of the word being the bond, a reality that enormously facilitated the execution of business and thereby enhanced its volume; on the other hand, a hostility – especially on the part of the traditional merchant banks – to innovation or any new ideas, a hostility that Grunfeld could only attribute to a deeply entrenched complacency, even arrogance.[35] It was a duality that, more for good than ill, he and Warburg would do much to destroy.

One did not have to be German to come to the City as an outsider and, although flourishing there, enjoy (so to speak) a decidedly ambivalent relationship with the City's inner circle. Take the careers of William Piercy, Harley Drayton and Brendan Bracken, each of whom was making a considerable mark by the 1930s. Piercy (born 1886) was brought up in London, the son of an engineer who lost his life in a works accident when Piercy was still a child. Accordingly, he left school at eleven in order to support his family, taking a series of jobs before in 1906 going to the timber brokers Foy, Morgan & Co. In 1910 he started studying part-time at the LSE and by the outbreak of war had begun an academic career teaching history and public administration. During the war he was mainly at the Ministry of Munitions, while afterwards he decided that he could not afford to be an academic and became general trading manager of Harrisons & Crosfield. Then from 1925 to 1933 he was joint Managing Director of the timber brokers Pharaoh Gane & Co, at which point disagreements between the directors persuaded him to leave and join the Stock Exchange. There he became a seriously rich stockbroker, first with Capel-Cure & Terry, then with Fenn & Crosthwaite, being much involved in the development of unit trusts. By this time he was a hugely experienced businessman, as well as very active in the Political Economy Club, and with Liberal beliefs that may have been starting to move leftwards, notwithstanding the fact that he sent his son to Eton. 'Without doubt he was capable of being devious,' was the considered view of John Kinross, who would come to know him extremely well; and although Piercy, as early as 1925, had had his name put down for the City Club by none other than Vivian Hugh Smith, the 'old' City never quite trusted this clever, wholly self-made man.[36]

Drayton (born 1901) was the son of a gardener with the London County Council, but was mainly brought up in the Croydon home of a Scottish sanitary inspector. In 1915, barely educated, he got a job as an office boy in Dashwood House at 69 Old Broad Street, home of the investment trusts ultimately controlled by Lord St Davids. At this stage, and for some time thereafter, he was still known as Harold Drayton –

'Harley' came later. By the 1930s it was apparent that he possessed not only an omnivorous appetite for acquiring financial information and an elephantine ability at retaining it, but also a sound strategic grasp of investment allied to a certain flair for taking risks and eschewing the obvious. During that decade he managed to nurse to gradual recovery most of the group's trust companies, following the disastrous slump, and shortly before the war he became Managing Director of the '117 Old Broad Street Group', as it was now called. Drayton was very much the protégé of Jack Austen, right-hand man of St Davids until the latter's death in 1938, and he had managed to see off the challenge of another coming man, Percy Moody, secretary in the 1930s of the group's largest investment trust, Premier. The group's historian explains succinctly where Moody went wrong: 'He, too, was well liked by J.S. Austen, but it appeared that his enthusiasm for the Territorial Army was rather excessive. The result was that he was frequently away on military matters when he might otherwise have been discussing group tactics over the weekend at Plumpton Hall. Harold Drayton did not make that mistake . . .' Plumpton Hall was Austen's country house in Suffolk, which Drayton would subsequently inherit. A resplendent future beckoned for the City's licensed buccaneer – liked, admired, more or less trusted, but never completely integrated into the inner circle – who also doubled as a country gentleman.[37]

The third outsider, undeniably on the make, was Bracken (also born in 1901). After an eclectic start to life – childhood in Ireland as the son of a well-to-do Tipperary builder, adolescence in Australia, a term as a pupil at Sedbergh at the age of nineteen and a half – he managed by his late twenties to become, as chief executive on behalf of Eyre & Spottiswoode, a leading newspaper proprietor. His group mainly comprised the *Banker* (which he founded in 1926), the *Financial News* (the *FT*'s main rival), the *Investors' Chronicle* and a half-interest in the *Economist*. At this stage, despite having accumulated a mass of information about many diverse subjects, he knew little about finance itself, but had identified it as his platform to social and political influence. A tall, striking figure, with his rather simian features and a shock of flaming-red hair, he was someone who 'beneath his confident and reckless manner', in the perceptive assessment of his biographer Charles Lysaght, 'concealed a sensitive and vulnerable inner self'. He may have been the original for Evelyn Waugh's Rex Mottram in *Brideshead Revisited*, but the future Minister of Information was always more interesting than that.[38]

At the *Financial News* itself, based from 1929 at 20 Bishopsgate, the

assistant editor Collin Brooks kept a diary in which his early view of
Bracken as 'a likeable, erratic fellow' soured by the early 1930s under the
pressure of the slump, which badly affected financial advertising. 'The
office is still astir with the impending dissolution of the paper and
Bracken's rat-like rushings from one expedient to another,' Brooks
recorded in February 1932, adding that according to the editor, Oscar
Hobson, 'he has quite lost his nerve'. Nevertheless, Bracken had a
courageous streak to him. On one occasion Lloyds Bank demanded that
the paper's 'Lombard Street' columnist, Einzig, be dismissed, on the
grounds of his persistent criticism of it, but Bracken flatly refused, in
spite of the paper's heavy reliance on Lloyds for a long-running
overdraft. Moreover, under his leadership the *FN* of the 1930s was a
lively, even sometimes iconoclastic paper, attracting many young and
talented journalists; but unfortunately – and predictably – its circulation
lagged badly behind that of the intensely respectable, intensely dull *FT*,
sometimes known as 'the stockbrokers' Bible'. In 1937 the *FT*'s
proprietor, Lord Camrose, wanted to change the colour of the paper
back to white, but his editor, Archie Chisholm, gave the firmest of
vetoes. He pointed out that young fellows travelling into the City liked to
be seen with such a distinctive paper, thereby identifying them as
'something in the City'. It was a franchise that as yet Bracken could only
envy.[39]

For one prominent self-made man, with little or nothing of the
buccaneer about him, the City proved a place of both opportunity and
frustration. Sir Gilbert Garnsey, fifth son of a Somerset butcher and
knighted for his wartime work, was able – according to one obituarist –
to 'quote imposing lists of figures and complicated accounts off-hand
when the occasion arose'. He also had a highly developed conceptual
grasp, a zeal for his profession and the ability to inspire his juniors.
'What use are you to me, Southall, unless you can do it as well as I
could?' one audit clerk would recall him asking impatiently. Unfortunately for Price Waterhouse, however, the senior partner throughout the
1920s was not Garnsey but Sir Albert Wyon, son of the chief engraver at
the Royal Mint and also knighted during the war. Wyon was the older
man, by fourteen years, and it was soon clear that he was holding back
the firm's progress – not just through blocking (to the exasperation of
Garnsey) a merger with Peats, but also through his generally unimagina-
tive, conservative, introverted approach to business at a time when the
opportunities for accountancy were hitherto unequalled in peacetime.
Eventually, by around the close of the decade, Wyon agreed that on 1
July 1932 he would hand over as senior partner to Garnsey. Five days

before he was due to take up the reins, Garnsey collapsed and – aged only forty-nine – died of a haemorrhage of the lungs. The reprieved Wyon stayed on as senior partner for another five years until his own death in 1937.[40]

It was, however, in the world of joint-stock banking that the balance between old City and new City – or closed City and open City – was most nicely adjusted. Throughout the inter-war period the 'Big Five' comprised Midland, Lloyds, Barclays, National Provincial and Westminster, of which Midland was the biggest. Its Chairman, McKenna, explained matters to Morand in 1933: 'None of these banks, except the Westminster, is of London origin. Thirty years ago they all came in from the provinces and now they have succeeded in eliminating the old system of private banks with six or seven partners.'[41] Spoken like a triumphant outsider, yet taking the Big Five as a whole, it is clear that in both the portentousness of their new City head offices and in the composition of their boards, there was a craving for respectability and acceptance rather than an instinctive assumption of natural superiority over old, outmoded City dynasticism. It is pretty clear that the City Establishment, for its part, continued to view the five banks as something of a necessary evil: the Court of the Bank of England remained obstinately closed to its representatives, while for a long time Norman's personal relations with McKenna and Goodenough (Chairman of Barclays) were notoriously difficult. In the larger relationship, the concessions were mainly one-way. In the old days, Holden may have half-seriously imagined rivalling or even supplanting the Bank of England as the main source of monetary power and influence, but none of his successors amongst the joint-stock men seem to have scouted the possibility. Rather, the process under way was much more that of absorption into the existing City Establishment, a process strengthened by the oligopolistic character of commercial banking in the wake of the great amalgamation movement between 1890 and the end of the war. Once Goodenough had gone (he died in 1934), and McKenna had reached a *modus vivendi* with Norman, there would be nothing to stop full-blown absorption, a far cry from the competitive iconoclasm of an earlier era.

Westminster Bank was perhaps the prime case in point. Once the original iconoclast, going back to its controversial origins in the 1830s, it had as Chairman for most of the 1920s the Rugby-educated Hugh Tennant. 'He spends five days a week in the City,' a press profile noted in 1924, 'but he retires for the week-end to Derbyshire, and somehow or other he brings Derbyshire to Lothbury. He will talk of shooting, fishing, anything except Big Banking . . .' By the time Arnold conducted his survey of *The Bankers of London* in 1938, he was able to refer to Westminster's 'reputation for having a very superior and aristocratic board of directors' (unlike Midland, which still retained a distinctly provincial, industrial element on its board). The then Chairman, the Hon Rupert Beckett, was 'of the old-established Yorkshire banking family', following Westminster's takeover of Beckett & Co in 1923, and as Chairman also of the *Yorkshire Post* was 'not without influence in the Conservative Party'. The Deputy Chairmen were the second Baron Hunsdon (a partner in Antony Gibbs) and Sir Malcolm Hogg, brother of Lord Hailsham; other directors included two former Viceroys of India and Lord Runciman, a Cabinet minister before, during and after the war; as many as seven out of the twenty-seven on the board had married the daughters of Lords; and as for educational background, 'one might be tempted to say that the directorships of the Westminster Bank were won at Eton' – or ten of them anyway.[42]

Inevitably, however, it was not an Etonian who undertook the unremitting, day-to-day graft of running a big clearing bank like the Westminster. Charles Lidbury, joint General Manager from 1927 and chief General Manager from 1930, was the son of a Cheshire schoolteacher and himself left school at the age of thirteen. Thereafter, by dint of intense effort, he had worked his way up from the very bottom of the banking ladder. His personality was forceful, occasionally domineering, and his monetary thinking was impeccably orthodox. By 1932, when Raymond Streat of the Manchester Chamber of Commerce was invited to lunch at the bank's head office, Lidbury was at the height of his powers. Streat found his host a 'tremendous thruster' and 'vigorous in his cross-examination', as Lidbury on the question of new industries 'maintained that the Banks were already doing all that was really necessary' and 'said he thought I had "swallowed" the Macmillan report too readily'. In short, 'he was downright and forthright to a degree', before he 'dashed off in great haste – I imagine that to be the style he affects – and left his calmer colleagues to see me off the premises'. Overall, Lidbury's efforts were appreciated, and in 1936, while still chief General Manager, he was elected to Westminster's board – a sign that the gulf between the gentlemen and the players was starting to close, albeit very slowly.[43]

All these outsiders – Warburg and Piercy, Drayton and Bracken, Garnsey and Lidbury – had one other thing in common: their sex. It was already over a century since Ann Alexander had taken over the running of her late husband's bill-broking firm, pending the coming of age of their son, but in the City of the 1930s it was simply inconceivable that a woman could attain a senior position. Nor was it even possible to become a member of Lloyd's or the Stock Exchange. In 1925, following an application for admission by a woman, the latter institution's solicitors advised the Committee that the Stock Exchange being a private body, not an incorporated society, it was therefore exempt from the Sex Disqualification (Removal) Act 1919; accordingly the application was refused. There matters rested until June 1936, when Mrs Mab Gosnell, connected with the firm Geo J. Ascott & Co of 20 Copthall Avenue, 'respectfully' applied for membership. The inevitable refusal came later that month, with no reasons given. Mrs Gosnell, taking the long view, acknowledged it tactfully: 'I fully appreciate that such an innovation has difficulties which time may or may not remove.'[44]

The traditional female route to City wealth – if rarely to influence – remained the better bet. In 1930 a nineteen-year-old called Marcia Christoforides, from Sutton, got her first (and in the event only) job, as secretary to the City-based Canadian financial adventurer Sir James Dunn. A year or two later, when the market picked up, she relied on his guidance to invest all her savings (some £150) in shares, which obligingly multiplied eightfold in value. She then got hold of a racing tip, sold all the shares and gambled the lot on a horse called Maid of Essex. This came in at 8–1, and thus fortified she became in due course not only Dunn's close associate in his Canadian steel interests but also his wife, after the financier's first wife had divorced him by consent. Ultimately she finished up as the widow of Lord Beaverbrook and a strikingly successful racehorse owner in her own right – not bad for a girl from the suburbs who would be recalled as 'not notable for intelligence' but possessing 'a curious magnetism'.[45]

*

'We have bought a little house from Bill Phipps called Furneux Pelham, not far from Bishop's Stortford,' Brand informed a friend in 1921. 'I think it is an extremely attractive place, and I hope we shall like it.' The actual address was The Hall, Furneux Pelham, Buntingford, Herts, so presumably it was not such 'a little house'; anyway, perhaps dissatisfied, by the 1930s Brand was living at Eydon Hall, Eydon, Rugby. Few leading merchant bankers did not have their own, usually ample country residence, where they could follow country pursuits. Jack Hambro, a top-notch shot, kept going the family estate at Milton Abbey in Dorset; Vivian Hugh Smith, as a leading figure in the National Hunt world, would be remembered for 'the pleasure he took in conducting visitors

around the paddocks at his Oxfordshire home, Tusmore Park'; while in
1925 the future Viscount Mersey was an appreciative guest of the
Schröders at Dell Park on the edge of Windsor Forest: 'Very friendly and
gemütlich. He has wonderful orchids and three sorts of claret served at
dinner, progressively better.'[46]

Nor did other prosperous City men stint themselves when it came to
rolling acres and all the trimmings. McKenna, for instance, persuaded
Lutyens to rebuild Mells Park in Somerset for him, and to landscape its
gardens, which with the house stood in 910 acres of land, complete with
an excellent shoot. Percy Mackinnon, Chairman of Lloyd's, lived at
Crockham Hill in Kent, a house recalled by his grandson John Gale as
having many bathrooms, 'a marvellous view over the Weald of Kent', a
large garden, a swimming pool and a farm; while in the 1930s, once
Gale's father reluctantly got established at Lloyd's, he lived in the Manor
House at Bletchingley in Surrey, 'a William-and-Mary house' with about
forty acres of land:

> When we moved to the Manor House the tennis court, running from east
> to west, was in my father's eyes wrongly placed for the sun: he had oaks
> and elms uprooted so that the court could run from north to south; and he
> had perfect turf laid. My father was obsessional about that turf: when he
> returned from the City on fine evenings he would walk out in his dark suit
> on to the tennis court and pace up and down, up and down, minutely
> examining the velvet green. Then he might go indoors and open a bottle of
> port . . .

Among stockbrokers, notable estates included those belonging to
Lancelot Hugh Smith (The Old Hall at Garboldisham in Norfolk) and
Mullens's Berdoe-Wilkinson (Knowle, near Cranleigh in Surrey), the
latter enjoying such an opulent way of life that each year he arranged a
cricket match between his outdoor staff and his indoor staff. Even
somewhat younger stockbrokers could aspire to the dream. 'They are
doing extremely well,' Sydney Moseley noted in March 1935 after
lunching with Ian Anderson and 'poker-faced Jack Paine', his partner.
'Jack told me he is buying a racehorse, and he yearns for a freehold
country estate; he is going away salmon-fishing and God knows what
else. That's the life, if you are a successful stockbroker . . .'[47]

The City's grandees also kept up the style, and mixed business with
pleasure, at their London homes. Even the austere Addis did not mind
putting on his bib and tucker occasionally:

> *17 July 1919.* Dinner at Robert Flemings in Grosvenor Square. Fine

house – great wealth – beautiful pictures – sumptuous dinner – lovely flowers – genial evening. Sir Guy Granet, John Bradbury ... about fourteen or fifteen in all.

18 May 1921. Dined with Robert Fleming. Sir Joseph Todd [Chairman of Central Argentine Railway], Keynes &c there. Great air of wealth but not much distinction about his house in Grosvenor Square.

7 November 1921. Dined with Lord Revelstoke to meet the Chancellor of the Exchequer, Sir Robert Horne, and Jack Morgan. Norman, Tiarks & Grenfell & Villiers of Barings also there. Drank Mouton Rothschild 1884 and 1844 Brandy.

17 November 1927. Dinner at Kindersley's, eighteen men or so, to meet Goldschmidt of the Darmstadter Bank. D'Abernon, Steel Maitland, Robert Horne, Goodenough & others. Splendid dinner. Splendid Moselle & 1864 Port. First rate. Good company, good fare, good evening ...

The London homes of these men seem to have made few concessions to changing mores or taste. 'Very old-fashioned and rather like a museum' was one contemporary comment, in 1927, on the Rothschild family home in Piccadilly; but the atmosphere there seems to have been positively exciting compared to the London home of Britain's richest man, Sir John Ellerman, the City-based financier who over the years had developed multifarious interests and holdings. Fairly soon after the war his new son-in-law, an American writer called Robert McAlmon, came to stay:

> The Audley Street house was, as Bryher [Ellerman's novelist daughter] warned me, 'a stuffy old museum', and conversation at meal-times was cautious and restrained so that servants would not overhear. The rooms, halls and staircase walls were lined with French paintings of the photographically sentimental and academic kind at their most banal ... In the dining-room were cow-pasture and woodland scenes; in the library was a glistening white statue of a high-bosomed young girl lifting eager lips to a cluster of grapes. There was also a painting of geese on the village downs ...

It was not a lifestyle that the City's rich young blades sought to emulate. Derrick Mullens, nephew of Sir John, became a partner in the family firm in 1932 at the age of only twenty-three, and for the rest of the decade he led a playboy life. He lived in a flat in King Street, off St James's Street; belonged to several clubs; and each summer would gather together some friends and drive his open Rolls-Royce to the South of France, where he could indulge in limitless gambling, especially *Chemin-de-fer*.[48]

Yet, for a classic metropolitan gentlemanly capitalist, neither old grandee nor young blade, the exemplar was surely that endearing if self-pitying jobber Roy Sambourne: bachelor, man about town, a faintly Bertie Woosterish figure. Throughout his life he lived at the Kensington home where he had been brought up by his parents, and he never knew what it was to do without a cook, a house maid and a parlour maid. But his main pleasures lay elsewhere: long hours with congenial friends and acquaintances at the Queen's Club or the Oxford and Cambridge Club, often leaving the City early in order to spend the afternoon there; meticulous visits to shops to get just the right pair of shoes (handmade, at Peal's in Oxford Street), shirt (from Wing's in Piccadilly) or hat (from Lincoln Bennett, similarly in Piccadilly); an outing to a new musical comedy, or an evening at the Savoy Hotel that included dancing as well as dining; perhaps above all, as *the* high point of the year, the Eton and Harrow match at Lords. On the eve of the encounter Sambourne would make a special trip to St John's Wood to make sure that everything was just so, especially the old-fashioned coach that he always hired for his family and friends. Then, as in 1928, came the two great days:

> *Friday, 13 July.* Off to Lord's. Eton win toss. Hard wicket. All out by 1 pm, rotten batting. We are 12 for excellent lunch. Harrow get lead of over 100. Many friends join us at various times, ices served all round. Home in Maud's [his sister's] car, on to Berkeley. Jolly party and dancing, break up at 1 . . . I am miserable over Eton's poor show and can only hope they make an effort tomorrow.
>
> *Saturday, 14 July.* Off to Lord's by 10.15, full of anxiety . . . We sit on coach. Nice breeze, big crowd, about the same as yesterday. All happy. Eton's wonderful batting, big score at lunch, 288 for 4. Back to coach early, big hitting and Eton declare, putting Harrow in at 5 to 4, with 308 to get. They go splendidly for the runs and never have I been so excited, consume iced coffee all afternoon. Last wicket falls at 7.15 and Eton have won by 28 runs. Floreat Etona, great cheering on both sides. Dine Claridges, all happy and tired. The end of a perfect day, thank God a million times.

From the mid-1920s there was also an almost annual Mediterranean cruise, which in 1927 included a stay in Venice. 'A wonderful city which surpassed expectations,' recorded Sambourne (a generally knowledge-able sightseer) before noting the downside: 'The sanitary arrangements, even at Danielli's, are vile. Why are foreigners so dirty?'[49]

Nevertheless, country houses on the one hand, Lord's or the Savoy on the other, in a sense mislead. Most of those who were 'something in the City' – if they really were something, and not just clerks – were far more likely to lead a thoroughly middle-class suburban or semi-suburban way of life, for the most part far removed from anything remotely resembling high society. Dundas Hamilton and Eileen Whiteing would recall growing up in this solidly comfortable but hardly glittering world. Hamilton's father was a Scottish-born stockbroker who had come to London around the turn of the century, joined the Stock Exchange and earned the Capel Court nickname 'Wee Hammie' on account of his diminutive size. He brought up his family in Hook Heath, near Woking, 'a very nice area in fact for that part of the world'. Hamilton (born 1919) explained why: 'Because the tennis club was in the road opposite and Woking golf-course and Worplesdon golf-course and Westhill golf-course were all in a kind of circle round and we had a small house which in due course we added to with a big enough garden to ride a bicycle in.' It was, in short, 'a marvellous, really idyllic kind of childhood'. Family values were further cemented by Hamilton's father not allowing his mother to use make-up: 'He thought that women who used make-up were not really proper people to be trusted.' And 'the one great sin in his eyes was anybody who broke their word.'[50]

As for Whiteing (born 1912), she grew up in the suburbs proper as the daughter of Henry Lawrence. For two or three years she lived in Waddon Court Road, on the outskirts of Croydon, but soon they moved to 'The Myrtles' in Park Lane, Wallington, a four-bedroom detached house. The paterfamilias was the typical, somewhat remote figure:

> My main memories of Father are that he was utterly undomesticated; that he lived for his life as a successful businessman in the City of London, where he was eventually managing director of his firm (D.A. Fyffe & Co, forage merchants of Eldon St, E.C.1) and regularly attended at the Corn Exchange; and that he refused to consider retirement until he was over seventy and had suffered two strokes . . .
> He was not remotely interested in art, books or music . . . and I must confess that I have still no real knowledge of his inner emotions or approach to life, as he always prided himself on 'keeping a stiff upper lip' . . . In London, among his business associates, he was known as 'The Man with the Smile', so I feel he must have been quite a popular figure. He also achieved high office in his Masonic life, which was a great source of pleasure and pride to him.

For all that ultimate remoteness, she draws a picture of a very real human being. Her father was extremely fond of animals, smoked a pipe and enjoyed going to the cinema; he 'prided himself on never wearing the same suit or pair of clothes two days running'; his newspaper was invariably the *Daily Mail*, 'which Father always took off folded under his arm to read during his train journey to the City'; and, possessing a sweet tooth, he 'always kept a fancy tin filled with delicious jellies, fondants, peppermint creams and all kinds of candies'. Family holidays were usually at Eastbourne, Worthing or Bognor Regis, staying in a boarding-house or private lodgings, and 'on holiday, Father always prided himself on getting up in time to take us out for a brisk walk before breakfast, in order to collect the newspapers'.[51] On that bracing constitutional he would have been unlikely to bump into Olaf Hambro or Lionel de Rothschild, and probably not even King George V.

*

The second Wednesday in September 1925 was one of Roy Sambourne's more philosophical days: 'The St Ex leads nowhere. The biggest man in the City has no position socially – & is looked askance at when his name is up for a club. With an Artist, a Writer, a Barrister or a Soldier it is vastly different & rightly so. But there it is & one must make the best of it.'

Such a belief may have comforted Sambourne, but it would hardly have been realistic even half a century earlier, let alone in the 1920s. The City may not have been universally loved or even admired, but realistically any lingering desire to impose social ostracism upon its leading figures had long gone. An invitation that Brand received in the mid-1920s from 'Bobbety' disguised no condescension. 'Do you want a loader for Saturday?' Lord Salisbury wrote from Hatfield House. 'I can easily get one. Do bring two guns, anyway. It *is* nice you can come.'[52]

By this time the increasingly impoverished British aristocracy was seeking seats on City boards with ever-greater urgency, and being given them almost as a matter of routine; so not surprisingly the City/aristocracy compact – one that arguably stretched back to the eighteenth century – became ever tighter.[53] For 'Lancie' Hugh Smith, with feet firmly planted in both camps, the only moment of inner turmoil came when (so the story goes) memorial services were thoughtlessly arranged for the same day for a Duke and a leading businessman, both of whom he had known. Which to attend? After taking advice, he plumped for the latter's service, on the grounds that more Dukes would attend it than the peer's. Society was even willing to embrace 'Louis XIV'. This was Louis Fleischmann, who before the war had been nicknamed thus on the Stock Exchange because, reputedly, he was only ever invited to a dinner-party if someone dropped out at the last moment. Between the wars, however, he not only won the confidence of Norman, but became a country gentleman (Chetwode Manor, near Buckingham) and increasingly involved with the Royal National Orthopaedic Hospital. Ultimately, the conventional obituary phrases would roll off the presses – 'Behind a somewhat austere manner he had a heart of gold . . . He was a charming host, with a keen sense of humour . . .' – with that cruel tag long forgotten.[54] This social acceptance of a one-time pariah symbolised something large and important. London's financiers may have taken a hard knock as a result of the First World War and the subsequent vicissitudes of sterling, but in comparison to the once-proud landed aristocracy and the once almost equally proud industrialists, they were not faring so ill.

An emblematic encounter took place in October 1931, when Raymond Streat was summoned by Robert Holland-Martin to Martins Bank in Lombard Street in order to discuss the wish of the Manchester Chamber of Commerce that its members should be able to do foreign business on a dollar basis. Held up on the tube, Streat arrived quarter of an hour late:

> Holland-Martin and two or three important-looking colleagues were waiting with ill-concealed impatience when I arrived. Their attitude was that they were pleased enough to see anybody representative of so important a trading centre as Manchester but could not for the life of them see what we were bothering about. They are convinced that the machine they run is perfect and that they themselves are equally beyond reproach. It is very hard to persuade such people to change their mental approach . . .[55]

PART THREE

1931–45

Now, the City was a place where Mr Banks went every day – except Sundays, of course, and Bank Holidays – and while he was there he sat on a large chair in front of a large desk and made money. All day long he worked, cutting out pennies and shillings and half-crowns and threepenny-bits. And he brought them home with him in his little black bag. Sometimes he would give some to Jane and Michael for their money-boxes, and when he couldn't spare any he would say, 'The Bank is broken,' and they would know he hadn't made much money that day.

P.L. Travers, *Mary Poppins* (1934)

CHAPTER THIRTEEN

Two Fingers

'Somehow I feel resigned – almost stunned by recent events,' Roy Sambourne recorded on Tuesday, 22 September 1931, with for once pardonable hyperbole. 'It has been a terrible strain & shock – & I shall have to economise rigorously. The Athenaeum & Garrick will have to go. With God's help we shall pull through but I am very anxious . . . I lunch cheaply at Slaters. . .'[1] The following morning Norman docked at Liverpool, to be told formally that Britain had, in his absence, been compelled to leave the gold standard. In London, on Thursday, he saw Baldwin and Snowden, but then retreated to the country for a long weekend to prepare himself for the ordeal of returning to his humbled fortress.

One old adversary could now afford to be generous – 'Out of the ashes the City of London will rise with undiminished honour,' Keynes declared in the *Sunday Express* on the 27th – but for Norman these were days of bereavement and even bewilderment. For the moment he could only clutch at the capsized nostrums of the past decade. 'Must have a big majority on the side of sound finance,' he advised Baldwin on the 28th about the soon-to-be-called general election, adding in the most time-honoured phrase that, in foreign eyes, 'this will restore confidence'; while next day, to a sympathetic correspondent, he stated that 'it is too early yet to say along what lines the difficulties of this country and of the world are to be solved, but you are not alone in thinking that the remedy lies in international action of one form or another'. He was sufficiently unmanned that he even had to be cajoled by his colleagues into agreeing to attend the next Basle meeting of the Bank for International Settlements, Norman arguing that he should resign his position there following the departure from gold. 'He is very "kindlich" at times,' noted Addis on the last day of a traumatic month.[2]

Perhaps it was not surprising that Norman, in what was already his twelfth year as Governor, now had to face yet another coup attempt at the Bank of England. 'He is a dear man,' Addis conceded on 13 October after a heart-to-heart in the train on the way back from Basle, 'but I think the time has come for him to go.' Just over a fortnight later, and probably in the immediate wake of a broadly negative report from Norman's specialist ('to continue indefinitely in these abnormal times is asking too much of yourself at your age'), Addis brought round the Committee of Treasury to his view: 'After prolonged discussion it was agreed to write Norman and tell him we had too many doubts about his health to justify us in asking him to carry on after April.' By the following Monday, however, the Committee's resolve had weakened. 'Some of us would like to see him retire,' Addis reflected, 'but I fancy he will get his own way in the end.' So he did, partly by dint of summoning Cecil Lubbock to Thorpe Lodge that evening and solemnly promising that he would not remain as Governor beyond April 1933. Not only that, but (in Lubbock's note of the conversation) 'he will be unwilling that any further extension should be suggested'. Two days later Lubbock saw Norman again: 'I have just been with the Governor,' Lubbock informed Addis, 'telling him of our opinion that we should let it be known, in our announcement, that this was the last time. He did not dissent from publication, but suggested it would come better in April, when the election [i.e. of Norman's successor from April 1933] took place . . .' The matter duly remained private; and by April 1932 Addis was on the way out (having reached retirement age as a Bank director), while internal opposition to Norman continuing indefinitely as Governor had significantly dwindled. There was no obvious successor, and perhaps his colleagues knew as well as Norman himself that he would have been, in the plausible surmise of one of his biographers, 'quite lost without his job'.[3]

*

Inevitably the winter of 1931/2 was a difficult, uneasy one in the City at large. The landslide election victory of the National Government on 27 October may have provided a fillip – being 'generally regarded as a victory for sanity and safeness', as Barings cabled to New York – but with the world still gripped by severe economic depression, the relief was only temporary. 'Well the day passes & a raw cold day it is,' Sambourne jotted on 16 November amidst sagging prices and enforced idleness. Perhaps he should have followed the example of the stockbroker Vernon Laurie, who two days later informed Colonel Francis Whitmore, his client and near-neighbour in the Essex countryside, that he had 'had a really good day's hunting yesterday from Does Gate corner', which had been 'some slight compensation for the general depression which has once more descended upon the City!' There were odd rallies, but gloom persisted in most of the markets for most of the time. There was also, just as spring came with its usual mood of irrational hope, a memorable moment in March 1932 when the wires announced that the Swedish 'match king', Ivar Kreuger, had killed himself in his Paris flat. 'Of course he had debts,' Norman privately observed soon afterwards, adding how he had 'noticed that it is not losses which drive people to despair, but debts'. In fact, the Stock Exchange reacted surprisingly calmly to the downfall of someone who had become a legendary figure in international business; but it did not help. 'Keynes said that pig trade will recover in six months and that farming will recover before the City,' Conrad Russell noted in April – a welcome prediction to someone who had once been a jobber and grown to hate it.[4]

Britain's joint-stock banking system remained resolutely stable in the midst of all this, but outside the powerfully capitalised 'Big Five' there was no shortage of covert support operations taking place on behalf of other, troubled banks. 'An acceptance credit was recently arranged for Cosach by the Anglo-South against nitrate which was to be stored in warehouses in the name of the Anglo-South,' Hyde of Midland recorded a week before Britain went off gold. 'This ran into large figures and had been participated in by most of the Accepting Houses.' It was an accurate summary. 'Cosach' was the large, City-backed Chilean nitrate company floated earlier in 1931; 'Anglo-South' was the Anglo-South American Bank, which had unwisely over-committed itself to what was becoming the increasingly unviable nitrate industry; and Hyde's reference to the accepting houses perhaps explained why Westminster Bank's Lidbury was so indignant the following June when the clearing banks were accused of 'not pulling their weight' in the rescue of Anglo-South, which had been going on, under the auspices of the Bank of England, over the previous nine months. The main clearers had contributed up to £1m each, and granted that this was 'almost certainly an entire loss', Lidbury was 'not prepared to contribute another penny'. Instead, the main burden passed to the Treasury; and although enough had been done in 1931/2 to prevent the collapse of either the London discount market or British credit in South America, eventually in 1936 Anglo-South became part of the Bank of London and South America (Bolsa).[5]

Three other rescue operations in spring 1932 involved even more 'inner' City houses. First, in March, the Bank of England advanced £100,000 ('on special terms – and on the security of family property') to what the Bank's historian cautiously describes as one 'of the great names'. Almost certainly it was Hambros, but unfortunately that bank's official history offers only one unhelpful sentence on the subject.[6] The following month it was the turn of Higginson & Co, whose American parent firm, Lee, Higginson, had been severely affected by the Kreuger collapse. Higginsons did manage to stay in business in London, unlike in New York, but only with the help of £340,000 from the Bank.[7] Finally, in May, there was a reprise rescue for Lazards, which because of serious problems in its Paris house had to be baled out to the tune of £2m, half coming from the Bank and half from National Provincial.[8] Olaf Hambro, Guy Granet, Bob Kindersley: each presumably was grateful that the concept of moral hazard was not too zealously applied.

Of wider consequence to the City was the reshaping of British economic and monetary policy in the wake of the 1931 crisis. 'There are few Englishmen who do not rejoice at the breaking of our gold fetters,' Keynes optimistically declared a week after that event. 'We feel that we have at last a free hand to do what is sensible. The romantic phase is over, and we can begin to discuss realistically what policy is for the best.' A few weeks later, in the preface to his *Essays in Persuasion*, Keynes still more memorably summed up the state of play:

> There is a lull in our affairs. We are, in the autumn of 1931, resting ourselves in a quiet pool between two waterfalls. Scarcely anyone in England now believes in the Treaty of Versailles or in the pre-war gold standard or in the policy of deflation. These battles have been won – mainly by the irresistible pressure of events and only secondarily by the slow undermining of old prejudices. But most of us have, as yet, only a vague idea of what we are going to do next, of how we are going to use our regained freedom of choice.[9]

Moreover, quite apart from the question of what the new policy should be, there was also the matter of *how* that policy should be arrived at. In the eyes of Ramsay MacDonald, it was high time that the Cabinet acquired a much greater degree of control in monetary areas, and accordingly, soon after the election, he set up a Cabinet committee on currency questions. But in practice he was thwarted: partly because the Treasury and the Bank were equally determined that between them they would keep control over these areas, and partly because three of MacDonald's most important colleagues – Baldwin, Snowden and Neville Chamberlain, the latter having succeeded Snowden as Chancellor after the election – successfully persuaded the rest of the Cabinet not only that 'liaison' with Norman 'could hardly be more close', but also that 'government control' of Bank policy was 'undesirable'.[10] Even so, as the first half of 1932 would show, the Treasury and the Bank could only maintain an omnipotent monetary axis provided they charted a new course that was satisfactory to their political masters. Back in 1925, or even during the crisis itself in 1931, the Bank's word had been well-nigh unanswerable; now, after the shattering blow to the Bank's prestige represented by the abandonment of gold, that could no longer be the case.

Protection was the first pillar of the 1932 settlement.[11] Broadly protectionist since 1930, the City had not been inclined in the interim to return to its traditional free-trade allegiance, as the economic crisis deepened. Norman may have been a resolute non-convert to protection-ism, telling Baldwin at the end of September 1931 that the National Government should 'leave out tariffs' when it went to the country on a ticket of 'sound finance'; so indeed it did, but once Chamberlain succeeded Snowden there was little doubt that tariffs were on the immediate agenda. Goodenough probably spoke for more thoughtful mainstream City opinion in his address to Barclays' shareholders in January 1932. He warned that 'a tariff system in Great Britain may prove unavoidable for a long time to come', on the grounds of 'the unreasonably high protectionist attitude adopted by other creditor nations'; but at the same time he emphasised that 'care should be exercised in the imposition of duties, and their effects will have to be carefully watched, as indiscriminate use of them would do us an immeasurable amount of harm'.[12]

The historic announcement – of a 10 per cent general tariff, although with temporary exemption for Empire goods – came from Chamberlain on the late afternoon of 4 February. 'The Government's tariff proposals were very favourably received in the City,' the *FT* reported of the response next day, and for its part asserted that 'British capital will be encouraged, foreign investment in our industries quickened and an enduring fillip given to confidence and economic recovery'. Significantly, it was not so much the intended reduction of imports, but rather 'the revenue-producing aspect that was accorded the best reception in the City'. Additional revenue, the City clearly believed, would help to achieve a balanced budget, keep up the value of sterling and keep down personal tax rates; whereas the reduction of imports was of little obvious benefit outside the manufacturing sector. Not everyone was reconciled. 'Tariffs lead to the twilight of civilisation and the deterioration of the moral code just as surely as, in the Myth, Wotan's condonation of the Rheingold robbery leads to the dimming of the old standards of faith.' Thus Cecil Baring, the third Lord Revelstoke, in a letter to the press some months later; while soon afterwards, also from 8 Bishopsgate, Villiers told a New York correspondent that of the 'many adverse factors' still in play, as important as any was 'the dwindling of international trade due to tariffs'.[13] Economic internationalism temporarily ended in the early 1930s, globally speaking, to be replaced by autarchism; but the City as a whole – thoroughly rattled, or perhaps merely defeatist – had little compunction about selling the pass.

What about sterling itself?[14] 'If there is any comforting thought to be derived from our present distress,' Norman wrote to a fellow-central banker on his first day back at his desk in September 1931, 'it is that we shall now have to collaborate more than ever before in order to restore and maintain an international Gold Standard.' Already, however, there was little support in the Treasury for a return to gold even in the mid-term; instead what now pervaded Treasury thinking on the subject was how to manage the sterling exchange in such a way as to foster the recovery of British industry – a nationalist orientation, in other words, quite unlike the internationalist assumptions that had underpinned the return to gold six years earlier. As with free trade, Norman found himself a somewhat beached figure even in the City. 'At least let us be in no hurry,' the old sage Gaspard Farrer privately argued in October about a possible return to gold. 'My own belief is that the trade of this country can be run without "fond shekels of the tested gold."' Norman persevered – trying to push Chamberlain in December towards a pro-return policy and attempting in January to sit on one of his directors, the former Treasury man Sir Basil Blackett, who had argued publicly in favour of a managed currency – but the tide was running all the other way, especially when sterling began to climb by the end of 1931 and raised political as well as Treasury fears of an adverse impact on British industry.[15]

McKenna, as he addressed Midland's shareholders at the end of January, must have enjoyed the feeling of being no longer out of the policy loop. Declaring that 'the time has gone by for the child-like belief that as long as a country is on the gold standard all is well,' and stating that 'harsh experience has shaken this faith rudely', he called instead for a 'managed currency' and 'deliberate, skilled and resolute monetary management'. By early March the Treasury had devised what it believed would be the appropriate mechanism for the management of sterling, and on 19 April the creation was announced of the Exchange Equalisation Account. Endowed with the authority to borrow up to £150m, and with the avowed aim of guarding against undue fluctuations in the value of the currency (in either direction, from a target of around

$3.50 to the pound), it received what the *FT* described as a 'cordial' reception in the City. The paper itself hoped that eventually there *would* be a return to the gold standard, but accepted that 'that will be at some time in the future which cannot be specified until the world has settled down'.[16] Many in the City may have shared that wish, but in terms of policy in the here and now – and indeed in the foreseeable future – there was no alternative to managed money.

In practice, and to the City's relief, there was a halfway house between economic internationalism and economic nationalism: namely, the British Empire, formal and informal, to which so much capital had flowed from the City, and which capital now needed to be protected.[17] Sir Harry Goschen, in his capacity as Chairman of Union Discount, pointed in this direction in January 1932: 'It is true that, from an international banking point of view, the London market has temporarily suffered a reverse by being driven off the gold standard. But that event may prove to be the turning-point in our overseas trade relations, particularly with our own kith and kin.' Chamberlain's tariff announcement the following month temporarily exempted colonial goods, and at the Imperial Conference held at Ottawa in August a system of imperial preference was formally agreed. It produced no chorus of praise from Threadneedle Street, where Norman remained an unabashed free trader, but the *FT* almost certainly mirrored City opinion generally as it hailed 'a very considerable achievement'.[18]

There was, moreover, another aspect to the imperial theme.[19] Three months after the departure from gold, Leo Amery had attended a dinner party where guests included Bracken and Boothby as well as three men (Strakosch, Niemeyer and Blackett) with a strong Bank of England connection. The main topic of discussion was 'the sterling area', a term just starting to come into use. 'Blackett's now a terrible enthusiast over the sterling area idea,' Amery recorded, 'which I put into his head not so long ago; more interesting, both Niemeyer and Strakosch accepted readily as the only practical step in the near future on the idea that universal world exchange stability is not permanently abandoned.' Lloyds Bank's monthly review picked up the ball in February 1932, arguing that the formation of a sterling bloc, already starting to emerge, 'would confirm the bill on London in its traditional position of the medium of world commerce, and would be an insurance against any loss of financial prestige and business due to the depreciation of the pound against gold'. Over the next few months it became increasingly clear that some sort of *de facto* sterling bloc was in existence, comprising most of the British Empire as well as the Baltic States, Egypt, Iraq and Argentina.

The Treasury as well as the City at large generally welcomed this development – essentially the result of the continuing hegemony in large parts of the world of British trade and/or credit – but Norman was initially reluctant to accept the concept of the sterling area, presumably seeing it as a rival to the gold standard, and somewhat slow to grasp its potential for helping to restore the City's international position. Accordingly, he ensured that the monetary side of imperial co-operation was deliberately downplayed at Ottawa. Keynes, as so often, subsequently called it right, if perhaps a little generously. 'The sterling area,' he remarked in 1944, 'was a brave attempt on our part to maintain the advantages of multilateral clearing to the utmost possible extent.'[20] It may not have been the world that Norman had known as a young man, or sought to re-create in middle age, but sterling's new lease of life as an international currency was in practice a crucial counterweight to the danger (as he would have seen it) of the City turning wholly in upon itself.

The final part of the new dispensation, and strictly for domestic consumption, was cheap money.[21] The departure from gold had pushed Bank rate to 6 per cent, where it stayed until February 1932, well into the period when sterling had started to stabilise or even improve. On the 11th of that month, as Norman adamantly insisted that no change be made, he came under strong attack from three of his directors – Sir Josiah Stamp (the eminent statistician-cum-businessman), Kindersley and Blackett. 'I feel convinced that we are now completely on the wrong tack, and I have never been so disturbed about the consequences,' Norman was informed by Stamp, who described himself as the Bank director 'mostly in close day-to-day touch with industry *in general* all over the country'. Kindersley was also concerned, in a reflection of changed times, to speak for interests beyond the City. Describing 6 per cent as 'an oppressive rate' and no longer justified, he went on: 'I feel we should be doing a great injustice to the community who are as a whole suffering severely from the present strain if we do not lower it. The responsibility is tremendous and weighs rather heavily on one.' These were two voices that Norman would not have found it easy to disregard, while as for the generally more heretical third dissenter, he would have been struck by Blackett's flat statement that 'criticism is rife all round', including from the Treasury. 'I am afraid,' Blackett continued, 'that if the 6% Rate is maintained much longer there will be a concentrated and formidable attack upon the Bank and also upon you personally. I do not mean an Evening Standard outburst, but serious criticism and condemnation from quarters usually friendly with the whole press unanimous against the Bank.'[22] A week later Norman at last abandoned his insistence that the rate must remain at 6 per cent until a further £80m of foreign currency credits had been repaid by the Bank, and the rate came down to 5 per cent. Over the next two months the Treasury was increasingly insistent that the rate must get down to at least 3 per cent, and by 21 April that had been achieved, with a further reduction (to $2\frac{1}{2}$ per cent) following on 12 May. The sources do not record the degree of reluctance with which Norman implemented these changes, but what is reasonably clear is that cheap money was a policy driven by the Treasury.

The final move downwards, witnessed by 'Autolycus', came on Thursday, 30 June:

> Half the House, or to be more exact, perhaps 10 per cent of the House, faced the Capel-court door underneath the Stock Exchange War Memorial awaiting the arrival of the Official Broker to the National Debt Commissioners [i.e. the Government broker], who was expected to announce a change in Bank Rate. Beforehand, the wagering varied between even money and 2 to 1 on a change.
>
> Mr Gosling came into the House at five minutes to twelve, accompanied by two of his partners. He mounted the bench, took off his hat, and made the usual little speech, holding up two fingers to indicate the new Rate, which immediately flashed out, without a tremor, from the electric indicators round the House.
>
> The Consol market cheered, and round the House there was half-hearted applause at this reversion to a Rate of which a good many men in the House have had no experience during their membership.[23]

So 2 per cent it was, for the first time since September 1897. Then, such a rate had been compatible – just – with adherence to the gold standard; now, it seemed wholly incompatible.

An obvious concomitant of low Bank rate was lower long-term interest rates, which was something that the Labour government had wanted to bring about before being overwhelmed by the 1931 financial crisis. In practice this meant a 'Conversion' of the 5 per cent War Loan, the giant stock created in 1917.[24] In March 1932 the Westminster's Lidbury wrote to his Chairman, on holiday in Cannes, about 'my main preoccupation':

> What will happen to us if the 5% War Stock is converted to approximately a 4% basis, which is now the talk of everybody in the City? All the learned jobbers; all the discount market and all the people of the type of Glendyne and Bernard Greenwell talk of the inevitability, if not

the imminence, of a conversion scheme of this character, which if it came about would immediately slice £250,000 a year from our income. Moreover, at that time we should not be able to re-invest on a better basis. Yet I cannot find any particular attraction in any switch at present prices, because I am not so entirely convinced as to the possibility of a complete conversion, having regard to the weight of the Stock.

Lidbury added that 'there is nothing in the world that gives anything like a comparable yield for the type and class of security'.[25] The detailed planning for conversion was undertaken by the Bank of England, and on 6 June Norman noted that $3\frac{1}{2}$ per cent was the rate he would be advising the government to convert the stock to. Just over a fortnight later he reached another important decision – that the converted stock would be, in effect, irredeemable. On Tuesday, 28 June it was announced that the Stock Exchange would open on the following Saturday: no reason was given, and the general assumption was that a conversion operation must be in the offing, especially as the competing attractions of Henley and Wimbledon meant that there must surely be a very good reason for throwing open the doors of Capel Court on a Saturday at the beginning of July.

Thursday the 30th duly ended the rumours. Within hours of Bank rate having come down to 2 per cent, Chamberlain stood up in the Commons and announced the terms of the conversion operation. As the news came over the wireless that evening, it must have been a bad moment for Percy Hart, Treasurer of Barclays. In recent weeks he had, like many in the City, made two false assumptions – that the stock was so huge that government would only be able to convert it piecemeal, and that it would not have the nerve to offer an irredeemable stock in exchange for a redeemable one. In consequence Hart had persuaded his Chairman, Goodenough, that the bank should sell its holding of $3\frac{1}{2}$ per cent Conversion Stock and acquire with the proceeds, at a little over par, 5 per cent War Loan. It was a disastrous error, and one for which Goodenough never forgave him. 'A little later,' Anthony Tuke would note in his house history of Barclays, 'I heard a whisper that the investor on the other end of this transaction was the Midland Bank, but I do not suppose that anyone dared to tell F.C.G. this . . .'[26]

'Holders of the Five per Cent War Loan will gasp this morning,' the *FT* declared on 1 July. 'Hardly one of them can have anticipated so deep a cut into the return, or so drastic an alternative.' That alternative was repayment in cash, and was available only to holders who specifically stated that they did not wish to convert by the end of September, whereas in previous operations the convention had been that holders of stock would receive cash unless they specifically opted to buy the new converted stock. From the start the patriotic drum was beaten loudly and insistently. Chamberlain's announcement, asserted the pink paper, 'represents the most magnificent gesture of confidence in the credit of Britain ever witnessed', and 'the operation is of the highest importance to national economy'. It would only work, however, if the big holders of War Loan showed the way. A couple of exasperated entries in Norman's diary showed one notable institution declining to do so, on the grounds of a higher responsibility to the interests of its depositors and shareholders. On 6 July: '11. McKenna. Why he can't or won't convert 5 War Loan. I urge. He jibs.' And on the 7th: '12.15. McKenna. I appeal to him to convert (along with all other bks). He refuses . . .' An acrimonious discussion followed, culminating in Norman – in a dramatic as well as important gesture – saying that he would buy £25m of Midland's £30m holding of the stock, with McKenna handsomely agreeing to convert the remaining £5m. That same day Norman also saw, at less expense to the Bank, leading figures from the discount houses: 'I urge inter alia that D. Mkt convert their 5 War Loan & promise not to penalise them for holding a long Stk'.[27] Overall, the tactics worked. From 12 July the government-run War Loan Conversion Publicity Bureau published each day a list of 'principal organisations', including leading City institutions, that had agreed to convert. The great majority of small holders did likewise over the next few weeks, and eventually £1,920m was converted out of the £2,085m total stock. The actual task of processing all these conversions represented a huge, if stressful achievement by the Bank of England, one that was important in helping it recover its collective morale after the public humiliation of the previous year.

Keynes, already gratified by the move to cheap money, praised the complementary conversion as 'a constructive measure of the very first importance'.[28] Why had such a large proportion of holders agreed to convert? Clearly there was some element of passivity, some element of patriotism, and some element of self-interest – and different commentators have given different weightings.[29] Analysing 'the public mind' at the time, Keynes persuasively sketched 'a peculiar combination such as could only exist, perhaps, in this country, of a keen desire to make the scheme an overwhelming success, both by personal and by communal action, with an unspoken conviction or at least a suspicion that the whole thing is in truth a bit of bluff which a fortunate conjunction of circumstances is enabling us to put over ourselves and one another'.[30] In the City itself, the role of Norman was undoubtedly crucial, with the conversion operation offering as it did the opportunity for a classic exercise in moral suasion. The stock may have become irredeemable, but a mixture of gubernatorial and national approval offered, in an essentially conformist milieu, an alternative means of redemption.

*

Protection, Exchange Equalisation Account, sterling area, cheap money: within a year of going off gold, the economic and monetary environment in which the City functioned had changed fundamentally. Taken as a whole, it was a changed environment that Keynes warmly welcomed, but in the *New Statesman* in September 1932 he warned that 'our own authorities, as typified by Mr Neville Chamberlain and Mr Montagu Norman, are not won over in their hearts from an ultimate return to gold as their goal and their ideal'. It was therefore a situation not without irony, he went on, that 'it will, in fact, be the doubting Mr Norman (doubting, not prejudiced, for he is an empiricist with whose scepticism dogma would be incompatible) who will have the first shot at trying to carry out the policy which is not his own choice'. The following month, at the bankers' dinner at Guildhall, Norman himself took refuge in a confessional mode in his speech: 'The difficulties are so vast,the forces so unlimited, so novel, and precedents are so lacking, that I approach this whole subject not only in ignorance, but in humility. It is too great for me.'[31] Looking through a glass darkly at this changed world, and indeed essentially out of sympathy with it, he refused to abandon his belief that economic internationalism remained the last best hope – and that it would have worked in the 1920s if central bankers had not been let down by politicians and their democracies.

The symbol, and to a significant degree the substance, of that economic internationalism was Germany, the country whose fortunes Norman had done so much to try to rebuild during his early years as Governor. Nor was it only the world, he believed, that needed a strong German economy, but also the City itself, granted the sheer extent of its financial and trading links with that country. Not surprisingly, then, Norman had supported Frank Tiarks of Schröders in the engineering of the Standstill Agreement, eventually reached in September 1931, which had saved the skins of the City's leading Anglo-German accepting houses. Equally unsurprisingly, in the winter of 1931/2, he backed Tiarks in the successful renewal of that agreement, having pointed out to him that 'it seems quite impossible that the £75 million due to this country from Germany should be repaid when it falls due', with the implication that there was therefore little alternative to renewal.

Germany's creditors in the City included the clearing banks as well as the accepting houses, although only for the latter was it a matter of life-and-death that the German credit agreement be renewed, and thus interest on the debts continue to be paid, with the ultimate hope of the debts themselves being repaid. It was not a situation that best pleased Lidbury – 'Why should we add, by sacrifice of interest which in fact we may take as a reduction of principal debt, to the fund of exchange available for the Accepting Houses to rob us by?' he asked in June 1932 of one particular proposal – but by the second half of that year there was a widespread feeling that Germany might be about to come right again.[32] The international agreement at Lausanne in July virtually ended the reparations saga, the economy was showing signs of picking up, and as for politics, the prevailing note of reports from Berlin tended to the sanguine.

'I feel quite certain that Hitler has missed his chance and the best he can hope for in the future is to become a party leader, but he will never become a German Mussolini,' argued a generally optimistic memorandum on the German position sent to Barings early in September. Two months later Sir Edward Reid of Barings was in Berlin himself (staying at the inevitable Hotel Esplanade, where English bankers always put up), from where he wrote to a colleague about the Chancellor, Franz von Papen: 'It is impossible for him and Hitler to come together. Von Papen is a "gentleman" in every sense of the word, wears collars that you would approve of, and so on, while Hitler has all the bad qualities of the so called lowest classes.' As for the possibility of the Austrian house-painter becoming Chancellor: 'It should have no very untoward results, as Hitler is more reasonable in action than in speech, and the Chancellor by himself does not have a very great amount of power.'[33] Yet again, the City grandee knew no more than the man on the Clapham omnibus about how the dice would tumble.

CHAPTER FOURTEEN
Dogs Barking

J.B. Priestley made his *English Journey* in the autumn of 1933: Southampton to Newcastle, Newcastle to Norwich. It finished with a frustrated author, anxious to get home to tea in Highgate, crawling down a fog-bound Great North Road just south of Baldock and relieving his feelings by meditating on what he had seen. He tried, in particular, to identify a culprit for the mass unemployment, but was all too aware of his disabling ignorance:

> My childlike literary mind always fastens upon concrete details. Thus, when the newspapers tell me that there is yet another financial crisis and that gold is being rushed from one country to another and I see photographs of excited City men jostling and scrambling and of bank porters and sailors carrying boxes of bullion, I always feel that some idiotic game is going on and that it is as preposterous that the welfare of millions of real people should depend on the fortunes of this game as it would be if our happiness hung upon the results of the Stock Exchange golfing tournament . . . On the rare occasions when really grown-up persons, such as economists and bankers and City men, condescend to mention their mysteries to me, I show a lack of comprehension and seriousness that brings a smile to these solemn faces. So I told myself, as I stared at the fog, that even in trying to think about these things, I was foolishly floundering out of my depth. But I risked it. Perhaps the enveloping fog gave me courage. I thought then how this City, which is always referred to with such tremendous respect, which is treated as if it were the very beating red heart of England, must have got its money from somewhere, but it could not have conjured gold out of Threadneedle Street, and that a great deal of this money must have poured into it at one time – a good long time too – from that part of England which is much dearer to me than the City, namely, the industrial North. For generations, this blackened North toiled and moiled so that England should be rich and the City of London be a great power in the world. But now this North is half derelict, and its people, living on in the queer ugly places, are shabby, bewildered, unhappy. And I told myself that I would prefer – if somebody must be miserable – to see the people in the City all shabby, bewildered, unhappy. I

was prejudiced, of course: simply because I belong to the North myself, and perhaps too because I like people who make things better than I like people who only deal in money. And then again, I reflected, it is much pleasanter either working or idling in the City, a charming old place, than it is in Bolton or Jarrow or Middlesbrough; so that the people there could stand a little more worry. Perhaps I would not have dragged the City into this meditation at all if I had not always been told, every time the nation made an important move, went on the Gold Standard or went off it, that the City had so ordered it. The City then, I thought, must accept the responsibility. Either it is bossing us about or it isn't. If it is, then it must take the blame if there is any blame to be taken. And there seemed to me to be a great deal of blame to be taken. What had the City done for its old ally, the industrial North? It seemed to have done what the black-moustached glossy gentleman in the old melodramas always did to the innocent village maiden.

In short, Priestley concluded this train of thought – one that almost certainly struck a sympathetic chord with many of his readers – 'it was all very puzzling. Was Jarrow still in England or not? Had we exiled Lancashire and the North-east coast? Were we no longer on speaking terms with cotton weavers and miners and platers and riveters?'[1]

Arthur Villiers of Barings perhaps accepted the charge. 'As far as conditions over here are concerned,' he told a New York correspondent in December 1932, 'there is no large change. Naturally we do not see the worst of the situation in London and the south of England.' That same year, even Norman was smartly upbraided by one of his directors, George Booth, whose Liverpool-based merchant and shipping house had an office near London Bridge dealing with the export of hides and skins. The Governor, noted Booth, 'said that the "dole" had been and still was England's ruin and that the English working man was being taught not to work. I had to tell him that he knew nothing about his subject . . .'

By habit and instinct deeply Conservative as well as conservative, fundamentally uninterested in questions of the day that did not immediately affect the markets, and strangely detached from much of British life, the inter-war City was typically for many years somewhat hostile towards the newly established BBC, on account of Reith's reputedly left-wing views. The City, with its unquestioned tradition of secrecy and cultivation of mystique, hardly helped itself in the dawning age of mass democracy. The Bank of England's custom, Harvey told Keynes during the Macmillan Committee's inquiry, was 'to leave our actions to explain our policy', adding that 'it is a dangerous thing to start to give reasons'. The Committee suggested that a more open approach would be desirable, but over the next few years little changed in terms of the Bank's relations – or rather, non-relations – with the press and outside world generally. Inevitably the result was to leave hostages to fortune, and in April 1932 there was an explosion in the Commons from that dissatisfied stockbroker, Bob Boothby:

> A statesman is judged by results. If his policy goes, he goes. It may be unfair, but there is a kind of rough justice about it. Mr Montagu Norman, on the other hand, is never called upon to explain or justify or defend his policy; and it is his policy which has been carried on for the last ten years. Governments may come and governments may go, but the Governor of the Bank of England goes on for ever. It is a classic example of power without responsibility . . .²

The accusation was slightly unfair, bearing in mind Norman's ordeal before the Macmillan Committee, but was essentially justified. The Bank – and the City – may have had a far from faultless story to tell, but it was a somewhat better story than many people imagined. For everyone's sake, it should have been told.

Predictably, most of the attacks came from the left. The 1931 financial crisis had created the instant, very powerful myth of 'the bankers' ramp', and within days of going off gold Beatrice Webb jotted down a private retrospective that few in the Labour Party would have disputed:

> Now, having dismissed the Labour government and exacted the 'economy' Budget and thrown the unemployed back on to Poor Law, the bankers advise the government to repudiate gold . . . It is, alas, not a very complimentary sidelight on the financial acumen of the Labour Cabinet, that not one of them saw through the little conspiracy of the City . . . But one step forward has been secured. We know now the depth of the delusion that the financial world has either the knowledge or goodwill to guard the safety of the country over whose pecuniary interests they preside. They first make an appalling mess of their own business, involving their country in loss of money and prestige, and then by the most bare-faced dissimulation and political intrigue they throw out one Cabinet and put in their own nominees in order to recover the cost of their miscalculation, by hook or by crook, from the community as a whole . . .

That winter, under the instigation of Vaughan Berry, Assistant Manager at Union Discount, left-wing sympathisers in the City formed the XYZ Club, with the aim of making the Labour Party more knowledgeable and sophisticated in financial questions. Early members included Davenport, Wansbrough, the metal merchant George Strauss and the stockbroker C.F. Chance; and the group's very name, as well as the anonymity of its papers delivered at semi-secret meetings, reflected an understandable nervousness about coming out as socialists in a world where everyone assumed that everyone else was right-thinking.[3]

By the end of 1932 the Labour Party, partly but by no means entirely due to XYZ influence, was apparently committed to nationalisation not only of the Bank of England but also of the main joint-stock banks, as well as to the creation of a National Investment Board. 'We must exercise control over the direction and over the character of new capital issues and the money market and of new capital developments in different parts of the country, and in different industries,' Hugh Dalton told that year's Labour Party Conference. During 1933 the banks had no alternative but to begin to defend themselves, so that by the autumn, when Francis Bland of Barclays gave his inaugural address to the Institute of Bankers, he (according to Lidbury) 'spent practically all the time in dealing with the various charges which had been made against the banks from time to time by the Socialists and others'. Soon afterwards, at a meeting of the Committee of London Clearing Bankers, 'a discussion ensued upon the attacks on the banks by the Socialist party and upon the possibility of taking any steps to meet these attacks', but no decision was reached. The cause of these bankers was hardly helped by Norman, who in October had been responsible for one of the great public-relations disasters. The occasion was the Lord Mayor's banquet at the Mansion House, when he finished his speech by quoting an Arab proverb: 'The dogs may bark but the caravan moves on.' He could probably have got away with it before 1931, but not after, and in the apt words of the Bank's historian, 'justly or unjustly his audience shuddered at an emphasis on Norman's contempt for his critics and his determination to hold defiantly – as it appeared – to his own unexplained course'. The consequence, again to quote Sayers, 'was to embitter criticism both of the Bank and of the Governor who was now regarded as its personification'.[4]

There was no shortage of pot-shots in 1934. Priestley published his reflections from Baldock. Wyndham Lewis asked: 'Has the Labour Party a Chinaman's chance of suppressing Mr Montagu Norman, much less the Joint Stock Banks? If it has, a Golden Age would be at hand.' And Thomas Johnston, a minister in the previous Labour government, contributed a polemic on *The Financiers and the Nation*, in which he argued that 'as an essential preliminary to any change towards Democracy in Finance, we must first shatter the delusion that the oracles of the present financial dispensation are to be obeyed with awe and reverence'. To encourage this shattering, he appealed to the bar of history: 'They were wrong about reparations from Germany and its effects. They were wrong when they advised Mr Churchill about the Gold Standard, and wrong when they pled in 1931 that the re-suspension of that standard would knock the bottom out of civilisation.'[5]

Perhaps most notably, on the wireless that spring, the Labour Party's leading academic economist, G.D.H. Cole, took the fight direct to a City defendant in the person of Brand. 'Should the Banks be Nationalised?' was the title of their discussion, and Cole insisted that, although he did not wish government 'to interfere with the day-to-day technical conduct of the business', nevertheless nationalisation was 'an essential part of the general policy of changing the economic organisation of society, and building up a new social order based on reason and justice'. He turned specifically to the Bank of England:

> In my view the present Directors, however honestly they may try to serve the interests of the community as they understand it, are by reason of their origin and point of view incapable of understanding those interests in the right way. They think of the prosperity of the City as the prosperity of Great Britain. They pay far too much attention to what they regard as sound finance, and far too little to industry and to the need to getting the biggest possible output of goods and doing all that can be done to prevent unemployment.

As for the joint-stock banks, Cole argued that in the context of a planned economy, 'a socialist joint-stock banking system will be the main means by which a Government can make its industrial plan effective over all the essential industries'. Brand's reply to this was twofold: 'I do not share your illusions as to constant efficacy of Governments.' And: 'Our great banks – I have been a Director of one [Lloyds] for many years – are in no sense political bodies. They give credit and loans, not on political but on banking grounds.' He added, sounding a note of compromise, that the banks would be prepared, if there was a Labour government, to extend credit to *other* nationalised industries – an offer that failed to persuade his adversary: 'I don't feel at all convinced that the bankers would play the game ... When a Socialist Government comes in and begins socialising industries, then the people who are now at the head of the banking system will think that the Socialist Government is leading the country to rack and ruin and they will therefore feel it their duty to oppose it.' Later in the discussion, after Cole had reiterated that he wanted the bankers to 'take their directions about the credit which they are to grant to industries from those who are responsible for the formulation of the industrial plan as a whole', Brand riposted that if this were tried, 'you would soon get into very deep water, and the new British banking system would soon lose the confidence of depositors and the esteem of the world, instead of being regarded as the best in existence'. In the final exchanges Cole insisted that his party's 'industrial plan' would 'not be held up because a few gentlemen in the City regard our schemes as financially unsound', while Brand sought to shift the blame elsewhere for the dismal economic situation of the past few years:

> It is Governments and Democracies who were responsible for the War, for the fantastic reparations settlement and for war debts, and not bankers. It is governments who raise tariff walls and put on quotas and exchange restrictions. It was Government action – both during and after the War – which has done more than anything else to ruin currencies and the world's monetary and credit system, and yet it is to Governments and to what you call 'democratic control' to which you propose to hand over everything including banking.

In Norman's eyes, after perusing the *Listener*, there was only one winner. 'I have read the debate with interest,' he told Brand, 'and conclude that you left Mr Cole upon his back!'[6]

Two months later however, in June 1934, Norman was informed that several well-disposed MPs were critical 'of the apathy and silence of the Commercial Banks and, though not so strongly, of the Bank of England itself, in the face of criticism and discussion of the monetary system'. The matter was discussed by the Committee of Treasury, and Kindersley formulated a scheme by which the Bank and the clearing banks would together sponsor the formation of a 'Bankers' Bureau' (as Norman called it), with the aim of publicly defending the banking system. Oscar Hobson, who had recently relinquished the editorship of the *Financial News* and would soon become City editor of the leftish *News Chronicle*, was chosen to head the putative bureau. It did not get very far. 'Of course Reggie [McKenna] is standing out,' Kindersley reported to Norman in late August, '& saying it is a trick of B of E to use the Bankers to shelter itself.' By early October, Norman himself noted, a briefly plausible initiative was virtually dead: 'Big 5 more & more divided: Midland hostile. N.P. doubtful: Barclays no Ch'man [after Goodenough's death]: Lloyds, Pease gone to N.Z., A. Harris [Deputy Chairman], not declared . . .' The following spring, after even Lloyds had abandoned ship, Norman read the last rites to Kindersley:

> How many thousand pities it was that your Bureau could not get going and that nothing since has been concocted to take its place. It is through

going abroad and through talking to foreigners that I am moved to say this. They seem to see capitalism in the dock and liable to sentence either from ignorance or from malevolence. Here in London we have the best machine in the world and we who are its cogs cannot even get together enough to educate the folk who live in the other towns or in the country on the value of London and of this machine to the whole of this island and to the world.

It was an eloquent admission, calling to mind nothing so much as Asquith's description three decades earlier of leading City men being 'as jealous of one another as a set of old maids in a Cathedral town'.[7]

The attacks did not only come from the left. Ezra Pound, writing from Rapallo at the start of 1935, sent Norman a published list of Social Credit nostrums, as approved by Major Douglas, and asked him to express a view on them. For instance: 'It is an outrage that the state shd run into debt to individuals by the act and in the act of creating real wealth.' And: 'If money is regarded as certificate for work done, taxes are no longer necessary.' It is unclear whether Norman even glanced at the questionnaire, and the following week his assistant secretary replied to Pound that it was not the Governor's 'practice to take part in public controversy in fields in which the Bank might be regarded as having a function to perform'. Pound's counter-reply was rather fuller. After stating that he was well aware that Norman 'did not make it a practice of entering public controversy or of publicly admitting the known facts of history and economics', he made a fair stab at goading his opponent:

> Nevertheless in view of the 'depressed areas'; the extent of human misery produced by the system you have stood for during your lifetime, perhaps the day is approaching when a departure from a fixed habit wd be advisable. Men not having a direct interest in the importation of Chinese eggs, in the anticipated commissions gathered on foreign loans that will never be paid, the suppression, *via* their Austrian catspaws, of honest experiment for the good of the people, have for a decade or more been gathering facts, and forming opinions. Even the unconscious participation or acquiescence in mass murder may in a future state of human opinion, be regarded as less than praiseworthy. In view of which things, may I ask you to reconsider your communication of the 12th inst in the interest perhaps even of the institution you head.

This time Norman's man did no more than merely acknowledge receipt. Pound tried again on 2 February – pretty much a rant, and dispiriting to read for an admirer of the poetry. 'Why don't you have a try while there's time' was one of the few coherent sentences. Third time round there was no acknowledgement, and the correspondence ceased. A year later it was Paul Einzig's turn to receive a blast. 'If you have any honest motive in printing it,' Pound wrote in justifying his decision not to renew his subscription to the *Financial News*, 'I cd do with an explanation of that.' The letter was addressed to Einzig at the 'Financial "News"', in 'Hell's lowest hole or London'.[8]

During the intervening year much had happened on a more important front, to the City's left. It began in February 1935 when Hugh Dalton, Labour's leading figure in financial matters and fond of quoting Lloyd George's famous description of the 'flapping penguins' of the square mile, made a pointed attack on the Bank of England: 'In the larger issues of central banking policy, it is idle to ask that there should be "no politics". Politics necessarily enter in. The only choice is between private politics, played by an irresponsible Governor, and public politics, played by accredited Ministers directing the Governor.' The problem, Dalton continued, was that 'Mr Norman has played private politics on many occasions' – sometimes 'anti-French and pro-German politics' unauthorised by the Foreign Office, sometimes 'pro-gold standard politics, even when the British Government has declared against a return to that discredited monetary system'. He concluded that 'such a dyarchy is bad both in theory and practice'; that, in short, 'someone must be master'. However, if Labour's apparent intention to nationalise the Bank of England went back to the 1920s, what was new was its policy of nationalising the banking system at large; and it was now that the combative Lidbury emerged strongly to fight the good fight. It was a fight, he told his Chairman in March, that involved more than just the writing of articles (although he did this also, in some profusion):

> There is no doubt that the general public is beginning to wake up to the dangers of the situation, but whether they realise sufficiently all the implications is another matter. I am sure you will agree that I am trying to do my part, because some time in May I have been invited to attend a week-end conference arranged by the Fabian Society to give them my case against the Nationalisation proposals. I shall feel rather like Daniel in the lion's den, but I have no doubt I shall amuse myself, if I do not succeed in convincing them!

At the conference on banking and finance, held at Maidstone, Lidbury duly made his pitch on behalf of the joint-stock banks. He defended them as apolitical, 'concerned only with the administration of the funds deposited with them by the general public'; argued that their nationalisation was wholly unnecessary; and insisted that 'the Profit and Loss account was the only real and safe criterion of the efficiency and safety of any bank'. The defining moment of the conference came as Lidbury slowly waved his finger to and fro, as he uttered the sacrosanct words 'Profit and Loss'. At which point F.W. Pethick-Lawrence, a former financial secretary to Snowden, turned to Vaughan Berry, sitting next to him, and said, 'Good God, I thought we were living in the twentieth century.'[9]

Lidbury was undeterred. Notes survive for a talk he was to give (audience unknown) later in 1935:

> History indicates that strongest have survived – Increase in facilities offered – Banks have marched with times – Demand for educational standard of staff is higher than ever before – Future must accentuate demand for most competitive and highly efficient banking services.
>
> English banking system – Not rigid – Not static – Not inelastic – Ally to need for adaptation to new and fresh conditions – Moves freely in conformity with economic demands. Is symbol for banking throughout the world.

The talk was apparently given on 12 November, just a few days before the general election. It was an election in which the City was virtually of one mind that a Labour victory would, in the words of an *FT* leader, 'be the immediate prelude to a crisis'. There was, however, little sense of panic, as the Bank of England's Basil Catterns told a correspondent in Canada a week before polling day: 'The Election does not seem to be exciting people very much and I understand that the Stock Exchange betting is 10 to 1 on the National Government, the latter certainly having got Labour on the wrong foot.' Labour duly crashed to a heavy defeat, and over the next year or two the nationalisation of the clearing banks (but not of the Bank of England) was quietly dropped from the party's policy.[10]

For its part the City did, towards the end of the decade, start to show some signs of becoming more concerned about its public image. The Stock Exchange, for example, decided in 1937 to set up a voluntary fund to help make good future losses sustained by the public at the hands of defaulters. At the Bank of England itself, Ruby Holland-Martin (an executive director) was given the job of speaking to the press. 'But though a most affable character,' recalled Douglas Jay (then working in the *Daily Herald*'s City office), 'he turned out to know more about horsemanship than public relations', with the result that Norman's rising star, Cameron Cobbold, was deputed instead 'and made a very much better job of it'. Anyway, there were limits. Shortly after the 1935 election Norman received a visit from two leading figures in the Co-operative Wholesale Society, in the course of which they claimed (Norman informed Stamp) to be 'so big and important' that they ought to have 'a seat on the Court'. It was a claim, noted Norman, 'which at present I do not think we need to take too seriously' – but at the same time he thought it best to cover himself by opening an account for the Co-op.[11]

CHAPTER FIFTEEN

No Fond Return of Gold

'This morning I saw a remarkable sight,' Geoffrey Madan (celebrated coiner as well as collector of *aperçus*, and reluctant City man) recorded in his notebook in March 1932:

I came up to the City in the Underground rather late, about half-past ten. At Bond Street a man got in whom I just know . . . He wore loose clothes, a ringed and jewelled tie, a crumpled black hat. His general presence made a most distinguished effect, suggesting all manner of romantic things: a Restoration poet, a historic French admiral, a bearded nobleman of Spain . . . This strange being was in a state of high tension. He lay back looking half strangled, as if fallen from a great height, or praying to be supported in some heavy trial; darted a glance away, focussing a distant passenger and slowly dropping his chin; glared round with the queer look of a man swelling with laughter and longing to share it with someone else; or groaned aloud in pain. The carriage was half-full. A woman rose to get out at a station. He started and stared in horror, lifting both hands with delicate fingers, and crooning a song as if to calm a child. Then he fell back, with forehead deeply lined, a flicker of splendid hands, and a magnificent eye very wide open. Two or three people recognised the Governor of the Bank. In the inestimable English tradition they smiled faintly, assumed all to be somehow for the best, and let it go at that.

The train scraped round the rails at the Bank station, and emptied itself. Last but one, out of the last carriage, strolled this enigmatic figure. He struck out now in some odd rhythm, half-jaunty, half-defiant; bent idly down to peer all round an empty carriage; then slid past a group of people at a double pace: only to halt for a leisurely and mournful study of an advertisement on a wall. At the end he paused again, gazing nobly into the distance, like some fine old Swiss guide watching the signs of a storm. Soon he strode on and mounted the escalator, alone, like the bridge of a ship, striking a glorious pose – portrait of an admiral in China seas . . . I thought of the Treasury saying, that the Bank of England acts like a commander in the days before strategy was thought of.

He had no ticket at the bar; and the same instinct which would not stare in the train, would not ask a question as he left the platform. As well demand a passport from a Czar. But the ticket was found at last, by its

380

imperial owner, stuck in the back of his soft dark hat. Still the drama continued; a chuckle, a tormented backward glance, a sudden scrutiny of forbidden entrances. At the top, one last proprietary gaze at the vulgar novelties which press on the old symbolic temple of Threadneedle Street. The traffic was in full flow: it was instantly reined back as he approached: three men saluted. But the mysterious grandee had already slipped and sauntered out of sight, chin in air.

It is a compelling cluster of images of a man who, as the 1930s unfolded, remained as instinctively secretive (what one of his advisers subsequently called his 'constant habit of not telling any one person the whole story') and as instinctively autocratic as ever. A young Hungarian economist called Thomas Balogh felt the full force of that latter trait. He had been asked by Strakosch to do some statistical work in the Bank on his behalf, and the story goes that when Norman saw Balogh going from desk to desk in the discount office copying down figures from papers, the Governor took him by the ear to the door and told him never to come back.[1] It was a humiliation that Balogh, for one, never forgot.

For Norman himself, it is true that life in the City was never quite the same again after 1931 – symbolised by his abandonment of the top hat, unless it was strictly necessary – but he still had an appetite for the work, an appetite fortified by his happy marriage in January 1933 to a much younger woman, cause among other things of some predictable Stock Exchange jokes about Bank rate going up (and down). Always there was one source of power and perhaps solace. 'Siepmann tells me,' Robert Bruce Lockhart noted in December 1932, 'that the Governor keeps no papers. His desk is bare. But in his left-hand drawer is a book with the entry, date and brief account of every conversation.' The entries recording his many interviews retained their laconic, sometimes sardonic streak, as on 26 May 1934: 'P.A. Carmine: as he asked in Letter of 24th: Swiss natural[d] 1912. Disc[t] and, post-war Exch Broker. Business gone: misery come: starvation coming.' Norman's own prospects were altogether more enviable, as from the mid-1930s any internal movement that it was at last time for a change of governorship seemed to wither away. He wanted, despite occasional protestations to the contrary, to continue; he alone knew where all the bodies were buried; and no plausible successor was yet in sight. At one point there was talk of Niemeyer, but on lunching at the Bank in November 1937, Addis found that Kindersley 'is strongly against on account of his German origin'.[2] That was becoming, in some quarters anyway, an increasingly damning indictment.

It was not only Norman whom the 1931 crisis had deeply affected, but also the Bank as a whole. Whereas in the old days, in the authoritative words of Sayers, 'discussion and decision were practically confined to the Governors and a handful of the Directors', by the time Norman returned in late September from his enforced break, 'the old Bank had been replaced by a regime in which the new caste of Advisers had won its place and senior officials, Governors, Directors and Advisers would be closeted together in discussion both of ultimate questions of policy and of the daily conduct of business in pursuance of the emerging policies'. Put another way, although the world of public relations may have remained a mystery, the Bank was now becoming a significantly more sophisticated, outward-looking institution. It was a development furthered the following year, when an internal report under Peacock's chairmanship endorsed the concept of appointing two full-time executive directors, of whom one would take responsibility for the staff and the other for the money markets. Henceforth the trend would be for the importance of the Court, and arguably also the Committee of Treasury, to diminish, as the key decisions and business were undertaken by what has been called 'an entourage or Cabinet' of some fifteen or twenty generally youngish, well-qualified people, operating mainly on the international side and reporting directly to Norman. One should not exaggerate the modernity of it all: Norman's own belief in the primacy of instinct, his dislike of theory and an at times almost mystical belief in the wisdom of the City's markets all remained strong, influencing not only the circle immediately around him but even subsequent generations at the Bank. 'The Economics Section,' Catterns told a former colleague in 1935, 'tell me that they are very happy; much used by Henry Clay and myself, not to mention Siepmann and Skinner: but I am told that the Governor has not yet heard of it!' Or, as Norman himself had, two years earlier, famously informed his eventual biographer: 'Mr Clay, we have appointed you as our economic adviser; let me tell you that you are not here to tell us what to do, but to explain to us why we have done it.'[3]

Whatever the loss of prestige suffered as a result of the events of 1931, Norman's Bank continued to exercise a large, even growing, degree of influence over most parts of the City. The major exception was the insurance sector, whether inside or outside Lloyd's. Traditionally the Stock Exchange and its member firms had comprised virtually as independent a community as that of Lloyd's, but by the 1930s this was no longer the case, especially as the long-term consequences of a vastly enlarged National Debt began to be institutionalised. In February 1932, for instance, it was inconceivable that Mullens could decide who should fill the shoes of Hugh Priestley without submitting its candidate to the

Governor's scrutiny. Ted Cripps, currently with W.A. Simpson & Co, was duly summoned: 'Long talk: satisfactory in all ways, eg manner, ideas, Natl Service capacity – but ?health'. Norman's main Stock Exchange concern was the gilt-edged market, an informal patronage vindicated by his adroit handling of the leading gilt jobbers and brokers during the conversion operation, but it was not confined to it. Take the last day of April 1934, when Panmure Gordon's Hon Evelyn Fitz-Gerald received the call for one o'clock: 'I beg him to give *careful* advice as to New Issue of Cent Mining Co. He admits suggestions of H-Davis [Richard Hart-Davis, another partner] have been rather "casual".' Norman added in his diary entry that his fear was that Central Mining might be 'persuaded to issue too cheap and so invite awkward rush', which would be 'bad for mining mkt'. Five hours later Fitz-Gerald returned with Hart-Davis: 'I refuse to discuss terms or price of issue but urge them to be careful of interests of Cent Mining so as to avoid criticism &c'. Later that year, in September, Norman and his deputy had a revealing conversation with the Stock Exchange's Chairman, Sir Archibald Campbell: 'We agree unofficially . . . that S Ex sh^d be open on Saturdays, as a rule. Their monopoly sh^d be exercised in interests of the Public – or their historic freedom may come to be lost. Precise date of opening again after summer is for discussion or compromise. We believe above to be unofficial view of Treas^y . . .'[4]

As in the 1920s, however, perhaps the prime example of Norman's moral sway over the City was in the area of the flotation of new issues of foreign loans, not wholly ruled out of court but in general much discouraged by the authorities. Baron Emile d'Erlanger came to see him in July 1932: 'Wishes to arrange advance to Holland 1 year. I most strongly protest. He will at once withdraw proposal & do nothing.' The following March it was the turn of that supremely well-connected stockbroker, Lord Charles Montagu: 'I say he cannot in any way sell or place French T Bills in London: contrary to Embargo'. Even Charles Hambro, a Bank of England director, received a fairly curt negative in March 1934: 'As regards your Turkish proposal, I think from your angle it is little less than silly. There is nothing to be said in favour of the Turks; they have nothing to do with you; and if they need financing for orders they place here it is up to the Government and not to the City.' Two years later Chamberlain announced the formation of the Foreign Transactions Advisory Committee to regulate foreign loans. Its Chairman was Lord Kennet (the former Sir Edward Hilton Young, editor of the *Financial News* in the 1920s) and its members included Catterns, who had recently become Deputy Governor at the Bank. This committee's establishment, the *Banker* noted, was part of a wider post-1931 trend 'of Government requests to the City, accepted in a spirit of loyalty and obedience'. Implicitly its establishment somewhat undermined the Bank's authority, but it did not stop Norman speaking his mind, as Micklem of Cazenove's discovered in November 1938: 'May they issue or place 1500^m Woolworth ord^y for a client in N.Y. value £4/5000^m. I say No No No but if they need official answer, they sh^d go direct to Kennet Com.'[5] It is unlikely that Micklem, with his keen sense of what was and was not feasible, pressed the matter with the higher authority.

The world ushered in by the Exchange Equalisation Account, or what has been called 'sterling's managed float', required rather more technical skills on the part of the Bank.[6] The EEA's task, in essence, was to execute official exchange-rate policy; and the principal method through which this was to be achieved was buying and selling in the foreign exchange and bullion markets. In 1937, five years after it had started, Norman explained to a meeting of the Empire's central bankers how it worked. On the one hand, he emphasised that in this field he was now 'an instrument of the Treasury', that 'the money in the Exchange Equalisation Account is public money', and that once Britain left the gold standard 'there took place an immediate redistribution of authority and responsibility' in which 'Foreign Exchange became a Treasury matter'. On the other hand, he continued:

> In managing the Exchange Equalisation Account, we are given an extraordinarily free hand . . . In actual practice it means that the Treasury are kept currently informed about the operations of the Account, chiefly by means of a Statement, which covers only one sheet of foolscap, and is rendered to them once a week . . . As to the general trend and outlook, the Treasury are kept in touch by regular personal contact with the Governors, and all questions of policy are discussed with the Treasury by the Governors alone . . . But the executive management of the Account is normally left entirely to the Bank, and beyond rendering the regular Statement *ex post facto*, we are not called upon to explain our interventions or our failure to intervene, nor to justify the complete discretion which the Treasury allow us in matters of day to day practice . . .

That same year, Siepmann, also analysing the Bank-Treasury relationship in the running of the EEA, stressed the 'readiness on the part of the Governor and of the Bank to be identified with an exchange policy which is never formulated, explained or justified, but which is all the time having cumulative effects that must eventually thrust themselves upon public attention'. Crucial to the working through of this relationship were the Friday afternoon meetings to review exchange-rate policy.[7] The regular attenders during the early, defining phase of the EEA were Harvey as Deputy Governor, Charles Hambro as an executive director, Charles Whigham of Morgan Grenfell, a clearing banker (often Cecil Ellerton of Barclays) and two Treasury officials. Inevitably there were tensions, but they seem to have been surprisingly few, with the Treasury in practice bowing to the Bank's new-found expertise in the foreign exchange market.

A sharply contrasting pair was primarily responsible for that expertise. Robert Hecht, son of the London Manager of the Anglo-Austrian Bank, had his early City training first with the Imperial Ottoman Bank and then with Lazards, before in 1904 he went to Brown Shipley, where he used his skills as a foreign exchange arbitrageur to start to build up a separate foreign exchange department. In 1910 he moved on to become London Manager of the Cassel-backed National Bank of Turkey; during the war he changed his surname to Kay, a gesture that came too late to stop his employers ditching him and thereby giving him a permanent chip on his shoulder; and in 1922, after some difficult years, he became London Manager of the reconstituted Anglo-Austrian Bank.[8] His candidature for that post was backed by Norman. 'He is a very "nice" man, gentlemanly, though rather timid and shy, but able,' the Governor assured the Bank of England man mainly responsible for the reconstitution, adding that 'his appearance is distinctly foreign but he is married to an Englishwoman'. Kay's career culminated in 1929, when the Bank of England decided that it needed to recruit its first foreign exchange specialist. His responsibilities substantially increased after 1931, with Britain going off gold and the subsequent creation of the EEA, and in January 1933 George Bolton was recruited from Helbert Wagg's foreign exchange department to assist Kay. In their shared office, Bolton would recall, 'apart from morning and evening greetings, I sat in dead silence for the rest of the month. Kay, as I eventually discovered, was completely out of sympathy with the Bank and all its officials and, for that matter, with the world.' Or to be more precise, he 'adored Norman but hated everyone else in the Bank'.[9]

The initiative rapidly passed to the quick-witted, iconoclastic Bolton:

> I soon became fully occupied, after discovering – to my astonishment – that the Bank had no knowledge or experience of, nor access to, the Exchange Markets, and was still trying to control fluctuating sterling exchange and money rates by gold standard methods . . . The techniques in

daily use were embryonic, consisting of a private line to Rothschilds to give
them the opportunity of selling or not selling South African Reserve Bank
gold at the fixing, and one line to a Foreign Exchange Broker who, though
honest, was in my experience the most incompetent Broker in the Market.
And so I became busy re-establishing my previous contacts and pressing for
reforms; this delighted Kay, provided that he was not expected to support
or promote my reckless ideas.

Bolton found that the prospect of 'working in the ruins of a totally
collapsed monetary system with no landmarks, framework or rules'
positively suited his temperament, and by 1934 he was making almost all
the running on the Bank's foreign exchange side:

> Kay had deliberately withdrawn from a world and an activity that he
> violently resented and so I became the unfortunate channel of communica-
> tion between the market and the Treasury. News, views, rumours and
> scandals multiplied in the atmosphere of the time as I expanded the range
> of contacts with all the European Central Banks by telephone, by personal
> relations through visits, correspondence and so on. I cultivated friendly
> relations with all foreign banks substantially engaged in foreign business,
> especially the Swiss and the New York metropolitan banks; the Foreign
> Exchange Office in consequence began to attract attention inside and
> outside the Bank.

Virtually making up the rules as he went along, Bolton was the right man
for the job. One of his young associates would remember him as 'a
dealer by nature', who habitually 'went *beneath* the market' and whose
firm belief was 'never let the market be static'.[10] As for Kay, one morning
in January 1936 he reached the top of St Swithin's Lane at his customary
time, stepped off the kerb and dropped dead. Bolton succeeded him as
principal of the Bank's foreign exchange department, and a major City
career was starting to take shape.[11]

The foreign exchange market, so active during the first half of the
1920s, picked up again after Britain's departure from gold. By 1939 it
comprised over 140 banks and other large financial institutions, brought
together each day by some thirty brokers who in effect acted as
telephonic intermediaries. One of those brokers was Astley & Pearce of
46 Bishopsgate, a firm started in 1931 by Geoffrey Astley and Vi Pearce,
who had previously been working for the foreign exchange brokers Percy
& Arnold De Beer; another was Godsells of 1 Great Winchester Street,
the creation of Wally Godsell, an East Ender who before the war had
been a docker; while a third was Souch Jefferys & Spillan, the first-
named being Freddy Souch, son of an accountant at Deutsche's London

branch. The dealing table was the centre of each broking firm's activity – a large, rectangular table around which half-a-dozen or so dealers sat, each with his own telephone and dealing board – but Wally Godsell was probably not alone in concluding many foreign exchange deals over a drink or two with bank dealers in Coates Wine Bar on London Wall.[12]

It was, Bolton recalled, a market with a less than salubrious reputation:

> There was widespread corruption, including the sharing of commissions between dealers in the banks and foreign exchange brokers, and the practice among brokers and dealers of taking foreign exchange positions on their own accounts; if a loss was made the original exchange contracts were then passed in the name of the bank which employed the dealer. At Christmas-time in London it was impossible to hire a 'District Messenger' as they were employed in trundling around the City cases of champagne, enormous hampers, turkeys, whisky and port, gramophones, etc – but these were for the clerks; the seniors received cheques and motor cars . . .
>
> I cannot stress too strongly the complete ignorance of the banks . . . of the consequences of the collapse of the gold standard and the emergence of a new breed of operators, undisciplined, remarkable in their capacity to take a short view, and without any long-term objectives . . . Many of these operators were European, mainly Central European, and the magnitude of their transactions completely overwhelmed the embryonic accountancy and control capacity of the banks they served . . .

Bolton himself did much from the mid-1930s to clean up this market, in particular exercising a direct form of quality control by giving the Bank's own business – which was very substantial – only to firms that he considered honest. The Bank was also instrumental in promoting the establishment of the Foreign Exchange Brokers Association, which oversaw a Bank-endorsed code of conduct. The central bank, furthermore, required London banks to do their foreign exchange business solely through Association members, and again Ellerton of Barclays was a helpful figure.[13]

The banks and other leading users of the market also had their own body, originally called the Committee of London Foreign Exchange Managers, but reconstituted in 1936 on a more formal, regular basis as the London Foreign Exchange Committee. 'Hitherto it has been simply a self-constituted body of technicians,' the Bank of England's Siepmann noted in October that year, 'without authority to impose its will or its rulings, and often unable even to take a decision.' Accordingly:

> We want to make it really representative of the market as a whole and

we want its rulings to have binding force. What has been done so far has been done not merely with our approval but on our initiative. On the other hand, we do not intend ourselves to do the job of remodelling the Committee nor do we mean to be represented on it. We are in the market but not of it. The Committee has been an extremely useful link, and indeed I don't know what we should have done if we had not been able to deal with the Chairman personally at short notice – leaving him to round up the market. The personnel of the Committee is good and strong enough. What needs to be improved is its status as a body, and its relationship to the big institutions with their (sometimes) self-important General Managers and their (generally) suspicious and competitive outlook towards one another.[14]

'In the market but not of it': it was a classic Bank position.

In both the foreign exchange and gold markets, Norman resisted as far as possible the spread of forward dealings, which he regarded as inherently speculative and destabilising.[15] It was an uphill, largely unavailing battle, for the general economic turbulence of the 1930s inevitably meant that in both markets there was considerable speculative activity. Indeed, the decade arguably represented the heyday of the London gold market, it being estimated that up to two-thirds of Europe's private gold hoards were physically located in the vaults of London's gold merchants.[16] A letter to Phillips of the Treasury in April 1935 was symptomatic of the problems faced by Norman:

> I want to try and avoid any attack on the pound, and at the same time I must try and avoid attacks on the European currencies: the two go together: and I include, of course, gold. To achieve anything I must start with the Clearing Bankers. If I can get agreement with them I can take the Houses next, then the foreign banks, and so forth. I am trying, you see, to leave the Exchange Market free but to keep dealings within the bounds of decency and honour.

A month later Norman had won the informal assurance of the clearing banks that they would assist the Bank's efforts to curtail speculation in both gold and foreign exchange, while by June the American banks in London were being persuaded to sign up along the same lines to what Catterns described to the Fed as 'a Gentleman's Agreement'. In the temporarily more austere climate that ensued, London's bullion brokers reduced their forward commitments, including those in silver, which was fortunate because later that year a sudden change of American purchasing policy in relation to that metal led to a crisis in the London silver market that might have had very serious consequences. Even so, there had been 'overtrading' (to use Norman's term), particularly on the part of one London broker, Sharps & Wilkins; and in January 1936, after the crisis had been resolved but before the forward silver market was re-opened, Catterns told a correspondent that he had 'found some difficulty in getting the brokers to accept the idea that what threatens, and limits their ability to retain the world market in London, is the extent of their contingent liabilities in relation to their resources'.[17]

The Bank now demanded regular information on this aspect, but ran into resistance from the silver brokers, who (led by Edgar Mocatta of Mocatta & Goldsmid) refused to be tied down to a specific figure beyond which their commitments could not go without notice to the Bank. Expressing the hope that the Bank would 'continue to receive regularly the particulars which have been given for some time past about the forward position', Catterns was otherwise reduced to little more than exhortation when he wrote to Mocatta in early February, with normal forward business about to resume in the market:

> Once again I wish to say that the chief concern of the Bank is that London should remain the world market for silver and should be adequately equipped for this purpose. We have no wish to pry or to control. In fact, it must be clearly understood that, if we are told what the commitments are, we do not thereby incur any kind of responsibility for deciding what they should be.

The forward march of bullion and foreign exchange business was irresistible, whatever the Governor's sensitivities, and over the next eighteen months the Bank itself not only plunged for a time into the forward dollar market but even actively co-operated with the Bank of France in the execution of that central bank's forward transactions.[18] After all, as Norman sometimes tacitly acknowledged, the Bank could hardly hope to influence the markets unless it too operated in the real, changing world.

The discount market was altogether more reassuringly familiar, although not without its serious problems in the context of cheap money and sharply reduced demand for bills of exchange.[19] 'If your firm and ours agree to unite,' Gilletts warned Jessel Toynbee in 1933 about a merger that in the event was not consummated, 'we shall, to use the language of metaphor, be launching a vessel into the open sea in the middle of a hurricane, and at a time when the weather forecast is of necessity omitted from the News Bulletin.' Three years later, at the Lord Mayor's Banquet, Norman lamented the 'sorry plight' of his 'friends' in the discount market: 'Their unique knowledge and tradition of bills is gradually disappearing. They are becoming mechanised. Their cunning is

being unused . . .' And a year later, on the same occasion: 'No part of the
financial machinery has suffered harder knocks than the Discount
market' – a statement that prompted the *Financial News* to observe
sympathetically that 'short-term rates of interest scarcely move and
signify nothing', that indeed 'we have a gap of $1\frac{1}{2}$% between short-term
money rates and our quite ineffective Bank Rate of 2%'.[20]

Norman himself continued during the 1930s to keep the closest
possible tabs on the market, especially through his Thursday afternoon
tea-parties for the market's representatives; and he was determined that
it should not go to the wall, against his instincts even accepting that it
should start dealing in short-dated government bonds (in competition
with jobbers in the gilt-edged market) in order to scratch a living. He
also, between September 1933 and February 1935, brokered three
gentleman's agreements between the discount houses and the clearing
banks, to ensure that the market was running at at least a modest profit.
The final agreement was especially significant, for this saw the clearers
consenting to stay out of the weekly Treasury bill auction, leaving the
field clear for generally very cosy arrangements between the discount
houses and the Bank, a cosiness fortified by the houses themselves
devising and implementing a firm 'syndicate' agreement 'to cover the
tender' on a quota basis. Rather less palatable to some of the houses was
Norman's determination to 'rationalise' the market, with £300,000
explicitly set as the minimum capital for each firm. By the end of 1938
the number of houses was down to eighteen (compared to twenty-four at
the start of the decade), after National Discount had absorbed Reeves,
Whitburn & Co and William P. Bonbright & Co had retired from the
fray. Gilletts, meanwhile, was also actively considering winding up its
business, and it was clear that the dreaded R-word still had a long way
to go.

The willingness of the clearing bankers to do Norman's bidding in
relation to the discount market reflected a relationship between themselves and the Bank that had been transformed since the more abrasive
era of Holden and Schuster. Norman saw the chairmen regularly,
conveyed his own and/or the government's views and/or requests to
them, and in a tacit reciprocal arrangement was increasingly regarded by
them as the sole channel for conveying their own wishes and problems to
government. Even McKenna, now more relaxed about monetary policy
and no longer quite the energetic, disconcerting presence he had been,
was on much better terms with the Bank. So much so, indeed, that in
April 1938 he took Norman into his confidence about the future at

17 *Montagu Norman outside Claridges, 1931.*

Members of the House:

drawn by John Kennedy ('Jonk'), a fellow-member of the Stock Exchange.

18 *Neville Durlacher*

19 *Roy Sambourne*

20 *Sir Archibald Campbell*

21 *Walter Landells ('Autolycus')* 22 *Ernest Shaw*

23 *Francis Moore*

24 *The Shadow of War: Frank Tiarks and Baron Bruno Schröder, late 1930s.*

25 ABOVE *Bank of England, 12 January 1941: the morning after a bomb had fallen on Bank underground station.* 26 BELOW *Mansion House, a few weeks later.*

27 *The flattened City: looking east from St Paul's Cathedral, c. 1942.*

COMING MEN

28 LEFT *Harley Drayton.*
29 BELOW *Clarence Sadd.*

Midland of Sir John Anderson, former Permanent Secretary at the Home Office. 'He says Midland Board,' noted Norman, 'has refused A, as Ch'man & Dep, because he is standoffish, with a swelled head: A can remain Director of Midland & do as he pleases or go to the devil.' More generally, a meeting of the Committee of London Clearing Bankers in November 1936, held at the Bank of England, saw a typical example of Norman politely but firmly raising his eyebrows: 'The Governor referred to the recent rise in Stock Exchange prices and the possibility of the existence of a position of over-speculation. While there was, in his opinion, no need at the moment for action he asked the bankers to watch the position carefully and to report to him in a month or two.'[21]

Occasionally his requests were refused – as over the question of the banks providing greater and more accurate detail in their monthly statements of assets and liabilities – but mainly Norman got his way. Various factors contributed to this relative ease of moral suasion: Norman's personal mix of charm and forcefulness; the death of Goodenough (in 1934) and the taming of McKenna; the absence of outstanding figures among other chairmen of the Big Five; the significant decline in banking profits during the 1930s, which probably had the effect of making the banks less assertive; and the sense in which, following their relatively untroubled survival of the world as well as national slump between 1929 and 1932, they had indisputably and permanently 'arrived' on the financial scene, whatever their provincial origins.[22]

Norman, characteristically, did not confine his attentions to the Big Five. In October 1932, for instance, he saw the Chairman of Martins, in order to 'suggest Nigel Campbell or Max Bonn or Gordon Munro and Gordon Leith (tho' a disagreeable fellow) as future Directors'; while the following year, when Edward (Ruby) Holland-Martin, of that same family bank, became an executive director of the Bank of England, it was the first time that a clearing banker had penetrated to the Court. Such a step would have been almost inconceivable twenty years earlier, but no one seems to have complained. Undoubtedly, however, the clearing bank that most concerned Norman in the 1930s was Glyn Mills, with its increasingly threadbare capital resources. From the mid-1930s he and the bank's Sir Herbert Lawrence considered, explored and ultimately rejected various merger possibilities, until by autumn 1938 the two were agreed that the best option was to take refuge under the Royal Bank of Scotland's umbrella. Martins made a late bid, but in the final summer of peace the partners of Glyns, the 'last private bank in Lombard Street', sold their capital to the Royal Bank.[23] The name lived on, but in terms of deposit banking in the City it was the end of a proud, defining tradition.

Henceforth, the onus of carrying on that 'private' tradition would in effect rest with the merchant banks. They themselves were hardly in great shape during the 1930s – indeed, as Edward Clifton-Brown of Brown Shipley rather wanly put it to Brown Brothers of New York in April 1936, 'We appreciate that conditions for private banks on both sides of the water have been greatly affected by recent developments, and the process of adjusting ourselves thereto has to be overcome in some way or other.' Traditionally the two main arms of merchant banking business were the issuing of foreign loans and accepting, neither of them flourishing activities during these largely difficult years.[24] As the floating of overseas loans almost dried up, and by 1938 'practically reached the vanishing point' according to one observer, there was an even more obvious incentive than in the 1920s for the merchant banks to move into the field of domestic new issues.[25] Morgan Grenfell, Helbert Wagg, Barings and Bensons had already to an extent made that move, and they were now joined by Hambros; even so, for most of them and a few others it was still a somewhat hesitant, provisional step, as they continued to hope and trust that the world would eventually return to its pre-1914 senses. On the accepting side, as world trade only stutteringly recovered from the slump and national governments became increasingly autarchic, there was much less money to be made than in the 1920s. Whereas in 1925 Kleinworts had led the way with acceptances outstanding of £17.6m, followed by Schröders on £13.9m, Hambros on £10.1m and Barings on £10m, by 1932 Kleinworts was still ahead, but only on £10.3m, followed by Hambros on £7.8m and Schröders on £5.5m; while six years later, at year-end 1938, it was Hambros that had forged ahead (£11.4m), followed by Kleinworts (£7.8m), Erlangers (£4.4m) and Schröders (£4.2m). Unlike Kleinworts and Schröders, the balance-sheet of Hambros was not full of frozen German credits, and the opportunity was there at least to look for new accepting business, especially in relation to the finance of domestic trade. It was a switch of emphasis specifically endorsed by Norman, who told the senior partner of Guinness Mahon in 1936 that 'he was most anxious to keep the accepting houses going'.[26]

Even with Norman's good (and generous) offices, not all survived. David Sassoon & Co and the E.D. Sassoon Banking Co merged as early as 1930; H.S. Lefèvre, the London Merchant Bank and Goschens & Cunliffe all reached the end of the road as merchant banks in the course of the decade; and Huths, once so rock-solid, finally gave up the ghost in

1936. 'You are already aware,' Norman informed the Treasury that March, 'of the great difficulties which have surrounded the business of this firm for some years past – difficulties which were increased by the quarrels of Mr Konig, the Senior Partner with the Administrator of German Property and the long liquidation arising therefrom. The commitments in London of the firm at the present time are about £1½ million of which it is expected that a third, or may be a half, will, alas, turn out not to be represented by their assets!' Most merchant bankers, however, survived, though largely in the doldrums. In January 1937 a recently retired partner of Norman's old firm, Brown Shipley, told the Governor that he was 'glad to be quit of Founders Court' and was 'not happy about their future'; six months later Antony Gibbs, still mired in nitrate, might have foundered, but for Norman agreeing to a temporary advance of up to £50,000. At Schröders, survival would not have been possible without not only the aid of Westminster Bank, but also the partners drawing on their own private resources – in which context, Tiarks nobly gave up polo on his Chislehurst estate; while at Kleinworts, which by 1939 was still owed almost £5m by firms on the Continent, the mass redundancies of the early 1930s were followed by a long period of relatively subdued business activity, with profits never reaching £200,000 and losses being made in two years out of seven.[27]

In general, with so much less business to go round, there tended to be a sharper edge to getting whatever business there was. Even Barings was not immune. 'We have the feeling that if it were perfectly agreeable to you we would rather like to have a first glimpse of any business suitable to the London market which you may obtain,' Evelyn Baring requested Kidder Peabody in New York in October 1936, after that bank had taken a recent 'share deal' to Cazenove's first. 'It might be,' he went on, 'that the business would be one which we should feel justified in handling direct.' Nevertheless, *among* the leading merchant banks, the old courtesies did not disappear. When Francis Rodd of Morgan Grenfell was approached the following year by Dresdner Bank to see whether Morgans would be interested in financing the Iraq government on the security of oil royalties, the decisive information was, Rodd noted, that it 'appeared that two substantial London banks had been interested in the business'. Accordingly, Rodd 'explained that if substantial London banks of the standing of M.G. & Co were already interested in the business, M.G. & Co would not wish to compete, since it was a tradition with such Houses that although they might participate in each other's business, they did not compete with one another to secure what appeared to be other people's business'.[28] Barings, as was fit and proper, duly did this rare foreign issue, of £1m for the Iraq government.

Norman kept quite as close an eye on the merchant banks as he did on the discount houses. Moreover, as Olaf Hambro and Emile d'Erlanger discovered in November 1932, when they were sent for the day after a Treasury letter to Hambros disapproving of the issue of debenture stock for Olympia Ltd, Norman's form of suasion could be surprisingly direct. 'I say that any such firms,' noted Norman after what seems to have been a one-way dialogue, 'who ignore Ch's request in Letter or Spirit not only embarrass me, but jeopardise goodwill of B of E towards their firms.' Three years later there was another encounter, when Norman's diary recorded him warning Olaf Hambro against doing anything 'unethical', to which Hambro riposted that 'Bankers must do what business they can'. As Rothschilds gradually began to recover from the Credit Anstalt disaster, Anthony de Rothschild quite often came to Norman's room to consult him about possible business ventures; while Rex Benson did likewise during eventually abortive merger discussions between Bensons and Higginsons – discussions that, Benson told Norman in December 1938, 'broke down because too little capital for *all* the business of Higginson & Benson'. Peacock of Barings even consulted Norman in December 1935 about whether he should become a vice-president of the Air League of the British Empire. 'My dear Peak,' replied Norman, 'personally I think it a most inadvisable job for you. It means publicity without any real advantage and the subject may lend itself to controversy both in and out of Parliament. Furthermore, it is too far from the middle of *your* road – either Pall Mall or Bishopsgate – to have effective claim on your kindheartedness.'[29]

There was rarely any doubt with Norman about who was inside his favoured circle and who outside, and if Peacock was definitely in, then the thrusting Philip Hill, self-made son of a West Country cab proprietor, was equally definitely out.[30] During the 1920s he had become a significant financial figure, first in the commercial property market and then as a promoter of companies, and by the mid-1930s Philip Hill & Partners was a very active issuing house (originally based in the West End), which was powerful enough to attract that sage practitioner and writer Hubert A. Meredith to its ranks. In June 1935 Norman discussed with a visitor the reconstruction of Tobacco Securities Co: 'Do I advise them to take Philip E Hill as Ch'man & Partner? I say No.' Some three years later Olaf and Charles Hambro came to Norman to discuss the possibility of 'liaison with Philip Hill', taking the form of 'perhaps joint issues', but 'anyway close cooperation'. Norman's view was predictable: 'I advise No 2'.[31]

Increasingly the Accepting Houses Committee (of which Philip Hill was not a member) was coming to be seen as *the* City club, and by the 1930s Norman had come to a bargain with it that broadly suited both parties. His side of the bargain was that members of the AHC would be given the finest rediscounting terms by the Bank and thus a significant commercial advantage; their side was an obligation to present their accounts to him on a regular basis. 'My dear Bob,' the remorseless Norman wrote to Kindersley in June 1936, 'I know your time must have been very crowded since you came home but all the same I should like to receive your balance-sheet one of these days. It seems to be the only one outstanding.'[32] Kindersley presumably grunted – and complied.

*

Cheap money was a key characteristic of the 1930s (Bank rate staying at 2 per cent from 30 June 1932 to 24 August 1939) and, it is generally agreed, did much to stimulate the British economy, especially in relation to the housing sector.[33] Norman himself was less than enthusiastic. Phillips of the Treasury informed Chamberlain in October 1932 that Norman regarded money rates as 'exceedingly low' and that 'he gave the impression that he holds the view that he is not committed to cheap rates except for the period of the Conversion operation and the Lausanne Conference'. The fundamental political reality, however, was that Chamberlain was settling in for a long spell as Chancellor; that he was convinced of the merits of the cheap-money policy that the Treasury was pushing hard; and that the Bank had effectively lost its former virtual autonomy over the making of monetary policy. Norman periodically warned, of course, about the inflationary and speculative consequences of excessively easy money, but so politicised had monetary policy become, as a result of the slump, that his warnings were little more than politely listened to. Moreover, monetary policy itself no longer had quite its old primacy, as Keynesian doctrines began – however patchily and however much resisted – to take hold for the first time on British economic policy as a whole. Addressing in 1933 what he called 'the control of the business cycle', Keynes argued that 'circumstances can arise, and have recently arisen, when neither control of the short-rate of interest nor control of the long-rate will be effective, with the result that direct stimulation of investment by government is a necessary means'.[34] Three years later there appeared his path-breaking *General Theory*. The world, or at least part of the world, was going rapidly macro-economic, and on past form (including Norman's almost atavistic distaste for economic theory) the City would struggle to construct an adequate response.

Generally, it did not try to, and was broadly content to follow the National Government, and Chamberlain in particular, along its very cautious, essentially orthodox and deflationary approach to economic policy. When Chamberlain in January 1933 declared his opposition to any notions of an imbalanced budget, he was applauded by the *FT*, which declared that he had been 'wise to lose no time in stating clearly this country will indulge in no financial chicanery'. That remained the *FT*'s position – and that of the larger, mute City that was its faithful constituency – but Robert Brand, the intellectual merchant banker, oscillated as ever between adherence to orthodoxy and admiration for Keynes. 'I am afraid, as you may remember from Macmillan Committee days,' he told Keynes in March 1933 after an important series of articles on the 'means to prosperity' by the latter in *The Times*, 'I don't altogether agree with you about Government expenditure, because I think the practical difficulties for anything *very large* are too great.' That summer Brand was more forceful, engaging in *The Times* in a vigorous correspondence against Bradbury, still a wholly unyielding pillar of monetary and economic orthodoxy. 'I would favour a kind of management both as regards cheap money and the sterling exchange which would work for rather than against a rise in the general price level,' he roundly declared, 'and if Lord Bradbury regards that as monetary manipulation to be condemned unconditionally, I fear we differ.' Norman complained to Kindersley, who in turn reported back to him in August. 'Seems to have had a show-down with Brand who now regrets the Letters to "Times",' recorded Norman. 'So does RMK who fully sees his personal responsibility to Bank for his partners words & letters on National & Bank Policy. Brand will write no more letters without RMK's agreement.' Three months later Brand himself said to Norman that he was 'sorry' for having stepped out of line.[35]

The other intermittent renegade was Sir Basil Blackett, the Treasury man who had become a Bank of England director. In the first week of 1934 he received a dressing-down from Norman: 'Our troubles & embarass[t] fr time to time by his writings & speeches in opposition to Chancellor's policy. Bk & all members of Court sh[d] support in public tho' they may urge & nag in private. He will consider.' So perhaps he did, and in May 1935 Norman noted with pleasure Blackett's response on being asked to go to China as financial adviser: 'He seems impressed

& pleased & well disposed – perhaps anxious to turn over a new leaf, towards orthodoxy.' Norman may have under-estimated his man, for when Blackett was killed in a German motoring accident that summer, he had been on his way to give an address in Heidelberg in which he was going to set out his full acceptance of the need for state planning in a modern economy – anathema to Norman, and indeed to almost everyone in the City who thought about such things.[36] It may not have been the most mourned death of the era.

Towards the question of public works, central at this time to policy-making debate, some of Norman's advisers (such as Clay) may have been supporters of such schemes, but Norman himself seems to have been broadly non-committal, certainly in public.[37] There can be little doubt that for several years his attitude, and that of the City generally, was negatively affected by the American 'New Deal' taking shape under Roosevelt. Even the *Financial News*, far more receptive than the *FT* to new ideas, was distinctly cautious. 'Let us not delude ourselves with the idea that we can follow America and the dollar,' it asserted in July 1933 about Roosevelt's plans for industrial recovery. 'We cannot afford it. And our circumstances differ materially. As a country to which export trade is of fundamental importance, the policy of indefinitely increasing costs, wages and prices in isolation is no good to us.' Between Norman and Roosevelt there was neither liking nor trust.[38] 'Old Pink Whiskers' was the American's unflattering epithet for the Governor, while Roosevelt reminded Norman of no one so much as Lloyd George, which in Norman's book was far from a compliment. By the mid-1930s, if not earlier, a deep ambiguity permeated Norman's frequent gazes across the herring pond. 'I agree that with America we must choose between friendship or enmity, avoiding war at all costs,' he told the Earl of Lytton in December 1934. 'When all's said and done the fact remains that as well as the need for friendship there is a peculiar opportunity for competition between the two countries in many fields!' The following April his tone was almost hysterical. America was the country 'on whom we *all* depend for international health,' he wailed to Addis, yet it was 'more autarchic than ever', being 'decoyed in one direction by a strange President & buffeted in the other by a wicked Congress'. And in June 1935, to a Canadian central banker, he flatly stated that America's monetary policy was 'too frequently conducted on the principle, "sweet are the uses of publicity"'.[39] It was an attitude that helped to make, above all in the field of exchange policy, for an often tormented relationship.

In that field, it remained a case of getting used to life without the gold standard. In January 1933 Gaspard Farrer probably reflected main-stream City opinion when, following a conversation at Brooks's, he wrote to John Hugh Smith of Hambros:

> Before the War life in this Country was thought impossible without the jingling, tingling, golden minted quid in our trouser pocket – we have learned better – I am afraid I certainly – and you too perhaps – will have our wings on before the World learns the lesson – but I do not want our Country again to be put at the risk of a capital flight – at the mercy of the French peasant and his stocking or the frightened American bank depositor.[40]

Over the next six months the situation moved yet further away from the almost unanimously desired ideal of a return to the pre-1914 world, as first Roosevelt (soon after becoming President) took the dollar off gold and then, during the futile World Economic Conference, held in London, he deliberately sabotaged the central bankers' hope of achieving a temporary agreement to stabilise the main currencies.[41] By the end of the summer it was clear that, for the time being, it was each currency for itself – prompting Brand to assert, in one of his letters to *The Times* that so vexed Norman, that 'the only wise course for us is a frankly opportunist policy, not "anchoring on" to any other exchange, but guiding our course according to circumstances'. Norman himself still hankered after the old days. 'Ultimately we expect to see a general return to the Gold Standard,' he informed an Australian correspondent in September 1933, 'because no other monetary system seems to afford the same assurance of stable monetary relations between different countries or the same safeguard against unsound financial policies.' He conceded, however, that 'for the present there would seem to be little chance of restoring the Gold Standard,' given that 'the economic relations of different countries are so unbalanced and exchanges are so much influenced by panic movements of funds'.[42]

In truth, there could be no going back: not only had Roosevelt dropped his bombshells, but there had also been a proliferation of exchange controls.[43] Moreover, over a year after the establishment of the Exchange Equalisation Account, it was starting to become no longer novel that the prime purpose of managing sterling was essentially domestic – in particular, that exporters were not handicapped by an unnecessarily high pound and that the cheap-money policy was not vulnerable to international flows of gold.[44] The demise of the international gold standard did not mean that gold itself suddenly became unimportant; quite the reverse, as faith in paper money almost universally withered. What it did mean, however, was that nations now formulated, for better or ill, national economic policies – and that meant that the power of central bankers almost everywhere waned, notwithstanding some phases of notable co-operation between them, as the politicians increasingly ran (or attempted to run) their national shows.

George Bolton, effectively in charge of the day-to-day operations of the Exchange Equalisation Account, was at the sharp end during the mid-1930s:

> The list of incidents affecting world politics, and therefore trade and economic activity, lengthened day by day: Mussolini's attempt to control Austria by a Tripartite Treaty between Italy, Hungary and Austria; the Sino-Japanese tension; the fearful wrangles in the U.S. Congress over silver and gold, and sanctions under the Johnson Act against defaulters on debt payments; daily evidence of the German intention to default on all indebtedness; the unenviable position of the Dollfuss Government in Austria, after espousing Fascism in an endeavour to avoid a Nazi takeover. In these agitated conditions the Governor's decision was that we should on every possible occasion buy gold and if, in pursuit of steadying the exchange markets, we should accumulate foreign currency, it must be exchanged and/or sold for gold at the first opportunity.
>
> The American Exchange Fund emerged, after the Gold Act [i.e. the Gold Standard Act of January 1934, pegging the price of gold at $35 per ounce] had become law, and plunged about in the exchange markets like a myopic elephant suffering from a secrecy mania, apparently unaware that its agents were already working for us and without reluctance becoming double agents. Cariguel [the Bank of France's exchange manager] and his deputies exchanged information with us, watched, and countered the operations of the Americans with whom we had no direct contact. A lamentable state of affairs from which no one profited except the professional exchange dealers . . .

Norman, still yearning for the lost certainties of the gold standard, could see little way out. 'For the last two or three years sterling has really been going from bad to worse,' he complained to Chamberlain at the end of 1934, 'and yet stabilisation seems to be as impracticable and remote as ever. I wish we could find a cure for the vicious circle of trade restrictions on the one side and unstable exchanges on the other.' Foreign exchange and gold markets remained turbulent during 1935, as the pace of disquieting world events declined to slacken, and in June Norman outlined to Canada's leading central banker the impediments to stabilisation. These included not only the large quantities of what Norman called '"panic" money', capable of wrecking such an agreement in the same way that they had wrecked the gold standard, but also the fact that 'the rest of the world' was not yet 'prepared to envisage the problem as a whole', in particular that 'your American neighbours show no sign of such a disposition'.[45]

Why did Norman, and most of London's leading bankers, want an agreement to stabilise the main currencies? Essentially it was a desire, which even politicians in Washington started to feel by 1936, to tame what were seen as the vagaries of almost incessantly turbulent and volatile markets; and that summer the deterioration of the French financial and exchange position gave the opportunity for a stabilisation accord to be reached between London, Paris and Washington. The Tripartite Agreement of September 1936 was a huge relief to Bolton and Cariguel – 'all we wanted was something that would bring relief, however temporary, to the emotion-charged exchange markets and diminish the movements of money and gold across the frontiers' – and, on the Bank of England's part, was largely the achievement of Bolton's contemporary, 'Kim' Cobbold. Under the agreement the three central banks pledged, in Bolton's words, 'to consult and inform each other of any technical situations in the foreign exchange and gold markets which might call for intervention to support a weak currency, and to collaborate on measures, necessarily temporary, to restore order to markets that had been out of control ever since the collapse of the World Economic Conference'. And: 'Under cover of this agreement the franc depreciated rapidly; I recall that the rate moved from about F75=£1 to F105=£1 and, after some fairly violent clean-up operations, markets settled down to the new regime and behaved much better than they had done in the past.' The Tripartite Agreement was, in short, 'the first sign of monetary sanity and, like a candle in a window, threw a flickering light on the gloomy scene of international monetary and political convulsions'.[46]

One of those monetary convulsions occurred in April 1937, when London's markets were reduced to a state of collapse by rumours that Roosevelt intended to reduce the price at which the American government bought gold, from $35 an ounce to $30. For the veteran financial journalist Hartley Withers, in the process of preparing the sixth edition of his classic treatise *The Meaning of Money*, the episode epitomised all that had gone wrong since the palmy days of its first edition in 1909:

> Then, one knew that the supply of money depended on the gold stock of the central bank, and movements of gold were evident and fully recorded: this dependence was not absolute and exact, but was regulated by authorities closely in touch with business sentiment, determined to

maintain the exchange value of the currency and working by recognized rules.

Now, all the sign-posts have been smashed. Gold is hidden away in Exchange Equalisation Funds, the operations of which the House of Commons has allowed the authorities to shroud in complete mystery. This secrecy may be justified on the ground of the necessity for mystifying speculators; but it means another patch of darkness where light once was. Those who manage these affairs, either as politicians, or as officials of a treasury or of a central bank, are, from the nature of their occupation, less closely in touch with the risks of ordinary business than those who used to emerge for a time from ordinary business life to manage money matters and then return to it.

Then, London was the world's financial and monetary centre, working with English calm (which our critics say, perhaps rightly, is another form of English stupidity) and with English honesty (not yet smirched by an unpaid American debt-charge), and with English tolerance and respect for the point of view of others. Now, the best that can be hoped is international co-operation in leadership, possibly guided by the Bank for International Settlements.

Then, the price of gold was regarded as fixed and immutable, and with it, the gold points of the exchanges, subject to slight variations due to fluctuating rates of interest and costs of shipment. Now, the price of gold and rates of exchange are playthings of politicians; and many very intelligent people are convinced that gold and its value, now almost entirely based on convention, are doomed to disappear. As to that, only a highly civilized world seems likely to be able to dispense with the gold convention; and in the last twenty years the forces of barbarism, expressing themselves in Jew-baiting, book-burning, suppression of free speech and glorification of war, have definitely advanced . . .'[47]

*

The events of 1931 and thereafter may have been a hammer-blow to hopes of permanently reviving pre-1914 economic internationalism, but that was far from meaning that the City tamely abandoned its influence, or even aspirations, in some of the most important parts of the world. In South America, for instance, although Chile almost totally and Brazil to a great extent moved during the 1930s largely out of London's economic and financial orbit, this was far from being the case in Argentina, so long a somewhat irrationally compelling magnate to British investors.[48] Few of those investors were happy early in the 1930s, as the imposition of exchange controls made it impossible for British-owned railway (and other) companies in that country to repatriate profits to London, but in 1933 Barings, with help from others, came up with an ingenious and successful scheme that led in October to the formation of the United Kingdom & Argentine (1933) Convention Trust, enabling the holders of blocked pesos to exchange them for negotiable sterling securities. The scheme had its critics – 'I told Mr Baring that the idea seemed to me wholly vicious and entirely bad,' Lidbury noted at a fairly early stage of the proceedings – but it was the necessary pre-condition to a series of government-authorised sterling loans that Barings and Morgan Grenfell issued on behalf of Argentina over the next three years.[49]

The one in early summer 1934, for £2.3m, was particularly taxing, and was made possible only by the goodwill of some powerful interests. Evelyn Baring put his Buenos Aires correspondent fully in the picture on 18 May:

> Walter Whigham of Flemings is, as you know, now Chairman of the Central Argentine Railway [headquarters in Coleman Street], and he is particularly well disposed to assist to the best of his ability any operation which may have for its purpose the reduction of the Argentine Government foreign exchange requirements. Crump of the Prudential has not the same incentive and is naturally more critical and apt to judge the operation on its merits. He says that the inclination of the British investor today tends more and more towards domestic issues where profits seem reasonably secure, owing to the tariffs which have been erected against the import of foreign goods. His view is that today the holder of any foreign Government security would accept repayment with alacrity and gladly sacrifice a proportion of his income for the opportunity of exchanging his foreign investment for one from which the difficulties of exchange and transfer were excluded. He said that on the whole, therefore, he could not consider the issue of an Argentine Government $4\frac{1}{2}$ Loan at 93 an attractive business proposition, but after thoroughly damping our spirits with opinions such as these he finished up by saying that he realised the importance of doing something for Argentina and that he would be prepared to assist in any reasonable operation provided he could see his way to being relieved of at least 50 per cent of his underwriting participation.

The job of placing the underwriting was put into the capable hands of Cazenove's, and Flemings took £400,000, the Pru £200,000, and those on £100,000 included the five big clearers (no problems this time from Lidbury), Bensons and Helbert Wagg. A relieved Baring reported to Buenos Aires on the 31st:

> Underwriting of the whole Conversion offer was done inside a day and was very well received. We had prepared the ground very thoroughly

before sending the prospectus round and our job was greatly facilitated by Walter Whigham of Flemings, who took a substantial amount for the Trust Companies in which he is interested and also did some valuable propaganda work throughout the City. In all there are no more than 30 Underwriters, and these are all influential firms who can well afford to hold the Stock for which they may be called upon to subscribe ... The press without exception was very favourable to the operation and even the 'Daily Express' forbore to criticise.[50]

The issue was far from fully subscribed by the public, but being underwritten, that did not affect the Argentine government, which at last saw its floating debt in London wiped out.

To Teddy Grenfell, writing to Mildmay of Barings at the end of June, the overall lesson was splendidly clear: 'The long negotiations and the efforts made to improve Argentine credit in London by the Conversion operation must confirm the feeling held for so long that the London Bankers are the best friend that Country has.' Norman would have concurred, and in 1935 a central bank was established in Argentina very much along the lines that Niemeyer had recommended during an official visit two years previously. 'It was interesting watching Niemeyer conduct a financial mission,' one of his colleagues had privately noted during the return voyage. 'He confined himself to talking to people – to anyone who had any claim to have his opinions considered. He was very affable, but always made it clear he was the great man.'[51] It was, for the Argentinians, the perhaps inevitable human price of financial dependence.

During the winter of 1934/5 Catterns of the Bank of England described Argentina as 'in effect in the sterling bloc' – which meant that that fortunate country belonged to something whose members comprised more than one-fifth of the world's population; were responsible for one-quarter of the world's exports; and enjoyed among themselves the huge advantage of stable exchange rates, as a result of holding their monetary reserves mainly in London and maintaining their local currencies at parities that had been established with sterling.[52] During the 1930s the City as whole, including Norman, increasingly warmed to the concept of the sterling area, not least because of the role it might play within the wider imperial purpose; and in July 1934 there was the considerable boost of Chamberlain's announcement that in principle he would be prepared to relax the embargo on foreign loans in the case of loans being floated in London on behalf of countries in the sterling area. 'The decision was rightly welcomed in the City,' the *Banker* recorded, adding that 'there is no doubt that the pound is strong enough to bear any new load of this kind, and our assumption of the leadership of the sterling area means that we must be prepared to withstand the effects of any disequilibrium within the area'.[53]

The belief that London could take the strain was fortified by the recent turmoil in the American banking system, and indeed as early as September 1933, only two years after Britain had gone off gold, Paul Einzig even argued that 'to some extent, London has already recovered her old financial supremacy, and the complete restoration of her old role as the world's leading banking centre is now considered to be only a question of time'. In truth, the sharp overall downturn in international business during the 1930s meant that the battle between London and New York as rival international financial centres could hardly yet be conclusively settled either way, but Einzig's view was an eloquent reflection of how, in the eyes of the City itself, 1931 did not *necessarily* presage London's decline and fall. Much would depend, it was generally believed, on how the members of the sterling area, not only Argentina, comported themselves. The override, however, was readily discernible: in the acute phrase of the economic historians Cain and Hopkins, 'financial imperialism without gold'.[54]

As so often over the previous half-century, London's approach to Australia epitomised this not uniformly successful policy.[55] That particular dominion *did* bite on the metropolitan bullet, adopting Niemeyer-style deflation from 1931 and then in May 1932 becoming part of the sterling area, the latter move being partly to try to ensure success of an imminent New South Wales conversion operation on the London capital market. Over the next few years the reward was not only successful conversions for New South Wales but also for the federal government itself. 'We are relieved and glad you are staying on,' Norman wrote in September 1933 to Stanley Bruce, who was acting as Australia's chief negotiator in London, 'and we like to think that we may continue the co-operation which we have begun, extending it perhaps to something wider than loan-mongering – Imperial unity, economic and financial.'[56]

New Zealand was, from London's standpoint, a rather less happy story during the 1930s.[57] There, orthodox deflationary policies during the first half of the decade resulted in the election in 1935 of a Labour government determined to shape an autonomous economic policy – sufficiently provocatively that by 1937 Norman was advising United Dominions Trust's Gibson Jarvie 'to avoid opening in NZ – too socialistic'. Equally exasperating was the fate of New Zealand's central bank, the Reserve Bank of New Zealand: established in 1933 broadly on the Bank of England model, it was nationalised by Labour in 1936.

Norman himself was just as keen in the 1930s as he had been in the 1920s to spread the gospel of central banking; and in May 1937, on the occasion of George VI's coronation, he organised in London an Imperial Conference of central bankers. For at least one of the representatives, however, it proved something of a disappointment, for although the delegates were treated to plenty of 'background papers' that had been prepared by the Bank of England, Norman himself was unwilling to go much beyond expressions of goodwill or engage in real exchanges of confidences. In particular, he had nothing to say about the darkening European political and diplomatic situation.[58] Presumably he assumed that it was not the business of the far-away Dominions.

The less than gruntled participant was Graham Towers, who two years previously had become the Bank of Canada's first Governor. There was perhaps a mutual sense of dissatisfaction (though not with Towers personally), for it was Canada that illustrated most clearly the limits to London's reach during the 1930s.[59] Back in 1932 a vigorous attempt was made to persuade Canada to join the sterling area, but such was that country's financial indebtedness to the United States that British pressure was firmly resisted. The following year gave London the opportunity to try a different route to the exercising of influence, when the Canadian government – faced by the problems of exchange management – decided that Canada needed its own central bank, leading to a commission of inquiry with two British representatives on it. One was Addis, who successfully pushed the inquiry into recommending the establishment of a privately owned central bank – in other words, like the Bank of England. 'I honestly think you may have provided for something which was not only badly needed but which may help to keep Canada free or freer from the rapacious clutches of New York and the Federal,' Norman congratulated Addis on his return from Canada in October 1933. The Bank of Canada opened its doors in March 1935, with the Anglophile Towers in the chair; but the election later that year of a government committed to nationalising the central bank led in 1936 to a fundamental change of status, one with which Norman was inevitably unhappy.

This change was partly fuelled by a strong feeling in Canada during the mid-1930s that its leading financial institution should not become merely a tool of London's wishes. 'Are we to have a Norman Conquest of Canada?' asked one prairie politician, while when Norman himself conceded to Towers in March 1936 that 'the belief in a "malign influence" is not easily dispelled', he added his hope that Towers would 'gradually convince your folk that the real aim of Central Bank co-operation is, and for the Bank of Canada can only be, the welfare of

Canada'. Overall, Canada remained in the American financial orbit, not
the British. A more tactful approach might have helped – perhaps
particularly on the part of Addis, who on his return from the inquiry had
publicly referred to Canada as a 'province' of the British Empire – but
the inescapable fact was that, in a Canadian context, it was the Yankee
dollar that now had the clout.[60]

In China likewise larger forces were at work, beyond the City's
control.[61] Addis in November 1933 looked back upon the China
Consortium's almost complete lack of business since assuming its present
form in 1922:

> The only rational policy was and is to withhold any external financial
> assistance from China until she has given some evidence of an intention to
> reform her internal administration, and to consolidate her indebtedness. To
> have lent money on any other pretext would only have served to annul one
> of the few remaining incentives to have set her house in order, and to
> pander to the communist hopes of an ultimate repudiation of all debts in
> arrear. In such circumstances the wisest and not the least difficult policy
> may be one of negation . . . Some day, perhaps quite suddenly, the long
> expected revival in China will come and the Powers combine for her
> reconstruction . . .

The recipient of this play-it-long advice was Vandeleur Grayburn of the
Hongkong and Shanghai Bank, which the following winter tried hard to
persuade Norman to put pressure on the Treasury to allow the London
flotation of a £5–6m sterling loan for China. '"This is only a pint when
China wants a hogshead to put their house in order,"' reported the
bank's London manager O.J. Barnes to Grayburn of Norman's attitude
in November 1934, adding that Norman 'felt that the proceeds of the
Loan would just "go down the drain"'. Norman was still gloomy the
following spring – telling Addis that China was 'giving long trouble and
insoluble problems' – but over the next eighteen months the situation
seemed markedly to improve. In the course of 1935 the new Chinese
dollar was linked to sterling, making the country a semi-member of the
sterling area; in 1936 Matheson & Co's Dallas Bernard, who that year
also became a Bank of England director, upliftingly described China as
'the only great undeveloped market in the world'; while in March 1937
the British Ambassador in Peking took the view that such was the
Chinese fear of Japan that the British were 'on a very good wicket here
and we ought to take full advantage of it'.[62] Over the next few months
Addis, in close liaison with the Bank of England, was to the fore in
instigating negotiations for a wave of sterling loans to China – loans

that, it was believed, would strengthen China's position within the sterling area and markedly reduce American financial influence in China itself.

Unfortunately Japan invaded in July 1937, and all bets were off. 'I feel confident that neither side will allow the trouble to develop beyond what they call a local affair,' Bernard optimistically surmised in August, on the grounds that 'Japan is in a very bad way economically and must nurse her resources', but by September he was reporting that 'both Japanese and Chinese bonds have fallen heavily on the London market, very little business is being put through and sales are matters of negotiation'. The Sino-Japanese war was under way, and in January 1938 Norman told Jack Morgan that 'it disgusts me that the rest of the world should have to sit by and watch these two Asiatic peoples destroying so much and prejudicing their future'. Britain remained neutral; but partly motivated by its investments in China being much greater than its investments in Japan, the decision was taken to give significant financial support (though much less than the United States was able to give) to the Nationalist government in China. This support included the establishment in spring 1939 of a £10m stabilisation fund to prevent undue fluctuations in the sterling value of the Chinese dollar, and during negotiations Norman bullied one of the fund's three backers, the Hongkong and Shanghai Bank, to come into line about the rate of interest being charged. Norman told Barnes's deputy that his bank 'should feel honoured at being chosen by the Government to act as their Agent' and added that 'he could easily find other means of raising the money'.[63]

The Japanese meanwhile, once so popular in the City in those Edwardian days of 'chrysanthemum' loans, retained a London financial presence. Some twenty years later the Yokohama Specie Bank's manager in the late 1930s, Hisaakira Kano, would return to London, with a small cocktail party being organised in his honour. 'Do you remember him?' Brigadier G.M.B. Portman, the chairman of a discount house, was asked in advance of the event. 'Yes – Very well,' the Brigadier replied. 'He used to chew glass when tight.'[64]

*

The Pru's Percy Crump reassured Evelyn Baring in 1934 that he 'realised the importance of doing something for Argentina'.[65] Did he and other powerful City figures also realise the importance of doing something for Britain, and in particular British industry?[66] During the 1920s the City had, undeniably, taken significantly more interest in British industry than it customarily had prior to the war; in 1930 Norman had made his famous call for a 'marriage' between 'the industry of the North and the finance of the South', though only 'provided that industry can satisfy finance that its house is in order'; now, during the 1930s as a whole, there was a further shift away from the City's traditional international orientation, whatever the lure of the sterling area. Domestic issues during this decade accounted, in terms of nominal value, for 74 per cent of new capital issues in London, compared to 63 per cent in the 1920s. Among investment institutions the London Trust was probably fairly typical in the way that the proportion of its investments (measured by book cost) that were made in Britain as opposed to overseas increased from 44.5 per cent in 1933 to 54.4 per cent in 1939. In the Stock Exchange the old, pre-1914 Miscellaneous market had become the much more prestigious Industrial market, dealing in the securities of over 1,700 companies by 1939 (a thousand more than in 1924), and on 1 July 1935 the *Financial News* reflected this growth of investment interest by initiating an ordinary share index in the thirty most actively traded industrial shares.[67] Ultimately becoming the FT 30, this index would for half a century be the most reliable, readily intelligible and oft-cited barometer of the London stock market's mood – and indeed of the City at large.

The main institutional symbols of the City's reputed resolve to consummate a marriage with industry were, of course, the Securities Management Trust and the Bankers Industrial Development Company – the latter formed by the Bank of England in 1929/30 with the somewhat grudging support of the main clearing and merchant banks, in order to help put British industry on a structurally more rational basis. By early 1932, not helped by the prevailing economic blizzard, little had been achieved. In the view of the President of the Federation of British Industries, Sir James Lithgow, industry was doing its bit with regard to rationalisation, but (he complained that February to Nigel Campbell, who was shortly to succeed Granet as Chairman of BIDC) the problem was that the Big Five 'look upon themselves as competitive with one another, not in the matter of rates, but in the matter of treatment of their customers', and 'they are therefore loath to incur what they conceive to be the obliquity of forcing bankrupt concerns into liquidation'. Unless this changed, he added, industrial rationalisation was a dead duck, for it was useless to expect 'relatively prosperous concerns to take steps, the benefits would be largely absorbed by the unfit'. A week later Norman even-handedly distributed blame when he discussed the problem with

Chamberlain: 'Trouble of Rational[n] of Industry: Bankers unhelpful: owners dug in'.[68]

Several inactive months later Norman received memos from both Campbell and Albert Pam of Schröders, also on the BIDC board. Campbell pointed out that among BIDC's shareholders 'there is a definite feeling that when they were asked to participate they did so under the distinct impression that it was more or less of a gesture'; argued that it was 'very questionable' whether BIDC was 'a suitable instrument for attending to the complicated work which every large industrial issue implies'; and noted that 'the more normal method would be to conduct the issue through Issuing Houses, but this naturally raises several very complicated questions'. So indeed it did, especially granted that the City's most prestigious issuing houses – the leading merchant banks – were hardly used to floating flourishing domestic industrial concerns, let alone ones that were virtually in the knacker's yard. Was the sensible alternative to look to government? Pam argued that 'whatever might be the cushion available, it could never be large enough to enable the Company [i.e. BIDC] to deal with all the industries in need of rationalisation'. However, as he well knew, one of Norman's main purposes in initiating BIDC had been to avert the possibility of the government engaging in large-scale industrial intervention; this possibility had diminished following the change of government in August 1931 but had not, Norman believed, permanently vanished. Accordingly, Pam asserted that 'it would be better in every way to be able to help the finance of one or two schemes which have been carefully studied rather than attempt too much'.[69] It was hardly a clarion call, and it set the tone for the Bank of England's muted but not entirely negligible aspirations in industrial reconstruction over the next seven years.

One of those targeted concerns was the mired Lancashire Cotton Corporation, whose management the Bank, in tandem with Barings, successfully shook up in the course of 1932. Its new Managing Director became Frank Platt, who in May 1933 visited Midland Bank's G.P.A. Lederer, successor to Parkes as that bank's cotton-industry specialist. Platt, noted Lederer, 'referred to the general conditions of the trade and outlined in skeleton form his idea of forming further combines so that the output could be regulated, but said nothing could be done without the co-operation of the Midland Bank'. Whereupon, 'he asked for our support, but I told him we were not likely to support another amalgamation of spinning mills on the lines of the Lancashire Cotton Corporation . . .' Over the following winter, Campbell – on Norman's instigation – tried to persuade the clearing banks to co-operate among themselves in order to bring about the scrapping of some ten million surplus spindles, but he did not get very far, with the banks professing to lack the means to drive through amalgamations in the cotton industry's spinning section. The other option was statutory compulsion, but that in Norman's eyes was a wholly unacceptable solution, striking at the very roots of private enterprise. At the end of January 1934 Streat of the Manchester Chamber of Commerce poured out the cotton industry's exasperation to the Bank's Henry Clay:

> When we go to the Government, they tell us the City will do everything we need; when we go to the City, they tell us that they can find finance only if we can show a profit. Back we go to the Government to ask for the compulsory powers without which it is impossible to make the industry profitable; and they tell us that when the whole two thousand of us are agreed on every detail of a complete re-organisation of the whole industry (which is impossible, especially without new capital which we cannot get), they will consider our request. Meanwhile they tell the City privately to head us off the demand for compulsory powers . . .[70]

Over the next year or two LCC's financial performance picked up, but the spinning section remained broadly unreconstructed.

Campbell was not perhaps the ideal front man for BIDC. On at least two occasions in the mid-1930s he went to see Lidbury, apparently in order to win the Westminster's support for proposals relating to the cotton industry, and found himself barely able to utter a coherent thought in the face of that tough-minded clearing banker's austere, disapproving gaze. 'I do not know what Mr Nigel Campbell could have had in mind when he came to see me,' Lidbury noted after one visit, 'or what the object of his visit was, but at any rate I do know that not only did it attain nothing but it also did not propose anything.' Nor was Campbell BIDC's only merchant banker who failed to impress. In November 1937 Peacock initiated a meeting with Lidbury in order to explain the proposed reorganisation of Combined Egyptian Mills, in which Westminster was a significant shareholder; but according to Lidbury, he 'was entirely vague, inexact and imperfectly informed upon the subject'.[71] Lidbury's own position – undeviating opposition to industrial intervention – was never in doubt, or tentatively expressed.

Steel was the other industry in which the Bank was closely, even more directly involved.[72] Several times in the 1930s, faced with the impossibility of going to the investing public for funds, it dipped into its own pockets: in 1932 a £0.5m advance, via BIDC, to enable a start to be made in constructing Stewart and Lloyd's new steelworks at Corby; in

1937 a £200,000 investment in an electric steelworks at Jarrow; the following year a £1.5m infusion into Richard Thomas's new works at Ebbw Vale; also in 1938 a £1m subscription to John Summers in Shotton for its new strip-mill. The case of Richard Thomas also involved the Bank organising a £4.5m whip-round in May 1938, after (the Bank's Ernest Skinner recalled many years later) 'Lloyds & Rothschilds got cold feet!' Lidbury did his best to decline the honour, but on 16 June informed his absent Chairman that he and the directors had decided that afternoon 'to accept the proposal of the Bank of England because it would be highly undesirable that Westminster Bank should incur the odium of standing out by itself and thus breaking up the arrangements which the Bank of England would otherwise complete'. Beckett's reply spoke for all victims of moral suasion:

> One regrets this departure into the realms of support for industrial concerns not on intrinsic merits but for outside reasons which we have to take on trust. The past management, which has so woefully miscalculated the financial requirements of the concern, does not inspire one with any confidence for the future. Also the manner in which Catterns [Deputy Governor] has handled the matter taking the Banks in detail & then holding up the possible reproach as to the invidious position of any one to resist, does not commend itself; though I suppose from his point of view it was the best if not the only way . . .[73]

Overall, the only authoritative assessment (by Tolliday) of the Bank's involvement with the steel industry during this difficult decade is one of strictly modified rapture. 'Profoundly orthodox in its economics', the Bank sought to encourage amalgamations but 'was not prepared to commit its own capital to a below-average rate of profit sector as the price of control in the short term in order to carry out restructuring and raise the level of profitability in the long term'; second, 'although Norman was able to assemble a powerful team of industrial advisers on general policy issues, he lacked the resources rigorously to reconstruct management at enterprise level'; and third, such was Norman's determination to keep industry out of the hands of the state that 'the Bank did not accept that industrial re-organisation required a central coordinating and guiding hand unless it arose from within the industry itself'.[74] Therefore, although the Bank's amalgamation schemes for the British steel industry were much better thought out than they were for cotton, most came to nought or achieved relatively little.

By 1938/9 a decision was looming about whether BIDC should be continued in 1940 for a further five-year period. In July 1938 Campbell expressed the view, doubtless unwelcome to Norman, that if it did have a future, it would have to be as a confidential helpmate to government, given government's increasing involvement in the previous two or three years in industrial matters. The following February Skinner (who had advanced within the Bank from being Norman's private secretary to becoming an industrial adviser) posed a series of questions, cumulatively giving the impression of nothing so much as treading on hot coals:

> To what extent are the Bank prepared to finance further schemes for industry: are they to be active or passive? Can they find the £50 million which one person has estimated to be necessary to put major industry straight?
> Can the B.I.D. [i.e. BIDC] or even a re-arranged S.M.T. do this work without heaping coals of fire upon the Bank? Industrial financing started as the tail of the dog!
> Or might or can the whole thing be taken sufficiently outside the Bank for it to be disassociated from the Bank in the public eye? Or since the Government might after all have to come in, ought not the Bank to stand completely aside from further ventures, or at least to tread warily, building up slowly but comprehensively?

Clearly there was some big thinking in the air, probably galvanised by the government's increasing industrial engagement, and McKenna called on Norman at the end of February to tell him that he was 'well disposed to idea of Bks finding £3–5m each as cap for a reconstituted BID with independent management towards needs of Iron & Steel'.[75]

Next day saw an illuminating exchange of views in the Committee of Treasury:

> *Walter Whigham:* Position of control which the Bank has had to assume is dangerous: renders them still more vulnerable to attacks from the 'Left'. City would assist sound concerns, if unsound, better that they should crash and reorganise. Each industry should work out its own salvation. Present tendency is to bolster up bad management.
> *Peacock:* Consider B.I.D. as carried on for some time useful but disturbed at its becoming more and more a Nursing Home . . . Summers ought never to have come here. Any company in good order able to obtain its finance from City, e.g. United Steel [the responsibility of Morgan Grenfell].
> *Norman:* Speaking broadly, the Bank's policy over the past years has proved to be a right one: Companies necessary in the public interest have been saved from extinction and Government intervention has been avoided. Unfortunate that control perforce lies here, but complaints in this

regard from certain quarters should not be taken as a reason for liquidation.

Over the next few weeks the opinion of Norman's advisers seems increasingly to have swung towards winding up BIDC. Such at least was the view of Clay, who in pointing out the extent to which economic circumstances had changed since BIDC was formed in 1930, put forward one particularly interesting argument:

> If the London capital market is to survive, it has to adjust itself to the loss of the greater part of what was formerly its chief business – overseas issues. The natural adjustment would be to devise ways of directing capital to new domestic uses. This adjustment is not likely to be effected if the Bank even gives the impression that it will take the responsibility of finding capital for industry in any case of difficulty, still less if the Bank or a Bank-controlled agency undertakes a large part of the work.[76]

Put another way, implied that shrewd Yorkshireman, it was time for the City to make the sort of structural 'adjustment' that it devoted so much rhetoric to calling on industry to make.

The Bank of England was also directly involved in three new industrial initiatives during the 1930s. One was the ultimately abortive Industrial Mortgage Corporation. The original idea seems to have come from Lloyds, which told Norman in March 1932 that the intention was 'to lend long money to small industries' and that it was an explicit response to the Macmillan Report. The plan was to get participation from other clearers, the Bank's reaction was broadly positive, and soon afterwards Streat recorded Lidbury's complaint that '"they" (the usual undesignated powers behind the throne) were thinking of a new industrial mortgage corporation but that it could not deal with small amounts which were too costly to look after and more suitable for private individual enterprise'. Later that year Rex Benson became involved, but fell out with Lloyds because his own scheme was too ambitious. 'I say I expect to subscribe to 1st Co wh is formed,' Norman told him in July, '& will carry out Macmillan Report & have so informed promoters.' Over the next year not a lot happened, and by October 1933 Norman was sufficiently concerned to send Niemeyer to Midland to try to persuade Hyde to give his bank's fuller support to the proposed scheme. It was not, Hyde emphasised to his visitor, a scheme that chimed in with the traditional lending precepts of English deposit banking:

> I reminded him that the Banks by retaining their right to call in the

money enabled them to exercise some control over the borrowers, whereas if the loans were made for a definite period of five years and the Corporation were not satisfied with the progress that the borrower was making they would have no right to exercise any control. Sir Otto said that he thought it would not be practicable for the Corporation to interfere during the period agreed to for the loan. He appreciated that this might mean that they were taking certain risks that the Banks were not prepared to take.

I referred to his suggestion that the introduction of business should come through the Banks, and I asked him whether this would not mean that he would only get such business as the Banks were not themselves prepared to take. He appreciated this point, but he still thought there would be room for the Corporation . . .

I asked him what his idea was regarding Capital, and he said that he was hopeful that each of the five big Banks would be prepared to take say £50/75,000 of the capital. I said this was much higher than we had in contemplation, as we regarded a contribution of say £20,000 as about as far as we wanted to go.[77]

By February 1934 Norman was sufficiently involved that he made a personal appeal to the Big Five for £50,000 from each.

Now, however, there was a new entrant in the lists, in the form of the Charterhouse Investment Trust, whose Nutcombe Hume made the journey to Frederick Hyde's office on the same day (1 February) that Norman issued his appeal. He submitted the skeleton prospectus for a new corporation to be devoted to mid-term industrial finance and told Hyde that Lloyds was already interested. 'The manner in which Mr Hume's scheme differs from some of the others that have been discussed,' Hyde noted, 'is that he does not want to confine the interest in concerns they finance to Debentures but also wants to be in a position to take either Preference or Ordinary shares.' Returning to the Midland five days later, Hume was at first encouraged to be told by Hyde and McKenna that their bank preferred his scheme to the one being endorsed by the Bank of England, but was then 'rather disappointed' when told that Midland was willing to subscribe only £5,000 to the minimum of £250,000 that he saw as necessary. For Norman, Charterhouse's apparently sudden emergence was heaven-sent, giving him the chance to withdraw the Bank's scheme, which almost certainly would be a source of resentment to the clearing banks. 'We are willing to drop whole idea,' he told Beckett on the 19th, 'as arranged with Bankers on the 1st, if Others will afford facilities claimed & relieve Whitehall of complaint.' It may well have been a close-run thing that the Bank was enabled to get off the hook, for the only leading joint-stock banks that agreed to become shareholders in the Charterhouse Industrial Development Co were Midland and Lloyds, which meant that Charterhouse Investment Trust itself had to find most of the eventual £200,000 capital. 'It was the first time,' Hume would legitimately boast a decade later, 'that a Company had been formed in the City for the express purpose of providing capital for smaller concerns in the form of share or equity capital'; but, as he would also reflect, 'the proposal was not received with enthusiasm in Banking Circles'.[78]

The Bank's other new industrial initiatives both came to fruition and were less tortuous sagas. Writing to a fellow-central banker in June 1935, Norman fairly summarised one of them:

> About a year ago the United Dominions Trust [part-owned by the Bank] formed, for political reasons and in co-operation with the Bank, a subsidiary called Credit for Industry in order to provide medium-term credit in small amounts (up to £50,000) for industrial concerns. This move complies with one of the recommendations of the Macmillan Committee and satisfies a need of which we have heard a great deal. How real is this need is open to doubt ...

The £250,000 nominal capital came from UDT, whose J. Gibson Jarvie was responsible for the name Credit for Industry, which was in existence by mid-1934. CFI, however, seems to have achieved relatively little over the rest of the decade, not helped by the fact that the clearing banks tended to poach its best customers.[79]

The final initiative seems in the first instance to have come Norman's way on 28 November 1935: '2.30. de Stein. Finance for Special Areas. Suggest an Arrang' with backing of all Trust Cos & will submit outline of Scheme. Says Jarvie too much of a Banker as opposed to investor.' The diarist James Lees-Milne would describe Edward de Stein (a successful financier who had started his own issuing house) as 'a peppery, fussy, schoolmasterish little man, with whom I should hate to have a row'; but as the owner of Lindisfarne Castle in north-east England, de Stein had at least some idea of what a depressed area, whose need for industrial diversification was becoming widely accepted, was like.[80] Within a few months legislation was pending to create the Special Areas Reconstruction Association Ltd, otherwise known as SARA.[81] Its somewhat unambitious remit would be to grant middle-term credits to undertakings in those areas, not exceeding £5,000 each, and Norman agreed to try to raise £100,000 capital from the banks. Lidbury was probably typical in viewing the proposal unenthusiastically, while accepting that 'the joint stock banks cannot, as a political desirability, avoid giving favourable response to the request to take up capital stock'.[82]

Eventually, in the course of 1936, the City as a whole (including insurance companies and investment trusts) subscribed half or even somewhat more of SARA's £1m capital. Over the next year or two SARA made only a very limited impact on the industrial situation in the Special Areas, not helped by Skinner in particular arguing forcibly that if it started lending to large as well as small businesses, then its shareholders would revolt, on the grounds that their money was being spent on financing their competitors. Likewise ensuring nugatory results was the insistence that SARA be run along strictly orthodox financial lines, above all the provision of loan capital at strictly market rates of interest. Overall, in the sober verdict of SARA's historian, 'the financial community did not develop a positive conception of its role with regard to new industry' – and what de Stein had called, in his appeal to would-be subscribers, a 'practical gesture' had, in practice, the stress firmly on the second word.[83]

Yet all that said, the City in the 1930s, at both an institutional and a personal level, was far more embroiled in the often intractable difficulties of British industry than it ever had been before. Among the clearers, Midland was especially concerned with trying to restore the fortunes of the Lancashire textile industry, as well as straighten out the appalling Royal Mail imbroglio; the two main industrial areas that preoccupied Lloyds were coal in the North-East and steel in south Wales; while for National Provincial, concerns about iron and steel were supplemented by the problems of the Yorkshire woollen trade.[84] For all three banks, these may not have been a wholly welcome set of preoccupations, arising as they did out of imprudent lending soon after the war, but (as in the 1920s) their involvement could not be gainsaid.

For the merchant banks, the main orientation was towards the iron and steel industry – for instance, Rothschilds and Dorman Long, Morgan Grenfell and United Steel, and Hambros and Consett Iron Co.[85] Or take a handful of individuals whose involvement went far beyond passive advice and/or execution. The Ostrer brothers (Isidore, Maurice and Mark) were financiers who effectively ran Gaumont-British – making films, distributing them and owning cinemas – before selling out to J. Arthur Rank in 1936.[86] Leo d'Erlanger joined the family bank after the war, developed what his biographer calls 'a passionate interest in the aviation industry', and during the 1930s was not only largely responsible for the formation of British Airways, but also did an enormous amount to ensure that such manufacturing concerns as de Havilland and Short

416

Brothers were adequately financed.[87] And the stockbroker Edward Beddington-Behrens became so concerned about Montague Burton's complete absence of long-term financial planning that, after his firm (Myers & Co) had made a £2m issue for the company, he got himself elected to the board as Deputy Chairman and oversaw the financial aspect of an ambitious development programme that led to the opening of 200 shops in only four years.[88]

The supreme case in this period, however, was that of another youngish stockbroker, Edward Lewis.[89] During the 1928 new issue boom his small, recently established firm, E.R. Lewis & Co, had acted as brokers to the Decca Record Co, which manufactured and sold many gramophones, but only a few gramophone records. This struck Lewis as poor strategy, and when the newly floated company – hitherto a rather staid family business – ran into problems the following year, he found the money to enable Decca to take over the Duophone Record Co. At this point he joined the board, and by the early 1930s was effectively in charge of a business that was hit, like so many others, by the slump. In 1933 Decca's bank was about to pull the plug, but agreed to give Lewis three weeks to find at least £120,000. With only two days to go there was still a significant shortfall, with few in the City showing much inclination to back Decca, before the situation was saved by Harley Drayton deciding to take a £40,000 punt. Lewis needed the money in order to buy an American record company, Brunswick, whose star turn was Bing Crosby; and the following year, with that purchase made, Lewis was able to form the American Decca Co. For almost another half-century Lewis remained the commanding figure at Decca in Britain; and, as a good City man, his approach was essentially personal. 'He would do business with you if he liked you, but not otherwise,' an associate recalled. Until the early 1960s things went swimmingly, but the turning-point in Decca's fortunes was the fateful decision not to sign up the Beatles – a decision that perhaps would have been different, had Lewis himself been exposed to Brian Epstein's charm.

Turning back to pre-Cavern days, the 1930s, it is the clearing banks that have been subjected to most criticism in relation to the City's alleged failure during those years to help – or to help sufficiently – British industry. Three main charges have been made against them: that their approach rarely went beyond disciplining and reconstructing management, when it should have embraced large-scale reorganisation and rationalisation; second, that their lending policies were unduly conservative, with a paramount emphasis on short-term loans and an undue obsession about liquidity; and third, that those lending policies were deliberately skewed against small and medium-sized firms. The considerable, inevitably sometimes conflicting literature on the subject makes it clear enough, overall, that while each charge has some substance, there is not only a body of evidence suggesting that the banks in practice often went beyond their traditional cautious precepts, but also a danger of overlooking the difficult economic environment in which the banking system – admittedly, a cartelised banking system – was operating. 'At a time of bad trade, and in an atmosphere charged with impatience and irritability, quite insufficient recognition has been given to what has been done and is still being done by the Joint Stock Banks,' an unrepentant Lidbury stated in February 1933 to a meeting of industrial managers. 'I am particularly impressed by the fact,' he went on, 'that apparently neither the compilers of the Macmillan Report nor the Government, nor the industrialists, nor the Press, desires the Joint Stock Bank to live and make a profit.' And he insisted that 'the ultimate risk should be borne by the owner of the equity, who is the owner of the fruit which should flow from the exploitation of the business', whereas 'the function of the Joint Stock Banks is to assist in the direction of the utilisation of credit, and I do not think that they fall short of their duty in this respect, but rather believe that through an exaggerated regard for the public duty they land themselves constantly into losses which a more commercial regard for themselves would lead them to avoid'.[90] Such rhetorical flourishes apart, Lidbury well knew that nothing mattered, in the end, so much as the profit-and-loss figures; and though it may have been an approach to banking that lacked commercial imagination as well as national vision, there was and is much to be said for stability in a banking system.

The other main area of the rumbling City/industry debate concerned the efficiency of the domestic capital market. Did there indeed exist a 'Macmillan gap' – that is, the absence of capital-raising facilities for medium-sized companies requiring capital of somewhere between £50,000 and £200,000? Charterhouse Industrial Development Co and Leadenhall Securities, the latter created by Schröders in 1935, were two of the more important City initiatives aimed at filling this proposed gap. Neither initiative, however, achieved very much before the outbreak of war. Leadenhall's ambitions may have been blunted by the knowledge that Norman viewed this venture of Schröders with little enthusiasm – privately describing it as an 'industrial and possibly speculative business' and warning his discount office that Schröders 'are, to some extent, assuming an unliquid commitment in a direction other than banking and accepting'. Several investments were made in smallish companies, and a handful of flotations undertaken, but the scope of business was significantly restricted by the proviso that loans were to be for a five-year period prior to the firm concerned going public. As for Charterhouse, there was, Hume would recall, 'much publicity' in the immediate wake of the establishment of CIDC in summer 1934: 'As a result some 300 proposals came in by the first post, and it looked at first as if the company would be overwhelmed with business. This, however, proved to be wrong, for nearly every one of these and subsequent applications failed in the tests the Directors considered to be essential . . .' So stringent seem to have been those 'tests' that, by the end of the 1930s, CIDC had examined over 7,000 propositions, of which only seventeen had it been able to go any way towards financing. Hume added, in his progress report to Midland in 1940, 'that where there was any credit-worthiness either in capital or character, the Banks covered the position'.[91]

Such complacency was not shared by the man behind the other noteworthy capital-market response to the Macmillan gap. This was an old rival of Hume's, John Kinross, who after cutting his teeth in the late 1920s with Gresham Trust decided in autumn 1933 to set up his own issuing house, Cheviot Trust. A hectic period ensued, and between 1934 and 1938 he was responsible – sometimes under the Cheviot label, sometimes not – for over a hundred issues. He practised quality control as conscientiously as possible and was insistent that costs be kept to less than 10 per cent of the amount of cash raised. During these years he took on approximately one out of every 400 proposals received – which, in Kinross's case, did *not* lead him to the conclusion that there was no unsatisfied legitimate demand. Such was also the perception of the economically very literate stockbroker William Piercy, who in 1938 argued in *British Management Review* that although an increasingly vigorous new issue market had seen the upper threshold of the Macmillan gap significantly reduced over recent years, the gap itself had not gone away.[92]

Nor was that all, for in the 1930s, even with Hatry behind bars and other unsavoury company promoters of the 1920s apparently extinguished by the slump, a decidedly mixed crew still operated the London market in British industrial new issues. Crucially, although such utterly reputable merchant banks as Barings, Morgan Grenfell and Lazards were indeed shifting their focus increasingly away from international and towards domestic matters, their impact as yet was only limited.[93] To take the figures for one year, 1937, the only merchant banks that managed to sponsor or co-sponsor as many as six issues were Barings and Helbert Wagg – whereas no fewer than five stockbroking firms achieved double figures entirely off their own bats, although admittedly almost all of them were smaller issues than those done by the merchant banks.[94] Put another way, it does seem likely that a mixture of prudence, habit and perhaps a certain disdain for what was still sometimes seen as second-class business combined to hold back the merchant banks from an unequivocal commitment to the domestic new issue market.

A revealing episode occurred in January 1935, following the death of Lord Riddell, Chairman of the *News of the World*. The Public Trustee approached Morgan Grenfell to discuss the possibility of the News of the World Ltd being converted into a public company and to ask whether Morgan Grenfell would do it. The answer was no. 'Although it was not so stated,' Charles Whigham noted, 'Mr Fass was quite aware that our refusal was due not only to the operation involving newspaper finance [with which Morgan Grenfell had always avoided getting involved] but that the newspaper in question was not a suitable one.' Whigham did, however, agree on Fass's behalf to canvas Peacock at Barings. It was not quite the thing for 8 Bishopsgate, either:

> Sir Edward said that he had no hesitation in saying that Barings would not themselves undertake such an issue. He thought the matter was of the greatest interest and importance. He agreed that it was unlikely that any of the first class houses would undertake the issue and that probably if a public issue were made the only method would be to employ a firm like Cazenoves or one of the other leading brokerage firms to handle it . . .

Cazenove's was indeed by this time a leading, high-class company broker – sponsoring or co-sponsoring as many as nineteen issues in 1937 – and others that were both active and highly regarded in this field included Cohen Laming Hoare, Panmure Gordon, Greenwells and Rowe, Swann & Co. There was also Myers & Co, the outfit run by Mossy Myers, which with one or two exceptions had a pretty good list and was responsible for a wide range of new industrial issues. Other broking firms were active but had the reputation of doing anything for a fee, though there were fewer of them than in the boom of the late 1920s – no doubt partly because, even when the new issue market was at its most active in the mid-1930s, there was nothing like the utterly indiscriminate bubble effect that had characterised the Hatry era.[95]

Many issues (probably between one-third and a half) were brought out by neither merchant banks nor stockbrokers, but by a variety of finance and issuing houses. Again, quality was far from uniform. Investment Registry and London Industrial Finance Trust were both, for example, perfectly sound if not particularly dynamic; but the same did not apply to Whitehead Industrial Trust, the creation of Arthur Whitehead, whose brilliance at persuading the chairmen of medium-sized businesses to plump for a Stock Exchange quotation was matched by an almost complete lack of interest in the quality and long-term prospects of those businesses. Like Philip Hill, Whitehead's offices were in the West End, but also like Hill the stock market was his indispensable vehicle. Whitehead himself, prior to establishing his own organisation in February 1936, had previously been the driving force at London Industrial and then tried but failed to persuade Kinross to sell half of Cheviot; he now, in Kinross's stern words, 'predictably proceeded to churn out the largest number of issues of any industrial issuing house'.[96] Yet even he, it seems, could not fill the 'gap' single-handed.

Many of the domestic industrial new issues were made not through the traditional method of inviting public subscription via a published prospectus, but by what was known as a Stock Exchange 'introduction', in effect a private placing direct on to the market, in the first instance, through the jobbers.[97] The appeal of this latter method was obvious, especially in terms of smallish issues and cutting down on advertising costs, but it tended to be open to abuse, especially in the bull market of the mid-1930s when the investing public came to feel – quite justifiably – that it was not getting a fair bite, or sometimes any bite, at the cherry. Matters came to a head in June 1935, after a private placing of £360,000 Bristol Aeroplane ordinary shares had been arranged by Cazenove's just before Baldwin announced in the Commons that the existing target for the RAF's front-line strength was to be doubled. The result was an immediate boom in the aeroplane market, leading to fat profits for some lucky Stock Exchange members when dealings began in the shares. Those members who had failed to acquire shares at the time of placing were probably even crosser than investors at large; and one of them may have been Walter Landells who, wearing what was usually his very uncritical hat as 'Autolycus', argued that 'it may be better, possibly, for everyone to have the chance of applying for shares on a prospectus, than to put down their names on lists of orders to buy at the opening price'.

The chorus of protest, from both within and without the House, prompted the Stock Exchange Committee in July to set up a special sub-committee to examine the whole question of these introductions. That autumn a series of leading members, especially brokers, was summoned to give evidence on the subject. A few conceded that there were legitimate grievances, but most did not. 'Any restrictions would prove harmful to the public as well as the Vendors and the Stock Exchange,' thought Charles Micklem of Cazenove's. Kit Hoare 'took the view that the only people who complained were those who had lost money'. E.W. Hamilton of Govett, Sons & Co 'considered that any grievance the public might have amounted to a flash-in-the-pan over certain issues'. R.S. Rogers of Keith, Bayley & Rigg (brokers who had been responsible for some introductions) 'said the grievance had been fostered by the newspapers' and 'thought it amounted purely to "sour grapes"'. And Fred Pitman of Rowe & Pitman agreed, saying that it was his firm's 'general opinion' that 'the agitation against the method of "introducing" shares had come from sources of which too much notice need not be taken,' those sources being 'the Press and disappointed "stags"'. The sub-committee reported in February 1936 and soon afterwards, in accordance with its recommendations, the Stock Exchange Committee publicly declared that it was 'desirable that all issues, particularly those of Ordinary Capital, should be made by Prospectus or Offer for Sale unless from a public standpoint the necessity or advantage of a private placing is indicated by the circumstances'. However, these were words only, unaccompanied by a change to the rules, and if anything the popularity of the method actually increased in the years before the war.[98] Even so, the very phrase 'the public standpoint' had its significance, for it was not one that the rulers of the Stock Exchange had traditionally been much given to employing.

The decision not to ban introductions allowed a classic Stock Exchange set-piece to be played out in October 1936. On Thursday the 15th, against a background of the motors section of the Industrial market being particularly bullish, four firms of jobbers were to start dealing at ten o'clock in a huge block of Morris Motors ordinary shares that had been acquired from Lord Nuffield. 'A frantic rush is expected,' noted 'The Diarist' in that morning's *FT*. It had been, he added, 'half-seriously suggested that to avoid a hopeless jam a section of the House should be marked off by Belisha beacons and that brokers be compelled to follow a one-way route around the besieged jobbers'. Soon after nine-thirty, when the Stock Exchange's doors opened, 'Autolycus' was in the thick of the action:

> As the time went on the crowds increased, until, at five minutes to ten o'clock the queue waiting for one firm reached for more than 50 yards, and it must have been pretty nearly ten deep. Somewhat similar conditions obtained around the other three firms. It was obvious, of course, that those nearest the front would get the cheapest shares.
>
> As the clocks struck ten there were loud cheers and immediately the buyers nearest to the jobbers who had the shares to sell were able to buy Morris Ordinary at 39s, up to a specified number of shares. The crowds

had now swollen to a degree that has never been seen around individual firms in the Stock Exchange before. There were violent swayings from side to side. Literally, one was off one's feet every now and then.

The heat and the noise were almost overpowering. Men threw up their arms, with extended fingers to show how many shares they wanted to buy. As one struggled nearer and nearer to the dealers who were selling the shares, so, vaguely, the quotation became known. It was in the highest degree tantalising to hear the price going up by sixpence every few minutes, without being able to buy shares at a particular figure, owing, of course, to the enormous pressure, not only in front, but all round.

When one got right up to the jobbers who were selling the shares, the price at which they could be bought was made certain. It took one man, I know personally, twenty very painful minutes to achieve this object.

Maybe this sketchy explanation will serve to let clients know how it was that their limits were executed at what must have been varying prices . . .

Nevertheless, despite all the personal discomfort and invidiousness of the situation, Landells was not inclined to criticise the Stock Exchange Committee, pointing out that if they had 'thrown technical obstacles in the way of doing the business' the upshot would only have been that Nuffield would have marketed his shares either in New York or on one of the provincial stock exchanges.

The *FT* itself was less sanguine – 'little can be done,' argued an editorial, 'to convince the general public that the Stock Exchange functions predominantly as an investment market proper when such an example of frenzied gambling as this is broadcast throughout the country' – but the Committee neither launched an inquiry nor amended its rules.[99] They may have been the most tumultuous scenes in the House since the introduction of American Marconis back in 1912, but in the eyes of most members that was far from being a signal to give even the lightest touch to the regulatory tiller.

*

The 1930s had its share of rogues, scoundrels and morally challenged creative financiers – though none perhaps in the Hooley or Hatry class. There were, for example, the 180 or so keepers of bucket shops, who as outside brokers were exempt from the rules of the Stock Exchange and were often engaged in share-pushing exercises that amounted to a systematic attempt to defraud the public. Not all these outside brokers were entirely villainous, and as a class they represented a twin threat: significant competition to the Stock Exchange, whose members were still not allowed to advertise, in effect a continuing form of quality control;

and an ominous reminder to the City as a whole that its own act must be cleaned up, lest London be compelled to go down the American road, where the establishment in 1934 of the Securities and Exchange Commission more or less ended self-regulation on Wall Street. In 1936 a Board of Trade inquiry into bucket shops and share pushers received full support from the Stock Exchange Committee, and the eventual outcome was the enactment in February 1939 of the Prevention of Frauds (Investment) Act, which just about killed off the bucket shops.[100]

Martin Harman – the self-styled 'King of Lundy Island' – would not have been seen dead in one of them. The first two decades of his City career had been spent with Lazards, his investment vehicle was the Rock Investment Co, his interests were far-flung, and in February 1930 Norman confessed to Hopkins of the Treasury that 'Harman is rather a friend of mine and a gorgeous buccaneer, but has great difficulty keeping his feet on the ground!' That same month Harman called on Norman, 'begging that Rock may open a/c here & receive advance of £15/20m [i.e. thousands] against a mixed parcel of Sec^s (inc Lundy)'. However, Norman continued, 'I say not reasonable & practical politics for Bk'. Harman's problems were only just beginning: in 1932 he failed with liabilities of £500,000; and later that year he was charged with 'fraudulent conspiracy' and sent to Wormwood Scrubs for eighteen months. 'He was a rugged, bull-headed man more suited to his island in the Bristol Channel than the City,' recalled one not unsympathetic confidant, the journalist Francis Williams. '"We hold the exposed positions," he said, "while your banker pals keep out of range. We get the casualties. They get the cash."'[101]

There was nothing bull-like about Claude Albo de Bernales. He came from a line of Basque-Spanish nobility and was an elegant, sophisticated figure, who spent freely on the good things of life. In a sense a more urbane version of Whitaker Wright, he had made his fortune on the goldfields of Western Australia, but by the 1930s was largely based in London, floating between 1932 and 1936 a whole series of intricately financed Western Australian investment corporations that together comprised the Commonwealth Mining & Finance Group. He enjoyed giving big lunches at the Great Eastern Hotel, where he would eloquently talk up the latest, usually specious reports about new fields being found; and on the whole he enjoyed a not unfavourable press, until in September 1936 the 'Midas' columnist on the *Financial News* – a stockbroker of high analytical intelligence called Harold Cowen – uncovered enough information and suspicious circumstances to pull the plug on the huge speculative gamble that was being orchestrated in the group. Thereafter the fortunes of de Bernales were on the wane, culminating in criminal proceedings during the 1940s.[102]

If de Bernales was on the way out, Denys Lowson was only just starting. His background was Winchester and Christ Church, he married in 1936 the younger daughter of the 1st Baron Strathcarron, and his speciality was the still very youthful field of unit trusts – a field regarded with much suspicion by the Stock Exchange, but broadly welcomed by the Bank of England on account of the original pioneer involvement of one of its directors, George Booth. In 1935 Lowson became Managing Director of Security First Trust, and over the next few years built up what became known as the Fifteen Moorgate group of unit trusts. As for his methods, one can only quote what would become the much-cherished words of his eventual obituary in *The Times*:

> Lowson began his career in the City before the [1939] war, when the standards of financial morality and duty to shareholders were less developed than they are today [1975]. He showed consistently that he was more concerned to turn situations to the advantage of himself and the interests he controlled than with his fiduciary duty to the companies of which he was a director. His reputation in this respect was established with the more respected leaders of the City early in his career and his methods never represented the best City practice.[103]

Indeed they did not – but that did not stop a long and profitable City career proceeding to unfold.

Yet nothing in the 1930s quite matched the pepper scandal.[104] John Harrison was a successful, middle-aged financier who was Chairman of the London Tin Corporation and specialised in floating tin companies. Several of his early flotations were distinctly inflationary, and he seems to have been regarded in the City with a mixture of mistrust and respect. During the first half of 1934 he hatched a scheme with Garabed Bishirgian, a leading Armenian-born commodity broker, whose goal was nothing less than to corner the world market in white pepper. To secure the necessary funds, Harrison acquired a small firm of commodity brokers, James & Shakspeare, and with the assistance of Cull & Co floated it that September. The word 'pepper' did not feature in the prospectus. In the event, the corner failed, not least because those attempting to perpetrate it overlooked the fact that black pepper was capable of being processed into white. Such was the almost unlimited credit that some of the leading Mincing Lane brokers had extended to James & Shakspeare that by the end of January 1935 it was not only that firm which was in trouble. There ensued an intense drama.

The bank most intimately involved was Midland, not least because McKenna was not only Chairman of Tobacco Securities Trust, a subsidiary of which had invested in James & Shakspeare, but was also himself a shareholder in that firm. As the storm broke, he was on a boat to South Africa, leaving Hyde to field alone a visit from Harrison (accompanied by three commodity brokers) on Thursday the 31st. Having been informed 'that the position of pepper was very critical' and that 'unless some steps were taken it was likely to lead to many failures amongst the Mincing Lane brokers', Hyde was asked whether 'a Pool might be formed to lift the surplus quantity of pepper off the market'. Hyde's immediate response was negative, on the grounds that 'I did not think that anyone would want to increase their finance against pepper under present conditions'. He promised, however, to sound out the other banks, and a meeting was arranged for the following afternoon. One of the banks contacted was Westminster, where R.E.W. Mount was in charge in Lidbury's absence on Standstill business in Berlin. Mount sent a representative, and reported on the outcome in his Friday evening despatch to Lidbury:

> L. [Lloyds] were not represented (their real reason being that they did not see why they should pull other people's chestnuts out of the fire!). The object of Mr H. [Hyde] seemed to be to ascertain the feeling of the various banks as to whether there was any disposition to form a pool to carry the position arising out of the forthcoming settlement on the 8th. It was, however, pointed out by him that the real trouble arose owing to the c.i.f. position which would immediately arise owing to the imminent arrival of various shipments of pepper, all of which was understood to be sold eventually to J. & S.
>
> Mr H. seemed disinclined to help in the matter, and inasmuch as they are believed to be very fully concerned, it did not seem obvious to the rest of the meeting why they themselves should enter into the suggested pool. Inasmuch as Mr H. did not himself formulate any plan, nothing was done. Obviously the M. [Midland] are very interested, but it was not emphasised! The trouble will probably boil over on Monday and the immediately succeeding days as the first boat is expected to arrive either on Sunday or Monday. The feeling is that the repercussions may be far reaching.

Midland's exposure was indeed not emphasised, for according to an account of the crisis that Westminster's James Greenhill sent to Lidbury some days later, at the meeting on the 1st, Hyde 'said that his Bank was concerned only with a few small advances', but 'it has since transpired that the Midland Bank admit to having advanced James & Shakspeare £100,000'.

Next day, Saturday the 2nd, the General Produce Brokers' Association formally appealed to the clearing banks to provide around £2m and thereby avert 'a most serious crisis', especially in Mincing Lane, where 'a large number of smaller Brokers and traders will be ruined'. 'There is a more hopeful feeling in Mincing Lane late this afternoon but what it rests upon is not known,' Mount informed Lidbury on Monday the 4th, and next afternoon the bankers assembled at the Clearing House to consider their response to the application for assistance. By this time the pepper market had formed an *ad hoc* committee, comprising representatives of Samuel Figgis & Co, C. Czarnikow Ltd, Lewis & Peat, Edward Boustead & Co, and Faure, Blattmann & Co (of whom Figgis and Lewis & Peat were both heavily committed), and the appeal to the bankers was reiterated, in the context of payment for £1.8m being due later that week. There was no joy for the Mincing Lane men, for behind closed doors 'the banks all agreed', Hyde recorded, 'that it was an improper thing to finance this pepper, especially having regard to the fact that the present price was an inflated one and the quantity of pepper to be dealt with represented several years consumption in this country and probably 2/3 years of the whole world consumption'. Hyde added that 'it was agreed generally that the banks would regard sympathetically the requirements of any of their own customers in order to avoid the failure spreading to a large number of brokers, but this would have to be on business lines'.[105] It sounded a crisp – and final – enough decision.

The bankers reckoned without Norman, who had been keeping closely in touch with the situation and indeed had known about the impending difficulties since the previous November. 'I do nothing leaving trouble to McKenna,' he had tersely jotted in his diary then. By Thursday the 7th, with James & Shakspeare going bankrupt and two commodity firms sinking in its wake, he saw no alternative but to step in. '1.15. Bkrs meeting – till 2 pm: then Lunch: then again till 4 pm.' Behind that flat entry lay a highly charged afternoon, on the occasion of the clearing bankers' regular quarterly meeting at the Bank of England. It is best told from the standpoint of the Westminster, whose Beckett and Tennant were both present on its behalf. 'The Governor intimated that it was his wish,' Greenhill wrote later that day to Lidbury, 'that assistance from the banks should be forthcoming, even if such assistance were given to those who had been gambling and those who were really not entitled, on their financial position, to receive such assistance'. Beckett and Tennant left the meeting at 3.30 in order to discuss the matter with Sir Malcolm Hogg, another Westminster director. Whereupon, Greenhill told Lidbury (whose vexation about the turn of events one can only imagine), 'it was decided that this Bank should conform to the wishes of the Governor and make the necessary advances', in Westminster's case up to £198,000 to four specific firms. 'I am afraid it is a case of force majeure,' continued Greenhill, 'and neither the Chairman, nor Mr Tennant nor Sir Malcolm Hogg, and certainly the General Managers, felt that Westminster Bank could undertake the responsibility of throwing into chaos a scheme which had been evolved by Mincing Lane to meet this crisis and which had received the backing of the Governor.' The outcome was the formation of a pepper pool, which ultimately had forty-one participants and which over the next six years disposed of over 20,000 tons of pepper. Perhaps Lidbury did not mind at the time, or perhaps he became reconciled, for in February 1941 he would write to B. Figgis, Chairman of the London Pepper Sales Control Committee, that the intervention of the banks in 1935 had 'had the desired effect of limiting the extent of damage already done and preventing what might have degenerated into a catastrophe'.[106]

In February 1936, a year after Norman had so adeptly twisted the bankers' arms, Harrison, Bishirgian and another associate were all found guilty of publishing a false prospectus and sent to prison. Two months later, Norman left no room for doubt when privately asked what Harrison should do when he came out: 'I say go far East, or far West: never show his nose in London: he can & sh^d have no moral standing & is not welcome here, ever.' The pepper scandal also had the effect of making Norman reconsider the Bank's traditional attitude of non-involvement in the commercial world east of Bishopsgate and Grace-church Street. 'You may remember our chance meeting at the end of the Mall about a month ago,' he reminded John Niven, Chairman of the Baltic Exchange, in November 1935, 'when I was so bold as to point a finger at the Brokers of Mincing Lane: my experiences of last winter, I told you, were enough to induce me to do so! You, on the other hand, gave me to understand that any changes in the arrangements of those Brokers were more your affair than mine.'[107] Norman did not push the matter unduly, but it was a significant sighter.

Arguably, however, the real losers from the affair were the two top men at Midland. Wilfrid Crick, co-author in 1936 of the bank's centenary history, would recall how in the absence of McKenna when the crisis broke it was left to Hyde 'to carry the can, and he never quite recovered from this'. As for McKenna himself, he found himself under a public cloud as early as 16 February 1935, when the *Economist* identified his shareholding involvement in James & Shakspeare and asked whether he had been 'personally privy' to the 'speculative manipulations' that had taken place in the pepper market. Of course he had not, and in relation to the proceeds of the James & Shakspeare issue he was able to assure the Official Receiver that 'pepper was never even mentioned to him'. He also, on 1 May 1935 after his return from South Africa, opened himself to Norman. 'An hour protesting pain, surprise & innocence as to any knowledge of or dealings in pepper,' Norman noted about what must have been, on both sides, an uncomfortable meeting.[108]

Although his senior directors talked him out of his offer to resign Midland's chairmanship, McKenna's zest for the job, and his hitherto supreme self-confidence in performing it, never quite recovered. For a decade and a half he and Hyde had successfully consolidated the remarkable achievement of their mutual mentor, Holden; now, with Barclays hard on Midland's heels, the years of assured dominance were drawing to an end, and the pepper fiasco cruelly symbolised the changing order.

CHAPTER SIXTEEN

Jitter Bugs

The City did not, on the whole, have an insuperable problem with the idea of authoritarian government. Early in 1933, for example, the Bank of England's Harry Siepmann assured the Treasury that if Portugal – which had recently come under Salazar's rule – 'wanted to borrow money in this market', it was 'sure to be given a sympathetic hearing at any time'. The Portuguese had, he went on, 'done marvellously well, and their country is being run by a man who, I suppose, is one of the three or four most eminent men in Europe'. He added that since 'the constitutional question was gone into long ago, and even the lawyers gave it a clean bill, there can be no kind of reason for digging it up again now'. Portugal was, however, merely a bit-player on the European stage compared to Germany, on whose economic recovery rested so many hopes. On 19 January 1933, the day after Siepmann's encouraging noises about Portugal, Sir Edward Reid in Berlin sent his latest assessment to Villiers at 8 Bishopsgate. Although the political situation was, as usual, 'obscure and unsatisfactory', the fundamentals were positive: 'Germany has come through so far, and has the enormous advantages of efficient industries, hardworking and law-abiding people, and an organised government . . . There is less reason now to doubt her coming through than there was a year or even eight months ago . . .' He did not deny, however, that there were 'many difficulties and uncertainties still ahead'.[1]

Twelve days later the front page of the *Financial News* had two main headlines: in the top left-hand corner: 'Kaffirs Higher Still'; in the top right-hand corner: 'Herr Hitler – Chancellor of Germany'. The main editorial was entitled 'Heil Hitler!' and began: 'If ever man had a right to chuckle, the little Austrian pocket-Mussolini has justification for chuckling today.' The paper then argued, however, that Hitler would be the prisoner of the non-Nazi majority in the Cabinet, indeed that 'it is, to say the least of it, highly unlikely that the Nazis would attempt to base their power on armed force'. The *FN*'s pink rival was almost equally comforting: 'Finance is left in the capable hands of Count Schwerin von Krosigle . . .'[2]

On 18 March 1933, some seven weeks after Hitler's elevation, Reid in Berlin sent Alec Baring a letter that was shown to Peacock, who in turn sent a copy to Norman. Reid's progress report sympathised with the new government's irritation about criticisms in the foreign press: 'Of course Jews have been molested, and a few people (including an American newspaper correspondent) knocked on the head, but these events were local and individual and the life of the great populace went on as usual . . . One sees a lot of swastika flags about and a lot of Nazis with collecting boxes standing at the corners of streets, but otherwise no change at all can be noticed.' Reid had also been listening to the views of German bankers, and he passed on their encouraging judgement that 'in all important matters Hitler has up to now been very sensible and has listened to the advice of those entitled to give it'. Nevertheless, he added on his own account, 'what one does not know is how he will be able to keep the discipline of his gang when the first enthusiasm has worn off and a new government appears to be as dull and humdrum as any other'. Three days later Reid wrote again. This time he was less sanguine about what had happened since the end of January: 'There has been a complete revolution here; more than a change of government, a change of regime.' Part of this revolution included the disappearance of freedom of speech, as well as the fact that 'the Jewish population feel very uncomfortable and have reason to do so'. Even so, 'Hitler himself now holds very sensible views, and he and most of his colleagues are doing their best to control the situation'. Two days later, on 23 March, Hitler successfully demanded the passing of the Enabling Act, effectively creating the Nazi dictatorship. In his report next day, Reid (by now in Frankfurt am Main) noted that Hitler's speech had made 'an excellent impression' and that 'he is well advised, and listens to his advisers, and his responsibilities have made a real man of him'. As for those obstinate stories in the foreign press about anti-Semitic atrocities, they were 'gross exaggerations', and Reid added that 'the removal of Jews from their public posts, which has occurred on quite a large scale, is largely justified'.[3]

It is easy, of course, to job backwards, and it is only fair to remember that Reid's concerns (like those of almost any City man) were primarily financial, not social or political. 'Over here most people feel that, in the long run, Germany may settle down and overcome its troubles successfully,' Alec Baring wrote at the end of March to an American correspondent, and most would have concurred with what was a wish as much as an opinion. Nor, anyway, were the larger, international politics of the situation as clear-cut as they would ultimately become. 'His attack on the Versailles Treaty will nowhere in the City be resented,' the *FT* asserted after a major speech by Hitler in May, and the City's view was widely shared. So too, at this stage, was its admiration for the senior dictator. 'The Renaissance of Italy: Fascism's Gift of Order and Progress' was the title of an *FT* special supplement the following month, which came complete with a signed photograph of a studious-looking Mussolini.[4] Over the next six years – as hope gave way to fear and then eventually to a slightly unsteady resolve – the City was rarely out of step with the national mood.

*

Within months of Hitler's rise to power the City had achieved a financial *modus vivendi* with the new, rather unsettling German regime. The first, and indispensable, step was the renewal for the second time of the 1931 Standstill Agreement, whereby the German banks agreed to continue to pay interest in return for the huge credits that had been made to them staying frozen. In the City there was some resistance from Midland, which felt that the two British delegates in Berlin – Tiarks and Brand – were trying to 'bounce' the London bankers as a whole into the renewed agreement. 'I have good hope,' Brand sought to reassure Hyde at the end of February 1933, 'that unless political disasters intervene, the Standstill creditors may be able in a year or two to dispense with the Standstill.' And he added, about the concessions over interest and discount rates that he and Tiarks had felt compelled to make, that 'very powerful interests in the new German government have opinions about interest rates and foreign debts decidedly different from those of bankers, and there seemed a considerable risk for the future in our adopting a completely uncompromising attitude'. Midland agreed to stay in the Standstill arrangements, and on 16 May all the City's bankers were shocked when the Reichsbank warned the Bank of England that Germany would henceforth be unable to pay in foreign currency the interest on all outstanding loans. Tiarks and Brand at once travelled to Berlin, lobbied extremely hard and were rewarded on 8 June when Standstill credits were excluded from the interest transfer moratorium on Germany's external obligations that was declared that day.[5]

For accepting houses like Kleinworts and Schröders, the continuing existence of the Standstill Agreement, broadly in the form as established in 1931, was integral to their very survival. There was also, from the point of view of these Anglo-German houses, a strong *emotional* commitment to the revival of the Germany economy – a revival that would, of course, enable the credits to be unfrozen and a welcome return to commercial and financial normality to be achieved. An illuminating episode occurred in late May 1933, when Schrobanco, the New York house of Schröders, insisted – directly against the wishes of Tiarks and Baron Bruno – on liquidating its German debts. For Schröders, that was an impossible option, in terms of both balance-sheet and sentiment. At a meeting of the Accepting Houses Committee, on 12 June, Tiarks could hardly have been more explicit about his long-term commitment to the German economy: 'He pointed out that the Standstill Agreement should not be looked upon as a basis for getting out of Germany, and that its true object was to tide matters over until the time arrived when it would become unnecessary, owing to the desire of credit givers to resume their ordinary operations of granting credits to German concerns.' It was a viewpoint which, as applied to the international banking stage, was wholly shared by Norman. 'I believe the interests of the B.I.S. [Bank for International Settlements], the Reichsbank and the Bank of England to be identical,' Norman informed a fellow-central banker that September. 'I do not think any of them should act without the others . . .'[6]

So it largely continued in 1934, as Hitler suppressed all opposition at home and engaged in a thorough policy of what has been aptly described as 'bloodcurdling warnings interspersed with conciliatory gestures'. Early in the year Norman defined 'a Hitlerite' in a positive way, being someone who 'accepts private initiative subject to public advantage'; while in early July he offered Sir James Grigg a revealing commentary about the very recent Night of the Long Knives:

> We [i.e. in London] are engrossed in the purging process by which Hitler is dealing with the Nazi Party: late as many think, and therefore more bloody; but maybe not too late to save and maintain a moderate situation. My friends declare that the lateness of Hitler has been due to his affection for the buccaneers and burglars who stood with him throughout the hard years, of whom he was loath to believe extreme intentions and still less disloyalty.

The sense is of reportage, but Norman did not distance himself from the interpretation. Later that month he was in New York, where a partner of Morgans summarised his latest thoughts: 'Monty says that Hitler and Schacht are the bulwarks of civilisation in Germany and the only friends we have. They are fighting the war of our system of society against communism. If they fail, communism will follow in Germany, and anything may follow in Europe.' Norman pinned quite unrealistic hopes on Hjalmar Schacht, who by August 1934 was Minister of Economics as well as President of the Reichsbank. Norman's congratulatory letter to him sounded a regretful note – 'financially as well as economically our affairs have come to be more and more dominated by politics' – but expressed the hope that 'in your double role you may somehow be able to surmount the difficulties ahead of you without abandoning those sound principles with which all through these years your name and policy has been associated'.[7]

Again, it is important to get the right historical perspective. Hugh Dalton a few months later would publicly note that Norman was 'rumoured' to be pursuing 'pro-Nazi politics'; but even as early as 1934 it would be true to say that Norman's stance was pro-German rather than pro-Nazi, even though he was still prepared, for the time being, to give Hitler himself the benefit of the doubt. In this stance, he broadly reflected as well as influenced City opinion as a whole. Certainly, there was little inclination yet in the square mile to ride the Russian horse as an alternative to the German. In April 1934, after H.G. Wells had mentioned to Brendan Bracken that Maisky, the Russian Ambassador in London, was complaining that he never met any bankers, Bracken sent on Wells's letter to Lidbury, and added: 'If you have no strong objection to Russians as such, it might be desirable to get Maisky to lunch – more especially if you still retain your view that we may go Bolshie after the next general election.' To which Lidbury replied: 'I am not sure that I ought to meet "M" at the office, but it might be that one evening next week I could perhaps arrange a little dinner at my Club ...'[8]

Interminable, highly complex negotiations in the course of 1934 ensured that the Standstill Agreement remained in place to underpin the pro-German orientation.[9] In January there was serious alarm when the British government seemed to be pursuing a policy of pressing for a unilateral Anglo-German clearing arrangement, with a view to protecting the interests of trade and financial creditors in Britain as a whole, not just the interests of the Standstill creditors. Such a clearing would, in practice, not only have disqualified German bills from being traded in the London discount market, thereby making impossible any renewal of the Standstill credits, but would also have been a severe blow to London's standing as a repository of overseas money and securities. Neville Chamberlain told his sister that the government's policy had 'put the City in a blue funk', but in the event the Germans promised to treat British creditors more considerately and the threat of a clearing was called off. As soon as June, however, it re-emerged, under the provocation of Germany being seemingly about to default on her long-term debts. 'He is fully alive to the dangers of a German clearing to you Standstill folk,' Norman reassured Tiarks on the 22nd about Chamberlain's attitude, 'and he realises that if there is trouble your blood may fall on his head. I have told him so a dozen times and he accepts it.'[10]

In early July an Anglo-German agreement did give some joy to the justly aggrieved British bondholders, and what Norman called 'the hated clearing' was again avoided. But yet again the ugly possibility raised its head in October, in the context of the British government wanting to do something for British traders (suffering from frozen commercial debts to Germany) to complement what had been done for British bondholders. Norman recorded McKenna on the 12th as 'angry but powerless & bitter agst Ch Ex', while Norman himself warned his colleagues later in the month that if the Standstill Agreement (which had been renewed again earlier in the year) was made untenable, then the Bank might need to organise the rescue of at least four Standstill creditors. An Anglo-German payments agreement, to help British traders, was reached at the start of November, and once again a more general clearing was avoided, to the disgust of the Foreign Office but palpable relief of the City, or at least of the Standstill creditors. From the viewpoint of British trade creditors it was not a particularly wonderful agreement, but such were Chamberlain's anxieties – 'horrible possibilities of the bankruptcy of some of the great English financial firms had been hanging over me ever since I took office and just lately they have been very menacing,' he confided at one point – and such was Norman's skill at playing upon those anxieties that perhaps such an outcome was inevitable.[11]

In February 1935, for the annual Standstill renewal, Tiarks and Brand were joined at their regular Berlin base, the Esplanade Hotel, by a new British delegate. 'If and when the Treasury asks for a liaison banker in the German matter,' Peacock had advised the Bank of England's Ruby Holland-Martin the previous autumn, 'we should have a good two-fisted fellow. I suggest Lidbury for your consideration.' For the moment, Lidbury was content to back up the two senior bankers, and the renewal proceeded smoothly enough. Two months later, in April 1935, the regular monthly meeting at Basle of the Bank for International Settlements happened to coincide with the conference at Stresa where Britain, France and Italy showed a united front in condemning Germany's repudiation of her Treaty of Versailles obligations. On his return Norman confided in Addis: 'There was only one subject of conversation from Boulogne back to Calais ... which seemed in everyone's thoughts – war, war, when, where, how. And practically today all due to Nerves: at least I believe it to be as remote as the Millennium. And so does Schacht . . .'[12]

Within months, however, the threat of war came not from Germany but from Italy. On 19 August, Roy Sambourne was the usual accurate, slightly hysterical barometer, at least of those not in the know: 'Feel worried re City. Thank God I have something put by – liquid so to speak . . . Market very flat on Abyssinia – very anxious . . .' A month and a day later, with the crisis having worsened and the British Foreign Secretary, Sir Samuel Hoare, having apparently committed Britain to taking part in collective intervention on behalf of the League of Nations, Sambourne's nerves were tauter still: 'We have had a very bad a/c – but it might have been worse. I am terribly anxious – Italy will say "No" & what then – God help us all . . .' However, those in the City a little closer to the centres of power than Sambourne would probably have concurred with Alec Baring, who a few days later, on 23 September, told one of his American correspondents that 'most people in their heart of hearts feel that the present crisis will in some way or other peter out without a major conflict'.[13]

So it was. On 2 October, with rumours rife on the Stock Exchange that Italy had invaded Abyssinia, 'Autolycus' caught the Capel Court mood, at its most inimitable:

> The apprehension that lurks at the back of most people's minds is that the League of Nations may consider it advisable to apply sanctions. Such a contingency, though apparently present in current circumstances, is regarded as likely to be fraught with consequences too grave for it to be lightly undertaken. The House was quite ready to be amused with the caption that appeared on a list of prices in the Consol market:-
>
> Italy 27 for 2
> Rain stopped play.

Italy invaded Abyssinia on the 3rd, and four days later 'Autolycus', in a column headed 'A Return of Confidence', recorded that 'majority opinion considers negligible the risk of the League applying military Sanctions'. Over the next two and a half months the City seems to have been almost solidly behind the Baldwin government in its various diplomatic twists and turns; while as for the imposition that autumn of financial sanctions, prohibiting the flotation of Italian loans or the opening of banking or other credits for Italian nationals, this according to the *Banker* in November 'left the City largely unmoved'. This was because 'most British banks had decided some time ago not to open fresh Italian credits and close down existing credit lines as quickly as they could', having 'done this simply because for the moment Italy was not considered a safe risk'.[14] By the end of 1935 the League of Nations, and accompanying notions of collective security, had lost almost all credibility – but few in the City lamented the fact.

Hitler's unopposed reoccupation of the Rhineland on 7 March 1936 confirmed that the dictators had an almost free hand. 'Herr Hitler has acted with his customary precipitancy,' the *FT* declared on the Monday morning after this Saturday jolt, before arguing that from the event 'may well emerge in the end a clearer prospect of European peace than has existed for a generation past'. On the Stock Exchange itself, the mood on the Monday was similarly calm, according to 'Autolycus':

> Strange as it may appear, the majority opinion seems to be rather pleased than otherwise at the abrupt turn which the politics of Europe have taken under the direction of Herr Hitler. That some step of this kind was bound to occur, it is generally agreed: that it would come quite so soon is the more matter for surprise.
>
> In no part of the House did I hear any suggestion of a European conflagration. Provided that people keep calm at the present time, it is considered that the action of Herr Hitler is likely to prove in the interests of peace rather than of war.

By Tuesday the 10th, Landells noted, Stock Exchange markets had 'all but regained their accustomed attitude of financial philosophy that was somewhat rudely shaken by the unexpectedness of Herr Hitler's action last Saturday'. Or, expressed more musically, 'the rattle of the sword in its scabbard died away to a quiet piano'.[15]

If, however, the City as a whole wanted peace above everything, and could not get very steamed up when what most saw as a legitimate grievance was redressed, that did not mean that the positively pro-German lobby (which from 1935 took institutional form in the Anglo-German Fellowship, of which Tiarks and Kindersley were both individual members) could operate without constraints. Early in 1936, during the run-up to the annual Standstill renewal, the opposition of Anthony Eden (who had succeeded Hoare) prevented Norman from pushing hard for Germany to become a member of the sterling bloc;[16] in May that year allegations in the House of Commons concerning credits and advances made to German borrowers outside the Standstill Agreement forced a formal denial from the clearing banks and accepting houses;[17] and later in the summer Norman conceded, following that parliamentary 'hullabaloo' (as he typically called it), that 'whatever the intrinsic attractions of the scheme, political conditions make impossible today any large

German refunding operation', given that 'the subject of German loans is so prickly that you could not be sure of a rational consideration'.[18] Nevertheless, the City was by this time sufficiently well disposed towards existing German loans. 'Personally I do not think Germany will default on these Bonds,' the stockbroker Vernon Laurie wrote in August 1936 to a client, Colonel Francis Whitmore, recommending German government $5\frac{1}{2}$ per cent Young Bonds. Laurie's reasoning was that such a default by Germany 'would be entirely contrary to her present desire to become a respectable first-class power once more'. The Colonel seems to have been reluctant, but a month later Laurie pushed the bonds again: 'Personally, I rather feel that while Germany is inclined to pick a quarrel with Russia, she will be careful to keep friends with the Western countries in Europe, particularly England, and any attempt to default on the Young or Dawes Loans would not be in accord with such a policy'. Eventually, in February 1937, Whitmore did buy £500 of the bonds at $41\frac{1}{2}$ – one gentlemanly capitalist's smallish but symbolic commitment to German prosperity and Anglo-German harmony.[19]

From July 1936 there was another theatre of attention. 'A survey of the situation in Europe is not encouraging,' Dallas Bernard of Mathesons observed two months later. 'In Spain we have a fight between Communism and Stability, say Fascism.' The City's attitude to the Spanish Civil War generally mirrored that of the British government: formally neutral, implicitly sympathetic to the nationalist side. In the case of Kleinworts that sympathy took a very tangible, if secretive form, with the bank's José Mayorga actively involved on behalf of one of Franco's leading supporters, Juan March, in hoarding and disbursing bullion in order to pay for Italian help. But in one country where there was little trouble about republicanism, Roy Sambourne's diary near the end of 1936 had a terse tone:

> 7 December (Monday). I dread the markets. I pray God all may go well & the King decide rightly. Markets weak – uncertainty – what will the King do.
> 9 December. Rumours of the King's abdication from Paris.
> 10 December. A late street – when the King's decision became known – by a broadcast at 4 pm in the House.

The market's reaction to the news was instantly bullish, and when Bruce Lockhart had lunch next day at Anthony de Rothschild's, he found the City 'relieved that Edward has gone'. His host quoted his brother, Lionel, who had apparently remarked, 'If anyone had said years ago that a King of England had abdicated and on the same afternoon there had been a boom on the Stock Exchange he would have been qualified for a lunatic asylum.' That same day, writing to New York, Villiers of Barings agreed that it had all turned out surprisingly well: 'Naturally the abdication of the King has been a very great disappointment, but we are very fortunate in having a successor who has an extremely nice wife and everybody is confident that they will be a success.'[20]

Standstill negotiations were rarely the stuff of front-page headlines, but they concerned the City rather more vitally. Towards the end of 1936, on one of his frequent trips to Berlin, Tiarks told 'Jerry' Pinsent of the British Embassy there that there had been (as Pinsent reported back to London) 'a kind of revolt of the Standstill creditors against his leadership, but that this had been followed by a meeting in which the matter had been discussed and a unanimous vote of confidence had been passed in him'. Tiarks at that point had 'contemplated that the Standstill would be renewed for another year with very little alteration'. If, however, Tiarks hoped for an easy ride in the 1937 renewal, he reckoned without one of his fellow-delegates. 'We cannot go on like this for ever,' Lidbury told his fellow-clearers on 11 January. 'It is unthinkable that we, as lenders at short term of other people's money, can be forced into the indefinite continuance of a semi-permanent arrangement which amounts practically to a forced and unrecognised funding.'[21]

The Joint Committee of British Short Term Creditors – comprising representatives from both the accepting houses and the clearing banks – met on the 18th. Proceedings began with a short statement from the clearers that they would renew the existing agreement only up to the end of June that year:

> On this letter being read [Kindersley reported to his partners, having stood in for the absent Brand] Tiarks at once asked Wardington [the former Beaumont Pease, and still Chairman of Lloyds] whether he could be given any explanation. Colin Campbell [Chairman of National Provincial] thereupon made a rather curious and rambling speech. He said that the Clearing Bankers had discussed the position very carefully and they felt that the time had come when a firm attitude should be adopted with the Germans and that the question of the bills circulating on the London market should be dealt with . . .
>
> Tiarks at once took up these remarks and said that he could understand a proposal being wanted from the Germans but he did not follow who else could deal with the situation. To this Campbell replied that the Clearing Bankers thought that the bills could not go on circulating if the Standstill was going to be renewed indefinitely without any [capital] reduction. Tiarks said that, of course, if necessary the Accepting Houses would take up their bills. Colin Campbell emphasised that his remarks were not

intended to be personal to Tiarks or his firm. The Clearing Banks thought
everyone should understand their attitude . . .
  It was agreed that the Clearing Banks' letter should be kept confidential
although it was feared that Einzig would hear of it . . .
  Tiarks felt the Americans ought to be told *now* what attitude the English
were going to adopt. Lidbury said this was equivalent to handing out the
information to Einzig . . .

According to a Treasury briefing shortly before the meeting, the
underlying concern of the clearers, with McKenna to the fore, was 'why
the Standstill creditors for 3 years have refrained from pressing for any
capital repayments and thus assisted to finance German rearmament'.
The same briefing noted that the German position was unyielding: 'They
regard it as quite impossible for capital repayments to be made'.
Eventually, shortly before the British delegates set out for Berlin early in
February, a compromise was reached: the aim would be to renew the
agreement for a further year, but to achieve a 5 per cent reduction on the
current amount of the Standstill (as opposed to the original wish of the
clearers for a 10 per cent reduction on the original amount).[22]
  Negotiations began on the 9th, and next day Pinsent reported to the
Treasury that he was finding Lidbury 'very unsatisfactory'. All that he
could get out of him were 'fire-eating remarks' to the effect that 'the
Germans were working a continuous swindle', that 'the quality of the
standstill credits was steadily deteriorating' and that 'he assumed that
H.M. Government would not let the City down'. Pinsent added, 'I dare
say that to some extent Lidbury was keeping up a pose.' A few days later
Lidbury and Brand returned from Berlin, in order to report to the Joint
Committee that Schacht was refusing to offer any cash payment at all.
During their few days in London before returning to Berlin, it became
clear not only that Norman was unwilling to fight on behalf of the
creditors against Chamberlain's reluctance to tackle the question of
capital repayments, but also that there was no serious quarrel with the
proposition that at all costs the position and authority of Schacht must
be upheld. By the end of February 1937 the agreement had been
renewed, with barely a concession made by the Germans. Dallas
Bernard, writing to Jardine Matheson in Hong Kong, offered a laconic
comment:

  It is amazing how this country can allow Germany to import materials
  for arms and munitions, side track British merchants and trade, allow them
  to withhold money rightfully belonging to British creditors while the
  country holds what you call the whip hand of the creditor party. While

holding this whip hand, we should certainly dictate to Germany what she should do and tell her where she gets off the rails.

So no doubt it seemed to some others as well, but to Norman and at least several other leading figures in the City there was a larger prize at stake, and still seemingly within grasp: Anglo-German co-operation, mainly through the good offices of Schacht, and a return to something like the world they had grown up in. Moreover, wishful thinking was by no means confined to paid-up members and supporters of the Anglo-German Fellowship, for as Bernard argued that spring, 'so far as Germany is concerned as far as I can make out they have no desire in the very least to embark at the present time on any Warfaring venture'.[23]

Yet Norman himself, contrary to what is sometimes assumed, was not *wholly* the prisoner of wishful thinking. A significant, very hush-hush development was under way from autumn 1936, for which the inside account comes from Bolton:

> The Governor, for reasons never revealed, let it be known to Siepmann, Catterns, Cobbold and Edward (Ruby) Holland-Martin that a war book might be prepared but that he was not to be officially informed or consulted. There was a very precise understanding that this was to be an entirely normal Bank precaution against an emergency never likely to happen: moreover, the circle in the know was to be the smallest possible, no secretaries were to be used and we must make doubly sure that nothing leaked to the Press, to Whitehall and especially not to Ministers. Siepmann and I had a series of discussions on strategy and tactics but conclusions were hampered by his conviction that no one could cater for chaos . . .
>
> In consequence, Cyril Hawker and I talked about the possibilities and, despite his personal revulsion against any idea that his hockey-playing friends in Bonn University would support or even welcome a Second World War, we began to hammer out a series of ideas to deal with the problems of financing our imports of basic necessities in time of war . . .
>
> After weeks of laboured consideration, Hawker and I decided to recommend a total mobilisation of resources, without any consideration of the rights of the individual, and comprehensive exchange control with the aim of conserving for as long as possible our exiguous foreign exchange purchasing power. The consequential interference with private business and financial life raised problems of great magnitude; although our self-imposed terms of reference appeared superficially to concern, say, the foreign exchange market, overseas finance, commodity markets, gold, portfolio investment etc., the execution of our projected measures would require official interference with practically every aspect of personal and institutional activity. But we plunged ahead undeterred . . .

By June 1937 a lengthy memorandum on 'War Measures' had been prepared, followed towards the end of the year by a rough draft of an Exchange Control Act.[24]

The Bank of England's willingness to countenance the possibility of war, and to think the unthinkable when it came to planning the financial execution of that war, owed much to Bolton personally and contrasted sharply with the Treasury's very conservative approach at this time to the same set of problems that the Bank was addressing.[25] 'I was continuously driven on by gloomy forecasts in the reports of those whom I knew and trusted in foreign banking,' Bolton would recall about his growing conviction that war was inevitable, on the basis of 'the information and warnings that I daily received from those deeply involved in European affairs', from men such as Albert Palache of Helbert Wagg, Louis Franck and David Keswick of Samuel Montagu, and Siegmund Warburg, as well as 'the many contacts I had through the foreign exchange market'. It was a tribute to the Bank that it largely gave Bolton his head and that its preparations for foreign exchange control in the event of war were therefore so advanced. What these preparations did *not* mean, however, was that Norman and those around him, let alone the City as a whole, either saw war as a foregone conclusion or were psychologically unready to go the extra mile to avoid it. Some of Norman's illusions may have gone – in October 1937 he described Germany and Italy as 'powers, whose international gospel professes to be the repelling of Communism, adopting in world affairs an attitude essentially similar to that of the Communist in domestic matters' – but he remained resolutely attached to that most understandable, not entirely ignoble of causes, appeasement.[26]

Schacht's 'position in Germany today was better than ever it was', Tiarks assured the Accepting Houses Committee on 4 November 1937, shortly before he lost his position as Economics Minister; Schacht did, however, remain President of the Reichsbank, and Tiarks and Norman continued to invest unrealistic hopes in him. At the same meeting, Brand argued in relation to Standstill that the customary bankers' renewal was the least bad policy, for 'as long as the service is maintained and the debts recognised it is doubtful whether the assistance of the British Government would amount to much and in the meantime the goodwill of the Germans would have been lost'. In February 1938, at about the same time as the agreement was being quietly renewed, Eden resigned as Foreign Secretary in protest at Chamberlain's conduct of foreign policy. 'Those who stand on the wrong side of 50 are generally for the Prime Minister,' was how the Bank's Siepmann gauged City reaction to this apparent demand for a stronger approach, whereas 'those who are younger are generally with Mr Eden'. One of Siepmann's colleagues, Cameron Cobbold, disagreed. He argued that though the 'vast majority' had 'a great regard for Eden' and that all their 'sentiments are in favour of its policy and of telling the dictators to go to the devil', nevertheless 'at the bottom of its heart' this majority 'feels that the League is a wash-out, that League policy has made us look silly, and that the best chance of recovering lost ground is to put sentiment aside and follow unattractive but solid, determined, common-sense Birmingham'. Addis for one agreed: 'My sympathies are with Neville Chamberlain. By all means enter to conversations with Mussolini: and Hitler too. Even if they fail as they well may they may help to clear the air.'[27]

A persistent thorn in the side of the appeasers was Paul Einzig's 'Lombard Street' column in the *Financial News*, and Norman at the start of March sent for one of the paper's directors, Guy Dawnay: 'Complaints fr abroad about one of Einzig's Articles: he will see what can be done'. On 13 March came the *Anschluss*, an event already largely discounted by the City. Arthur Villiers of Barings, writing the previous month to Kidder Peabody in New York, had correctly anticipated the general City reaction:

> Many people have felt that in the long run Austria and Germany will become one country or at least have a very close association, but the bullying way in which Hitler has behaved is disturbing. After all, though, he is only behaving as he has done on various occasions before! It is most unfortunate that circumstances have brought Italy and Germany together and one must hope that something will occur to break this friendship.

Admittedly a meeting was held at Lazards – attended by such City reprobates as Falk and Boothby – in order to organise a public protest, but even then Brand found himself being hauled in by Norman to apologise for having made the facilities available.[28]

Irrespective of opinion, everyone knew that Hitler's next move would be in the direction of Czechoslovakia. Over the next six months the pace of rumours flying around the City rarely abated – a typical one was that if only Chamberlain would back Czechoslovakia, then high-ranking officers in the German Army were prepared to bump Hitler off – but Norman, suffering from shingles, was seldom at his desk to hear them. On one occasion during the summer when he was in London, he mentioned to Chamberlain the desire of Schacht (as recently expressed to him in Basle) that British foreign policy should take more account of the attempt that he – Schacht – was making to moderate the Nazis.

Chamberlain's response to Norman was brusque: 'Who is Schacht? I have to deal with Hitler.' Norman and Schacht had formed their alliance in the 1920s, the age of the banker, but that age had gone. Norman, and other bankers who thought like him, could do little more than give their full support to Chamberlain, whom in a letter to General Smuts on the last day of August 1938 he described as 'not being deluded like an ostrich but rather in his wisdom has been facing facts and, in spite of what may be thought of the autarchic rulers, trying bravely to reach a solution with them on all outstanding questions'.[29] Over the years, 'facing facts' had always been the highest City wisdom; and the new, rapidly looming fact was Hitler's designs upon Czech territorial integrity, at a time when Britain was unprepared – in almost every sense of the word – for war.

'The Stock Exchange and the great majority of its clients refuse to believe that there will be war in Europe,' asserted 'Autolycus' on 9 September. Three days later came Hitler's intensely aggressive anti-Czech speech at Nuremberg, and shortly afterwards it was announced that Chamberlain was to fly to see him at Berchtesgaden. Markets rallied on the first day of their meeting, Thursday the 15th, and 'in the Stock Exchange', according to 'Autolycus', 'nothing but satisfaction and pleasure were expressed at what is recognised as a brave grasp of a situation which evidently held an even greater measure of gravity than most of us had realised'. As for the larger issue, Arthur Villiers was, as earlier in the year, in line with representative City opinion: 'The Germans are behaving as only Germans can behave, but unfortunately our friends the Czechs have not an entirely blameless record as regards their treatment of minorities . . . Nothing can excuse the speeches of Goering and Hitler but it is difficult to believe that such a large minority [i.e. the Sudeten Germans] can remain part of Czechoslovakia if they prefer to be Germans.' Over much of the next week, following Chamberlain's return, the skies seemed reasonably blue, as the Czechs reluctantly submitted to Anglo-French demands that major territorial concessions be made to Hitler. The closest reading of the City during these days came from 'Dives' in the *New Statesman*:

> Although the City as a whole supports Mr Chamberlain's policy of scuttle, it must not be assumed that anybody welcomes the prospect of temporary peace with dishonour. As far as I have been able to check up City opinion, I find that even reactionary and Die-hard Conservatives feel humiliated by the abject submission of a British Prime Minister to the German Dictator . . . A few, who see the ruin of Stock Exchange business if Herr Hitler maintains this tension for another twelve months, are even

regretting that the 'show-down' has been postponed. However, if there is to be peace with dishonour it is generally assumed that there will be no disarmament.

By the time these words appeared, however, Chamberlain was about to begin another round of talks with Hitler. 'A day of acute tension & weakening prices,' Roy Sambourne recorded on Friday the 23rd, as 'grave news' started to come through from Godesberg. 'No hope of a settlement – but it is almost desperate,' he added ungrammatically but feelingly.[30] Hitler had ratcheted up his demands, and by the weekend war seemed inevitable.

The *FT*'s editorial on Monday the 26th was reasonably tough – 'If such demands, and their manner, are successful there can be little prospect of security in Europe' – but the mood of the Stock Exchange, and one particular jobber, was encapsulated in Sambourne's diary: 'The markets collapse all round – very heavy falls indeed . . . Home & have my cocktail with a heavy heart'. Tuesday was even worse for Sambourne – 'Nothing but a miracle can save us' – though there was a late rally when entirely unsubstantiated rumours spread round the Stock Exchange that not only had Hitler given the Czechs an extra fortnight to consider their reply, but that riots had broken out in Berlin. Most of Wednesday the 28th was little better. 'Gloom settled over the City and it was the worst day experienced since August 1914,' Bernard reported to Hong Kong, though according to 'Autolycus' there was the odd hopeful fresh rumour in the markets, such as 'that the Pope had intervened'.[31]

With London in a state of high tension, and trenches being dug in Hyde Park, representatives of the Committee of London Clearing Bankers spent the day in Staffordshire, inspecting the buildings of the Trentham Park Amusement Hall as a possible site for an emergency central clearing house in the event of war. Meanwhile, the Accepting Houses Committee met at four o'clock at 16 Bishopsgate, home of H. S. Lefèvre & Co. Early on it was stated that the discount market was not functioning properly and that the clearing banks were not buying bills, but most of the meeting comprised a general discussion about what to do if war broke out. But then, at about a quarter to five, just as the meeting was ending, a telephone call came from Kleinworts to Cyril Kleinwort, who was able to announce to the others that news had been received from the House of Commons that Chamberlain would shortly be flying to Munich. The news had already led to stirring after-hours scenes outside the Stock Exchange, according to 'The Diarist' in the next day's *FT*:

Within a minute or two of Mr Chamberlain's surprise announcement in Parliament brokers and their clerks came rushing into Throgmorton-street from every entrance.

An outburst of vociferous bidding spread like a tidal wave from Shorter's Court round the corner eastwards into the Oil, Industrial and Kaffir markets, spending its force among the few remaining Rhodesian and West African jobbers. Telephones were overwhelmed. You had to wait two or three minutes before the 'dialling tone' could be got on the automatic instruments. Trunk calls were virtually unobtainable.

Or as Sambourne – probably not one of those jobbers making an opportunistic turn in the street – rhetorically asked about the wonderful news: 'How can I tell you what happened then? Prices soared . . . I pray it may be the end of all the tension in Europe.'[32]

'A Chance for Reason' was the *FT*'s leader headline on Thursday the 29th, with the paper describing Chamberlain's 'efforts to preserve the peace' as having 'assumed heroic proportions'. According to 'Autolycus', the Stock Exchange's slogan for the day was 'The war is over!', though there was an uncertain start: 'Everyone was agog to hear what the first price might be. As the market filled up, so the curiosity increased, the first price being awaited with undisguised interest. A shout of laughter arose when somebody made $1\frac{1}{2}$ to 2 in Venterspost.' That hiccup over, through the invoking of a speculative Kaffir stock, markets were buoyant, ahead of the Munich Conference starting that afternoon. Sambourne, and no doubt many others, underwent a private agony – 'I am still very anxious. How will it end?' – but the following morning's *FT* had the headline that almost everyone in the City wanted: 'Midnight Pact at Munich'. The accompanying editorial stated that 'dismemberment is a painful thing for a proud country to contemplate', but 'it possesses the one virtue, that it will have spared countless millions the horrors of a war more intense and destructive even than that of 1914–18'. That Friday a mood of massive relief pervaded the City. On the Stock Exchange, according to 'The Diarist', there was 'heartfelt thankfulness and a paean of praise for the Prime Minister'; in Lloyd's, shortly after noon, the Chairman, Stanley Aubrey, mounted the Rostrum and, after two strokes on the Lutine Bell, announced, to prolonged applause, that the Committee of Lloyd's was sending a congratulatory message to Chamberlain; while Sambourne, having thanked God 'a million times', returned home to Kensington and gave his servants 'a Pint of champagne to celebrate'. One wily City bird had called it right. 'Chamberlain returned from Munich bringing "Peace with honour",'

Addis noted at the end of this historic day. 'The Consols I bought two days [ago] at 66 are today quoted 75!'[33]

Over the following week there was a chance for reflection. The only minister to resign was Duff Cooper, and according to 'The Diarist' on Tuesday, 3 October, his protest 'reflects a point of view which has had a good many exponents in the City'. Almost certainly, however, 'Autolycus' that same day, in his almost euphoric post-Munich assessment, was closer to the City pulse: 'Many ups and downs, many hopes and disappointments are inevitable, but the optimist will look forward to such peace in Europe as shall make this continent a more secure and abiding resting place for industry, capital and enterprise than it has been within the memory of most of us.' The Stock Exchange as a body sent an official congratulatory message to Chamberlain, while Philip Hill gave 550 guineas to the Westminster Hospital in thanksgiving for the preservation of peace – the sum denoting fifty guineas for each company of which he was chairman. Yet perhaps the last City word on what would become one of the most myth-laden episodes of modern British history should go to Morgan Grenfell's Lord Bicester, the former Vivian Hugh Smith. Neither an Anglo-German intimate of Norman's nor a friend of the appeasers, he wrote to New York on the 6th, warning that Hitler was a 'fanatic' and that Goering and Goebbels were 'gangsters'.[34] He would not have played it differently from Chamberlain; but unlike some, he did not imagine that Munich was more than a stay of execution.

*

During the months immediately after Munich, the City – like the rest of the country – did not quite know what to think. 'Anthony Rothschild believes that out of this crisis will come a rejuvenation of England,' Bruce Lockhart noted at the end of October 1938. 'He agrees with me no use cursing and blaming; at same time he is against the frightful complacency of the Chamberlainites and wants a strong line.' Villiers of Barings preferred to accentuate the positive with less qualification. 'Rightly or wrongly,' he observed on 5 November, 'people here are feeling rather happier about politics, both internal and external. The more the Czechoslovak question is ventilated the more people realise that the Czechs are not angels and certainly have not the gift of tact when handling other races.' He added that 'people are beginning to believe that the natural place for Germany to trade is in Eastern Europe'. A few days afterwards, however, occurred the *Kristallnacht*, prompting

447

Dallas Bernard of Mathesons to report to Hong Kong that 'the country recoils with horror, and doubts if it is possible to live in friendliness with a regime that not only permits but apparently organises such a persecution'.[35]

In December the monthly 'Securities for Investment' circular sent out by Rowe & Pitman (Lancie Hugh Smith's firm, featuring three Hons out of eleven partners on its notepaper) reflected the City's exasperation with the European situation:

> Once again the cup of market recovery, filled by expanding trade in America, has been dashed from our lips by the dictators, who are becoming more and more skilled in the art of frightening the investor. If the leaders of Germany and Italy were only half as expert in speculation as in political gambles, they could easily prop up their tottering national finances by means of market operations timed to coincide with each hair-raising 'coup de théâtre'.
>
> The certainty of uncertainty nowadays makes investment prophecy a luxury. It is easy to draw up predictions for the long run; but in the long run, as Mr J.M. Keynes has observed, we are all dead. Meanwhile market forecasting has become a morbid study of hate and fear, of tyranny and fanaticism . . .

At about the same time the journalist and broadcaster Sydney Moseley reflected how 'businessmen want peace passionately, without being prepared to pay its price'; and he asked his friend Bill Citron, a member of the Stock Exchange, how the House was 'taking this supreme crisis in our affairs'. Citron responded with an evocative description of institutional *ennui*:

> Markets round the House all in a state of complete idleness. Here and there small groups discussing the day's sport, and as I passed the Reuter tape some sportsmen were intently studying the weather forecast, in order to make up their minds whether 'goals' for next Saturday should be bought or not.
>
> As the clock struck three, the Yankee market strolled towards the Shorter's Court door and there awaited the opening cables from New York. For fully five minutes silence was the most prominent feature, and then somebody bid ½ for steel . . . The proceedings were then somewhat enlivened by the rendering of 'Three cheers for the Red, White, and Blue' – a song which was taken up by the entire House.
>
> Somebody bid a half for steel . . .
>
> More yawns, more discussions of sport, more 'goals' and then – suddenly – a large commotion in the centre of the market. An elderly

gentleman, complete with top hat and winged collar, goes in the market to try and deal; a jobber, over-wrought perhaps at the sight of a genuine dealer, suddenly leans forward and rips the unfortunate gentleman's collar; there is a roar, and the whole market surges forward. The top hat is whipped off, disappears, and a moment later appears looking something like the sort of hat one puts on scarecrows. The collar is torn in two, and later the owner of the excellent articles is hurled, smiling because he is frightened to do anything else, out of the main door.

Silence ... Somebody bids a half for steel.

The boys in the market seem to be getting a little restive, and suddenly two rival jobbers start pushing one another; again the collar game, and the jobber appears minus one. He goes out of the House amid cheers, and then somebody bids a half for steel.

It is all getting rather monotonous again when the jobber who had some minutes previously left the House minus his collar appears in the market wearing a new one. I thought to myself at the time that this was rather 'walking where angels fear to tread', and my fears proved correct when he was again seized, and the collar again torn off, but by way of reminder the man's braces were forcibly removed as well.

The 'boys' had now tired of this sport, and continued by singing and dancing the 'Lambeth Walk', a number which seemed rather appropriate.

Somebody bid a half for steel – and then $\frac{5}{8}$, $\frac{3}{4}$, buy steel, figure buy Chrysler, and so on. The market was suddenly alive, cables were coming in every second, dealers shouting; play was forgotten and business was the keynote, and so as the bell struck four o'clock and I rushed out into the street market I realised what a strange place the Stock Exchange is, and how many phases one can see in just an hour ...

'This is how stockbrokers get rid of their inhibitions – if they have any!' commented Moseley after receiving his friend's account. 'And yet they will be among the first to volunteer when the time comes.'[36]

Norman continued to see no reason why that time should come. A letter to Schacht, in early November 1938, encapsulated what would be his attitude almost until the sirens sounded:

> You and I are no doubt in agreement that European prospects have improved since Godesberg and München where our Prime Minister, alongside the helpful attitude of your Führer, showed a courage and initiative which is not usual or easy in a highly democratic country. We may well be thankful to have escaped war, certainly for a short and, I hope, for a long period. It is in the early future that the habit of reason and reasonableness and give-and-take should surely replace alarm and threats as the international method.

In mid-December Schacht paid what was theoretically a private visit to London (seeking support for a scheme to assist the emigration of German Jews), but Norman arranged for him to see ministers and others unofficially. Some of those others included leading City figures, such as Lord Bearsted, whom Siegmund Warburg warned not to have any truck with someone who was seeking only to 'improve his own personal position with the Nazi government'. Not surprisingly, assessments by Einzig and Norman differed as to the success or otherwise of Schacht's visit. 'The hope that he might be able to rally the pro-Nazi and pro-German influences in the City failed to materialise,' the tireless anti-appeasement journalist wrote some months later, adding that 'most of the bankers who in the past had agitated in favour of humouring Germany by granting her new credits had either changed their views or considered it expedient not to express those views in public'. Norman, however, writing to Schacht's daughter the day after he had put her father on to the boat train at Liverpool Street Station, declared that Schacht had 'found here a real welcome from everyone he saw and no one made a disagreeable remark'.[37]

Even before Schacht's visit, Norman had cleared it with Chamberlain that he himself would be paying a reciprocal 'private' visit to Berlin, in order to attend – as a godparent – the christening of Schacht's grandson. The Foreign Office was not told. 'We heard tonight that that mountebank Montague [*sic*] Norman is off to Berlin,' Halifax's private secretary, Oliver Harvey, exploded on 2 January 1939. 'Such a visit can only do harm – by encouraging the pro-German proclivities of the City, by making American and foreign opinion think we are doing another deal with Germany behind their backs – another example of the P.M.'s pro-Nazi tendencies – and finally in Germany itself where it will be regarded as proof of our anxiety to run after Hitler.' By Tuesday the 3rd, news of Norman's impending trip had leaked to the press and was on the front pages, being given a City reception that, admittedly according to Einzig, 'could not, with the best will imaginable, be described as favourable'. Early on Wednesday, the day of intended departure, Norman received a letter from the Foreign Office seeking to deter him. He steamed round at eleven, 'in a rage' according to Harvey, and said that the visit had been 'agreed long since with PM – Ch Ex – N. Henderson – H.J. Wilson . . .'[38] At 1.45 p.m. he caught the Dover train from Cannon Street Station, thereby neatly side-stepping the pressmen gathered at Victoria for the two o'clock train.[39] By the time he reached Berlin on Thursday morning, Ernest Bevin was publicly warning about the harm that his visit might be doing 'to the cause of Democracy and

Freedom' and declaring that 'we shall never get peace whilst we allow this financial underworld to operate against the interest of the public'. There also appeared, on the Friday, a very hostile cartoon by Low in the *Evening Standard*.

Norman himself, presumably oblivious, at once called in on the British Embassy and, according to the official account, 'said that apart from a visit of courtesy to Dr Schacht he was of opinion that, private visits from personalities such as himself who warmly supported the Prime Minister's policy of appeasement, did nothing but good and were like straws thrown into a stream in order to test which way the current was running'. The christening took place that Thursday afternoon in the Reichsbank building – the little boy's first name was Norman – and the godfather was back in the Reichsbank for most of Friday, before dropping in on the Embassy prior to catching the night train to Basle. He told Pinsent that he had spent most of his time with Schacht and Reichsbank officials, that at lunch he had met a few German bankers and industrialists, and that he had not seen any members of the German government. None of the conversations, Pinsent reported back to London, 'was concerned with any concrete proposals, nor has the Governor "done any business", as he put it'. And, 'the Governor said that he had always been in favour of establishing and extending contacts with the more moderate elements in Germany and doing anything which might serve to strengthen their hand'.

Back in London the following week, Norman reported to Ashton-Gwatkin at the Foreign Office. 'He considers S.E. Europe to be a natural field for the development of German trade,' the official noted. 'He was not optimistic about the possibility of finding a solution to the European question; but he does not believe in the likelihood of war this year.'[40] As usual, Norman also reiterated how he was pinning his hopes on Schacht to be a restraining influence – but unfortunately, on the 20th, the President of the Reichsbank received the order of the boot from his Nazi masters. Some weeks later Norman penned a tribute to his long-standing friend, describing him as 'full of courage and resource', 'a true internationalist', someone who sought 'to support London as the essential money market of Europe', and 'the sane man among a party of dangerous totalitarians'.[41] Whatever the validity of the judgements, they were the words of one almost impotent central banker about another.

Norman and Schacht were a rather more amenable pair than Tiarks and Lidbury. 'I tried to get you yesterday to discuss a few ideas I have about the new Standstill and was sorry to hear that you had left London for the Christmas holidays,' Tiarks wrote from 145 Leadenhall Street on

23 December 1938 to Lidbury at his country home at Melbury Abbas in Dorset. Tiarks's letter, asking for a meeting on Friday the 30th, reached Lidbury on Christmas Day and received a pretty cool reception: 'I am on Holiday and not returning to town until Sunday night while on Monday – the first business day of the year – I must devote the day, like all good Clearing Bankers, to the compilation, study & consideration of the year's Results . . .' Lidbury added that he 'had not expected that questions arising upon the expiry of the so recently prolonged agreement at end May would present themselves for hasty consideration over the turn of the year'. Furthermore, 'I had indeed thought that the present political situation rendered any general discussion premature or inopportune'. Tiarks, for whom barbed remarks tended to be water off a duck's back, formally put forward his plan at the start of 1939, by which (as he had explained to the Accepting Houses Committee a few weeks earlier) all acceptances were to be 'taken out of the Standstill and dealt with under individual agreements between creditors and debtors'. The response from Lidbury was predictably negative: 'Any general discussion both premature & inopportune. The present period of international tension cannot be utilized to further a *permanent* settlement. The May agreement may in my view best be continued as it is for a year without discussion unless the Debtors make proposals.' And more generally: 'Proposals of Creditors have dangers. I fear the "German mind" & think we should hesitate to give the Debtors opportunity to turn Creditors over actions (or proposals) to the detriment of Creditors.'[42]

Tiarks's plan was dead in the water, which was particularly unfortunate for accepting houses like his own and Kleinworts at a time when the outstanding Standstill bills were becoming ever more unpopular in the London market, particularly with the clearing banks. Accordingly, those accepting houses to which major Standstill debts were still owed had no alternative but to take up on their own account increasing quantities of the Standstill bills – a considerable drain on their already stretched resources. One of Tiarks's allies in formulating his Standstill plan had been Hermann Abs, who as foreign manager of Deutsche Bank was closely involved in Standstill matters. In mid-February he paid an uncomfortable visit to Lidbury. 'As Mr Abs continued to discourse upon the "improved quality of the bills",' his host noted afterwards, 'I took occasion to exhibit to him a couple of handfuls of German Standstill paper out of our portfolio, all of which he was forced to admit, with the exception of two small bills for trifling amounts, were the most vicious type of "kite".' Half a century later the great German banker would recall a happier visit, also in February 1939, to Kindersley at Lazards.

With characteristic directness, Kindersley apparently declared that he hated the Germans, but would make an exception of Abs, because he was 'the only one I know from your country who knows the art of understatement'.[43]

Generally, putting aside individual interests and prejudices (even beliefs), it was the City's usual lack of imagination that made it so difficult for it to grasp what Hitler was about. Finance and ideology tend to mix badly, and during these anxious, febrile times the City constantly found itself coming up against the limits of rationality and not knowing where to turn next. Typical – including in its sense of being at the mercy of events – was the assessment that Sydney Parkes, joint chief General Manager of Lloyds Bank, offered at the end of January 1939 to a business friend abroad. After noting that 'everyone in the City' had recently had 'a very bad dose of what the Home Secretary calls the "jitter bug"', so much so that 'the topic of conversation at every table, in business and out of business, seems to be war, the preparation for war and the defence against war', Parkes took comfort in what he saw as the underlying logic of the situation: 'My own impression is that the internal position of Germany is exceedingly bad and that Hitler and company at the present time have got all that they can do to look after that position, to provide their people with the necessaries of life and to keep them reasonably quiet'. A month later, under 'long questionings' from Joseph Kennedy at the American Embassy, Norman too saw matters largely through the prism of commonsensical economic rationality: 'I say Jews, Palestine, Spain need to clear up before daylight ahead. Germany & Italy good for 3–6 m. France & UK for a year or more financially. War not inevitable at all. Trade needed, to wh US tariff principal bar.'[44]

It was a prism that Norman shared with Tiarks. 'Germany's own economic difficulties, Tiarks thought, had had a most salutary effect on her attitude,' Pinsent in Berlin noted after a conversation with him on 1 March. 'His business friends laugh at the idea that Germany *could* go to war in her present state.' Three days later Tiarks was in Cologne to address the Anglo-German Fellowship. 'As soon as we are all convinced that in future Germany and England can again work together and not against each other,' he asserted, 'I see no reason why, with a view to increasing German foreign trade credit facilities, London acceptance credits should not once again reach their previous level; there are many London houses who wish to maintain this old service in financing German trade, but if they are to do so, the machinery must be kept intact.' And he added that, in order to re-establish mutual confidence, it was necessary 'to end the race in the world's armaments'. Chamberlain uttered similar sentiments soon afterwards, declaring that a period of tranquillity in Europe beckoned; and though by 14 March there were some concerns in the City as to the Czech situation, 'Autolycus' assured his readers that 'the general impression heard in every market of the House maintained that the Czecho trouble would blow over'.[45]

On the 15th, however, Hitler annexed what remained of Czechoslovakia. Initially, when the news came through, the Stock Exchange tried to shrug it off – 'Autolycus' referring to 'the prevailing impression among members that nothing serious will come of the Czecho development' – but later that day, after the House had closed, Chamberlain took a tough line in Parliament. Prices fell next day, and 'Autolycus' began his column memorably on Friday the 17th: 'Herr Hitler, had he ever been a member of the Stock Exchange, London, might have better understood what he obviously failed to appreciate at the present time: to whit, that a bargain is a bargain.' That evening Chamberlain made a much-applauded speech in Birmingham in which he denounced what Germany had done. 'There can be no doubt now that Mr Chamberlain's sweeping condemnation of Herr Hitler involves a major reorientation in British foreign policy,' the *FT* declared on Monday the 20th. 'It could not have been otherwise.'[46]

Less than a fortnight later, on Friday the 31st, there was announced the Anglo-French guarantee to Poland, the pivotal point of the year's diplomacy. For most of that day the markets were dull, waiting for Chamberlain's afternoon statement. When it came, it (according to that evening's stock market report) 'met with general approval and imparted firmness to prices at the close'. 'The Diarist' agreed, noting that 'the Prime Minister's statement put new heart into the Stock Exchange'. The *FT*'s editorial too was generally positive, seeing in the statement 'evidence of a determination on the part of the British and French governments which is the best hope for the maintenance of some degree of stability'; but at the same time the paper insisted that the pledge to Poland did not rule out 'the possibility of a just political settlement', in other words with Germany.[47]

If the City's mood had stiffened, it could not yet quite believe that there was not a way out. Indeed, perhaps it would not even require a settlement. 'I still do not see war,' was Dallas Bernard's private assessment in mid-April. 'There are many factors operating against that, for instance insufficient food in Germany, shortage of oil, bad railway situation, undigested Czechs, undigested Austrians who are now less sympathetic towards the Nazis than they were . . .' Or, in the flat, matter-of-fact words of Addis about City fears at this time that war was imminent: 'I am not convinced.'[48]

Nevertheless, the City – and the national – temper had changed, and during the spring and early summer of 1939 this gave a rather different context to Anglo-German financial relations. 'It is peculiarly unsuitable at this moment to contemplate giving any uncompensated advantages to Germany,' Lidbury observed, two days after the occupation of Prague, about the Standstill position, after noting that 'there is no repudiation the Nazi Government will not make when it suits it'. Over the next two months the clearing banks were again at odds with the accepting houses: the former wanted a substantial repayment of principal, preferably 10 per cent, while the latter as usual preferred to be more emollient towards the Germans and thus favoured a straightforward renewal, in effect a strategy of playing for time. Schröders and Kleinworts in particular remained in a thoroughly uncomfortable position, as the discount market increasingly cold-shouldered Standstill bills, and indeed Kleinworts had to go to the Westminster in April for a £1m loan. In the end an agreed British position was reached – Standstill to be renewed, though under the threat of being terminated after six months unless the Germans made a substantial cash payment – but as late as mid-May, while final negotiations were going on in Berlin, Lidbury (briefly in London) was compelled to cable to Tiarks there, about the latest proposals coming from Berlin, that all the clearing banks had 'the gravest objections to the institution of any three year lines of any sort or kind', with the clear implication that Tiarks needed further stiffening.[49]

That the Anglo-German houses still wanted to continue as much as possible, and as late as possible, with a business-as-usual approach was graphically shown during the summer when Kleinworts entered into a £330,000 credit agreement with Krupps. Equally instructive in its way was the controversial case of the 'Czech gold'. This was the work of Einzig, who from mid-May was engaged in a brilliant, relentlessly sustained exposure of how the Bank for International Settlements had successfully instructed the Bank of England to hand over to the Reichsbank a gold deposit of some £6m belonging to the Czechoslovak National Bank. Einzig's campaign caused considerable embarrassment not only to the British government but also to the Bank of England, which of course was represented on the BIS. Had the British directors known in advance about the decision? If so, had they agreed to it? There were other questions involved as well, and the Bank of England emerged from the episode with its reputation somewhat damaged – partly the result, Einzig himself subsequently reckoned, of its unwillingness to depart from its time-honoured policy of 'never explain, never apologise'.

With the controversy at its height, in early June, one of the Bank's directors, Sir Alan Anderson, offered some thoughts to Norman about the state of public opinion on the question. As so often in the 1930s, the sense is of bankers and other men of commerce (Anderson himself was in shipping) finding it hard to adjust to a new, in many ways rebarbative world: 'What they [i.e. the public] must settle is whether they wish – in finance – to maintain the machinery of international discussion instead of force. If they do then the umpire must be left free to decide & sometimes he will decide against us . . .'[50]

The City at large, and the Stock Exchange in particular, was prey to many mood swings during this last summer of peace. As ever, 'Autolycus' faithfully recorded them. On 5 June: 'Fear of possible shocks still lurks in men's minds, but, for all that, it is very noticeable how rarely one hears the name of Hitler mentioned in the markets of today.' Four days later: 'Hitler, Goering, Goebbels, Danzig, massing of troops – these old familiar symptoms of Stock Exchange depression came again into evidence in the markets yesterday afternoon.' On the 16th: 'The hope that Russia will come in on the side of this country and of France remains in the air.' In the air was where that hope remained, though on 4 July, just after lunch, 'a rumour, swift as a flash of fire, ran round the House to the effect that the Anglo-Russian Pact had either been signed, or was on the point of being concluded', and 'prices went up with a rush'. Even without that pact being signed, the Danzig situation seemed to stabilise during July, and on the last day of the month that other regular *FT* stock market columnist, 'The Diarist', wrote buoyantly of how 'confidence appears to be gradually returning to the Stock Exchange'. A striking paragraph followed:

> The democratic circle is in the ascendant and the autocratic Axis in semi-eclipse. Mars, which recently approached us closer than for a generation, is now in forced retreat. According to one of the best-known of Stock Exchange philosophers: 'Almost before this year is out we shall be more concerned with what we can do to save Germany from economic disaster than with worrying about the prospect of war'.[51]

If the desire for peace, and the propensity for clutching at straws, remained strong, the underlying attitude was now tougher, less compromising – in the City as elsewhere. It was a toughness that at last came from the top. In early June the passionately pro-Hitler Duke of Buccleuch asked Norman to call on him at Grosvenor Gardens. 'I reserve my opinion, contrary to his, that Hitler and Co are liars,' was Norman's summary of the conversation. Later that month, while continuing to deny the inevitability of war, Bernard put it well: 'Compared to a year ago we are vastly stronger as a nation, but today we have commitments in the east of Europe which we must live up to. A year ago there were none.' The tone was similar on 14 July: 'The great difficulty seems to be to convince the Axis Powers that this country means business.' And on the 25th, after an unofficial meeting between trade representatives of the British and German governments had led to a denial by Chamberlain that there was any proposal for a loan to Germany, 'Autolycus' noted that 'the reported conversation between Mr R.S. Hudson and Dr Wohltat had no particular influence over prices, but it gave rise to a good deal of comment – some of it polite'.[52]

This tougher attitude did not, however, prevent one City man from making an eleventh-hour bid for peace.[53] E.W.D. Tennant of 9 Mincing Lane (where the chemical merchants C. Tennant, Sons & Co had their offices) had been strongly pro-German since shortly after the war. He had a good business connection there and during the 1920s had been an early supporter of Hitler, getting to know him and von Ribbentrop before the Nazis came to power. In November 1933 Tennant had even arranged for Ribbentrop to meet Baldwin. By 1935 his friendship with Ribbentrop had cooled, because of the Jewish question, but on 10 July 1939 he wrote to ask if he could come and see him. Ribbentrop's reply invited Tennant to his home near Salzburg on the 26th. Shortly before he was due to travel, Tennant approached the British government with a plan offering 'financial compensation' to Germany 'in exchange for a satisfactory relaxation of tension'. Tennant's scheme lacked nothing in ingenuity, for it involved 'the offering to credit Germany with an "imaginary" sum say of £100,000,000', which in turn would lead to a stock market boom all over the world, enabling Germany to be credited with the profit that it would have made via its imaginary loan in benefiting from that boom. 'I have personally discussed the question of foreign credits with Hitler,' Tennant pointed out, 'and he became all worked up at the idea of taking on further commitments involving him in finding more foreign-exchange to pay the interest.' The plan received a cool reception in Whitehall; but Tennant, undeterred, still made his way to the home of the German Foreign Minister. There he got little joy from his old friend, with Ribbentrop stressing Hitler's anger against England and his feelings of being let down. In his official report on the visit, however, Tennant did append his own thoughts: 'The united, dynamic, very young German nation is something tremendous which is definitely there, and we should, I feel, make more effort to understand it, work with it and accept it. It is now too late to attempt to dam up this terrific force.' He also, pointedly, quoted Ribbentrop's last words to him as they parted: 'Goodbye, and let us remember your English proverb "It is never too late to mend."'[54]

An implicit coda to Tennant's unavailing mission occurred soon afterwards, on 7 and 8 August, when a party of British businessmen (including Sir Edward Mountain, Chairman of Eagle Star, and Sir Robert Renwick of the stockbrokers Greenwells) went to a house near Bredstedt in order to have conversations with Goering.[55] The British party was significantly more critical of German foreign policy than Tennant had been; but although it was stressed that Hitler had broken his word given at Munich, and that that had been responsible for changing the British mood, it was also emphasised that the British conversations with Russia were merely prudent and 'should not be interpreted as showing any sort of sympathy with the Russian method of Government'. For his part Goering did little more than talk vaguely about the reciprocal recognition of the two countries' colonial claims and possessions – but that was sufficient for the businessmen to promise that the door was still open to comprehensive Anglo-German talks.[56] Again, in the event nothing came from this private initiative, but it was indicative that it happened at all.

None of which prevented the City from achieving an impressive degree of readiness in case of war breaking out.[57] Catterns, Cobbold, Bolton and Hawker were all key figures at the Bank of England in this respect, as was the Chief Cashier Kenneth Peppiatt. A major physical concern was gold, and in April 1939 Peacock asked the Bank whether it would be willing to store gold to the value of £2.5m currently held by Barings on behalf of that bank's customers. The vaults at Barings, he said, were old, security was not first-class, and anyway there were plans to evacuate London in the event of an emergency. Ruby Holland-Martin, however, turned down the request, on the grounds that not only was the Bank of England already at full stretch dealing with gold, but also that other banks and accepting houses would demand the same facilities as Barings, if its request was accepted. The Old Lady was indeed at full stretch, and during the summer it shipped to Canada a huge amount of both its old gold and that belonging to customer central banks. 'We took enormous risks,' according to Bolton, 'and when the war actually began we had about £500,000,000 of gold afloat in ships of 5,000 tons upwards'; happily, 'we did not lose one bar of gold throughout this period'.[58]

In general, Bolton also recalled, 'during the last few months of "peace" we were busily engaged in organising the banking system and the City to meet the strains of war' – and inevitably this brought the chief general managers of the clearing banks very prominently into the fray.

Bolton, not the easiest of men to impress, was struck by these managers' 'complete co-operation and single-minded devotion to the objectives of ensuring the survival of the country irrespective of their own banking interests', and he paid particular tribute to Lidbury as 'a tireless and dedicated man who was more than willing to do everyone's work and, indeed, even to think for them'. Cobbold, also in retrospect, agreed: 'Lidbury was an awkward chap, but when he got moving he could shift mountains. Ellerton [of Barclays] was his charming expert self, but without Lidbury's gun-fire I do not think we should easily have got the banks lined up before the outbreak of war.'[59] This involved establishing the appropriate machinery for exchange control; ensuring that the clearing system (to be transferred to Trentham Park in Staffordshire) would work smoothly; and a thousand and one other matters, often very tricky in relation to the many bank customers with substantial overseas business interests. Overall, the contrast was stark compared with that summer exactly a quarter of a century earlier, when the City had stumbled into war in an almost wholly unprepared way. Then there had been another 'awkward chap' among the clearing bankers, but Holden had been given less of a chance to 'shift mountains' and thereby earn the City's gratitude.

The final weeks were played out in an atmosphere of depressed markets, stagnant business and many City men being at the seaside rather than behind their desks. 'When I got back last Friday,' Parkes of Lloyds noted on Tuesday, 8 August, 'I found a certain feeling of nervousness in the City putting war on a 50/50 basis, but, personally, I still feel reasonably optimistic.' Next day Roy Sambourne described the 'news of Poland' as 'most disquieting', but as 'Autolycus' so judiciously put it on Friday the 11th, 'business conditions after today are not likely to hold important interest for those who, going North tonight, will find something fresh to Grouse about'. The following week saw the Stock Exchange at a virtual standstill. Sambourne's diary entry for Wednesday the 16th was staccato in the extreme – 'No business. Gloomy outlook. Germany adamant. Italy backing her. What will happen?' – while that same day, according to 'Autolycus', 'the Little Mining Market introduced a darts board by way of diversion, but the rest of the House seemed too languid to bother about anything except discussion of the political situation'. And on Thursday, while 'the strained situation in Poland and Danzig clamped down any spirit of enterprise that might otherwise have been attracted by the fall in prices throughout most departments', not only did 'the Little Mining Market play off its darts handicap', but 'the Sea Scouts benefitted to the extent of five or six pounds from the sale and distribution of fragrant lavender sachets'.[60]

By Tuesday the 22nd the betting, according to 'Autolycus', remained open: 'One body of Stock Exchange opinion holds stoutly to the view that there will be no war; another maintains that conditions have so closely approached the precipice that, short of another miracle or a similar happening, nothing can prevent a clash of arms. A third party frankly admits that it is impossible to tell what may happen.' On that day, however, the Stock Exchange – like the rest of the City – had to take on the chin the news of the just-announced Nazi-Soviet Pact. Parliament was recalled, and Norman cut short his holiday on the Isle of Man. On Thursday the 24th the *FT*'s leader ('Resolute and Calm') warmly described the City's endorsement of the Cabinet's communiqué about defending Poland, minimum prices were introduced for gilt-edged stock, and Bank rate was doubled to 4 per cent. Had the chance of 'another Munich miracle' entirely disappeared? 'Nobody in the House,' asserted 'Autolycus' late that day, 'attempts to minimise the extreme gravity of the situation or the intensification of the crisis. But the opinion is quietly expressed, here and there, round the markets, that the position, even at this twenty-third hour, does not wholly preclude the possibility of peace being preserved in Europe.' That little tinge of optimism persisted on Friday the 25th. 'A feeling of greater confidence in the maintenance of peace spread through the Stock Exchange after lunch,' noted 'The Odd Man' (deputising for 'The Diarist'), 'and this most anxious week comes to its end on a relatively firm note.' It was not an optimism that Sambourne shared. 'I am bewildered,' he wrote on the Thursday. 'Parliament meets. Preparations being hastened on all fronts. What a mess we have made of it.' And on Friday: 'Is Germany mad? God could not let her succeed.'[61]

By the following week there was little that most in the City could do other than watch and wait. 'Days pass with no relief from the tension,' the bill broker Ronald Gillett wrote to his mother, 'but that is better than having war. The City looks very depressing with every other building lined with sandbags, and many buildings empty through the evacuation of businesses and staffs to the country.' According to 'Autolycus', the Stock Exchange on Tuesday the 29th was calm enough: 'People refused to sell. In spite of the appearance of the City streets, holders decline to be sandbagged out of their shares.' Wednesday was another phlegmatic day on the Stock Exchange – 'Autolycus' attributing the market's 'cool confidence' to 'a growing conviction that whatever happens now will be the prelude to a firm and lasting settlement in the future' – but Thursday the 31st was rather different. Sambourne, as usual, eschewed under-statement:

> Alas after a good start – & the usual St Ex optimism – we get a bombshell. Evacuation of Children – Calling-up of Navy – practically complete mobilisation. Prices begin to fall & intense gloom prevails. The Stock Exchange to be closed tomorrow. Still one or two optimists still are to be found. I have practically – God help me – given up all hope.

The closure of the Stock Exchange was intended to be only temporary, in the context of the evacuation of children, but 'Lex' of the *Financial News* did not exaggerate when he observed on Friday morning that 'a grim Tchekovian gloom hangs over Throgmorton Street'.[62]

Germany invaded Poland that day, 1 September. On Saturday, while the British government eventually made up its mind to send an ultimatum to Germany, Norman replied to someone called H. Lipschutz, who had asked him how he could hasten the process of naturalisation. 'I have to admit,' Norman's letter ended, 'that there is nothing I can now do towards giving effect to your suggestions. And, while I have been searching, the sands of peace have been running out . . . so that there is no more for me to say . . . except to wish you well.' The ultimatum expired at 11 a.m. on Sunday the 3rd, and a quarter of an hour later Chamberlain was speaking on the wireless. 'From now on,' a mordant Norman announced to his secretary during that lovely sun-lit day, 'we shall be simply rubber stamps.'[63]

CHAPTER SEVENTEEN

All Blasted

'Office hours have been reduced to 10.0 am to 2.0 pm!' Ronald Gillett informed his mother three days after Chamberlain's dispirited announcement. The lack of activity at the family firm of bill brokers at 52 Cornhill was typical, as the outbreak of war immediately and severely curtailed the City's activities. All Stock Exchange bargains had to be done for cash, with no 'carrying over' from one fortnightly account to another; all new issues required Treasury sanction; the mainstream accepting business of the merchant banks virtually dried up; and the commodity markets were closed. 'The City is depressing beyond description,' Brendan Bracken lamented in November 1939, the third month of war. 'I go there for about an hour a day and I depart feeling like Job in the depth of his woes.' There were exceptions – the psychologist Anthony Weymouth visited Billingsgate Market early on a Thursday morning that same month and discovered 'a scene of feverish activity', full of 'porters carrying boxes of fish' (invariably on their heads) and 'hurrying, jostling, shouting fish-salesmen' – but most in the City shared Bracken's *ennui*.[1]

It was, during these early weeks and months of the war, a boredom tinged with apprehension. No stranger to anxiety, Roy Sambourne let himself go in his diary. On 14 September: 'I fear that it is all up with the Poles. What will happen then? God alone knows. What can we do? God help us.' On 3 October: 'We have let ourselves in for this war & God alone knows what the end of it will be. America may stand by us – but Germany have been too diabolically clever.' And on 8 December: 'I am very despondent over the War. Germany are arrogant & strong & I think that England has made a mess of her Politics. It dates back to Eden's fatal blunder of sanctions against Italy.'[2] Re-creating the City mood at any one time is never easy, and for the 'Phoney War' it is peculiarly difficult. Recalling the national mood, Harold Macmillan would justifiably assert that there was a smell of peace in the air – but to what extent it permeated the square mile it is almost impossible to say.[3] Certainly there is little firm evidence that it did, either in an extensive or a significant way. 'None could wish more than I for a speedy outcome,'

Norman wrote to a Japanese banker during the first week of war, 'when it may be hoped that men of goodwill and principle in all nations will be able again to co-operate constructively and effectively.'[4] Norman, however, knew as well as anyone that the terms of trade with Hitler had fundamentally changed; and, with its deeply conformist streak, the City as a whole was most unlikely to break ranks with the albeit somewhat queasy consensus that this was a war that had to be fought.

Inevitably the City's daytime population shrank. Not only was there military call-up, but many members of staff engaged in routine work also evacuated bomb-threatened London, as wealthy City partners made good use of their liberal supply of country houses in order to accommodate them. Morgan Grenfell, for example, went to Haresfoot near Berkhamsted in Hertfordshire; Hambros to The Hyde near Luton; and Rowe & Pitman to Mount Clare at Roehampton in Surrey. 'New Court in wartime was a fortress manned only by a small garrison of men whose presence in the City was necessary to keep the place going,' Palin recalled of Rothschilds. 'The young men had been called up; the women and those of the older men whose jobs could be done conveniently in the country were evacuated to the mansion at Tring in Hertfordshire where the second Lord Rothschild [Natty's son Walter] had kept his entomological collection.' He added that 'in the Dividend Office coupons and drawn bonds were still taken in over the counter but were then immediately conveyed to Tring for processing'. In the case of Hambros, two bank messengers – one from 41 Bishopsgate, the other from The Hyde – would meet each afternoon at Cockfosters tube station in order to exchange despatch cases.[5]

The Bank of England also evacuated much of its administrative side, to Whitchurch in Hampshire; the evacuees included the 275 women of the Dividend Preparation Office, waved off on 3 September at Waterloo Station by Norman himself. The financial core of the Bank's activities, however, stayed firmly put; and during the autumn this proved to be a key factor in the determination of the gilt-edged jobbers in resisting the Stock Exchange Committee's apparent wish to move the floor of the House to the Denham film studios in Buckinghamshire, on which the option on a lease had been obtained prior to the outbreak of war. 'The physical difficulties of a general concentration of Members at Denham are obvious,' conceded the Committee, but argued that 'it is essential that as effective a Market as possible be established at the earliest possible moment after the City has been evacuated.' Such was the gilt market's umbilical cord to the Bank of England and its transfer facilities that it flatly riposted that it would 'make arrangements of its own' rather than move to leafy Bucks. As tended to be the case in Stock Exchange matters, the gilt men had their way, and the idea was quietly dropped.[6]

How to pay for the war?[7] An important letter in October 1939 from the Bank of England director Sir Alan Anderson to the Deputy Governor, Catterns, reflected an appreciation that the social and political climate would not permit a repeat of the *rentier*-friendly policy of the First World War:

> Some City friends of mine have been talking to me about a hope and a fear that possess them. In this time of stress when rich and poor have gladly offered themselves and have been forced to offer themselves as soldiers they hope that the City will not ask the State to pay 4% or 5% for the money it needs. They fear 90% of the Stock Exchange would say that money today is worth 4% or 5% and would stop at that and as a sequel the non monied man in the street would be confirmed in his impression that conscription applies to him and not to the rich.

Norman broadly agreed with Anderson and his friends that this time round it must be a 'cheap money' war – but was naturally uncomfortable with the high-tax implications of such a policy. On 2 November, shortly after Bank rate had returned to 2 per cent, he told Sir Horace Wilson at the Treasury that in his view 'taxation has been pushed very near if not quite to the limit'.[8] The larger argument, however, prevailed, and in the closing weeks of 1939 Norman was instrumental in persuading the City about the virtues of what the *Economist* would shortly dub the 'Three Per Cent War'. So it was, with issues done mainly on a 'tap' basis via the Government brokers, Mullens & Co.

The war was also paid for through individual savings, as well as large institutional funds, and here the key initial role was played by Kindersley, long-standing Chairman (later President) of the National Savings Committee. Kindersley was deeply wedded to the voluntary approach to savings, but Keynes published two articles in *The Times* in mid-November in which he argued that reliance on voluntary savings would not only fail to reduce consumption but would also be inflationary. Accordingly, he argued for compulsory savings, in the form of deferred pay. The City's reaction was largely hostile, but when Keynes towards the end of February 1940 published his pamphlet *How to Pay for the War* – elaborating his ideas and seeking 'an advance towards economic equality greater than any which we have made in recent times' – he found support from a surprising quarter. One of the pamphlet's recipients was Norman, who invited his old antagonist to the Bank on 8 March. The conversation went well, and soon afterwards Keynes privately noted that, 'after long estrangement', his scheme had achieved the welcome by-product of 'a personal reconciliation' with Norman. Kindersley remained resolutely opposed to the compulsory approach, but the fiscal arguments were moving inexorably the other way.[9]

Exchange control was, from the City's standpoint, the other fundamental aspect of financial policy during the war – an aspect that included the consolidation and institutionalisation of the sterling area, eventually including a still reluctant Canada.[10] 'Major holdings of sterling (those who held reserves in sterling and could maintain exchange control) were invited into a novel imperial nexus where all internal transactions were free, all external ones tightly controlled, and capital outflow virtually forbidden in the interests of the whole,' is how Middlemas describes what he rightly terms 'a flexible and remarkably unbureaucratic system', which was essentially the achievement of the Commonwealth's central banks under the Bank of England's 'consultation and tutelage'.[11] British implementation of exchange control was, of course, the responsibility of the Bank itself, which as before the war continued to set the pace – in terms of making exchange control effective – while the Treasury dragged its heels.

'Suddenly everyone was on our doorstep with questions of bewildering complexity,' one of the Bank's young men, Leslie O'Brien, would recall:

> We made up rules as we went along and we made them fast under the pressure of insistent enquiry and the threat of unjustified loss for the enquirer. To those in the Bank who liked the challenge, and that was most of us, the exchange control was highly stimulating. Many of us excelled ourselves, even over-reached ourselves, as never before. Long hours meant nothing in such a vibrant community which for some years worked and slept in Threadneedle Street. As the machine necessarily expanded with new offices being created, promotions and appointments came thick and fast and they caused some uneasiness, if not jealousy.

Elsewhere in the Bank, O'Brien added, 'there was little of our excitement to be found', with 'numerous women' having 'taken over jobs formerly the male preserve as men were released for war service'.[12] Moreover, if exchange control was a rare, not universally popular opportunity for capable, ambitious young men like O'Brien to circumvent the rigid Bank of England hierarchy, it also represented a potentially dire threat to the ranks of foreign exchange brokers, as London's foreign exchange market was unceremoniously closed on the outbreak of war. The Bank softened the blow partly by recruiting some seventy-five brokers to come and work in the Bank on the exchange control side, partly by selecting four firms to be retained as sub-offices of the Bank in case its telephones were put out of action. Overall, the guiding spirit was one of flexibility, and Harry Siepmann – in day-to-day charge of exchange control – already had on the wall of his room, before war broke out, what became a celebrated notice: 'Freedom is in danger. Defend it with all your might.' At the same time, building on Bolton's important preparatory work before the war, there was a determination not to allow any loopholes. Either way, exchange control now represented an important rationale for the Bank's existence – and over the ensuing years, an important element of its authority in the City.

In many ways, exchange control mirrored the larger triangular relationship between government, central bank and City. In the fourth week of war, the Chancellor, Sir John Simon, wrote to Norman asking him to ensure that the clearing banks restricted their advances to such winning-the-war purposes as the needs of armaments and the export trade. Norman duly passed on Simon's letter to Colin Campbell, Chairman of the Committee of London Clearing Bankers; and thus was established what would become the firm unwritten rule that all communications between the Treasury and the clearing banks were, in either direction, mediated by the Bank of England. By early November, citing 'the settlement of rates of interest and other terms of borrowing' during recent weeks, Dalton was asserting to the Commons that 'as compared with the last war the control by the government and by the Treasury over the Bank of England and over the whole financial machine in the City of London, has developed to a very great extent, indeed to an extent which is very seldom frankly admitted and is not always generally recognised'. The government itself may not have been willing as yet to make such claims, but according to Dalton, 'as between the Treasury and the Bank of England in particular the relationship has been completely revolutionised', in that 'the Governor of the Bank of England is to a much greater extent than is openly admitted or legally recognised, today the agent and servant of the Treasury rather than an independent financial dictator as has been the case in the past'. Typically, Dalton over-stated his case – there had already been a significant shift in the disposition of power between Bank and Treasury during the inter-war period – but war did make a difference. Nor, in the course of the first winter, was it only the Treasury to which Norman found himself having to be subservient. In late February for example, shortly before an issue of War Loan, he saw someone from the dreaded Ministry of Information. 'He is settling details for next week,' Norman noted wryly, '& I promise to obey his orders!'[13]

The new dispensation did not appeal much to a forceful spirit like Lidbury. Late in 1939, in the context of attacks from Einzig as well as the Labour Party on the unwillingness of the banks to reduce call money rates to their pre-war level (in turn meaning that the Treasury had to pay half a per cent more on its weekly borrowings), Lidbury grumbled feelingly to Peppiatt at the Bank of England:

> If the Banks are to run their own business successfully reasonable scope should still be left for the interplay of the forces of Supply and Demand. The Treasury is now in virtual command of both, and will doubtless use its power increasingly as the War goes on. Why introduce undue stresses and strains in the financial structure by imposing a Call Money Rate which at the moment is out of touch with reality?

As the war went on, however, most of the City's leading clearing bankers settled comfortably enough into the role they had been assigned as *de facto* civil servants. 'One thing which is impressing all of us,' Sydney Parkes of Lloyds informed his bank's New York representative in March 1940, 'is the clever way in which the Treasury is handling the financial situation; by having a closed economy they have control of the situation which is being handled very skilfully.'[14]

Norman was not entirely dismayed, for if war undoubtedly reduced the Bank's power *vis-à-vis* the Treasury, it equally strengthened it in relation to the rest of the City. On 29 January an entry in the journal of the bill brokers Smith St Aubyn said much: 'Governor of Bank sent for Wyse [R.C. Wyse, Chairman of the London Discount Houses Committee] and told him he expected 100% Conversion into the new 2% five year Bond. The market had been buying with a view to *dissenting*.' Norman had his way, and Wyse himself was dead within the week. In another field, Norman's diary entry for 1 March, when he and Catterns saw R.P. Wilkinson, Deputy Chairman of the Stock Exchange, could not have been terser: 'No fortnightly settlements'. The question was closed. In war, as in peace, he remained the indispensable source of guidance as to appropriate or inappropriate behaviour. Early in May 1940 he received a call from Helmut Schroder, only surviving son of Baron Bruno. 'Sh^d he serve, without waiting to be called up – or sh^d he mind the Schroder concerns & claim exemptions,' was how Norman noted his visitor's dilemma. He may not initially have expressed a view, but three weeks later – after a Parliamentary question had been asked about the allegiance of the no-longer-umlauted Schroder – he most certainly did, when Helmut came again. 'He swears to be neither seen nor heard in any way by anybody anywhere,' Norman recorded.[15] A lengthy exile from the City beckoned, just as it had for Helmut's father a quarter of a century earlier.

Helmut did not miss much business – or fun – at 145 Leadenhall Street. The historian of Schroders summarises succinctly why few of the City's sectors suffered as much from the war as did its merchant banks:

> Foreign-drawn bill business disappeared because of the problems of international transfers, while the securing of supplies by government bulk purchasing from the Dominions and through Lend Lease [from 1941] all but eliminated the need for acceptance finance for British trade. Foreign exchange dealing, a significant source of revenue for some merchant banks in the 1930s, disappeared as an activity at the beginning of the war because the accepting houses were omitted from the official list of authorised dealers, but even when they secured recognition there was little business to be done. Issues for private borrowers became rare events as the capital market was reserved for funding the wartime requirements of the state . . .

In almost all the merchant banks, accordingly, it was 'care and maintenance' that preoccupied the partners, at least for the first two years of the war, and not the getting of business. Inevitably it was the prestige of not only the individual houses that suffered, but also their umbrella body, the Accepting Houses Committee. Colonel Bertram Abel Smith of M. Samuel & Co became that body's new Chairman in spring 1940, and soon afterwards called on the Governor. 'We agree that Ass" must eventually be purged & reconstituted – must gain prestige – must come to terms with Cl Bkers Com,' Norman noted.[16]

Most of the firms in the discount market were similarly gloomy during the early stages of the war, as its traditional commercial bill business almost vanished. 'What hope for reasonable profits for small discount Houses?' one bill broker asked Norman after less than two months. 'Very little during the war' was the discouraging reply. One firm, Gilletts, finally made up its mind that it would call it a day, with the doors to close on 1 July 1940, the maturity date of the $4\frac{1}{2}$ per cent Conversion Loan in which it had made heavy purchases in 1937. A special meeting of shareholders was called for the spring, in order to give this plan the nod, but the day before the meeting, the Bank of England privately told the discount houses that they must convert all their holdings of this loan or go out of business. Norman's threat, Ronald Gillett would recall, 'brought into the question a patriotic motive' – and in this potentially invidious situation, the shareholders decided that the firm must continue. The young Ronald, son of Sir George, had been almost the only member of the family wanting the firm to go on, and in due course he became that rare thing in the discount, or indeed any other, market: a visionary figure.[17]

None of these various local difficulties mattered tuppence in comparison to the war itself. 'It is the general feeling here that our affairs must be prosecuted with more vigour, both economically and militarily,' Parkes of Lloyds reflected in early December, while when Norman saw Sir John Simon on a Wednesday evening in the New Year, their encounter produced a classic diary entry: '6. Ch. Ex. hot air!' Norman had no time for Simon, whom he saw as neither dynamic nor trustworthy, and he may well have been pushing at about this time for Sir Josiah Stamp to replace him, though there are conflicting recollections about this. Of course, it was hard during the early months of 1940 not to succumb to a certain mood – semi-complacent, semi-fatalistic – of being in the lull before the storm. On 8 April the *Financial News*'s 30-Share Index stood at 70.6, just above what it had been on the last day of peacetime trading – a relative buoyancy caused mainly by the realisation that the cheap-money regime initiated in 1932 was going to continue for the foreseeable future. The following day, however, the 'Phoney War' ended, and with it that somnolent lull. 'Bad news on arrival in City,' Roy Sambourne recorded, by his standards calmly. 'Germany has invaded Norway & Denmark – the latter without a struggle. Prices naturally are weak all round. No business. We must have lost quite a good deal. Intense anxiety.'[18]

The news gave an added impetus to the need to get the financial mechanism right for the conduct of the war, and in two key areas – savings and exchange control – Keynes intensified his efforts. In fact, both questions were starting to go his way, and he could afford to be generous. 'The real trouble is, of course, that in thinking his movement can be adequate he has got the order of magnitude quite wrong,' he wrote to Brand on 3 May about Kindersley's voluntary savings campaign, adding that Brand's distinguished partner 'never had much of a head for figures!' Five days later, having submitted a lengthy memorandum on exchange control, Keynes went to the Bank of England to discuss the subject with Clay, Siepmann and Bolton. The ensuing conversation, he told Clay next day, 'was one of the most heartening I have enjoyed for a long time', for 'it was extraordinarily agreeable to discover for once people in executive positions who were in a drastic state of mind, seemed completely competent and equal to their job and were *not* enjoying living in a perpetual twilight, dim and incomplete'. On a copy of Keynes's letter, Norman scribbled some words that would once have seemed unimaginable: 'He must come again: his support of Exch policy will be most important under new Cabinet. Treas^y have neither time nor knowledge to help – but feel bound to interfere!'[19] Politically, the old guard – dominant since Lloyd George's fall in 1922 – was on the way out; and by the time Norman scribbled his words, Churchill had, on the evening of Friday, 10 May, become Prime Minister. What is striking, however, is that Keynes by this time did *not* see Norman's Bank of England as part of that old guard. Again, this was unimaginable from an earlier, return-to-gold perspective – and, among other things, a reflection of how much the Bank had changed since the trauma of 1931.

Not that Norman himself, for understandable reasons, was wholly ecstatic about the change of national leadership. 'Now I know that I shall never cross the threshold of No. 10 again,' he accurately predicted on hearing the news. It was news that came within hours of Hitler's invasion of the Low Countries, prompting a predictable tumble of Stock Exchange prices. The war was getting serious, and on Monday the 13th the one o'clock radio news was, for the first time, broadcast live in the Stock Exchange – an innovation that was greeted enthusiastically. That same day 'Autolycus' took the pulse about the coalition government – including Labour politicians – that the new Prime Minister had shaped over the weekend:

> Stock Exchange views on the composition of the new Cabinet, if they cannot be called enthusiastic in support of some of the Ministers, may be summed up in the statement that Mr Churchill has done as well as he could with the material at his disposal. Sympathy is generally expressed with Mr Chamberlain. The driving power of Mr Winston Churchill is not questioned, and it is driving power, according to the general view, that the country requires at this crisis.

Yet, away from the public prints, many members perhaps shared Sambourne's forebodings. 'Prices fall all round,' he noted the following evening in a far from Churchillian frame of mind. 'The news gets worse & worse. Italy practically certainly to fight against us – America will do nothing – Germany's might is overwhelming – & I do not see how the French and English can stop them . . . So with a heavy heart I go home on a No 9 bus . . .'[20]

The series of catastrophic military reverses could only deepen this jobber's gloom:

> 22 *May*. The news is terrifyingly critical & serious . . . Prices fall all round.
> 28 *May*. The ghastly news reaches me in the City that the King of the

Belgians has capitulated . . . It is all so fearful that one can scarcely realise it. Prices naturally fall . . .

18 June. Churchill's speech [in the Commons, invoking the 'finest hour']. Heartening in a way – but what a change of tone – 5 short weeks has seen a debacle.

20 June. One of our worst days in City. Prices fall heavily everywhere except gilt edged . . . I should like to chuck it.

For a heavy speculator like the Canadian financier Jimmie Dunn, these were bad days indeed. During these weeks, with France being overwhelmed and shares falling drastically in value, the stockbroker Mossy Myers called for payment of loans, and Dunn was unable to comply. At least one City friend refused to help, before he found some much-needed relief when Claud Serocold of Cazenove's agreed to carry the loans due to his firm. By Friday, 21 June, the 30-Share Index was down to 52.9, and the following day France obtained her wretched armistice. 'The Stock Exchange, frankly, did not like either the French armistice terms or their implications,' noted 'Lex' as the Index slid further to 50.4 on Monday the 24th. 'Lex' saw no comfort in the short-term future, but argued that 'the equity shareholder's day will come, when Britain has re-exerted her control of European history, with decisive effect'. Tuesday saw the Index holding relatively steady at 50.3, helped by a late rally on the strength of an impending speech by Churchill. But even he failed to restore spirits; and on Wednesday the 26th, amid ill-founded rumours of Stock Exchange closure or at the least a suspension of dealings in industrial securities, the Index for the only time in its life dipped below the half-century mark to finish at 49.4. Meeting its shareholders that same dog-day afternoon was the Globe Telegraph & Trust Co, with the octogenarian Earl of Midleton in the chair. His reported remarks may have been somewhat platitudinous ('The year had been a very difficult and anxious one, and at the moment there was no cheerful prospect ahead'), but none could deny the historical perspective he brought to bear; for as St John Brodrick, he had been Financial Secretary to the War Office back in the 1880s. And he added sagely: 'With the world in its present state it was impossible to make any forecast of the future prospects.'[21]

The day of 26 June 1940 was in fact one of the outstanding purchasing opportunities of the century; and with the investment trusts earlier than most to appreciate that possibility, the Index gradually began to recover. Writing on 6 July to John Martin, a Bank of England director who spent the war in South Africa ensuring regular gold supplies from there, Norman reviewed the political situation in a couple of striking sentences:

The P.M. devotes all his energy and imagination and courage to conducting the war (anyway till 10 p.m.), Attlee and Greenwood are obstacles to quick decisions, good administration and any smell of economy. Chamberlain [who had become Lord President of the Council] is *the* worthy, balanced and effective Minister all round; much abused but sitting tight and gradually (I pray) coming back into his own.[22]

Norman was writing at the very time that Chamberlain and his closest followers were being publicly indicted as the *Guilty Men*, with a Gallup Poll revealing that majority opinion wanted the former Prime Minister to leave the government – which, as it happened, he soon did, on account of a mortal illness. Norman could hardly hope to be within the Churchillian loop, but these two sentences are a graphic reminder of how far outside it he was.

In the same letter, Norman noted how difficult it had become 'to collect a weekly Court' and mentioned that Catto had gone 'to the Treasury as Adviser'. This was the highly capable Thomas Catto, ennobled in 1936 as Lord Catto of Cairncatto, a Morgan Grenfell partner who earlier in 1940 had succeeded Lord St Just (the former Teddy Grenfell) as a Bank of England director. Catto was Norman's choice to be financial adviser to the new Chancellor (Sir Kingsley Wood, who had replaced Simon), and at the Treasury he would not only forge a close alliance with Keynes – the two men being dubbed 'Catto and Doggo' – but do much to protect the Bank's interests. It was also in July 1940 that the regulations were introduced, dealing with special accounts and blocked sterling, that at last made exchange control really effective. By then, moreover, there had been the introduction by the Treasury of what were called Treasury deposit receipts (TDRs), which were unpopular with the discount houses, in that they were in essence Treasury bills issued direct to the banks on a telephonic 'tap' basis; but they proved a very effective form of government borrowing.[23]

All such financial considerations soon seemed petty. 'Life is going on in a normal way here,' Sir Edward Reid of Barings wrote to New York on 28 August, 'except that air raid alarms make us lose a little sleep at nights. The German losses are, however, satisfactorily heavy and the damage which they are doing to us seems to be considerably less than what our Air Force is able to inflict on them. Thus we are all quite cheerful.' Six days later, on the first anniversary of the war beginning, Roy Sambourne recorded the latest from the floor of the House: 'Air raid warnings 10.20–11.30 & 3–4 pm. No business. Mac makes a mess of VOC. Queen walks through at 12.30. Great reception.'[24] A stirring moment, but the old grimy, historic City – Herman Melville's 'Cindery City of Dis' – was about to disappear for ever.

*

The first bomb on the City had already fallen: on 24 August, landing on St Giles's Churchyard in the Barbican. A few days later bombs landed in Old Change and Paternoster Row, but it was the massive bombardment of the Docks and East End on Saturday, 7 September that made Londoners generally realise that the Blitz had truly begun.[25] The following night there were more bombs, and in the words of the Dean of St Paul's, Walter Matthews, 'once more we could see from the roof a great conflagration in the east, which spread for many miles along the horizon, while nearer at hand there were smaller fires all round the Cathedral'. St Augustine's in Watling Street took a direct hit, with those on the roof of St Paul's seeing its spire first bend and then collapse into the nave below. Nor was Mammon immune, as the Bank of England discovered on the Monday night. Norman ruefully described to Martin 'our so-called barrage':

> A No. 1 bomb fell in Threadneedle Street a few yards from our outside wall and made a hole about 15' × 20'. It really did little damage except to glass, gas mains, etc. Another bomb fell on our roof, happily at a very strong point close to the corner of Lothbury and Tokenhouse Yard, which smashed the telephone exchange, kitchens and a bit of the two top storeys on that side. And a shell which was fired at Ealing – or some such friendly spot – but never exploded, came through the roof near the corner of Princes Street and Lothbury and smashed the ceiling and the water pipes and made a mess but did no other harm . . .

During these early nights of bombing, and days of inspecting the damage, Virginia Woolf was an aghast witness. 'And then,' she wrote to a friend on Wednesday the 11th, 'the passion of my life, that is the City of London – to see London all blasted, that too raked my heart. Have you that feeling for certain alleys and little courts, between Chancery Lane and the City? I walked to the Tower the other day by way of caressing my love of all that.'[26]

Over the next two months, until the Luftwaffe temporarily concentrated on the provinces, few parts of the City were entirely unaffected. The raid on the night of 10 October was particularly destructive, with St Paul's taking its first direct hit and many bombs falling on Cornhill. Five nights later the Dutch Church in Austin Friars was almost totally destroyed. The art critic James Pope-Hennessy visited the scene:

> Except for the traces of three Gothic arches outlined upon the east wall, no one would guess what sort of a building stood here. The Austin Friars is not a picturesque ruin: its slender pillars and great fourteenth-century windows, its elegant Gothic arcades, were not strong enough to stand up to high explosive, and there is now nothing upon its site but pieces of stone, lengths of sodden planking, smashed tiles, red telephone books hurled from a nearby office by the bomb blast, a mound of curled lead (as elaborate as Richard II drapery), and a stack of iron railings.

Almost a month later, on the night of 12 November, 32 Lombard Street, the London home of Guaranty Trust, took a direct hit, and with much of the building reduced to rubble the firm was given hospitality by Glyn Mills. During that autumn each firm and institution worked out its own way of coping. At the Cornhill head office of Lloyds, at any one time several hundred staff were staying round the clock, while fire squads did fortnightly turns of duty. At Kleinworts, turns were taken at firewatching, and the men played poker long into the night. At Bensons one morning, after bombs during the night had destroyed nearby buildings, the staff looked at the surrounding rubble and unanimously decided that they had been mistaken in appointing each other as executors.[27]

For all concerned, the daily inconvenience was considerable, as Norman described to Martin towards the end of October:

> You may not realise it, but for us one of the great troubles now is travel. The stations in London are for ever being bombed and closed for some days or else the tracks and perhaps bridges are busted – or again the bus roads in and out of London become unusable. Instead of an hour morning and evening from door to door many of our folk take two or three hours and may have to walk a good step: troublesome and hard on the individuals and getting worse with the shorter days and blackout.
>
> Our higher floors are hardly used and most work is done below ground, where mercifully there are several floors of huge desolate vaults. And soon perhaps as many as 1,000 men and women will be working two or three days running and sleeping here for one or two nights and then going off and staying at home for a couple of days. In this way travel should be ever so much reduced and, along with it, weariness and wet skins and all the ills and miseries of winter.

Norman himself was now sleeping at the Bank two or three nights each week – and occasionally a lowly member of staff would sight that still alert and vital figure wearing a dressing-gown emblazoned with a dragon.[28]

'On Sunday night,' Virginia Woolf recorded on the first day of 1941, 'as I was reading about the great fire, in a very accurate detailed book, London was burning. Eight of my city churches destroyed, & the Guildhall.' It was not only Guildhall that was badly damaged and eight of Wren's churches that were razed to the ground on the dreadful night of 29 December; the destruction also included much of the area around St Paul's (including the book trade centred on Paternoster Row), the textile warehouses there and in the Wood Street area off Cheapside, and most of the buildings in Cannon Street. R.C.M. Fitzhugh, a firewatcher on the roof of Guildhall, would never forget what he saw:

> The block bounded by Brassishaw Hall, Fore Street, Aldermanbury, and Basinghall Street appeared to be one solid mass of flame. St Stephen's, Coleman Street, was soon enveloped in flames, and we could see the steeple and weather-cock fall. Fires were everywhere in the City area. From time to time, heavy high explosive bombs or land mines were dropped . . . There would be the sound of something rushing through the air – then a brilliant flash would light up the entire sky and horizon and be followed within two or three seconds by the most resounding explosion . . .

Overall, the night *could* have been worse – 'St Paul's Cathedral, built by Sir Christopher Wren, her great dome towering above the capital of the Empire, is burning to the ground as I talk to you now,' Ed Murrow misleadingly informed his American listeners – but even so, it *should* not have been as catastrophic as it was. Many of the firms whose premises were destroyed had failed to employ firewatchers; most of those buildings could perhaps have been saved, had firemen been able to effect an entrance; while, even more frustratingly, the water supply failed early in the night.[29]

'Gigantic German Attempt To Set The City of London Ablaze' was the headline of the *Evening News* on Monday the 30th. That morning, in the company of another off-duty air-raid warden, Leo Townsend attempted to walk the City's streets:

> We emerged from a splinted Bank station into smoke-laden air, heavy with disaster. Traffic had ceased. Cheapside was sealed off; Lombard Street and Queen Victoria Street were impassable. A tangled skein of entrails, fire hoses twisting, interweaving among dust and débris, snaked up King William Street, coiled along Princes Street, as though a monster had been disembowelled. Firemen, their smarting eyelids circular with

strain and red against their blackened faces, rubbed away grimy sweat on
the cuffs of smoke-soaked uniforms. In Moorgate flakes of black snowed
the atmosphere, swam and dipped above our heads, rising on a cushion of
hot air, tilting and fluttering down upon us as we walked. Some streets
were cordoned off, but otherwise the steel Civil Defence helmets slung on
our backs provided a passport to undisturbed wandering. However the
way proved heavy going; mounds of sodden rubble often altered our
course, we avoided lakes of mud strewn with islands of broken brick.
Scarcely a door was on its hinges, not a pane of glass intact. No shops were
open; those who would normally have been buying and selling found it all
they could do to reach the site of the premises they worked in. Many had
decided it was useless to attend that day, others had arrived to find there
was nothing left to attend to. Occasional small groups of people stood
talking in low voices.

The air grew heavier, thickening with soot; our feet stumbled among the
undergrowth of charred wood, the steaming masses of warehouse goods,
the sprawling tubes issuing from pump and hydrant. Piles across the
roadway gave off a smell of burning rubber and smouldering cloth. Fires
leaped within the gaping skins of buildings, smoke bloomed from shattered
window-sockets. Grim and weary, the A.F.S. [Auxiliary Fire Service] still
laboured, shouting to each other in desultory parched phrases that echoed
against hollow façades. They had worked at full stretch throughout the
long night, dealing with flames which had seemed then to be raging from
one end of the City to the other, illuminating the scene like glaring
daylight, driving vast migrations of sparks through narrow streets. These,
such as Ave Maria Lane, had become tunnel-like infernos and were gutted
almost from end to end. Known buildings were rendered indistinguishable,
except when a spurt of fire licked a church tower into sudden prominence.

We entered Finsbury Square, where flames blazed torchlike through the
shell of an unattended house. As we plodded over the smoking wreckage J.
became uncomfortably aware of the possibility of unexploded bombs
beneath our feet.

The destruction persisted along City Road; over the mossy green of
Bunhill Row Fields breakers of flame still leaped into the black spume from
another deserted house, the flickerings on the grave-stones adding to the
desolation. I have heard from City Wardens that, in the nights that
followed, the rubble strewn streets were dead and strangely silent, no
whisper even from the wind among the empty husks and fallen walls, no
life except the soundless shadows of rats.

Another witness recalled the bewilderment that still prevailed on the
Tuesday morning. 'Numbers of City workers walked about with dazed
and stunned looks,' Charles Graves observed. 'They were the people who
had arrived the previous morning and found that their place of

employment was gutted and were coming back on the following day simply because they had nothing better to do.' On 10 January 1941 it was reported that the thirty or so pillar-boxes that had disappeared under the City rubble had at last been dug out.[30] Next day a bomb landed on Bank underground station, killing 117 people who had been taking shelter down on the platform. It also caused, almost directly in front of the Royal Exchange, a vast crater, which for almost a year could be traversed only by a hastily erected Bailey bridge.

Among those tending the wounded at Bank station was a Hungarian doctor. He paid his tribute: 'You English cannot appreciate the discipline of your people. I have not found one hysterical, shouting patient.' The Blitz, of course, speedily created its own myths, which subsequent revisionist accounts have sought – with only partial success – to strip away. In terms specifically of the City's higher echelons, we have no more than a few clues about underlying morale and attitudes during the winter of 1940/1. On 8 December the US military attaché in London recorded in his diary how he had been told that the City was 'ready for appeasement at any time', apparently not least on the grounds that it had 'no hold on Churchill', who had been failing to express sufficient concern for the Empire. Eleven days after that noteworthy but unsubstantiated assessment, writing to one of his partners while convalescing in Devon, the prominent City solicitor Harry Clifford-Turner declared that 'as long as we can just tick over and keep body and soul together, if we can save our skins and I can get better it will not be long before we will get back to the old position for there will be a tremendous lot of reconstruction work to do'. Early in the New Year a visiting American politician, Wendell Wilkie, was struck by the country's cohesion. 'He is amazed,' Harold Nicolson noted, 'that Big Business are as determined on victory as anybody. They know that it means their ruin, but even Montagu Norman had said to him, "Ruin? Go to hell. We must win."'[31]

What was, however, starting to dismay Norman was a growing awareness that one of the major costs of war would be a huge shift in international financial relations. As he wrote to Brand after a year and a half of the conflict: 'I have never realised so strongly as now how entirely we are in the hands of American "friends" over direct investments, and how much it looks as if, with kind words and feelings, they were going to extract them one after another!' Away, however, from *haute finance* – where surely the dominant attitude was that, at almost whatever cost, the war was something that had to be seen through – the pervasive atmosphere was one of sheer, unheroic tedium, as the clock seemingly went backwards. Over thirty years later, one of Norman's minions would remember without any misplaced nostalgia 'those airless vaults it was part of our fate to endure, on one of those nights which were a mixture of extended hours of work, interrupted by meals, with an occasional spice of danger but mostly made up of hours and hours of empty boredom'.[32]

It was during the autumn of 1940 that George Orwell wrote his marvellous extended essay, *The Lion and the Unicorn*, published in February 1941. 'If we can survive this war,' he argued, 'the defeat in Flanders will turn out to have been one of the great turning-points in English history':

> In that spectacular disaster the working class, the middle class and even a section of the business community could see the utter rottenness of private capitalism. Before that the case against capitalism had never been *proved*. Russia, the only definitely socialist country, was backward and far away. All criticism broke itself against the rat-trap faces of bankers and the brassy laughter of stockbrokers. Socialism? Ha! ha! ha! Where's the money to come from? Ha! ha! ha! The lords of property were firm in their seats, and they knew it. But after the French collapse there came something that could not be laughed away, something that neither cheque-books nor policemen were any use against – the bombing. Zweee – BOOM! What's that? Oh, only a bomb on the Stock Exchange. Zweee – BOOM! Another acre of somebody's valuable slum-property gone west. Hitler will at any rate go down in history as the man who made the City of London laugh on the wrong side of its face.

In the same essay, Orwell also looked forward to a post-war socialist future, in which the economy was planned and hereditary privilege was wiped out: 'The Stock Exchange will be pulled down, the horse plough will give way to the tractor, the country houses will be turned into children's holiday camps, the Eton and Harrow match will be forgotten . . .'[33]

For the nabobs of the City it was hardly an inviting prospect, but one who barely lived long enough to fear it was that patron of literature, the senior partner of Rowe & Pitman. 'Lancelot Smith died at circa 70,' Roy Sambourne recorded on 26 March. 'He was a rich successful man. Rather snobby I fear – & he would have had little use for me . . . I do not think somehow that he will be much missed. I *may be wrong*.' Three days later, on the 29th, Virginia Woolf – her mind affected at least in part by the destruction of her beloved City – drowned herself in the River Ouse. A memorial service for the not entirely beloved Lancie Hugh Smith was held on 1 April at the Savoy Chapel (Norman among those present), but it was another fortnight before Virginia Woolf's body was found and identified.[34]

In the interim, on 7 April 1941, Kingsley Wood presented the first modern, essentially Keynesian budget. Among other things it sought to implement Keynes's policy of compulsory loans from earnings, praised by the *FT* as an 'ingenious scheme' that the Treasury was now putting into effect 'in the simplest way through existing machinery'. Everyone, as usual, had one eye cocked upwards, and on the 16th there occurred what became known as 'The Wednesday', when a thousand tons of incendiaries and high explosives rained down on the City during one night. St Paul's was the particular target – the architectural writer J.M. Richards, who was also a firewatcher at the Cathedral, would call it 'the roughest night of all' – but Wren's masterpiece survived. Three days later Sambourne was less than happy about the British retaliation: 'I am terrified over what the consequences to London will be after our raid on Berlin. We are fools & fools we shall remain . . . God only knows how we can win this war. Germany so far has been triumphant everywhere.'[35] His fears about what would happen to London were justified, for the City's very worst night still lay ahead. It came on 10 May, when almost all the surviving buildings near St Paul's succumbed, there was huge devastation in several other parts of the City, and the London Commercial Sale Rooms, for so long the epicentre of the Mincing Lane commodity trades, were razed. Up to that night the City had been at least as much a commercial as a financial centre; subsequently it would be predominantly financial in character. It was one of the less obvious ways in which Hitler's bombs ripped the heart out of the old City.

*

Over the next few years the war was the City's constant backdrop. In late May 1941, as the nation celebrated the sinking of the *Bismarck*, the phlegmatic response at Lloyd's was to ring the Lutine Bell the traditional once, in order to indicate that a ship had been lost, and not twice, for good news. The news itself, however received, did not prevent the prominent City figure Sir Hugo Cunliffe-Owen, a man with fingers in many pies, from calling on Norman soon afterwards to vent his anxieties. 'Most unhappy about Politics & Strategy,' Norman noted. 'Wants professional War Cabinet of all arms & Dominions. And Alexander instead of Churchill.' In fact, the turning-point of the war was at hand – albeit one would not have known it from the Stock Exchange's reaction. 'Markets,' reported 'Lex' after some serious head-scratching on

23 June, 'spent the morning endeavouring to make up their minds whether the German aggression against Russia was a bull or a bear point', until 'having given the matter their due consideration, the majority of members concluded that whatever happened we could hardly be worse off as a result of Hitler's latest summersault'.[36] Accordingly, the 30-Share Index inched up fractionally to 71.8. Thereafter, however, equities steadily pushed upwards. The Index stood at 79.7 at the end of 1941, 93.7 at the end of 1942, and 103.1 at the end of 1943.

But if the Blitz was over, and the destiny of the war seemed increasingly assured, that did not mean there was an end to the firewatching. Early in 1941 Midland's head office in Poultry had been approached by the City Remembrancer to provide volunteers to help keep watch over Guildhall, a task proudly described four years later:

> With the available Corporation Staff and some others, the 200 odd bankmen were blended into ten well balanced and efficient squads, each squad taking duty from 5 p.m. to 9 a.m. every tenth night. Many are the stories that could be told of the various squads as they gradually acquired proficiency at fire appliance drill, at knot tying, and climbing vertical ladders – the prospect of which at first made many a heart beat faster – and as 'First Aiders' ... There at the Guildhall, altogether for 1350 nights, there was a *charitable* approach to every question of the day: a really unselfish *comradeship* enjoyed; and an exhilarating though regulated *conviviality* practised in varying degree. None who served regrets the experience: all now treasure the pleasantest memories, and thrill to the knowledge that their allotted task in the years of greatest peril to our nation, linked them as individuals with the stirring episodes enacted at Guildhall in bygone centuries.

Firewatching was one of the war's many egalitarian aspects. In a Christmas letter in 1942 to a member of staff serving abroad, Alan Welsford of Slaughter and May remarked how it had 'given us all a great opportunity of getting to know each other much better than is possible in ordinary peacetime circumstances', adding that it was 'exceedingly good' for a partner such as himself 'to get thoroughly put on the spot by a junior office boy at the office billiard table'. Welsford himself was middle-aged, but on the whole the City's workforce during the war comprised the old and the very young. This inevitable skewing, added to the physical wreckage, created almost a sense of a ghost town, and on a Saturday afternoon in March 1942 James Lees-Milne took a melancholic stroll:

I walked through the devastated area to the north of the cathedral. It was like wandering in Pompeii. The sun was shining warm and bright. There was not a breath stirring, only the seagulls wheeling and skirling over the ruins. Not a sound of traffic when I was in the midst of the isolation. From one spot there is waste land visible as far as the eye can roam. It was most moving. Unfortunately the ruins are not beautiful, too like scarred flesh, and as yet untoned by time. I do pray they will at all costs keep the Wren spires, even if they must clear away the shells of the naves. I walked past the ruins of Christchurch Newgate, St. Giles's Cripplegate, St. Vedast, St. Lawrence Jewry, St. Benet's, St. Mary-le-Bow (when I last saw this church about a year ago it still had its roof on though badly damaged. A subsequent raid has evidently finished it off) and so on . . .[37]

About one-third of the City's 675 acres had been reduced to a bombsite, and for so long did most of them remain in that state that it almost became accepted as the natural order of things.

The fortunes of war affected countless individual City destinies. For example, Harley Drayton, still in his thirties when hostilities began, was able for most of the duration to stay firmly put in 117 Old Broad Street, achieving complete dominance over the investment trusts based there, whereas two potential rivals were both lost to military duties. One, Percy Moody, had already lost ground in peacetime on account of his unwise keenness on the Territorial Army. The other, Denzil Carlisle, was not only the son of a well-known figure in the investment trust world, but was also 'tall, popular and handsome' and 'renowned for his liking of the very strong Capstan Full Strength cigarettes which he always resisted manfully until mid-day'. However, on return from the war, Carlisle found his competitors, above all Drayton, 'now entrenched in the top seats', and as a result 'he never realised his full potential'.[38]

The story was not dissimilar at the stockbrokers Phillips & Drew. There, the members of the old family firm mainly went off to the war, whereas Sidney Perry (himself too old for war service) and his team were barely affected, with one of its members having a crippled arm, another being half-Italian and thus out of military contention, and a third being a Quaker. By the end of the war, Perry and his team had gone a long way towards capturing the firm as a whole. Or contrast the fortunes of Albert Martin and Algy Belmont at another stockbroking firm, Cazenove's.[39] Martin, who had come in 1899 as the office boy, was some forty years later an indispensable figure, especially in relation to the nuts-and-bolts of new issues. Towards the end of the war he became a partner – the first in the firm to have risen all the way through the ranks. Belmont, the son-in-law of Kindersley and nicknamed 'Electric Whiskers' on account of his short temper as well as his enormous black moustache, was expected to become senior partner in due course – until he was accidentally killed in the Hyde Park black-out while doing a tour of inspection of his anti-aircraft batteries.

Terence Higgins was more in the Martin mould. The son of a Jermyn Street shirtmaker, and brought up modestly at Pinner, his break came in 1942 at the age of only sixteen, when he got a berth at Lloyd's (where he ultimately became a leading underwriter) because his father had made shirts for the two Service sons of an established underwriter there. For George Tite, the mordant correspondence clerk at Rothschilds so memorably evoked by Palin, the war meant not opportunity, but the end of everything; and at some point after it had broken out, he made the ultimate statement by hanging himself.[40]

During the early summer of 1941 it seemed likely that Norman also would be making an exit. His seventieth birthday was due to fall on 6 September, taking him past the normal retirement age for a Bank of England director, and on 19 May he noted that he had seen George Booth 'on behalf of a meeting after Court last week, to ask if I w^d ascertain if Catto c^d be released fr Treas^y & if he w^d stand for early Election [i.e. to resume his Bank directorship, which he had given up on going to the Treasury], with object of Govr next year'. Norman, as ever, did not relish the prospect of retirement, and he told Booth that the question should be held over until Peacock's return the following month from the United States. At about the time that Peacock returned, Norman was fortified by hearing Anderson's opinion that 'as regards next year's succession' the question of age was 'immaterial compared with lasting independence of Bk'; while soon afterwards, on 1 July, Peacock told Norman that, when 'pressed for personal opinion' by the Chancellor, he had expressed the view that the seventy-year rule 'might likely be suspended'.[41] That may or may not have been Peacock's independent view, but he would certainly have known Norman's wishes in the matter. These wishes prevailed, for later that month the Court agreed not to apply the seventy-year rule in his case, and Norman remained Governor.

There was, however, a vacancy on the Court, following Stamp's death in April after a bomb had landed on his house in Kent. On Booth's initiative, the bold decision was taken to approach Keynes. After Kingsley Wood had given his consent to the idea, Norman went to the Treasury on 5 September (the day before his own birthday) to pop the question. That was on a Friday afternoon, and after thinking over the matter during the weekend (and remarking to his mother that if he was not careful he would become a bishop next), Keynes told Norman on Monday afternoon, when the latter returned to the Treasury to get his answer, that he would be delighted to accept. On the 15th, Norman put Martin in the larger picture:

> I may tell you that there has been much coming and going about broadening the base of the Court: in other words, about introducing someone who may be held to represent Labour or the Trade Unions. The trouble is that, while we are willing to have (so to speak) a 'Coalition' Court, being under a Coalition Government, it has proved impossible to find the required representative who would commend himself with any reality or, I may say, decency. Therefore, as a sort of compromise, which in itself is valuable and may be a great advantage, we are shortly proposing the name of John Maynard Keynes to fill the vacancy caused by the tragic death of Stamp.[42]

Two days later Keynes lunched with Norman at the Bank, and on the 18th the public announcement was made. 'I fear you will soon be a KCB and quite lost,' the Cambridge economist Joan Robinson chided Keynes, who replied: 'Look on me hopefully as fifth column.' To Falk, the new director conceded that the 'old villain [i.e. Norman] loves his *institution* more than any doctrine', but added that in terms of the Bank as a whole 'the balance of sympathies and policies is widely reoriented'. Two other remarks by Keynes at this richly symbolic moment are also worth recording. 'At last orthodoxy has caught up with me.' And: 'I do not know if it is I or the Old Lady who has been made an honest woman of.' On 9 October there was a slightly tart tone to Norman's diary – '11.20. J.M. Keynes. 1st Court, hob nobbing and Lunch' – while three weeks later he told Martin that 'we are receiving some enlightenment and much enlivenment from Keynes, who certainly seems to have a mind which never rests and is always seeking after some new thing'. Keynes himself went to the Bank most Thursdays, for a Court meeting followed by lunch. After one visitation he left with Booth, slumped back in the car they were sharing, and declared: 'I do enjoy these lunches at the Bank: Montagu Norman, always absolutely charming, always absolutely wrong!'[43]

On the same day that Keynes made his début at Court, the Bank prepared a memorandum on its relations with government – a memorandum written very much with a view to use in future controversy, especially the question of whether the Bank should be nationalised. Essentially it was a prepared defence, arguing that the relationship was in fundamentals the same in war as it had been prior to war, in that on the one hand 'the Government, through the Treasury, seeks continuously the advice of the Bank, both on technical and wider questions, but retains undivided responsibility for major questions of policy', while on the other hand 'the Bank remains the confidential adviser and the administrative agent'. The defence ended with a classically empirical statement: 'Like many of the institutions that form the mainstay of this country, the Bank has reached its position by a process of growth and whilst, in theory, it may seem to be open to criticism on this ground or that, in practice – like the Common Law of England – it works.' Anxiety levels about the Bank's future were clearly rising, and Norman reiterated to Martin at the end of October that the election of Keynes as a director was not in itself enough in terms of broadening the Court, and that 'what we have now need to find is another candidate or two (of a Leftish tinge) for next spring'. By December the name of the leading pottery manufacturer Josiah Wedgwood, from a traditionally 'leftish' family and author of *The Economics of Inheritance*, was in the frame, and Kingsley Wood promised to find out on Norman's behalf whether he was a member of the Labour Party. Presumably the enquiries were satisfactory, for Wood agreed in January 1942 that Norman could approach Wedgwood.[44] That spring he duly became a director, replacing the over-age Cecil Lubbock.

Norman himself, however, was increasingly pessimistic that such changes of personnel would be enough to prevent the Bank from having to undergo a fundamental change in its status. Indeed, in March 1942 he frankly told the Committee of Treasury that 'in his view it had seemed for a long time past increasingly likely that some form of nationalisation would be applied to the Bank, not long after or even during the war, whatever the political party in power'. Furthermore, he believed that 'the interests of the Country and Empire and the maintenance of the credit structure and of a valuable tradition would be best served by the conversion of the Bank into a public utility corporation; and perhaps the sooner the better'. But as he added, 'no action could be taken for the time being, owing mainly to the personality of the present Chancellor, without whose determined support no such conversion was possible'. Although he did not spell it out, presumably Norman's thinking was that if nationalisation was going to happen anyway, it was better for the Bank that it was done before rather than after a Labour government was elected. Predictably, however, his mood fluctuated on the nationalisation question. Towards the end of that year, while similarly addressing some of his close colleagues in the Bank, he noted with some resignation how 'all decisions on policy were in fact taken in Whitehall' and, in terms of the Court, referred to 'the presence, in Lord Keynes [ennobled earlier in 1942], virtually of a Treasury representative'. Yet in September 1943, speaking at the *Economist*'s centenary lunch, his attitude was more robust. 'Norman was very short,' Raymond Streat observed. 'He traced the community of interest over the 100 years between the *Economist* and the Bank of England – both privately owned but both, he thought, rather the better able on that account to serve the public interest.'[45] His heart, in short, was not obeying his head – a not unusual Norman occurrence.

The old crispness did not desert him in his eighth decade. 'Shall we have the rare pleasure of seeing you next Tuesday and Wednesday?' he asked one of his directors, Lord Craigmyle, in April 1942. In July that year, Craigmyle was for once in London rather than his Galashiels home, arguing in the House of Lords strongly against the folly of allowing independence for India without adequate safeguards for British interests. Norman responded sympathetically, telling Craigmyle that 'the post-Cripps prospects for the Eastern Banks and for British business in India are meagre'. Always – even in war – there were functions to attend, most of them unwelcome, and Norman spent a Saturday afternoon in October 1942 having tea at Mansion House with the King, the Queen, Mrs Roosevelt, Ernest Gowers '& half a dozen Goats'. Still, at least they were probably Protestant goats, for the Lord Mayor was Lieutenant-Colonel Sir John Laurie. However, his period of office was almost up, and Norman had spent much of 1942 in something of a state about who would succeed him. This had included a private meeting with Laurie on 22 May: 'The next L Mayor falls to be a Jew (Pullitzer) & the 2^d in order likewise (Samuel): w^d they be wise to elect a Jew? I say NO.' The same diary entry recorded Norman's reasons as being 'bait for Hitler' and 'Black market'. Two more diary entries in September pick up the story. On the 17th: 'L. Mayor to make appt for Joseph (2^d on List of 2 Jews for L Mayor) who has heard that I oppose Election of Jew – wh I deny. I say any respectable person can make app^t to see me thro' my Sec.' And four days later: 'Ch Ex. N° 11 . . . A Jew for Ld Mayor? No.'[46] All to no avail, for Sir Samuel Joseph became Lord Mayor in November 1942 – almost a century after David Salomons had been the first Jew to attain that position.

The bee continued to buzz in Norman's bonnet, for that same month, when Leo Amery sat between Norman and Kingsley Wood at a big Mansion House lunch, Norman was 'somewhat embarrassingly audible, in view of a very Jewish looking old boy sitting opposite, in voicing his preference for Christian over Jewish Lord Mayors'. Knowledge of the Holocaust had been available in Britain since the summer, but Norman's anti-Semitism seemed to intensify with age. Ironically, when Geoffrey Madan had spotted him 'at third-class guichet at Liverpool Street Station' in December 1941, the Governor had looked 'like an old Rumanian Jew begging for alms'. Never the most equable of men, Norman was also getting testier, not helped by deteriorating health during much of 1943. His private secretary that year was Leslie O'Brien, who had succeeded Maurice Parsons. 'I went in to bat on a wicket that could hardly have been stickier. Norman hated losing Parsons and showed it by the impatient way he yelled for "O'Brien" from time to time. Nevertheless his feline charm, principally exercised on women, occasionally was lavished on me.'[47]

Some of that irascible charm was turned on the discount market, which Norman continued to nurse and which, perhaps to its own surprise, did not in the end do too badly out of the war. Commercial bill business may have collapsed, but with the volume of 'shorts' – short-dated government stocks – being pumped up in order to finance the war, that gave them plenty to deal in and hold. Even so, Norman was determined to continue with the market's consolidation, and in mid-1941 the Bank let it be known that it was looking for every dealer member of the market (apart from its own pet house, Seccombe, Marshall & Campion) to have resources of at least £500,000. Cater & Co and Brightwen & Co had already fused soon after the start of war, thereby becoming by far the largest of the private discount houses, and in July 1941 Cater, Brightwen & Co grew further by absorbing the oldest house, Roger Cunliffe, Sons & Co, which had preserved its identity unchanged since 1819. Other houses were also looking round for new partners, and John Parsons of Gilletts wrote illuminatingly in September 1941 to Arthur Penn of King & Shaxson:

> It has always been my hope that if ever I were personally involved in an amalgamation leading to a public company it would be possible to agree that the directors themselves would continue to run the business and tour the market each morning in the same way as the partners in a private firm do today. The personal touch I believe to be vital and would do a great deal to enhance the position and credit of the company and help to make business life pleasant ...

That fusion failed to happen, but the following year Gilletts did acquire Hohler & Co – a small discount house, one of whose two major partners had been killed in the war – at no apparent cost to that congenial routine. The war's final merger was in September 1943, when Cater Brightwen absorbed Daniell, Cazenove & Co. 'I blame Musker [Sir John

Musker, Chairman of Cater Brightwen] friendly-wise for having helped
to reduce Houses from 12 to 11,' Norman recorded that month. 'He
agrees: didn't realise it.' Back in 1933 there had been as many as twenty-
two houses, and presumably Norman had not wished to rationalise to
less than a round dozen. The following year, 1944, the market took on a
new institutional form, as the London Discount Market Association,
with 'Gus' Ellen of Union Discount as its first Chairman. Norman called
him his 'true and faithful servant', and almost all vestiges of the discount
market's independence were lost.[48]

There was also consolidation in the Stock Exchange. At the outbreak
of war there had been 796 member-firms, but by July 1942 as many as
114 had gone completely as the result of merger, while a further 110 had
made temporary arrangements with other firms that more often than not
ultimately became permanent. During the first two years of war the
overall volume of business declined by as much as 80 per cent, but from
1942 there was a perceptible revival. Given the huge increase in
government debt (which tripled between 1939 and 1945), it might have
been expected that most of this business would have been in gilts. In
practice, however, the gilt-edged market had a somewhat downbeat war,
for the government tended to bypass it and instead target its securities
directly at the public and institutions.[49] Moreover, there was a distinct
shift of investment appetite towards equities, especially after 1941 when
the imposition of income tax at 10s sharpened the desire for higher yields
than were obtainable from gilts.[50] The 30-Share Index climbed steadily
up; in 1944 Hargreaves Parkinson, editor of the *Financial News*,
published his influential treatise, *Ordinary Shares*, which directly
anticipated the post-war 'cult of the equity'; and increasingly the
emphasis was on identifying what were known as 'recovery stocks',
those with good prospects in peace. The authorities, however, remained
a stumbling-block to business-getting innovation. When in 1941 a young
stockbroker called Gerald Ashfield, attached to Strauss Turnbull, started
his own unit trust – probably the first stockbroker to do so – the Stock
Exchange Committee refused the application by Practical Investment Co
for inclusion in the general register of agents. Ashfield was compelled to
beat a temporary retreat, but in the end this innate conservatism stopped
neither him nor the unit trust movement.[51]

As an institution, the Stock Exchange was more on the defensive than
it had been at any time since being subjected to a royal commission in the
1870s. George Orwell was not alone in expecting it to become redundant
in a planned post-war economy, while in terms of stockbroking's
perceived contribution to the current war economy it must have been

disconcerting that that profession was ranked only forty-sixth in the order of reserved occupations – with the fact that stockbrokers came just after flower-sellers an additional humiliation. In July 1942, when the Stock Exchange Committee submitted a memorandum to the Treasury Committee under Lord Kennet that was considering the question of releasing manpower from the financial sector, the opportunity was taken to make some broad propaganda points:

> We have not failed to move with the times. To a far greater extent than most public Institutions we have retained our flexibility of organisation and our ability to adjust ourselves to ever changing circumstances. We have been successful in avoiding that rigidity which in so many directions has clamped a dead hand on enterprise. The standard of service rendered by stockbrokers has been revolutionised during the last generation . . . With our long experience of international trading, our unrivalled legal system and our immense prestige for honest dealing, we ought to be able to re-create great markets in London in the future, and in this work The Stock Exchange has a vital part to play. Such markets bring to this country directly and indirectly very large earnings in the aggregate, and we shall need every penny of such earnings in the New World after the war.[52]

It was not only the Stock Exchange itself that was increasingly concerned to uphold the market's reputation. Later in 1942 Norman summoned the Chairman, R.B. Pearson, and was broadly satisfied by what he heard: 'In spite of talk in the papers there is *no* speculation – No buying on borrowed money: practically no half com[n] men at work. I can give this assurance [to the Kennet Committee?]. He sh[d] abolish $\frac{1}{2}$ com men.' Not long afterwards, in May 1943, the Committee was compelled to act decisively in a clear case of insider trading. It had emerged that Edward Gayler, financial editor of the *Sunday Dispatch*, was in cahoots with two partners (including the senior partner) of the brokers Crews & Co as well as a half-commission man attached to the brokers Hurst-Brown, Buckmaster & Peter Hicks. The half-commission man, R.M. Pearson, gave his side of the story:

> With regard to his fore-knowledge of Mr Gayler's articles Mr Pearson said that if he suggested a share as cheap and if Mr Gayler subsequently said 'I have looked into it and entirely agree with you' then he thought that probably it would be mentioned in the next articles. He added, however, 'Mr Gayler was not in my pocket'. When questioned as to the propriety of his speculative dealings, he replied that speculation was rampant in the Stock Exchange and he did not see why he should be left out of it.

Pearson, not being a member, got off scot-free, but the senior partner was expelled and the other was suspended for five years.[53]

In all sorts of ways the world was changing – away from the buccaneers and towards greater regulation – and someone who disagreed strongly with that drift was the obstinate Jimmy Palmer-Tomkinson of Cazenove's, a major operator in gilts and a member of the Stock Exchange Committee since 1927. In 1941 he had argued successfully against the compulsory marking of bargains done on behalf on non-members ('Through all Stock Exchange history a bargain has been the private concern of the firms who do the bargain. No one in the world has the faintest right to know even that a bargain has been done . . .'), but by August 1943 his intemperately expressed hostility to the restrictive activities of the Capital Issues Committee was compelling Norman to ask his partner Claud Serocold 'to do nothing but bring peace & goodwill from Tomkinson toward the C.I.C.', with Norman adding to Serocold the instruction, 'his visit not to be mentioned'. However, even the urbane Serocold was unable to moderate Palmer-Tomkinson's wrath, and by the end of the year Norman and Peacock came to the conclusion that the latter should approach Pearson in order 'to evict Tomkinson fr Com^tee – in agreement with C. Serocold'.[54] But the bid to unseat Palmer-Tomkinson failed, for he remained on the Committee (shortly to become the Stock Exchange Council) for four more years.

The floor of the Stock Exchange remained an all-male preserve, but in March 1942 the Committee considered a request from two firms, Haley & Co and A. Sherriff & Co: each, being short of staff, wished to introduce a lady (Mrs Miller and Mrs Judd respectively) as settling-room clerks. A month of deliberation ensued, and on 20 April there took place a historic 12–11 vote 'in favour of women clerks being admitted to the Settling Room only as a war measure'. If that was a minor chink in one wall of prejudice, another wall was wholly intact. 'Here comes another fucking Jew!' A.R. Barton exclaimed just over a fortnight later, at 12.15 on Thursday, 7 May, when he looked up and saw another member, John Michael, while he was answering a call in the telephone room. Michael at once lodged a complaint, on the grounds that Barton, whom he described as having been 'so drunk he should not be allowed in the Stock Exchange', had sworn in front of the female telephone attendants. 'I had a severe attack in the morning of Kidney Trouble owing to having stones, and took Gin to relieve the pain,' was Barton's rather lame defence, and he was warned as to his future conduct. Nor was any action taken later that year, in December 1942, when another Jewish member, the elderly Leopold A. Abrahams, made his complaint: 'I wish to most strongly protest against the practice of Horse Play in the Oil Market, of which today I have been the victim, being forcibly thrown to the floor, receiving cuts on my nose and head injuries; apart from the dangers of these practices, I feel that it lacks decorum and lowers the prestige of the Institution.'[55]

Also getting no joy, in September 1943, was Captain Norman Chivers, last heard of in 1931:

> I have the honour to apply for the cash value [worth some £400] of my nomination. I was elected a member in 1927, and was a very happy man, as always, until I was suspended for a technical matter occurring every day, but that tragedy, to me, is passed. I have read and re-read Nomination Rule in conjunction with a Member of long standing. The conclusion was obvious, my Nomination value was mine, and I should have applied before, but the rule could be construed that the Committee could take it if they wished. I am not like an expelled or hammered Member, in fact my suspension caused me heavy loss, apart from breaking my spirit . . . I am a sick man from recurring wound troubles, and need cash for expenses etc . . . I apologise for pencil and scrappy paper.

The unyielding reply was that 'under Rule 28, you have no right of nomination as your application for re-election was rejected'. Chivers tried one more time – 'from a humane point of view I am only asking for my own money,' he asserted, before describing his 'unhappy but truthful application' as 'so desperately urgent' – but the earlier reply was merely confirmed.[56]

*

No one cared about poor Chivers, but quite the reverse was the case with the City's troubled merchant banks. 'Eclipse of the Merchant Banker' was the title of Paul Bareau's generally gloomy overview in the *Banker* in August 1941. Looking ahead to the post-war world, however, he contended that 'no doubt the character of their business will undergo considerable changes, but this prospect should hold no terrors for institutions which have always given proof of the greatest resilience and adaptability'. Specifically, he pointed to the prospect of their continuing to possess 'a degree of initiative and capacity for immediate decision which are not easily found in joint-stock concerns'. It was a prognosis sharply at odds with that of George Bolton, who in a February 1942 memorandum gazed ahead with his usual confident certainty:

The Clearing Bank will be in a stronger and more powerful position at the end of the war compared with other London banks and accepting houses. Their functions as the accredited agents of the Treasury during the war will have tended to attract business previously performed by expert private organisations. This increased competitive power will continue, as not only will the Clearing Banks remain the agents of Exchange Control but foreign exchange will become largely a simple matter of service to customers and not a mystery whose secrets are shared only by adepts. There would appear to be little room for successful competition to give customers a better banking service either at home or abroad and therefore the revival of the old conception of the foreign banker appears improbable, although there may be individual examples due entirely to the personal element. The private Houses may also have difficulty in avoiding unfavourable criticism based on comparative credit ranking. But it is possible that the merchant banks may regain their original status of merchants, provided that they leave banking to their deposit bankers and develop their foreign connections with a bias towards merchanting and not banking.[57]

Throughout the rest of the war, conventional wisdom in the City tended to favour the more pessimistic analysis. At the same time, there was a strong disinclination to leave for dead what had once been such a notable – and profitable – activity.

Naturally, circumstances varied from merchant bank to merchant bank. 'Rex Benson – to say he goes to Wash[n] ?next week – as a Soldier: Firm left desolate: Guy in Wilts: Con in So'ton: but no business!' Norman's diary entry in January 1941 accurately summed up the state of play in one house. In the context of war, it was a significant help to a merchant bank's situation if there was already a strong tradition of doing investment business on behalf of well-off – or reputedly well-off – individual clients. Kleinworts, for example, had no such tradition and suffered accordingly, whereas Barings, with its connections deep into British society, prospered in this area. 'We are in financial straits,' Lady Diana Cooper wrote to 8 Bishopsgate from the Dorchester in 1942. 'Can you help us out by selling our worst shares? If I don't get £2000 soon they will put me in jug.' Hambros was another house faring not too poorly – with Olaf successfully cultivating inland acceptances – whereas by contrast, and presumably unbeknown to Kindersley and Brand, Peacock called on Norman in October 1943 to ask why Lazards had 'a bad smell & reputation'. There were also problems at Brown Shipley. E. Clifton Brown, the Governor's former partner, called on Norman in December 1942. 'Firm's position: I say lack of Cap . . . He is angry & hurt and inclined to threaten.' At this time Norman was also worried about Morgan Grenfell's inadequate capital (down to £1.5m), and over the next few weeks he seems to have devised the idea of a merger between it and Brown Shipley. However, although Bicester proved amenable, Brown did not, and the idea was abandoned. Instead, Morgan Grenfell fortified its position by acquiring (despite Norman's initial opposition and against competition from Hambros) Cull & Co, whose elderly partners were keen to sell out.[58]

There is no doubt what was *the* great might-have-been of these difficult years. It began when Norman saw Anthony de Rothschild in December 1941: 'Seems overwrought & worried: Lionel seriously ill & future uncertain'. Lionel, an inveterate cigar-smoker, died the following month, and it was left to Anthony to carry on alone. The precise financial position of Rothschilds at this time remains a mystery, but in April 1942 Norman told Cobbold 'in all secrecy of R's dependance on Bk – wh is a bar to more freedom to Acc Hses'. Later in 1942 there were three of the most pregnant entries in all of Norman's diaries:

> *8 September*. Pam [Albert Pam of Schroders]. Why sh^d not Schroders, Rs & Barings amalgamate? Or why sh^d not Barings take over the other 2?
>
> *10 September*. ERP [Peacock of Barings]. ?BB & Co + JHS & Co + NMR & S: he will consider.
>
> *2 October*. ERP. BB & Co not willing, after consideration, to join with JHS & Co, whose methods are impossible & unpopularity great – nor with NMR & S who are entirely a *Jewish* family concern.

Of course, even if Peacock had been willing to transform 'the Trinity' into a single deity, it is far from certain that it would have been a runner. It is, nonetheless, a supremely tantalising moment in City history. Over the next few months Norman continued to note regular visits from Anthony de Rothschild. 'He shows an improving position but has a long way to go.' And: 'They must go very slow.' Pam, meanwhile, would call again in August 1943, when there was another tantalising Norman entry: 'Future of Schroders: I mention Roth^s, Brandts, Browns, wh he will consider'. Nothing came of it, nor of Pam's own idea later in the year of a merger with Guinness Mahon.[59] For better or worse, most of the hallowed names would still be in place when the war ended, even if some of their businesses were in distinctly poor shape.

There were no such traumas for the far better capitalised, less exposed clearing banks.[60] 'Because of the Government hand in every channel of life,' Parkes of Lloyds observed in 1941, 'almost in complete control of industry and the main customer of industry, banking is easy.' He reiterated the point later in the war: 'Today we have few problems –

lending is easy and the work is light.' Indeed, 'I sometimes wish I had more to do than I have on many days at present.' For one clearing banker, the easy life was constitutionally impossible. When Lidbury's London home was destroyed in 1941, he quartered in the basement of Westminster's head office in Lothbury, and (in his biographers' words) 'he remained there until the war ended, on hand to inspect immediately any London branch damaged by enemy action, prodding rubble with his walking stick to find anything worth salvaging'. It was unlikely that Lidbury found a soulmate in his fellow-clearing banker Clarence Sadd, who in June 1943 became Midland's 'Director and Chief of Executive' – in effect Chief Executive. After entering the bank's service in 1898 as a fifteen-year-old, he had risen through provincial branches before coming to head office in 1933. He possessed a keen sense of publicity, on behalf of himself as well as the bank, and was reputed to have leftish political sympathies, even aspirations. John Kinross recalled meeting this 'exceedingly ambitious man' at a dinner in Leicester in the late 1920s: 'He opened the conversation by enquiring if I read the Bible, to which I replied "not very often". "That's a pity," he said, "I get all my best business phrases from it."' Kinross added that 'during the next twenty years I saw a certain amount of Sadd and for a time I had a differently worded letter from him on my birthday each year – a typical Sadd gimmick'.[61]

In the same month that he became Chief Executive, Sadd's Chairman, McKenna, fell ill, and the question of the succession became pressing.[62] From his sick-bed McKenna pressed his senior director, Sir Thomas Royden, to take over – 'It is not a commercial mind that is wanted but a statesman's, and you have statesmanship in a high degree' – but Royden preferred to stay in the background. McKenna died on 6 September, and over the next week and a half Norman's diary recorded the outcome:

7 September. 11.45. Stanley Christopherson [Midland's octogenarian Deputy Chairman]: favours Sadd as M^{c}K's succ^r: Sadd is unwilling. I say the 2 posts sh^d not be combined.

3.15. Sir Thomas Royden, following my talk with Christopherson. Chris ch'man 'for the duration'. Royden will *not* be d^y but a nonentity will be found: Woolton [the Minister of Food] ch'man post-war: Sadd keeps his present position unchanged. I agree.

14 September. 3.45. S. Christopherson. No alternative to Sadd as his N° 2 [i.e. to be Deputy Chairman]. I warn him of poss. discontent among other ch'men.

16 September. 3.30. Clarence Sadd. i. recounts some sayings of McKenna over the last few days of his life & will send me short note about them. ii.

we agree at all times & in all conditions to consult & cooperate & play ball together.

Christopherson, then, was to be the stop-gap Chairman, with Sadd combining the roles of Chief Executive and Deputy Chairman. Over the next three weeks there were further manoeuvrings, against a background of Christopherson being confined to bed with what Sadd described to Norman as a 'bad heart'. Sir John Anderson came to see Norman in order to put in a bid for Midland's post-war chairmanship, but on the day that he did so the Chancellor, Kingsley Wood, died, and Anderson succeeded him. Midland's board, anyway, wanted Anderson no more than it had done in 1938, with Cunliffe-Owen condemning him to Norman as 'arbitrary and rude'. Woolton (of 'pie' fame) was much, though not unanimously, preferred; and by early October he had informally agreed to keep himself free, should the chairmanship become vacant.[63] As for Sadd, he had for the time being that most enviable of things: a free hand.

Moreover, as a self-proclaimed progressive, he embraced the future – a future that many in the City, including Norman, feared. In December 1942 the Beveridge Report was published, laying the foundations of the post-war Welfare State. The *Financial News* adopted a fairly favourable tone towards it, but not so the *FT*, declaring that 'the Beveridge plan, in its main outlines, is that of the Trades Union Congress'. Over the next year and a half, the City tried hard to have a restraining influence on post-war welfare and employment commitments, but generally found itself in an uncomfortably isolated position as the 'reconstruction' process gathered momentum.[64] It was difficult for the City not to feel under threat. Even a Tory radical like Boothby, in his prognosis of *The New Economy* that lay ahead after the war, anticipated not only a nationalised Bank of England, but also 'the transformation of the banking system from a private profit-making concern into a public service'. In February 1943 Norman invited to lunch the Home Secretary, Labour's Herbert Morrison, and presumably hoped to exercise his feline charm. Their topic of conversation, no doubt chosen by the guest, was the unhappy one of the 1931 financial crisis. 'He charges Bk with plot against Labour and dole,' Norman recorded without comment.[65] Integral to the domestic side of the reconstruction process was that old chestnut, the relationship between finance and industry. Ernest Bevin in particular, as a former member of the Macmillan Committee, helped to propagate the view that the City in the past had let down industry and that it was time for a fresh start in that vexed relationship. Above all, that meant at last doing something satisfactory about the 'Macmillan gap' – the provision of capital to medium-sized firms. Much would turn on how it was filled.

Back in December 1941, almost two years after BIDC had in effect been wound up, the Bank's Henry Clay was starting to look ahead to the question of long-term finance for British industry after the war. He argued that the London capital market was unsatisfactory in its present form: its costs were too high, it was geared almost entirely towards providing a market for existing concerns, and 'there is no industrial financing concern on which borrowers can fall back'. Accordingly, he suggested the establishment of such a concern – an institution that, he presciently noted, 'would have to take an equity interest so that profits might offset losses'. Almost certainly it was helpful that Clay became a member in July 1943 of a committee on post-war domestic finance, which the Bank had set up four months earlier under Niemeyer's chairmanship. The committee was not entirely convinced of the economic value of what it was doing: Niemeyer defined 'the misfits' of industry as 'too small for issues, too disorganised, ill-advised' and argued that in post-war Britain 'these misfits will have a political importance disproportionate to their real importance'. That autumn, however, his committee proposed the establishment of an institution, capitalised at £50m, that would provide, in Niemeyer's words, 'temporary finance for some who later go to the market' and 'permanent finance for others (mainly small) who cannot get to the market'. The capital would have to come from the clearing banks, but as Niemeyer observed, 'if such a scheme is to keep Whitehall from more Governmental forms of industrial finance, it has got to be substantial and demonstrably so.'[66]

If Norman was sceptical, as he may well have been, that scepticism disappeared once he became aware, as he did by early December, of apparently competing Board of Trade schemes that, according to the faithful Skinner, were a 'bureaucratic monster'. Over the Christmas period Norman was in tacit alliance with the Treasury's Sir Wilfrid Eady about formulating a proposal that would be acceptable to government, and on 7 January 1944 he explained his thinking to his new friend, Sadd. '*My purpose*,' Norman stated frankly, '*is to satisfy Whitehall*: to keep them out of the Banking Business and free of malevolence towards the Bankers – which at this moment are stakes worth playing for.' Appended to Norman's letter was a draft prospectus. Two new institutions were now envisaged. One, aimed at larger firms, was to have capital of about £30m (supplied by the insurance companies and investment trusts) and in many ways was to be a retread of BIDC, with industrial restructuring its aim. The other, with capital of some £20m mainly to come from the clearing banks, was to be directed at the provision of finance for rather smaller businesses. The latter was far the more contentious proposal.[67] Above all, would the banks wear it?

In persuading them to do so, the Bank received valuable softening-up support from Eady, who on 10 February lunched at National Provincial with that bank's Chairman, Colin Campbell, who was also Chairman of the Committee of London Clearing Bankers, and its chief General Manager, Ernest Cornwall. 'Campbell thought it would have to be done but Cornwall nearly had a fit,' Niemeyer recorded afterwards on the basis of what he had been told by Eady. 'It is quite plain that Eady more or less indicated unpleasant alternatives propounded by Whitehall, if the Banks did not play.' Over the next few weeks the clearers suggested a compromise solution – of individual subsidiaries to do business with small firms – but received no encouragement from the Bank. By mid-March Lidbury was complaining bitterly to his Chairman about the consequences for the clearing banks of what he called 'the present political ferments', in particular the 'indirect levy on the resources of the commercial banks for the subsidising of commercial and industrial "adventures" in the interests of the "full employment" campaign'. Although Anthony Tuke of Barclays was more pragmatic – arguing that the banks had no alternative but to find the 'least objectionable' way to proceed, given that the Bank of England was seemingly 'more nearly allied to the Government than to the clearing banks' – it was Lidbury who, at the end of March, had his way in formulating a strongly worded response to the Bank from the clearers as a whole. After a stout denial that the 'gap' even existed, and an assertion that after the war the banks would be competing 'far more fiercely' for lending business than before the war, there followed a paragraph that only he could have penned:

It is obviously undesirable to countenance the raising of hopes and expectations of people whose request for financial assistance will not, and cannot, satisfy the scrutiny and examination dictated by common business prudence. It may be feared that this class may constitute the unsatisfied demand.

Even so, the clearing banks did concede that 'notwithstanding the reasons which support their belief that existing credit facilities do, in actual practice, cover all requirements which are able to provide economic justification, there may be considerations of a public nature of sufficient psychological importance to render it expedient that a further organisation should be formed'. That did not mean, however, that they could 'look with equanimity on a project which may saddle them with substantial losses made outside their own control'.[68] Put another way, though there was no derailing the reconstruction train, Lidbury wanted to make sure that he was in the signal box keeping the lights set on red.

The other key aspect of reconstruction, from the City's point of view, was the nature of the international financial order that would emerge from the war.[69] There may at a personal level have been a rapprochement between Keynes and Norman, but within a few months of Keynes becoming a director of the Bank in September 1941, it was clear that in a larger sense there remained a gulf between the two men. Believing that 'the post-war world must not be content with patchwork', Keynes that autumn pushed hard the concept of a Clearing Union, essentially as a means of achieving multi-lateralism by means of international agreement rather than traditional *laissez-faire*. The Bank's instinctive response was to view this approach as not only unrealistically Utopian, but also a threat to the future of the sterling area. Early in December 1941, looking ahead to the post-war world, Norman asserted to Martin in South Africa that 'nothing is more important in my view than that the Commonwealth should hang together as closely as, if not more closely than, they are now doing and should maintain the Sterling Area, to which with advantage might be added some more adherents when the time comes'. Soon afterwards, Keynes tried personally to persuade Norman of the merits of his plan, describing it as 'a bold bid to combine the great historical advantages of the XIX Century Gold Standard with modern ideas and the requirements of the post-war world'. Norman declined to be seduced, but in practice the Bank could do little other than (in Cobbold's words at the end of December) 'allow J.M.K.'s stuff to percolate where it will'.[70]

The Bank may have feared Keynes's inclination to accept without question the fact of post-war American economic and financial dominance – Leo Amery discovered in January 1942 that Norman 'shares my anxieties as to American ambitions to make the British empire a lebensraum for their exports' – but during the rest of the war it was Keynes, not the Bank, who made the running on the British side. By February 1944, with the Bank continuing to uphold the claims of the sterling area as against the plans for an international monetary fund that Keynes and the Americans were developing – and anyway naturally resentful of any new organisation apparently designed to go above existing structures of central banking co-operation – Keynes exploded. 'The Bank is not facing any of the realities,' he told the Chancellor (Anderson), explaining that it was failing to allow either 'for the fact that post-war domestic policies are impossible without American assistance' or 'for the fact that vast debts and exiguous reserves are not, by themselves, the best qualification for renewing old-time international banking'. Early in March, writing to Beaverbrook, he almost went over the top:

> Twice in my life I have seen the Bank blindly advocating policies which I expected to lead to the greatest misfortunes and a frightful smash. Twice I have predicted it; twice I have been disbelieved; twice it has happened . . . My conviction is that here is a third occasion. The Bank is engaged in a desperate gamble in the interests of old arrangements and old-fashioned ideas, which there is no possibility of sustaining. Their plan, or rather their lack of plan, would, in my firm belief, lead us into yet another smash.[71]

Third time round, however, Keynes's fears were exaggerated, for nothing – not even Bank of England obstruction – could stop the International Monetary Fund from being established.

Even as Keynes remonstrated, his old adversary was no longer in the game. Over the previous year Norman's health had palpably started to deteriorate, sharpening the question of the succession.[72] One possibility was Niemeyer, but Churchill (who would never forget the return to gold) ruled him out. Another was Cobbold, who was very much Norman's protégé and, like Niemeyer, had become an executive director shortly before the war, but he was not yet forty – in City terms, almost a babe. Norman himself came to accept in the course of 1943 that the sands of time really were running out, and he agreed to retire in 1945. Probably at the instigation of Keynes, Kingsley Wood pushed the idea of Towers, of the Bank of Canada, becoming the next Governor; and in June 1943 Norman reluctantly consented to send Peacock to Canada to sound Towers out. 'Peacock was extraordinarily persuasive,' he would recall, 'but at the end of our talk he said that when I retired at the end of five years "we will find you some directorships in London". It was fairly clear that what the Bank wanted was a caretaker governor who would quietly disappear at the end of his term.' Not surprisingly, Towers added, 'I found the prospects singularly unattractive.' Nevertheless, his hat remained in the ring – until, first, Kingsley Wood died, and then, on 21 October, the Committee of Treasury formally decided that Towers was unsuitable, on the grounds of his 'essentially "dollar" background', and being 'publicly committed to post-war plans which many of us feel would prejudice the international position of sterling'. Or, as Norman tersely put it in his diary that day, Towers was altogether 'too much JMK & $'. In his place, the front-runner now emerged as Catto, whom Norman trusted and whom he believed would – with his range of contacts in government as well as in the City – best protect the interests of the Bank. Catto himself, still based in the Treasury, was agreeable, but Norman recorded on 7 January 1944 that Anderson at No 11 was 'undecided & may be going to sound Colleagues'.[73]

Barely a week later Norman's health at last decisively gave way, and the situation suddenly became urgent. He was diagnosed as having pneumococcal meningitis, his doctors determined that he must not continue as Governor, and towards the end of March he accepted their verdict with infinite reluctance. 'It's not going back that will kill me,' he told Peacock. The new Governor, formally elected at the meeting of the Bank of England's stockholders on 15 April, was Catto, with Anderson having been given little time to canvas other possibilities, though there is no reason for thinking that he was not happy enough with the choice. 'It seems that everything is falling about my ears,' Norman wrote, the day before the stockholders met, to the Bank's chief accountant. 'I am as good as gone, and have to find some way of avoiding the qualities of a vegetable.' Nor was his mother, still going strong at ninety-six, inclined to look on the bright side: 'They should have let him finish his twenty-five years.' And, reputedly, she added: 'I do wish I could find him a job.'[74]

*

The end was also fast approaching for Roy Sambourne. His spirits had generally improved with the upturn in the fortunes of war, but early in 1944 he was taken ill and did not return to action – or, in practice, inaction – until 5 April: 'To City & enter St Ex after 13 weeks. Greetings from all & sundry – very flattering. Things not going too well. I leave before 1 pm & lunch Ox & C.' During the rest of the year he was rarely in the City, though occasionally he would travel up from Nymans in Sussex, where he was staying for the duration with his brother-in-law Lennie Messel, a less than welcoming host. 'To City – fog & train late – no business – and most disheartening,' he recorded five days before Christmas. 'We do nothing.'[75] The diary ends abruptly at the end of 1944, and Sambourne died in a London nursing home a year and a half later.

While that minor City career was petering out during the course of 1944, the historic house of Schroders was trying to decide if it had a future in the post-war world. The crux was the attitude of the younger partners, Helmut Schroder and Henry Tiarks, on whose resolve or otherwise the firm's future would depend. 'At this juncture in our lives,'

Schroder wrote to Tiarks (who was away, recovering from tuberculosis) in June, 'I think it is vitally important to our own happiness that we should make up our minds quite definitely, once and for all, that to run J.H.S. & Co is what we want to do more than anything in the world. That we want to and can deal with and master awkward folk and awkward unpleasant situations and enjoy doing it. Before you decide to return to 145, do please assure me that you know your own answers convincingly, unswervingly and without regard to what you might conceive would please your father or me.' Tiarks's reply was unequivocal: if their generation were to decide to 'throw away the vantage point of an organisation (however battered) which it has taken our fathers and grandfathers and us 100 years to establish, and which stands for something in the minds of businessmen in nearly every country', it would be nothing less than a breach of duty. Briefly, at about the same time, the possibility was refloated (this time by 8 Bishopsgate) of a merger with Barings, but it came to nothing; and it was clear that the fate of Schroders would lie in the hands of two youngish men with a tried and trusted City pedigree.[76]

Siegmund Warburg also had a fine banking pedigree, but in most City eyes remained far from tried or trusted. It was on the face of it a hammer blow when in January 1945 the New Trading Co's other leading figure, the brilliant Harry Lucas, died at the age of only thirty-nine, having failed (unlike Tiarks) to recover from tuberculosis. Quite apart from his creative input, Lucas with his background in the discount market had added much to Warburg's City credibility. 'I deeply appreciate your sympathy,' Warburg wrote from 82 King William Street (tel: Mansion House 7703) to Reid of Barings, thanking him for his 'kind words of condolence'. The sentiments were no doubt sincere – but as his fellow-director Sir Andrew McFadyean accurately recalled some twenty years later, the cardinal fact was that 'dual control' had now ended and 'Siegmund could fashion the bank as he desired, and carry out the work for which he had trained himself'. Almost certainly there were no such mixed feelings for that other exponent of the free hand, Clarence Sadd, when it was decided that Midland's new Chairman from February 1945 was to be not Woolton (by now Minister of Reconstruction and presumably unavailable), but instead the Marquess of Linlithgow. A former Viceroy of India, he knew nothing about banking; and, in the understated words of Midland's historians, 'this relative lack of experience obviously strengthened the decision-making position of his vice-chairman', Sadd, who soon afterwards was knighted.[77]

By this time, Norman's successor had got his feet properly under the table.[78] Catto, sixty-five when he became Governor, had had a remarkable life: his father was a shipwright; he left school at fifteen; and before the First World War he became a successful merchant, mainly in the Near and Middle East. During the war he was Chairman of the British Food Mission, before spending most of the 1920s in Calcutta as head of the Calcutta-based merchanting firm Andrew Yule & Co, in which Morgan Grenfell had a large interest. In 1929 he returned to London to head the London firm (originally George Yule & Co, but renamed Yule, Catto & Co in 1920) and also become a partner in Morgan Grenfell. He was created a Baron in 1936. In all, he was (as the Bank of England's Humphrey Mynors would put it) 'a leading example of the Scottish boy of comparatively humble origin who rose to the top rank in the City of London through a combination of innate qualities and of grasping opportunities wherever they offered'. Catto had a memorable physique, which Raymond Streat encountered in 1945: 'One of the smallest men I have met. Dapper, alert, sharp-eyed, Scots accent.' Or, as Mynors nicely as well as shrewdly described him: 'In appearance he was very short of stature, with a fresh complexion and clear blue eyes. His open countenance and quiet manner perhaps tended to conceal his shrewdness and skill as a negotiator . . .'[79]

O'Brien, fresh from his battering at the hands of Norman, was the new Governor's private secretary for a year:

> He had never before been at the head of such a large, diverse and highly skilled organisation and I would guess that he never fully comprehended its ramifications or attempted to make full use of the instrument which had been placed in his hands. He had spent a lifetime relying on himself and doing most things for himself. So far as possible this was how he wanted to continue, regarding the Bank services in some respects as competing rather than collaborating with him. He always took impish delight in any failure of the Bank to live up to its high reputation, seeing it, I suspect, as evidence that Bank performance was inferior to Catto performance. I guess shortness of stature had something to do with this, but he was a delightful man to work for, equable, direct and unfailingly courteous so that in no time my nervous dyspepsia became nothing but a memory.

O'Brien also noted that it was hard for the Bank's permanent officials, like himself, not to feel that Catto had 'a rather exaggerated respect for Treasury opinion and quality'. Few, however, could deny the sheer depth of Catto's commercial experience, the soundness of his judgement, or the appropriateness of the fact – at this particular juncture in the Bank's history – that he was neither a government stooge nor a deeply entrenched member of the City Establishment. In January 1945, six months after the Bank had celebrated its 250th anniversary and Catto had taken the opportunity to reaffirm publicly that its purpose in relation to government was 'to give independent and candid advice based upon experience', Keynes in London assured Brand in Washington that 'Catto is very decidedly getting his hand on the helm, much quicker and more firmly than I felt confident of, and is a great success'.[80] Having won his City spurs (and Norman's confidence) in the 1930s by helping to sort out the Royal Mail situation, Catto perhaps felt that any other task was relatively straightforward.

Shortly after he became Governor, the long-running discussions about the post-war monetary and trading order culminated in the United Nations conference at Bretton Woods in July 1944, when the basic principles were established of an International Monetary Fund designed to stabilise exchange rates and a Bank for Reconstruction and Development (the future World Bank), designed to provide long-term loans. Catto and the Bank of England, however, remained only bit-players in the process, with Keynes from his Treasury base continuing to be the dominant figure on the British side. All that could be done was to attempt to exercise a restraining influence. 'I am anxious that it should be made clear from the very beginning that the proposed institution is not intended for relief purposes,' Catto wrote to the Treasury a month before Bretton Woods, about the proposed Bank for Reconstruction and Development. 'Unless the institution is run on a strictly commercial basis, its resources will gradually be frittered away and the high ideals of its intentions will end in disaster and recrimination.' He added that he 'should like to make another plea that the institution should be called something other than a bank'. That particular plea fell on deaf ears, but the Governor did manage to secure at Bretton Woods what became known as 'the Catto clause' – in effect, a reluctant acceptance by the United States that, even in a world run by the almighty dollar, other nations had the right, as a last resort and in consultation with the IMF, to vary their exchange rates. 'Bolton will have told you all about Bretton Woods,' Brand in Washington wrote to Catto after it was all over. 'I did what I could in the case of the Bank, generally aiming at getting the conference to be sufficiently conservative. Some people on the American side and in other quarters had, to my mind, many inflated ideas as to the immense sums of money that ought to be available at once for international lending.' Brand added that Bolton, representing the Bank of England, 'was not in a very easy position, but he acquitted himself admirably'.[81]

Overall, the City's response to Bretton Woods was polite rather than enthusiastic. The *FT* expressed anxiety about whether the Bank for Reconstruction and Development would make its loans selectively, pointing out that 'the creditworthiness of the borrower as well as the nature of the work helps to determine the ultimate fate of the loan and of the lenders' money', while the *Financial News* strongly criticised the system of IMF quotas, on the grounds that they gave the United States 'such a figure as will make her attitude, at any future moment, decisive to all intents and purposes'. Parkes of Lloyds, however, reflected privately that 'on the whole I think a very good job has been done and I think it augurs well for the future that the powerful countries amongst the Allies are honestly endeavouring to restore economic sanity to the world'. He did not deny, nevertheless, 'the leaning there is over here in certain quarters in the direction of bilateral trade treaties instead of multilateral'. It was a leaning with which Catto sympathised to only a limited extent. 'It is sheer madness,' he declared the following spring in a note on commercial policy, 'to think the Empire can create a cave where we take in one another's washing and ignore the rest of the world! ... The countries we sell to are not necessarily the countries from which we buy, and if we begin unilateral trading we return to *barter, the survival of the fittest* and *more war!*'[82] The implications of the choice were financial as well as commercial. Put another way, was the whole world to be the City's oyster, as it had been before 1914 and even up to 1931? Or, with the dollar now conclusively paramount in global terms, was it more sensible, if less glorious, to rely almost solely on the sterling area?

On the domestic side of post-war reconstruction, the new Governor had by now successfully brought the clearing banks into line. The nub was the proposed Industrial and Commercial Finance Corporation. 'Such a company, concerned only with industrial matters and independently managed,' ran Skinner's briefing for Catto ahead of the latter's crucial first meeting with the clearers on 11 May 1944, 'would not only make a good public appeal but would be a wise step for the Banks to take and go a long way towards allowing them to get on with their legitimate business in peace.' At the meeting itself, Catto emphasised that 'a new organisation for each Bank would be quite impracticable' and that what was needed was a larger organisation showing to the public 'that the banking entity are anxious to play their part in the finance of small businesses'. Edwin Fisher of Barclays reluctantly agreed:

> We all feel that we can do this ourselves – rightly or wrongly – Banks would be able to advise if they had applications which they could not deal

with. I think there may be political reasons but if unorthodox banking must be done I think there is much to be said for the formation of a separate institution with the help of the Bank of England. If you have a separate company it does preserve the reputation of British Banking from the imputation that they are getting into a system of continental banking . . .

To which Catto remarked that 'there is no suggestion that this should not be run on a strictly commercial basis'. The outcome of the meeting was a committee to draft specific proposals for government approval – a committee in which the most powerful figures were Niemeyer on behalf of the Bank, determined that the ICFC should happen, and Lidbury, whose private view remained that 'the damn thing isn't wanted'.[83]

Niemeyer had his way, not least in the context of that summer's landmark White Paper on full employment, which to the City's relief did not include the establishment of a National Investment Board. Necessarily, the implicit price of that exemption was a more whole-hearted commitment to industry on the part of the banks, a logic that even Lidbury was unable to evade. Detailed proposals went to government, via Catto, in October; and in January 1945 Anderson announced in Parliament the intended formation of the Finance Corporation for Industry, aimed at large businesses, alongside the much more politically charged ICFC, which would specialise in supplying medium- and long-term capital for small- and medium-sized business, in amounts ranging from £5,000 to £200,000. The Big Five would be the ICFC's main shareholders (contributing £11m out of £15m), and Anderson emphasised that neither new institution would be subject to government direction. 'Even if it can be regarded as little more than a gesture,' the *Financial News* asserted about the ICFC after the announcement, 'the gesture is a sympathetic one and indicative of the best intentions.'[84]

Who would chair it? The Bank of England's first choice was Sir Geoffrey Vickers, but on his declining the position, an offer was successfully made to William Piercy. That self-made City man, latterly as a stockbroker, had had a very successful war, heading up the British Petroleum Mission to Washington and then with deft timing moving from the Liberal to the Labour camp as Attlee's principal assistant. His main day-to-day colleague, it was eventually decided during the summer of 1945, would be another self-made financier, John Kinross, who before the war had advocated such an institution and soon after the parliamentary announcement wrote to the Bank pushing his claims for a berth. From his Hertfordshire farm, where he spent much of the war, Kinross also sent a copy of his application to Sadd – presumably in the hope that the latter would help to roll his log – and asked Midland's Vice-Chairman to accept 'fresh eggs & a roasting chicken'. As for the board, each of the main shareholders appointed one director. Westminster asked the merchant banker Edward de Stein (of SARA repute) if he would do the honours. Purely 'as a matter of public service', de Stein accepted. 'I do not believe that the Company will be a success,' he added to Westminster's Chairman, and Beckett agreed: 'I fear that many projects of this nature which have a political origin will prove that such an emanation does not produce successful financial or commercial results.'[85] Such negative sentiments merely echoed those of Westminster's chief General Manager, the almost wholly unreconstructed Lidbury.

Few imagined that the impending post-war world would not be more heavily regulated than had previously been the case in peacetime. A touchstone was the Cohen Committee on Company Law, which was set up by the Board of Trade and began to take evidence in 1943. One witness that year was the reform-minded financial journalist Hargreaves Parkinson, a strong advocate of the compulsory disclosure of any transfers to secret or inner reserves. 'Would you in that respect draw any distinction between trading or commercial companies on the one hand, and banking, insurance and investment companies on the other?' he was asked. 'That is a very delicate question. Personally I should not draw such a distinction, but I am afraid that would bring the wrath of the banks and insurance companies down upon me.' On another area of disclosure, Captain Nutcombe Hume, Managing Director of the various Charterhouse organisations, disdained ambivalence:

> I think if the remuneration of the chairman of banks and of some of the other great national enterprises in this country were made available to the public at large – because you cannot confine such information to the shareholders only – in the annual reports of those companies, it would create a quite wrong impression in the minds of a very large number of people that they were being paid more than they should get. I do not think the average member of the public can properly assess what is the right rate of remuneration for the leading executives, particularly of the big companies.

In the course of 1944 it remained a moot point whether the Cohen Committee would advocate a fundamental overhaul of company law. Harold Brown, a former senior partner of the solicitors Linklaters & Paines and according to that firm's historian 'a recognised expert on company law', strongly hoped not. 'There are black sheep in the flock,' he conceded to the committee, but during his forty years in the City he had been 'impressed mainly by the honesty and high standard of conduct generally displayed by those controlling and carrying on business in this country', which he added made for 'a pleasant contrast to the standards which seem to prevail in some foreign countries'.[86]

In the event, the Cohen Report of June 1945 did lead to far-reaching changes – in particular, the compulsory consolidation of accounts – while accepting that it remained for the Stock Exchange alone to decide which issues should or should not come to the market. It was, from the Stock Exchange's standpoint, a vital endorsement, at a time when the popular mood was running all the other way. 'Some people, it was declared, think of the House as a gambling casino,' reported 'Autolycus' regretfully, in the wake of a meeting of the Stock Exchange's shareholders near the end of the war. 'Others regard it as a place where the public, if they deal, are bound to lose money. Such impressions, it was claimed, might be met by the appointment of a well-paid Public Relations Officer who would instruct the public in the service, and the value, of the Stock Exchange.'[87]

The final year of war was not, in general, a happy time in the City. The flying bombs began to hit London in June 1944, and over the next few months there was considerable destruction in the City. For instance, 31 Old Jewry took a direct hit on 6 October, and Freshfields turned to the Bank of England for temporary sanctuary. As late as March 1945 Lees-Milne was recording that 'three hundred people' had been killed by a rocket attack 'in the City'. Nor, despite the 30-Share Index continuing to rise (up to 116 by the end of the year, representing a remarkable recovery in real as well as nominal terms), was there a lot to occupy the days. When Lionel Fraser returned to Helbert Wagg early in 1945, he found that 'life seemed crushingly dull' and that 'the City had not got back into rhythm'. Moreover, the sense of gloom was compounded by a widespread pessimism about the City's future. 'At the beginning of this year we had a little business to do and managed to sell two issues,' Evelyn Baring rather mournfully informed New York in March 1945. 'They were both very successful, but the profit from our point of view was insignificant. However, I suppose we have got to expect that in this new world.' Still, even in this dreaded new world, high-level contacts would presumably continue to matter. 'Lunched at New Court with Tony Rothschild,' Churchill's private secretary, 'Jock' Colville, noted on 4 May. 'Lord Bennett [former Prime Minister of Canada], Sir Basil Brooke [Prime Minister of Northern Ireland] and Colonel Vickers were the other guests.'[88]

Three days later the European War at last ended. Tuesday the 8th was

VE Day, and 'Autolycus' recorded that 'not a few members' came to town to make sure for themselves that the Stock Exchange really was closed for business. 'Other people who came to the City,' he went on, 'were a fair number of country cousins, who wandered round the Bank of England and the Mansion House, listened to the blaring of the canned music and sympathised with the bank staffs.' He added that 'the visitors could hardly fail to have been impressed by the City's decorations'.[89] The relief was sincere and palpable – the following week a packed Stock Exchange held a thanksgiving service – but unlike 1918, there was no assumption of a ready return to a golden past.

CHAPTER EIGHTEEN

Ultimately for the Best

'As you know,' Sydney Parkes of Lloyds wrote on 5 June 1945 to his man in New York, 'we are about to face all the distractions of a General Election, but I do not think your friends on your side of the Atlantic need feel that we are going to lose our present leader. Whilst there may be a turnover of many seats in Parliament, the general opinion is that the Conservatives will finish with a majority, though heavily reduced, over all parties.' Polling day was exactly a month later, and the *FT* declared on that hopeful Thursday morning that 'the Stock Exchange as a whole has become more and more convinced that Mr Churchill will be put in power again, and takes a cheerful view accordingly'. Even in the City, though, there were signs that a quiet social revolution was already under way. On 3 July, following some discussions over the telephone, J. Lyons & Co wrote to Lord Ashburton at Barings enclosing 'some specimen menus for the proposed luncheon service to your personnel in the Grill Room at our Throgmorton Restaurant to which there is a separate entrance'. Sittings would be of 'about 100 each' and specimen menus revealed a main course on Mondays of braised ham and spinach with potatoes, or pilchard salad, followed by chocolate pudding or ice cream. The caterers added that they understood that 'you would desire us to serve luncheon on your own premises as soon as conditions allow'. Barings replied on the 9th (four days after polling but still over a fortnight before the results were due to be declared), to the effect that the firm desired to have three sittings daily, starting on 30 July, and that it would supply luncheon vouchers to its staff for these meals.[1] All in all, hardly an earth-shattering innovation, but it did show that even the City's oldest merchant bank was starting to appreciate that the times were changing.

'Autolycus', approaching the end of his marathon stint on the *FT*'s front page, was as usual the City's bell-wether, as the declaration loomed. On 10 July he confessed to 'lurking uncertainty', but by the 19th, with exactly a week to go, he and the Stock Exchange as a whole were far more confident: 'That Mr Churchill and his party will be returned is practically taken for granted. The point of uncertainty is the sum of the majority, and upon this will turn the behaviour of prices when the issue of the poll becomes known.' The characteristic cheeriness was maintained over the next few days. 'It may be reiterated,' he asserted on Monday the 23rd, 'that Stock Exchange expectation looks for the return of Mr Churchill and the Conservative Party with a working majority. Confidence in this opinion is widely spread.' And next day: 'Certain it is that no sign exists in the Stock Exchange of apprehension in regard to the outcome of the General Election.' The *FT*'s front-page headlines were similarly optimistic – 'Cheerful Market Tone Maintained' on the Tuesday, 'Market Steadiness Well Maintained' on the Wednesday, and 'Firm and Confident Tone of Markets' on the Thursday itself – but at the last Landells, and his beloved markets, had got it wrong. 'Opposition Majority of 210' was the altogether less comforting main headline in the *FT* on Friday the 27th, while an unabashed 'Autolycus' started his column by noting that 'the impossibility of calculating the incalculable result of a General Election is once more demonstrated'.[2] The unthinkable was a reality; Labour had achieved real political power for the first time.

There immediately ensued some vigorous whistling in the dark. 'It must be hoped the victors will not allow their great majority to persuade them to extremist courses such as would aggravate world anxiety' (*FT*). 'The responsibility of office is a sobering thing, and Mr Attlee's general conduct of affairs is hardly likely to be irresponsible and revolutionary' (*FN*). Evelyn Baring wrote to New York on Saturday the 28th summarising reaction at 8 Bishopsgate: 'I need hardly say that the result came as a complete surprise to all of us . . . Anyway, we are in for an interesting time. A new era has started which may be less comfortable than that to which we have been accustomed in the past.' He added, however, that 'the wish of the people of England has been made very evident and should the administration not succeed this wish may in due course be reversed'. Baring's colleague Arthur Villiers was also inclined to look on the bright side, when it came to his turn early in August to send the latest City news and views to Kidder Peabody: 'Taking rather a long view, many sensible people feel that the Labour Party, having been in opposition for so long, had become very irresponsible and that the only cure for this is the responsibility of office . . . People generally are inclined to take the view that, all things considered, what has happened may be ultimately for the best . . .' A similar pragmatism imbued at least one prosperous underwriter at Lloyd's. 'To my astonishment,' John Gale would recall about returning to England after the election, 'I found that my father welcomed the Labour victory. "There might have been trouble if they hadn't got in", he said. I never asked how he voted.'[3]

On 6 August, less than a fortnight after the election, came Hiroshima. The event went unrecorded in the pages of the *FT*, but Villiers wrote two days later to New York that 'we hope that the new bomb will make the Mikado pack up'.[4] Nagasaki followed, and the Second World War was finally over. Thirty-one years after the guns of August had signalled the abrupt end of the City's golden age – an age that Montagu Norman had tried in vain between the wars to re-create – the square mile found itself at its lowest peacetime ebb in living memory.

Notes

ABBREVIATIONS

AHC	Records of Accepting Houses Committee (Guildhall Library)
Addis	Papers of Sir Charles Addis (School of Oriental and African Studies Library)
BB	Baring Brothers Archive (at ING Barings)
BoE	Bank of England Archives
Bolton	Unpublished autobiography of Sir George Bolton (now deposited at Bank of England Archives)
Brand	Papers of Lord Brand (Bodleian Library)
DBB	David J. Jeremy (ed), *Dictionary of Business Biography* (1984–6)
FN	*Financial News*
FT	*Financial Times*
HSBC	HSBC Group Archives
JM	Records of Jardine, Matheson & Co (Cambridge University Library)
JS	Centre for Metropolitan History, *The Jobbing System of the London Stock Exchange: An Oral History* (Collection held at British Library National Sound Archive)
Kleinwort	Records of Kleinwort, Sons & Co (Guildhall Library)
Lloyds	Lloyds TSB Group Archives
MG	Records of Morgan, Grenfell & Co (at Deutsche Morgan Grenfell)
Macmillan	Committee on Finance and Industry: Report and Minutes of Evidence (Parl Papers, 1930–1, Cmd 3897)
NW	NatWest Group Archives
PRO	Public Record Office
SE	Records of the London Stock Exchange (Guildhall Library)
SSA	Records of Smith, St Aubyn & Co (Guildhall Library)
Sambourne	Diary of Roy Sambourne
Sayers	R.S. Sayers, *The Bank of England, 1891–1944* (Cambridge 1976, two volumes and appendixes)

All references are published in London unless otherwise stated.

CHAPTER ONE

1. Records of Frederick Huth & Co (Guildhall Library), Ms 22,305, 14 April 1871; records of Accepting Houses Committee (Guildhall Library), Ms 29,295, vol

1, 5 Aug 1914.

2. Records of National Discount Co (Guildhall Library), Ms 18,130, box 2, 20 Jan 1915.

3. Accounts of the crisis and its resolution include: Richard Roberts, *Schroders: Merchants & Bankers* (1992), pp 152–5; Sayers, pp 66–78; Teresa Seabourne, 'The Summer of 1914' in Forrest Capie and Geoffrey E. Wood (eds), *Financial Crises and the World Banking System* (1986).

4. *FT*, 14 Aug 1914.

5. Addis, 14/32, 7 Aug 1914; records of Gillett Brothers & Co (Guildhall Library), Ms 24,700; SE, Ms 14,606, 21 Aug 1914; Ronald Knox, *Patrick Shaw-Stewart* (1920), p 101; Stephen McKenna, *Reginald McKenna, 1863–1943: A Memoir* (1948), p 235; *War Memoirs of David Lloyd George, I* (1933), p 111.

6. Cameron Hazlehurst, *Politicians at War* (1971), p 173; Sir Austen Chamberlain, *Down the Years* (1935), pp 105–6.

7. The fullest treatment of this episode is in John Peters, 'The British Government and the City-Industry Divide: The Case of the 1914 Financial Crisis' in *Twentieth Century British History* (1993).

8. PRO, T 170/28, 26 Aug 1914, T 172/128, 9 Sept 1914; BoE, G 15/59, 25 Aug 1914.

9. PRO, T 170/56, 5 Aug 1914, T 170/57, 6 Aug 1914, T 170/28, 15 Aug 1914, T 172/162 (Grenfell); *Hansard*, 26 Aug 1914, col 71.

10. PRO, T 172/136, 24 Aug 1914.

11. HSBC, 158/3, 24 Sept 1914.

12. Records of Morgan, Grenfell & Co (Guildhall Library), Ms 21,799, fo 122; *War Memoirs*, pp 113–14; PRO, T 170/56, 5 Aug 1914; Michael and Eleanor Brock (eds), *H.H. Asquith: Letters to Venetia Stanley* (Oxford, 1982), p 312.

CHAPTER TWO

1. Addis, 14/175, 9 Aug 1914; Reginald Pound and Geoffrey Harmsworth, *Northcliffe* (1959), p 478, *FT*, 25 May 1915; BB, Dep 33.15, 14 Aug 1914.

2. *Economic Journal*, Sept 1914, p 484; Kathleen Burk, 'Money and power: the shift from Great Britain to the United States' in Youssef Cassis (ed), *Finance and Financiers in European History, 1880–1960* (Cambridge, 1992), p 362.

3. The best overview is Kathleen Burk, 'The Treasury: from Impotence to Power' in Kathleen Burk (ed), *The Transformation of British Government, 1914–1919* (1982).

4. BB, Dep 33.16, 16 March 1915; records of London Chamber of Commerce (Guildhall Library), Ms 16,623, vol 1, 29 April 1915; E.V. Morgan, *Studies in British Financial Policy, 1914–25* (1952), p 187; SSA, Ms 14,894, vol 25, 14 April 1915, 30 Sept 1915; PRO, T 176/13, Part 1, 6 Dec 1925.

5. Sayers, pp 79, 81 for details.

6. HSBC, 158/6, 12–13 Nov 1914.

7. Lady Victoria Hicks Beach, *Life of Sir Michael Hicks Beach* (1932), vol II, pp 320–1; *Bankers' Magazine*, March 1915, p 497.

8. Richard Roberts, *Schroders: Merchants & Bankers* (1992), p 160.

9. MG, private letter books, no 12, 7 Aug 1914; *Lord Riddell's War Diary*,

1914-1918 (1933), p 72; Derek Wilson, *Rothschild* (1988), pp 329–30; records of Morgan, Grenfell & Co (Guildhall Library), Ms 21,799, fo 79.

10. Kathleen Burk, 'A Merchant Bank at War: The House of Morgan, 1914–18' in P.L. Cottrell and D.E. Moggridge (eds), *Money and Power* (Basingstoke, 1988).

11. Philip Ziegler, *The Sixth Great Power: Barings, 1762–1929* (1988), pp 328–32; BB, 204071.

12. MG, letter book of E.C. Grenfell, 21 Jan 1915; *Bankers' Magazine*, March 1915, p 497; *Riddell*, p 60; *War Memoirs of David Lloyd George, I* (1933), p 114; *Riddell*, p 370.

13. *War Memoirs*, p 114; *Riddell*, p 94, A.J.P. Taylor (ed), *Lloyd George: A Diary by Frances Stevenson* (1971), p 53.

14. John Ramsden (ed), *Real Old Tory Politics: The Political Diaries of Sir Robert Sanders, Lord Bayford, 1910–35* (1984), p 20; Robert Skidelsky, *John Maynard Keynes: Volume One, Hopes Betrayed, 1883–1920* (1983), p 306; Lady Cynthia Asquith, *Diaries, 1915–1918* (1968), p 457; J.A. Gere and John Sparrow (eds), *Geoffrey Madan's Notebooks* (1981), p 27; Lord Beaverbrook, *Politicians and the War, 1914–1916, Volume I* (1928), p 155. In general on McKenna, see also: Stephen McKenna, *Reginald McKenna, 1863–1943: A Memoir* (1948); *DBB*, Edwin Green, 'Reginald McKenna', vol 4, pp 33–7.

15. MG, Grenfell, 24 Aug 1915; Stephen McKenna, p 237; Kathleen Burk, *Morgan Grenfell, 1838–1988: The Biography of a Merchant Bank* (Oxford, 1989), p 130; MG, Grenfell, 14 Jan 1916; Beaverbrook, p 153.

16. Morgan Grenfell, Ms 21,799, fos 99–100; BB, Dep 33.16, 7 July 1915; Stephen McKenna, p 237; MG, Grenfell, 25 Nov 1915; SSA, Ms 14,894, vol 25, 29 Sept 1915; Martin Horn, 'External Finance in Anglo-French Relations in the First World War, 1914–1917' in *International History Review* (1995), p 66.

17. SSA, Ms 14,894, vol 25, 1 Nov 1915; Hicks Beach, vol II, p 346; SSA, Ms 14,894, vol 25; MG, Grenfell, 26 Nov 1915; BB, 101949, 29 June 1916.

18. Sayers, pp 89–91.

19. HSBC, 158/20, 29–30 Nov 1915, 3 Dec 1915, 8 Dec 1915.

20. Andrew Boyle, *Montagu Norman: A Biography* (1967), p 103; records of Brown, Shipley & Co (Guildhall Library), Ms 20,111, vol 4, 17 Sept 1917; Boyle, pp 104–5.

21. Strong Papers at Federal Reserve Bank of New York: Diary of European Visit, 1916.

22. Kenneth Mouré, 'The Limits to Central Bank Co-operation, 1916–36' in *Contemporary European History* (1992), p 262.

23. Records of Balfour, Williamson & Co (University College London, Manuscripts and Rare Books), box 10, 11 Feb 1915; Judy Slinn, *Clifford Chance: Its Origins and Development* (Cambridge, 1993), pp 81–2; Kleinwort, Ms 22,033, vol 2, fo 151.

24. BB, Dep 33.16, 9 Feb 1915, Dep 33.18, 7 Sept 1917; Ranald Michie, 'Dunn, Fischer & Co in the City of London, 1906–14' in *Business History* (1988), p 212; Edgar Jones, *True and Fair: A History of Price Waterhouse* (1995), p 110.

25. *FT*, 7 Dec 1991.

26. BoE, G 15/113, 15 Feb 1919.

27. Sayers, p 616; BB, Dep 33.16, 11 June 1915; Frank H.H. King, *The History*

of the Hongkong and Shanghai Banking Corporation: Volume II (Cambridge, 1988), p 598; Balfour Williamson, box 10, 12 May 1916, box 11, 11 April 1918.

28. Sir William Nott-Bower, *Fifty-Two Years a Policeman* (1926), pp 271–3; SSA, Ms 14,894, vol 27, 13 June 1917; MG, Grenfell, 19 June 1917.

29. Siegfried Sassoon, *Memoirs of an Infantry Officer* (1965, pbk), pp 207–8; Vera Brittain, *Testament of Youth* (1979, pbk), pp 365–6.

30. SSA, Ms 14,894, vol 27, 7 July 1917; Addis, 14/35, 7 July 1917; MG, Grenfell, 7 July 1917; BB, Dep 33.17, 11 July 1917.

31. BB, Dep 33.15, 7 Aug 1914; *FT*, 12 May 1915, *FN*, 8 May 1915; *FT*, 14 May 1915; Ronald Palin, *Rothschild Relish* (1970), pp 94–5.

32. Slinn, *Clifford Chance*, p 90; Aytoun Ellis, *Heir of Adventure: The story of Brown, Shipley & Co, merchant bankers, 1810–1960* (1960), p 148; SE, Ms 14,600, vol 101, 26 Feb 1917; Hurford Janes and H.J. Sayers, *The story of Czarnikow* (1963), p 66; Roberts, *Schroders*, pp 362–3, 365–6.

33. *FT*, 10 May 1915; SE, Ms 19,515, vol 4, no 293; *FT*, 13 May 1915, 25 May 1915; SE, Ms 14,600, vol 98, 15 Nov 1915, 21 Dec 1915, 26 Jan 1916.

34. SE, Mss 14,600, vol 101, 26 Feb 1917, 6 March 1917, 9 March 1917, 19,515, vol 4, no 309, 19,297, vol 21, 17 April 1912 (Dent's letter of 27 June 1918 attached).

35. Addis, 14/33, 25 Feb 1915, 14/34, 21 Sept 1916; Roberts, *Schroders*, pp 363–6; Morgan Grenfell, Ms 21,799, fo 108; Roberts, *Schroders*, p 156.

36. Morgan Grenfell, Ms 21,799, fo 107; John Vincent (ed), *The Crawford Papers* (Manchester, 1984), pp 344–5; *FT*, 25 May 1915; Michael and Eleanor Brock (eds), *H.H. Asquith: Letters to Venetia Stanley* (Oxford, 1982), p 292.

37. Sir Almeric Fitzroy, *Memoirs* (1925), vol II, p 569; *FT*, 21 May 1915; Kurt Grunwald, ' "Windsor-Cassel" – The Last Court Jew' in *Leo Baeck Institute, Year Book* (1969), p 160; Jamie Camplin, *The Rise of the Plutocrats* (1978), p 290.

38. BoE, ADM 34/4, 30 May 1916, 6–7 June 1916, 27 June 1916.

39. BoE, ADM 34/4, 24 Oct 1916, 8 Nov 1916, 17–18 Nov 1916, 22 Nov 1916.

40. BoE, M 6/64, 10 Nov 1916, ADM 34/4, 29 Nov 1916; Skidelsky, *Keynes*, vol 1, p 335; *FT*, 12 Dec 1916; BoE, ADM 34/5, 12 Jan 1917; *FT*, 9 Jan 1917, *FN*, 12 Jan 1917; Robert C. Self (ed), *The Austen Chamberlain Diary Letters* (Cambridge, 1995), p 41.

41. MG, Grenfell, 30 June 1916; BB, 204071; Addis, 14/35, 29 March 1917; Sayers, pp 93–4.

42. BB, Dep 33.17, 30 May 1917.

43. Sayers, pp 99–109 gives the authoritative account of the quarrel.

44. Sayers, p 105; BoE, G 15/31, fos 30, 32, ADM 34/5, 18 July 1917, G 15/31, fos 34–42.

45. BoE, G 15/31, fo 42; BB, Dep 33.17, 15 Aug 1917; BoE, G 15/7, 29 Aug 1917.

46. BoE, ADM 34/5, 12 Sept 1917, 10 Oct 1917, 18 Oct 1917; Morgan Grenfell, Ms 21, 799, fo 121; BoE, ADM 34/5, 20 Nov 1917, 12 Dec 1917.

47. BoE, ADM 34/6, 27 Feb 1918, 22 March 1918; Morgan Grenfell, Ms 21, 799, fos 121, 123.

48. BoE, ADM 34/6, 24 April 1918; SE, Ms 14,600, vol 103, 13 May 1918, 21

May 1918; *The Times*, 15 July 1918; BB, Dep 33.19, 13 Aug 1918; PRO, T 176/
13, part 1, 18 Feb 1929; Sir Henry Clay, *Lord Norman* (1957), p 113.
  49. Brand, file 12, 3 Oct 1918; Balfour Williamson, box 11, 5 Oct 1918.
  50. R.P.T. Davenport-Hines, *Dudley Docker* (Cambridge, 1984), esp chapters
5–7; Scott Newton and Dilwyn Porter, *Modernization Frustrated* (1988), chapter 2.
  51. *Round Table*, Dec 1916, pp 52–6, 62–3; *Economic Journal*, Dec 1917, pp
518–19.
  52. Davenport-Hines, *Docker*, pp 133–54 gives the fullest account.
  53. PRO, BT 55/32, 27 June 1916, 5 July 1916, 31 Aug 1916; BB, Dep 33.17, 10
Aug 1916, 19 Aug 1916.
  54. Roberta Allbert Dayer, *Finance and Empire: Sir Charles Addis, 1861–1945*
(Basingstoke, 1988), p 88; Davenport-Hines, *Docker*, p 141; *FT*, 17 May 1917;
BOLSA Collection (UCL), D1/31, 9 Aug 1918.
  55. *Economist*, 9 Feb 1918.
  56. *Economist*, 19 Jan 1918, 9 Feb 1918; SE, Ms 14,600, vol 103, 7 Jan 1918.
  57. Sayers, pp 597, 628–31; Elizabeth Hennessy, 'The Governors, Directors and
Management of the Bank of England' in Richard Roberts and David Kynaston
(eds), *The Bank of England* (Oxford, 1995), pp 194–5.
  58. BoE, G 15/31, fo 95c, G 15/111, fos 5, 7a, 11, 13, 21.
  59. BoE, G 15/112, fo 66, ADM 34/6, 28 March 1918, 25 April 1918.
  60. Elizabeth Johnson (ed), *The Collected Writings of John Maynard Keynes:
Volume XVI* (1971), p 31.
  61. *Daily Express*, 4 Feb 1918.
  62. Sayers, pp 236–41; A.R. Holmes and Edwin Green, *Midland: 150 Years of
Banking Business* (1986), pp 129–32.
  63. PRO, T 1/12267/50326, 18 March 1918, 20 March 1918.
  64. *The Times*, 17 July 1918.
  65. *Edinburgh Review*, July 1918, pp 44, 48.
  66. The classic account of the Cunliffe Report and all that derived from it
remains D.E. Moggridge, *British Monetary Policy, 1924–1931: The Norman
Conquest of $4.86* (Cambridge, 1972). See also, on the Cunliffe Report specifically:
R. Boyce, 'Creating the Myth of Consensus: Public Opinion and Britain's Return to
the Gold Standard in 1925' in Cottrell and Moggridge, *Money and Power*, pp
174–5; Ross E. Catterall, 'Attitudes to and the Impact of British Monetary Policy in
the 1920s' in *Revue internationale d'histoire de la banque* (1976), pp 29–42.
  67. PRO, T 1/12238/47228, T 185/1, 11 March 1918, 19 March 1918, 8 April
1918, 6–7 May 1918; Addis, 14/36, 6–7 May 1918.
  68. Sayers, Appendixes, p 58; *The Times*, 30 Oct 1918; Boyce, 'Creating the
Myth', p 175.
  69. *The Times*, 31 Oct 1918; *Economist*, 2 Nov 1918; *Bankers' Magazine*,
March 1919, p 371.
  70. BB, 101951, 4 Jan 1918; Ziegler, pp 323–4; *Economic Journal*, Dec 1918, p
386; Dayer, p 85; *Economic Journal*, Dec 1918, p 397.
  71. *FT*, 9 May 1945; Balfour Williamson, box 11, 11 Nov 1918; Addis, 14/36,
11 Nov 1918; Bryher, *The Heart to Artemis* (1963), p 190.
  72. C.H. Rolph, *London Particulars* (Oxford, 1980), pp 151, 153, 197–9.

CHAPTER THREE

1. Georgiana Blakiston (ed), *Letters of Conrad Russell, 1897–1947* (1987), pp 59–60, 62; JS, several versions.

2. BB, Dep 33.20, 9 April 1919; Susan Howson, *Domestic Monetary Management in Britain, 1919–38* (Cambridge, 1975), p 10.

3. *Sunday Express*, 26 Jan 1930. In general on Hatry, see: P.S. Manley, 'Clarence Hatry' in *Abacus* (June 1976), pp 49–60; *DBB*, David Fanning, 'Clarence Charles Hatry', vol 3, pp 110–14; *Banker*, May 1985, pp 78–9.

4. SSA, Ms 14,894, vol 29, 29 Sept 1919; S.J. Diaper, 'The History of Kleinwort, Sons & Co in Merchant Banking, 1855–1961' (Nottingham PhD, 1983), p 376; SE, Ms 19,515, vol 5, nos 336, 343, 348.

5. Sayers, Appendixes, pp 51–4 reprints the memorandum of staff grievances.

6. BoE, G 15/113, ADM 34/8, 15 Feb 1919, G 15/113.

7. *Journal of the Institute of Bankers*, April 1919, pp 124–7; Elizabeth Johnson (ed), *The Collected Writings of John Maynard Keynes: Volume XVII* (1977), p 12; *Lord Riddell's Intimate Diary of the Peace Conference and After* (1933), p 47; *Economic Journal*, December 1953, p 764; L.E. Jones, *Georgian Afternoon* (1958), p 114; Colin Cross (ed), *Life with Lloyd George: The Diary of A.J. Sylvester, 1931–45* (1975), p 75.

8. BB, 101953, 12 Jan 1920; BoE, G 35/1, 16 Jan 1920; *Punch*, 14 Jan 1920.

9. Archives of N.M. Rothschild & Sons, XI/111/101, 29 April 1919.

10. The definitive overview is John Atkin, 'Official Regulation of British Overseas Investment, 1914–1931' in *Economic History Review* (1970).

11. Brand, file 12, 26 May 1919, file 16, 27 May 1919; BoE, ADM 34/9, 29 Jan 1920.

12. Roberta Allbert Dayer, *Finance and Empire: Sir Charles Addis, 1861–1945* (Basingstoke, 1988), chapter 5.

13. BoE, G 35/1, 11 Nov 1919; Brand, file 12, 10 June 1919; Addis, 14/36, 24 Dec 1918; BB, 200256, 7 Jan 1925.

14. Sir Charles Petrie, *The Life and Letters of The Right Hon Sir Austen Chamberlain* (1940), vol 2, p 141.

15. Susan Howson, 'The Origins of Dear Money, 1919–20' in *Economic History Review* (1974), pp 90–2.

16. SSA, Ms 14,894, vol 29, 16 March 1919, 28 March 1919; BB, Dep 33.20, 9 April 1919; BoE, G 35/1, 5 June 1919; Russell Ally, *Gold and Empire: The Bank of England and South Africa's Gold Producers, 1886–1926* (Johannesburg, 1994), pp 56–61.

17. Brand, file 16, 6 Sept 1919; PRO, CAB 27/72, 25 Sept 1919.

18. SSA, Ms 14,894, vol 29, 6 Nov 1919; BoE, G 35/1, 6 Nov 1919; *FN*, 31 Jan 1920, *FT*, 24 July 1919; Robert C. Self (ed), *The Austen Chamberlain Diary Letters* (Cambridge, 1995), p 128; Sayers, p 117.

19. PRO, T 172/1384, 25 Feb 1920; BoE, ADM 34/9, 9 March 1920; Self, p 130. In general, on the rise to 7 per cent and immediate aftermath, see Howson, 'Origins', pp 100 ff.

20. Robert Skidelsky, *John Maynard Keynes: Volume Two, The Economist as Saviour, 1920–1937* (1992), p 40; *FT*, 16 July 1920; BoE, G 3/176, 17 July 1920.

CHAPTER FOUR

1. Addis, 14/37, 11 Nov 1919, 14/38, 1 April 1920; Andrew Boyle, *Montagu Norman: A Biography* (1967), p 140; Addis, 14/39, 7 July 1921, 14/40, 27 Sept 1922.

2. Emile Moreau, *The Golden Franc* (Boulder, Colorado, 1991), p 51; Marguerite Dupree (ed), *Lancashire and Whitehall: The Diary of Sir Raymond Streat* (1987), vol 1, pp 32–4; *Lloyds Bank Review*, April 1968, pp 33–4; Duncan Crow, *A Man of Push and Go: The Life of George Macaulay Booth* (1965), p 168; BoE, G 15/241 (Beyen), G 35/3, 6 July 1922.

3. Kleinwort, Ms 22,033, vol 2, fo 70; Addis, 14/38, 15 July 1920, 14/454, 28 Sept 1926. In general, on the ending of the two-year tradition, see Sayers, pp 647–8.

4. BoE, G 35/3, 17 Feb 1922, 13 March 1922, 31 Oct 1922; Addis, 14/41, 5 Nov 1923, 20 Nov 1923; BoE, ADM 34/13, 20 Feb 1924, G 35/4, 30 Nov 1924.

5. BoE, ADM 34/11–13; L.E. Jones, *Georgian Afternoon* (1958), pp 122–3.

6. Philip Ziegler, *The Sixth Great Power: Barings, 1762–1929* (1988), p 339; *FT*, 14 March 1921; BoE, ADM 34/11, 10 Oct 1922, G 3/178, 21 Dec 1922, 23 Dec 1922; *FT*, 5 May 1923, 28 Oct 1926; SSA, Ms 14,894, vol 29, 28 Dec 1919.

7. Records of Morgan, Grenfell & Co (Guildhall Library), Ms 21,799, fo 92; Richard Meinertzhagen, *Diary of a Black Sheep* (1964), p 311; Kleinwort, Ms 22,033, vol 2, fo 130; BoE, ADM 34/11, 29 July 1922, G 3/179, 22 May 1923; Kleinwort, Ms 22,033, vol 2, fo 141; Sayers, p 269.

8. On Kleinworts after the war, see: Stefanie Diaper, 'Merchant Banking in the Inter-War Period: The Case of Kleinwort, Sons & Co' in *Business History* (1986); Jehanne Wake, *Kleinwort Benson: The History of Two Families in Banking* (Oxford, 1997), chapter 7.

9. Morgan Grenfell, Ms 21,799, fo 136; BoE, ADM 34/9, 30 June 1920; Quintin Gilbey, *Fun was my Living* (1970), pp 105, 107; Stefanie Diaper, 'The Sperling Combine and the shipbuilding industry: merchant banking and industrial finance in the 1920s' in J.J. van Helten and Y. Cassis (eds), *Capitalism in a Mature Economy* (Aldershot, 1990); Wake, p 227.

10. Richard Roberts, *Schroders: Merchants & Bankers* (1992), chapter 7.

11. BoE, ADM 33/25; MG, private letter books, no 25, 2 Feb 1922.

12. BB, 200256, 19 April 1922, Dep 33.20, 12 Feb 1919.

13. In general on Peacock, see *DBB*, John Orbell, 'Sir Edward Robert Peacock', vol 4, pp 559–67.

14. BB, Dep 33.21, 23 May 1922, Dep 33.22, 9 Nov 1923, 26 Feb 1924.

15. For an overview of Rothschilds after the war, see Niall Ferguson, *The World's Banker: The History of the House of Rothschild* (1998), pp 984–91.

16. BB, Dep 33.20, 20 May 1919; Ronald Palin, *Rothschild Relish* (1970), p 118.

17. Allen, Harvey & Ross scrapbook (Cater Allen records); MG, private letter books, no 25, 7 April 1922; BB, 101954, 28 Jan 1921.

18. BoE, ADM 33/25–6; *The Times*, 21 July 1954; Brand, file 44, 3 May 1921; Roberts, *Schroders*, pp 368–72. On Kindersley and Brand, see also *DBB*, D.E. Moggridge, 'Robert Molesworth Kindersley, 1st Lord Kindersley of West Hoathly', vol 3, pp 596–7, Kathleen Burk, 'Robert Henry Brand, 1st Lord Brand of Eydon', vol 1, pp 437–40.

19. Kleinwort, Ms 22,033, vol 2, fo 29; S. Japhet, *Recollections from my Business Life* (1931), p 122.

20. Roberts, *Schroders*, p 188; BB, Dep 33.22, 3 Oct 1923; Brand, file 49, 1 March 1923; Kleinwort, Ms 22,033, vol 2, fo 6; HSBC, 347/6, 10 Nov 1924.

21. Addis, 14/38, 6 May 1920, 14/41, 7 Nov 1923; BB, Dep 33.23, 25 Nov 1924.

22. Francesca Carnevali and Leslie Hannah, 'The Effects of Banking Cartels and Credit Rationing on U.K. Industrial Structure and Economic Performance since World War Two' in Michael D. Bordo and Richard Sylla (eds), *Anglo-American Financial Systems: Institutions and Markets in the Twentieth Century* (Burr Ridge, Ill, 1995), p 66.

23. *DBB*, P.E. Smart, 'Frederick Crauford Goodenough', vol 2, pp 603–6, Edwin Green, 'Reginald McKenna', vol 4, pp 33–7.

24. Information from Leslie Hannah, based on interviews with Barclays' directors; BoE, ADM 34/9, 20 Sept 1920; Kleinwort, Ms 22,033, vol 2, fo 6; Addis, 14/43, 31 March 1925; BoE, G 35/4, 3 Dec 1923; J.A. Gere and John Sparrow (eds), *Geoffrey Madan's Notebooks* (Oxford, 1981), p 14; *The Times*, 15 Sept 1943; BoE, ADM 33/27.

25. Nicholas Davenport, 'Keynes in the City' in Milo Keynes (ed), *Essays on John Maynard Keynes* (Cambridge, 1975); *DBB*, D.E. Moggridge, 'John Maynard Keynes, 1st Lord Keynes of Tilton', vol 3, pp 588–91.

26. Robert Skidelsky, *John Maynard Keynes: Volume Two, The Economist as Saviour, 1920–1937* (1992), p 231; BB, Dep 33.18, 14 Sept 1917; Skidelsky, pp 41–3.

27. BoE, G 3/180, 30 Jan 1924; Eric Street, *The History of the National Mutual Life Assurance Society, 1830–1980* (1980), pp 29–31; BB, 101957, 18 Jan 1924; MG, private letter books, no 31, 25 Oct 1924.

28. Addis, 14/397, 26 Oct 1921.

CHAPTER FIVE

1. Andrew Boyle, *Montagu Norman: A Biography* (1967), p 152.

2. BoE, G 3/179, 26 Feb 1923; Robert Skidelsky, *John Maynard Keynes: Volume Two, The Economist as Saviour, 1920–1937* (1992), pp 123–4.

3. Frank C. Costigliola, 'Anglo-American Financial Rivalry in the 1920s' in *Journal of Economic History* (1977), pp 911–34; György Péteri, 'Central Bank Diplomacy: Montagu Norman and Central Europe's Monetary Reconstruction after World War I' in *Contemporary European History* (1992), pp 248–9.

4. Brand, file 37, 2 Jan 1923, 4 Jan 1923.

5. BoE, G 35/1, 3 Dec 1920.

6. BoE, G 35/2, 5 Jan 1921; Sayers, Appendixes, p 75; BoE, G 3/178, 7 Feb 1922, 22 March 1922.

7. Péteri, pp 239–40; Costigliola, p 918.

8. BoE, G 35/3, 9 Aug 1922.

9. BB, 101954, 9 June 1921, Dep 33.21, 10 Aug 1922, Dep 33.22, 30 May 1923.

10. BoE, ADM 34/13, mid-Jan 1924; Richard Roberts, *Schroders: Merchants & Bankers* (1992), pp 198–9.

11. Philip Ziegler, *The Sixth Great Power: Barings, 1762–1929* (1988), pp

351–4; Anne Orde, 'Baring Brothers, the Bank of England, the British Government and the Czechoslovak State Loan of 1922' in *English Historical Review* (1991).

12. BB, 101955, 21 Jan 1922, 200343, 1 Feb 1922, 17 Feb 1922, 200344, 16 March 1922, Dep 33.21, 5 Aug 1922; Ziegler, p 353.

13. Sayers, pp 174–83 gives a helpful overview of the City and Germany during these years.

14. BoE, G 30/9, 30 May 1922, G 35/4, 9 April 1923, G 3/180, 10 Jan 1924. On Schacht generally, see John Weitz, *Hitler's Banker: Hjalmar Horace Greeley Schacht* (New York, 1998).

15. BoE, G 3/180, 31 March 1924.

16. Péteri; pp 254–7; Costigliola, pp 919–20.

17. Péteri, p 254; BoE, G 3/180, 2 June 1924.

18. BB, Dep 33.22, 8 July 1924; BoE, ADM 34/13, 7 Oct 1924; Addis, 14/42, 1 Oct 1924; *FT*, 1 Oct 1924, 14 Oct 1924; BB, Dep 33.23, 14 Oct 1924; *FT*, 16 Oct 1924, 15 Oct 1924.

19. BoE, G 3/177, 14 May 1921; Brand, file 53, 30 May 1922; BoE, ADM 34/13, 9 July 1924; *DBB*, R.P.T. Davenport-Hines, 'Charles Birch Crisp', vol 1, p 825; S.J. Diaper, 'The History of Kleinwort, Sons & Co in Merchant Banking, 1855–1961' (Nottingham PhD, 1983), p 222; BB, 204071.

20. John Atkin, 'Official Regulation of British Overseas Investment, 1914–1931' in *Economic History Review* (1970).

21. BB, Dep 33.22, 25 Feb 1924; MG, private letter books, no 31, 2 Feb 1925; Frank H.H. King, *The History of the Hongkong and Shanghai Banking Corporation: Volume III* (Cambridge, 1988), pp 113–16.

22. Brand, file 80, 11 March 1925; *Midland Bank Limited Monthly Review*, Oct–Nov 1924, p 3; Ziegler, p 349.

23. Roberts, *Schroders*, p 213; Kathleen Burk, *Morgan Grenfell, 1838–1988: The Biography of a Merchant Bank* (Oxford, 1989), pp 87–90.

24. Addis, 14/41, 25 Oct 1923; BB, Dep 33.22, 15 July 1924.

25. Bernie Schedvin, 'E.G. Theodore and the London Pastoral Lobby' in *Politics* (1971); Bernard Attard, 'Australian Financial Diplomacy, 1914–39' in Carl Bridge and Bernard Attard (eds), *Between Empire and Nation* (Melbourne, 1999). For further background, see Bernard Attard, 'Politics, Finance and Anglo-Australian Relations: Australian Borrowing in London, 1914–1920' in *Australian Journal of Political History* (1989).

26. SE, Ms 14,609, vol 7, 8 June 1920; Schedvin, p 33; BB, Dep 33.21, 28 June 1921; BoE, G 15/182, 1 Dec 1923; Schedvin, pp 38–9.

27. Russell Ally, *Gold and Empire: The Bank of England and South Africa's Gold Producers, 1886–1926* (Johannesburg, 1994), pp 90–1, 113–18, 91, 66; BoE, G 3/177, 31 May 1921, G 3/178, 9 Nov 1922; Ally, p 70.

28. Kleinwort, Ms 22,033, vol 2, fo 70; Rachel Gibbs, *Pedigree of the Family of Gibbs* (1981), p xx; records of Antony Gibbs & Sons (Guildhall Library), Mss 11,042, vol 2, 29 Jan 1921, 11,115, vol 2, 31 March 1921; BB, Dep 33.21, 17 May 1921; Antony Gibbs, Ms 11,115, vol 2, 24 May 1921; BB, 101954, 9 June 1921; records of Morgan, Grenfell & Co (Guildhall Library), Ms 21,799, fos 132, 131; BB, Dep 33.21, 4 July 1922; Kleinwort, Ms 22,033, vol 2, fos 162, 164; Addis, 14/42, 3 July 1924. In general on Herbert Gibbs, see *DBB*, R.P.T. Davenport-Hines, 'Herbert Cokayne Gibbs, 1st Lord Hunsdon', vol 2, pp 555–8.

29. Winston Fritsch, 'The Montagu Financial Mission to Brazil and the federal economic policy changes of 1924' in *Brazilian Economic Studies* (1985); P.J. Cain and A.G. Hopkins, *British Imperialism: Crisis and Deconstruction, 1914–1990* (1993), pp 161–4.

30. Morgan Grenfell, Ms 21,799, fo 138; BoE, G 3/177, 3 Dec 1921; Roberts, *Schroders*, p 203; Roberta Allbert Dayer, *Finance and Empire: Sir Charles Addis, 1861–1945* (Basingstoke, 1988), p 161; Fritsch, pp 285, 288–9; Addis, 14/42, 2 April 1924.

31. PRO, FO 371/3690, 21 March 1919, 9 April 1919; *Daily Mail*, 29 April 1919; King, p 94. See more generally: King, pp 85–98; Cain and Hopkins, pp 244–7.

32. NW, 2469, 24 Jan 1924; Brand, file 77, 4 April 1924; BB, Dep 33.22, 12 Feb 1924; *The Times*, 14 Feb 1924.

33. HSBC, 347/5, 23 July 1923; BB, Dep 33.22, 3 Aug 1923.

34. FT, 4 July 1919; FN, 22 Jan 1934. Ranald C. Michie, *The London Stock Exchange: A History* (Oxford, 1999) provides the most authoritative survey of the inter-war market.

35. Senior partner's speech to mark the firm's eightieth birthday in August 1955.

36. Ranald C. Michie, *The City of London: Continuity and Change, 1850–1990* (Basingstoke, 1992), p 104; BoE, ADM 34/14, 15 April 1925, ADM 34/9, 2 Feb 1920; David Wainwright, *Government Broker: The Story of an Office and of Mullens & Co* (1990), pp 64–5, 68.

37. *Sociological Review*, Jan 1924, p 10; Nicholas Davenport, *Memoirs of a City Radical* (1974), p 18.

38. FT, 21 Jan 1921; BoE, ADM 34/10, 28 Nov 1921, G 30/8, 25 April 1922, 6 Oct 1922; R.P.T. Davenport-Hines, *Dudley Docker* (Cambridge, 1984), p 153.

39. SE, Ms 14,603, vol 8, 14 Dec 1922; BB, Dep 33.21, 18 Nov 1922; Michie, *City*, pp 135–6.

40. Donald Cobbett, *Before the Big Bang: Tales of the Old Stock Exchange* (Portsmouth, 1986), p 56; FT, 7–10 July 1924.

41. *Sunday Express*, 26 Jan 1930.

42. *DBB*, R.P.T. Davenport-Hines, 'Gerard Lee Bevan', vol 1, pp 321–4; HSBC, 347/5, 13 Jan 1921, 19 May 1921; FT, 25 July 1921; HSBC, 347/5, 8 Aug 1921, 13 Jan 1922; FT, 1 Feb 1922; BoE, G 30/8, 2–3 Feb 1922; HSBC, 347/5, 3 Feb 1922; FT, 17 Feb 1922; H. Osborne O'Hagan, *Leaves from my Life* (1929), vol II, p 339. See also: P.S. Manley, 'Gerard Lee Bevan and the City Equitable Companies' in *Abacus* (Dec 1973).

43. SE, Ms 14,600, vol 113, 14–28 May 1923.

44. *DBB*, Oliver M. Westall, 'Cuthbert Eden Heath', vol 3, pp 136–41; BoE, ADM 34/12, 1 Oct 1923; D.E.W. Gibb, *Lloyd's of London* (1957), pp 264, 271; Gibb, pp 284–91; Andrew Brown, *Cuthbert Heath* (Newton Abbot, 1980), pp 134–41; Harold Nicolson, *Some People* (1958 edn), p 38.

45. BB, Dep 33.21, 18 Nov 1922; H.W. Phillips, *Modern Foreign Exchange and Foreign Banking* (1926), pp 54–5; Bolton; Roberts, *Schroders*, p 187; FT, 30 Jan 1920; Martin Gilbert, *Winston S. Churchill: Volume V Companion, Part I* (1979), p 28.

46. Phillips, pp 67–8, 70.

47. Phillips, p 69; records of Brown, Shipley & Co (Guildhall Library), Mss

20, 118, vol 2, 4 April 1921, 20,110, vol 1, 22 April 1921, 20,118, vol 2, 25 Aug 1922, 20,110, vol 1, 30 Aug 1922.

48. Roberts, *Schroders*, pp 371–2; W. Lionel Fraser, *All to the Good* (1963), p 71.

49. Wallis Hunt, *Heirs of Great Adventure* (1960), vol II, p 142.

50. Michie, *City*, p 45; Cain and Hopkins, pp 31–48.

51. Cecil Beaton, *The Wandering Years: Diaries, 1922–1939* (1961), pp 59–60.

52. Significant versions and/or interpretations of this narrative include: Sidney Pollard (ed), *The Gold Standard and Employment Policies between the Wars* (1970); D.E. Moggridge, *British Monetary Policy, 1924–1931: The Norman Conquest of $4.86* (Cambridge, 1972), pp 37–97; Sayers, chapters 6 and 7; R. Boyce, 'Creating the Myth of Consensus: Public Opinion and Britain's Return to the Gold Standard in 1925' in P.L. Cottrell and D.E. Moggridge (eds), *Money and Power* (Basingstoke, 1988); Skidelsky, chapters 5 and 6.

53. BoE, G 3/176, 6 Sept 1920; Sir Henry Clay, *Lord Norman* (1957), p 292; BoE, ADM 34/9, 28 Dec 1920, ADM 34/10, 2 Nov 1921.

54. *Journal of the Institute of Bankers*, Dec 1921, pp 382–3, 386; Brand, file 62, 25 Aug 1922.

55. *Midland Bank Limited Monthly Review*, July–Aug 1923, pp 3–4; SSA, Ms 14,894, vol 33, 5 July 1923.

56. *Nation and Athenaeum*, 14 July 1923, 21 July 1923; BoE, G 3/179, 19 July 1923; *The Times*, 7 Aug 1923.

57. BoE, G 35/4, 8 Oct 1923; Sayers, p 131; BoE, G 3/179, 15 Oct 1923, ADM 34/12, 23 Oct 1923; BB, Dep 33.22, 24 Oct 1923.

58. BoE, G 3/179, 13–14 Nov 1923; Antony Gibbs, Ms 11,042, vol 1, 18 Dec 1923; David Marquand, *Ramsay MacDonald* (1977), p 298.

59. Skidelsky, pp 153–64 gives a typically incisive but nuanced analysis.

60. Skidelsky, p 161; Dayer, p 160; BoE, G 3/180, 30 Jan 1924; BB, Dep 33.22, 31 Dec 1923.

61. Donald Moggridge (ed), *The Collected Writings of John Maynard Keynes: Volume XIX, Part 1* (1981), pp 159, 161–2.

62. Philip Snowden, *An Autobiography* (1934), vol 1, pp 613–15; BoE, G 3/180, 30 Jan 1924; MG, private letter books, no 30, 2 April 1924.

63. BoE, G 3/180, 16 April 1924, ADM 34/13, 13 June 1924; Richard Roberts, '"A special place in contemporary economic literature": the rise and fall of the British bank review, 1914–1993' in *Financial History Review* (1995), p 48; *Midland Bank Limited Monthly Review*, June–July 1924, p 3; Addis, 14/42, 18 June 1924.

64. PRO, T 160/197/F7528/02/1, 27 June 1924, 3–4 July 1924; Robert C. Self (ed), *The Austen Chamberlain Diary Letters* (Cambridge, 1995), p 254.

65. BoE, ADM 34/13, 7 July 1924; PRO, T 160/197/F7528/02/2, 10 July 1924; BoE, G 35/4, 3 Dec 1923.

66. PRO, T 160/197/F7528/02/2, 11 July 1924.

67. Addis, 14/407, 25 July 1924.

68. BoE, G 3/181, 16 Oct 1924; MG, private letter books, no 31, 25 Oct 1924; BoE, G 3/182, 27 Oct 1924, G 35/4, 18 Nov 1924.

69. Addis, 14/43, 8 Jan 1925, 21 Jan 1925.

70. BoE, G 35/5, 24 Jan 1925; Addis, 14/43, 26–8 Jan 1925; PRO, T 160/197/F7528/02/3, 28 Jan 1925; BoE, OV 32/1, 13 Feb 1925.

71. *The Times*, 22 Jan 1925, 30 Jan 1925, 7 Feb 1925, 28 Jan 1925; Martin Gilbert, *Winston S. Churchill, Volume V: 1922–1939* (1976), p 96.

72. Moggridge, *British Monetary Policy*, pp 261, 270–2; Gilbert, *Churchill, Volume V*, p 96.

73. Gilbert, *Churchill, Volume V*, pp 97–8.

74. Addis, 14/43, 23 Feb 1925; PRO, T 176/13, part 1, 4 March 1925; BoE, G 3/183, 7 March 1925.

75. *Daily Express*, 12 March 1925; PRO, T 176/13, part 1, 12 March 1925; Sir Frederick Leith-Ross, *Money Talks* (1968), p 95.

76. BoE, G 3/183, 7 March 1925; *The Times*, 5 March 1925; *Midland Bank Limited Monthly Review*, Feb–March 1925, pp 1–4.

77. Records of London Chamber of Commerce (Guildhall Library), Ms 16,623, vol 2, 6 March 1925; *Round Table*, March 1925, pp 259, 262, 270.

78. P.J. Grigg, *Prejudice and Judgement* (1948), pp 182–4; Skidelsky, p 200; BoE, ADM 34/14, 19–20 March 1925; Addis, 14/43, 20 March 1925.

79. Addis, 14/43, 3 April 1925; Moggridge, *British Monetary Policy*, p 86; Gilbert, *Churchill, Volume V*, p 100.

80. BB, 200256, 28 April 1925; BoE, ADM 34/14, 28 April 1925; Gilbert, *Churchill, Volume V Companion*, p 472; FT, 29 April 1925; *The Times*, 29 April 1925.

81. Moggridge, *British Monetary Policy*, p 228.

82. *Nation and Athenaeum*, 21 Feb 1925.

83. *Economic Journal*, June 1924, p 169.

CHAPTER SIX

1. Brand, file 75, 1 May 1925; BoE, G 3/183, 8 May 1925, G 3/182, 17 July 1925.

2. BB, Dep 33.23, 7 Aug 1925; BoE, G 3/182, 25 July 1925, G 3/184, 27 July 1925; *The Collected Writings of John Maynard Keynes: Volume IX* (1972), pp 220, 223.

3. *Nation and Athenaeum*, 2 May 1925; *Manchester Guardian*, 15 Oct 1925; Robert Skidelsky, *John Maynard Keynes: Volume Two, The Economist as Saviour, 1920–1937* (1992), pp 335–7.

4. Insightful overviews include: Sidney Pollard, *The Development of the British Economy: 1914–1980* (1983 edn), pp 137–41; Patrick K. O'Brien, 'Britain's Economy between the Wars: a Survey of a Counter-Revolution in Economic History' in *Past and Present* (May 1987), pp 121–3.

5. BoE, G 35/5, 23 Nov 1925.

6. PRO, T 176/13, part 1, 3 Dec 1925; Addis, 14/43, 3 Dec 1925; BoE, G 15/7, 4 Dec 1925; Sayers, p 216.

7. FT, 3 May 1926.

8. FT, 4 May 1926; SSA, Ms 14,894, vol 36, 3 May 1926; Addis, 14/44, 4 May 1926; BOLSA Collection (University College London, Manuscripts and Rare Books), B 64, 4 May 1926; information from Jehanne Wake; Brand, file 76 ('Emergency Orders'); FT, 6 May 1926; BB, 101959, 10 May 1926.

9. Addis, 14/44, 12 May 1926; FT, 13 May 1926; *The Times*, 24 June 1926; MG, private letter books, no 34, 23 July 1926; BoE, ADM 34/15, 7 Nov 1926.

10. *Midland Bank Limited Monthly Review*, Jan–Feb 1927, pp 1–6; BoE, G 35/7, 18 Sept 1927; BB, 101961, 25 Oct 1928.

11. Keith Middlemas (ed), *Thomas Jones, Whitehall Diary: Volume II, 1926–1930* (Oxford, 1969), p 98; Martin Glibert, *Winston S. Churchill, Volume V: 1922–1939* (1976), pp 237–8; John Barnes and David Nicholson (eds), *The Leo Amery Diaries, Volume I: 1896–1929* (1980), p 552; P.J. Grigg, *Prejudice and Judgement* (1948), p 193; Lord Moran, *Winston Churchill: The Struggle for Survival, 1940–1965* (1966), pp 303–4.

12. R.S. Sayers, 'Bank Rate in Keynes's Century' in *Proceedings of the British Academy* (1979), p 201; Addis, 14/47, 6 Feb 1929; *Daily Mail*, 8 Feb 1929; BoE, G 15/7, 12 Feb 1929, 19 Feb 1929; BB, 202040, 16 April 1929.

13. The extensive literature includes: Sir Henry Clay, *Lord Norman* (1957), pp 272–317; Sayers, chapter 14; W.A. Thomas, *The Finance of British Industry, 1918–1976* (1978), chapters 2–4; Steven Tolliday, *Business, Banking and Politics: The Case of British Steel, 1918–1939* (Cambridge, Mass., 1987); Duncan M. Ross, 'The clearing banks and industry – new perspectives on the inter-war years' in J.J. van Helten and Y. Cassis (eds), *Capitalism in a Mature Economy* (Aldershot, 1990); Michael Collins, *Banks and Industrial Finance in Britain: 1800–1939* (Basingstoke, 1991), pp 69–86; W.R. Garside and J.I. Greaves, 'The Bank of England and industrial intervention in interwar Britain' in *Financial History Review* (1996); Duncan M. Ross, 'Commercial banking in a market-oriented financial system: Britain between the wars' in *Economic History Review* (1996); W.R. Garside and J.I. Greaves, 'Rationalisation and Britain's Industrial Malaise: the Interwar Years Revisited' in *Journal of European Economic History* (1997).

14. BB, Dep 33.22, 25 May 1923; BoE, ADM 34/14, 17 Sept 1925.

15. Sayers, pp 314–18; Philip Ziegler, *The Sixth Great Power: Barings, 1762–1929* (1988), pp 342–4.

16. BB, 202043, 8 Aug 1927; Garside and Greaves, 'The Bank of England', pp 74–7; BoE, ADM 34/17, 24 April 1928.

17. Specific studies include: Jeffrey H. Porter, 'The Commercial Banks and the Financial Problems of the English Cotton Industry, 1919–1939' in *Revue internationale d'histoire de la banque* (1974); J.H. Bamberg, 'The government, the banks, and the Lancashire cotton industry, 1918–39' (Cambridge PhD, 1984); J.H. Bamberg, 'The Rationalization of the British Cotton Industry in the Interwar Years' in *Textile History* (1988).

18. HSBC, 30/122, 31 Jan 1928; *Journal of the Institute of Bankers*, March 1928, p 151; Sayers, p 319; BoE, ADM, 34/17, 14 Nov 1928, SMT 2/240, 19 Dec 1928, 5 Dec 1928; *Nation and Athenaeum*, 2 Feb 1929; BoE, SMT 2/240, 5 Dec 1928.

19. DBB, J.R. Edwards, 'Sir Francis D'Arcy Cooper', vol 1, pp 781–5, Edgar Jones, 'Sir Basil Edgar Mayhew', vol 4, pp 207–10, Michael Bywater, 'Sir William McLintock', vol 4, pp 68–75.

20. BoE, ADM 34/17, 18 Dec 1928; MG, private letter books, no 39, 14 Jan 1929.

21. BB, 202043, 8 Aug 1927; Ziegler, pp 342–6.

22. Kathleen Burk, *Morgan Grenfell, 1838–1988: The Biography of a Merchant Bank* (Oxford, 1989), pp 91–3; Robert Jones and Oliver Marriott, *Anatomy of a Merger* (1970), pp 89–127, 130–7; Richard Roberts, *Schroders: Merchants & Bankers* (1992), pp 207–9; Jehanne Wake, *Kleinwort Benson: The History of Two Families in Banking* (Oxford, 1997), p 239; Roberts, p 378; Wake, p 294.

23. Ziegler, pp 344–5; Stefanie Diaper, 'Merchant Banking in the Inter-War Period: The Case of Kleinwort, Sons & Co' in *Business History* (1986), p 59.

24. *DBB*, J.W. Scott and Francis Goodall, 'Frederick Alexander Szarvasy', vol 5, pp 427–9; Goronwy Rees, *St Michael: A History of Marks and Spencer* (1969), p 64.

25. *DBB*, J. Max Keyworth, 'Sir Arthur Wheeler', vol 5, pp 759–62, Laurie Dennett, 'Sir Hubert Nutcombe Hume', vol 3, pp 388–90.

26. *The Times*, 4 Nov 1965; *DBB*, R.P.T. Davenport-Hines, 'Guy Payan Dawnay', vol 2, pp 30–3, Robert Murphy, 'Isidore Ostrer', vol 4, pp 492–6.

27. Edward Beddington-Behrens, *Look Back Look Forward* (1963), pp 80–2.

28. BB, 101961, 10 May 1928.

29. HSBC, 30/122, 16 Oct 1928; *FT*, 13 Nov 1928; *Investors' Chronicle*, 12 March 1949.

30. *DBB*, Jenny Davenport, 'Sir Edward Roberts Lewis', vol 3, pp 757–60; *Issuing House Year Book and Financial A.B.C.* (1929).

31. John Kinross, *Fifty Years in the City* (1982), pp 73, 50–2, 73–4.

32. *Lloyds Bank Monthly Review*, Jan 1934, pp 10–11.

33. In the continuing absence of a proper biography of Hatry, the most helpful accounts of his career remain P.S. Manley, 'Clarence Hatry' in *Abacus* (June 1976) and *DBB*, David Fanning, 'Clarence Charles Hatry', vol 3, pp 110–14.

34. MG, private letter books, no 37, 12 April 1928; BoE, ADM 34/14, 21 Oct 1925; Wake, pp 238–40; *Author* (autumn 1993), p 100; Francis Williams, *Nothing So Strange* (1970), p 90.

35. Fanning, p 111; extract from private memoir by R.C.F. Besch; BB, 202040, 8–9 April 1929; David Kynaston, *Cazenove & Co: A History* (1991), p 117; BB, 202040, 10 April 1929.

36. Stanley Chapman, *The Rise of Merchant Banking* (1984), p 179. However, in BoE, G 3/194, 14 Feb 1929, Cecil Lubbock puts the total of London acceptances at year-end 1928 significantly higher, at around £260m.

37. Andrew Boyle, *Montagu Norman: A Biography* (1967), p 197; Brand, file 78, 29 Oct 1926; BoE, G 3/187, 23 Oct 1926, ADM 34/15, 13 Dec 1926.

38. See P.J. Cain and A.G. Hopkins, *British Imperialism: Crisis and Deconstruction, 1914–1990* (1993) for a sophisticated treatment of City and Empire in the 1920s; BoE, G 3/191, 15 Feb 1927.

39. BoE, ADM 34/14–17.

40. On Loewenstein, see: Hubert A. Meredith, *The Drama of Money Making* (?1931), pp 297–306; William Norris, *The Man who Fell from the Sky* (1987); Ziegler, pp 340–1; Roberts, *Schroders*, pp 209–10.

41. MG, private letter books, no 18, 12 Oct 1917; Williams, p 89; BB, 200378, 3 Sept 1926, 200379, 28 Jan 1927; Meredith, p 304.

42. Ziegler, p 350; J.M. Atkin, 'British Overseas Investment, 1918–1931' (London PhD, 1968), pp 173–4; BB, Dep 33.23, 31 Dec 1925; Anthony Sampson, *Anatomy of Britain* (1962), p 385; Roberts, *Schroders*, pp 203–5; BB, 202040, 8 March 1929.

43. See Cain and Hopkins, chapter 7, for the fullest treatment.

44. T. Jackson, *The Origin and History of the Drayton Group* (Croydon, 1991), p 20; David Wainwright, *Henderson: A History of the life of Alexander Henderson, first Lord Faringdon, and of Henderson Administration* (1985), p 36; BOLSA Collection (UCL), B 64, 26 May 1925.

45. Burk, p 301.

46. Bernard Attard, 'The Bank of England and the origins of the Niemeyer mission, 1921–1930' in *Australian Economic History Review* (1992), pp 68–71.

47. BoE, G 3/191, 25 March 1927, 6 April 1927.

48. Casey quotations (July 1928) from Bernard Attard, 'Australian Financial Diplomacy, 1914–39' in Carl Bridge and Bernard Attard (eds), *Between Empire and Nation* (Melbourne, 1999); Attard, 'The Bank of England', p 71; W.J. Hudson and Jane North (eds), *My Dear P.M.: R.G. Casey's Letters to S.M. Bruce, 1924–1929* (Canberra, 1980), p 469.

49. Addis, 14/45, 8 Feb 1927; Cain and Hopkins, pp 246–51; JM, Semi-Official Letters, London to Hong Kong, 6 Sept 1928, 17 April 1929.

50. Ziegler, p 351; Brand, file 74, 6 April 1926; BB, 101959, 10 Nov 1926; BoE, ADM 34/14, 20 May 1925; BB, 200257, 15 Feb 1927.

51. Roberts, *Schroders*, pp 194–6; BB, COF/05/14/4, 13–23 Sept 1926.

52. Diaper, p 64; John Orbell, *Baring Brothers & Co., Limited: A History to 1939* (1985), p 78; NW, 7442, 26 Feb 1929.

53. Sayers, pp 191–3; Burk, pp 136–8.

54. BB, 101959, 15 March 1926; Ziegler, p 354; MG, private letter books, no 35, 30 Oct 1926, 27 Oct 1926; Ziegler, p 354.

55. Sayers, p 193; BoE, G 3/182, 19 Nov 1926; Sayers, p 194. In general on the Italian stabilisation loan, see: Sayers, pp 193–5; Burk, pp 138–9.

56. BoE, G 35/7, 26 Oct 1927; BB, 200257, 5 Oct 1927; HSBC, 347/7, 22 Dec 1927; MG, private letter books, no 37, 22 Dec 1927.

57. See especially Sayers, pp 183–9; Kenneth Mouré, 'The Limits to Central Bank Co-operation, 1916–36' in *Contemporary European History* (1992), pp 265–73.

58. BoE, G 3/184, 9 Sept 1925; Sayers, pp 337–41; BoE, G15/241, 30 April 1960 (Kershaw).

59. BoE, G 3/191, 23 June 1927; Emile Moreau, *The Golden Franc* (Boulder, Colorado, 1991), pp 51, 238, 256, 258, 430, 479, 525.

60. Clay, pp 260–6; Sayers, pp 195–9. See also: R.H. Meyer, *Bankers' Diplomacy: Monetary Stabilisation in the Twenties* (New York, 1970), pp 100–37; Stephen V.O. Clarke, *Central Bank Co-operation, 1924–31* (New York, 1967), chapters 6 and 7.

61. Moreau, pp 444, 447; Addis, 14/46, 24 Feb 1928, 27 Feb 1928; Moreau, p 449; Addis, 14/46, 28 Feb 1928.

62. Clay, pp 265–6.

63. BoE, ADM 34/17, 27 Nov 1928.

64. BB, 202040, 18 Feb 1929; BoE, G 3/195, 7 March 1929, 28 March 1929; BB, 101961, 10 May 1928.

65. Ziegler, pp 356–7.

66. BB, 202040, 28 Feb 1929, 8 March 1929, 200729, 13 April 1929, 202040, 16 April 1929; Ziegler, p 357.

67. Ranald C. Michie, *The City of London: Continuity and Change, 1850–1990* (Basingstoke, 1992), chapter 2, gives a pioneering account of the 'Commercial City'.

68. Economist Intelligence Unit, *The London Metal Exchange* (1958), pp 104–10.

69. Hugh Barty-King, *The Baltic Exchange* (1977), pp 329–40.

70. Gordon D. Hodge, *56 Years in the London Sugar Market* (1960), p 36.

71. MG, private letter books, no 36, 2 June 1927; HSBC, 347/7, 6 July 1928; BoE, EID 4/30; Kynaston, p 104.

72. MG, private letter books, no 35, 20 Oct 1926; Brand, file 76, 30 June 1927; BoE, G 3/191, 14 Dec 1927.

73. BoE, ADM 34/15–17.

74. BoE, G 35/6, 21 Sept 1926; Sayers, pp 243–8, 147–8; BoE, G3/191, 5 May 1927.

75. Diaper, p 66.

76. BB, Dep 22.XXIII; Roberts, *Schroders*, pp 185–6; BoE, EID 4/86, item 10.

77. For more generally on the discount market, see: Sayers, pp 272–83; G.A. Fletcher, *The Discount Houses in London* (1976), pp 37–43. See also BoE, G 15/62, Tiarks memo of 25 April 1927.

78. BoE, ADM 34/9, 1 April 1920; George and Pamela Cleaver, *The Union Discount: A Centenary Album* (1985), p 59; *DBB*, Gordon A. Fletcher, 'Lawrence Henry Seccombe', vol 5, pp 102–6.

79. Sayers, p 282; BoE, G 3/191, 23 Nov 1927.

80. Clay, pp 304–12; Sayers, pp 648–51.

81. Addis, 14/43, 7 Oct 1925; BoE, G 35/5, 18 Oct 1925; Addis, 14/44, 8 July 1926; BoE, G 35/5, 1 Nov 1925.

82. BB, 101959, 22 July 1926; Addis, 14/44; BoE, ADM 33/26 (Trotter); Clay, p 307; BoE, G 35/6, 10 Oct 1926.

83. Addis, 14/454, 28 Sept 1926.

84. Sayers, p 650; Addis, 14/46, 7 June 1928; Clay, p 310.

85. BB, 202044, 6 Sept 1928, 101961, 22 Oct 1928, 25 Oct 1928.

86. Sayers, pp 620–1; Clay, p 311; Addis, 14/456, 17 May 1928.

87. For more on Strakosch, see J.D.F. Jones, *Through Fortress and Rock: The Story of Gencor, 1895–1995* (Johannesburg, 1995), chapters 6–7.

88. BoE, G 35/7, 28 Nov 1927; Addis, 14/46, 22–3 Feb 1928.

89. *FT*, 14 July 1925.

90. *The Private Diaries of Sydney Moseley* (1960), pp 264, 266, 269, 273, 282, 285–6; H.E. Raynes, 'The Place of Ordinary Stocks and Shares (as distinct from Fixed Interest bearing Securities) in the Investment of Life Assurance Funds' in *Journal of the Institute of Actuaries*, March 1928, with the Eliot quotation on p 46.

91. Roberts, *Schroders*, p 393; Skidelsky, p 340; *FT*, 16 April 1929.

CHAPTER SEVEN

1. BoE, G 1/511, 19 April 1929; Addis, 14/47, 19 April 1929; BB, 200427, 17 May 1929.

2. *FN*, 4 Oct 1929; records of Antony Gibbs & Sons (Guildhall Library), Ms 11,042, vol 1, 21 Feb 1929; Keith Middlemas, 'The Party, Industry, and the City' in Anthony Seldon and Stuart Ball (eds), *The Conservative Century* (Oxford, 1994), p 452; BoE, ADM 33/8, Skinner recollections of Norman, June 1958; MG, private letter books, no 40, 19 Nov 1929.

3. *Economist*, 15 June 1929; BB, 200427, 25 June 1929; BoE, G 1/515, 28 June 1929.

4. *Banker*, Feb 1926, pp 162–3; *The Times*, 25 July 1929; *FN*, 26 July 1929; PRO, T 176/13, Part 2, fo 46; *Daily Herald*, 30 July 1929.

5. For a revealing interview with Hatry, see *Evening Standard*, 19 April 1929.

6. Hubert A. Meredith, *The Drama of Money Making* (?1931), pp 308–9.

7. BoE, ADM 34/18, 28–9 May 1929, G 3/195, 1 June 1929; Meredith, p 310; BoE, ADM 34/18, 5 June 1929, 11 June 1929.

8. *DBB*, David Fanning, 'Clarence Charles Hatry', vol 3, p 112; Lloyds, B 1403a/2, 8 Aug 1929.

9. BoE, G1/506 (Addis), 21 Aug 1929, 31 Aug 1929.

10. BoE, G 1/506 (Addis), 4 Sept 1929, G 15/7, 4 Sept 1929, ADM 34/18, 9 Sept 1929.

11. BoE, G 15/7, 4 Sept 1929.

12. On Hatry's downfall, see (in addition to works already cited): W.J. Reader, *A House in the City: A Study of the City and of the Stock Exchange based on the Records of Foster & Braithwaite, 1825–1975* (1979), pp 150–4; Edgar Jones, *True and Fair: A History of Price Waterhouse* (1995), pp 143–4.

13. Lloyds, B 1403a/2, 19 Sept 1929.

14. The Marquess of Winchester, *Statesmen, Financiers and Felons* (1935), pp 269–70; SSA, Ms 14, 894, vol 39, 20 Sept 1929; *FT*, 21 Sept 1929; HSBC, 347/7, 24 Sept 1929; BoE, G 3/195, 27 Sept 1929, ADM 34/18, 30 Sept 1929.

15. SSA, Ms 14, 894, vol 39, 26 Sept 1929; *FT*, 27 Sept 1929; *FN*, 27 Sept 1929.

16. PRO, T 176/13, part 1; *Evening Standard*, 27 Sept 1929; *Daily Express*, 27 Sept 1929; *Daily Herald*, 27 Sept 1929; BoE, ADM 34/18, 30 Sept 1929.

17. Sayers, pp 360–3 gives the background.

18. *FN*, 4 Oct 1929; BoE, G 1/515, 12 July 1929.

19. *Daily Express*, 27 Sept 1929; BoE, G 15/7, 30 Sept 1929; Alan Bullock, *The Life and Times of Ernest Bevin: Volume One* (1960), p 418; BoE, ADM 34/18, 2 Oct 1929, G 3/195, 4 Oct 1929; *FT*, 4 Oct 1929.

20. Peter Clarke, *The Keynesian Revolution in the Making, 1924–1936* (Oxford, 1988), p 104.

21. BB, 200427, 23 July 1929; Oliver M. Westall, *The Provincial Insurance Company, 1903–38* (Manchester, 1992), p 360.

22. *FN*, 24–5 Oct 1929, 29–30 Oct 1929; JS, no 17.

CHAPTER EIGHT

1. Sidney Pollard, *The Development of the British Economy: 1914–1980* (1983 edn), p 141; Robert Skidelsky, *John Maynard Keynes: Volume Two, The Economist as Saviour, 1920–1937* (1992), p 343; records of Morgan, Grenfell & Co (Guildhall Library), Ms 21,799, fo 136; BB, 200427, 13 Dec 1929; records of Brown, Shipley & Co (Guildhall Library), Ms 20,110, vol 2, 30 Jan 1930; Frank Holt letter courtesy Davina Walter (grand-daughter); David Kynaston, *Cazenove & Co: A History* (1991), p 125.

2. BoE, G 1/503, 16 Jan 1930, ADM 34/19, 25 Jan 1930.

3. Sayers, pp 352–9 covers fully the foundation and early years of BIS.

4. BoE, G 15/7, 4 Sept 1929, G 3/197, 6 March 1930, 13 March 1930.

5. H. Montgomery Hyde, *Norman Birkett* (1964), p 284; John Kinross, *Fifty Years in the City* (1982), p 57; *The Times*, 25 Jan 1930; *Sunday Express*, 26 Jan 1930; Hyde, p 285; BoE, G 1/511, 23 Dec 1943, 30 Dec 1943; *DBB*, David Fanning, 'Clarence Charles Hatry', vol 3, p 113.

6. BoE, G 3/197, 13 Feb 1930; NW, 7258, 20 Dec 1929, HSBC, 347/7, 23 Dec 1929, NW, 7258, 30 Dec 1929; W.J. Reader, *A House in the City: A Study of the City*

and of the Stock Exchange based on the Records of Foster & Braithwaite (1979), pp 154–6; R.G. Walker, 'The Hatry Affair' in *Abacus* (June 1977).

7. BoE, ADM 34/18, 20 Nov 1929. In general on UDT and its impact, see Sue Bowden and Michael Collins, 'The Bank of England, industrial regeneration, and hire purchase between the wars' in *Economic History Review* (1992).

8. Stimulating discussions of the City and industrial rationalisation are to be found in: William H. Janeway, 'The Economic Policy of the Second Labour Government, 1929–31' (Cambridge PhD, 1971); Steven Tolliday, *Business, Banking and Politics: The Case of British Steel, 1918–1939* (Cambridge, Mass., 1987); J.H. Bamberg, 'The Rationalization of the British Cotton Industry in the Interwar Years' in *Textile History* (1988); W.R. Garside and J.I. Greaves, 'The Bank of England and industrial intervention in interwar Britain' in *Financial History Review* (1996), 'Rationalisation and Britain's Industrial Malaise: the Interwar Years Revisited' in *Journal of European Economic History* (1997).

9. BoE, G 3/195, 16 Sept 1929, 14 Aug 1929, ADM 34/18, 2 Oct 1929.

10. Sayers, p 325, *DBB*, R.P.T. Davenport-Hines, 'Sir Charles Bruce Gardner', vol 2, pp 480–4; J.H. Bamberg, 'The government, the banks, and the Lancashire cotton industry, 1918–39' (Cambridge PhD, 1984), p 60.

11. BoE, G 3/196, 8 Jan 1930; Sir Henry Clay, *Lord Norman* (1957), pp 326–7; Sayers, p 326; John Vincent (ed), *The Crawford Papers* (Manchester, 1984), p 531.

12. BoE, SMT 2/53, 22 Feb 1930, 5 March 1930, G 3/196, 17 March 1930, 21 March 1930, ADM 34/19, 18 March 1930, SMT 2/53, 25 March 1930, 2 April 1930.

13. For a fuller analysis of Norman's response, see: Sayers, pp 230–2; Susan Howson, *Domestic Monetary Management in Britain, 1919–38* (Cambridge, 1975), pp 66–7.

14. Addis, 14/48, 12 Feb–5 March 1930; Roberta Allbert Dayer, *Finance and Empire: Sir Charles Addis, 1861–1945* (1988), p 211.

15. Studies of the Macmillan Committee include: Scott Gordon, 'Two Monetary Inquiries in Great Britain: The Macmillan Report of 1931 and the Radcliffe Report of 1959' in *Journal of Money, Credit, and Banking* (Nov 1972); Brian Griffiths, 'Two Monetary Inquiries in Great Britain: Comments' in *Journal of Money, Credit, and Banking* (Feb 1974); Sayers, pp 360–73; Peter Clarke, *The Keynesian Revolution in the Making, 1924–1936* (Oxford, 1988), chapters 5–9.

16. Brand, file 30, 8 Nov 1929, file 27, 22 Nov 1929.

17. BoE, ADM 34/18, 26 Nov 1929, G 3/196, 7 Jan 1930; Sayers, Appendixes, pp 117–71; BoE, G 1/426, 19 Dec 1929.

18. Macmillan, qq 494, 580–3 (Goodenough), 1162, 1164, 1216, 1224, 1308, 1526 (Kindersley).

19. NW, 7299, 13 March 1930; Macmillan, qq 2203 (Pease), 2502 (Payton).

20. Donald Moggridge (ed), *The Collected Writings of John Maynard Keynes: Volume XX* (1981), pp 91, 140–1; Alan Bullock, *The Life and Times of Ernest Bevin: Volume One* (1960), p 429.

21. BoE, G 1/425, unrevised evidence of Norman, 26 March 1930, qq 3332–5, 3338, 3344, 3383–9, 3403, 3405–6, 3459–62, 3507–8, 3511–16. For the revised version, see Sayers, Appendixes, pp 172–87.

22. Clarke, p 129; BoE, G 3/197, 27 March 1930; Sayers, p 369; BoE, G 15/241, 18 Dec 1957 (Brand).

23. Addis, 14/48, 31 March 1930; Sayers, pp 368–71; BoE, G 3/196, 2 April 1930.

24. Anne Olivier Bell (ed), *The Diary of Virginia Woolf: Volume 4* (1982), p 208.

25. Addis, 14/48, 7 May 1930, 22 May 1930; BoE, G 3/196, 26 June 1930; *FT*, 23 June 1930; SE, Ms 14,609, vol 9, 13 May 1930.

26. Anne Olivier Bell (ed), *The Diary of Virginia Woolf: Volume 3* (1980), p 199; Nicholas Davenport, *Memoirs of a City Radical* (1974), pp 35–6; *The Times*, 4–5 July 1930, *FT*, 5 July 1930; *The Times*, 9 July 1930, 12 July 1930. For an alternative version of Cooke's death, see Andrew Lycett, *From Diamond Sculls to Golden Handcuffs: A History of Rowe & Pitman* (1998), pp 45–6.

27. On the City's shift from free trade, see: Robert W.D. Boyce, *British Capitalism at the Crossroads, 1919–1932* (Cambridge, 1987), pp 253–4; Tim Rooth, 'The Political Economy of Protectionism in Britain, 1919–32' in *Journal of European Economic History* (1992), pp 62–5. Anthony Howe, *Free Trade and Liberal England: 1846–1946* (Oxford, 1997), chapter 8, puts the issue in a long-term, post-Edwardian perspective.

28. *FT*, 5 July 1930; Boyce, p 254.

29. Peter Love, 'Niemeyer's Australian Diary and other English Records of His Mission' in *Historical Studies* (1982). See also Bernard Attard, 'The Bank of England and the origins of the Niemeyer mission, 1921–1930' in *Australian Economic History Review* (1992).

30. BB, 200534, 8 Aug 1930.

31. Love, pp 267–73.

32. *Economist*, 30 Aug 1930; BoE, G 3/197, 11 Sept 1930; Attard, pp 67, 82.

33. BoE, SMT 2/53, 4 April 1930, SMT 9/1, 11 April 1930.

34. BoE, SMT 9/1, 16 June 1930; Bamberg, 'Rationalization', p 92, 'The government, the banks', pp 195–6; BoE, SMT 9/1, 25 Aug 1930, 1 Sept 1930.

35. BoE, SMT 2/55, 13 Oct 1930; BB, 200484, 3 Nov 1930, 20 Nov 1930; L.E. Jones, *Georgian Afternoon* (1958), p 120.

36. BoE, SMT 2/55, 18–19 Dec 1930.

37. Macmillan, q 7988.

38. Brand, file 29, 14 Aug 1930.

39. Brand, file 31, 31 Oct 1930, 30 Oct 1930, 5 Dec 1930.

40. BoE, G 3/197, 1 Oct 1930; BB, 200534, 8 Oct 1930. In general, on the growing sense of crisis during the closing months of 1930, see Philip Williamson, *National Crisis and National Government: British Politics, the Economy and Empire, 1926–1932* (Cambridge, 1992), pp 133–42.

41. BoE, SMT 9/1, 17 Nov 1930; MG, private letter books, no 42, 27 Dec 1930; W.N. Medlicott, *Contemporary England: 1914–1964* (1976, pbk), pp 245, 249.

42. Addis, 14/49, 7 Jan 1931; Brown, Shipley & Co, Ms 20,110, vol 2, 22 Jan 1931; Williamson, p 200.

43. BoE, ADM 34/20, 26 Jan 1931, G 3/198, 27 Jan 1931; Addis, 14/49, 27 Jan 1931, Williamson, p 200; Brand, file 30, 30 Jan 1931.

44. BoE, G 1/143, 2 Feb 1931, ADM 34/20, 5 Feb 1931.

45. Boyce, p 300.

46. SE, Ms 14,600, vol 125, 2 March 1931.

47. Addis, 14/48, 15 Oct 1930; Brand, file 28, 1 Jan 1931; Sayers, p 372.

48. Macmillan, qq 9078–9 (Granet), 9121–2, 9183–4 (Norman).

49. Kathleen Burk, *Morgan Grenfell, 1838–1988: The Biography of a Merchant*

Bank (Oxford, 1989), p 97; *FT*, 26 March 1931; Bamberg, 'The government, the banks', p 119.

50. BB, 200537, 17 April 1931, 20 April 1931.

51. Sayers, p 547; Bamberg, 'Rationalization', p 94, 'The government, the banks', p 217; also on Platt, see *DBB*, J.H. Bamberg, 'Sir Frank Platt', vol 4, pp 716–22.

52. BoE, G 3/198, 2 March 1931, 17 March 1931; Richard Roberts, *Schroders: Merchants & Bankers* (1992), p 206; *FT*, 30 March 1931.

53. On Booth and/or the early history of unit trusts, see: BoE, ADM 33/24; Duncan Crow, *A Man of Push and Go: The Life of George Macaulay Booth* (1965), especially pp 175–8; Sayers, pp 535–6; Adrienne Gleeson, *People and their Money: 50 Years of Private Investment* (1981); Karin Newman, *Financial marketing and communications* (Eastbourne, 1984), pp 143–6; *DBB*, R.P.T. Davenport-Hines, 'George Macaulay Booth', vol 1, pp 380–3.

54. SE, Ms 14,600, vol 125, 6 May 1931.

55. BoE, G 3/198, 30 April 1931, OV 32/7, 5 May 1931.

CHAPTER NINE

1. NW, 7387, 7 Jan 1931; BB, Dep 22.XXIII.

2. Accounts of the Credit Anstalt failure and its impact on the City include: Sir Henry Clay, *Lord Norman* (1957), pp 375–7; Sayers, p 389; Robert W.D. Boyce, *British Capitalism at the Crossroads, 1919–1932* (Cambridge, 1987), pp 332–3; Diane B. Kunz, *The Battle for Britain's Gold Standard in 1931* (Beckenham, 1987), pp 46–8, 54–9; P.L. Cottrell, 'The Bank of England in its International Setting, 1918–1972' in Richard Roberts and David Kynaston (eds), *The Bank of England* (Oxford, 1995), pp 95–9; Niall Ferguson, *The World's Banker: The History of the House of Rothschild* (1998), pp 993–5.

3. Cottrell, p 99; Kunz, p 48; NW, 7387, 28–9 May 1931; BoE, ADM 33/25.

4. For further detail about the City and Germany in 1931, including the Standstill Agreement, see: Clay, pp 377–83, 448; Sayers, pp 503–7; Stefanie Diaper, 'Merchant Banking in the Inter-War Period: The Case of Kleinwort, Sons & Co' in *Business History* (1986), pp 67–70; Boyce, pp 334–9, 344; Richard Roberts, *Schroders: Merchants & Bankers* (1992), pp 250–7; Jehanne Wake, *Kleinwort Benson: The History of Two Families in Banking* (Oxford, 1997), pp 242–4.

5. BoE, ADM 34/20, 10 June 1931, 19 June 1931.

6. Sayers, p 503; BoE, G 3/198, 1 July 1931.

7. BoE, G 3/198, 6 June 1931, 13 June 1931; records of Heseltine, Powell & Co (Guildhall Library), Ms 23,267, vol 3, 26 May 1931, 17 June 1931, 19 June 1931.

8. BoE, G 15/7, 18 June 1931, 25 June 1931, 29 June 1931.

9. The most authoritative assessment is Peter Clarke, *The Keynesian Revolution in the Making, 1924–1936* (Oxford, 1988), pp 212–18. See also, on the identification of the 'Macmillan gap', Richard Coopey and Donald Clarke, *3i: Fifty Years Investing in Industry* (Oxford, 1995), pp 9–10.

10. BoE, G 1/425, 23 June 1931, 26 June 1931; Brian Griffiths, 'Two Monetary Inquiries in Great Britain: Comments' in *Journal of Money, Credit, and Banking* (Feb 1974), pp 111–12; BoE, G 1/504, 15 July 1931.

11. Macmillan, pp 161–74; *FT*, 15 July 1931.

12. Sayers, pp 530–1; Andrew Boyle, *Montagu Norman: A Biography* (1967), p 264.

13. BoE, G 35/7, 18 Sept 1927; Roberta Allbert Dayer, *Finance and Empire: Sir Charles Addis, 1861–1945* (Basingstoke, 1988), p 192; Addis, 14/49, 17 July 1931.

14. *FT*, 15–16 July 1931; BoE, ADM 34/20, 15 July 1931.

15. Wake, p 244; Roberts, *Schroders*, pp 265, 252–7; BB, 200489, 31 July 1931, 12 Aug 1931; Laurie Dennett, *Slaughter and May: A Century in the City* (Cambridge, 1989), p 184.

16. There is an extensive literature on the 1931 financial crisis. Important contributions include: Clay, pp 383–98; Sayers, pp 391–415; Philip Williamson, 'A "Bankers Ramp"? Financiers and the British Political Crisis of August 1931' in *English Historical Review* (1984); Forrest Capie, Terence C. Mills and Geoffrey E. Wood, 'What Happened in 1931?' in Forrest Capie and Geoffrey E. Wood (eds), *Financial Crises and the World Banking System* (Basingstoke, 1986); Boyce, pp 339–66; Kunz, pp 77–146; Kathleen Burk, *Morgan Grenfell, 1838–1988: The Biography of a Merchant Bank* (Oxford, 1989), pp 148–56; Philip Williamson, *National Crisis and National Government: British Politics, the Economy and Empire, 1926–1932* (Cambridge, 1992), pp 259–424; William H. Janeway, 'The 1931 sterling crisis and the independence of the Bank of England' in *Journal of Post Keynesian Economics* (winter 1995–6).

17. Kunz, p 77; Robert Skidelsky, *John Maynard Keynes: Volume Two, The Economist as Saviour, 1920–1937* (1992), p 393; Kenneth Young (ed), *The Diaries of Sir Robert Bruce Lockhart, Volume One* (1973), p 178; SSA, Ms 14, 894, vol 41, 22 July 1931.

18. Kunz, p 82.

19. BoE, ADM 34/20, 27 July 1931; Kunz, p 107; *FT*, 29 July 1931.

20. The Royal Mail literature includes: P.N. Davies and A.M. Bourn, 'Lord Kylsant and the Royal Mail' in *Business History* (1972); Edwin Green and Michael Moss, *A Business of National Importance: The Royal Mail Shipping Group, 1902–1937* (1982); Dennett, pp 187–91; Edgar Jones, *True and Fair: A History of Price Waterhouse* (1995), pp 145–57.

21. *FT*, 21 July 1931; Jones, pp 154–5; P.N. Davies, 'Business Success and the Role of Chance: The Extraordinary Philipps Brothers' in *Business History* (1981), p 225.

22. BoE, ADM 34/20, 29 July 1931; PRO, 30/69/260 (MacDonald Papers), 30 July 1931.

23. Sayers, p 395; Williamson, 'Bankers Ramp', p 773.

24. Norman and Jeanne MacKenzie (eds), *The Diary of Beatrice Webb: Volume Four* (1985), p 249; Addis, 14/49, 5 Aug 1931; PRO, 30/69/260, 5 Aug 1931.

25. Sayers, p 395; BoE, G 3/210, 6 Aug 1931, ADM 34/20, 6 Aug 1931.

26. BoE, ADM 34/20, 10 Aug 1931, G 3/210, 10 Aug 1931, G 8/60, 11 Aug 1931; BB, 200489, 11 Aug 1931.

27. *FT*, 13 Aug 1931; Addis, 14/49, 12 Aug 1931; BoE, G 3/210, 12 Aug 1931; Addis, 14/49, 13 Aug 1931; Thomas Jones, *A Diary with Letters, 1931–1950* (Oxford, 1954), p 11; BoE, G 3/210, 17 Aug 1931.

28. BoE, G 3/210, 18 Aug 1931; SSA, Ms 14,894, vol 41, 18 Aug 1931; Burk, p 150.

29. PRO, PREM 1/96, fo 44; *The Times*, 15 Aug 1931; *FT*, 21 Aug 1931; BoE, G 3/210, 20 Aug 1931; Burk, p 150.

30. Addis, 14/49, 22 Aug 1931.

31. *Beatrice Webb*, p 253; Addis, 14/49, 23 Aug 1931; Burk, p 153.
32. Burk, p 152; *DBB*, John Orbell, 'Sir Edward Robert Peacock', vol 4, pp 565–6; Boyce, p 451.
33. Boyce, p 354.
34. BoE, G 8/60, 24 Aug 1931; Addis, 14/49, 24 Aug 1931; SSA, Ms 14,894, vol 41, 24 Aug 1931; *FT*, 25 Aug 1931; *Beatrice Webb*, pp 254–5.
35. Francis Williams, *Nothing So Strange* (1970), p 101; *FT*, 26 Aug 1931; PRO, 30/69/1314, 25 Aug 1931.
36. Such is the persuasive interpretation put forward in Williamson, 'Bankers Ramp'.
37. Samuel Brittan, *The Treasury under the Tories, 1951–1964* (1964), p 308.
38. Addis, 14/49, 25–6 Aug 1931; BoE, G 8/60, 2 Sept 1931, G 3/210, fos 285, 285a.
39. *FT*, 12 Sept 1931; *Bruce Lockhart*, p 185; *FN*, 14 Sept 1931.
40. *SE*, Ms 14,600, vol 126, 14 Sept 1931.
41. *FN*, 16 Sept 1931, 18 Sept 1931; Williamson, *National Crisis*, pp 413–15.
42. Kunz, p 135; PRO, PREM 1/97, 18 Sept 1931, fos 84–9.
43. *FT*, 21 Sept 1931.
44. BoE, G 1/515, 20 Sept 1931; *FT*, 21 Sept 1931; *FN*, 21 Sept 1931; *The Times*, 21 Sept 1931.
45. BB, 200534, 21 Sept 1931; MG, private letter books, no 44, 21 Sept 1931; Skidelsky, p 397; Anne Olivier Bell (ed), *The Diary of Virginia Woolf: Volume 4* (1982), p 45.
46. Sonia Orwell and Ian Angus (eds), *The Collected Essays, Journalism and Letters of George Orwell: Volume I* (1968), pp 93–4.

CHAPTER TEN

1. H.M. Tomlinson, *Gallions Reach* (1952, pbk), p 8; J.B. Priestley, *Angel Pavement* (1937, Everyman edn), p 27.
2. Percy Harley, *My Life in Shipping, 1881–1938* (1938), p 82. By far the most thorough treatment of the post-1914 commercial City, among recent historians, is provided by Ranald C. Michie, *The City of London: Continuity and Change, 1850–1990* (Basingstoke, 1992), chapter 2.
3. Michie, p 30; J.H. Dunning and E.V. Morgan, *An Economic Study of the City of London* (1971), p 32; David Kynaston, *The City of London, Volume I* (1994), p 139.
4. Collin Brooks, *Something in the City: Men and Markets in London* (1931), pp 104–224.
5. *The Post Office London Directory* (1927), p 264; records of London Chamber of Commerce (Guildhall Library), Ms 16,639, Annual Report of London Fur Trade Association, Dec 1934.
6. Anon, *A Short History of Bradbury Greatorex and Co Ltd* (197?), p 5. See, in general, S.D. Chapman, 'The Decline and Rise of Textile Merchanting, 1880–1990' in *Business History* (1990).
7. Charles G. Harper, *The City of London Guide* (1927 edn), pp A12, A25, A76, A91. On the question of how many people worked in the City, see Michie, pp 13–15.
8. Anon, *History of Chas. Hope & Son* (1948), p 8.
9. H.V. Morton, *When You Go To London* (New York, 1933), pp 56–7.

10. F.D. Ommanney, *The River Bank* (1966), p 23; C.H. Rolph, *Further Particulars* (Oxford, 1987), pp 39–48; Bolton.

11. For a brief overall survey of change and continuity in the City's character, see David Kynaston, 'A Changing Workscape: The City of London since the 1840s' in *London Journal* (1988).

12. W. Lionel Fraser, *All to the Good* (1963), pp 37–8; Virginia Woolf, *The Waves* (1964, pbk), p 79; Ommanney, p 24.

13. H. Macdonald, 'A Merchant Looks Back' in Ian Norrie (ed), *The Book of the City* (1961), pp 145–6; James Bone, *The London Perambulator* (1925), p 129.

14. Edward Liveing, *A Century of Insurance* (1961), pp 180–5; Harold Clunn, *The Face of London* (1932), p 24.

15. For an authoritative guide to the subject, see John Booker, *Temples of Mammon: The Architecture of Banking* (Edinburgh, 1990).

16. Richard Roberts, *Schroders: Merchants & Bankers* (1992), p 183; Nikolaus Pevsner, *London: Volume One, The Cities of London and Westminster* (Harmondsworth, 1957), p 195; *Banker*, April 1926, p 385.

17. Booker, p 236; Kathleen Burk, *Morgan Grenfell, 1838–1988: The Biography of a Merchant Bank* (Oxford, 1989), pp 100–1; *Banker*, April 1926, pp 382–6.

18. Newman Flower (ed), *The Journals of Arnold Bennett, 1921–1928* (1933), pp 275–6; A.R. Holmes and Edwin Green, *Midland: 150 Years of Banking Business* (1986), pp 171, 175, Booker, p 235; Pevsner, p 236, Booker, p 235.

19. *Banker*, Sept 1933, p 234, June 1939, p 370.

20. For a notably insightful account, see I.S. Black, 'Imperial visions: rebuilding the Bank of England, 1919–1939' in F. Driver and D. Gilbert (eds), *Imperial Cities: Landscape, Display and Identity* (Manchester, 1999).

21. Herbert Baker, *Architecture and Personalities* (1944), p 124; Sayers, Appendixes, pp 338–42; *Banker*, Aug 1937, pp 198–202; James Lees-Milne, *Prophesying Peace* (1984, pbk), p 185; Pevsner, pp 164–5; Baker, p 128.

22. Pevsner, pp 250, 209; Vanessa Harding and Priscilla Metcalf, *Lloyd's At Home* (1986), p 133; Clunn, *Face of London* (1951 edn), p 43.

23. Pevsner, p 225; Corporation of London (Stuart J. Murphy), *Continuity and Change: Building in the City of London, 1834–1984* (1984), p 64; *Banker*, Jan 1928, p 118; Priestley, p 5; *The Post Office London Directory* (1926), p 397; Alastair Ross Goobey, *Bricks and Mortals* (1992), pp 23–4.

24. Robert Thorne, 'The Setting of St Paul's Cathedral in the Twentieth Century' in *London Journal* (1991), p 117; Richard Trench, *London Before the Blitz* (1989), pp 4, 12, 142, 163–4. Trench's book is a marvellously evocative – and poignant – reconstruction of the pre-1940 City.

25. Harper, p 5; Stephen Graham, *Twice Round the London Clock* (1933), p 22.

26. Anne Olivier Bell, *The Diary of Virginia Woolf: Volume 5* (1984), p 119; Nigel Nicolson (ed), *The Letters of Virginia Woolf: Volume VI* (1980), p 186; *Diary of Virginia Woolf: Volume 5*, pp 132, 203–4, 217.

27. Clunn, *Face of London* (1932 edn), p 40; *FN*, 22 Jan 1934.

28. John Summerson, 'The Victorian Rebuilding of the City of London' in *London Journal* (1977), p 164.

29. Unpublished memoir by Jack Smeaton (Slaughter and May records).

30. Ommanney, pp 19–22, 29.

31. David Kynaston, *Cazenove & Co: A History* (1991), pp 117–21; David

Wainwright, *Government Broker: The Story of an Office and of Mullens & Co* (1990), pp 67–8.

32. W.J. Reader and David Kynaston, *Phillips & Drew: Professionals in the City* (1998), pp 10–11.

33. Ronald Palin, *Rothschild Relish* (1970), pp 2–4, 20–5, 53–4, 95, 64, 7.

34. Elizabeth Hennessy, 'The Governors, Directors and Management of the Bank of England' in Richard Roberts and David Kynaston (eds), *The Bank of England* (Oxford, 1995), p 204; *The Old Lady*, spring 1981, p 28; Frank H.H. King, *The History of the Hongkong and Shanghai Banking Corporation: Volume III* (Cambridge, 1988), pp 318–19.

35. BoE, E 1/5.

36. Palin, p 63; Michael Bonavia, *London Before I Forget* (Upton-upon-Severn, 1990), pp 108–9.

37. Charles Short, *Morgan Guaranty's London Heritage* (1986), p 34; George and Pamela Cleaver, *The Union Discount: A Centenary Album* (1985), pp 55–6.

38. M.C. Reed, *A History of James Capel & Co* (1975), p 83; Jehanne Wake, *Kleinwort Benson: The History of Two Families in Banking* (Oxford, 1997), pp 217–19.

39. Judy Slinn, *Clifford Chance: Its Origins and Development* (Cambridge, 1993), pp 113–15; BB, 202617.

40. Cathy Courtney and Paul Thompson, *City Lives: the changing voices of British finance* (1996), p 60; Wake, pp 245–6, 296.

41. Ommanney, p 29; BB, 200606.

42. Reed, p 83; Reader and Kynaston, p 11; Berry Ritchie, *A Touch of Class: The Story of Austin Reed* (1990), pp 67–73.

43. BB, 200463, 31 Dec 1924, 5–6 Jan 1925.

44. Graham, p 20; Holmes and Green, p 173; J.R. Winton, *Lloyds Bank, 1918–1969* (Oxford, 1982), pp 89–90; Wake, p 246.

45. Kynaston, *Cazenove*, pp 129–30; Cleaver, pp 66–7.

46. Robert Dougall, *In and Out of the Box* (1973), p 41; T. Jackson, *The Origin and History of the Drayton Group* (Croydon, 1991), p 45; Elizabeth Hennessy, *A Domestic History of the Bank of England, 1930–1960* (Cambridge, 1992), pp 53–4.

47. BB, 200463; S.J. Diaper, 'The History of Kleinwort, Sons & Co in Merchant Banking, 1855–1961' (Nottingham PhD, 1983), p 367; Judy Slinn, *Linklaters & Paines: The First One Hundred and Fifty Years* (1987), p 122; HSBC, LOH II 735, E.J. Davies report on London office, 31 Dec 1936; Sayers, p 617.

48. NW, 7290; Eric Street, *The History of the National Mutual Life Assurance Society, 1830–1980* (1980), p 106; Palin, p 94; HSBC, G.W. Stabb interview.

49. BB, 200463, Dec 1927, 200606, 2 July 1928, 4 July 1928.

50. BB, 200606, 5 April 1928; Winton, pp 84–5; Leslie O'Brien, *A Life Worth Living* (privately published, 1995), pp 1–6, BoE, G 15/650, 'Notes by Lord O'Brien', c 1987.

51. Courtney and Thompson, pp 16–17, 37.

52. Cecil Beaton, *The Wandering Years: Diaries, 1922–1939* (1961), pp 67–72.

53. Brian Johnston, *It's Been a Lot of Fun* (1974), pp 52–4.

54. In general on Eliot and the City, see: Lyndall Gordon, *Eliot's Early Years* (Oxford, 1977), pp 99–100; Winton, pp 38–40; Robert Crawford, *The Savage and the City in the Work of T.S. Eliot* (Oxford, 1987), p 44.

55. Valerie Eliot (ed), *The Letters of T.S. Eliot: Volume I, 1898–1922* (1988), pp 164, 168; Michael Holroyd, *Lytton Strachey: Volume II* (1968), p 365; *Letters, Volume I*, p 597; Andy Bull, 'In retreat from the unreal City', *Independent*, 19 May 1990.

56. Herman Melville, *Israel Potter* (1925 edn), p 255; Priestley, p 204.

57. Charles F.G. Masterman, *England after War: A Study* (1922), pp 51–2.

CHAPTER ELEVEN

1. Hubert A. Meredith, *The Drama of Money Making* (?1931), p 254.

2. Nigel Nicolson (ed), *The Letters of Virginia Woolf: Volume III* (1977), pp 243, 442; John Kinross, *Fifty Years in the City* (1982), p 47.

3. Lord Carrington, *Reflect on Things Past* (1988), p 20; Osbert Lancaster, *Pillar to Post* (1938), p 62, *Homes Sweet Homes* (1939), p 70.

4. The source for much of this and the next paragraph is Ranald C. Michie, *The London Stock Exchange: A History* (Oxford, 1999).

5. Financial News, *The Stock Exchange: An Investor's Guide* (1933), p 22.

6. F.E. Armstrong, *The Book of the Stock Exchange* (1934), p 167.

7. Michie.

8. Unpublished reminiscences of Sir George Aylwen; Donald Cobbett, *Before the Big Bang: Tales of the Old Stock Exchange* (Portsmouth, 1986), p 34; W.J. Reader, *A House in the City: A Study of the City and of the Stock Exchange based on the Records of Foster & Braithwaite, 1825–1975* (1979), p 176.

9. W.J. Reader and David Kynaston, *Phillips & Drew: Professionals in the City* (1998), pp 2–3; SE, Ms 14,600, vol 135, 19 Dec 1938; David Kynaston, *The City of London, Volume I* (1994), p 282.

10. Addis, 14/48, 30 Sept 1930; BB, 200780, 25 Jan 1939.

11. E.W. Swanton, *Gubby Allen: Man of Cricket* (1985), pp 58, 142, 230.

12. *The Collected Writings of John Maynard Keynes: Volume VII* (1973), pp 155–6; JS, no 37.

13. David Wainwright, *Government Broker: The Story of an Office and of Mullens & Co* (1990), pp 79, 68, 70, 72; JS, no 21.

14. Wainwright, pp 70–1, 65, 81.

15. See Andrew Lycett, *From Diamond Sculls to Golden Handcuffs: A History of Rowe & Pitman* (1998) for a full account of how this distinctive firm operated.

16. Nicholas Davenport, *Memoirs of a City Radical* (1974), pp 18–19; BoE, G 3/180, 15 March 1924.

17. Davenport, p 20; Andrew Lycett, *Ian Fleming* (1995), p 71.

18. John Pearson, *The Life of Ian Fleming* (1966), pp 74–5.

19. David Kynaston, *Cazenove & Co: A History* (1991), pp 98–9.

20. W. Lionel Fraser, *All to the Good* (1963), p 207; Andrew St George, *JOH* (1992), p 60; Kynaston, *Cazenove*, pp 99–107.

21. Denzil Sebag-Montefiore, *The Story of Joseph Sebag and Co and its Founding Families* (1996), pp 13, 15, 19, 21, 28, 42; Cobbett, p 22.

22. Hugo Vickers, 'Ralph Vickers' in *Independent*, 16 Sept 1992; interview with Harold Cowen, c 1988; David Cannadine, 'Churchill and the Pitfalls of Family Piety' in Robert Blake and Wm Roger Louis (eds), *Churchill* (Oxford, 1993), p 13; Hugo Vickers, 'John Spencer Churchill' in *Independent*, 9 July 1992.

23. SE, Ms 14,600, vol 126, 18 Jan 1932; Robert Skidelsky, *John Maynard Keynes: Volume Two, The Economist as Saviour, 1920–1937* (1992), p 694; Lewis Whyte, *One Increasing Purpose* (1984), pp 63, 27; Oliver M. Westall, *The Provincial Insurance Company, 1903–38* (Manchester, 1992), pp 381–3.

24. E.K.H. Karslake, 'A Short History of Chase, Henderson & Tennant' in Elizabeth Hennessy, *Stockbrokers for 150 Years: A History of Sheppards and Chase, 1827–1977* (1978), pp 51–3; Davenport, pp 38–41. On Boothby in the City, see also Robert Rhodes James, *Bob Boothby: A Portrait* (1991), pp 93–4.

25. Kynaston, *Cazenove*, p 134; Reader and Kynaston, *Phillips & Drew*, pp 8–18.

26. *The Times*, 23 Nov 1973; Hennessy, p 31; B.H.D. MacDermot, *Panmure Gordon & Co, 1876–1976: A Century of Stockbroking* (1976), pp 57–8, 60.

27. SE, Ms 14,600, vol 126, 12–26 Oct 1931.

28. Meredith, pp 225–30.

29. Cobbett, pp 56–7; JS, no 12; Cobbett, pp 51, 53–4.

30. Most of this and the following paragraph derives from Cobbett, pp 52, 62, 73, 66, 30–1.

31. Kynaston, *Cazenove*, p 106.

32. SE, Ms 14,600, vol 134, 1 Nov 1937.

33. Michie, *London Stock Exchange* gives a detailed analysis of the inter-war jobbing system. On the jobbing system more generally, see Bernard Attard, 'The Jobbers of the London Stock Exchange: An Oral History' in *Oral History* (1994). See also, forthcoming, Bernard Attard, 'Making a Market: The Jobbers of the London Stock Exchange, 1800–1986'.

34. JS, no 17.

35. JS, no 12; Cobbett, pp 23–4; JS, no 28.

36. SE, Ms 14,600, vol 128, 9 Dec 1932–9 Jan 1933.

37. JS, no 21.

38. *The Times*, 1 June 1982.

39. JS, no 1.

40. JS, no 26.

41. David Higham, *Literary Gent* (1978), pp 11–12; Cobbett, pp 46–7.

42. Cobbett, pp 44–6, 116; Cowen; JS, no 12.

43. Sambourne's life, outside as well as inside the City, is detailed in Shirley Nicholson, *An Edwardian Bachelor: Roy Sambourne, 1878–1946* (1999).

44. Nicholson.

45. The quotations in the remainder of the chapter are all from Sambourne's diaries.

CHAPTER TWELVE

1. Addis, 14/38, 4 May 1920; Cathy Courtney and Paul Thompson, *City Lives: the changing voices of British finance* (1996), p 194; Ronald Palin, *Rothschild Relish* (1970), pp 30–1.

2. L.E. Jones, *Georgian Afternoon* (1958), pp 118, 120–1, 134–5, 143–4.

3. Francis Williams, *Nothing So Strange* (1970), p 121; Nicholas Davenport, *Memoirs of a City Radical* (1974), pp 42–3.

4. Brand, file 80, 8 May 1924; Percy Arnold, *The Bankers of London* (1938), p 105.

5. *DBB*, R.P.T. Davenport-Hines, 'Sir Herbert Alexander Lawrence', vol 3, pp 667–74, 'Guy Payan Dawnay', vol 2, pp 30–3, Richard Reed, 'Colin Frederick Campbell, 1st Lord Colgrain', vol 1, pp 580–1.

6. The most helpful historical study of the investment trust movement as a whole is Youssef Cassis, 'The emergence of a new financial institution: investment trusts in Britain, 1870–1939' in J.J. van Helten and Y. Cassis (eds), *Capitalism in a Mature Economy* (Aldershot, 1990).

7. T. Jackson, *The Origin and History of the Drayton Group* (Croydon, 1991), chapters 1–3; Jehanne Wake, *Kleinwort Benson: The History of Two Families in Banking* (Oxford, 1997), pp 299–301.

8. BoE, G 35/7, 7 Nov 1927; *The Directory of Directors* (1931); Bo Bramsen and Kathleen Wain, *The Hambros* (1979), pp 389, 391.

9. J. Leighton-Boyce, *Smiths the Bankers, 1658–1958* (1958), p 310; *The Times*, 18 Feb 1956; MG, private letter books, no 33, 18 Dec 1925; *DBB*, Kathleen Burk, 'Vivian Hugh Smith, 1st Lord Bicester of Tusmore', vol 5, pp 223–4.

10. On this quartet, see: Kathleen Burk, *Morgan Grenfell, 1838–1988: The Biography of a Merchant Bank* (Oxford, 1989), pp 99–100, 159; Dominic Hobson, *The Pride of Lucifer* (1990), pp 75–6; David Kynaston, *Archie's Last Stand* (1984), pp 29–31, 138.

11. Burk, *Morgan Grenfell*, p 157.

12. *The Directory of Directors*; Andrew Lycett, *Ian Fleming* (1995), pp 65–70.

13. Eleanor Adlard (ed), *Robert Holland-Martin: A Symposium* (1947) provides a telling portrait of a significant City figure.

14. Wake, pp 231–6; BoE, ADM 34/24, 12 June 1935; Thea Thompson, *Edwardian Childhoods* (1981), p 143.

15. John Gale, *Clean Young Englishman* (1988, pbk), p 29; Lord Rothschild, *Meditations of a Broomstick* (1977), p 17. See Niall Ferguson, *The World's Banker: The History of the House of Rothschild* (1998), pp 995, 1009–13 on Rothschilds during these three decades.

16. David Newsome, *A History of Wellington College, 1859–1959* (1959), p 361.

17. Wake, chapter 8.

18. *The Memoirs of Lord Chandos* (1962), pp 113–47.

19. *The Times*, 5 Jan 1996.

20. Courtney and Thompson, p 36.

21. Grey Papers (University of Durham), 202/6, 5 Dec 1914; MG, private letter books, no 38, 25 Sept 1928; *DBB*, R.P.T. Davenport-Hines, 'Arthur Morton Grenfell', vol 2, pp 652–3 for Grenfell's inter-war career.

22. Wake, pp 293–4, 302–3, 311; Ben Pimlott (ed), *The Political Diary of Hugh Dalton, 1918–40, 1945–60* (1986), p 157; BoE, ADM 26/9, 8 Oct 1935.

23. Paul Morand, *A Frenchman's London* (1934), pp 282–4.

24. Hugh Barty-King, *The Baltic Exchange* (1977), pp 342–6; Gordon D. Hodge, *56 Years in the London Sugar Market* (1960), p 28.

25. *Banker*, Oct 1933, pp 29–30.

26. MG, private letter books, no 31, 6 Feb 1925; Denzil Sebag-Montefiore, *The Story of Joseph Sebag and Co and its Founding Families* (1996), p 42; BoE, ADM 34/21, 2 Feb 1932, G 3/199, 4 March 1932; Jones, pp 142–3.

27. M.C. Reed, *A History of James Capel & Co* (1975), p 75; Roger Fulford, *Glyn's, 1753–1953* (1953), p 231; A.C. Pointon, *Wallace Brothers* (Oxford, 1974), p

66; HSBC, S.E. Franklin, 'Samuel Montagu & Co: A brief account of the development of the Firm' (1967 typescript).

28. Lycett, p 60; MG, private letter books, no 40, 14 Oct 1929.

29. Philip Ziegler, *The Sixth Great Power: Barings, 1762–1929* (1988), p 358; BB, 200832, 2 July 1937.

30. DBB, John Orbell, 'Sir Edward Robert Peacock', vol 4, pp 559–67; Daphne Pollen, *I Remember, I Remember* (1983), p 229.

31. DBB, Cyril A. Kidd and Simon Katzenellenbogen, 'Sir Alfred Chester Beatty', vol 1, pp 230–3; A.J. Wilson, *The Life and Times of Sir Alfred Chester Beatty* (1985), pp 197–8, 207–8.

32. Peter Brackfield, 'Singer & Friedlander Limited' in *Bowring Magazine* (summer 1978); personal information.

33. There have been two major biographical studies of Warburg: Jacques Attali, *A Man of Influence: Sir Siegmund Warburg, 1902–82* (1986); Ron Chernow, *The Warburgs: A Family Saga* (1993), esp chapters 28, 33, 38–40, 42–9. See also FT, 20 Oct 1982.

34. Sebag-Montefiore, p 52; BoE, ADM 34/23, 15 Oct 1934. On Sir Albert Stern, see *The Times*, 3 Jan 1966; there is also much about his younger years in Shirley Nicholson, *An Edwardian Bachelor: Roy Sambourne, 1878–1946* (1999).

35. FT, 11 Jan 1945, 15 Jan 1945; Chernow, pp 548–9, FT, 23 Nov 1987; interview with Henry Grunfeld, 2 Feb 1989.

36. DBB, Martin Chick, 'William Stuckey Piercy, 1st Lord Piercy of Burford', vol 4, pp 684–9; John Kinross, *50 Years in the City* (1982), p 120; Piercy Papers (LSE), 11/5, 2 Dec 1925.

37. In general on Drayton's career, see: Antony Hornby, 'Harold Charles Gilbert Drayton' in E.T. Williams and C.S. Nicholls (eds), *The Dictionary of National Biography, 1961–1970* (Oxford, 1981), pp 309–10; DBB, John Hibbs, 'Harley Charles Gilbert Drayton', vol 2, pp 173–6; Jackson, inc p 51 about Moody.

38. Charles Lysaght, *Brendan Bracken* (1979), p 88. See also on Bracken, Andrew Boyle, *Poor Dear Brendan: The Quest for Brendan Bracken* (1974).

39. David Kynaston, *The Financial Times: A Centenary History* (1988), pp 102–16, 130.

40. Edgar Jones, *True and Fair: A History of Price Waterhouse* (1995), pp 122–9.

41. Morand, pp 286–7.

42. NW, 7299, 5 Sept 1924; Arnold, pp 68–75.

43. DBB, Geoffrey Jones and Margaret Ackrill, 'Sir Charles Lidbury', vol 3, pp 783–5; Marguerite Dupree (ed), *Lancashire and Whitehall: The Diary of Sir Raymond Streat* (1987), vol 1, pp 143–4.

44. SE, Mss 14,600, vol 116, 6 July 1925, vol 133, 22 June 1936, 27 July 1936.

45. Colin Vines and Richard Griffiths, 'Marcia Beaverbrook' in *Independent*, 31 Oct 1994.

46. Brand, file 52, 17 Nov 1921; *The Times*, 29 Aug 1963; Leighton-Boyce, p 310; Viscount Mersey, *A Picture of Life, 1872–1940* (1941), p 327.

47. Jane Brown, *Lutyens and the Edwardians* (1996), pp 219–21; Gale, pp 26, 31; Andrew Lycett, *From Diamond Sculls to Golden Handcuffs: A History of Rowe & Pitman* (1998), p 57; David Wainwright, *Government Broker: The Story of an Office and of Mullens & Co* (1990), p 81; *The Private Diaries of Sydney Moseley* (1960), p 345.

48. Addis, 14/37, 14/39, 14/45; Mersey, p 337; Robert McAlmon, *Being Geniuses Together* (1938), pp 1–2; Wainwright, pp 79–80.

49. Apart from the two Lord's quotations from Sambourne's diary, the detail in this paragraph is derived entirely from Nicholson, *An Edwardian Bachelor*.

50. National Life Story Collection (British Library National Sound Archive), 'City Lives', C 409/008.

51. Eileen Whiteing, *Anyone for Tennis? Growing up in Wallington between the wars* (Sutton, 1979), pp 21–2, 33, 49–50.

52. Sambourne, 9 Sept 1925; Brand, file 71.

53. David Cannadine, *The Decline and Fall of the British Aristocracy* (1990), pp 417–20.

54. Lycett, *Diamond Sculls*, p 57; Jones, p 136; *The Times*, 1 Jan 1955, 5 Jan 1955.

55. *Lancashire and Whitehall*, vol 1, p 103.

CHAPTER THIRTEEN

1. Sambourne, 22 Sept 1931.

2. *Sunday Express*, 27 Sept 1931; Thomas Jones, *A Diary with Letters, 1931–1950* (Oxford, 1954), p 13; BoE, G 3/198, 29 Sept 1931; Addis, 14/49, 30 Sept 1931.

3. Addis, 14/49, 13 Oct 1931; Andrew Boyle, *Montagu Norman: A Biography* (1967), p 277; Addis, 14/49, 28 Oct 1931, 2 Nov 1931, 14/424, 2 Nov 1931, 4 Nov 1931; Boyle, p 278.

4. BB, 200534, 29 Oct 1931; Sambourne, 16 Nov 1931; records of Heseltine, Powell & Co (Guildhall Library), Ms 23, 267, vol 3, 18 Nov 1931; *National Westminster Bank Quarterly Review*, Nov 1968, p 64; Georgiana Blakiston (ed), *Letters of Conrad Russell, 1897–1947* (1987), p 117.

5. HSBC, 30/99, 14 Sept 1931; NW, 9338, c 1 June 1932. In general on the Anglo-South rescue, see Sayers, pp 263–7.

6. Sayers, p 531; Bo Bramsen and Kathleen Wain, *The Hambros* (1979), p 380.

7. Sayers, p 531; Vincent P. Carosso, *Investment Banking in America: A History* (Cambridge, Mass., 1970), pp 317–19.

8. Sayers, p 531; BoE, ADM 34/21, 24 May 1932.

9. *Sunday Express*, 27 Sept 1931; John Maynard Keynes, *Essays in Persuasion* (1931), p ix.

10. Philip Williamson, *National Crisis and National Government: British Politics, the Economy and Empire, 1926–1932* (Cambridge, 1992), pp 497–9.

11. Tim Rooth, 'The Political Economy of Protectionism in Britain, 1919–32' in *Journal of European Economic History* (1992), pp 87–95.

12. Jones, p 13; *The Times*, 22 Jan 1932.

13. FT, 5–6 Feb 1932; Daphne Pollen, *I Remember, I Remember* (1983), p 232; BB, 200534, 9 Aug 1932.

14. For helpful accounts of the creation of the EEA, see: Susan Howson, *Domestic Monetary Management in Britain, 1919–38* (Cambridge, 1975), pp 80–8; Williamson, pp 499–500.

15. BoE, G 3/198, 28 Sept 1931; BB, Dep 33.24, 19 Oct 1931; Addis, 14/50, 27 Jan 1932.

16. *Midland Bank Monthly Review*, Jan–Feb 1932, pp 1–4; *FT*, 21 April 1932.
17. This is a governing theme of the pioneering survey by P.J. Cain and A.G. Hopkins, *British Imperialism: Crisis and Deconstruction, 1914–1990* (1993).
18. *FT*, 22 Jan 1932, 22 Aug 1932.
19. On the creation of the sterling area, see: Sir Henry Clay, *Lord Norman* (1957), pp 409–11; Cain and Hopkins, pp 79–82.
20. John Barnes and David Nicholson (eds), *The Empire at Bay: The Leo Amery Diaries, 1929–1945* (1988), p 224; *FT*, 8 Feb 1932; Sayers, p 449; Donald Moggridge (ed), *The Collected Writings of John Maynard Keynes: Volume XXIV* (1979), p 162.
21. On the coming of cheap money, see: Sayers, pp 423–5, 429–30; Howson, pp 86–8.
22. BoE, ADM 33/34, 11–12 Feb 1932.
23. *FT*, 1 July 1932.
24. Accounts include Clay, pp 457–8, Sayers, pp 430–47.
25. NW, 7299, 10 March 1932.
26. A.W. Tuke and R.J.H. Gillman, *Barclays Bank Limited, 1926–1969* (1972), p 34.
27. *FT*, 1 July 1932; BoE, ADM 34/21, 6–7 July 1932.
28. Robert Skidelsky, *John Maynard Keynes: Volume Two, The Economist as Saviour, 1920–1937* (1992), p 433. For an interpretation downplaying the conversion operation in terms of its impact on long-term interest rates, see Forrest H. Capie, Terry C. Mills and Geoffrey E. Wood, 'Debt management and interest rates: The British stock conversion of 1932' in *Applied Economics* (1986).
29. These commentators include: Howson, pp 88–9; Shekhar Das, 'The 1932 War Loan Conversion con trick' in *Investors Chronicle*, 23 Dec 1983.
30. Sayers, p 447.
31. *New Statesman*, 17 Sept 1932; *Banker*, Dec 1932, p 161.
32. BoE, G 3/198, 16 Oct 1931; NW, 9338, 2 June 1932. In general, on the renewal of Standstill in 1932, see Sayers, pp 507–8, Richard Roberts, *Schroders: Merchants & Bankers* (1992), p 257.
33. BB, 200551, 6 Sept 1932, 11 Nov 1932.

CHAPTER FOURTEEN

1. J.B. Priestley, *English Journey* (1934), pp 409–11.
2. BB, 200534, 8 Dec 1932; Duncan Crow, *A Man of Push and Go: The Life of George Macaulay Booth* (1965), p 168; Judy Slinn, *Linklaters & Paines: The First One Hundred and Fifty Years* (1987), p 137; Sayers, pp 379–83; Robert Rhodes James, *Bob Boothby: A Portrait* (1991), p 141.
3. Norman and Jeanne MacKenzie, *The Diary of Beatrice Webb, Volume Four* (1985), pp 259–60; Douglas Jay, *Change and Fortune* (1980), p 60, Ben Pimlott, *Hugh Dalton* (1985), p 223.
4. Jim Tomlinson, 'Attlee's inheritance and the financial system: whatever happened to the National Investment Board?' in *Financial History Review* (1994), pp 141–3; NW, 7299, 14 Nov 1933, 9338, 7 Dec 1933; Sayers, pp 460–1.
5. Wyndham Lewis, *Men Without Art* (1934), p 246; Thomas Johnston, *The Financiers and the Nation* (1934), p 201.
6. *Listener*, 4 April 1934; BoE, G 3/201, 16 April 1934.

7. Sayers, p 382; BoE, ADM 34/23, 16 July 1934; Sayers, p 383; BoE, ADM 34/23, 3 Oct 1934, G 3/202, 16 March 1935; David Kynaston, *The City of London, Volume II* (1995), p 421.

8. Derrick Byatt, 'The Bank's Pound Notes' in *The Old Lady*, June 1990, pp 54–5; Einzig Papers (Churchill College, Cambridge), 1/18, 23 March 1936.

9. Nicholas Davenport, *Memoirs of a City Radical* (1974), p 95; *Banker*, Feb 1935, pp 104–11; NW, 7299, 19 March 1935; Elizabeth Durbin, *New Jerusalems: The Labour Party and the Economics of Democratic Socialism* (1985), p 167.

10. NW, 20028, 12 Nov 1935; *FT*, 4 Nov 1935; BoE, ADM 23/1, 8 Nov 1935; Tomlinson, p 142.

11. SE, Ms 14,600, vol 134, 5 July 1937; Jay, p 68; BoE, G 3/203, 25 Feb 1936.

CHAPTER FIFTEEN

1. J.A. Gere and John Sparrow (eds), *Geoffrey Madan's Notebooks* (Oxford, 1981), pp 101–2; BoE, G 15/241 (Kershaw); Alec Cairncross, *The Wilson Years: A Treasury Diary, 1964–1969* (1997), p 33.

2. Andrew Boyle, *Montagu Norman: A Biography* (1967), p 280; Kenneth Young (ed), *The Diaries of Sir Robert Bruce Lockhart, Volume One* (1973), p 237; BoE, ADM 34/23, 26 May 1934; Sir Henry Clay, *Lord Norman* (1957), pp 316–17; Roberta Allbert Dayer, *Finance and Empire: Sir Charles Addis, 1861–1945* (Basingstoke, 1988), p 309.

3. Sayers, p 417; Clay, pp 314–15, Elizabeth Hennessy, 'The Governors, Directors and Management of the Bank of England' in Richard Roberts and David Kynaston (eds), *The Bank of England* (Oxford, 1995), p 196; John Fforde, *The Bank of England and Public Policy, 1941–1958* (Cambridge, 1992), pp 1–2; BoE, ADM 23/1, 8 Nov 1935; Paul Bareau, 'The Financial Institutions of the City of London' in The Institute of Bankers, *The City of London as a Centre of International Trade and Finance* (1961), p 15.

4. BoE, ADM 34/21, 2 Feb 1932, ADM 34/23, 30 April 1934, 21 Sept 1934.

5. BoE, ADM 34/21, 12 July 1932, ADM 34/22, 22 March 1933, G 3/201, 8 March 1934; *Banker*, Nov 1936, p 106; BoE, ADM 34/27, 22 Nov 1938.

6. On the workings of the EEA, see: Susan Howson, 'The Management of Sterling, 1932–1939' in *Journal of Economic History* (1980) and *Sterling's Managed Float: The Operations of the Exchange Equalisation Account, 1932–39* (Princeton, 1980); Richard Roberts, 'The Bank of England and the City' in Roberts and Kynaston, p 172.

7. Clay, pp 437–8; Sayers, p 469; Howson, 'Management of Sterling', p 16.

8. *Banker*, Feb 1936, pp 154–5; Aytoun Ellis, *Heir of Adventure: The story of Brown, Shipley & Co* (1960), p 148; Bolton.

9. BoE, ADM 33/26 (Bolton); Bolton.

10. Bolton; BoE, ADM 33/27 (Hawker).

11. In general on Bolton, see: Richard Fry (ed), *A Banker's World* (1970); *DBB*, R.P.T. Davenport-Hines, 'Sir George Lewis French Bolton', vol 1, pp 364–9.

12. William M. Clarke, *Inside the City* (1979), p 175; *Exco International News*, July 1989, Nov 1990.

13. Bolton; *A Banker's World*, pp 20–1; Roberts, 'Bank of England and the City', p 172.

14. BoE, ADM 25/11, 27 Oct 1936.

15. Sayers, p 470; Howson, *Sterling's Managed Float*, p 46.

16. *Futures*, Feb 1985, p 66.

17. BoE, G 3/202, 27 April 1935, 29 May 1935, ADM 23/1, 8 June 1935, ADM 34/24, 16–31 Dec 1935, G 3/203, 16 Jan 1936, ADM 23/1, 24 Jan 1936.

18. BoE, ADM 23/1, 3 Feb 1936; Sayers, p 470.

19. Guides to the discount market in the 1930s include: *Banker*, May 1944, pp 79–84; W.M. Scammell, *The London Discount Market* (1968), pp 208–19; R.S. Sayers, *Gilletts in the London Money Market* (Oxford, 1968), pp 87–108; G.A. Fletcher, *The Discount Houses in London* (1976), pp 43–53; Sayers, pp 536–44; Roberts, 'Bank of England and the City', p 164.

20. Records of Gillett Brothers & Co (Guildhall Library), Ms 24,692; George and Pamela Cleaver, *The Union Discount: A Centenary Album* (1985), pp 69–70.

21. Michael Moran, 'Finance Capital and Pressure-Group Politics in Britain' in *British Journal of Political Science* (1981), pp 394–5; BoE, ADM 34/27, 7 April 1938; NW, 9339, 5 Nov 1936.

22. Sayers, pp 556–7. In general on commercial banking in the 1930s, see: A.R. Holmes and Edwin Green, *Midland: 150 Years of Banking Business* (1986), chapter 8; Michael Collins, *Money and Banking in the UK: A History* (1988), chapters 7–8; Duncan M. Ross, 'Commercial banking in a market-oriented financial system: Britain between the wars' in *Economic History Review* (1996).

23. BoE, ADM 34/21, 21 Oct 1932; Hennessy, p 196; Sayers, pp 250–2; Roger Fulford, *Glyn's, 1753–1953* (1953), p 234.

24. Records of Brown, Shipley & Co (Guildhall Library), Ms 20,110, vol 2, 2 April 1936; Stefanie Diaper, 'Merchant Banking in the Inter-War Period: The Case of Kleinwort, Sons & Co' in *Business History* (1986), pp 67–75.

25. Richard Roberts, *Schroders: Merchants & Bankers* (1992), pp 268–9.

26. Roberts, *Schroders*, pp 188, 267; Diaper, p 73.

27. Diaper, p 73; BoE, G 3/203, 11 March 1936, ADM 34/26, 5 Jan 1937, G 3/204, 2 July 1937; Roberts, *Schroders*, pp 263–5; Diaper, p 73.

28. BB, 200641, 23 Oct 1936; MG, miscellaneous business offered files, no 20, 6 May 1937.

29. BoE, ADM 34/21, 8 Nov 1932, ADM 34/24, 18 July 1935, ADM 34/25, 26 Oct 1936, ADM 34/27, 8 Nov 1938, 2 Dec 1938, 6 Dec 1938, G 3/202, 16 Dec 1935.

30. *DBB*, T.A.B. Corley, 'Philip Ernest Hill', vol 3, pp 235–9.

31. BoE, ADM 34/24, 19 June 1935, ADM 34/27, 8 Nov 1938.

32. Richard Roberts, 'What's in a Name? Merchants, Merchant Bankers, Accepting Houses, Issuing Houses, Industrial Bankers and Investment Bankers' in *Business History* (July 1993), p 32; BoE, G 3/203, 23 June 1936.

33. For a discussion of the effects of cheap money, see Patrick K. O'Brien, 'Britain's Economy between the Wars: A Survey of a Counter-Revolution in Economic History' in *Past and Present* (May 1987), pp 123–8.

34. Susan Howson, *Domestic Monetary Management in Britain, 1919–38* (Cambridge, 1975), p 95; Robert Skidelsky, *John Maynard Keynes: Volume Two, The Economist as Saviour, 1920–1937* (1992), p 501.

35. *FT*, 30 Jan 1933; Brand, file 198, 20 March 1933; *The Times*, 24 July 1933, 29 July 1933; BoE, ADM 34/22, 3 Aug 1933, 20 Nov 1933.

36. BoE, ADM 34/23, 4 Jan 1934, ADM 34/24, 8 May 1935, G 1/506 (Blackett); *The Times*, 16 Aug 1935.

37. On the somewhat opaque matter of Norman and public works, see Sayers, pp 462–3, Howson, *Domestic Monetary Management*, p 95.
38. *FN*, 4 July 1933. On Norman and Roosevelt, see: Boyle, p 288; Ian M. Drummond, *The Floating Pound and the Sterling Area, 1931–1939* (Cambridge, 1981), p 181.
39. BoE, G 3/201, 29 Dec 1934; Addis, 14/459, 14 April 1935; BoE, G 3/202, 19 June 1935.
40. BB, Dep 33.24, 20 Jan 1933.
41. Patricia Clavin, '"The Fetishes of So-Called International Bankers": Central Bank Co-operation for the World Economic Conference, 1932–3' in *Contemporary European History* (1992).
42. *The Times*, 24 July 1933; BoE, G 3/200, 15 Sept 1933.
43. On this proliferation, see Drummond, p 260.
44. Howson, 'Management of Sterling', p 55.
45. Bolton; BoE, G 3/201, 29 Dec 1934, G 3/202, 19 June 1935.
46. Bolton.
47. Hartley Withers, *The Meaning of Money* (sixth edition, 1937), pp 263–4.
48. On Chile and Brazil, see: P.J. Cain and A.G. Hopkins, *British Imperialism: Crisis and Deconstruction, 1914–1990* (1993), pp 165–8; Robert Greenhill, 'Investment Group, Free-Standing Company or Multinational? Brazilian Warrant, 1909–52' in *Business History* (1995), p 101. On Argentina, see: Sayers, pp 523–4; Cain and Hopkins, pp 157–61.
49. David Kynaston, *Cazenove & Co: A History* (1991), pp 148–9; NW, 7375, 8 Feb 1933.
50. BB, 200647, 18 May 1934, 31 May 1934.
51. BB, 200647, 28 June 1934; Marguerite Dupree (ed), *Lancashire and Whitehall: The Diary of Sir Raymond Streat* (Manchester, 1987), vol 1, p 234.
52. BoE, ADM 23/1, fo 66. On the sterling area in the 1930s, see: Cain and Hopkins, pp 83–105; P.J. Cain, 'Gentlemanly imperialism at work: the Bank of England, Canada, and the sterling area, 1932–1936' in *Economic History Review* (1996), pp 337–8.
53. *Banker*, Sept 1934, pp 170–1.
54. *Banker*, Sept 1933, p 182; Cain, 'Gentlemanly imperialism', p 338; Cain and Hopkins, p 83.
55. Cain and Hopkins, pp 119–26, is complemented by Bernard Attard, 'Australian Financial Diplomacy, 1914–39' in Carl Bridge and Bernard Attard (eds), *Between Empire and Nation* (Melbourne, 1999).
56. BoE, G 3/200, 22 Sept 1933.
57. Cain and Hopkins, pp 135–7.
58. BoE, ADM 34/26, 5 Oct 1937; Sayers, pp 516–18, 525–7; BoE, ADM 33/24 (Towers, 22 May 1968).
59. On Canada and the City in the 1930s, see: Sayers, pp 514–15; Dayer, pp 248–9; Cain and Hopkins, pp 138–43; Cain, 'Gentlemanly imperialism'.
60. BoE, G 3/200, 12 Oct 1933; Cain, 'Gentlemanly imperialism', p 353; BoE, G 3/203, 12 March 1936; Cain, 'Gentlemanly imperialism', p 351.
61. Accounts of this complex story include: Dayer, pp 274–306; Frank H.H. King, *The History of the Hongkong and Shanghai Banking Corporation: Volume III* (Cambridge, 1988), chapters 7–8; Cain and Hopkins, pp 251–9.

62. HSBC, F 4.5, 8 Nov 1933, L 2.25, 9 Nov 1934; Addis, 14/459, 14 April 1935; Cain and Hopkins, p 235; Dayer, p 300.
63. JM, semi-official correspondence, London to Hong Kong, 12 Aug 1937, 10 Sept 1937; BoE, G 3/205, 14 Jan 1938; HSBC, L 2.25, 7 March 1939.
64. Allen, Harvey & Ross scrapbook (Cater Allen records), internal note, 3 Nov 1959.
65. BB, 200647, 18 May 1934.
66. In addition to the works already cited about the City (banking system and capital market) and its relationship with British industry, see two important contributions by Duncan M. Ross: 'Information, Collateral and British Bank Lending in the 1930s' in Youssef Cassis, Gerald D. Feldman and Ulf Olsson (eds), *The Evolution of Financial Institutions and Markets in Twentieth-century Europe* (Aldershot, 1995); 'The "Macmillan gap" and the British credit market in the 1930s' in P.L. Cottrell, Alice Teichova and Takeshi Yuzawa (eds), *Finance in the Age of the Corporate Economy* (Aldershot, 1997).
67. Steven Tolliday, *Business, Banking and Politics: The Case of British Steel, 1918–1939* (Cambridge, Mass., 1987), p 183; issue figures from Ranald C. Michie, *The London Stock Exchange: A History* (Oxford, 1999); River and Mercantile Trust collection (University College London, Manuscripts and Rare Books), London Trust records, E 4/2; Richard Lambert, 'Capturing the market's mood' in *FT*, 1 July 1985.
68. BoE, SMT 2/55, 19 Feb 1932, ADM 34/21, 26 Feb 1932.
69. BoE, SMT 2/56, 4 July 1932, 18 July 1932.
70. HSBC, 30/127, 18 May 1933; J.H. Bamberg, 'The Rationalization of the British Cotton Industry in the Interwar Years' in *Textile History* (1988), pp 95–6; BoE, SMT 2/276, 1 Feb 1934.
71. NW, 7491, 21 Sept 1933, 7508, 17 March 1936, 9 Nov 1937.
72. The definitive account is Tolliday, *Business, Banking and Politics*. See also Clay, pp 345–9, Sayers, pp 547–50.
73. BoE, ADM 33/8, 6 Feb 1971; NW, 7672, 16 June 1938, 20 June 1938.
74. Tolliday, pp 269–71.
75. BB, 200739, fos 197–9, 209–10; BoE, G 14/55, 2 Feb 1939, ADM 34/28, 28 Feb 1939.
76. BoE, G 14/62, 1 March 1939, 3 April 1939.
77. BoE, ADM 34/21, 2 March 1932; *Lancashire and Whitehall*, vol 1, p 143; BoE, ADM 34/21, 28 July 1932; HSBC, 30/99, 25 Oct 1933.
78. HSBC, 30/99, 1 Feb 1934, 6 Feb 1934; BoE, ADM 34/23, 19 Feb 1934; HSBC, 30/152, 23 Feb 1945. In general on Charterhouse Industrial Development Co, see also: Laurie Dennett, *The Charterhouse Group, 1925–1979: A History* (1979); Holmes and Green, pp 182–3.
79. BoE, G 3/202, 20 June 1935. See Ross, 'The "Macmillan gap"' for an assessment of CFI's impact.
80. BoE, ADM 34/24, 28 Nov 1935; James Lees-Milne, *Prophesying Peace* (1984, pbk), p 233; *The Times*, 4 Nov 1965.
81. Carol E. Heim, 'Limits to Intervention: The Bank of England and Industrial Diversification in the Depressed Areas' in *Economic History Review* (1984).
82. NW, 9339, 6 Feb 1936.
83. Heim, pp 550, 538.
84. Duncan M. Ross, 'The clearing banks and industry – new perspectives on the

inter-war years' in J.J. van Helten and Y. Cassis (eds), *Capitalism in a Mature Economy* (Aldershot, 1990), p. 57.

85. BoE, ADM 34/22, 31 May 1933; Kathleen Burk, *Morgan Grenfell, 1838–1988: The Biography of a Merchant Bank* (Oxford, 1989), pp 162–6; Bo Bramsen and Kathleen Wain, *The Hambros* (1979), p 395.

86. *DBB*, Robert Murphy, 'Isidore Ostrer', vol 4, pp 492–6.

87. *DBB*, John King, 'Leo Frederic Alfred d'Erlanger', vol 2, pp 80–3.

88. Edward Beddington-Behrens, *Look Back Look Forward* (1963), pp 86–9.

89. On the Lewis story, see: E.R. Lewis, *No C.I.C.* (1956); *DBB*, Jenny Davenport, 'Sir Edward Roberts Lewis', vol 3, pp 757–60; T. Jackson, *The Origin and History of the Drayton Group* (Croydon, 1991), p 37.

90. NW, 7320, 14 Feb 1933.

91. Roberts, *Schroders*, pp 270–2; HSBC, 30/152, 23 Feb 1945, 30/29, 7 Feb 1940.

92. John Kinross, *Fifty Years in the City* (1982), pp 71–84; Richard Coopey and Donald Clarke, *3i: Fifty Years Investing in Industry* (Oxford, 1995), p 12.

93. John Orbell, *Baring Brothers & Co., Limited: A History to 1939* (1985), pp 83–5; Burk, pp 160–6; Kynaston, *Cazenove*, pp 155–6. See also Roberts, *Schroders*, pp 388–93 on Helbert Wagg and corporate finance in the 1930s.

94. Kynaston, *Cazenove*, p 158.

95. MG, miscellaneous business offered files, no 19, 24 Jan 1935; Kynaston, *Cazenove*, p 158; interview with John Kinross, 1 Sept 1988.

96. Kinross, pp 81–2.

97. Barnard Ellinger, *The City* (1940), pp 300–7.

98. Kynaston, *Cazenove*, pp 152–5; SE, Ms 14,609, vol 13, 23 Oct 1935–13 Nov 1935.

99. *FT*, 15–16 Oct 1936; SE, Ms 14,600, vol 133, 19 Oct 1936.

100. The three main sources for this paragraph are: Karin Newman, *Financial marketing and communications* (1984), pp 63–4; Donald Cobbett, *Before the Big Bang: Tales of the Old Stock Exchange* (Portsmouth, 1986), pp 99–103; Michie, *London Stock Exchange*.

101. BoE, G 3/196, 8 Feb 1930, ADM 34/19, 20 Feb 1930; Francis Williams, *Nothing So Strange* (1970), p 88. See also Alan Jenkins, *The Stock Exchange Story* (1973), p 88.

102. R.T. Appleyard and Mel Davies, 'Financiers of Western Australia's Goldfields' in R.T. Appleyard and C.B. Schedvin (eds), *Australian Financiers* (Melbourne, 1988), pp 175–86; David Kynaston, *The Financial Times: A Centenary History* (1988), pp 127–8.

103. *DBB*, R.P.T. Davenport-Hines, 'Guy Payan Dawnay', vol 2, p 31; *The Times*, 11 Sept 1975.

104. Accounts include: *The Memoirs of Lord Chandos* (1962), pp 140–3; Anon, *Two Centuries of Lewis & Peat, 1775–1975* (1975), pp 45–7; Sayers, pp 544–6; Holmes and Green, p 195.

105. HSBC, 30/99, 31 Jan 1935; NW, 7357, 1–7 Feb 1935; HSBC, 30/99, 6 Feb 1935.

106. BoE, ADM 34/23, 26 Nov 1934, ADM 34/24, 7 Feb 1935; NW, 7357, 7 Feb 1935, 25 Feb 1941.

107. BoE, ADM 34/25, 1 April 1936, G 3/202, 26 Nov 1935.

108. BoE, ADM 33/27; *Economist*, 16 Feb 1935; Holmes and Green, p 195; BoE, ADM 34/24, 1 May 1935.

CHAPTER SIXTEEN

1. BB, 200726, 18 Jan 1933, 200631, 19 Jan 1933. In general on the City and Germany in the 1930s important accounts include: Sayers, pp 507–12, 561–71; Neil Forbes, 'London banks, the German standstill agreements, and "economic appeasement" in the 1930s' in *Economic History Review* (1987); Scott Newton, 'The "Anglo-German Connection" and the Political Economy of Appeasement' in *Diplomacy and Statecraft* (1991); Richard Roberts, *Schroders: Merchants & Bankers* (1992), pp 257–62; P.J. Cain and A.G. Hopkins, *British Imperialism: Crisis and Deconstruction, 1914–1990* (1993), pp 93–105; Scott Newton, *Profits of Peace: The Political Economy of Anglo-German Appeasement* (Oxford, 1996), chapters 3–5.

2. *FN*, 31 Jan 1933; *FT*, 31 Jan 1933.

3. BB, 200631, 18 March 1933, 21 March 1933, 24 March 1933.

4. BB, 200641, 30 March 1933; *FT*, 18 May 1933, 19 June 1933.

5. HSBC, 30/194, 27 Feb 1933; Roberts, *Schroders*, pp 258–9.

6. Roberts, *Schroders*, pp 241, 258; records of Accepting Houses Committee (Guildhall Library), Ms 29, 295, vol 3, 12 June 1933; BoE, G 3/200, 30 Sept 1933.

7. W.N. Medlicott, *Contemporary England: 1914–1964* (1976, pbk), p 338; BoE, G 3/201, 23 Jan 1934, 4 July 1934; Ron Chernow, *The House of Morgan* (New York, 1990), p 394; BoE, G 3/201, 23 Aug 1934.

8. *Banker*, Feb 1935, p 107; NW, 7410, 19–20 April 1934.

9. Forbes, pp 578–82, Roberts, pp 259–60.

10. Forbes, p 579; BoE, G 3/201, 22 June 1934.

11. BoE, G 3/201, 4 July 1934, ADM 34/23, 12 Oct 1934; Forbes, p 581.

12. BoE, ADM 24/1, 16 Oct 1934; Addis, 14/459, 14 April 1935.

13. Sambourne, 19 Aug 1935, 20 Sept 1935; BB, 200641, 23 Sept 1935.

14. *FT*, 3 Oct 1935, 7 Oct 1935; *Banker*, Nov 1935, p 81.

15. *FT*, 9–11 March 1936.

16. On the tantalising question of Germany and sterling, there is suggestive evidence in BoE, G 3/202, 20 Nov 1935, fo 652, 23 Dec 1935, fo 747, ADM 34/25, 10 Jan 1936, G 3/203, 15 Jan 1936, fo 50.

17. NW, 9339, 7 May 1936; Brand, file 191, c 18 May 1936.

18. BoE, G 3/203, 11 Aug 1936, 2 July 1936.

19. Records of Heseltine, Powell & Co (Guildhall Library), Ms 23,267, vol 3, Aug 1936, 23 Sept 1936.

20. JM, semi-official correspondence, London to Hong Kong, 4 Sept 1936; Jehanne Wake, *Kleinwort Benson: The History of Two Families in Banking* (Oxford, 1997), pp 249–54; Sambourne, 7 Dec 1936, 9–10 Dec 1936; Kenneth Young (ed), *The Diaries of Sir Robert Bruce Lockhart, Volume One* (1973), p 361; BB, 200641, 11 Dec 1936.

21. PRO, T 160/818/12681/05/4, 18 Jan 1937, Pinsent to Waley (I am indebted to Scott Newton's ground-breaking work on the City and appeasement for guiding me to this and other PRO sources relating to the three years before the outbreak of war); NW, 7439, c 8 Jan 1937.

22. Brand, file 192, 20 Jan 1937; PRO, T 160/818/12681/05/4, 14 Jan 1937, Waley memo; HSBC, 30/102, 2 Feb 1937.
23. PRO, T 160/818/12681/05/4, 10 Feb 1937, Pinsent to Waley; JM, semi-official correspondence, London to Hong Kong, 4 March 1937, 30 April 1937.
24. Bolton.
25. Sayers, pp 567–8.
26. Bolton; BoE, G 3/204, 20 Oct 1937.
27. Accepting Houses Committee, Ms 29,295, vol 4, 4 Nov 1937; BoE, ADM 26/9, 25 Feb 1938, 28 Feb 1938; Addis, 14/56, 4 March 1938.
28. BoE, ADM 34/27, 2 March 1938; BB, 200756, 16 Feb 1938; BoE, ADM 34/27, 24 March 1938.
29. *The Private Diaries of Sydney Moseley* (1960), p 371; Andrew Boyle, *Montagu Norman: A Biography* (1967), p 304; BoE, G 3/205, 31 Aug 1938.
30. FT, 9 Sept 1938, 16 Sept 1938; BB, 200756, 15 Sept 1938; *New Statesman*, 24 Sept 1938; Sambourne, 23 Sept 1938.
31. FT, 26 Sept 1938; Sambourne, 26–7 Sept 1938; FT, 28 Sept 1938; JM, semi-official correspondence, London to Hong Kong, 29 Sept 1938; FT, 29 Sept 1938.
32. NW, 9341; Accepting Houses Committee, Ms 29,295, vol 4, 28 Sept 1938; FT, 29 Sept 1938; Sambourne, 28 Sept 1938.
33. FT, 29–30 Sept 1938; Sambourne, 29 Sept 1938; FT, 30 Sept 1938, 1 Oct 1938; Sambourne, 30 Sept 1938; Addis, 14/56, 30 Sept 1938.
34. FT, 3–4 Oct 1938; Chernow, p 434.
35. *Bruce Lockhart*, p 406; BB, 200756, 5 Nov 1938; JM, semi-official correspondence, London to Hong Kong, 11 Nov 1938.
36. BB, 200729, Dec 1938; *Moseley*, pp 376–8.
37. BoE, G 3/205, 7 Nov 1938, G 1/418; Ron Chernow, *The Warburgs: A Family Saga* (1993), p 484; Paul Einzig, *World Finance, 1938–1939* (1939), p 250; BoE, G 3/205, 19 Dec 1938.
38. John Harvey (ed), *The Diplomatic Diaries of Oliver Harvey, 1937–1940* (1970), pp 234–5; FN, 4 Jan 1939; *Harvey*, p 235.
39. The main sources on Norman's visit to Berlin are: BoE, G 1/419, ADM 34/28, 4–6 Jan 1939; PRO, FO 371/23000 (Pinsent reports).
40. PRO, FO 371/23000, fos 245–6.
41. BoE, G 3/206, 18 March 1939.
42. NW, 7464, 23 Dec 1938, c 27 Dec 1938; Accepting Houses Committee, Ms 29,295, vol 4, 7 Dec 1938; NW, 7464, 16 Jan 1939.
43. Stefanie Diaper, 'Merchant Banking in the Inter-War Period: The Case of Kleinwort, Sons & Co' in *Business History* (1986), p 71; NW, 7465, 15 Feb 1939; National Life Story Collection (British Library National Sound Archive), 'City Lives', C 409/040.
44. Lloyds, HO/GM/Par.4, 31 Jan 1939; BoE, ADM 34/28, 27 Feb 1939.
45. PRO, FO 371/23001, 2 March 1939, Pinsent memo; NW, 7464, 4 March 1939; FT, 15 March 1939.
46. FT, 16–17 March 1939, 20 March 1939.
47. FT, 1 April 1939, 3 April 1939.
48. JM, semi-official correspondence, London to Shanghai, 21 April 1939; Roberta Allbert Dayer, *Finance and Empire: Sir Charles Addis, 1861–1945* (Basingstoke, 1988), p 311.

49. NW, 7465, 17 March 1939; Diaper, p 71, Forbes, p 585, Roberts, p 262; NW, 7465, 10 May 1939.

50. Wake, p 255; Paul Einzig, *In the Centre of Things* (1960), pp 186–94; BoE, G 1/506, 3 June 1939.

51. *FT*, 5 June 1939, 9 June 1939, 16 June 1939, 5 July 1939, 31 July 1939.

52. BoE, ADM 34/28, 7 June 1939; JM, semi-official correspondence, London to Shanghai, 29 June 1939, 14 July 1939; *FT*, 25 July 1939.

53. Newton, *Profits of Peace*, pp 122–3.

54. PRO, PREM 1/335, fos 29–82.

55. Newton, *Profits of Peace*, pp 123–4

56. PRO, FO 371/22991, fos 37–79.

57. On these preparations, see: Sayers, pp 567–71, 575–81; Elizabeth Hennessy, *A Domestic History of the Bank of England, 1930–1960* (Cambridge, 1992), pp 83–9.

58. BoE, G 1/505, 25 April 1939 (Holland-Martin memo); Bolton.

59. Bolton; BoE, ADM 33/6, 19 Sept 1974.

60. Lloyds, HO/GM/Par.4, 8 Aug 1939; Sambourne, 9 Aug 1939; *FT*, 11 Aug 1939; Sambourne, 16 Aug 1939; *FT*, 17–18 Aug 1939.

61. *FT*, 22 Aug 1939, 24–6 Aug 1939, Sambourne, 24–5 Aug 1939.

62. Records of Gillett Brothers & Co (Guildhall Library), Ms 24,693, 29 Aug 1939; *FT*, 30–1 Aug 1939; Sambourne, 31 Aug 1939; *FN*, 1 Sept 1939.

63. BoE, G 3/206, 2 Sept 1939; Boyle, p 309.

CHAPTER SEVENTEEN

1. Records of Gillett Brothers & Co (Guildhall Library), Ms 24,693, 6 Sept 1939; Charles Lysaght, *Brendan Bracken* (1979), p 167; Anthony Weymouth, *A Psychologist's War-Time Diary* (1940), pp 99–100.

2. Sambourne, 14 Sept 1939, 3 Oct 1939, 8 Dec 1939.

3. See Scott Newton, *Profits of Peace: The Political Economy of Anglo-German Appeasement* (Oxford, 1996), chapter 6 for an exploration of the question.

4. BoE, G 3/206, 8 Sept 1939.

5. Ronald Palin, *Rothschild Relish* (1970), p 143; Bo Bramsen and Kathleen Wain, *The Hambros* (1979), p 398.

6. Elizabeth Hennessy, *A Domestic History of the Bank of England, 1930–1960* (Cambridge, 1992), pp 7–12; SE, Mss 14,600, vol 136, 2 Oct 1939–vol 137, 20 Nov 1939.

7. Sayers, pp 584–8 gives an accessible overview. For the definitive treatment of war finance, however, see his *Financial Policy, 1939–45* (1956).

8. BoE, G 1/506, 11 Oct 1939, G 1/69, 2 Nov 1939.

9. D.E. Moggridge, *Maynard Keynes: an economist's biography* (1992), pp 629–34; BoE, G 1/15 (press cuttings).

10. For details of the Bank's implementation of exchange control during the war, see Sayers, pp 570–1, Hennessy, pp 85–107.

11. Keith Middlemas, *Power, Competition and the State: Volume I* (Basingstoke, 1986), pp 26–7.

12. Hennessy, p 90, BoE, G 15/650, 'Notes by Lord O'Brien', c 1987.

13. BoE, G 1/69, 26 Sept 1939, G 15/7, fo 74, ADM 20/29, 28 Feb 1940.

14. NW, 7516, 28 Dec 1939; Lloyds, HO/GM/Par.2, 6 March 1940.

15. SSA, Ms 14,894, vol 50, 29 Jan 1940; BoE, ADM 20/29, 1 March 1940, 9 May 1940, 31 May 1940.

16. Richard Roberts, *Schroders: Merchants & Bankers* (1992), p 274; BoE, ADM 20/29, 13 June 1940.

17. BoE, ADM 34/28, 31 Oct 1939; R.S. Sayers, *Gilletts in the London Money Market* (Oxford, 1968), p 118, Gillett Brothers, Ms 24,692; DBB, J.S.G. Wilson, 'Ronald Brodie Gillett', vol 2, pp 564–5.

18. Lloyds, HO/GM/Par.5, 4 Dec 1939; BoE, ADM 20/29, 3 Jan 1940; Sayers, p 592, John Colville, *Footprints in Time* (1976), p 73; Sambourne, 9 April 1940.

19. Brand, file 198, 3 May 1940; BoE, G 1/15, 9 May 1940.

20. Andrew Boyle, *Montagu Norman: A Biography* (1967), p 311; *FT*, 14 May 1940; Sambourne, 14 May 1940.

21. Sambourne, 22 May 1940, 28 May 1940, 18 June 1940, 20 June 1940; Lord Beaverbrook, *Courage: The Story of Sir James Dunn* (Fredericton, New Brunswick, 1961), p 146; *FN*, 25–7 June 1940.

22. BoE, G 1/510, 6 July 1940.

23. BoE, G 1/510, 6 July 1940; DBB, R.P.T. Davenport-Hines, 'Thomas Sivewright Catto, 1st Lord Catto of Cairncatto', vol 1, pp 616–20; Hennessy, p 95; J.R. Winton, *Lloyds Bank, 1918–1969* (Oxford, 1982), pp 104–5, W.M. Scammell, *The London Discount Market* (1968), p 224.

24. BB, 200820, 28 Aug 1940; Sambourne, 3 Sept 1940.

25. Richard Trench, *London Before the Blitz* (1989) is a wonderful account of the City during (as well as before) the Blitz.

26. Trench, p 24; BoE, G 1/510, 18 Sept 1940; Nigel Nicolson (ed), *The Letters of Virginia Woolf: Volume VI* (1980), p 431.

27. James Pope-Hennessy, *History under Fire* (1941), p 4; Charles Short, *Morgan Guaranty's London Heritage* (1986), p 57; Winton, pp 100–1; Jehanne Wake, *Kleinwort Benson: The History of Two Families in Banking* (Oxford, 1997), pp 259, 317.

28. BoE, G 1/510, 24 Oct 1940; Hennessy, p 15.

29. Anne Olivier Bell (ed), *The Diary of Virginia Woolf: Volume 5* (1984), p 351; Trench, pp 122, 27; Leo Townsend, 'The Morning After' in Ian Norrie (ed), *The Book of the City* (1961), p 191.

30. *Evening News*, 30 Dec 1940; Townsend, pp 188–90; Philip Ziegler, *London at War, 1939–45* (1995), p 144; *Evening News*, 10 Jan 1941.

31. Ziegler, p 170; Newton, p 185; Judy Slinn, *Clifford Chance: Its Origins and Development* (Cambridge, 1993), p 115; Nigel Nicolson (ed), *Harold Nicolson: Letters and Diaries, 1939–45* (1967), p 142.

32. Brand, file 197, 28 March 1941; Hennessy, pp 15–16.

33. Sonia Orwell and Ian Angus (eds), *The Collected Essays, Journalism and Letters of George Orwell: Volume II* (1968), pp 104–5, 99.

34. Sambourne, 26 March 1941; BoE, ADM 34/30, 1 April 1941.

35. *FT*, 8 April 1941; Trench, p 28; Sambourne, 19 April 1941.

36. *The Book of the City*, p 115; BoE, ADM 34/30, 10 June 1941; *FN*, 24 June 1941.

37. HSBC, 255/21, 11 July 1945; Laurie Dennett, *Slaughter and May: A Century in the City* (Cambridge, 1989), p 201; James Lees-Milne, *Ancestral Voices* (1984, pbk), p 35.

38. T. Jackson, *The Origin and History of the Drayton Group* (Croydon, 1991), pp 38–9, 51.

39. W.J. Reader and David Kynaston, *Phillips & Drew: Professionals in the City* (1998), pp 27–31; David Kynaston, *Cazenove & Co: A History* (1991), pp 82, 106, 168.

40. National Life Story Collection (British Library National Sound Archive), 'City Lives', C 409/027; Michael Bonavia, *London Before I Forget* (Upton-upon-Severn, 1990), p 125.

41. BoE, ADM 34/30, 19 May 1941, 27 June 1941, 1 July 1941.

42. Duncan Crow, *A Man of Push and Go: The Life of George Macaulay Booth* (1965), p 167; BoE, ADM 34/30, 5 Sept 1941, 8 Sept 1941, G 1/510, 15 Sept 1941.

43. Donald Moggridge (ed), *The Collected Writings of John Maynard Keynes: Volume XXII* (1978), p 409; Moggridge, p 664; Paul Bareau, 'The Financial Institutions of the City of London' in The Institute of Bankers, *The City of London as a Centre of International Trade and Finance* (1961), p 16; BoE, ADM 34/30, 9 Oct 1941, G 1/510, 31 Oct 1941; Sayers, p 602.

44. BoE, G 15/7, 9 Oct 1941, G 1/510, 31 Oct 1941, ADM 34/30, 22 Dec 1941, ADM 20/31, 15 Jan 1942.

45. BoE, G 15/7, 18 March 1942, 16 Dec 1942; Marguerite Dupree (ed), *Lancashire and Whitehall: The Diary of Sir Raymond Streat* (Manchester, 1987), vol 2, p 144.

46. BoE, G 1/509, 9 April 1942, 31 July 1942, ADM 20/31, 24 Oct 1942, 22 May 1942, 17 Sept 1942, 21 Sept 1942.

47. John Barnes and David Nicholson (eds), *The Empire at Bay: The Leo Amery Diaries, 1929–1945* (1988), p 842; J.A. Gere and John Sparrow (eds), *Geoffrey Madan's Notebooks* (Oxford, 1981), p 70; Leslie O'Brien, *A Life Worth Living* (privately published, 1995), p 21, BoE, G 15/650, 'Notes by Lord O'Brien', c 1987.

48. *Bank of England Quarterly Bulletin*, June 1967, p 145; *Banker*, May 1944, pp 79–84, Aug 1941, pp 76–7; Gillett Brothers, Ms 24,692, 12 Sept 1941; Sayers, *Gilletts*, pp 119–20; BoE, ADM 34/32, 23 Sept 1943; George and Pamela Cleaver, *The Union Discount: A Centenary Album* (1985), p 82.

49. The first half of this paragraph is drawn mainly from Ranald C. Michie, *The London Stock Exchange: A History* (Oxford, 1999); see also *Banker*, Aug 1941, p 91.

50. *FT*, 13 Aug 1945.

51. SE, Mss 14,600, vol 138, 28 July 1941–vol 139, 6 Oct 1941; interview with Gerald Ashfield, 20 Nov 1997.

52. *Independent*, 26 Jan 1991; SE, Ms 14,600, vol 139, 6 July 1942.

53. BoE, ADM 20/31, 2 Nov 1942; SE, Ms 14,600, vol 141, 17 May 1943, 27 May 1943.

54. SE, Ms 14,600, vol 139, 10 Nov 1941; BoE, ADM 34/32, 17 Aug 1943, 2 Dec 1943.

55. SE, Mss 14,600, vol 139, 16 March 1942, 20 April 1942, 11 May 1942, 14 May 1942, vol 140, 14 Dec 1942.

56. SE, Ms 14,600, vol 141, 27 Sept 1943.

57. *Banker*, Aug 1941, pp 82–7; BoE, ADM 14/3, 19 Feb 1942.

58. BoE, ADM 34/30, 28 Jan 1941; Wake, p 256; BB, 202800/22; Bramsen and Wain, pp 399–400; BoE, ADM 34/32, 15 Oct 1943, ADM 20/31, 8 Dec 1942;

Kathleen Burk, *Morgan Grenfell, 1838–1988: The Biography of a Merchant Bank* (Oxford, 1989), pp 168–9, BoE, ADM 34/32, 18 Jan 1943, 25 Jan 1943.

59. BoE, ADM 34/30, 2 Dec 1941, ADM 20/31, 15 April 1942, 8 Sept 1942, 10 Sept 1942, 2 Oct 1942, 23 Oct 1942, ADM 34/32, 21 Jan 1943, 10 Aug 1943; Roberts, p 277.

60. A helpful contemporary overview is 'Bankers as Civil Servants', *Banker*, Aug 1941, pp 77–82.

61. Winton, p 104; *DBB*, Geoffrey Jones and Margaret Ackrill, 'Sir Charles Lidbury', vol 3, pp 783–4; *The Times*, 3 Oct 1962, A.R. Holmes and Edwin Green, *Midland: 150 Years of Banking Business* (1986), p 207; John Kinross, *Fifty Years in the City* (1982), p 43.

62. See Holmes and Green, pp 206–7, for an alternative account of the succession to McKenna.

63. Holmes and Green, p 206; BoE, ADM 34/32 7 Sept 1943, 14 Sept 1943, 16 Sept 1943, 21–3 Sept 19, 5 Oct 1943.

64. *FT*, 2 Dec 1942. In general on the City and reconstruction, see: Middlemas, pp 73, 98; Scott Newton and Dilwyn Porter, *Modernisation Frustrated* (1988), pp 104–6.

65. Robert Rhodes James, *Bob Boothby: A Portrait* (1991), p 312; BoE, ADM 34/32, 23 Feb 1943

66. BoE, ADM 14/8, 11 Dec 1941; John Kinross and Alan Butt-Philip, *ICFC, 1945–1961* (1985), 7, 9–10.

67. John Fforde, *The Bank of England and Public Policy, 1941–1958* (Cambridge, 1992), p 710; BoE, SMT 2/308, 7 Jan 1944. There are three principal accounts of the formation of ICFC: Kinross and Butt-Philip, pp 7–59; Fforde, pp 704–27; Richard Coopey and Donald Clarke, *3i: Fifty Years Investing in Industry* (Oxford, 1995), pp 13–28.

68. Kinross and Butt-Philip, p 22; Coopey and Clarke, p 22; Kinross and Butt-Philip, pp 314–23.

69. Important contributions to the literature include: L.S. Pressnell, *External Economic Policy Since the War, Volume I: The Post-War Financial Settlement* (1986), pp 66–261; Fforde, pp 31–73; Moggridge, pp 670–795; P.J. Cain and A.G. Hopkins, *British Imperialism: Crisis and Deconstruction, 1914–1990* (1993), pp 270–2; P.L. Cottrell, 'The Bank of England in its International Setting, 1918–1972' in Richard Roberts and David Kynaston (eds), *The Bank of England* (Oxford, 1995), pp 110–13.

70. Fforde, p 37; BoE, G 1/510, 3 Dec 1941; Fforde, p 44; Moggridge, p 676.

71. *The Empire at Bay*, p 762; Moggridge, p 734.

72. See the account in Sayers, pp 653–4.

73. BoE, ADM 33/24 (Towers notes, Sept 1974); Sayers, p 654; BoE, ADM 34/32, 21 Oct 1943, ADM 34/33, 7 Jan 1944.

74. Boyle, pp 322–4; BoE, Norman to Stapley, 14 April 1944, G 15/241, 30 April 1960 (Kershaw).

75. Sambourne, 5 April 1944, 20 Dec 1944.

76. Roberts, pp 277–9.

77. *FT*, 11 Jan 1945; BB, 200824, 16 Jan 1945; Sir Andrew McFadyean, *Recollected in Tranquillity* (1964), p 148; Holmes and Green, p 207.

78. The fullest account of Catto's life and character is to be found in *Thomas*

Sivewright Catto, Baron Catto of Cairncatto: A Personal Memoir and a Biographical Note (Edinburgh, 1962), compiled anonymously but with a significant input from the Bank of England.

79. *Thomas Sivewright Catto*, p 119; *Lancashire and Whitehall*, p 245; *Thomas Sivewright Catto* p 118.

80. O'Brien, pp 22–3; BoE, G 15/650, 'Notes by Lord O'Brien', c 1987; Philip Geddes, *Inside the Bank of England* (1987), p 36; Brand, file 198, 18 Jan 1945.

81. BoE, ADM 14/14, 15 June 1944; Brand, file 197, 12 Aug 1944.

82. *FT*, 24 July 1944; *FN*, 25 July 1944; Lloyds, HO/GM/Par.2, 9 Aug 1944, 25 Sept 1944; BoE, G 18/3, 20 March 1945.

83. BoE, SMT 2/308, 8 May 1944; Kinross and Butt-Philip, pp 324–7; Kinross, p 116.

84. Kinross and Butt-Philip, p 51.

85. *DBB*, Martin Chick, 'William Stuckey Piercy, 1st Lord Piercy of Burford', vol 4, p 686; HSBC, 30/152, 17 Feb 1945; Kinross and Butt-Philip, p 56.

86. *Committee on Company Law Amendment: Evidence and Minutes* (Parl Papers, 1944–5, Cmd 6659), qq 2512, 5306; Judy Slinn, *Linklaters & Paines: The First One Hundred and Fifty Years* (1987) pp 175–6.

87. W.T.C. King, *The Stock Exchange* (1947), pp 78–9; *FT*, 4 May 1945.

88. Judy Slinn, *A History of Freshfields* (1984), p 157; James Lees-Milne, *Prophesying Peace* (1984, pbk), p 174; W. Lionel Fraser, *All to the Good* (1963), p 172; BB, 200861, 23 March 1945; John Colville, *The Fringes of Power* (1985), p 597.

89. *FT*, 9 May 1945.

CHAPTER EIGHTEEN

1. Lloyds, HO/GM/Par.2, 5 June 1945; *FT*, 5 July 1945; BB, 200832, 3 July 1945, 9 July 1945.

2. *FT*, 10 July 1945, 19 July 1945, 23–7 July 1945.

3. *FT*, 27 July 1945; *FN*, 27 July 1945; BB, 200861, 28 July 1945, 8 Aug 1945; John Gale, *Clean Young Englishman* (1988, pbk), p 84.

4. BB, 200861, 8 Aug 1945.

Acknowledgements

I am grateful to the following for allowing me to reproduce material, including copyright material: Victoria Allison; The Bank of England; Anthony J.E. Besch; The British Library National Sound Archive; Edward Brooks; The Centre for Metropolitan History; Rupert Crew Ltd (*The Wandering Years*); Deutsche Morgan Grenfell; Dresdner Kleinwort Benson; Valerie Eliot (*The Letters of T.S. Eliot, 1898–1922* and *Collected Poems, 1909–62*, both published by Faber & Faber); The Federal Reserve Bank of New York; HSBC Holdings; A.M. Heath & Co Ltd on behalf of Mark Hamilton as the Literary Executor of the Estate of the Late Sonia Brownell Orwell, and Martin Secker & Warburg Ltd; David Higham Associates (*London Particulars*); ING Barings; Archie Jessep; Lloyds TSB Group; The London Investment Banking Association; Macmillan Ltd (*The Collected Writings of John Maynard Keynes*); Matheson & Co; NatWest Group; Mrs Ronald Palin; N.M. Rothschild & Sons; The School of Oriental and African Studies and the Addis family; Slaughter and May; University College London, Manuscripts and Rare Books; Davina Walter; Weidenfeld & Nicolson (*Memoirs of a City Radical*); the Executors of the Estate of Virginia Woolf, Hogarth Press and the Society of Authors; Gillian Wyatt.

The following kindly supplied illustrations: The Governor and Company of the Bank of England (jacket, 1, 11, 17); Deutsche Morgan Grenfell (15); Guildhall Library, Corporation of London (16, 25–27); HSBC Holdings (12, 29); ING Barings (3–9); Lloyds TSB Group (14); NatWest Group (10, 13); Schroders (24); Roger Young and Tom Jackson (28). In cases where it proved impossible to trace the copyright holder, the publishers will be pleased to receive any information.

As ever, I am indebted to many curators, archivists and fellow-historians. They include Melanie Aspey, Bernard Attard, John Booker, Kathleen Burk, Youssef Cassis, Henry Gillett, Edwin Green, Leslie Hannah, Roy Harris, Elizabeth Hennessy, Derek Keene, John Keyworth, Sara Kinsey, Rosemary Lazenby, Fiona Maccoll, Sarah Millard, John Orbell, Rob Perks, Dilwyn Porter, Richard Roberts, Duncan Ross, Susan

Snell, Jehanne Wake and Jane Waller. The Guildhall Library was, as usual, extremely helpful. I am also grateful to Stephanie Zarach for her assistance in connection with Slaughter and May's records; to Michael Burns for devilling for me in New York; to Iain Black for giving me an advance look at his study of the rebuilding of the Bank of England; and to Ranald Michie for doing likewise with his forthcoming history of the Stock Exchange – a history that will transform our understanding of that key institution. I owe a particularly great debt to Shirley Nicholson. She told me about the existence of Roy Sambourne's diaries, encouraged me to peruse them, and generously allowed me to plunder her forthcoming biography of Sambourne. His diaries are a marvellous source (not only about the City), and I am enormously grateful to her.

There are other thanks to offer: to the Authors' Foundation for a grant; to Deborah Rogers for being a supportive agent, and her assistant Stephen Edwards; to Amanda Howard for typing my tapes; to Neil Bradford for designing the illustrations; to Mandy Greenfield for copy-editing; to Jo North for proofreading; to Marie Lorimer for the index; and, above all, to Jenny Uglow, my editor at Chatto, and her colleagues there, including Jonathan Butler, Mary Gibson, Alison Samuel, Rowena Skelton-Wallace and Stuart Williams, as well as Will Sulkin at Pimlico.

An old friend, Harry Ricketts, made encouraging noises about the City while we discussed *Debits and Credits* and related matters. Lucy and our three children – Laurie, George and Michael – have been a refreshing counterpoint to solitary hours at the desk. And finally, I am grateful to all those (some of them mentioned above) who have been undismayed by the prospect of an extra helping of this particular plum pudding.

London, winter 1998/9

Index

A. E. Ashford & Co 98
A. Sheriff & Co 489
A. Spurling & Co 311
Abdication 438–9
Aberconway, Lord 181
Abrahams, Leopold A. 489–90
Abs, Hermann 323, 452–3
Abyssynia 436
acceptance business 70, 75
  volume 49, 143, 392; losses 74;
  merchant banks 74, 227, 392;
  joint-stock banks 75, 195; German
  commitments 150–1, 452, 455; Big
  Five 163–4; commissions 163;
  failure to establish central clearing
  house 195; liquidity requirement
  227
Accepting Houses Committee 3, 195,
  232, 395, 433, 442, 445, 452, 468
accountants, inter-war 134–5
Addis, Sir Charles 40, 61, 68, 79,
  92, 148, 173, 205, 228, 277,
  296–7
  1914 financial crisis 4–5; and First
  World War 10, 27, 34, 50; and
  female employment 25, 286; and
  Stock Exchange anti-German
  feeling 30; and bank
  amalgamations 46; criticises
  clearing bankers 47, 75, 76; and
  industrial unrest 54; and German
  post–war reconstruction 56;
  disparages US politicians 59–60;
  and Norman 64, 67, 155, 166,
  167, 202, 216, 234, 357–8; urges
  adoption of common monetary
  policy 67; and Keynes 77–8; and
  Dawes Loan 84; and Canada 86,
  405, 406; and foreign loans 86,
  91; Brazilian mission 90, 91; and

Herbert Gibbs 90; and China 91,
  406; dines out 91, 323, 348–9;
  supports deflationary policies 103;
  urges return to gold standard 103;
  and a managed currency 107; and
  gold standard 109–10, 113, 120,
  121; and Bank rate 117, 122, 125,
  130, 177–8, 193; and general
  strike 126, 127; German
  reparations committee 158; and
  Bank governorship 165, 166–7,
  168, 202, 357–8, 381; and Bank
  specialist advisers 169; and
  Macmillan Committee 202; 1931
  financial crisis 213, 214, 236, 238,
  240, 241, 244; retirement 358; and
  impending war 443, 454; and the
  Munich Conference 446–7
Adelaide House 267–8
Ahern, Terrence 309, 312, 317
Aiken, Conrad 291
Akroyd, Bayly 93
Akroyd & Smithers 93, 184, 313
Alexander, Ann 346
Allen, G.O. (Gubby) 297
Allen, Harvey & Ross 72–3
Allied Newspapers 137
Amalgamated Industrials 54
amalgamation movement 44–6, 492,
  500
American Exchange Fund 399
Amery, Leo 129, 204, 230, 363,
  485, 497
Anderson 499, 504
Anderson, Sir Alan 68, 122, 165,
  168, 204, 456, 464, 482, 499
Anderson, Sir John 391, 494, 504
Andreae, Herman 70, 141, 162,
  331–2
Anglo-Austrian Bank 327, 385

Davenport, Nicholas 94, 203–4,
299–300, 304, 305, 325–6, 372
David A. Bevan & Co 297, 306
David Sassoon & Co 392
Davidson, J.C.C. 173
Davison, Henry P. 17
Dawes Plan 83, 84, 150, 158
Dawnay, Guy 327, 443
Dawnay, Day & Co 137, 327
Dawson, Christopher 93–4
de Bernales, Claude Albo 424
de Stein, Edward 415, 416, 505
de Trafford, Rudolph 242
dear–money policies 62, 63, 104,
125
Debenhams 161
Decca 138, 417
Deloitte, Plender, Griffiths & Co 285
Denmark 59, 469
Dent, Alfred (Alfred Schacht) 29–30
Dent, Palmer & Co 69
d'Erlanger, Baron Emile 73, 383, 394
d'Erlanger, Leo 416–17
Deterding, Sir Henri 135
Deutsche Bank 40, 323, 452
devaluation 242–3
Dingwall, Kenneth 306
directorships, multiple 326–7, 329,
331
disclosure 32–3, 505
discount market
and Bank of England 11, 164–5,
390, 486; crises 389–90, 445, 468;
and clearing banks 390, 445;
rationalisation 390, 486–7; short-
dated government stocks 390, 486;
wartime business 468, 486
Discount Market Committee 164
Dixie, Alexander Archibald Douglas
Wolston 306
Dixon, J.G.G. 179
Docker, Dudley 39, 40
dollar-sterling exchange rate 60
domestic new issues 203, 392, 408
capital market response 135–7,
226–7, 418–20; merchant banks
135–6, 160, 392, 393, 409, 419,
420; issuing houses 136–7, 138–9,
226, 420–1; boom 137–40; and
Hatry 140–3; and the Macmillan
report 226–7; 'introductions'
421–2; offer by prospectus 421,
422; *see also* Bankers Industrial

Development Company
Dougall, Robert 285
Dowling, S.W. 253–4
Drayton, Harley 342–3, 417, 481
Dresdner Bank 75, 393
Drew, David 305
Duguid, Charles 91
Duncan, Sir Andrew 190
Dunn, Sir James 23, 347, 471
Durlacher, Esmond 314
Dutch banking crisis 244

E. Johnston & Co 90, 290
E. R. Lewis & Co 417
E. B. Savory & Co 297
Eady, Sir Wilfrid 495, 496
Eastwood & Holt 257
Eaton, Colonel Sir Richard 296
economic internationalism 205, 362,
363, 368, 401
Economic Journal 40, 49
economic liberalism 79
economic nationalism 362, 363
Economist 48, 77, 104, 174, 206,
232, 343, 464, 485
on the BST 42; criticises Bank 42;
pepper scandal 428–9
Economy Committee 214–15, 220,
225
E. D. Sassoon Banking Co 392
Eden, Anthony 437, 442, 443
Edgar, Sir Mackay 70, 71
Edward Boustead & Co 427
Edward de Stein & Co 137
Edward VIII 438–9
Einzig, Paul 344, 377, 443, 467
1931 financial crisis 243, 244;
on 'Jewish conspiracy in
international finance' 337; London
recovers financial supremacy 404;
and Schacht's visit to England 450;
exposes Czech gold controversy
455
Eliot, T.S. 171, 249, 290–1
Ellen, Edgar C. (Gus) 487
Ellerman, Sir John 50, 349
Ellerton, Cecil 385, 387, 459
Ellis & Co 96, 97, 98
English & International Trust 328
English & New York Trust 328
equities 487
Erlangers 68–9, 73
new issues 160; acceptance

National Shipbuilders 218
nationalisation 124, 173, 373, 374,
 377, 378, 484
naval mutiny (Invergordon) 243
Nelke, Paul 5, 29
Nelke & Phillips 303
New Deal 397
new issue boom 137–41
New Statesman 305, 368, 444–5
New Trading Company 341, 500
New Zealand 120, 404–5
Newman, R.L. 15, 43
News Chronicle 375
News of the World 420
Nickisson, J.L. 311–12
Nicolson, Sir Arthur 19
Nicolson, Harold 477
Niemeyer, Sir Otto 108, 113, 121,
 129, 169, 363, 381, 498
 Chamberlain Committee 109; and
 gold standard 115, 119; and
 Churchill 116, 118; and Bank rate
 117–18; on Bank/government
 relations 117, 118; Australian
 financial crisis 205–7; Brazilian
 financial crisis 224; conduct of
 financial missions 403; and
 Industrial Mortgage Corporation
 413, 414; and post–war domestic
 finance 495; and ICFC 504
Niven, John 428
Nivison, John 148
Nivisons *see* R. Nivison & Co
Norman, Montagu 300, 349, 405
 joins Bank of England 20; and
 Strong 21; and McKenna 32, 110,
 128, 345, 390–1; on wartime
 financial conduct 32; and Bank/
 Treasury relations 33, 384, 466,
 467, 484–5; and Bonar Law/
 Cunliffe dispute 35; and Cunliffe
 36, 37; Deputy Governor 36; and
 Bank internal reform 42, 43–4;
 and staff grievance committee 55;
 and Keynes 57, 77, 79, 107,
 464–5, 469–70, 482–3, 497;
 foreign loans 59, 85–6, 90, 91, 92,
 144–5, 152, 186, 219–20, 383,
 384; backs anti-inflationary
 measures 60; and Bank rate 61,
 62, 63, 102–3, 105, 117, 125,
 130, 178, 180, 192, 199, 364–5;
 becomes Governor 62, 63; anti-

Semitism 64, 337, 485–6;
 character 64, 65–6; charm 64, 80,
 391, 486; impressions of 64, 65–6,
 380–1; and governorship 67, 68,
 166, 167–8; City authority 68–9,
 467; and Huths 70, 393; and
 Goodenough 76, 345;
 internationalism 79; urges payment
 of war debt 79; and central
 banking 80, 81, 153–4, 187, 225,
 405; supports reconstruction loans
 81; and German reparations 82–3;
 and German loans 83–4, 437–8;
 and sterling bloc 83, 364, 403,
 437; and industrial unrest 84; and
 Russian loans 84, 149; deprecates
 US loans to Australia 87; and
 South African gold producers 88;
 and gilt-edged market 93, 383;
 and BST 94; and credit insurance
 98; and gold standard 102, 108–9,
 112, 113, 114, 115–16, 119, 120,
 122, 199, 362, 398; and
 politicisation of monetary policy
 104; and amalgamation of Bank
 and Treasury notes 108–9; and
 Labour governments 108, 173; and
 general strike 127; and Churchill
 128–9, 470; and City/industry
 relations 131, 132, 133, 134, 135,
 198–9, 209–10, 217, 408–9; and
 Armstrong Whitworth & Co 132;
 and Hatry affair 141, 176, 180,
 188–9; and London's subservience
 to New York market 143; and
 Australia 147, 206, 404; approves
 Italian fascism 152; and the Long
 Island 'Club' 153; confidence in
 Schacht 154, 442, 443–4,
 451; 'club' of central bankers 155,
 187; and Romanian reconstruction
 loan 155–6; and Balkan loans 156;
 and US speculative fever 157; and
 merchant banks 161–2, 394,
 491–2; and joint-stock banks
 162–3; and Pease 162; and
 discount market 164–5, 389–90,
 468, 486–7; and Anderson 165;
 and Trotter 165–6; recruits
 specialist advisers 169; and
 Macmillan Committee 181–2,
 198–202, 216; and BIS 187, 357,
 433; and hire-purchase finance

189; and rationalisation 189–90,
191, 192, 200, 217–18; and BIDC
191, 192, 202, 217, 409; and
industrial initiatives 191–2, 202,
207, 209–10, 217, 408–9, 411–12,
412–13, 414, 415, 418, 495; and
SMT 191; breakdown 194; and
unemployment 200; instinctual
behaviour 201–2, 381, 382; re-
election as governor 202; and LCC
207, 209–10; 1931 financial crisis
212, 213, 220–1, 223, 224, 230–1,
232, 234, 236, 239, 357; and
Credit Anstalt crisis 222; maintains
German credit 223; and Brazil
224; and Macmillan Report 225–6;
and German financial crisis (1931)
228–9; and Lazards rescue 228;
and Hambros 328–9; and New
Trading Company 341; promises
to step down in 1933 358; and
Kreuger 359; on losses and debts
359; and protectionism 361; and
free trade 363; and War Loan
conversion operation 366, 367;
retains belief in economic
internationalism 368; and
Standstill Agreement 368, 433,
435, 440; and 'dole' 371;
Boothby's criticism of 372;
criticisms of 373, 376, 377; and
Bankers Bureau 375–6; sent Social
Credit nostrums by Pound 376;
autocratic behaviour 381; marriage
381; secrecy 381; moral suasion
382–3, 391, 394; and the EEA
384; and Kay 385; curtails
speculation in gold and foreign
exchange 388; resists forward
dealings 388; and clearing banks
390, 391; and acceptance business
392; and Philip Hill 394–5; and
Accepting Houses Committee 395;
and cheap money policies 395; and
Blackett 396–7; and Roosevelt
397; and US monetary policy 397;
and impediments to stabilisation
399–400; and New Zealand 404;
and Canada 405–6; and China
406; and Japan 407; and Harman
424; pepper scandal 427, 428,
429; and Nazi Germany 433–4;
pro-German stance 433–4; Second

World War 435–6, 442, 449, 453,
460, 461, 462–3, 473; wartime
banking arrangements 441, 474;
favours appeasement 442, 451;
German 'Communism' 442; and
Italy 442; and Einzig 443; and
Schacht's visit to England 450;
visits Berlin 450–1; and Hitler
456; and war finance 464; and Sir
John Simon 469; and the conduct
of war 471–2, 479; and growing
US financial dominance 477; and
shift in international financial
relations 477; retirement 482, 498,
499; and Court candidates 484;
and nationalisation 484; and
mayoral succession 485; and
market reputation 488; and
Rothschilds amalgamation 492;
and Midland succession 493–4;
and post-war domestic finance
495–6; succession 498–9
note issues, amalgamation of 108–9
Nuffield, Lord 422, 423
Nugent, Christopher 47

O. T. Falk & Co 304
O'Brien, Leslie 287, 465, 486, 501
O'Hagan, H. Osborne 97–8
Old Broad Street Group 327–8, 343
Ommanney, Francis 258–9, 260,
271–3, 282
Onyon, Henry 56
Orpen, Ronald 318, 320
Orwell, George 246–7, 478, 487
Osborn, Percy 282
Ostrer, Isidore 416
Ostrer, Mark 416
Ostrer, Maurice 416
Ostrer Bros 137
outside brokers 315–17, 423–4

Paget-Cooke, Oliver 204
Paine, Jack 348
Palache, Albert 442
Palgrave, Sir Robert Inglis 49
Palin, Ronald 275–6, 279, 323, 463
Palmer, H.G. 69
Palmer-Tomkinson, Jimmy 489
Pam, Albert 71, 192, 409, 492
Panmure Gordon & Co 306, 383,
420
Paris Peace Conference 57

THE FINANCIAL NEWS *Map of* THE STOCK EXCHANGE